Economics of
Social Issues

Economics of Social Issues

Seventeenth Edition

Ansel M. Sharp
University of the South

Charles A. Register
Florida Atlantic University

Paul W. Grimes
Mississippi State University

 McGraw-Hill
Irwin

Boston   Burr Ridge, IL   Dubuque, IA   Madison, WI   New York   San Francisco   St
Bangkok   Bogotá   Caracas   Kuala Lumpur   Lisbon   London   Madrid   Mexic
Milan   Montreal   New Delhi   Santiago   Seoul   Singapore   Sydney   Taipei

McGraw-Hill
Irwin

ECONOMICS OF SOCIAL ISSUES
Published by McGraw-Hill/Irwin, a business unit of The McGraw-Hill Companies, Inc., 1221 Avenue of the Americas, New York, NY, 10020. Copyright © 2006, 2004, 2002, 2000, 1998, 1996, 1994, 1992, 1990, 1988, 1986, 1984, 1982, 1980, 1979, 1976, 1974 by The McGraw-Hill Companies, Inc. All rights reserved. No part of this publication may be reproduced or distributed in any form or by any means, or stored in a database or retrieval system, without the prior written consent of The McGraw-Hill Companies, Inc., including, but not limited to, in any network or other electronic storage or transmission, or broadcast for distance learning.

Some ancillaries, including electronic and print components, may not be available to customers outside the United States.

This book is printed on acid-free paper.

1 2 3 4 5 6 7 8 9 0 DOC/DOC 0 9 8 7 6 5

ISBN 0-07-298435-X

Publisher: *Gary Burke*
Executive sponsoring editor: *Paul Shensa*
Editorial coordinator: *Heila Hubbard*
Senior marketing manager: *Martin D. Quinn*
Lead producer, Media technology: *Kai Chiang*
Project manager: *Dana M. Pauley*
Production supervisor: *Gina Hangos*
Lead designer: *Matthew Baldwin*
Senior media project manager: *Susan Lombardi*
Media project manager: *Ellyn Zydron*
Supplement producer: *Gina F. DiMartino*
Developer, Media technology: *Brian Nacik*
Cover design: *Cheryl Carrington*
Cover illustrator: *Frank Miller*
Typeface: *10/12 Palatino*
Compositor: *Cenveo*
Printer: *R. R. Donnelley*

Library of Congress Cataloging-in-Publication Data

Sharp, Ansel Miree, 1924–
    Economics of social issues/Ansel M. Sharp, Charles A. Register, Paul W. Grimes.—
17th ed.
      p. cm.
    Includes bibliographical references and index.
    ISBN 0-07-298435-X (alk. paper)
    1. Economics. 2. Social problems. I. Register, Charles A. II. Grimes, Paul W. III. Title.
HB171.5.S5498 2006
    330—dc22

                                   2005041786

www.mhhe.com

Preface

Welcome to the 17th edition of the first textbook to introduce the social issues approach to the teaching of economic principles. Over the years, our revisions to each edition of *Economics of Social Issues* have attempted to reflect the important societal trends and public debates current at the time. Currency and relevance are the motivations behind the major changes that previous users will quickly find in this volume. Although the specific topics and organization of the material continue to evolve, at least one thing remains a constant: our basic teaching objectives designed to produce economically literate citizens. These objectives are to (1) create student interest in the study of economics and (2) provide a framework of basic analytical tools useful in the understanding of social issues. To reach these objectives, we first introduce and discuss the important aspects of a contemporary social issue. Next, we develop the economic concepts and principles germane to the issue. Finally, we apply these principles to the issue to resolve it. The issues throughout the text are arranged so that basic economic concepts are logically developed and an understanding of these concepts is reinforced through repeated use and application. Enough flexibility is built in, however, to give instructors the ability to experiment with different sequences of topics and chapters. As always, we carefully choose relevant social issues that not only stimulate classroom discussion but also lend themselves to helping students learn the important basic principles of economics.

WHAT'S NEW

Our primary goal throughout the revision process was to enhance the uniqueness of our pedagogical approach to teaching basic economic concepts while continuing to improve the overall quality of our final product. We feel we succeeded in doing this and hope that both our new and our long-time users will agree.

Those familiar with previous editions of the book will find a number of modifications and additions incorporated into the 17th edition. The most obvious change is in Chapter 2. With the Soviet Union receding into the pages of history, we received numerous recommendations from reviewers and long-time adopters to replace our discussion of the Soviet transition with an exploration of the experiences of the People's Republic of China. On the basis of these suggestions, China is now the focal point of Chapter 2, where the examination of the differences between command economies and market-based economies is used to illustrate the power of the marketplace to answer society's basic economic questions. The basic instructional goals of the chapter remain the same, only the example has changed. Given the ongoing controversies about China's role in the global economy, we believe this change will make Chapter 2 more relevant for today's college student.

We have retained the same number and sequence of chapters for the 17th edition and, although the primary instructional objectives of the text have not changed, we have revised each chapter to reflect the current public discourse and debate on the topics at hand. For example, in Chapter 6 on the economics of education, students are presented with recent research findings concerning the effects of vouchers and charter schools on student performance. In Chapter 10 on international trade, we have added a discussion of the currently popular protectionist argument about the need to prevent outsourcing of service sector jobs overseas. Chapter 10 also reflects the recent expansion of the European Union to its current 25 members. Our chapter on public finance, Chapter 14, has been updated to account for recent tax reform measures, and the comparison of U.S. tax rates to those in other countries has been updated and expanded. In the discussion of the incidence of tax burdens, Chapter 14 now introduces students to the concept of price elasticity of demand, a concept missing from the last several editions of the text. Readers will also find that Chapter 16 on Social Security includes the latest forecasts for the trust fund balance and discusses the 2003 Medicare Modernization Act. There are many other changes throughout the text that are too numerous to list here and, of course, each chapter was thoroughly revised and updated with the latest statistics and data available at press time.

Again, the end of each chapter includes an updated list of recommended World Wide Web sites relevant to the particular social issues discussed in that chapter. These sites were chosen on the basis of their content and ability to provide students with additional information or alternative points of view. Please visit our enhanced Web site created and maintained by Margaret A. Ray and hosted by McGraw-Hill/Irwin. This site provides hyperlinks to each Web site listed at the end of each chapter, as well as links to articles and information that supplement our textbook material. Furthermore, self-tests designed to enhance the resources found in our companion *Study Guide* are available to students. The URL for our Web site is www.mhhe.com/economics/sharp17.

Without question, however, the most important change is that the 17th edition marks the first edition in which founding author Ansel Sharp has not taken an active role. We have each known Ansel for some 25 years now. We have known him as professor, as mentor, as coauthor, and most significantly as dear friend. Ansel being no longer actively involved leaves us with very big shoes to fill. At the same time, through 25 years of observing his exemplary professionalism, it is our hope that we can fill those shoes, keeping *Economics of Social Issues* as current, interesting to students, and analytically sound as it has always been.

THE SOCIAL ISSUES PEDAGOGY

To those instructors who are contemplating the adoption of a social issues approach to teaching economic principles, we would like to call your attention to the following research article: "The Social Issues Pedagogy vs. the Traditional Principles of Economics: An Empirical Examination," *The American Economist*, vol. 41, no. 1, Spring 1998. This paper was written by Paul along with Professor Paul S. Nelson of the University of Louisiana at Monroe. It presents the results of a controlled experiment comparing the learning of students enrolled in a social issues–oriented course that used a previous edition of this book with students who took traditional principles of economics courses and used a standard encyclopedic text. The results are encouraging in that no significant difference was found between students in the social issues course and students enrolled in the traditional macroeconomics principles course, after controlling for student demographic characteristics, prior experiences, and academic aptitude. Furthermore, the results strongly indicate that the students in the social issues course had a higher probability of course completion relative to those in the control group. In this era, in which student retention is becoming more important, we strongly believe that this result suggests an important positive spillover benefit of our pedagogical approach that those who design economics courses and curriculum should consider.

Acknowledgments

First, we would like to thank former author Richard H. Leftwich for all his contributions to past editions of this book. Much of the credit for the success of the social issues pedagogy belongs to him. The author team also extends its sincere appreciation to the author of the *Study Guide* and *Instructor's Manual*, Margaret A. Ray of Mary Washington College, for her diligent work in revising and updating these important companions to our book. Margaret has also provided insightful comments and suggestions throughout the last several revisions of the textbook. We also wish to thank her for applying her expertise in economic education to the development and maintenance of the Web site. Margaret's hard work has proved instrumental in the success of this important enhancement of our efforts.

Many of the features included in this edition are based on suggestions made to us in conversation or in writing by the following users or previous reviewers of our book:

Ron Adams
California State University, Chico

Ugur Aker
Hiram College

John E. Altazan
University of New Orleans

Sally Andrews
Linn-Benton Community College

Michael W. Babcock
Kansas State University

Joe G. Baker
Southern Utah University

Louis E. Bauer
Concordia University, Portland

Walter Baumgartner
State University of New York—College at Oneonta

Alexandra Bernasek
Colorado State University

David Blanchard
University of Wisconsin at Oshkosh

Jeanne Boch
Augsburg College

James Bolchalk
Mount Union College

Dr. Lawrence P. Brunner
Central Michigan University

Donald Bumpass
Sam Houston State University

Heather Campbell
Arizona State University

Perry A. Cash
Chadwick University

Edward Cearny
Coastal Carolina University

Daniel S. Chiremba
Queens College of The City University of New York

Elchanan Cohn
University of South Carolina

Basil Cooil
Tompkins Cortland Community College

Harry L. Cook
Southern Oregon State College

Douglas W. Copeland
Johnson County Community College

Edward J. Deak
Fairfield University
Lori Dickes
Lander University
Bruce R. Domazlicky
Southeast Missouri State University
Douglas P. Dotterweich
East Tennessee State University
James H. Dukes
University of West Florida
Dr. Douglas Dyer
University of Central Texas
Allen Early
West Texas State College
Robert C. Eisenstadt
University of Louisiana–Monroe
Ed Ford
University of South Florida
Charles R. Fraley
College of Mount St. Joseph
Dan Fuller
Weber State University
Dan Gallagher
St. Cloud State University
James Gapinski
Florida State University
Neil Garston
California State University–Los Angeles
David E. R. Gay
University of Arkansas
John Grabner
University of St. Francis
Gregory Green
Idaho State University
Joe Green
Dixie State
Steven A. Greenlaw
Mary Washington College

George H. Hand
Southern Illinois University
Charles Harrington
University of Southern Indiana
Robert B. Harris
Indiana University—Purdue University at Indianapolis
Sydney Hicks
Interfirst Bank of Dallas
Linda Hill
Idaho State University
Doug Hodo
University of Texas at San Antonio
William W. Howard
Phoenix College
Gail Hoyt
University of Kentucky
John Jambura
Eastern Oregon State College
William Kern
Western Michigan University
Douglas Kinnear
Colorado State University
Robert Kirk
Indiana University—Purdue University at Indianapolis
Howard Kittleson
Riverland Community College
Joseph Krislov
University of Kentucky
Barry Krissoff
Western Michigan University
Michael J. Kuryla
Broome Community College
Vince LaFrance
Messiah College
Howard D. Leftwich
Oklahoma Christian College

E. Victor Maafo
North Carolina Central University
K. T. Magnusson
Salt Lake Community College
Shahreh Majin
University of Western Michigan
Margaret Malixi
California State University, Bakersfield
Jim Mangum
Louisiana Technical University
James Marsden
University of Kentucky
Thomas McCann
University of Louisiana–Monroe
James McClain
University of New Orleans
Douglas McNeil
McNeese State University
Charles Meyerding
Inver Hills Community College
Lanse Minkler
University of Connecticut at Storrs
Thomas Mitchell
Southern Illinois University at Carbondale
Jeff Moore
University of Houston
Clair E. Morris
United States Naval Academy
Roland Mullins
Arkansas State University
Dave Nagao
Sacramento City College
Ken Nair
West Virginia Wesleyan University
John Neal
Lake-Sumter Community College
Paul S. Nelson
University of Louisiana–Monroe

Cliff Nowell
Weber State University
Ronan O'Beirne
American Institute of Computer Sciences
Thomas Parsons
Massachusetts Bay Community College
Janie Phelps
Mississippi State University
Wayne Plumly
Valdosta State University
George M. Radakovic
Indiana University of Pennsylvania
Padmapriya Rajagopalan
Purdue University
John Reifel
Grand Valley State University
Mary Sack Rittenhouse
University of Nebraska at Kearney
Rose Rubin
University of Memphis
Fred Ruppel
Eastern Kentucky University
Michael Sattinger
State University of New York at Albany
John L. Scott
Northeast Louisiana University
Harold M. Seeberger
Heidelberg College
Laurence Seidman
University of Delaware
Carl Simkonis
Northern Kentucky University
Robert Smith
Louisiana State University
John Somers
Portland Community College
Lee C. Spector
Ball State University

T. D. Stanley
Hendrix College
Gary Stone
Winthrop College
Amy Stritikus
University of Nebraska at Kearney
Terry P. Sutton
Southeast Missouri State University
Millicent Taylor
Carson-Newman College
Sonia Walgreen
University of Massachusetts at Dartmouth
James M. Warner
Gustavus Adolphus College

Philip F. Warnken
University of Missouri
Dennis Weidenaar
Purdue University
Rudolph B. Wuilleumier
Eastern Kentucky University
Shiu-fang Yu
Texas State University
Anthony Zambelli, J.D.
University of Redlands
Martha Zenns
Jamestown Community College

Furthermore, a special appreciation is again extended to Marybeth F. Grimes, Reference Librarian at Mississippi State University, for her expert help and research in identifying and compiling our lists of World Wide Web sites for each chapter. Thanks are also extended for her help in locating various economic data sources and updating our lists of recommended reading and citations.

We also wish to thank the employees of McGraw-Hill/Irwin for their expert help in preparing this edition, including our editor, Paul Shensa. Finally, thanks are extended to Heila Hubbard and Monica Escalares for editorial advice and assistance. We, however, are responsible for all errors of fact and theory.

Charles A. Register

Paul W. Grimes

Contents

Alleviating Human Misery
The Role of Economic Reasoning

Chapter outline

Checklist of economic concepts

- Labor resources
- Capital resources
- Technology
- Production possibilities curve
- Opportunity costs
- Opportunity cost principle
- Increasing opportunity costs
- Marginal social cost
- Marginal social benefit
- Cost-benefit analysis
- Gross domestic product, current dollar
- Gross domestic product, real
- Gross domestic product, real per capita
- Gross domestic product, per capita
- Price index numbers
- Lesser developed countries
- Developed countries

Argentina may produce enough food to feed a population equivalent to that of the United States, but little has reached 1-year-old Debora Santana, who lay in a rusty hospital cradle with an IV drip attached to her rake-thin arm.

Her single, jobless mother took Debora to a children's hospital in northern Tucuman province after she became listless, refusing to eat the little food offered. She arrived suffering from diarrhea and parasites and weighed less than 13.2 pounds, nearly half what an average child her age should.

Debora, her stomach bloated, looked up from the iron cot with dark, scared eyes. Mother and daughter had been living on a bowl of noodle soup daily and an herbal tea called mate.

"It's a disgrace this is happening in Argentina," said Mirta, a nurse in the dingy ward of broken tiles as she looked over the bed. She echoed the anger and shame Argentines feel at the plight of a crisis-wracked nation that a few years ago was a beacon of middle-class prosperity in Latin America.

In the latest of hundreds of often fatal cases of malnutrition, Debora was a "grade three," the most extreme when body weight is some 40 percent lower than normal.

Argentina, with a population a tenth of that in the United States, produces annually the equivalent of 2 tons of grains for each of its inhabitants. But a slump worse than the 1930's U.S. depression has made millions of families so poor they depend on state aid to feed their children.

"Argentina has food for everyone but there is a problem of distribution. It's incredible Argentina has come to this point. It's a disgrace," said Economy Minister Roberto Lavagna.

Debora has, so far, survived. But in the last few months, five children died from malnutrition at the same run-down hospital as Argentina's social welfare and health systems collapse from the strain of a four-year recession combined with endemic state corruption.

Health groups say that one in five children nationwide is malnourished. Dozens of child deaths nationally and images of kids with the bloated stomachs that come from severe protein deficiency have sparked a crisis of conscience.

"I sometimes have to remind myself this is not Africa, this is Argentina," Mirta said.

Argentina, with its legacy of state welfare and pride of having one of the highest standards of living in the region, has long said it is different from the Third World.

But the news from Tucuman and other provinces has reminded people how far their nation—vying economically with Canada 70 years ago—has fallen. Deaths from malnutrition in Argentina are nothing new—before this year's crisis, national charity Red Solidaria estimated several children died daily from malnutrition.

But the sheer scale of the crisis has shocked even hardened doctors. Official data this year is not available but doctors in Tucuman say their number of malnutrition cases has doubled.

A currency devaluation in January that doubled basic food prices from noodles to cooking oil only added to poverty. Imported hospital supplies such as syringes tripled in price.

One of the places worst hit was Tucuman, a region of over a million people and one of the world's biggest lemon exporters.

At the children's hospital, some 200 mothers milled by the emergency entrance. Some babies wailed in the heat. Others with the red-streaked hair caused by malnutrition slumped over their mothers' shoulders with listless eyes, motionless.

"It's the babies that don't cry that you worry about," said one doctor, who asked to remain anonymous.

A few miles away, Rosario Vargas, 18, stood by a wooden shack with her 18-month-old daughter who weighed 17.5 pounds—9 pounds underweight. Neither one had eaten for 24 hours. For breakfast she gave her daughter herbal tea.

"There are some days we eat nothing," Rosario added. Her daughter had sunken eyes that seemed to stare into space.

Source: Alistair Scrutton, "Children Starve in National Crisis," *South Florida Sun-Sentinel*, December 10, 2002, p. 25A.

WORLD POVERTY AND ECONOMICS

Some two-thirds of the world's population go to sleep hungry at night. The World Bank estimates that perhaps as much as one-quarter of the world survives on no more than $1 per day. Outright famine regularly occurs in various parts of the world—recent examples being the mass starvation of an estimated 1 million people in Ethiopia during the drought of 1984–1985; the estimated 3 million who died, mostly from disease and malnutrition in Congo between 1998 and 2003; the ongoing catastrophe in North Korea that has led many to consume grass and tree bark; and the 6 million Sudanese fleeing to the Darfur region from the country's ongoing civil war that the United Nations says are all currently at risk of starvation. Most of the hungry have no protection from the summer's heat or the winter's cold. They receive little or no medical care and live in unsanitary surroundings. Infant mortality is high, and life expectancy is low. While in the United States 8 infants out of each 1,000 live births die before reaching their fifth birthday, the rate explodes to more than 1 in 10 in places such as Ethiopia, Haiti, Pakistan, and Tanzania. At the opposite end of life, the typical Ethiopian can expect to die about 35 years earlier than his or her contemporary in the United States. Recognition that the misery of poverty is the lot of a majority of the world's population leads us to ask the questions: Why is it so? What are the causes? How can it be alleviated? This in turn leads us directly into the province of economics. An assessment and an analysis of poverty problems require an explicit understanding of the very foundations of economic activity. In this section, we sketch out these foundations.

Our Insatiable Wants

Economic activity springs from human wants and desires. Human beings want the things necessary to keep them alive—food and protection from the elements of nature. We usually want a great many other things, too, and the fulfillment of these wants and desires is the end toward which economic activity is directed.

As nearly as we can tell, human wants in the aggregate are unlimited, or insatiable. This is true because once our basic needs are met, we desire variety in the way they are met—variety in foods, in housing, in clothing, and in entertainment. Additionally, as we look around, we see other people enjoying things that we do not have, and we think that our level of well-being would be higher if we had those things, too. But perhaps most important, want-satisfying activity itself generates new wants. A new house generates wants for new furnishings—the old ones look shabby in the new setting. A college or university education opens the doors to wants that would never have existed if we had stayed on the farm or in the machine shop. To be sure, any one of us can saturate ourselves—temporarily, at least—with any one kind of good or service (like ice cream or beer), but almost all of us would like to have more than we have of almost everything and higher qualities of purchases than we now can obtain.

Our Limited Means

The fundamental economic problem is that the means available for satisfying wants are *scarce* or limited relative to the extent of the wants. The amounts and qualities of goods and services per year that an economic system can produce are limited because (1) the resources available to produce them cannot be increased by any great amount in any given year and (2) the technology available for production is subject to a limited degree of annual improvement.

An economy's *resources* are the ingredients that go into the making of goods (like automobiles) and services (like physical examinations). Production is similar to cooking. Resources (ingredients) are brought together; technology is used to process these resources in certain ways (mixing and cooking them); and finally a good or service results (a cake, perhaps). Some outputs of production processes are used directly to satisfy wants. Others become inputs for additional production processes. The resources available in an economy are usually divided into two broad classifications: (1) labor and (2) capital.

Labor resources consist of all the efforts of mind and muscle that can be used in production processes. Included are the ditchdigger's effort along with that of the heart surgeon and the university professor. There are many kinds and grades of labor resources; their main common characteristic is that they are human.

Capital resources consist of all the nonhuman ingredients that go into the production of goods and services. They include both natural and man-made ingredients of production. Ingredients such as land that is usable for agriculture or as

labor resources
The physical and mental efforts of an economy's people that are available to produce goods and services.

capital resources
All nonhuman ingredients of production. Capital resources can be further divided into natural and man-made categories.

space for production facilities, rivers, forests, and mineral deposits are all examples of natural capital resources. Man-made capital resources include factories and tools and machinery built up over time as well as semifinished materials such as sheets of steel and business inventories.

Resources are always scarce relative to the sum total of human wants. Consider the U.S. economy. The U.S. population is about 290 million. Most U.S. citizens want more things than they now have. Can the economy increase next year's production enough to fulfill all these wants? Obviously not. The labor force available from the present population cannot be increased substantially in either quantity or quality very quickly. Both may be increased over time by increasing the size of the population and through improving the education and training of the general population, but this increases total wants, too. The stocks of buildings, machines, tools, raw and semifinished materials, and usable land are not susceptible to rapid increases either; instead they are accumulated slowly over time.

technology
The know-how and the means and methods of production available within an economy.

Technology refers to the known means and methods available for combining resources to produce goods and services. Given the quantities of an economy's labor and capital resources, the better its technology, the greater the annual volume of goods and services it can turn out. Usually improvements in technology in an economic system result from increasing the scope and depth of its educational processes and from an ample supply of capital that provides a laboratory for experimentation, practice, and the generation of new ideas.

The Capacity of the Economy to Produce

Gross Domestic Product

The fundamental economic problem facing any society is scarcity: That is, in no society does there exist the resources and technology necessary to produce enough goods and services to fully satisfy all wants and desires. In much of the world, scarcity translates directly into the type of grinding poverty that was described in the introduction to this chapter. And even in relatively wealthy countries like the United States and Canada, while scarcity results in abject poverty for comparatively small minorities of the overall populations, even those at the top of the income spectrums, no doubt, feel that their overall level of well-being could be enhanced by higher quantities and qualities of existing goods and services or by

gross domestic product (GDP)
The market value of all final goods and services produced within an economy during a specific time period. GDP ignores the issue of whether ownership of the resources used for the production is domestic or foreign.

greater invention and innovation of new products. It is scarcity that forces each society to make economic choices as to how its resources can be best used. As a guiding principle, most economists define the best use of resources as that use which most fully satisfies the wants and desires of an economy's people. Put slightly differently, throughout our analysis, we assume that the goal of an economic system is to minimize the effects of scarcity or, more positively, to maximize social well-being. A first step in determining how well an economy is doing relative to this goal is to ascertain how effectively the economy is translating its labor and capital resources into goods and services. To this end, we wish to quantify, in dollar terms, the production of goods and services within an economy. Our primary measure of production is **gross domestic product (GDP),** which measures the total market value of all final goods and services produced within an economy during a specific time period.

As is true with any type of accounting, the measurement of national production using GDP can be quite misleading unless we have a clear understanding of what is, and what is not, measured by GDP. First, it is essential to bear in mind that GDP is measured in terms of market values or market prices. As such, increases in GDP can come about either through increases in the production of goods and services or simply through increases in average prices. The impacts of the two clearly have different effects on social well-being. Second, it is important to remember that GDP measures the total value of production taking place within a country, regardless of who might own the resources used in production. For example, even though Toyota Camrys are produced with capital resources owned by a Japanese company, the fact that the cars are built in Kentucky causes them to be considered part of U.S. GDP. From the opposite perspective, Chevrolet Impalas, being built in Canada, are not considered part of U.S. GDP even though Chevrolet is a division of an American firm. Finally, since we hope to use GDP as a first approximation of how well an economy is doing in fulfilling the goal of maximizing well-being, it is important to note that GDP is a measure of the dollar value of production only, which indicates nothing about who actually benefits from that production. Sometimes in the popular press GDP is referred to as the "economic pie." And if one wishes to assess how well an economy is doing in satisfying wants and desires, it is essential to know the size of the pie that is available for consumption. Equally important, however, is the number of people the pie must be distributed among and how evenly the pie is distributed. We take up each of these issues in detail later in this chapter.

Production Possibilities

Given an economy's available stocks of resources and level of technology, the combinations of goods and services that can compose its GDP are practically limitless. For simplicity, suppose that it produces only two items—food and education—and that all of its resources are devoted to producing these two items. The curve *AE* in Figure 1.1, called the **production possibilities curve,** represents all the maximum possible combinations of food and education that can be produced during one year. Thus, GDP might consist of 100 million tons of food per year if no education is produced as shown by point *A,* or 100 million student-years of education if no food is produced as shown by point *E.* Of course, there is no reason to devote all resources to producing one or the other of the two items, and thus a combination such as 90 million tons of food and 40 million student-years of education, as shown by point *B,* or any other combination along *AE* is possible. Equally possible is a combination like *F,* which yields a GDP of 50 million tons of food and 40 million student-years of education. This combination is clearly inefficient, however, because with the same stocks of resources and level of technology, the economy could produce up to 90 million tons of food without having to cut production of education below the 40 million student-year level. To be operating below the production possibilities curve indicates that either some of the economy's resources are not being used (called unemployment) or not being used to their fullest extent (called underemployment), or the economy is not using the best available technology.

production possibilities curve
Graphical representation of the maximum quantities of two goods and/or services that an economy can produce when its resources are used in the most efficient way possible.

FIGURE 1.1 **Production Possibilities Curve for an Economy**
Curve *AE* shows the maximum combinations of food and education that the economy's available resources and existing techniques of production can produce annually. Combinations such as *F* imply unemployment of resources or inefficiency in production. Those such as *G* are not attainable without increases in the quantity or quality of the economy's resources or an improvement in its production technology.

If the economy is originally producing combination *D* and then moves to combination *C*, the opportunity cost of the additional 8 million student-years of education is the 10 million tons of food that must be given up to produce it.

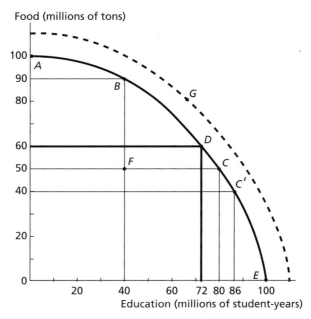

Operating below the curve would be of little consequence were it not for the fundamental economic problem of scarcity. That is, operating below the production possibilities curve makes the already difficult problem of scarcity worse.

Combinations of goods and services like *G*, lying above the production possibilities curve, while desirable, are not attainable given the economy's current stock of resources and level of technology. Over time, perhaps, production can be pressed to the higher level indicated by the dashed curve, but only if there is an increase in either the quality or the quantity of productive resources or an improvement in the level of technology. Outward shifts in the production possibilities curve are a graphical depiction of economic growth. We address the requisites for such growth briefly later in this chapter, but the concept of economic growth will be considered in detail in Chapter 13.

The Opportunity Cost Principle

Have you heard the expression "There is no such thing as a free lunch"? Actually, this is a simple way of expressing one of the most important concepts in economics, the **opportunity cost principle.** Suppose the economy is producing combination *D*, containing 60 million tons of food and 72 million student-years of

opportunity cost principle
The true cost of producing an additional unit of a good or service is the value of other goods or services that must be given up to obtain it.

education. Now let the output of education be increased to 80 million student-years. What is the cost to society of the additional 8 million student-years of education? The opportunity cost principle embodies an often overlooked but obvious point: If society's resources are initially fully and efficiently used as is true at *D,* an increase in the production of one good or service can come about only if the production of another good or service is reduced. In this sense, the true cost or opportunity cost to society of the additional 8 million student-years of education is the 10 million tons of food that must be forgone. An economy's ability to produce is limited by its resources and technology, and so more of one product necessarily means less of another or others.

The downward slope of the production possibilities curve shows the opportunity cost principle, or trade-off in production, that exists when an economy is operating at maximum efficiency. A quick glance at the production possibilities curve further indicates that this trade-off of food for education is not constant, however. That is, while the move from *D* to *C* requires society to give up 10 million tons of food for the additional 8 million student-years of education, the next 10 million tons of food given up releases only enough resources to produce an additional 6 million student-years of education (shown as the move from *C* to *C′*). In opportunity cost terms, it is becoming more costly for the economy to shift production from food to education. It is this **increasing opportunity cost** of production that gives the production possibilities curve its convex, or bowed-out, shape.

increasing opportunity cost As more of a particular good or service is produced, the cost in terms of other goods or services given up grows. This gives the production possibilities curve its bow shape.

The increase in opportunity costs as the economy concentrates more of its resources on producing education is due to the fact that all resources are not perfectly substitutable for one another. Suppose the economy is initially at point *A* on the production possibilities curve, producing only food, but then decides to produce some education as well. The cost in terms of forgone food is likely to be relatively low initially since the first resources to be taken out of production of food tend to be those resources that are least effective in producing food. That is, the first labor resources taken from food production will likely be those farmers and farm laborers who are not very good at farm life; the first land to be converted to school yards and university campuses is likely to be least fit for agricultural pursuits, and so on. As production of education is expanded further, resources of greater value in food production are increasingly drawn into educational pursuits, and thus relatively more food must be given up. The same would be true with all resources—not simply labor and land. This is especially true in a modern and quite complex economy in which there is a high degree of specialization among many, if not most, productive resources. The more specialized and less easily substituted an economy's resources are, the more extreme will be the bow in its production possibilities curve.

The Optimal Combination of Goods and Services

All combinations of food and education along the production possibilities curve *AE* in Figure 1.1 imply that the economy is producing as much of the two goods as possible, given its technology and scarce resources. But which of these combinations is best, or optimal? To answer this, recall that the primary goal we established for an economy was to maximize social well-being. Thus, the best combination is that which increases social well-being as much as possible. To see how we might, at least abstractly, arrive at this optimal combination, suppose that the economy is initially at combination *A* on the production possibilities curve, producing only food. What happens to well-being as the economy begins to move down the production possibilities curve toward point *B* and starts producing some education as well? For the shift to be consistent with the goal of maximizing social well-being, the public must be better off after the shift than it had been before. To make this determination, first consider the negative side of the shift. With each successive student-year of education produced, a certain amount of food must be given up. We call this the opportunity cost of the additional unit of education or, in slightly different terms, the **marginal social cost (*MSC*)** of the education. On the positive side, however, the shift in production gives society access to newly produced education, and the enhanced social well-being from each successive student-year of education is called the **marginal social benefit (*MSB*)** of the new schooling.

To determine whether each successive student-year of education between *A* and *B* should be produced, **cost-benefit analysis** can be applied. In general terms, cost-benefit analysis indicates that expansion of an activity serves to enhance well-being when it yields greater benefits than costs. Applying cost-benefit analysis in this context, we can conclude that each additional student-year of education should be produced as long as its marginal social benefit is at least as great as its marginal social cost.

Movements along the production possibilities curve then can be evaluated based on a comparison of marginal social benefits and costs. Any movement for which *MSB* > *MSC* of necessity improves social well-being, while the reverse would lead to falling well-being. With these tools we can get a better handle on the question of the optimal combination of goods and services. Suppose that for each successive student-year of education from *A* to *B*, social well-being is, in fact, enhanced since *MSB* > *MSC*. What about further movements down the curve? If these first increments in the production of education yielded greater benefits than costs, why would this not continue to be true as even more of the economy's resources are devoted to education? Unfortunately, this will not be the case indefinitely because with each increase in the production of education and the corresponding fall in the production of food, the benefits of further shifts to education decline while the costs rise. From society's perspective, the greatest marginal benefit from education no doubt comes as the public moves from illiteracy to basic, functional literacy. Especially in modern society, anyone who is unable to read and do simple arithmetic will have great difficulty making a significant contribution to GDP. Beyond basic literacy, while additional years of education clearly add to well-being, their addition is likely to be, on average, of declining value. Thus, as production is shifted from food to education, the greatest marginal value is found for the early increments in education. In other words, as more education is produced and consumed, the *MSB* from additional education falls.

---

marginal social cost (*MSC*)
The true cost (opportunity cost) borne by society when the production of a good or service is increased by one unit.

marginal social benefit (*MSB*)
The true benefit to society of a one-unit increase in the production of a good or service.

cost-benefit analysis
A technique for determining the optimal level of an economic activity. In general, an activity should be expanded so long as the expansion leads to greater benefits than costs.

On the cost side, recall that the production possibilities curve is bow-shaped due to the concept of increasing opportunity cost of production. In this context, as we expand the production of education, the value of the food that we must give up rises—that is, the *MSC* of education increases. As we move down the production possibilities curve, then, any gap between *MSB* and *MSC* that might initially exist tends to narrow. Once we reach the combination at which *MSB = MSC*, no further shifts in production will lead to increasing well-being. To go beyond this point would imply that we produced and consumed an increment in education which was not worth what it cost. Consequently, the optimal combination of goods and services is defined as that combination where the marginal social benefit of production just equals marginal social cost. How does a complex modern economy arrive at this combination of goods and services and the allocation of resources embodied in it? This question is the basis for Chapter 2.

Assessing Well-Being Using GDP

Adjusting GDP for Inflation

GDP was not created to be used as a measure of overall well-being; rather, its primary use is simply as a gauge of the value of production that takes place within an economy. Before it can be used to even roughly assess the overall well-being of a county's inhabitants, a number of adjustments must be made. First, when we are evaluating an economy's performance over time, we must take into account that an increase in GDP, far from indicating a general improvement in well-being, may simply result from an increase in the average level of prices—inflation. In an economy that produces only food and education, calculating GDP requires that the quantity of food produced be multiplied by the average price of food, making the same calculation for education and adding the total values together. Consequently, if we look at data for a series of years and find that GDP in dollar terms is rising, we cannot be certain whether the economy's production is increasing or whether average prices are rising. If the increase in GDP is due to increasing production, overall well-being may be increasing, but if the increase in GDP is due either entirely or predominately to inflation, overall well-being may be declining.

To see the effect of inflation on GDP, consider a very simplistic economy in which only one good, bread, is produced. Suppose that during 2003, the economy produces 1,000 loaves which are sold for $1 each. GDP for this economy in 2003 is simply $1,000 (1,000 times $1). Now suppose that during 2004 the economy continues to produce 1,000 loaves, but due to inflation each loaf sells for $2. GDP for 2004 is $2,000. Thus, between 2003 and 2004, GDP doubles even though the production of bread remains unchanged. The entire increase in GDP is due to inflation.

To correct for inflation, the entire series of GDP *numbers at price levels for each year* must be converted to a "base" year price level. Suppose we use 2003 as the base year and want to convert 2004 GDP to 2003 prices. The relationship between 2003 and 2004 can be depicted with price index numbers. In percentage terms, the price index for each year is calculated by dividing each year's price level (or

TABLE 1.1   Calculating Real GDP Using a Price Index

Year	(1) Production of Bread (Loaves)	(2) Price of Bread	(3) GDP in Current Dollars (1) × (2)	(4) Price Index Percentage and Decimal Forms	(5) Real GDP (2003 Dollars) (3)/(4) (in Decimals)
2003	1,000	$1.00	$1,000	($1/$1) × 100 = 100, or 1.00	$1,000
2004	1,000	2.00	2,000	($2/$1) × 100 = 200, or 2.00	1,000

average price level if more than one item is produced) by the price level that existed in the base year, then multiplying by 100, as in Table 1.1. Thus, the price index for 2003 is 100 (2003 price of $1 divided by the base year price, also 2003, of $1, then multiplying by 100). Likewise the price index for 2004 is 200, indicating that the average price in 2004 is 200 percent of the average for 2003. Once price index numbers are created for each year, the GDP data can be corrected for inflation by dividing each year's GDP in current dollars by that year's price index, after converting the index to decimal form. That is, 2003's inflation-corrected GDP is equal to its current dollar GDP of $1,000 divided by the 2003 price index of 1, in decimals, or simply $1,000. Inflation-corrected GDP for 2004 is found in the same way and is also $1,000 since current-dollar GDP in 2004 is $2,000 but the price index for the year is 2. When current-dollar GDP is corrected for inflation, the result is **real GDP.** In this example, while current-dollar GDP doubles between 2003 and 2004, real GDP remains constant, reflecting the fact that production is unchanged. In this way, real GDP shows us what is happening over time to the economy's real production of goods and services.

Adjusting GDP for Population

When we look at a series of GDP data, we must correct the series for the misleading effects of inflation. A second adjustment that must be made, regardless of whether we are considering a series of GDP data or simply one year's GDP, concerns the number of people that GDP must be spread among. That is, GDP in China is many times that of Switzerland, but since China's GDP must be spread among so many more people, the average level of well-being of the Swiss population is many times that of the Chinese population.

Adjusting GDP for differences in population requires that GDP be divided by the population of the country in question. But which GDP value, GDP in current prices or real GDP, should we use in the calculation? This depends on the data that we are analyzing. If we are looking at the performance of a single economy over time, the appropriate measure would be inflation-adjusted (real) GDP divided by the population, since prices are not likely to remain constant over time. This would be called **per capita real GDP.** Alternatively, if we are analyzing a country's GDP data for only one year, the appropriate measure would be GDP in current prices divided by the population, known simply as **per capita GDP.** For any one country, per capita real GDP for a series of years indicates whether the performance of the

real GDP
GDP in current dollars corrected for inflation. The correction requires dividing each year's GDP in current dollars by that year's price index, in decimal form.

per capita real GDP
Real GDP divided by population.

per capita GDP
GDP in current dollars divided by population.

TABLE 1.2   U.S. Gross Domestic Product in Current and Real Dollars, 1980–2002

Source: *Economic Report of the President*, February 2004, available at http://www.gpoaccess.gov/eop/index.html, Tables B-1, B-3, and B-34.

(1) Year	(2) GDP, Current Dollars (Billions)	(3) Price Index	(4) GDP, Real 2000 Dollars (Billions)	(5) Population (Millions)	(6) GDP, Real per Capita (2000 Dollars)
1980	2,789.5	54.06	5,160.0	227.7	22,661.40
1981	3,128.4	59.13	5,290.7	230.0	23,003.04
1982	3,255.0	62.73	5,188.9	232.2	22,346.68
1983	3,536.7	65.21	5,423.6	234.3	23,148.10
1984	3,933.2	67.66	5,813.2	236.3	24,600.93
1985	4,220.3	69.71	6,054.1	238.5	25,384.07
1986	4,462.8	71.25	6,263.6	240.7	26,022.43
1987	4,739.5	73.19	6,475.6	242.8	26,670.51
1988	5,103.8	75.69	6,743.0	245.0	27,522.45
1989	5,484.4	78.56	6,981.2	247.3	28,229.68
1990	5,803.1	81.59	7,112.5	250.1	28,438.62
1991	5,995.9	84.44	7,100.7	252.5	28,121.90
1992	6,337.7	86.39	7,336.1	256.9	28,556.25
1993	6,657.4	88.38	7,532.7	260.3	28,938.53
1994	7,072.2	90.26	7,835.4	263.4	29,747.15
1995	7,397.7	92.11	8,031.4	266.6	30,125.28
1996	7,816.9	93.85	8,329.1	269.7	30,882.82
1997	8,304.3	93.41	8,890.2	272.9	32,576.77
1998	8,747.0	96.47	9,067.1	276.5	32,839.91
1999	9,268.4	97.87	9,470.1	279.3	33,906.55
2000	9,817.0	100.00	9,817.0	282.4	34,762.75
2001	10,100.8	102.37	9,866.9	285.3	34,384.29
2002	10,480.8	103.95	10,082.5	288.2	34,984.39

economy, in terms of the average well-being of its inhabitants, is improving. When our intent is to roughly compare differences in well-being between countries at one point in time, per capita GDP is most useful.

In Table 1.2 we track the performance of the U.S. economy for the period 1980 through 2002 as an example of how per capita real GDP is calculated and used to shed light on changes in potential well-being. Current-dollar GDP is listed in column (2). The price index is found in column (3), in percentage terms, and uses 2000 as its base. Column (4) gives real GDP and is obtained by dividing column (2) by column (3), after converting the price index to decimals.

The first item of interest in Table 1.2 is the fact that real GDP declined during 1982 and 1991, even though current-dollar GDP increased during each of these years. This indicates that while actual production was falling in these years, the falls in production were more than offset by price increases, reinforcing the need to adjust current-dollar GDP for the effects of inflation. In each of these years, fewer goods and services were available for consumption than had been available in the preceding year. When the nation's output of goods and services declines in this way, we say that the economy is in *recession*. Sometimes, however, the economy is in recession even though this may not be immediately obvious when looking at annual data on GDP. This occurred most recently in 2001. We experienced declining production during three quarters of that year, yet, as Table 1.2 shows, both current-dollar and real GDP increased for the entire year. What happened, of course, was that while production fell during nine months of 2001, that fall was more than offset by the increases in production that took place during the remaining three months of the year. Consequently, while both current-dollar and real GDP increased for 2001, it was still a year in which a recession occurred.

Graphically, during the recessionary years of 1982, 1991, and 2001, the U.S. economy operated below the production possibilities curve, indicating that the average well-being of the population was lower than its potential. A rough estimate of average well-being can be found by dividing real GDP by population, giving real per capita GDP, as in column (6). Here again we find declines during the recessionary years of 1982 and 1991. More interestingly, even though both current-dollar and real GDP increased during 2001, per capita real GDP does show a decline, additional confirmation of that year's recession.

Table 1.3 reports data on population, GDP in current prices, and per capita GDP for selected countries in 2002 (ignore the other data in the table for now). Here, we use current-dollar GDP rather than real GDP since we are considering only one year's data. To maintain consistency, GDP for all countries is converted to U.S. dollar values. We arbitrarily classify a country as lesser developed (LDC) if its per capita GDP is less than $6,500 per year and as developed (DC) if its per capita GDP is greater than this level. Data of this sort provide direct insight into the economic problem of scarcity and allow for a rough international comparison of average well-being.

GDP in the United States during 2002 was roughly $10.5 trillion. That is, during 2002 there was about $10.5 trillion in goods and services available for consumption by the country's 288 million citizens. Dividing GDP by the population yields a per capita GDP of $36,366. Thus, if U.S. national production were equally divided in 2002, each member of the public would have had about $36,000 of goods and services at his or her disposal. Compare this with the plight of the average citizen in an LDC. In Zambia, for example, the per capita GDP is only $363 per year. And poverty of this nature is not simply an isolated problem, but rather commonplace in much of the world. Whereas scarcity in DCs is primarily a problem of not having all wants and desires satisfied, in much—or even most—of the world, scarcity translates into the type of grinding poverty noted in the introduction to this chapter. Finally, bear in mind that the problem of poverty that plagues much of the world is not simply an academic abstraction. Rather, as is pointed out in Table 1.3, it translates directly into early death. While an individual fortunate enough to be born in a DC in 2002 could count on an average life of 79 years, his counterpart born in an LDC would likely leave this life 16 years earlier.

TABLE 1.3   Per Capita GDP and Population, Actual and Growth Rates, Population Density, Annual Growth Rate of Real GDP, and Life Expectancy in Selected Countries

Source: World Bank, *World Development Indicators Online,* available at https://publications.worldbank.org/commerce.

Country	Population Estimate 2002 (Millions)	Annual Rate of Population Increase	Population Density per Square Kilometer (2002)	Per Capital GDP* (2002)	Percentage Annual Growth Rate of Real GDP	Life Expectancy at Birth, Latest Available Dates
Lesser developed						
Chile	16	1.2	21	4,115	2.1	76
China	1,28	0.7	137	992	8.0	71
Colombia	44	1.6	42	1,851	1.6	72
Egypt	68	1.8	67	1,354	3.0	69
El Salvador	6	1.7	310	2,228	2.1	70
Ethiopia	6.9	2.2	67	90	2.7	42
India	1,050	1.5	352	486	4.6	64
Indonesia	212	1.3	117	816	3.7	67
Kenya	31	2.0	55	393	1.0	46
Mexico	101	1.4	53	6,307	0.9	73
Nigeria	133	2.2	146	327	−0.9	45
Peru	27	1.5	21	2,116	4.8	70
Philippines	80	2.1	268	976	4.4	70
South Africa	45	1.2	37	2,296	3.0	46
Thailand	62	0.7	120	2,062	5.4	69
Venezuela	25	1.8	28	3,757	−8.8	74
Zambia	10	1.7	14	363	3.3	37
Average		1.5			2.4	63
Developed						
Canada	31	0.9	3	22,739	3.3	79
France	60	0.5	108	24,034	1.2	79
Germany	82	0.2	236	24,000	0.2	78
Italy	58	0.0	196	20,451	0.4	78
Japan	127	0.1	348	31,417	0.3	82
Singapore	4	0.8	6,827	20,893	2.2	78
Sweden	9	0.3	22	26,894	1.9	80
Switzerland	7.0	0.8	184	36,626	0.0	80
United Kingdom	59	0.3	246	26,520	1.8	77
United States	288	1.1	31	36,366	2.4	77
Average		0.5			1.4	79

*At market prices (U.S. dollars).

TABLE 1.4   The Distribution of Income within an Economy

	Annual Income Family A	Annual Income Family B	Annual Income Family C	Annual Income Family D	Annual Income Family E	Annual Income of All Families	Average Annual Family Income
Alpha	$2,000	$2,000	$2,000	$2,000	$ 2,000	$10,000	$2,000
Omega	0	0	0	0	10,000	10,000	2,000

Adjusting GDP for Distribution

The data in Table 1.3 indicate that much of the world's population suffers from a degree of misery that is probably unintelligible to those of us living in DCs. Yet, even the dire circumstances reflected by the data understate the true extent of human misery that afflicts so many, because average measures of well-being such as per capita GDP fail to take into account the unequal distribution of GDP within a country. Consider again Zambia with its per capita GDP of $363. Clearly, life would seem to amount to mere subsistence for a Zambian earning only $363 per year. Yet, most Zambians would dearly love to earn this "average" amount of income. In Zambia, with its very limited GDP, the problem of human misery is greatly complicated by the very uneven distribution of GDP. While a fortunate few earn many times more than $363 per year, the majority of Zambians have annual incomes far below this average figure.

What is meant by the distribution of GDP, or the distribution of income as it is more commonly known, may be best understood by considering a simple example. Suppose that there are two economies, Alpha and Omega, each composed of five families, A through E. Further, suppose that in Alpha each of the families earns $2,000 per year, while in Omega families A through D have no income and family E earns $10,000 per year, as presented in Table 1.4. In each economy, then, the annual income for all families, or GDP, is $10,000 and the average income is $2,000. Do these facts suggest that the people of each economy are equally well off? Obviously not. Simply looking at averages is quite misleading in this case since, although GDP levels are the same, the distribution of GDP differs so markedly between the two countries.

In the real world, of course, it is unlikely that either the perfectly equal distribution of Alpha or the perfectly unequal distribution of Omega will exist. But with a little reflection on Table 1.4, a way of evaluating actual distributions of GDP becomes apparent. That is, why is the distribution of income in Alpha considered to be perfectly equal? The answer is straightforward: Each of the five families controls the same share of Alpha's income ($2,000). Put differently, each of the five families represents one-fifth, or 20 percent, of Alpha's population, and at the same time, each of the five controls one-fifth, or 20 percent, of Alpha's GDP ($2,000/$10,000). Thus, perfect equality exists when each 20 percent "chunk" of an economy's families controls 20 percent of the economy's income.

TABLE 1.5   The Distribution of Income in Selected Countries

Source: World Bank. *World Development Indicators Online*, available at https://publications.worldbank.org/commerce.

Country (Year of Study)	Total Income or GDP Controlled by Each Group of Families				
	Poorest 20 Percent	Second 20 Percent	Third 20 Percent	Fourth 20 percent	Richest 20 Percent
Lesser Developed					
Chile (2000)	3.3%	6.6%	10.5%	17.4%	62.2%
China (2001)	4.7	9.0	14.2	22.1	50.0
Colombia (1996)	3.0	6.6	11.1	18.4	60.9
Egypt (1995)	9.8	13.2	16.6	21.4	39.0
El Salvador (2000)	2.9	7.4	12.4	20.2	57.2
Ethiopia (2000)	9.1	13.2	16.8	21.5	39.4
India (2000)	8.9	12.3	16.0	21.2	41.6
Indonesia (2002)	8.4	11.9	15.4	30.9	43.3
Kenya (1994)	5.0	9.7	14.2	20.9	50.2
Mexico (2000)	3.1	7.2	11.7	19.0	59.1
Nigeria (1996)	4.4	8.2	12.5	19.3	55.7
Peru (2000)	2.9	8.3	14.3	21.5	53.2
Philippines (2000)	5.4	8.8	13.1	20.5	52.3
South Africa (1993)	3.3	5.8	9.8	17.7	63.3
Thailand (2000)	6.0	9.5	13.6	21.2	53.1
Zambia (1996)	4.2	8.2	12.8	20.1	54.8
Average	5.2	9.2	13.4	20.2	52.2
Developed					
Canada (1994)	7.5	12.9	17.2	23.0	39.3
France (1995)	7.2	12.6	17.2	22.8	40.2
Germany (2000)	8.5	13.7	17.9	23.0	36.8
Italy (1995)	6.5	12.0	16.8	22.7	42.0
Japan (1993)	10.6	14.2	17.6	22.0	35.7
Singapore (1982–93)	5.1	9.9	14.6	21.4	48.9
Sweden (2000)	9.2	14.0	17.6	22.7	36.6
Switzerland (1992)	6.9	12.7	17.3	22.9	40.3
United Kingdom (1991)	6.6	11.5	16.3	22.7	43.0
United States (2000)	5.4	10.7	15.7	22.4	45.8
Average	7.4	12.4	16.8	22.5	40.9

How closely do existing economies come to perfect equality? Are there systematic differences in income distribution between LDCs and DCs? Answers to these questions are found in Table 1.5, which reports data on income distribution for selected LDCs and DCs. (You will note that, as is customary, Table 1.5 ranks each economy's families from poorest to richest rather than in randomly chosen 20 percent groups.)

To see the impact of the distribution of GDP on individual well-being, again consider Zambia. Recall that Zambia has a per capita GDP of $363, which was suggested to understate the degree of poverty felt by Zambians. If GDP were equally distributed, that is, if all Zambians earned $363 per year, then each 20 percent chunk of Zambian families would control approximately 20 percent of Zambian GDP. Yet, as Table 1.5 points out, this is not the case. As miserable as their plight would be with a perfectly equal distribution of income yielding a 20 percent share of GDP for the "poorest" families, in reality these families control only 4.2 percent of Zambian GDP. Thus, if the meager Zambian GDP were equally distributed, giving meaning to the per capita GDP value of $363, the families making up the poorest 20 percent grouping would find their income increasing by about a factor of 5 (rising from 4.2 to 20 percent).

This is not to suggest that all Zambians earn less than the average of $363. Such cannot be the case if the average is properly calculated. Table 1.5 indicates that while a majority of Zambian families are truly impoverished, some families are relatively rich. Note the share of Zambian GDP controlled by the richest 20 percent of families. The 54.8 percent share of national income controlled by this group indicates that the degree of human misery brought on by Zambia's extremely limited GDP is greatly worsened by the fact that this limited GDP is very unequally distributed.

Is this situation unique to Zambia? Unfortunately not. As the averages for the shares of GDP controlled by each group of families for the different countries indicate, the degree of income inequality in LDCs is much greater than in DCs. This is not to suggest that the DCs have distributions that approximate perfect equality. In fact, some may feel that the degree of income inequality that exists in DCs is unacceptably high. The importance of Table 1.5 is that the data indicate that the degree of inequality that exists appears to be significantly greater in LDCs than in DCs. Given this, it may be concluded that the degree of human misery reflected by average measures of well-being such as per capita GDP fails to describe accurately the misery suffered by much of the world's population.

CAUSES OF POVERTY AND REQUISITES OF ECONOMIC GROWTH

The economic roots of world poverty become reasonably clear from an examination of the foundations of economic analysis. In some cases, an economy may be operating to its potential, that is, operating on its production possibilities curve, and yet pervasive poverty is still the rule. Often mentioned as problems in this regard are pressures from the size and growth of an economy's population. Whether population pressures are the primary problem, when an economy's production possibilities are such that even achieving maximum output results in excessive poverty, remedial action must be directed toward economic growth. Pushing the production possibilities curve outward requires improvement in either the quality and quantity of a nation's labor and capital resources or an improvement in the overall level of technology—and occasionally an improvement in both. In other cases, poverty results from relatively inefficient production methods. Here remedies should be targeted toward returning the economy to its production possibilities curve. These topics are the focus for the rest of this book; we briefly introduce them here.

Quality of the Labor Force   Almost without exception, LDCs have labor forces that are not very well educated and thus not very productive relative to DCs. For example, whereas the adult illiteracy rate in the United States is only about 1 percent, the rate rises above 50 percent in countries like Haiti and Ethiopia. Education is the key to improvement in the quality of a country's labor force. As literacy rates increase, so do the possibilities for upgrading the skills of the labor force. A broad-based primary education system is a prerequisite for literacy, and literacy is, in turn, a basic foundation for economic growth. Beyond the primary level, secondary and higher education are important in improving labor force quality in that they develop workers who are more capable of problem solving and innovation. Clearly, development of a comprehensive educational system is essential to providing rising living standards. Equally clearly, developing such a system is difficult in a society whose population lives close to, or at, a subsistence level.

Stock of Capital and Capital Accumulation   Small amounts of available capital resources and, thus, low capital-to-labor ratios translate directly into low labor productivity and poverty. Countries with limited mineral deposits, meager supplies of tools and machinery, and poorly developed transportation and communications networks usually have low per capita GDPs. Capital accumulation is necessary if a country is to break out of a poverty prison. But capital accumulation requires that some of a country's annual output of consumer goods and services be sacrificed in favor of production of capital goods and development of resources. As is true with the development of an educational system, this is particularly difficult when many of a country's citizens suffer from malnutrition or even starvation.

Technology   A trip through the countryside and a visit to the industrial production sites in a poor country typically reveal very primitive techniques of production. Failure or inability to adapt to modern production techniques translates directly into low productivity and poverty. Unfortunately for LDCs, to some extent, technological development goes hand in hand with capital accumulation and the development of educational systems. High levels of technology are seldom developed in poor countries.

Efficiency   In many poor countries, available resources are neither fully nor efficiently used. Often, traditional ways of doing things block adaptation of new and efficient production techniques. For example, it is easy to find poor countries naturally endowed with potentially productive agricultural land but which, based on traditional tenure systems, hold the land in units too small to allow for maximum efficiency. In other countries, rigid wage systems make it uneconomical for potential employers to hire the entire labor force, leading to unemployment.

Population   Are population pressures serious threats to living standards? Evidence on this issue is presented in Table 1.3. Consider first the issue of population and the density of population. Does the absolute level of a country's population or its density preclude a high level of well-being? The answer is no on both counts. While India and China are examples of LDCs with very large populations, the United States and Japan are examples of DCs with both high levels of well-being and relatively large populations. In addition, many of the LDCs listed in Table 1.3 have relatively small populations. As for the concentration of population, known as *population density,* consider Ethiopia and Singapore. Ethiopia, truly one of the most impoverished countries on earth, has a low 67 persons per square kilometer, while Singapore, with a per capita GDP many times that of Ethiopia, is home to about 6,800 people per square kilometer. Similar outcomes exist for the relatively wealthy and densely populated United States and Japan and for the relatively poor, less densely populated Zambia, Chile, and Argentina. Finally, what of pressures from population growth? The evidence here is mixed. Whereas some LDCs such as Kenya, Nigeria, and Venezuela have both relatively high rates of population growth and economies that have been recently stagnant, just the opposite is true elsewhere. As examples, consider Egypt, Ethiopia, and the Philippines, which each recorded relatively high GDP and population growth rates recently.

What may we then conclude with respect to the impact of population pressures on poverty? Perhaps the most defensible conclusion would be that while population pressures are not the fundamental cause of world poverty, excessive population growth does tend to complicate the problem of scarcity. At the very least, we know that if overall well-being is to increase, real GDP must grow more rapidly than population.

CAN GOVERNMENTS HELP?

What, if anything, can governments do to help solve world poverty problems? Over the last few decades, populations have looked increasingly to their governments to solve their problems for them. Governments, in turn, have accepted more responsibility for solving the economic problems of their populations. Unfortunately, people often expect more of their governments than those governments can provide. And governments often promise more than they are able to deliver.

Governments of LDCs

The single most important decision that government must make with respect to economic development concerns the extent to which economic decision making will be influenced by government. The options range from little or no government involvement to decision making based entirely on government dictate. As will be discussed in Chapter 2, the ongoing movement away from extreme government interference in economic decision making that is sweeping through eastern Europe, China, and Vietnam indicates that economic development may be enhanced by reducing the economic role of government. To see this, return to Table 1.3 and note China's remarkable average annual rate of growth in real GDP of 8 percent, greater than any country listed in either the LDC or DC groups. Although it may seem paradoxical, the governments of many LDCs, rather than being vehicles for economic improvement, are burdens to development. In general, economic development tends to reach its potential when private parties, rather than government, are allowed to own economic resources and decide the use for those resources. Economists refer to this as *private property rights*. Equally important, resource owners must be allowed to reap the benefits of well-made decisions on resource use, and they must also be allowed to suffer the penalty of poorly made decisions. Governments of LDCs, then, would well serve the development interests of their people by making sure that their involvement in economic activity is limited to those areas where the economy, left to its own devices, clearly fails to achieve desired development goals. In this regard, the governments of LDCs should pursue policies that improve the quality of the labor force, enhance capital accumulation, raise levels of technology, increase efficiency, and, perhaps, slow population growth. This is a tall order—more easily said than done.

In most countries where literacy rates are high, governments have assumed responsibilities for primary education. In many countries this responsibility has been extended to secondary and even to higher education. Insofar as it can, the government of an LDC would be well advised to emulate these countries. But universal education does not come easily or without cost. The establishment of an educational system is a slow, expensive task. Physical facilities must be built, and a corps of teachers must be trained. LDCs find it very difficult to divert resources from the provision of subsistence goods to the provision of education. The immediate opportunity cost of additional education is high for a hungry population.

Most government help in the capital accumulation process will be indirect rather than direct. Governments cannot create new capital resources directly, but they can establish an economic climate favorable to capital accumulation. They can pursue monetary and fiscal policies conducive to economic stability. They can enact tax laws that provide special incentives for capital accumulation. It is also important that those who engage in saving and investing in new capital equipment be allowed to reap the rewards for doing so. In many instances, capital accumulation is discouraged because revenue-hungry governments tax away the returns that accrue from it.

Government officials in LDCs often speak glibly about such things as raising the levels of technology and increasing the operating efficiencies of their economies. One of the most positive things they can do in this respect is to press development of social infrastructure to the maximum extent that their resources will allow. For example, transportation networks and communications networks contribute greatly to efficiency. So do energy and power systems.

Sparked by governmental activities, some positive action appears to be under way in certain parts of the world concerning population control. For example, in India, Thailand, and China, massive government educational efforts for birth control and family planning have been made. In any case, during the past couple of decades trends in world population growth appear to have turned downward.

Governments of DCs

Since World War II, the economically advanced countries of the world have provided some economic assistance to LDCs, partly for humanitarian reasons and partly in hopes of obtaining ideological allegiance from the LDCs. In this regard, there has been much rivalry between communist countries and those of the Western world. Some aid to LDCs has been channeled through international agencies such as the World Bank. At the same time, individual countries have conducted aid programs of their own. Basically, aid takes two forms: (1) loans and grants and (2) technical assistance.

Loans and grants generally are expected to help the recipient countries improve their labor forces, accumulate capital, improve their technological capabilities, and increase the efficiencies of their production processes. They are used to build educational facilities and for sanitary engineering purposes. They help construct power plants, cement plants, communications and transportation facilities, agricultural facilities, and the like. They are also used to import such things as fertilizer, raw and semifinished materials, industrial equipment, agricultural equipment, and spare parts.

Technical assistance helps in upgrading labor force skills and in advancing the technologies of the recipient countries. Much technical assistance is turned toward increasing the productivity of agricultural resources, improving educational systems, and raising standards of public health. In addition, advisors from the DCs often assist in getting industrial projects under way.

The World Bank is an organization through which DCs can jointly assist LDCs. It provides both low-interest loans from funds supplied by the DCs and technical assistance to low-income countries. Loans are made for a variety of projects, large and small, public and private. Bank officials require that the projects for which loans are made show every promise of paying off both the principal and the interest. The World Bank has been quite successful in this respect but has often been criticized as being too stingy with its loans.

Summary

Abject poverty is without question the major economic problem of the world. This has always been so, but it has become the focus of great concern for nations and for large numbers of persons in recent years. To understand its causes and achieve its possible alleviation, an understanding of the nature of economics and economic activity is necessary.

Economic activity is generated by the wants of human beings, which seem to be insatiable in the aggregate. The means available in any economy for satisfying the wants of its population are scarce. They consist of the economy's resources—its labor and its capital—along with its available technology. The supplies of resources, together with the level of technology available, determine the maximum GDP that the country can produce to satisfy wants. Dividing a country's GDP by its population yields its per capita GDP, which is a rough measure of its citizens' average well-being. Further insight into actual well-being is achieved when the distribution of GDP is taken into account, as well.

The basic elements of economic activity and economic analysis provide insight into the causes of poverty. Poverty stems from low labor force qualities, little capital for labor to work with, low levels of technology, inefficiencies in the use of resources, and, in some instances, excessive rates of population growth. To break out of the poverty trap, a country must make progress in attacking some or all of the causes. But it is unlikely to make much progress unless it achieves a marked degree of political and economic stability.

Developed countries can and do assist LDCs as they strive to improve their economic lots. Aid takes two basic forms: (1) loans or grants and (2) technical assistance. Individual DCs have independent aid programs. They also engage in joint aid programs through such organizations as the World Bank.

Discussion Questions

1. GDP measures the total value of production within an economy during a specific time period. What adjustments must be made to GDP before it can be used as a rough measure of social well-being?

2. Explain how GDP and real GDP differ.

3. Using a production possibilities curve, explain the opportunity cost principle.

4. Using a production possibilities curve, explain the concept of increasing opportunity costs.

5. What would a linear (straight-line) production possibilities curve imply?

6. Often it is blithely stated that "a country should pull itself up by its own bootstraps." From the standpoint of shifting the production possibilities curve outward, improving educational systems is an example of this. Referring to the data for LDCs in Table 1.3, discuss the practical problems of such a recommendation for a very poor country.

7. Production possibilities curves are typically assumed to be convex, or bowed out. Explain the economic implications of this shape.

8. Cost-benefit analysis is one of the most versatile tools in economic analysis. Suppose the end of the semester is approaching and you have to begin preparing for exams. Explain how you might use cost-benefit analysis to maximize your grade point average.

9. Make up an example that shows that GDP can increase even though real production is falling within an economy between two years.

10. If the goal of public spending is to shift the production possibilities curve of an economy outward, which of the following proposals would seem most likely to succeed: the purchase of a nuclear-powered aircraft carrier; a "hot meals" program for the elderly; a job training program for unemployed workers?

11. Suppose an economy produces only food and housing. Draw and explain the characteristics of its production possibilities curve. Show and explain the impact on the curve of (*a*) a new technology that improves food production only; (*b*) a new invention that improves both food and housing production.

12. Using the concepts of marginal social benefit and marginal social cost, explain how the optimal combination of goods can be determined in an economy that produces only two goods.

13. From a standpoint of evaluating a country's economic performance over time, does it matter what year one chooses as the base year in calculating a price index?

14. Using the data of Table 1.3, calculate the GDP (not per capita GDP) of both the United States and China. If both economies continue to grow at their current rates, as listed in Table 1.3, when would the Chinese economy overtake the U.S. economy in terms of GDP?

Additional Readings

Bello, Walden, with Shea Cunningham and Bill Rau. *Dark Victory: The United States and Global Poverty.* 2nd ed. Oakland, CA: Food First Books, 1999.
Discusses the role the United States and other industrialized countries have had in global poverty.

Collier, Paul, and David Dollar. *Globalization, Growth, and Poverty: Building an Inclusive World Economy.* Policy Research Report. Washington, DC: World Bank; New York: Oxford University Press, 2002.
This World Bank report includes charts on world poverty, worldwide household inequality, wage growth by country group, GDP, and population density.

Haggard, Stephan. *Developing Nations and the Politics of Global Integration.* Washington, DC: The Brookings Institution, 1995.
Focuses on East and Southeast Asia and Latin America's international trade policies.

Kincaid, A. Douglas, and Alejandro Portes, eds. *Comparative National Development: Society and Economy in the New Global Order.* Chapel Hill: University of North Carolina Press, 1994.
Group of essays that discusses international economic development.

Landes, David S. *The Wealth and Poverty of Nations: Why Some Are So Rich and Some Are So Poor.* New York: Norton, 1999.
This bestseller presents the wealth and poverty of countries from a historical perspective and shows why Europe, and thus the United States, became the world's richest geographical area.

Meier, Gerald M., and James E. Rauch, eds. *Leading Issues in Economic Development.* 7th ed. Oxford, England: Oxford University Press, 2000.
Provides a thorough treatment of the major issues in economic development.

Mittleman, James H., and Mustapha Kamal Pasha. *Out from Underdevelopment Revisited.* New York: St. Martin's Press, 1997.
Discusses underdevelopment of the Third World and strategies for development.

Salvatore, Dominick, ed. *World Population Trends and Their Impact on Economic Development.* Contributions in Economics and Economic History, number 82. New York: Greenwood Press, 1988.
Fourteen essays that cover economic development, migration, population growth, status of women, and other topics.

Van De Walle, Dominique, and Kimberly Nead, eds. *Public Spending and the Poor: Theory and Evidence.* 2nd ed. Baltimore: Johns Hopkins University Press, 2000.
This book is an excellent analysis of the relations between public spending programs and the plight of the poor from an international perspective.

Weibe, Keith, Nicole Ballenger, and Per Pinstrup-Andersen, eds. *Who Will Be Fed in the 21st Century? Challenges for Science and Policy.* Baltimore: The Johns Hopkins University Press, 2001.
Contributors discuss how technological advances could affect the supply of food and how poverty could affect the demand for food.

Wolff, Edward N. *Economics of Poverty, Inequality, and Discrimination.* Cincinnati: South-Western College Publishing, 1997.
Although most of this book deals explicitly with poverty in the United States, Chapter 3 is a thorough treatment of income inequality from an international perspective.

World Development Report. New York: Oxford University Press, annual.
Outstanding source for data on development issues. Includes data on income, population, life expectancy, health status, and educational attainment (as well as other topics) for well over 100 countries.

World Wide Web Resources

Economic Growth Resources
www.bris.ac.uk/Depts/Economics/Growth/

Site includes links to statistical datasets, surveys, research papers, and other general matters related to economic growth and development.

Food and Agriculture Organization of the United Nations (FAO)
www.fao.org

The FAO is mandated to raise international nutritional levels and to improve the living conditions of the world's poor. Provides links to nutrition, sustainable development, economics, and other issues.

The Hunger Project
www.thp.org/bar.htm

The Hunger Project is a strategic organization committed to ending world hunger. Includes links to their programs, coming events, reports, and newsletters.

The Hunger Site

www.thehungersite.com/cgi-bin/WebObjects/CTDSites

The Hunger Site is the "world's first 'click to donate' site." Users click on a button, and donations of food, paid for by sponsors, are distributed around the world.

InterAction: American Council for Voluntary International Action

www.interaction.org/

InterAction is a coalition of over 160 nonprofit organizations, based in the United States, working to help the world's poor. The Web page includes a mission statement, a search engine, a library, a calendar of events, and other topics.

United Nations Capital Development Fund (UNCDF)

www.uncdf.org/

UNCDF is a partner in the UNDP Development Group. UNCDF works to reduce poverty in least developed countries through a variety of innovative approaches in both local governance and microfinance initiatives.

United Nations Children's Fund (UNICEF)

www.unicef.org

Provides links to its publications, donations, programs, research and evaluation, and *The State of the World's Children 2002*.

The World Bank Group

www.worldbank.org

The World Bank provides financing for economic development projects in the less developed countries. Topics include news, publications, development topics, economic research, projects, and data and statistics.

Economic Systems, Resource Allocation, and Social Well-Being
Lessons from China's Transition

Chapter outline

Checklist of economic concepts

- Economic systems
- Economic systems, mixed
- Economy, pure market
- Economy, pure command
- Economy, transitional
- Market
- Market, competitive
- Market, monopolistic
- Market, imperfectly competitive
- Demand
- Demand, law of
- Quantity demanded, changes in
- Demand, changes in
- Supply
- Supply, law of
- Quantity supplied, changes in
- Supply, changes in
- Price, equilibrium
- Shortage
- Surplus

In 1978, China embarked upon the greatest economic experiment in modern history. Deng Xiaoping launched a bold effort to reform China's economy and open economic ties with the noncommunist world. This effort involved injecting more market economics into China's moribund communist system and creating Special Economic Zones (SEZs) to stimulate trade with western countries. These policies have created something akin to a modern-day gold rush, with western businesses investing heavily in China. Despite setbacks like Tiananmen Square, the look and culture of southern China has fundamentally and probably irreversibly changed by these events.

Driven by the twin engines of foreign investment and exports, China has grown at a spectacular rate in recent years. Since 1990, China's growth has been in the double digits. This feat has been achieved while running a trade surplus, attracting a tremendous flow of foreign investment, and keeping inflation generally under control. No other country has been able to simultaneously achieve all of these economic marks.

In addition to growing at a rapid pace, the level of development in China has also increased. Per capita income is still low, but Chinese industry has surged forward. In less than two decades, China has been transformed from a near stone age economy to a full-fledged industrial power. China has gone from having virtually no trade to being one of the world's ten largest exporters. Increasingly, its exports have become more sophisticated. Advanced export categories, such as electronic products, have surged. Surprisingly, 80 percent of China's exports are manufactured products; the United States cannot match that figure.

Most notably, if China is able to continue to keep foreign investment and exports high and, as a result, enjoy strong growth, it will become the world's largest economy early in the next century. This is not to suggest, however, that China's economy will be the equal of the world's big three economies—the United States, Japan, and the European Union—in all respects. For decades to come, China will face regional disparities and other development problems that the big three have overcome. Nonetheless, China is certain to become an ever more important player in the world economy.

Source: Greg Mastel, *The Rise of the Chinese Economy: The Middle Kingdom Emerges* (Armonk, NY: Sharpe, 1997), pp. 3–4.

As noted in Chapter 1, few decisions influence social well-being more directly and forcefully than choices concerning the way in which governments organize their countries' economies. Economics is a science, a social science to be sure, but a science nonetheless. As such, experimentation is an important means toward understanding economic principles. In a social science, many of our most important experiments would not satisfy the conditions of true experiments, such as having randomly assigned control groups and the like, but these experiments do offer insights that theory alone can only be suggestive of. Perhaps the clearest and single most important of these economic experiments concerns the role of government in the economy that played out during the 20th century. More precisely, during this period, the world witnessed a clear competition between two very different economic organization choices. While the economies of the world entered the 20th century at various stages of industrialization, the benefits of the market orientation were becoming well understood globally. This was to quickly be called into question, however, by political events occurring in Russia as World War I drew to a close. With the Bolshevik Revolution of 1917–1918, Czarist Russia was overthrown and the new USSR was formed. The move from a market orientation was complete by 1930 because by then Soviet strongman Joseph Stalin had essentially eliminated all vestiges of market-based resource allocation in the USSR in favor of strict centralized planning in which all resource-use decisions were made by the state.

This approach to economic organization proved popular in many parts of the world. Most notably, this system was adopted in the world's most populated country, China, in 1949. The roots of Chinese civilization stretch back well before the Common Era. Rulers came and went throughout the centuries, but the economy of the country, while relatively underdeveloped, had always been characterized by elements of a market orientation. This orientation changed in 1949 following the Communist Party's success, led by its charismatic leader Mao Zedong, in pushing the Guomindang government of Chiang Kai-shek into internal exile in Taiwan. As will be discussed in more detail later in the chapter, Mao followed, for the most part, the Soviet example of centralized planning. China would not be the last to take this route. Shortly after, North Korea and Vietnam, to name just two prominent examples, were to follow. By the end of the century, however, the global economic landscape was left with only a couple of examples of strict centralized planning, notably, Cuba and North Korea. The experiment was clearly reaching its conclusion.

What lessons can be learned from the 20th century's experiment with centralized economic planning? By focusing on the Chinese example, we will attempt to answer this question. In doing so, we will first ask how resources are allocated in differing types of economies. Then we will more directly address the all-important question of how well the differing types of allocation mechanisms serve the interests of a country's citizens.

ECONOMIC SYSTEMS

Within any country, organizational arrangements develop that serve as a framework within which economic decisions are made. In general terms, these organizational arrangements specify who determines what is produced with the country's scarce resources and who benefits from well-made decisions, as well as who suffers from poorly made decisions. It is important to stress from the beginning that the choice of an organizational arrangement does not determine whether decision making and planning will occur but rather *who* will decide and plan. Historically, answers to this question range from private parties to a mix of private parties and the state, to the state entirely. The extent to which the state is involved in the economy is determined by the choice of an economic system, which can be thought of as falling on a continuum with the pure market economy at one extreme and the pure command economy at the other.

Pure Market Economy

pure market economy
Economic system based on private ownership and control of resources, known as private property rights, and coordination of resource-use decisions through markets.

There are two essential elements of the **pure market economy:** (1) private ownership of the economy's resources, known as private property rights, and (2) *decen-tralized* decision making coordinated through markets. Within the pure market, or capitalist economy, private individuals, businesses, and combinations of the two are allowed, with minor interference, to engage in whatever voluntary exchanges they feel best maximize their well-being. If offered a job for $10 per hour, the individual may choose whether to accept it or turn it down depending on such factors as the value placed on his or her time and the availability of alternative sources of income. Similarly, a business owner decides whether to hire more or fewer workers, to seek more or less capital, and to increase or reduce production. The key is that within a pure market economy, choices surrounding the use of resources are left to private resource owners, who are expected to make decisions that best suit their goals and aspirations. Once this myriad of decisions is made, coordination of the decisions takes place within markets. (Note the absence of any discussion of government in this process, with the implicit exception of legal enforcement of property rights.)

Pure Command Economy

pure command economy
Economic system characterized by state ownership and/or control of resources and centralized resource-use decision making.

At the opposite end of the continuum of economic systems is the **pure command economy.** This economic system is everything capitalism is not. That is, the pure command economy is characterized by state ownership and/or control of economic resources and by centralized planning. Decisions concerning what and how to produce are made by central authorities through binding directives to producers (deals that are too good to refuse!). Given the centralization of decision making, alternative means of coordination of decisions such as reliance on markets is not necessary. And the resulting extremely expanded role of government should be obvious; who else can play the role of central planner?

Mixed Systems

mixed systems
Economies that combine elements of the pure market and pure command economies.

Although examples of economies at or at least near the two extremes of pure market and pure command have existed, such as the United States during the first half of the 1800s and the USSR during its existence, most present-day economies lie somewhere between these two extremes. We refer to these as **mixed systems** in the sense that they have elements of both extreme types of economies. The key in determining where a specific mixed economy falls on the continuum between the pure command and pure market orientations is the extent to which private parties own and/or control a country's resources and the extent to which these parties are free to make resource allocation decisions without governmental interference. Nearer the pure market end you find countries like the United States, Japan, and Canada, for example, since in each the extent of government ownership and control of resources and decision making is relatively limited. Conversely, in countries like Sweden and France, the footprint of government in the economy is much greater, though each is certainly not a command economy because, again, most resources and resource allocation decisions remain in the hands of private parties.

transitional economy
A nation which is in the process of replacing an economic system of command and control with one based on market principles.

Beginning with the reforms undertaken by the Chinese Communist Party in 1978 which led to their declaration in 1982 that China would become a "socialist market economy," a new type of mixed economy was created: the **transitional economy.** While being mixed in the sense of having elements of both command and market economies, these are systems that have made official commitments to move in the direction of market orientation. Of course, China is not the only example of the transitional economy. Following a similar path are Vietnam and the 15 independent republics in eastern and central Europe created by the collapse of the USSR in 1991. Each, of course, faces its own unique problems of transition and is at a different point in the transitional process. Further, the extent of change and the degree of success from these changes vary from country to country, though none have proved more successful than China. Regardless, transition is difficult and does not happen overnight. The special problems of transition are discussed in more detail later in this chapter.

Although most present-day economies do not satisfy fully the criteria of either the pure market or the pure command economy, these polar cases are useful in analyzing the way in which resources are allocated within existing mixed economies and the impact these differing allocation mechanisms have on social well-being. The extent to which outcomes of this analysis apply to any particular mixed system is dependent on how closely the economy satisfies the conditions of the pure market or pure command classification. That is, an economy in which individuals own and/or control most resources and in which most economic decisions are made in a decentralized fashion can be expected to yield results that conform closely to the pure market model. Conversely, when most resources are publicly owned or controlled and most decision making is centralized, expect outcomes that more closely mimic those of the pure command economy.

RESOURCE ALLOCATION IN A MARKET ECONOMY

When the buyers and sellers of a product or service interact with one another and engage in exchange, a market exists. The geographic area of any market is simply the area within which the two parties are able to transfer information about and ownership of whatever is being exchanged. Some markets are local, some national, and still others international. Markets within the capitalist economy serve to coordinate the infinite number of decisions concerning resource allocation made by the owners of those resources. For example, in the last couple of decades, the development and application of digital technology has made possible compact disc and DVD players as cost-effective substitutes for phonographic turntables and VCRs.

And consumers' desire for digital technology, as you are no doubt aware, has been explosive. Left behind, of course, are items like turntables and VCRs, which are now viewed by most as being old-fashioned. Clearly, both the existing producers of turntables and VCRs as well as the many new compact disc and DVD manufacturers were well-advised to reallocate their efforts to the production of digital products and away from turntables. How did this happen? As you will see, this and the infinite number of other decisions about resource allocation and reallocation are brought together through markets.

Market Structure

The quality of market-based resource allocation decisions is in large part determined by the degree of competition that exists within the market economy. At one end of the spectrum, markets fall into the purely competitive classification. At the other, they are classified as purely monopolistic. The markets of any market economy can be found at or near each extreme, but most tend to fall firmly in between.

Purely Competitive Markets

purely competitive market
A market in which there are a large number of mobile buyers and sellers of a standardized product. Further, the price of the product is free to move up or down, and there are no obstacles preventing firms from entering or leaving the market.

For a market to be **purely competitive** it must exhibit five important characteristics. First, there must be enough buyers and sellers of the product so that no one of them acting alone can influence its price. To illustrate, consider the individual consumer buying a loaf of bread in a supermarket or an individual farmer selling wheat at a grain elevator. Second, each seller must be offering a standardized product. This condition is met when consumers are as happy to buy the product from one seller as from any other, understanding that there really is no difference between the items offered by the different sellers. Third, the product price must be free to move up or down without interference from government or any other party. Fourth, buyers and sellers must be mobile. This means that any buyer is free to move among alternative sellers and buy from whoever will sell at the lowest price. Similarly, sellers must be free to move among all potential buyers and sell to that individual who is willing to pay most for the product. Fifth, sellers must be free to leave the industry if they wish, and potential sellers must be free to enter if they feel they can produce the product more efficiently than existing sellers.

Few markets in the United States are purely competitive in the sense of rigorously fulfilling all five requirements, but some come close. Perhaps closest to pure competition in the United States is agriculture. The market for agricultural products certainly satisfies the first, second, and fourth characteristics of the purely competitive market, although it fails to fulfill the third and fifth. Since 1933, the government has often been actively involved in establishing and maintaining prices in agricultural markets, violating the third characteristic of pure competition. And the extremely large amount of money necessary to effectively enter this market probably poses a significant barrier to entry, violating the fifth characteristic.

Purely Monopolistic Markets

purely monopolistic market
A market in which there is only one seller of a product. The monopolist has substantial control over price and is often able to prevent potential sellers from entering the market.

A **purely monopolistic** selling market, at the opposite end of the spectrum, exists when there is but one seller of a product. The seller is able to manipulate the product price to his or her advantage. Typically, the monopolist is also able to block potential competitors from entering the market—often with government help. When markets are controlled by a single seller, the consuming public usually suffers in the form of higher prices and lower quantities and/or qualities of the good or service. With a little reflection, you may be able to recall an example of the negative effects of monopoly. Perhaps, if you are old enough or come from a small town, you recall a time when there was only one firm offering videotapes for rent in your community. Eventually, numerous competitors opened up shop. How did the new competition change things? If your town is representative, you probably saw greater variety in tapes available, lower rental rates, and perhaps the advent of multinight rentals as the new competitors attempted to gain the allegiance of the former monopolist's captive customers. Competition among sellers typically benefits consumers. Given that consumers, taken as a whole, are society, the existence of monopoly tends to keep the market economy from achieving its maximum level of social well-being. As such, the problems posed by monopoly are significant enough to warrant the thorough treatment given in Chapter 8. Although examples exist, pure monopolies fortunately are rare in the United States.

Imperfectly Competitive Markets

imperfectly competitive markets
Markets that fall between the purely competitive and purely monopolistic extremes; they may exhibit characteristics of either or both of these extremes.

Most markets in the United States fall somewhere between the purely competitive and purely monopolistic extremes. These markets are called **imperfectly competitive,** and the performance of such a market is dependent on the degree to which the market diverges from the extremes. That is, markets that do not fully satisfy the conditions of pure competition but come close to doing so can be expected to perform much the same as those that are purely competitive; those markets that are almost pure monopolies will likely yield outcomes not too dissimilar from those of pure monopoly.

Market Forces

demand
The quantity of the product that consumers are willing to purchase at various prices, other things being equal. The other things that must remain equal are (1) the consumers' incomes, (2) the prices of goods related in consumption, (3) the consumers' tastes, (4) the consumers' expectations, and (5) the number of consumers.

Markets bring together or coordinate all the decisions that economic factors make within the capitalist economy. You may have heard this referred to as the *forces of demand and supply.* To fully understand the market economy, you must have a solid understanding of how demand and supply interact to answer the question of how a market economy's scarce resources are allocated. Before we enter into that discussion, however, it is vitally important to bear in mind that the description of markets that follows assumes a very high degree of competition. As alluded to above, the virtue of markets as allocators of scarce resources is not independent of the degree of competition that exists in individual markets. For the remainder of this chapter, we present the market model in its ideal form. Circumstances in which the performance of markets is less than optimal are the basis for much of the remainder of this book.

Demand

The **demand** for a product refers to the maximum quantities of the product that consumers are willing to purchase at various prices, other things being equal. Consider the demand for Pepsi in your town, Collegetown, USA. Suppose that

TABLE 2.1	Price (Dollars)	Quantity (Six-Packs per Week)
A Demand Schedule for Pepsi in Collegetown	$1.50	1,500
	2.00	1,000
	2.50	500

FIGURE 2.1   A Demand Curve for Pepsi in Collegetown
The price-quantity demanded combinations of Table 2.1, plotted graphically, form the demand curve for Pepsi, *DD*. The demand curve shows the quantities of Pepsi that the consumers are willing to purchase at various prices, other things being equal.

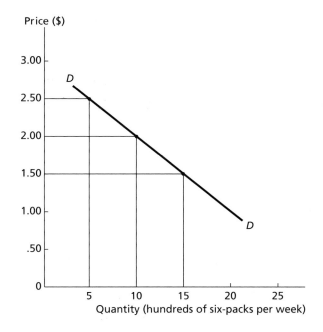

during one week, the consumers of Pepsi in Collegetown are willing to purchase 1,500 six-packs if the price is $1.50 per six-pack; 1,000 six-packs if the price is $2.00; or 500 six-packs if the price is $2.50. Each of these price-quantity combinations is listed in the demand schedule in Table 2.1 and then plotted as a demand curve in Figure 2.1. The demand schedule and curve each have several characteristics that are of great importance.

First, it is incorrect to refer to any of the individual price-quantity combinations listed above as demand. The quantity of a product that consumers are willing to purchase at a specific price, reflecting one point on a demand curve, is properly referred to as the quantity demanded at that price. That is, demand refers not to a specific price-quantity combination but to all the price-quantity combinations taken together. In this way, the demand for Pepsi in Collegetown is properly reflected in the entire demand curve or schedule.

Second, demand relates to the quantities of the product that consumers are actually willing to purchase at various prices, not merely the quantities of the product that consumers would like to consume. Each of us probably desires an expensive, oceanfront home, but unless we are actually willing to purchase such a house at its market price, we do not demand it in the economic sense of the term.

Third, demand reflects the quantities of the product that consumers are willing to purchase during some specific period of time. For example, the demand schedule and curve presented accurately depict the demand for Pepsi in Collegetown during one week. It makes little sense to discuss the quantity of Pepsi demanded at a specific price unless the period of time in which the purchases may take place is specified.

Fourth, it is assumed that customers will desire more of a product when its price is low than when it is high. Although this may seem to be nothing more than common sense, it serves as the often-overlooked basis of much that is done in economics. Formally, this inverse price-quantity demanded relationship is called the **law of demand** and states that the lower the price of a product, the larger will be the quantity demanded; and the higher the price, the smaller will be the quantity demanded, other things being equal. It is the law of demand that gives the demand curve its negative slope.

It is important to note that the law of demand does not simply state that the quantity demanded is greater when the price is low than when the price is high. The law states that this inverse price-quantity demanded relationship holds *only with other things being equal.* Although many factors could be listed as the other things that must be equal or held constant, the five most important are (1) the consumers' incomes, (2) the prices of goods related in consumption, (3) the consumers' tastes, (4) the consumers' expectations, and (5) the number of consumers.

Changes in the Quantity Demanded Versus Changes in Demand

From the information given previously, we know that the consumers of Collegetown are willing to purchase 1,000 six-packs of Pepsi per week when its price is $2.00 per six-pack. This quantity demanded is identified as point *A* on the original demand curve *DD* in Figure 2.2.

Should the price of Pepsi increase to $2.50, the consumers would reduce the amount they wish to purchase to 500 six-packs per week. That is, when the price rises to $2.50, the consumers move to the left on their demand curve to point *B,* which reflects a quantity demanded of 500 six-packs per week. Such a movement along one demand curve, brought about by a change in the price of the product, is called a **change in quantity demanded.** It is important to understand that this movement is not a change in demand. The consumers are merely moving from one price-quantity combination, or quantity demanded, to another in response to a change in the price of Pepsi.

A **change in demand** is said to occur when the entire demand schedule and curve change. For example, Figure 2.2 includes the original demand curve of Figure 2.1 (labeled *DD*) and two new curves, D_1D_1 and D_2D_2. Along demand curve D_1D_1, the consumers desire less Pepsi at each price than is the case along demand

law of demand
The lower the price of the good, the larger will be the quantity demanded; and the higher the price, the smaller will be the quantity demanded, other things being equal.

change in quantity demanded
A movement along one demand curve, brought about by a change in the price of the product.

change in demand
A shift to an entirely new demand curve, brought about by a change in one or more of the factors assumed to be held constant.

FIGURE 2.2   A Change in the Quantity Demanded versus a Change in Demand
The movement along *DD* from *A* to *B* is brought about by a change in the price of Pepsi and is called a *change in the quantity demanded.* A shift in the entire demand curve to either D_1D_1 or D_2D_2 is called a *change in demand* and is brought about by a change in one of the factors assumed to be held constant when the demand curve is drawn.

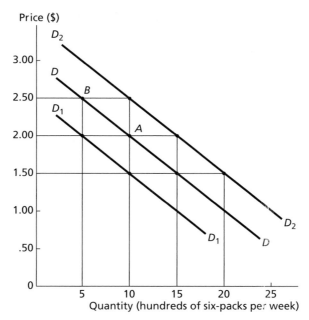

curve *DD.* Thus, a shift in demand from *DD* to D_1D_1 is referred to as a decrease in demand. Demand curve D_2D_2 indicates just the opposite, so a shift from *DD* to D_2D_2 is called an increase in demand. You should note that in each case the entire demand curve shifts, and this is what distinguishes a change in demand from a change in quantity demanded.

Changes in demand occur when one or more of the five factors assumed to be held constant changes. Before proceeding to the discussion of how changes in the constants lead to changes in demand, however, you must fully understand the distinction between a change in quantity demanded and a change in demand. If the price of the product rises or falls, consumers will adjust the quantity demanded per unit of time. Graphically, this adjustment is represented by a movement along one demand curve and is called a change in the quantity demanded. By contrast, if one or more of the five factors assumed to be held constant changes, consumers move to an entirely new demand curve, and this is called a change in demand. Do not confuse the two.

Changes in Consumers' Incomes   A change in demand may come about due to a change in the incomes of consumers. Suppose that initially demand curve *DD* in Figure 2.2 applies and the price of Pepsi is $2.00 per six-pack. At this price, the quantity demanded is 1,000 six-packs per week. Now suppose that the incomes of consumers rise. With incomes on the increase, it is likely that consumers will be willing to purchase more Pepsi, even if the price remains $2.00. Perhaps now they are willing to buy 1,500 six-packs. Similarly, had the initial price been $1.50, the increase in incomes might have caused consumers to increase the amount they wished to buy from 1,500 to 2,000 six-packs per week. Thus, when incomes rise, demand increases from DD to some higher level such as D_2D_2. Conversely, had incomes fallen, demand would have decreased to some lower level such as D_1D_1. In this example, an important assumption is implicitly made. Specifically, it is assumed that Pepsi is a **normal good.** A good is said to be a normal good if its demand increases as incomes rise and decreases as incomes fall. Although most goods satisfy this condition and are considered to be normal, there are goods for which the demand-income relationship is just the reverse. Such goods are known as **inferior goods** and exhibit demands that decrease as incomes rise and increase as incomes fall. Examples of inferior goods might include hot dogs, generic goods of all sorts, public transportation, and rabbit-ear antennae for television sets.

Changes in the Prices of Goods Related in Consumption   Regarding the demand for a particular good, the prices of two types of related goods are important. First, the prices of **substitute goods** must be considered. In simplest form, goods are considered to be substitutes if they satisfy the same consumer need or desire. More formally, goods are substitutes if an increase in the price of one leads to an increase in the demand for the other. Assuming that Pepsi and Coke are substitutes and starting from an initial position at point A in Figure 2.2, what would be the impact on the demand for Pepsi of a doubling in the price of Coke? Given that the two are substitutes, the rising price of Coke could be expected to increase the demand for Pepsi to some higher level such as D_2D_2 as consumers substitute Pepsi for the now more expensive Coke. Just the opposite would occur if the price of Coke were to fall.

Another type of related good whose price must be held constant is **complementary goods.** Complementary goods are used in combination, such as hot dogs and hot dog buns or cars and gasoline. The impact of a change in the price of a complement is just the opposite of that for substitutes. With complementary goods, the demand for the good in question decreases as the price of the complement rises. Again, returning to Collegetown, suppose that Pepsi and potato chips are complements. A decrease in the demand for Pepsi might be caused by an increase in the price of chips, but why? When the price of chips increases, the quantity of chips demanded must, of necessity, decline. Since consumers use the two products in combination, and it is known that they are purchasing fewer bags of chips, it follows that they will demand less Pepsi as well. Just the opposite can be expected when the price of chips falls.

Changes in Consumers' Tastes   When a demand curve is drawn, the consumers' tastes must be held constant. The way in which changes in this factor lead to changes in demand requires little discussion. Put simply, when tastes change in favor of a good, its demand increases, while demand decreases when the reverse occurs. Changes in tastes can occur for a variety of reasons, such as advertising

normal good
A good whose demand increases as incomes rise and decreases as incomes fall.

inferior good
A good whose demand decreases as incomes rise and increases as incomes fall.

substitute goods
Two goods for which an increase in the price of one leads to an increase in the demand for the other.

complementary goods
Two goods for which an increase in the price of one leads to a fall in the demand for the other.

or increased information about the product or its substitutes. Pepsi and Coke regularly enlist the services of famous music and film industry stars to advertise their products. To the extent that consumers associate these famous faces with the products, the advertising campaign can be expected to increase demand. At least this is what the makers of Pepsi and Coke have in mind.

Changes in Consumers' Expectations   The fourth category of demand controls concerns the consumers' expectations with regard to the future. How would you respond if you believed that the price of Pepsi would double in the next week? You probably would buy more Pepsi this week, that is, increase your demand for Pepsi this week, and store it so that you do not have to purchase as much next week at its higher price. If the consumers of Collegetown exhibit the same degree of common sense as you, an increase in the demand for Pepsi such as that from DD to D_2D_2 might accompany an expected future price increase, whereas a decrease in demand can be anticipated when consumers expect future price decreases.

Changes in the Number of Consumers   The final factor that must be held constant concerns the number of consumers in the group being considered. For example, an increase in the demand for Pepsi in Collegetown may come about purely due to an increase in the size of the consuming population of the city at the start of each fall semester. Similarly, a decrease in the demand for Pepsi can be expected each summer as many of the students leave the city.

The key to this factor, as with each of the others, is that if the factor changes, the entire demand curve shifts, and such a shift is known as a change in demand.

Supply

supply
The quantity of a product that sellers are willing to sell at various prices, other things being equal. The other things that must remain equal are (1) the cost of production, (2) the prices of goods related in production, (3) sellers' expectations, and (4) the number of sellers.

The **supply** of a product refers to the maximum quantities of the product that sellers are willing to sell at various prices, other things being equal. Suppose that the firms that produce and sell cars in the United States are willing to sell 250,000 cars per year when the price of a car is $5,000; 500,000 per year when the price is $10,000; and 750,000 when the price is $15,000. These price-quantity combinations are presented as a supply schedule in Table 2.2 and as a supply curve in Figure 2.3. As was true for demand, the supply schedule and curve have several important characteristics.

First, each of the price-quantity combinations listed in the supply schedule and graphed along the supply curve SS is properly referred to as a quantity supplied at a specific price. For example, the quantity supplied is 250,000 cars per year when the price is $5,000. These individual price-quantity combinations do not by themselves represent the supply of cars; rather, the supply of cars is represented by all of these individual price-quantity combinations taken together. Thus, the supply of cars is represented by the entire supply schedule in Table 2.2 or the entire supply curve in Figure 2.3.

Second, supply refers to the quantities of the good that sellers are willing to sell at various prices during some specified period of time. As was true on the demand side, it makes little sense to identify a specific quantity supplied unless the time period in which the sales are to take place is specified. For this reason, the supply information presented here reflects the sellers' intentions during one year.

TABLE 2.2
A Supply
Schedule for Cars
in the United
States

Price (Dollars)	Quantity (Cars per Year)
$ 5,000	250,000
10,000	500,000
15,000	750,000

Third, the positive slope of supply curve *SS* indicates that the quantity of cars offered for sale increases as the price of cars increases. The reason for this is simple: As the price increases, it becomes more profitable to sell cars, which encourages existing sellers to produce and sell more cars. This is a fundamental economic principle known as the **law of supply,** which states that the higher the price of the product, the larger will be the quantity supplied; and the lower the price, the smaller will be the quantity supplied, *other things being equal.*

It is once again the case that the *other things being equal* part of the law is crucial. As was the case with demand, the supply schedule and curve presented above accurately depict the intentions of the car sellers only if certain other factors are held constant. On the supply side, the most important other factors that must be equal are (1) the cost of production, (2) the prices of goods related in production, (3) the sellers' expectations, and (4) the number of sellers of the product.

law of supply
The higher the price of the product, the larger will be the quantity supplied; and the lower the price, the smaller will be the quantity supplied, other things being equal.

FIGURE 2.3   A Supply Curve for Cars in the United States
The price-quantity supplied combinations of Table 2.2, plotted graphically, form the supply curve for cars, *SS.* The supply curve shows the quantities of cars that the sellers are willing to place on the market at various prices, other things being equal.

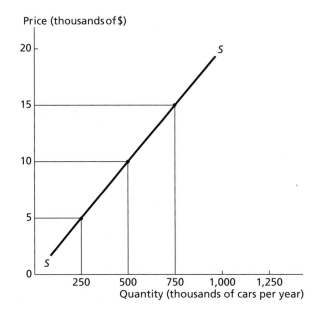

FIGURE 2.4   A Change in the Quantity Supplied versus a Change in Supply
The movement along *SS* from *A* to *B* is brought about by a change in the price of cars and is called a *change in the quantity supplied*. A shift in the entire supply curve from *SS* to either S_1S_1 or S_2S_2 is called a *change in supply* and is brought about by a change in one of the factors assumed to be held constant when the supply curve is drawn.

Changes in the Quantity Supplied versus Changes in Supply

Point *A* on supply curve *SS* in Figure 2.4 indicates that the sellers are willing to sell 500,000 cars per year if the price is $10,000 per car. Should the price increase to $15,000, the sellers will move to point *B* on *SS*, increasing the quantity that they are willing to sell to 750,000 per year. Such a movement along one supply curve due to a change in the price of the product is called a **change in the quantity supplied,** not a change in supply.

change in the quantity supplied
A movement along one supply curve, brought about by a change in the price of the product.

A **change in supply** occurs only when one or more of the four factors listed above changes. For example, there might be an increase in the supply of cars from *SS* to S_2S_2 or a decrease in supply from *SS* to S_1S_1 due to a change in the supply constants. The key is, if the price of the good changes, there is a change in the quantity supplied, which is depicted as a movement along one supply curve, whereas a movement to an entirely new supply curve is referred to as a change in supply and is brought about by a change in one or more of the four factors assumed to be held constant.

change in supply
A shift to an entirely new supply curve, brought about by a change in one or more of the factors assumed to be held constant.

Changes in the Cost of Production   Suppose supply curve *SS* in Figure 2.4 accurately reflects the intentions of car sellers and that the price is initially $10,000. At this price, the sellers are willing to sell 500,000 cars per year. What would happen if, for whatever reason, it became more expensive to build cars? Individual sellers would likely find it to be no longer profitable to keep production at previous levels, and some sellers might even choose to cease operations altogether. Regardless, we can be certain that when the cost of producing cars increases, the supply of cars will decrease to some lower level such as S_1S_1. Changes in the cost of production can come about in a variety of ways, two of which deserve special note. First, production cost changes are often due to advances in technology. If a new robot is developed that improves the efficiency of the production process, such an efficiency gain will be translated into a fall in the cost of production. A second common cause of production cost changes concerns input prices. When the price of steel, plastic, or labor increases, the cost of producing cars increases and can be expected to cause a fall in supply.

Changes in the Prices of Goods Related in Production   A change in supply may come about due to a change in the price of a good that is related in production. Minivans may be thought of as a good that is related in production to cars since, with only slight modification, the facilities used to produce cars can be used to produce minivans. Similarly, corn and milk are related in production since the land that is used to grow corn can be typically used to raise dairy cows. You should note that what is needed here is for the goods to be produced using similar inputs; it is not required that the consumer view the two goods as being related.

How might a change in the price of minivans influence the supply of cars? When the price of minivans increases, it becomes relatively more profitable to produce minivans and, consequently, the producers of cars are likely to shift some of their efforts into the production of minivans. In other words, an increase in the price of a good that is related in production can be expected to cause a reduction in the supply of the good in question. The reverse holds as well; that is, a fall in the price of minivans will likely result in an increase in the supply of cars.

Changes in Sellers' Expectations   Supply curve *SS* reflects the intentions of car sellers when they expect the future to be unchanged. If, however, the sellers believe that the price of cars is going to rise in the near future, we will probably witness a decrease in the supply of cars today. Would you sell as many cars today if you felt you could get an additional $1,000 for them next month? Conversely, an expected fall in the price of cars will typically lead to an increase in supply today as sellers attempt to sell the product before its price falls.

Changes in the Number of Sellers   In the past 25 years, we have seen the entry of a large number of firms into the U.S. auto market. Most of the firms have, of course, been foreign, but their impact has been much the same as it would have been if they were domestic. Specifically, the increase in the number of sellers has greatly increased the supply of cars. This is the typical case. When the number of sellers increases, supply increases as well. Were we to witness a fall in the number of firms selling cars in the next 25 years, the result would undoubtedly be a decrease in supply.

The key to this factor, just as with the previous three, is that if the factor changes, there is a movement to an entirely new supply curve, and this movement is referred to as a change in supply.

FIGURE 2.5   Competitive Market Price Determination

The demand and supply curves together show how the equilibrium price of a product is determined in the market. If the price is above equilibrium, surpluses occur, and the sellers undercut each other's prices until the equilibrium price is reached. If the price is below equilibrium, shortages occur, and the buyers bid against each other for the available supplies, driving the price up to the equilibrium level. At the equilibrium, there are neither surpluses nor shortages.

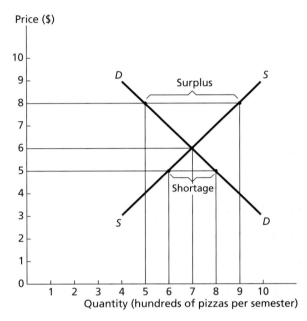

Competitive Market Equilibrium and Social Well-Being

Equilibrium Price and Quantity Purchased

The price of a product in a competitive market is determined by the interaction of buyers and sellers. To see how this works, return to Collegetown and consider the market for pizza during a typical semester, as detailed in Figure 2.5.

At a price of $6, the sellers are willing to sell 700 pizzas per semester. Why exactly 700 pizzas? The resources used to produce and sell pizza have many other uses. The pizza shops and their equipment might, for example, be used as bakeries, and the employees clearly could offer their employment elsewhere. It can be reasonably assumed that the owners of these resources will offer them for employment where they receive the greatest return. The quantity of resources devoted to producing pizza, then, and the resulting number of pizzas offered for sale reflect the value to the resource owner of using his or her resources in the production of pizza, relative to all other possible employments. When the price of pizza is $6 per pie, the resources necessary to produce and sell 700 pizzas will be drawn away from other production processes because they yield a greater return to their owners in producing pizza than in any of their other possible employments. As the supply curve indicates, if the price of pizza rises, new resources will be brought into pizza production from other production processes because those resources now offer their owners an increased return if used to produce pizza, given the rising price of pizza.

At the same time, Figure 2.5 indicates that at a price of $6, consumers wish to buy 700 pies per semester. Once again, the consumers have a nearly infinite number of ways to spend their incomes. When the price of pizza is $6 per pie, they decide that the $4,200 necessary to purchase and consume 700 pizza pies ($6 times 700 pies) could not be used to purchase anything else that would give them more satisfaction than the pizzas. If this were not true, they would not be willing to buy 700 pies at this price.

At a price of $6, then, the intentions of the sellers and consumers exactly coincide. That is, the owners of the resources necessary to produce 700 pizzas feel that no other employment of their resources will yield to them a greater return than can be had by producing pizza. And the consumers feel at this price, the expenditure of $4,200 on pizza yields greater satisfaction than a similar expenditure on any other good or goods. When the intentions of the sellers and buyers coincide in this fashion, we say that $6 is the **equilibrium price** of pizza and 700 is the **equilibrium quantity purchased.**

equilibrium price
The price at which the sellers of a product wish to sell exactly the same amount as the consumers wish to buy. As such, the equilibrium price indicates when consumers feel that precisely the correct share of the economy's scarce resources is devoted to producing the product.

equilibrium quantity purchased
The quantity of the product that is actually exchanged at the equilibrium price.

This concept of equilibrium price is particularly important. At this price, and only at this price, the consumers of pizza want to buy exactly the number of pizzas that sellers wish to sell. Put differently, only at this price do consumers feel that producers are using precisely the right amount of the economy's scarce resources to produce pizza. If this were not true, we could not say that their interests coincide with those of the producers. This outcome is of paramount importance in that the generally accepted goal for an economy is the minimization of the effects of resource scarcity, that is, the maximization of social well-being. The market economy leads to this outcome by ensuring that scarce resources are used where they are most highly valued by the consuming public. And who is in a better position to identify the amount of resources that should be used in each production process than the consuming public? Typically, then, an equilibrium price, by indicating when consumers are satisfied with a particular allocation of resources, indicates that unique allocation of resources that maximizes social well-being. To see this more clearly, consider what happens when price is not at its equilibrium.

Effects of a Price above Equilibrium

If the price is not at the equilibrium level, market forces are set in motion that move the price toward that level. Suppose, for example, that the price of pizza rises from $6 to $8. The sellers can be expected to increase the quantity supplied because pizza is now relatively more profitable to produce. That is, sellers can be expected to draw additional resources from other production processes and devote them to producing pizza because these resources can now earn a greater return in producing pizza. This is shown as a movement along *SS* to the 900-pizza quantity-supplied level.

But how will consumers react to the higher price? As price rises from $6 to $8, individual consumers can be expected to shift some of their purchasing power from pizza to other goods because these other options are now relatively cheaper. As depicted, at the price of $8 per pie, the consumers are willing to purchase only 500 pizzas during a semester. Consequently, when pizza is priced at $8 per pie, there is a surplus of 400 pies per semester.

From a standpoint of resource allocation, what does a surplus of 400 pizzas imply? Consumers are simply saying that when pizza is priced at $8 per pie, the resources necessary to produce the 400 surplus pizzas would be better used (add more to social well-being) in producing some other good or service. A surplus implies that consumers feel that too much of the economy's scarce resources is being devoted to a particular production process and, thus, they would prefer having those resources reallocated to another production process. How will this reallocation take place? When there is a surplus of any product, each seller who is unable to sell all that he or she has produced has an incentive to cut the price a bit below the existing price, because such a price advantage will enable the seller to dispose of his or her own surplus more easily. As long as a surplus exists, each of the pizza makers is likely to undercut his or her competitors in this fashion. Thus, if the price of pizza is above its equilibrium, market forces will cause the price to fall. And the price can be expected to continue falling until the surplus is completely eliminated. Figure 2.5 indicates that the surplus is eliminated when the price again returns to its equilibrium. In other words, the price of pizza can be expected to stop falling when the quantity of pizzas that the sellers wish to sell is equal to the quantity the consumers wish to buy. In this way, the market operating on its own ensures that the consumers' desire to have those resources that were used to produce the surplus pizzas released to be used in another production process is met.

Effects of a Price below Equilibrium

Now consider a price below equilibrium. When the price of pizza is $5, the consumers desire 800 pizzas per semester, while the sellers are willing to sell only 600, indicating that a shortage equal to 200 pizzas exists. Shortages of any good or service imply that consumers wish to have a larger share of their economy's scarce resources devoted to producing the product. In this situation, individual consumers have an incentive to offer the seller a bit more than $5 per pie to increase their chances of actually being able to purchase a pizza. For example, you call the local pizza shop to place an order and are told that the price is only $5, but unfortunately, due to a shortage, the pizza cannot be delivered until the next day. How do you respond? Given that the friends you have invited for dinner are knocking at the door, you call the pizza shop back and offer $7 if the pizza can be delivered immediately. To your satisfaction, but not surprise, before your friends have time to complain, the pizza arrives.

Whenever a shortage exists, market forces are put into action that tend to drive the price of the product up. As the price edges upward, the shortage becomes increasingly less severe as individual sellers respond to the rising price by increasing their production of the product. This process continues until the shortage is eliminated. That is, until the market once again reaches its equilibrium price.

In this way, other things being equal, the market operating on its own brings about the reallocation of resources that consumers desire because the shortage indicated that consumers felt more of the economy's scarce resources should be devoted to producing pizza. In other words, if left alone, the forces of demand and supply tend to ensure that social well-being, as reflected in consumer preferences, is maximized. This is not to say that market-determined outcome always maximizes social well-being. In certain circumstances, which are considered in detail in later chapters, the market fails to maximize well-being on its own. These circumstances, though important, are uncommon enough to be properly considered exceptions to the rule rather than the rule.

RESOURCE ALLOCATION IN A COMMAND ECONOMY

As indicated earlier in this chapter, the choice of an economic system is not a choice to have or not have decision making and planning; rather, the particular economic system selected simply indicates who will make resource-use decisions and plans. In the market economy, the consumer is king. That is, consumers decide what allocation of resources between competing production processes maximizes their well-being. Markets then coordinate this information and bring about any needed reallocation. None of this applies in the command economy, as can easily be seen by considering the example of China between 1949 and 1978.

Centralized Planning

With Japan's crushing defeat in World War II, China, under the leadership of the newly hailed war hero, Chiang Kai-shek, regained control over a number of its coastal and northern provinces that Japan had occupied since the 1930s. Chiang's popularity quickly began to fade, however, as the ministers he dispatched to manage the region proved brutal, vicious, and extremely corrupt in their dealings with the local population. From the time of the Japanese occupation, Chiang's archrival, Mao Zedong and his Communist followers had been, following the 3,000-mile Long March which cost many their lives, growing in strength in Yanan, where one of Mao's cardinal rules was that his group must do all that they could to support local peasant farmers in their farming activities as well as in the development of local infrastructure projects. Mao's emphasis on working with local peasants caused many in the West to initially see his movement as little more than much-needed agrarian reform. With the support of the masses, Mao's Communists succeeded in forcing Chiang's government to flee to Taiwan, establishing the Republic of China there in 1949. At the same time, China fell fully into the hands of Mao's Communist Party and the People's Republic of China, with its capital in Beijing, was founded.

Political control and economic control are, however, two very different things, and Mao, while a masterful politician, was not an economist. Fortunately, or unfortunately depending on one's perspective, Mao had an economic model and several decades of experience with it, from the USSR, to follow. Since the revolution of

1917, the Soviets had developed and implemented an economic system that very closely mimicked the pure command orientation. That is, nearly all vestiges of markets and market allocation of resources were eliminated, private farming gave way to mass collectivization and communes, and all major industrial production processes became government owned and operated. As you will recall, in a pure market economy, resources are owned by private parties who decide how they wish to use their resources and then this plethora of resource-use decisions is co-ordinated through markets. Lacking markets, how and who could provide this co-ordination for a country? Who was to decide what to produce, how to produce, and for whom to produce? The Soviet solution to the problem was to create an enormous centralized planning apparatus. With a few important modifications, China adopted this approach.

Mao and the Communist Party initially took a gradualist approach to establishing a command economy in China. This gradual approach was to be abandoned, however, by 1958, when Mao introduced the Great Leap Forward. Between 1958 and 1961, strict, all-encompassing centralized planning, much like that in the former Soviet Union, was introduced in China. During this period, the communists both consolidated their control over the country and replaced, in its entirety, what had been a rudimentary market-oriented economy with one of a near-pure command orientation. All, or nearly all, economic resources came under the ownership and control of the central government. Farmland was divided into enormous tracts operated by communes, some 25,000 by 1960, each of which had as many as 5,000 households and which grew even larger over time. Similarly, all major industry came under the ownership and control of the central government. As in the USSR, resource-use decisions were dictated by, in the Chinese case, the State Planning Commission, which operated through a labyrinth of more than 50 ministries and bureaus and regional and local commissions, each assigned the task of over-seeing the production of a specific set of goods. The problem for the planners, as mind-numbing as it seems in retrospect, was to determine both the desired quantities of each good or service to be produced and the appropriate technique to employ for each. For example, the planners had to decide how many cars would be produced, what those cars would look like, what types of factories and machinery would be used to produce the cars, who would manage the factories, who would work in the factories, what materials would be used, and, finally, who would, given government-set prices, be allowed to purchase the cars. And these questions had to be answered for each of thousands, if not millions, of production processes; quite a daunting task, indeed.

In broad, general terms, the State Planning Commission approached this task in the following way. The commission first developed a general plan which determined the quantities of each major production process it thought appropriate for the development of the country. Along with these production directives, resources were allocated as the commission felt appropriate to render each desired production level. This outline then filtered down through the ministries, bureaus, and regional and local commissions until finally reaching the commune or production facility. At that point, the managers of the enterprises gave input as to what they saw as the plan's shortcomings back up the chain of command with additional input being added at each step, until finally reaching the State Planning Commission. It was at this point that, operating with the full support of the Communist Party, the State Planning Commission developed the final and binding plan for each production process. These plans were developed often on a multiyear basis (five-year plans were common) and carried the full force of law.

To what extent may we expect that such an allocation mechanism serves to maximize social well-being? This question turns on the answer to a separate and much simpler question: Who is the best judge of what gives a person satisfaction, the state or the individual? Within the market economy it is assumed that the individual is in most cases the best judge. In the context of China's centralized planning mechanism, the state is thought to be the better judge. Fortunately, the answer to this question can be found by simply considering what China's experiment with centralized planning yielded. That is, China operated as a command economy, more or less, from 1949 through 1978. We can arrive at a defensible answer to the question by considering the problems China encountered with centralized planning and, subsequently, how the economy has performed since transition to its current market orientation which began in 1978.

Problems with Centralized Planning

While China's experiment with centralized economic planning spans the period 1949–1978, insight into both the problems of planning and the promise of transition can be had by realizing that this roughly 30-year period had three rather distinct phases. The initial phase lasted from 1949 to the onset of Mao's Great Leap Forward in 1958. During this early period, centralized planning was in its infancy, meaning that the enormous communes that were to become the hallmark of Communist China's agricultural sector were just beginning to be established, and in industry, whereas enterprise owners were losing actual ownership of their property, they were allowed, in most cases, to retain significant control of the firm's operations. From 1949–1957, then, China could be said to have retained some degree of market orientation.

The Great Leap Forward (1958–1961) was Mao's first attempt to eliminate all vestiges of markets from the Chinese economy, replacing market allocation of resources with strict, centralized planning. It was during this period that agriculture became dominated by massive communes and all major industries came under the direct control of the State Planning Commission, as discussed in the previous section. Interestingly, this proved disastrous, especially for agricultural production, which fell so dramatically that between 1958 and 1962, China experienced its most severe famine in modern history, resulting in the deaths of an estimated 25 million individuals.

Given the experience of the Great Leap Forward, pragmatists at the highest echelons of the Communist Party, most notably Premier Zhou Enlai, wrested some degree of power from Chairman Mao and took steps to, modestly, decentralize economic planning. For example, between 1962 and 1965, farmers were once again allowed to operate small private plots outside the control of the communes. Similarly, in industry, unreasonable output targets were relaxed. This liberalization, which essentially returned some degree of market orientation to China, was successful, and by 1965 the economy returned to the growth that it had experienced prior to the failed Great Leap Forward.

By the end of 1965, however, Mao, with his considerable political skills, launched the third phase of China's experiment with centralized planning with his Cultural Revolution which lasted until shortly after his death in 1976. During this period, the economy reverted to a nearly pure command orientation with its strict centralized planning. Not unexpectedly, economic performance declined.

Between 1949 and 1978, but especially during the Great Leap Forward and the Cultural Revolution, China operated as a near-perfect model of a command economy. What was the outcome? Our best estimates suggest that GDP per capita would have been about two times greater in 1992 than it turned out to be, had these two periods of near pure command not occurred.[1] Clearly, the command economy and centralized planning have a number of shortcomings. Here we address three that seem most problematic.

Informational Requirements

Consider the task of the State Planning Commission. They are charged with (1) determining what goods and services to produce and in what quantities; (2) deciding on the appropriate production technology to employ for each production process; (3) ascertaining the appropriate resources, along with the efficient levels of each, to be used in each process; and (4) deciding how the output of the various production processes would be distributed among the people. As daunting as this seems already, remember, we are talking about an economy with more than a billion citizens and one which produces hundreds of thousands, even millions, of goods and services. Further, this planning was being done prior to the advent and spread of modern, high-speed computers and networks. Lacking the required information, the inevitable outcomes were production bottlenecks that left some goods semifinished and thus in short supply while surpluses of other products existed. In addition, since the production targets given the farms and firms were quantity-based only, the quality of finished goods suffered severely. This problem can perhaps be summarized by asking, How are the planners to know what land is best for growing grain crops versus raising farm animals or what workers are best suited to be farmers versus production line workers?

Incentives for Efficient Production

Even if we assume that the planners of China's command economy somehow had all of the information they needed to create a reasonable plan, they faced perhaps an even more insidious problem of providing incentives for efficient production. This can be best seen on the agricultural commune. Suppose a commune has 1,000 farmers each of whom completes his or her shift for each workday during the year.

---

[1]See Gregory C. Chow, *China's Economic Transformation* (Malden, MA: Blackwell Publishers, 2002), p. 144.

When the crop is harvested, it is sold to the government at a price set by the pricing commission. The commune keeps this revenue less the actual costs of producing the crop (seed, fertilizers, fuel, equipment, and the like) less any share taken by the government. The revenue that remains with the commune is then paid out to the individual farmers as their annual income. The division of the revenue is based strictly on a point system in which a day's work counts as one point. Since, in this example, each farmer completes each workday throughout the year, each receives the same share of the revenue left to the commune at the end of the year. Because there are 1,000 farmers, each receives 1/1,000th of the revenue the commune is allowed to keep.

Now, consider what happens to an individual farmer, tainted by his or her remembrance of market incentives, who decides in the following year to work twice as hard, though still working the same number of days as all of his or her co-farmers. Clearly, output would rise, giving rise to some additional revenue being returned to the commune at the end of the next harvest. Suppose this additional revenue amounts to $2,000. What happens to the additional revenue? As with the revenue from the prior year's harvest, this year's revenue, including the additional revenue resulting from the individual hard-working farmer's efforts, is paid out to the commune's farmers based on the number of shifts each worked, that is, on the number of points each accumulated during the year. Since each worked the same number of days, each farmer again receives 1/1,000th of the entire revenue the commune has to pay out. What happened to our enterprising farmer? The commune received an increment in revenue of $2,000 for his or her additional work, and for that additional work, he or she received an increase in income of 1/1,000th of the commune's increase in revenue, or $2. That is, even though our hard-working farmer's additional effort brought in an additional $2,000 to the commune, $1,998 of this was paid out to the commune's other farmers who worked no harder than they had in the year prior.

And, in reality, as weak as the incentive for hard work embodied in this example is, imagine a more realistic example in which there are 10,000 farmers in a commune. In this case, one farmer choosing to work twice as hard would be *rewarded* by an increase in income of 1/10,000 of the added revenue. Would you work twice as hard if you knew that nearly all of the additional revenue your work provided would be paid out to others who didn't join you in working harder? Clearly this payment system did not provide much of an incentive for individual farmers to produce efficiently.

Similar incentive problems existed in the industrial sector of China's command economy. Consider first the workers. They are assigned to specific jobs by local labor bureaus. No doubt, there is some attempt to match workers to appropriate jobs, but often enough, the plum jobs were given, independent of ability or training, to well-connected individuals. Perhaps more important, however, once given a job, that job was typically that worker's job for his or her entire working life. Further, the pay for the job typically remained constant over time. As such, you have a problem much like that on the commune: Where is the incentive to work hard?

More important in the industrial context, however, are the incentives facing managers. Managers are given production goals and the resources needed to meet those goals by the State Planning Commission. Four problems are immediately apparent here. First, as you will recall from the discussion of how production targets are set, managers have input into the process, allowing them to argue down the target below what a plant operating at peak efficiency might produce. Equally important, since the manager is given resources by the State Planning Commission, where is the incentive to economize on the use of resources? Third, since, as mentioned above, the targets were quantity-based, the target was considered met if the required number of items was produced, independent of the quality of those items. Finally, managers were charged with deciding on appropriate investments for the firm to make in terms of plant, equipment, and processes. If a particular investment is made and proves successful, there is little or no reward for the manager. On the other hand, if an investment proves unsuccessful, the manager is punished. In such an environment, what types of investments are likely to be chosen? A rational manager would always choose those investments which, while being perhaps of little positive value, offer little risk of actual failure.

Heavy Industry versus Consumer Goods

As was true in the USSR, the Chinese Communist Party under the leadership of Chairman Mao had an unquenchable thirst for increasing production in the heavy industry sector of the economy. But, of course, if we assume that the economy that Mao inherited in 1949 was on its production possibilities curve, a shift toward greater production in the heavy industry sector could only come about if resources were shifted out of other sectors of the economy. What other sectors? The answer is obvious: consumer goods and light manufacturing. This decision is responsible for China's development of a world-class military and many useful elements of civilian infrastructure such as transport systems and dams. However, as we learned in Chapter 1, there is no such thing as a free lunch. In this case, the increased emphasis on heavy industry directly led to the opportunity cost of reduced production levels, reduced quality in production, and reduced choice among the entire array of consumer goods. The logical outcome of this has been well reported in the Western press often taking the form of extreme shortages in consumer goods resulting in ever-present long lines as consumers queued to attempt to get those items that they felt would yield greatest satisfaction.

Taken together then, it is easy to see that the command economy, with its reliance on centralized planning, is unlikely to fulfill an economy's productive potential. It is equally important to note, however, that each problem addressed above exists in a market economy. That is, all economies have to face the question of the enormous amount of information needed for efficient operation, how to provide incentives for efficient production, and what the mix of goods produced should be. Remember, the choice of an economic system is not a choice of whether there should be resource-use planning or not but, rather, who should make those choices. In the market economy, individual, private parties own and control most resources and decide how and where they should be used. If they wish to get the most from their resources, they will find the employment that yields them the greatest return. Further, hard work will maximize the resource owner's return. Finally, the enormous amount of information that is required need not reside in any one planning commission; rather, it resides in small bits within the minds of the market economy's citizens and is then brought together, as needed, when these citizens interact in markets. Put simply, in a well-structured market economy, and this is the beauty of this orientation, the problems faced by the central planners of a command economy tend to be automatically taken care of.

THE NEW CHINESE ECONOMY

China's Transition to a Market-Oriented Economy

After consolidating its power in 1949, the Communist Party entered into a period of economic experimentation involving an attempt to organize a near-pure command economy. The experiment reached its logical conclusion in the Cultural Revolution of the late 1960s and 1970s, ending in failure marked by subpar economic growth resulting from an extreme lack of incentives for efficient production, low-quality products, and public discontent with the government's strict authoritarian policies which gave them little control over their own economic destinies and starved them of consumer goods in favor of a concentration on heavy industrial manufacturing. Further, both the Chinese leadership and people saw around them the successes of their more market-oriented neighbors like Singapore, Hong Kong, Taiwan, Japan, and South Korea. It was clear by the mid-1970s that the experiment with command orientation was a failure. What was not clear, however, was how the command structure could devolve, especially since the strict ideologues, including Chairman Mao, remained in firm control of the Communist Party. China's fortunes and future were to be inexorably changed in September of 1976 when Mao, the father of Communist China, died. It was his death, more than any other single factor, that led to the end of China's experiment with the command structure.

Following a brief but bitter struggle between Mao loyalists and their more pragmatic colleagues, the pragmatists took control of the Communist Party, installing Deng Xiaoping as chairman in 1978. It was Deng, along with his allies, who started the process of transitioning China from its command orientation to what, by 1992, would be officially designated a "socialist market economy." And this has not been a transition in name only. As evidence, consider that, by 2000, fully 80 percent of the Chinese economy was market driven. Of course, such change did not occur overnight. In fact, the relatively slow, step-by-step approach taken during the transition is probably responsible for the success that China has enjoyed. Deng referred to this methodical conversion from command to markets as "crossing the river while feeling the rocks." That is, for Deng, the market has many virtues, but also pitfalls. So the wisest course to take is to launch reform in small, experimental ways, across the economy, identifying and expanding those that work, while rejecting those that do not. This approach both insured success and avoided unnecessary dislocation. To see how Deng's pragmatic approach was implemented consider reform as it played out in agriculture and industry.

Agricultural Reform

The Cultural Revolution showed clearly the inefficiencies involved with the collectivized, communal approach to agriculture. It was in agriculture that the first moves to a market orientation for China began. In 1978 some communes were allowed to experiment with what was known as a household responsibility system in which individual households were allocated a specific plot of land. The household was required to deliver a specified quantity of output to the commune but was allowed to keep for consumption or sale in local markets any output they produced over and above that required by the commune. The outcome of the experiment was immediately obvious: Total production increased dramatically as farmers now had an incentive to work efficiently. No doubt, a large part of the success of these experiments is due to the fact that a great many Chinese farmers were old enough to remember when the agricultural sector was market driven (the early 1950s and again in the early 1960s following the failed Great Leap Forward). Given the early success of the household responsibility system in its limited trials, the program was extended such that by 1980, nearly all of Chinese agriculture was operating in this fashion. That is, by 1980, agriculture in China had returned to a market orientation. To be sure, government retained ownership of the land, but this distinction soon became moot as well. While in the early days of reform, households just held leases to the land for a specified period of time, when reform was fully entered into, these leases became permanent and transferable; thus, while the government retained formal ownership, that ownership was, effectively, in name only.

How complete is the transition of Chinese agriculture to market orientation? One statistic tells the story: Today less than 1 percent of Chinese agricultural production results from command-oriented state farms. It can be honestly concluded that China's agricultural sector is now very near the pure market end of the spectrum of economic systems.

Industrial Reform

Industrial reform proved a tougher nut to crack than agriculture both because it effectively required a complete overhaul of the industrial sector and because so many party loyalists wished to hold on to the bureaucratic, managerial, and favored positions that they had held, in some cases, for decades. As opposed to agriculture, there really were no existing industrial managers who had knowledge of how to effectively manage a market-driven enterprise and no industrial workers who had ever had the benefit of having their compensation tied directly to their efforts. Even so, small steps toward reform began in 1978 when a few state-owned enterprises were allowed increased autonomy with respect to production, marketing, and investment decisions. As was the case in agriculture, these firms flourished, leading to an expansion of the reforms to other state-owned enterprises. By 1980, 45 percent of the total production arising from state-owned enterprises came from the reformed firms which, in steps, were given more autonomy. Most important, perhaps, with respect to their increased autonomy, these firms were now allowed to retain any profits earned, less a fixed tax paid to the government, and, further, were given control over hiring and firing of employees. So successful were these trials that by the end of 1981, 80 percent of China's state-owned enterprises were brought into the experiment, to one degree or another.

Similar to the household responsibility system in agriculture, a contract responsibility system was put in place in the reforming state-owned enterprises which, by 1987, allowed all state-owned enterprises to retain any profits earned, in excess of the fixed tax required by government. These retained profits could then be used to reward effective managers and workers. The next logical step was taken in 1997 when the Communist Party decided that all state-owned enterprises would be restructured into shareholding companies. Small and medium-size firms' shares were sold to their managers and workers, who could trade the shares among themselves. For the large enterprises, shares were allowed to be sold to those both inside and outside the companies and even to those outside China. A relatively small minority of these firms, because of their financial health, have shares actively traded in Shanghai, Hong Kong, and even New York. The only exception to this move to the modern, market-oriented, shareholding corporate model has been for a few, very large state enterprises that the Communist Party retains a controlling interest in because they view these as being essential to both the Chinese economy and Chinese security. As in agriculture, today, industrial China is very market oriented and the results have been, as will be discussed in the following section, nothing short of astounding.

With respect to both agriculture and industry, then, by 2004, China had nearly completed its transition to a market-oriented economy. One last element of this transition that has not been mentioned explicitly is reform of the price system. Implicitly, however, one sees that the rigid, centrally determined price system of the command economy has been replaced, by and large, by market-determined prices. In agriculture, this is seen in the fact that the household responsibility system allows households to sell their surplus in local markets where prices are determined, much as they are in farmer's markets in the United States, by the forces of supply and demand. Similarly, the contract responsibility system in place in industry gives the new shareholding firms the right to market their products as they see fit. Of course, they face competition from both other domestic producers and imports, so again, the forces of supply and demand are at work when prices for industrial products are established.

Now we turn our attention to the most important question of them all: How well has China's transition worked?

China's Transition to Markets: What Are the Facts?

Transition of the Chinese economy toward its current hybrid, socialist market economy following the death of Chairman Mao in 1976 was the pragmatic Communist Party leadership's response to the shortcomings of centralized planning. Has this worked? That is, how has the Chinese economy performed since the reform movement began? Table 2.3 compares China's economic performance between 1980 and 2002 with that of other high-growth Asian economies (including Vietnam, which has also been in transition to a market orientation), the average of all low-income countries (as defined by the World Bank), and the United States. The data suggest clearly that its experiment with market reforms has been nothing short of a stunning success for China.

TABLE 2.3   China's Economic Performance since Reform

	1980	1985	1990	1995	2000	2002	Average Annual Growth
GDP*							
China	164	272	398	700	1,040	1,210	9.56%
South Korea	149	217	342	489	620	680	7.21
Singapore	27	37	55	84	114	113	6.87
Vietnam	NA	11	14	21	29	33	6.53
Low-income	468	577	740	911	1,110	1,210	4.41
United States	4,770	5,560	6,520	7,340	8,960	9,200	3.04
GDP per capita†							
China	167	259	350	581	824	944	8.24
South Korea	3,910	5,322	7,967	10,849	13,199	14,280	6.13
Singapore	11,093	13,332	17,898	23,803	28,295	27,254	4.24
Vietnam	NA	188	211	284	369	413	4.59
Low-income	300	329	376	417	462	482	2.21
United States	21,000	23,383	26,140	27,713	31,730	31,891	1.93
Crop production‡							
China	66	86	102	125	152	159	4.15
South Korea	79	92	99	106	114	134	2.98
Singapore	587	380	121	57	48	48	−9.59
Vietnam	66	83	100	130	176	186	4.83
Low-income	71	85	99	116	133	134	2.96
United States	90	106	103	103	122	113	1.92
Industry value added§							
China	40	65	100	223	356	424	11.40
South Korea	36	56	100	147	194	212	8.56
Singapore	54	70	100	155	228	215	6.67
Vietnam	NA	79	100	177	291	352	9.25
Low-income	58	72	100	130	158	172	5.07
United States	80	88	100	113	135	NA	2.35

*In billions of constant 1995 U.S. dollars. †In constant 1995 U.S. dollars. ‡Indexed to 1989–1991 production levels. §Indexed to 1990 production levels.

Consider first the two summary aggregate measures of economic performance, real GDP and real GDP per capita, focusing especially on the average annual growth rates in these variables. Put simply, in terms of both of these key measures of economic performance, China has led the world in the 22-year period, 1980–2002. And, while taking into account the caveats of per capita GDP as a measure of well-being as discussed in Chapter 1, it is clear that the primary beneficiaries of this extraordinary rate of growth has been the Chinese people who have seen their per capita real GDP rise from a meager $167 in 1980 to well over $900 in 2002, an average annual growth rate of more than 8 percent.

While real GDP and real per capita GDP give us an overall view of China's performance, it is also informative to consider the two disaggregated indices of performance in Table 2.3; the production of food crops and industrial value added (a measure of industrial output). Note that the crop production measure for each country is indexed to the production levels that existed in that country between 1989 and 1991. That is, the crop production index value for China in 1980 of 66 indicates that China's agricultural output in 1980 was about two-thirds of its production during the 1989–1991 reference period. Similarly, the industrial production values in each year are measured relative to what was produced in each country in 1990, indicating that China, in 2002, had an industrial production level that was an astounding 424 percent of what that country produced just 12 years earlier. Considering the average annual growth rates, again we see that China has easily outperformed other Asian economies, a composite of all low-income economies, and the United States in terms of both agricultural and industrial production during the period.

It seems abundantly clear that China's transition toward a market-oriented economy has been a remarkable success. The reinstitution of markets and market incentives along with the reorganization of Chinese enterprises has, once again, shown the world the power of market orientation in advancing a country's economic growth and the well-being of its population. While China remains a relatively poor country, it should be noted that the World Bank has estimated that should China and the United States continue to grow at the rates that they have experienced since 1980, the Chinese economy will surpass that of the United States in terms of overall GDP by the year 2020. Of course, given the more than 1 billion persons living in China, even then, the average well-being of Americans will remain much greater than that of the typical Chinese citizen. Further, it is near folly to assume that we can even reasonably project growth rates for any country out as far as 2020. However, it is reasonable to assume that, given the extremely strong economic footing that China's pragmatic leaders have put the country on, the economic future for China is indeed extremely bright.

Before moving on to consider problems that transition has and may yet bring to China, it is important to note that the success of the Chinese transition doesn't necessarily mean that all countries attempting to transition to markets will be equally successful. Table 2.3 shows the success of China in its transition and also points out that Vietnam, another country in the midst of transition, has fared rather well. At the same time, while not listed in Table 2.3, most of the 15 republics spawned by the dissolution of the Soviet Union in 1991 have performed far worse than has either China or Vietnam. As an example, the new Russian Federation has seen its real per capita GDP fall from about $4,300 in 1990 to roughly $3,200 in 2002, for an average annual decline of 2.3 percent. This is not to say that Russia and the other former Soviet republics will not, in the longer term, benefit from transition, just that transition in and of itself is not an immediate cure-all for the damage done to an economy by years of centralized planning. It is informative, however, to ask briefly why countries like China and Vietnam have thrived during transition while the former Soviet republics, as a group, have performed so much more poorly. One answer seems obvious: Transition in both China and Vietnam took place within a context of political stability, while transition in the former Soviet republics happened as an outgrowth of the political collapse of the Soviet Union. It seems fair to conclude that transition is a difficult process and one that has a much greater likelihood of success if accompanied by a high degree of political stability. As such, the task facing the former Soviet republics has been much greater than that facing either China or Vietnam because the former had to simultaneously rebuild both the economic and political systems; a tall order indeed.

Problems of Transition in China

The discussion above might cause one to conclude that China's transition has been and will remain painless. This is not the case. China has faced several significant problems on the road to transition and potentially faces others. Here we discuss some of the most obvious and pressing problems.

Unemployment and Inflation

As has been found with all economies in transition to a market orientation, China quickly encountered significant problems with unemployment and inflation. By the mid-1990s, inflation was running 15 to 20 percent per year and it was estimated that upwards of 100 million workers were unemployed. Similar problems have been identified in the former Soviet republics during their early transitional years. Of course, it should be recognized that, to a large extent, these are problems that are predictable when a country moves from the inefficiencies of years of centralized planning to markets. That is, for example, China has closed a great many formerly state-owned enterprises which simply would never be able to compete with either efficient private firms or firms that remained state owned but which were able to adjust to the newly competitive environment. The predictable outcome is unemployment. Similarly, well-intentioned state planners had typically kept the prices of basic necessities like food crops and simple housing at unreasonably low levels. Thus, when markets were left to price items based on their demand and supply, prices rose. Fortunately for China, it appears that with respect to inflation, and to a lesser extent unemployment, the worst has passed. Inflation has fallen from its peak in the mid-1990s to an average of less than 1 percent since 2000. The unemployment picture is also improving, but at a much slower pace. This is as would be expected, however, since reemployment often requires retraining and relocation, neither of which happens instantaneously.

Corruption

As seems to be the case in all transitional economies, China experienced a great deal of corruption following its first steps toward market orientation. Reform in China left many local government officials in a position to extract bribes from those wishing to do business since these officials retained control over much of the still state-owned assets. Similarly, bribery became a necessary tax imposed to receive the permits and licenses necessary for many new entrepreneurs to operate. Perhaps a good way of looking at this type of corruption is as the last gasps of the dying centralized planning period. As was true for unemployment and inflation, however, the latest evidence suggests that corruption is fading and the economic landscape of China is becoming more open, free, and transparent. This is not to say that corruption no longer exists, but simply that it is becoming less of an everyday and necessary part of doing business.

Population Pressures

China is home to the world's largest population, with about 1.3 billion citizens. Worse, for much of the past century, China's population growth was extreme, regularly on the order of 3 percent per year. As early as 1950, Chairman Mao argued that rapidly increasing China's population was to be pursued as an economic goal so as to provide for both workers to develop the economy and a military to defend it. By the time of transition, however, China's leaders had already begun to realize the truism that the well-being of a population can only be increased if the population grows less rapidly than does the production of goods and services. That is, if GDP is growing at 3 percent per year and population at more than 3 percent, GDP per capita must be falling. With this understanding, China entered into a new era of population planning, summarized by the slogan "One Couple, One Child" in the early 1970s. Within this program, individuals were encouraged to marry later and families that limited themselves to one child received regular child care allowances while those which had more than one child were often taxed. The popular press, internationally, has reported on more extreme measures and the behaviors that China's population planning activities have led to. It is beyond the scope of our analysis to go into these issues in detail. What is important for us, however, is to note that the policies have been successful. That is, currently, China has a population growth rate of just less than 1 percent, which is about half that of the typical developing country and only slightly greater than that of the typical developed country.

The Desire for Democracy

Although the success of China's transition causes most ordinary Chinese citizens to be, on the whole, happy with the direction that their country is taking, there have been increasing calls for more direct participation in political processes. As the Chinese people grow in wealth and education and become more exposed to the world, it can be expected that their desires for more democratic institutions will also increase. Of course, China remains in the control of the Communist Party, and, like any other government, the Communists are not eager to cede control. Ever pragmatic, however, the current generation of Communist leaders have shown a willingness to allow modest political reforms which are, increasingly, giving the ordinary Chinese citizen input into political decision making. This can be best seen in two examples. First, consider the highest legislative body in China, the National People's Congress. To understand the change that is taking place in the People's Congress requires a bit of background. Since the Communists took power in 1949, local officials at the village or city block area have been directly elected by the people. These officials then elected the representatives for the next higher level of government and so on until finally, members of the National People's Congress were selected. So, while the People's Congress was clearly not directly elected by the public, there was, even prior to transition, some very limited degree of what we would call democracy. Unlike democracy, however, prior to transition, the People's Congress served as little more than as a rubber stamp for the policies that the Communist Party wished to pursue. Since the early 1980s, the National People's Congress has become emboldened, regularly rejecting directives from the

Communist Party leadership. To their credit, party leaders have increasingly deferred to the Congress.

The second example of the expanding degree of democracy in China occurred in the country's rural areas following the elimination of the commune system. During the commune era, each commune's leaders not only organized farming but were in charge of most local infrastructure activities such as road building, water supplies, education, and the like. With the collapse of the communes, there was initially no one in place to provide for these necessary civic functions. People in villages decided to take on the tasks themselves, directly electing the equivalent of mayors and others charged with overseeing these tasks. Far from disallowing these elections and demanding centralized control, China's central government has served to protect and even encourage this type of local democracy, realizing its social usefulness.

This is not to say that China is a democratic country. Indeed, it is far from it because the Communist Party retains ultimate control. However, it would be equally misleading to fail to see the steps that the Communist Party has taken in loosening its grip on the everyday lives of China's citizens. As economic development continues and the Chinese people become richer, more educated, and more exposed to the rest of the world, they will, no doubt, desire increasing degrees of political freedom to match their newfound economic liberty. Whether the Communist Party will continue to prove to be as pragmatic in dealing with political change as they have with economic change is yet to be seen. If they do not, significant social conflict could lie in China's future.

Summary

One of the most important economic decisions (if not *the* most important) a country must make in dealing with the fundamental problem of resource allocation concerns the choice of an economic system. Economic systems range from the pure market economy to pure command. The key differences between the two surround the issues of resource ownership and/or control and the mechanism through which resource allocation decisions are made.

Within a market economy, the economy's scarce resources are owned and controlled by private parties. This is referred to as the institution of private property rights. Equally important, within a market economy, resource allocation decisions are made by private owners and then these decisions are coordinated within markets. Within free markets, the forces of demand and supply operate to ensure that equilibrium prices and quantities are established at which neither shortages nor surpluses exist. Put differently, markets operating on their own tend to ensure that production is carried to the point where social well-being is maximized, given that the equilibrium reached is one in which the desires of consumers and producers exactly coincide. Should consumers' desires change, indicating that they would prefer either more or less of a given good or service, the market reacts to bring about the desired change. Circumstances in which markets fail to maximize social well-being, treated in detail in the following chapters, occur infrequently enough to be considered exceptions to the rule rather than the rule.

A command economy is one in which resources are owned, or at least directly controlled, by the state. Further, decisions about resource allocation are made directly and with the force of law by the state. Put simply, within the command economy, resources are allocated based on the preferences of the planners rather than on the preferences of the public. Given this, social well-being is maximized only if the planners know better than the public what mix of goods and services yields maximum satisfaction.

China's recent experience with both the command and market types of economic systems argues loudly in favor of market orientation. From the advent of the People's Republic of China in 1949 through the late 1970s, with minor exceptions, the Communist Party adopted the Soviet model of the command economy with its pervasive public ownership and/or control of most economic resources and extreme centralized planning. By the time of Chairman Mao's death in 1976, pragmatists in the Communist Party had begun to see the shortcomings of the command orientation. Later estimates suggest that this period of command cost the Chinese people in the sense that, had markets been allowed to exist during this period, per capita GDP in 1992 would have been about two times as great as it turned out to be. The inefficiency of the command orientation is also made plain when you look at the explosive, world-leading economic growth that China has enjoyed since it began its return to market orientation in the late 1970s. This is not to say that transition in China, or anywhere else for that matter, has been and will continue to be easy. China has had to address serious problems of inflation and unemployment, corruption, population pressures, and the public's growing desire for democratic change. It appears that, with the exception of the desire for democratic change, the Chinese government has weathered the storm. Time will tell whether the leaders of the Communist Party in China will prove as pragmatic in dealing with the public's desire for increasing input into political issues as they have with respect to economic reform. If the Communist Party is capable of this, China's future is indeed quite bright.

Discussion Questions

1. Compare and contrast the pure market and pure command economic systems. Where does the United States fit on this continuum?

2. One of the important characteristics of the purely competitive market is that there must be free entry to and exit from the market. Why is this condition necessary?

3. Suppose that initially the market for new cars in an area approaches being purely competitive. Describe the changes consumers might notice if that market becomes more monopolistic.

4. The outcomes for consumers are expected to be quite different if a market is purely competitive rather than purely monopolistic. List some of the differences you would expect and explain your choices.

5. Without reference to a diagram, explain the difference between a change in demand and a change in quantity demanded.

6. Discuss: "Recently the price of gas went up, and at the same time the quantity of gas purchased increased. This is a clear violation of the law of demand."

7. List and explain the factors we typically hold constant when drawing a demand curve. What additional factors do you think could be added to the list?

8. List and explain the factors that we typically hold constant when drawing a supply curve. What additional factors do you think could be added to the list?

9. With reference to a supply-and-demand diagram, explain why the equilibrium reached by a market typically reflects a well-being–maximizing production level of the good or service.

10. Suppose that during this year there is a very large personal income tax cut. Show and explain the effects you would expect on the market for new cars.

11. Explain why the transition from a command economy to a more market-oriented economy often entails a difficult period of transition.

12. Using the Chinese experience as the example, argue the benefits of the pure market economic system relative to the pure command system.

13. Discuss the three major problems embodied in the near-pure command system that existed in China from 1949 to 1978.

14. Discuss the economic reforms that were put in place after 1978 in China concerning agriculture and industry. Relying on the data presented in Table 2.3, how well has the Chinese economy responded to these reforms?

15. Most of the republics created by the fall of the USSR in 1991 have moved, to one degree or another, toward the market approach to economic organization. These economies have had varying degrees of success, but none has done as well as China. Why might this be the case?

16. The Chinese leader perhaps most responsible for putting China on the path to market reform is Deng Xiaoping, whose approach to reform is summarized in the saying "crossing the river while feeling the rocks." What does Deng mean by this, and to what extent do you think China's success in reform is due to this approach?

Additional Readings

Carson, Richard L. *Comparative Economic Systems*, 2nd ed. Armonk, NY: Sharpe, Inc., 1997.
Excellent and accessible text on the topic of economic systems. This book is especially interesting because of its emphasis on the role of government and the institution of private property rights.

Chow, Gregory C. *China's Economic Transformation*. Malden, MA: Blackwell, 2002.
A thorough and accessible treatment of China's economic history with special emphasis on the command era and the country's recent transition to market orientation.

Chow, Gregory C. *The Chinese Economy.* New York: Harper and Row, 1985.
While dated, this book offers a very clear and easy-to-read analysis of the functioning of the command economy that existed in China prior to its transition.

Finance and Development, September 2000.
Provides a very thorough treatment of the problems faced by transitional economies as well as an up-to-date summary of the various countries' performance since their transitions began.

The Journal of Economic Perspectives, Winter 2002.
A thoughtful and accessible symposium on the problems the transitional economies have faced and are continuing to face as they evolve into mixed-market economies.

Klein, Lawrence, and Marshall Pomer, eds. *The New Russia: Transition Gone Awry.* Stanford, CA: Stanford University Press, 2001.
Russian and American economists provide essays on how and why the Russian reforms since 1991 have failed to stabilize the economy.

Mastel, Greg. *The Rise of the Chinese Economy: The Middle Kingdom Emerges.* Armonk, NY: Sharpe, 1997.
Offers a thorough analysis of both the roots of reform in China and the problems facing China and rest of the world in integrating China into the world economy, and suggests some ways to address these problems.

Putterman, Louis. "Effort, Productivity and Incentives in a 1970s Chinese People's Commune." *Journal of Comparative Economics* 14 (1990), pp. 88–104.
This article clearly lays out the incentive problem that plagued Chinese agriculture during the command era.

Rosefielde, Steven. *Comparative Economic Systems: Culture, Wealth, and Power in the 21st Century.* Malden, MA: Blackwell, 2002.
Addresses the question of how ethics, culture, and politics affect the world's major economic systems.

Schmookler, Andrew. *The Illusion of Choice: How the Market Economy Shapes Our Destiny.* Albany: State University of New York Press, 1993.
Describes how the market economy affects all aspects of life.

World Bank. *China: 2020.* New York: Oxford University Press, 1997.
Offers an analysis of where China's reforms are likely leading the country, concluding with the now famous statement that, should the United States and China continue to grow at the rates they have recently experienced, China's GDP will surpass that of the United States by 2020.

World Development Report, 1996: From Plan to Market. New York: Oxford University Press, 1996.
A thorough treatment of the problems and promise of transitional economies. Includes a great deal of summary data on transition.

World Wide Web Resources

The CATO Institute

www.cato.org/home.html

A private institution founded to support "public policy based on individual liberty, limited government, free markets, and peace." Provides links to various free market–related sites and publications.

CIA World Factbook 2003

www.odci.gov/cia/publications/factbook/index.html

Gives demographic, environmental, geographic, and governmental information for all the countries in the former Soviet Union, as well as other countries.

Jerome Levy Economics Institute of Bard College

www.levy.org

A nonprofit institution devoted to the study of market-based public policy. Provides links to economic forecasts and other market-related sites and publications.

The National Council on Economic Education

www.ncee.net/index.html

Nonprofit organization that promotes economic literacy in the United States and abroad. Major producers of economic education material for grades K through 12. Their "Economics International" program is involved in bringing economics education to the former Soviet republics.

Government Control of Prices in Mixed Systems

What Are the Actual Outcomes?

Checklist of economic concepts

- Price ceilings
- Price floors
- Rent controls
- Minimum wages
- Derived demand
- Marginal revenue product of labor
- Marginal product of labor
- Marginal revenue
- Law of diminishing returns
- Substitution effect
- Income effect

It was one of many price controls brought in during the grim, panicky period between the attack on Pearl Harbour in 1941 and America's move to a full wartime economy in 1943. The housing market was seen as another thing that needed to be rationed or, at least, regulated—alongside rubber, petrol, coffee and shoes. By 1947 all these controls were phased out, except property-price regulations. Most cities have since scrapped these market distortions; the capital of capitalism has not.

Only one-third of New York City's 2m rental apartments are free of some kind of price restraint. A city board sets annual increases and administers an ever more complicated system. In some buildings, people live in similar apartments but pay wildly different levels of rent. In others, lone grandmothers sit in huge apartments, aware that moving would mean paying more for a smaller place elsewhere.

The oldest controls cover pre-1947 buildings (including any number of lovely houses on the city's most fashionable streets): these have average rents of $500 a month. A second tier, covered by rent stabilization, rent for $760. Unregulated apartments cost an average of $850, but this number is deceptive, since it includes the worst buildings in the outer boroughs.

Technically, new construction is free from these constraints. In fact, a complex system of tax inducements persuades most clever builders "voluntarily" to agree to rent-stabilization restraints. Not surprisingly under these conditions, building is anaemic; even with the largest surge in construction since the 1960s, the number of building permits issued in the past year will add less than 1% to New York's housing supply. Needless to say, in such a sclerotic system, the poor suffer most.

…

It is hard to find any economist who supports rent restraints. Price controls, even if laboriously tweaked, inevitably produce inefficiencies, reduce supply and cause bad side-effects. Black markets and bribery thrive. Building maintenance is often ignored. Landlords and tenants find themselves in poisonous relationships, since they are linked by law rather than by voluntarily renewable contracts. Unscrupulous property owners go to dangerous lengths to evict tenants in order to get higher-paying replacements; as a result, tenant-protection laws have been enacted that make it almost impossible to evict even a scoundrel.

Meanwhile, a vast bureaucracy has grown up to administer the price controls, supported by volunteers and litigators. The property owner who misses a filing deadline, or has his paperwork mislaid, can be blocked from even permissible rent increases. Given all this, most sane New Yorkers would rather eat their money than join the rentier class.

Oddly enough, for those landlords adept at navigating the system, returns are likely to be unaffected by price caps, as long as properties were acquired after they had been imposed and the potential for income is understood.

Indeed, although the press depicts the fight over price restraints as tenants versus landlords, it is more accurate to see it as tenants paying a below-market rent versus tenants who, in effect, pay the cost of this subsidy, says Peter Salins, the provost of the State University of New York and co-author of a book on New York's housing market (*Scarcity by Design*, Harvard University Press, 1992).

Who, then, are the lucky tenants? According to another study by Mr. Pollakowski, most benefits go to tenants in lower and mid-Manhattan, where the residents are relatively wealthy. The city's poorer folk, most of whom live in the outer boroughs, receive little or nothing. Perhaps the strongest argument offered by supporters of rent control is that it promotes stability; but, typically long-term tenants in unregulated markets receive similar concessions, since it is in a property-owner's interest to retain dependable renters in his buildings.

Mr. Salins says the members of the state legislature are well aware of all the basic arguments about the evil effects of price controls on the property market. They believe even more strongly, however, that voters do not like getting socked with rent increases. For New York's politicians, it is a time of small thoughts.

Source: "The Great Manhattan Rip-Off," *The Economist,* June 5, 2003.

The distinguishing feature between the pure market economy and a mixed system is that government is often actively involved in the individual markets of the latter. One common way in which government involves itself in mixed systems concerns the way in which prices are determined.

As was detailed in Chapter 2, prices in market-oriented economies tend to be set by the forces of demand and supply. Should the supply of an item increase relative to its demand, its price will fall. Alternatively, when demand rises relative to supply, price can be expected to rise. And it is this free movement of prices, in response to demand and supply conditions, that serves to allocate resources in the way in which the public wishes.

Suppose, for example, that two new alternative formats for watching television become available—high-definition and progressive scan—which are initially roughly equal in price and quality. Before long and for whatever reason, the public strongly prefers high-definition. What would be the expected market reaction? That is, would the public's desire for more high-definition machines and, of course, fewer progressive-scan devices be satisfied? As presented in Chapter 2, the answer is clearly *yes!* The process is simple: The demand for the high-definition devices would increase, driving the price of the items up. This increasing price for the devices initially induces existing producers to increase their own outputs. And, in the longer run, new investment into this industry can be expected as other, previous producers of perhaps related products are attracted into high-definition production by the lure of the relatively high prices and resulting profits. In each case you should see this analysis as a simple application of the laws of supply and demand. And, more importantly, you should see that the consumers, in fact, win—they get the additional high-definition devices that they wanted.

But what about the progressive-scan market? Just the opposite is happening, of course. The price for these devices will be falling in response to the falling demand. The falling prices induce existing producers to either cut their outputs or perhaps even discontinue producing the progressive-scan devices completely. Again, the consumers win—they wanted fewer progressive-scan devices, and the market, operating through freely moving prices, brought about the reallocation of resources that the public wanted.

Prices in mixed systems are not, however, always a simple response to demand and supply conditions. In fact, throughout history, and in nearly every market-oriented economy today, prices for certain goods and services have been and are under the legal control of government. Sometimes they set minimum prices that must be paid for a particular good or service, effectively making it illegal to sell the item below this price. In other circumstances, legally binding maximum prices are set by government. In many circumstances, the intention of government is to benefit some specific group of either producers or consumers who otherwise might be negatively affected were the market allowed to determine prices in accordance with demand-and-supply conditions. And in most of these cases, it is probably fair to conclude that government's intentions are laudable. For example, when world agricultural markets are such that an extreme surplus of dairy products exists leading to market prices which might force a large segment of the domestic dairy industry out of business, governments attempt to protect dairy farmers through a minimum permissible price for milk. And such a policy would likely have public support, at least from a humanitarian if not economic perspective. Similarly, when apartment rents appear to be outpacing the incomes of the working poor, government implementation of rental rate freezes or maximum rents certainly doesn't seem indicative of a government which cares little about the lives of its people.

What we must address is whether these types of policies—well intentioned or not—are effective. That is, can government control of prices improve upon the functioning of the market? You should be on the lookout here for two important lessons that have applications in nearly every area of government economic action: (1) When government takes action in a market, the market reacts. And this reaction, in many cases, serves to simply negate much of what the government action was designed to accomplish. (2) As with all human actions, unexpected and often negative consequences result from government intervention in markets. This is not to say that such intervention has no beneficial effects but rather that one should not necessarily feel that government price-setting activities can be a panacea for market outcomes which we dislike.

To consider these issues, we look at two of the most common examples of government determination of prices, rent controls and the minimum wage. Before we launch into this, we need to refine the definitions of government action that we have been using.

PRICE CEILINGS AND FLOORS

price ceiling
Maximum allowable price for a good or service, usually set by a government.

Price ceilings, or maximum prices, have been put into effect from time to time by government for two primary purposes. First, they have been established across-the-board in an attempt to hold inflation in check. Also, they have been used on a selective basis to keep the purchase of certain items within the reach of those at the lower end of the income scale. This latter purpose may also have an anti-inflationary intent. We will concern ourselves in this chapter with selective price ceilings, using rent controls as an illustration.

Rent controls have been used extensively in metropolitan areas of many countries as a device to hold housing costs in check for low-income groups. During the 1970s alone, more than 200 U.S. cities enacted some type of rent control. The most well known example of such controls in the United States is undoubtedly that of New York City, which has had rent controls in effect since World War II. Taking the cake internationally, however, is Paris, France, where rent controls have existed, to some extent, since the late 1700s. On a much smaller scale, it is common for a university to set rental rates on university apartments at relatively low levels to help alleviate problems encountered by low-income students.

price floor
A minimum allowable price for a good or service, typically set by a governmental unit or by a group of sellers.

When **price floors,** or minimum prices, are set for particular items, the intent of the government usually is to increase the incomes of those who sell the item. A classic example is that of minimum-wage legislation. The Fair Labor Standards Act of 1938 established the first federal minimum wage of 25 cents per hour for workers in designated industries. By 1981, the minimum had increased to $3.35 per hour. For the remainder of the decade, however, the minimum remained unchanged. Given a rising general level of prices throughout the 1980s and 1990s, those earning the minimum found that while their wage remained constant, their purchasing power was eroding. This situation eventually led to an increase in the minimum to its current level of $5.15 per hour in 1997. Further, not only has the minimum increased over the years, but the percentage of workers covered by it has also increased such that currently in excess of 80 percent of nonagricultural workers are covered. Finally, many state governments have enacted minimum-wage laws of their own to cover workers not covered by federal minimums.

Minimum-wage laws have had wide support from the general public. They apply, of course, to workers at the lower end of the income scale and were enacted to combat what Congress identified as "labor conditions detrimental to the maintenance of the minimum standard of living necessary for health, efficiency, and general well-being of the workers."

RENT CONTROLS

Almost everyone looks with disfavor on slums. In certain areas of most cities, one sees housing conditions that are distressing to say the least. Several families may be using the same bath and toilet facilities. Some families live in units that are not well-lighted or well-ventilated. Two or more families may be living in the same apartment. The buildings and apartments may be in various states of disrepair. Why do people live in them? Usually these are as much as lower-income families can afford. Or, if you have tried to find an apartment in Manhattan recently, you know that they may be all that is available. Why do these problems occur? Do the rent controls that have been operative in places such as New York City serve the best interests of lower-income groups? An examination of housing demand, supply, and pricing will help us evaluate the housing problems of the poor.

Demand

The demand for housing originates in households—families and unattached individuals—living in the economic system. Within the constraints of the incomes available to them and the prices they must pay for different goods and services, households choose what goods and services, and how much of each, they will purchase. Presumably, each household allocates its income among different goods and services such that a dollar's worth of housing contributes the same to its well-being as a dollar's worth of anything else it buys. If a dollar's worth of something else, say, food, were more valuable to the household than a dollar's worth of housing, the household would gain satisfaction by shifting some of its expenditure away from housing to food. On the other hand, if a dollar's worth of housing were more valuable than a dollar's worth of food, the household would gain in well-being by purchasing less food and more housing.

How does this translate into a demand curve for housing? In Figure 3.1, suppose that the market-determined rental rate is $500 per month. At this price, and assuming that households are spending their incomes so that a dollar's worth of housing makes the same contribution to household well-being as a dollar's worth of anything else, they purchase a total of 10,000 units of housing per year. What would happen to the quantity of housing demanded if rents rise to $600 and the other factors that influence demand remain unchanged? At the higher rent level, a dollar's worth of housing is a smaller quantity of housing than before; consequently, the contribution that a dollar's worth of housing makes to household well-being is smaller than it was before the rent increase. The contribution of a dollar's worth of any other item to household well-being thus is greater than that of a dollar's worth of housing. Rational households will shift dollars from housing to other items, reducing the amount of housing consumed to some level like 8,000. You may be asking, but mustn't these people be living somewhere? That is, can the public simply rent 2,000 fewer apartments this year than last? Of course they can. Some will take in roommates who once held their own apartments. In other cases, the relatively young might move back in with family. And many other possibilities exist, indicating that the demand for housing can and does respond very much like the demand for most goods and services. The entire demand curve *DD* is made up of such points as *A* and *B*, at which households consider that they are buying the correct amounts of housing relative to other goods and services at various prices for housing.

FIGURE 3.1 **Demand for and Supply of Housing**
The demand for housing *DD* shows the value of a unit of housing to households at various alternative quantities. If the quantity available is 10,000 units per year, the value of a unit to households is $500. If 11,000 units are available, the value of a unit becomes $400.

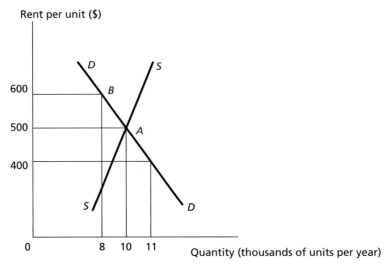

One more point should be made before we leave the concept of the demand for housing. The demand curve *DD* shows that when households take 10,000 units of housing, a unit of housing is worth $500 to them. That is, they believe the amount a unit contributes to their total well-being is the same as the contribution to their well-being made by $500 worth of any other good or service they consume. Similarly, if only the smaller amount of 8,000 were taken by them, they would value a unit of housing at $600. In general terms, the less we have of any given item, the more we value a unit of it.

Supply

The supply of housing available is not very responsive to price and/or rent levels over relatively short time spans. The supply curve tends to be sharply upward sloping, as shown by *SS* in Figure 3.1. The reason for this is evident. Most of the housing supply in any given year consists of the stock of existing units. In the course of a year, the amount by which this stock is likely to be increased or decreased is relatively small.

Nevertheless, some variation in the quantity supplied will occur in response to price changes. Consider, for example, the entire complex of housing units in New York City. The space they occupy is highly valuable for business purposes. A decrease in housing rental rates relative to what the space could earn if converted to business uses would cause some conversion to occur and decrease the number of housing units available. This can also work the other way around. An increase in housing rental rates relative to what the space could earn in business uses may result in conversion of some business space to housing units. It may also result in some construction of new housing units.

Price

Suppose that in a given city the demand curve for housing is *DD* and the supply curve is *SS*, as in Figure 3.2. The equilibrium rental rate is $500, and the number of housing units occupied is 10,000. Over time, economic growth and rising household incomes increase the demand for housing to D_1D_1. In the absence of rent controls, the short-run impact of the increase in demand is a rise in rental rates to $600 and an increase in the units made available to 11,000. Given the inability to build new housing units quickly, most of the new housing made available will result from converting buildings to housing uses from their former, perhaps commercial, uses.

The rise in rental rates will make investment in housing units more profitable, and in the long run—say, a period of five years or more—such additional investment will increase the supply of housing to S_1S_1 as new housing units are constructed and further conversions from other uses occur. Rental rates will fall to some value like $525, and the number of units rented will rise to 12,500. In the city as a whole, due to both space limitations and the alternative of using property for business purposes, it is highly unlikely that increases in supply can keep pace with increases in demand. Thus, the final rental rate, $525, will most likely exceed the original rental rate of $500. In other localities in which space is a much smaller problem and in which business competition for space is much less, the final rental rate may be even closer to the original rate.

The Effects of Rent Controls

In the United States, following World War II, numerous cities elected to continue rent controls established during the war. These controlled rates were maintained to some degree, although over time they have crept gradually upward. The purpose of the controls has been to keep the price of housing within the reach of lower-income groups. But what are the *actual* effects of the controls?

Most importantly, they generate a housing shortage. In Figure 3.2, as demand increases from *DD* to D_1D_1 with the supply curve at *SS*, if rents are not allowed to rise above $500, a shortage of 3,000 units develops. Not all households looking for apartments are able to find them. Some individuals and even families are forced to share living quarters. Numerous households take in boarders. Many young adults are forced either to delay leaving the family home for their own places or to return to the family home. Not all households desiring to add to their living space are able to do so. Much time is wasted in futile searches for apartments. Those whose employment is in the central city and who cannot find housing there are forced to outlying areas from which they must commute. This is the inevitable outcome of price ceilings. Whenever price ceilings have been set below the market equilibrium, shortages have quickly become apparent. Today in New York City, for example, those seeking rent-controlled housing frequently scan the obituaries looking for recently freed-up space.

FIGURE 3.2 **Effects of an Increase in Demand for Housing**
If the demand for housing units is *DD* and the supply is *SS*, the equilibrium level of rent is $500 and the equilibrium quantity occupied is 10,000 units. An increase in the demand to D_1D_1 increases the rent to $600 and the quantity occupied to 11,000. The increased profitability of producing housing causes supply to increase over time to S_1S_1, increasing the units occupied to 12,500. If, however, rent controls are enacted when the rental rate is $500, the long-run increase in housing supply would not take place, resulting in a shortage of 3,000 units over time (from 10,000 to 13,000).

In the second place, the cost of housing is not kept down for everyone. In the normal turnover of housing units—some households vacating their apartments and others renting them—it becomes common to make under-the-table payments to landlords for the privilege of a new lease. For those seeking housing, the search time required is a cost to the searchers. Many, if not most, of those forced to commute find their costs increased in at least three ways: (1) higher rents, (2) direct costs of commuting, and (3) the value of the time lost in commuting. Only those ensconced in housing before the controls were put into effect and who did not move after they became effective can be sure that the controls will not raise their housing costs. Such protection from rising rents for those who have lived in controlled apartments for long periods of time would seem to be exactly what the controls were put into effect for. Unfortunately, many who receive these benefits could hardly claim them on the basis of financial need. For example, it has been reported that a judge in New York City's housing court, whose job it is to enforce the city's rent control program, rents a two-bedroom apartment for less than $100 per month, which, if it were not rent-controlled, would bring well over $1,000 per month. Examples of this nature abound.

In the third place, the long-run profit inducements that would shift the supply curve to the right to S_1S_1 are eliminated by the rent controls. The rising household incomes that serve to increase the demand for housing also increase the demand for other goods and services. These are not subject to price controls. The industries producing these alternatives become relatively more profitable than the housing industry, in which investors cannot capture higher returns from households. Consequently, investors in real estate are provided with profit inducements to increase the space available for business relative to the space available for housing. In Paris, France, for example, between 1914 and 1950, almost no new rental housing units were constructed even though both the population and household incomes were rising. Further, it is even possible that the rent controls may cause the supply curve for housing units available to decrease in the long run, leaving even fewer housing units available than existed before rent controls were put into effect. This, no doubt, leads to an increase in the population of the homeless since less housing and homelessness must be inextricably linked. It is no fluke that, of major U.S. cities, 6 of the 10 with the highest rates of homelessness also have rent controls in effect.

In the fourth place, landlords faced with rent controls tend to allow the quality of their properties to deteriorate. For any given type of good or service, lower quality sold at the same price per unit is equivalent to an increase in the price when the quality is not decreased. So quality deterioration is a disguised means of securing at least some price relief. The enactment of minimum housing standards by a municipality may block landlords from this escape route; however, omnipresent slums in cities with longstanding rent controls indicate they are not always a resounding success.

Finally, the enforcement of rent controls means that for present housing supplies, the rental level of housing units is held below households' valuation of those housing units. For example, in Figure 3.2, after the increase in demand to D_1D_1, the quantity of housing supplied with rent controls at $500 is 10,000 units. But for this quantity of housing, the value of a unit to households is $800. The price of housing is not allowed to reflect the value that households place on a unit of it. In other words, resources of necessity become seriously misallocated since the price of housing no longer reflects the public's value of housing.

What, then, can be said concerning the government's attempt to keep housing affordable for those of modest means through rent controls? Clearly, some win— those who are fortunate enough to occupy a rent-controlled unit. Even these folks, however, don't tend to win in the longer term since the limited potential for profit for the landowners often leads them to allow the units to decay. Many others, of course, directly lose. Especially hard hit are those who cannot find adequate housing as the rent controls necessarily lead to housing shortages. Others are negatively affected as they expend precious time either searching for housing or commuting ever-longer distances from the central cities where they work. Still others are hurt by having to make under-the-table payments to unscrupulous landlords for access to housing. Finally, one is left to question whether, as the example of the judge living in a rent-controlled apartment attests, those who do win in the sense of acquiring such an apartment are the ones the policy was designed to help. In each case, one can see the two points made earlier with respect to government action in the mixed market economy: (1) markets may react to government action in ways that offset the intended impacts of that action, and (2) government actions may involve consequences that are clearly unintended.

MINIMUM WAGES

The establishment by law of minimum hourly wage rates is looked upon favorably by a large majority of those in our society. Most see minimum-wage rates as a means of helping those at the lower end of the income scale raise their wage rates and thereby raise their incomes. There is apparently a philosophical belief in our society that those who are willing to work should not find themselves living in poverty. Yet at its current level, the minimum wage fails to keep even a family of three (one working for the minimum) out of poverty. What are the economic effects of the minimum? Is it a good means of improving the lot of the working poor? Does the minimum serve to improve the distribution of income in the economy? Before we can answer these questions, we need an understanding of how the market for the peculiar commodity called labor functions.

Market Demand for Labor

The demand for unskilled labor by the employers of the economy is given in Figure 3.3. It should be noted that whereas the horizontal axis is labeled in the standard way, the vertical axis measures the wage rate since the wage rate is the price of labor per hour. There is an important difference, however, between the demand for labor by employers and the demand for a good or service by consumers. Specifically, consumers demand a good like orange juice because they receive satisfaction directly from consuming the product. Employers do not demand labor for the same reason. Employers demand labor not because they directly receive satisfaction from labor but because employing labor leads to satisfaction indirectly, in the form of increased revenues, when they sell the products that are produced by labor. For this reason, the demand for labor is said to be an indirect or **derived demand.** In other words, the demand for labor is derived from the demand for the product being produced.

derived demand for labor
The demand for labor is said to be dependent on, or derived from, the demand for the product being produced.

The demand curve for labor in Figure 3.3 is downward sloping, just as the demand for a good such as orange juice would be. Such a negatively sloped demand curve for orange juice suggests that the value placed on an additional unit of orange juice by the consumer declines as more orange juice is consumed. The demand for labor is downward sloping for exactly the same reason. The negative slope of the demand for labor indicates that, in terms of extra revenues, the value of an additional worker to the employer declines as more labor is hired.

It seems reasonable to argue that a fifth quart of orange juice consumed during a week yields less satisfaction than the fourth, but why would the same be true for units of labor? That is, why might a fourth unit of labor add less to the satisfaction

FIGURE 3.3 The Market Demand for Unskilled Labor

The market demand for unskilled labor shows the quantities of labor that employers in the economy are willing to hire at various wage rates. It is important to note that the law of demand holds for labor. That is, the quantity of labor demanded by employers falls as the wage increases, other things being equal.

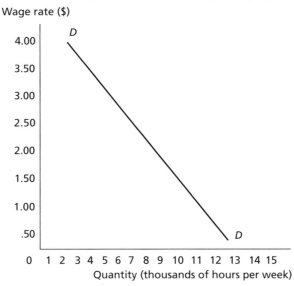

(revenues) of the employer than the third? To answer this question, detailed consideration must be given to the way in which a firm's revenues change as the firm's employment changes. Thus, we must shift away from the demand for unskilled labor by all employers, as presented in Figure 3.3, and consider the demand for unskilled labor by one employer.

The Demand for Labor by One Employer

marginal revenue product of labor
The increase in revenue that accrues to the firm when an additional worker is hired; indicates the value of the worker to the firm.

marginal product of labor
The increase in output due to hiring an additional worker.

marginal revenue
The increase in revenue from selling an additional unit of the product.

When a unit of labor is hired by a firm, a certain amount of additional output is produced, which is converted into additional revenue for the firm once the output is sold. The increase in revenue due to hiring one additional unit of labor is called the **marginal revenue product of labor** and indicates the value the firm places on the additional unit of labor. Our goal, then, is to determine why the marginal revenue product of labor declines as more labor is hired. The marginal revenue product of labor has two parts: (1) the increase in output due to hiring the additional unit of labor, called the **marginal product of labor,** and (2) the increase in revenue for the firm when each of the additional units of output is sold, called the **marginal revenue.** Given this, if the marginal revenue product of labor is to decline as additional labor is hired, at least one of these two components must be declining.

Consider first the marginal revenue, which indicates the amount of revenue the firm brings in when it sells each additional unit of its product. If the firm is purely competitive, marginal revenue is simply the market-determined price for the good. A characteristic of the purely competitive market structure is that no single firm has any control over the market price. Thus, the marginal revenue of a purely competitive firm does not change as it sells additional units of its product. Consequently, if the marginal revenue product of labor is to decline, the decline must be due to a declining marginal product of labor. The answer has now been found. Economists are so confident that the marginal product of labor declines as additional units of labor are hired that they refer to this phenomenon as the **law of diminishing returns.** This law states that as additional units of a variable input such as labor are added to a given amount of a fixed input such as capital, the resulting increases in output (the marginal product of labor) will *eventually* decline. Stating the law as fact, of course, does not make it so. An example should, however, convince even the most skeptical reader.

Table 3.1 details a typical situation for a firm that sells hamburgers when various quantities of labor per hour are hired. Labor is the variable input for this firm, and its capital consists of its building, tools, and equipment. When the firm hires no workers, total production is, of course, zero hamburgers, as given in column (2). When the first worker is hired, total production rises to five hamburgers per hour. Thus, the first worker contributes five units of production, which is given as that worker's marginal product in column (3). The firm operates in a purely competitive market, so the marginal revenue or price is constant at 50 cents per burger, as indicated in column (4). Finally, column (5) reports the marginal revenue product of each unit of labor. The first worker increased production by five units, each of which sold for 50 cents. Thus, the first worker's marginal revenue product is $2.50.

Suppose now that a second worker is hired. Total production rises to 25 burgers, indicating that the second worker's marginal product is 20 units. Why does the second worker add more to production than the first? Think about the way in which the firm would have to operate were it to have but one employee. This worker would have to be a jack-of-all-trades, first taking a customer's order, then scrambling to the supply area for the needed ingredients, then scrambling to the preparation area and to the grill. Once the beef patty is cooked, the worker must assemble the burger and again scramble (now short of breath) back to the counter to serve the customer. Put simply, with only one worker (or perhaps only a few workers), there is too little labor for the amount of capital that the firm has at its disposal. In other words, the firm's capital is underutilized. When the second worker is hired, the available capital can be used much more efficiently through the specialization of labor. For example, perhaps one worker concentrates on taking customer orders and gathering ingredients, while the other worker actually prepares the burgers. Such specialization of labor often yields increasing returns to labor initially and serves as the justification for modern assembly line processes.

Returning to Table 3.1, you see that the same situation holds true for the third worker. Eventually, however, just the opposite occurs. Experience teaches that just as capital can be underutilized, leading to the possibility of increasing marginal returns to labor, capital eventually becomes overutilized. When this occurs, diminishing returns to labor follow. For the hamburger shop, this occurs with the addition of the fourth worker. When this worker is hired, total production rises from 50 burgers per hour to 70. The marginal product of the fourth worker is

law of diminishing returns
As additional units of a variable input are added to a given amount of a fixed input, the resulting increases in output eventually will decline.

TABLE 3.1
Total Production, Marginal Product, Marginal Revenue, and Marginal Revenue Product for the Hamburger Shop

(1) Units of Labor	(2) Total Production	(3) Marginal Product	(4) Marginal Revenue	(5) Marginal Revenue Product $MRP = (3) \times (4)$
0	0			
		5	$.50	$ 2.50
1	5			
		20	.50	10.00
2	25			
		25	.50	12.50
3	50			
		20	.50	10.00
4	70			
		10	.50	5.00
5	80			
		5	.50	2.50
6	85			
		1	.50	.50
7	86			

20 units, which is 5 less than the marginal product of the third worker. Diminishing returns of this nature come about for a variety of reasons, the most obvious being that the burger shop itself is equipped to accommodate only a certain number of workers comfortably. As more workers are hired, they may have to share their tools with other workers or wait their turn to use capital equipment. Common sense dictates that regardless of the size of the firm, if additional workers are continually hired, eventually a new worker will do little more than get in the way. Just as your mother probably told you, "Too many cooks spoil the soup."

Diminishing returns for labor may also come about due to the overspecialization of labor. Although requiring each worker to be a jack-of-all-trades is clearly inefficient, specialization can go too far. If specialization goes to the point where the extent of a particular worker's job is simply squirting ketchup on buns all day, the worker will likely become bored, easily distracted, and perhaps even a bit resentful. The result is clear—reduced efficiency or, in other words, diminishing returns to labor.

Regardless of the exact cause of the fall in efficiency, we can be sure that it will eventually occur. The outcome of the diminishing returns is equally clear: The value to the firm of additional units of labor falls. The third worker has a marginal revenue product of $12.50; thus, this worker is worth $12.50 to the firm. When the fourth worker is hired, the marginal revenue product and thus the value of the fourth worker falls to $10. The same will be true for each unit of labor hired beyond the third. As additional units of labor are hired by a firm, the value placed on each new worker eventually declines due to the law of diminishing returns.

Now that the question of why an additional unit of labor may be valued less highly by the firm than a previously hired unit has been answered, the firm-level discussion of the demand for labor must be tied into the discussion of the demand for labor by all employers as presented in Figure 3.1. This requires two steps. First, as you have probably guessed, the marginal revenue product of labor is the firm's demand for labor. A demand curve simply indicates the value placed on each unit of a good or service by the purchaser. Marginal revenue product (*MRP*) is the firm's valuation of labor; thus, it is the firm's demand curve for labor. Plotting the data on the marginal revenue product of labor from Table 3.1 gives the demand for unskilled labor for the hamburger shop in Figure 3.4. Please note that the figure includes data for only the third through the seventh workers. The reason for this is that if the hamburger shop is managed rationally, it would never hire fewer than three workers. Why? The third worker is more valuable—has a greater *MRP*, that is—than either of the first two workers. Thus, if it is rational to hire the first and second workers, it must be rational to hire at least three.

The second step requires a tie between one firm's demand for labor and the demand by all firms. That is, there may be 100 or even 1,000 firms similar to the hamburger shop. In such a case, how is the demand for labor by one firm linked to the demand for labor by all firms? If your common sense suggests that all that must be done is to sum the individual firm demands, then you are right. The procedure is quite simple; for each wage, each individual firm's quantity demanded is added to the quantity demanded by all of the other firms to form the quantity demanded of labor by all firms. In this way, the demand for labor by all employers, as represented by Figure 3.3, may be thought of as the summation of the individual demands for labor by the individual employers in the economy.

Market Supply of Labor

The supply of labor refers to the quantities of labor, in terms of hours, that workers are willing to offer at various wage rates, other things being equal. As such, the supply of labor curve indicates what happens to the hours of work offered by an economy's workers when there is a change in the wage. For example, suppose there is a general wage increase. In such a situation, what will happen to the number of hours that workers are willing to work? There is a temptation to conclude that the number of hours increases as the wage increases, but this temptation should be resisted. In fact, the number of hours offered by workers may increase, decrease, or remain the same as the wage increases. The reason for the uncertainty is that a wage change puts two offsetting effects into action.

substitution effect
The change in the hours of work that occurs in response to a wage change, other things being equal.

The first is called the **substitution effect** and is defined as the change in the hours of work that occurs when there is a wage change, other things being equal. The substitution effect takes into account the fact that people have numerous ways in which to spend their time other than working. For simplicity, suppose that we group all these alternative uses of time into a category called leisure. Thus, the individual can spend his or her time working or consuming leisure. The only other point needed for an understanding of the substitution effect is the realization that

FIGURE 3.4   The Demand for Unskilled Labor by One Firm
The demand for labor for an individual firm is given by the marginal revenue product of labor, which measures the increase in firm revenues due to hiring additional units of labor.

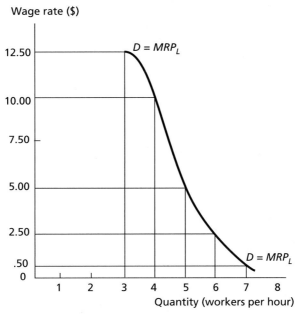

the wage rate is nothing more than the price of leisure time. For example, if the wage is $5 per hour and a worker chooses to work one hour less than normal—that is, if the worker chooses to consume one additional hour of leisure—the worker must give up, or pay, $5 to do so. Now consider the substitution effect of a wage increase. A wage increase amounts to an increase in the price of leisure and, as such, leads to a reduction in the quantity of leisure demanded by the individual. Since less leisure is being consumed, the individual of necessity is choosing to work more. Consequently, the substitution effect causes the hours of work offered to increase as the wage increases and would, on its own, give a positively sloped supply of labor curve.

Before drawing the conclusion that the supply of labor is positively sloped, however, recall that a second and offsetting effect is put into action when there is a wage change. This is called the **income effect** and is defined as the change in hours of work that occurs when there is a change in income, other things being equal. The income effect treats leisure as a normal good. Recall that a normal good is one for which demand rises as income rises. Given a wage increase and the accompanying income increase, the demand for leisure can be expected to increase. With the demand for leisure increasing, the hours of work offered tend to decline in response to the income effect of the wage increase. Thus, the income effect of a wage increase, on its own, gives a negatively sloped supply of labor curve.

income effect
A measure of the change in the hours of work that occurs when there is a change in income, other things being equal.

FIGURE 3.5 **The Supply of Labor for the Entire Economy**
The supply of labor shows the number of hours of labor that individuals are willing to offer at various wage rates. The steep positive slope indicates that a wage rate increase will coax some additional hours but not a great increase in the number of hours offered.

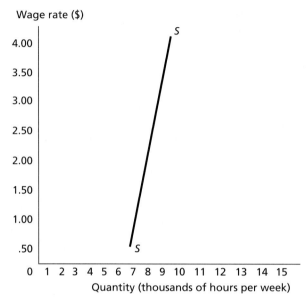

Which of the two effects dominates? If the substitution effect is dominant, the supply of labor is positively sloped, while a dominant income effect gives a negatively sloped supply. Clearly, this is not a question that can be answered theoretically. Fortunately, a great deal of research has been conducted on the issue, resulting in a general conclusion that suggests the supply of labor is very slightly positively sloped. When there is a general wage increase, then, the number of hours offered will increase, but only slightly. Such a supply of labor curve is drawn in Figure 3.5.

The Labor Market

Figure 3.6 brings together the demand for and supply of unskilled labor in the economy. Once this is done, it becomes clear that the labor market behaves much like any other market. For example, if *DD* and *SS* are the initial market demand and supply curves, there is an equilibrium wage and quantity hired of $5.00 and 9,000 hours per week, respectively. Note that at this wage there is neither a surplus of labor (unemployment) nor a shortage. Just as in any other market, the equilibrium indicates that the intentions of the buyers (firms) are the same as the intentions of the sellers (workers). In other words, at this wage the firms are willing to hire exactly the number of hours of labor that the workers desire to offer.

Before we continue, it is important to understand why the employers desire 9,000 hours of labor at the equilibrium wage of $5.00. A rational employer will hire a worker only if the worker adds more to revenue than to cost. The addition to

FIGURE 3.6   A Competitive Labor Market

A competitive market without discrimination will result in a market wage equal to the workers' marginal revenue product. In this case, marginal revenue product is $5.00 per hour, and 9,000 hours of labor will be hired.

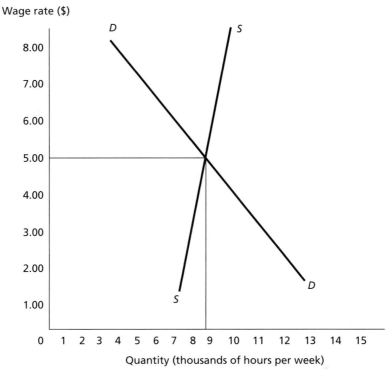

Wage rate ($)

Quantity (thousands of hours per week)

revenue is given by the marginal revenue product or the demand for labor curve. The addition to cost, on the other hand, is given by the wage rate. Thus, the rational firm increases employment up to the point where the wage rate equals the demand for labor. Figure 3.6 indicates that this occurs at the 9,000-hour level of employment. For each unit of labor up to the 9,000-hour level, the marginal revenue product is greater than the wage, indicating that these workers are profitably hired. Were employment to be carried even one unit beyond 9,000, however, the firms would be losing money on the additional worker since the worker would be adding more to cost than to revenue.

The Effects of the Minimum Wage

Figure 3.7 shows the standard or traditional analysis of the impact of a minimum wage. Starting from the equilibrium wage of $5, suppose a well-meaning Congress, concerned with the low incomes of unskilled workers, enacts a minimum wage of $6 per hour. What is the impact of the program? Consider the impact of the program on the demand for and supply of labor separately. Employers must now pay $6 for each unit of labor hired. Given that a rational employer will hire a worker only if the worker's marginal revenue product is greater than the wage, we

FIGURE 3.7 The Effect of a Minimum Wage, Standard Analysis

Within the standard analysis, the effect of a minimum wage set above the equilibrium wage is to lead to a surplus of labor. In this case, a minimum established at $6 leads to a surplus of 750 hours per week. This surplus is, of course, known as unemployment.

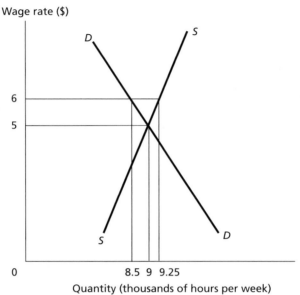

can be sure that quantity of labor demanded will fall in response to the wage increase. Recalling that the demand for labor represents the marginal revenue product of labor, we see in Figure 3.7 that the quantity of labor demanded will fall to 8,500 hours when the wage rises to $6. The reason for this is clear—for each unit of labor between the 9,000-hour and 8,500-hour levels of employment, the wage rate is greater than the marginal revenue product of labor.

This situation is further complicated by the supply reaction to the minimum wage. Specifically, the effect of the minimum is to increase the quantity of labor supplied from 9,000 hours to 9,250 hours. At the minimum wage of $6, then, there is a surplus of labor equal to 750 hours per week. That is, at this wage, there are 750 hours of employment that workers wish to provide but are unable to provide. This is the inevitable conclusion of government-established price floors in the standard analysis. Whenever such minimum prices are set above the market equilibrium, they result in a surplus called *unemployment*.

From this traditional theoretical perspective, it is clear that the establishment of a minimum wage leads to some unemployment, but what about increases in an existing minimum wage? A bit of insight suggests that the analysis just presented is equally applicable to a minimum-wage increase as it is to the initial establishment of a minimum. For example, suppose that the existing minimum of $6 was increased to $7. What would be the result of such a policy? The quantity of labor demanded would fall further, the quantity of labor supplied would increase further, and the two taken together would lead to even more unemployment.

Complicating this unemployment effect is the likelihood that many of those who will be working for the minimum wage are teenagers. To the extent that teenagers lose employment opportunities due to the minimum, they also lose two of the most valuable assets they need as they enter the world of work—job experience and on-the-job training. Here we have a clear application of the opportunity cost principle: teenagers who lose employment due to the minimum wage will have lost, forever, early job experience and the accompanying training that they will so desperately need as they enter the job market as adults.

Given the unemployment effect of the minimum, may it be concluded that minimum wages fail to make economic sense? Such a decision must rely on analysis of the benefits and costs of the program. The costs are clear, but what are the benefits? Returning to Figure 3.7, we note that the minimum generated a good deal of unemployment, yet not all the workers lost their jobs. In fact, 8,500 hours of labor remained employed. These workers clearly benefited from the establishment of the minimum, given that they earn more for their labor. Further, if these workers are from the lower end of the income distribution, the fact that they are earning more suggests that the minimum may tend to improve the distribution of earnings in the economy as a whole.

Given that the minimum wage involves costs and benefits, to properly evaluate the minimum wage or any increase in the minimum, we must answer three questions: Is the minimum an effective antipoverty tool? By how much does the unemployment rate rise when the minimum wage is increased? And to what extent does the minimum wage improve the distribution of income in the economy? Relatively little research has been conducted on the first of these questions. One way to address this issue is to consider how the minimum wage relates to the earnings of average workers and to the poverty line as presented in Table 3.2. The first column shows the minimum and its periodic changes since 1980. The second column presents the ratio of the minimum wage to the average hourly earnings of production workers. Finally, the last column shows how the minimum wage relates to the poverty line.

Consider first the minimum wage relative to average earnings. In 1980, a full-time, year-round worker earning the minimum brought home 47 percent of what the typical production worker earned. Obviously, this percentage varies year-to-year since the minimum only changes periodically while average wages drift upward. But what's particularly interesting is that, even with the 1997 increase in the minimum to $5.15 per hour, by 2003, the minimum had fallen to only 34 percent of average earnings.

Similarly, consider the minimum and its ability to move low-income earners out of poverty. In 1980, a family of three in which one person was a full-time, year-round minimum-wage worker had earned income which left them at 98 percent of the poverty line. That is, in 1980, the minimum was nearly capable of moving a family of three out of poverty. By 2003, that same family had fallen to only 73 percent of the income necessary to be considered "not poor" by the government's

TABLE 3.2
The Minimum Wage Relative to Average Earnings and the Poverty Level

Sources: www.census.gov/ hhes/poverty/threshld/ thresh01.html and www.bls.gov/ces/ (see Series Report CES0500000006).

	Minimum Wage ($)	Minimum as a Percentage of Average Earnings	Minimum as a Percentage of Poverty Level
1980	3.10	47	98
1981	3.35	46	96
1982	3.35	43	91
1983	3.35	42	88
1984	3.35	40	84
1985	3.35	39	81
1986	3.35	38	80
1987	3.35	37	77
1988	3.35	36	74
1989	3.35	35	70
1990	3.80	38	76
1991	4.20	41	80
1992	4.25	40	79
1993	4.25	39	77
1994	4.25	38	75
1995	4.25	37	73
1996	4.75	40	79
1997	5.15	42	84
1998	5.15	40	82
1999	5.15	39	81
2000	5.15	37	79
2001	5.15	35	76
2002	5.15	34	75
2003	5.15	34	73

official definition. As an antipoverty tool, then, it seems that the minimum is not particularly potent.

In contrast to the first question, a great deal of research has been directed toward considering the unemployment impact of increasing the minimum wage. Although the outcomes of these studies differ in significant regards, two results are commonly found. First, in terms of increased unemployment, teenagers appear to be more frequently harmed by the minimum than any other group of workers since they work in disproportionate numbers for the minimum wage. In fact, increases in the minimum appear to have little or no effect on the employment rate of adult workers. Beyond this, the research suggests that a 10 percent increase in the minimum is associated with an increase in the teenage unemployment rate of perhaps a bit less than 1 percent. For example, if the teenage unemployment rate is initially 12 percent and the minimum wage is increased by 10 percent, teenage unemployment can be expected to rise to about 12.5 percent. Importantly, however, some particularly new research suggests that even this unemployment effect of the minimum may be overstated. Specifically, *some* recent research, which we

FIGURE 3.8   The Effect of a Minimum Wage, Alternative Analysis
Within the alternative analysis, a minimum wage is expected to result in little or no unemployment as long as the wage remains in the indeterminate range, in this case, from $5 to $6 per hour.

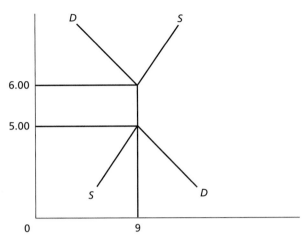

will refer to as the alternative analysis, suggests that for comparatively modest increases in the minimum wage, no negative effect on unemployment might be reasonably expected. Suppose as in Figure 3.8, for example, the initial equilibrium wage is $5 and Congress establishes a minimum of $6. What is the employment effect? Clearly there isn't one. That is, both before and after the minimum is put into place, 9,000 hours of labor are employed.

This is clearly an artifact of the peculiar way in which both the demand and supply curves of Figure 3.8 are drawn. Consider first the demand curve. The vertical portion suggests that so long as wages fall within the range of $5 to $6, the quantity of labor demanded is unchanged. Why might this be true? Several possibilities have been advanced by proponents of this view. It has been suggested, for example, that firms simply offset the higher wage for labor by perhaps allowing longer queues during peak hours, improving the operating efficiency of the firm, or raising prices on items they sell for which consumers are not particularly price-sensitive. Further, a rational firm might simply incur the additional wage costs and maintain employment, at least in the short term, to avoid the hiring and training costs associated with employing new workers at some later date.

The supply side of Figure 3.8 is a bit easier to grasp. The vertical portion in this case suggests that wages can vary anywhere from $5 to $6 with no impact on the quantity of labor supplied. Again, why might this be the case? One possibility is that many of the workers at this low level of earnings are part-time employees for whom a specific number of hours is more important due to other time constraints than is the wage, at least within a narrow range of wages. Alternatively, using the analysis presented above, it may be that for a range of wages, the income and substitution effects exactly or at least nearly exactly offset, leaving hours of work offered insensitive to wage changes.

What do we make of the alternative analysis of the minimum wage presented in Figure 3.8? It suggests that so long as wages remain in the vertical range of the demand and supply curves, a minimum wage is expected to have little or no impact on employment. It is too soon, however, in the development of the literature on this subject to simply throw over the standard approach, though the alternative does seem capable of explaining the limited research findings of no significant negative employment effect of the minimum wage. A cautious conclusion might be that there is likely to be a negative employment effect due to the minimum wage, especially among teenagers, but that this effect is probably rather slight.

Research into the third question is also quite informative. Specifically, the evidence suggests that the minimum wage has little impact on the distribution of income in our society. The primary reason for this outcome is that many of the individuals benefiting from the minimum wage are teenagers from middle- and upper-income families. For example, when the minimum was $3.35 per hour, it was estimated that only about 10 percent of those earning the minimum were heads of households living in poverty. As a policy designed to help the working poor, then, the minimum wage may be poorly targeted.

What may we now conclude about the minimum wage? First, some individuals clearly benefit from the minimum. The primary beneficiaries are those who remain employed and have their earnings increased in response to the minimum. Second, however, it is equally clear that other individuals lose when a minimum wage is established or increased. Especially hard hit are teenagers who lose their jobs and the accompanying experience and training in response to the minimum, though the alternative approach suggests that this effect may not be as great as previously thought. Third, the minimum wage appears to be a poor means of improving the distribution of income in the economy since it typically is established at low levels compared to average earnings and the poverty line and, further, since many of its recipients are not poor. At this point, a final decision concerning the desirability of the minimum wage must be left to each of us. These outcomes, however, are clearly not exactly what Congress had in mind when it enacted the minimum wage.

Summary

Governments within mixed economies have regularly supplanted the market determination of prices with legally instituted prices. In some cases, governments dictate that goods and services may not be sold for more than a specific price—price ceilings. In other cases, just the opposite happens and governments set minimum acceptable prices—price floors. In most of these circumstances, the goal of government is to "protect" either the producers or the consumers of the good or service from what are thought to be burdensome or unfair market-determined prices. And, in many of these cases, there is wide support for the government action.

When government sets prices, however, two important principles must be kept in mind. First, markets tend to react to government price setting in ways that, to some extent, offset or negate the intended action. Second, there are often unintended consequences of the government price-setting actions.

These two points can be clearly seen by considering the cases of rent controls and minimum wages. Concerned about keeping housing affordable, governments often institute price ceilings on rents. And some clearly benefit—those who are able to find and keep a well-maintained, rent-controlled apartment. But what other outcomes do rent controls create? First and most importantly, as with all price ceilings set below the equilibrium market level, housing shortages are generated. Further, the incentive to maintain property is reduced since invested monies cannot be recouped by the landowners and worse yet, over time, the incentive to build new housing units is either reduced or actually eliminated. Finally, it is not at all clear that those for whom the program was enacted actually are the ones who benefit by being able to occupy a well-maintained, rent-controlled apartment.

Minimum wages—a price floor for labor—are often enacted by governments as a means of helping the working poor. What are the actual outcomes? Again, some win—those who keep their jobs at the new higher rate of pay. Unfortunately, others are not so lucky. As with any price floor set above the market-determined price, the minimum necessarily leads to a surplus of labor, unemployment. Especially hard hit are teenagers who disproportionately work for the minimum and if unemployed lose the opportunity to attain job experience and training that they will so desperately need later in life. Finally, it should be noted that the minimum wage seems poorly targeted since so few of those working for the minimum are in fact heads of households. In the case both of rent controls and of the minimum wage, one is left to ask, "Might there be better ways to help those of modest means?"

Discussion Questions

1. Define and give examples of price floors and price ceilings.
2. Define the term *marginal revenue product of labor.* What are the two components of this, and why is it said to reflect the firm's demand for labor?
3. Explain why the demand for labor is said to be a derived demand.
4. Explain the concepts known as income and substitution effects. How do these relate to the supply of labor?
5. When governments impose prices in an attempt to help some particular group of producers or consumers, there are often unintended consequences. Use the case of rent controls to show this.
6. In what sense might minimum wages actually hurt those who are intended to be helped?
7. What effect would you expect minimum wages to have on the attainment of job experience and training of the young?

8. Within the context of the alternative approach to minimum wages, there is little or no unemployment effect. Explain this.

9. Why might a rational firm, in response to an increase in the minimum wage, not choose to reduce employment?

10. What effect would you expect rent controls to have on: (1) the availability of housing in the short run, (2) the availability of housing in the long run, and (3) the quality of housing available?

11. If minimum wages and rent controls create significant inefficiency in the market, why do they remain so popular publicly?

12. Minimum wages and rent controls are implemented in an attempt to help those of modest means. Suggest better alternatives.

13. Suppose that Congress enacts a large personal income tax cut that effectively increases the wages of workers nationally. Relying on income and substitution effects, would you expect workers to offer more hours of their labor to their employers in response to the tax cut?

Additional Readings

Burkhauser, Richard V., Kenneth A. Couch, and David C. Wittenburg. "Who Minimum Wages Bite: An Analysis Using Monthly Data from the SIPP and CPS." *Southern Economic Journal*, July 2000, pp. 16–40.
A modern analysis of the standard, or traditional, view of the unemployment effects of the minimum wage. Also offers a critique of the alternative approach.

Card, David, and Alan B. Krueger. "Minimum Wages and Employment: A Case Study of the Fast-Food Industry in New Jersey and Pennsylvania." *American Economic Review,* September 1994, pp. 772–793.
Offers the first comprehensive explanation and analysis of the alternative approach to the minimum wage's unemployment effect.

Card, David, and Alan B. Krueger. *Myth and Measurement: The New Economics of the Minimum Wage.* Princeton, NJ: Princeton University Press, 1995.
A thorough treatment of Card and Krueger's alternative approach to the minimum wage's "unemployment effect."

Grimes, Paul W., and George A. Chressanthis. "Assessing the Effect of Rent Control on Homelessness." *Journal of Urban Economics*, January 1997, pp. 23–37.
A thoughtful article showing statistically the correlation between the establishment of rent controls and homelessness.

Jackson, Raymond. "Rent Control and the Supply of Housing Services: The Brookline Massachusetts Experience." *American Journal of Economics and Sociology,* October 1993, pp. 467–475.
Based on the rent control program of one city, the authors document that rent controls lead to a decline in the total supply of housing available in the short run and also lead to a deterioration of the housing stock in the longer term.

Levin-Waldman, Oren M. *The Case of the Minimum Wage: Competing Policy Models.* Albany: State University of New York Press, 2001.
Explores the history of the minimum wage in the United States and examines how economic models are being used by politicians to argue this issue.

McCloskey, Donald N., ed. *Second Thoughts: Myths and Morals of U.S. Economic History.* New York: Oxford University Press, 1993.
A very useful and thoughtful book in general. Especially interesting is the chapter entitled "Can Price Controls Work?"

Neumark, David, and William Wascher. *Do Minimum Wages Fight Poverty?* Cambridge, MA: National Bureau of Economic Research, 1997.
Argues that the minimum wage benefits some low-income families while hurting others. Minimums simply redistribute income among low-income earners rather than from high to low earners.

Rockoff, Hugh. *Drastic Measures: A History of Wage and Price Controls in the U.S.* Cambridge, England: Cambridge University Press, 1984.
Has an excellent account of the price controls in the United States, from Colonial times through the 1980s.

Tucker, William. *Zoning, Rent Control and Affordable Housing.* Washington, DC: The Cato Institute, 1991.
Discusses the mechanics of rent control, the history of rent control in New York City, and suggestions beyond public housing.

World Wide Web Resources

American Enterprise Institute for Public Policy Research (AEI)
www.aei.org/default.asp?filter=all

The AEI is a think tank dedicated to conducting economic policy research. Type in "government control on prices" in their quick search box to see what publications their members have written.

Cato Institute
www.cato.org/pubs/pas/pa-274es.html

The Cato Institute's Policy Analysis provides an article on how rent controls affect housing affordability.

The Concise Encyclopedia of Economics: Price Controls
www.econlib.org/library/Enc/Pricecontrols.html

This article, written by Hugh Rockoff, is part of the online *Concise Encyclopedia of Economics,* part of *The Library of Economics and Liberty* collection of online resources.

Employment Policies Institute
www.epionline.org/index_mw.cfm

Employment Policies Institute is a research organization dedicated to studying entry-level employment issues. Discusses the difference between the minimum wage and the living wage, and the history of the minimum wage. Provides links to publications and other issues.

Minimum Wage Laws in the United States

www.dol.gov/esa/minwage/america.htm

Sponsored by the U.S. Department of Labor. Describes the minimum wage in the 50 states, American Samoa, Puerto Rico, Guam, and the Virgin Islands.

Pollution Problems
Must We Foul Our Own Nests?

Checklist of economic concepts

- Demand
- Supply
- Opportunity costs
- Cost-benefit analysis
- Marginal social costs
- Marginal social benefits
- Externalities in consumption
- Externalities in production
- Market failure
- Pollution rights markets

Washington—One of every three lakes in the United States, and nearly one-quarter of the nation's rivers contain enough pollution that people should limit or avoid eating fish caught there.

Every state but Alaska and Wyoming issued fish advisories covering some and occasionally all of their lakes or rivers in 2003, according to a national database maintained by the Environmental Protection Agency and updated every year.

Though the number of advisories rose to 3,094, up from 2,814 in 2002, according to figures released Tuesday, EPA Administrator Mike Leavitt said the increase was due to more monitoring, not more pollution.

Minnesota, which has an extensive monitoring system and more than 10,000 lakes, once again had the most advisories at 1,114, up 130 from 2002.

Nearly all the advisories involve contaminants such as mercury, dioxins, PCBs, pesticides and heavy metals, including arsenic, copper and lead. Currently they cover 35 percent of the nation's lake acreage and 24 percent of river miles.

Leavitt said mercury pollution from industry is decreasing, though he cited figures only as recent as five years ago. Primary sources of mercury pollution include coal-burning power plants, the burning of hazardous and medical waste and production of chlorine. It also occurs naturally in the environment.

The advisories cover fish caught during recreational and sport fishing, not deep-sea commercial fishing or fish farming operations.

"It's about trout, not tuna. It's about what you catch on the shore, not what you buy on the shelf," Leavitt said. "This is about the health of pregnant mothers and small children, that's the primary focus of our concern."

But he also acknowledged that virtually every acre of lakes and mile of rivers could eventually be covered by advisories.

Since pollution is found in fish nearly every time a state looks for it, the EPA assumes that whenever a state does that kind of monitoring it will wind up issuing a fish advisory, he said.

"I want to make clear that this agency views mercury as a toxin. Manmade emissions need to be reduced and regulated. There has been an appropriate, heightened public concern," Leavitt said.

This year, 44 states had a fish advisory for mercury, a persistent substance that affects the nervous system. Two more states, Montana and Washington, added statewide advisories to warn of the potential widespread contamination of fish.

Servings of fish caught by family or friends and not covered by an advisory should be limited to one six-ounce portion a week, according to the Food and Drug Administration.

The latest figures troubled frequent critics of the Bush administration, including environmentalist groups such as the Sierra Club, the National Wildlife Federation and Natural Resources Defense Council. They want stricter limits imposed on mercury pollution from coal-fired plants.

Earlier this month an environmental advocacy coalition released a report citing EPA figures to claim that 76 percent of fish samples collected from 260 bodies of water exceeded the agency's exposure limits for children under 3.

"Sadly, America's women and children are paying for the administration's procrastination," said Carl Pope, executive director of the Sierra Club, which noted that state advisories now cover 13 million acres of lakes and three-quarter million miles of rivers.

"This listing clearly indicates that we are moving in the wrong direction on mercury pollution," said Sen. Jim Jeffords, I-Vt., a senior member of the Senate Environmental and Public Works Committee.

Jeffords and President Bush have each proposed ways of regulating mercury and other pollution from coal-fired power plants. Jeffords would have the government force industry to reduce mercury emissions by 90 percent by 2008; Bush wants to cut mercury emissions by 70 percent by 2018.

The EPA, after being sued by NRDC, plans to issue by mid-March the nation's first regulations for the 48 tons of mercury a year from power plants.

Source: "Toxin Warnings Grow for U.S. Fish," The Associated Press, 2004.

Most of us are concerned about environmental problems, but we are not quite sure what we can do about them. As individuals, we seem to believe that we can do little. In fact, we are likely to add to the problems by thinking that our own bit of pollution is just a drop in the bucket.

Public reaction to pollution varies a great deal. At one extreme are those who object to anything that decreases the purity of the air and water or that mars the natural beauty of the landscape. At the other extreme are those who seem not to value clean air, water, and natural beauty at all. Most of us are between these two extremes.

A sensible attack on pollution problems requires the use of economic analysis along with inputs from other disciplines—especially the natural sciences. In particular, economic analysis can help us (1) understand why and under what circumstances economic units pollute; (2) determine the impact of pollution on resource allocation and social well-being; (3) determine the extent to which pollution control should be exercised; and (4) evaluate alternative antipollution activities of the government. Before we can fully apply economic analysis to the problem of pollution, however, two additional steps are needed. First, we must come to a clear understanding of what constitutes pollution. Having done this and since one of our primary goals concerns determining the impact of pollution on resource allocation and social well-being, we must pull together and extend what we have learned about these topics thus far.

WHAT IS POLLUTION?

We will not make much progress in an economic analysis of pollution until we are familiar with both the nature of the environment in which we live and what it is that constitutes pollution of that environment. Let's consider these two concepts in turn.

The Environment and Its Services

The environment is easily defined. It consists of the air, water, and land around us. These elements provide us with a variety of important services, including a habitat in which to live and resources with which to produce goods and services.

The services of the environment are used by production units and household units as they engage in activities of various kinds. Production units lay heavy claims on the environment's resources, but they may also make use of its habitat and amenity characteristics.

As production units engage in the process of transforming raw and semifinished materials into goods and services that will satisfy human wants, there are at least three ways in which the environment can be affected. First, some of the environment's stocks of exhaustible resources may be diminished. These include coal, petroleum, and many mineral deposits. Second, it is called upon for replaceable resources like timber, grassland, oxygen, and nitrogen. Third, it is used as a place to dispose of the wastes of the production and consumption processes—as a gigantic garbage disposal.

Recycling of Wastes and the Concept of Pollution

The pollution problem arises primarily from the use of the environment by producers and consumers as a dumping ground for wastes. We litter the countryside with cans, paper, and the other residues of consumption and production. We dump the emissions from our automobiles and factories into the atmosphere. We empty sewage and residue from production directly and indirectly into streams, rivers, and lakes.

As wastes from production and consumption are dumped into the environment, nature sets recycling processes in motion. Animals use oxygen, giving off carbon dioxide wastes. But plants use carbon dioxide, giving off oxygen wastes. Dead plant and animal life is attacked by chemical elements that decompose it, restoring to the soil elements that the living organisms had withdrawn from it. Iron and steel objects rust and disintegrate over time. So do wood and other matter. Wastes that can be decomposed in air, water, and soil are said to be biodegradable. But some wastes are not biodegradable, for example, aluminum containers such as beer cans.

Recycling—the transformation of wastes into raw materials that are again usable—requires variable lengths of time, depending on what it is that is being recycled. It takes many years for a steel pipe to rust away. Wood varies a great deal in the time it takes for its complete disintegration. But many plant and animal products require only a very short time to decompose.

Pollution consists of loading the environment with wastes that are not completely recycled, are not recycled fast enough, or are not recycled at all. It involves a diminution of the capacity of the environment to yield environmental services. Pollution occurs when recycling processes fail to prevent wastes from accumulating in the environment.

Common Forms of Pollution

Pollution is as old as civilization itself. Wherever people have congregated, their wastes have tended to pile up more rapidly than the forces of nature can digest them. As long as the world was sparsely populated and no permanent cities existed, no great problems were created. When the extent of pollution in one locale imposed costs on the people living there that outweighed the costs associated with moving, they simply moved to a new location. Then, given time, natural recycling processes could in many cases take over and restore the excess wastes to usable form.

When towns and cities came into existence, pollution raised more serious problems. How could body wastes from humans and animals, as well as refuse from the daily round of living, be disposed of? Until fairly recent times it was not disposed of in many instances—levels of sanitation were unbelievably low, and levels of stench were unbelievably high. As the density of the world's population has increased and as it has become more difficult to move away from pollution problems, the human race has increasingly turned its attention toward the development of control measures. But in order to control pollution, it must be identified as accurately as possible in its various forms.

Air Pollution

In the processes of production and consumption, five major kinds of wastes are dumped into the atmosphere. Most result from combustion and have caused local problems for a long time. Since there are millions of cubic miles of atmosphere to absorb these wastes, however, air pollution has not caused great concern until the last few decades. These wastes are carbon monoxide, sulfur dioxides, nitrogen oxides, hydrocarbons, and particulates.

Carbon monoxide, an odorless, colorless gas, makes the atmosphere a less hospitable habitat for animal life. In concentrated amounts, it causes dizziness, headaches, and nausea in humans. Exposure to a sufficiently high concentration for a few hours can be fatal. In 2001, some 82 percent of the carbon monoxide emissions into the atmosphere in the United States came from transportation sources, and another 2 percent came from industrial sources of one kind or another.[1]

Sulfur dioxides constitute a second major source of atmospheric pollution. Where they are heavily concentrated, they cause damage to both plant and animal life. Dioxides result largely from the combustion of fuel oils and coal. Consequently, high levels of concentration are most likely to occur where these are used for the generation of electricity and for residential heating.

A third atmospheric pollutant is nitrogen oxides. These can cause lung damage in human beings and may also retard plant growth. The main sources of this pollutant are automobiles and stationary combustion processes such as those used in generating electric power.

---

[1] U.S. Department of Commerce, Bureau of the Census, *Statistical Abstract of the United States, 2003*, Table 373.

Hydrocarbons constitute a fourth kind of waste emitted into the air. At their present concentration levels, no direct harmful effects have been attributed to them. However, they combine with nitrogen oxides and ultraviolet rays of the sun to form petrochemical smog. The smog may produce breathing difficulties and eye irritation for humans. In addition, it speeds up the oxidation processes to which paints and metals are subject, resulting in substantial damage to industrial plants and equipment. Almost 50 percent of hydrocarbon emissions in the United States comes from industrial sources, and another 40 percent comes from automobiles.

A fifth air pollutant consists of a heterogeneous mixture of suspended solids and liquids called particulates. These are largely dust and ash. The major source of particulates, however, is fuel combustion in stationary sources and in industrial processes. Open fires used to burn trash and garbage also make their contributions. Particulates lower visibilities.

Water Pollution

Water pollution is ordinarily measured in terms of the capacity of water to support aquatic life. This capacity depends on (1) the level of dissolved oxygen in the water and (2) the presence of matter or materials injurious to plant and animal life.

The level of dissolved oxygen is built up through aeration of water and through the photosynthetic processes of plant life in the water. It is destroyed in the decomposition of organic matter that originates in or is dumped into the water. The oxygen needed for decomposition purposes is referred to as biochemical oxygen demand (BOD). The level of dissolved oxygen available for supporting aquatic life, then, depends on the balance between aeration and photosynthesis on the one hand and on BOD on the other.

The level of dissolved oxygen is affected by several factors. First, it tends to be higher the greater the amount of a given volume of water exposed to the atmosphere. In nature, fast-running streams, rapids, and waterfalls contribute to aeration. Artificial aeration is frequently accomplished by shooting streams of water through the air. Second, it tends to be higher the greater the amount of photosynthesis that occurs in the water. In some instances, the amount of photosynthesis that occurs in aquatic plant life may be reduced by air pollution. In this way, air pollution may be a source of water pollution. Third, it tends to be higher the lower the temperature of the water—use of water for cooling by firms such as steel mills, oil refineries, and electricity-generating plants raises the temperature of the water and lowers its capacity to hold dissolved oxygen. Fourth, organic wastes that create BOD come from both domestic and industrial sources, so the level of dissolved oxygen varies inversely with the amounts that are dumped. The decomposition of such wastes can be greatly facilitated, and BOD can be correspondingly reduced, by chemical treatment of such wastes before they are discharged into streams, rivers, lakes, or oceans.

The capacity of water to support aquatic life is reduced when various kinds of materials and matter are dumped into it. Among these are toxins that do not settle out of the water and are not easily broken down by biological means. Mercury is a toxin that has created problems of contamination in various types of fish. Phenols, herbicides, and pesticides have also contributed greatly to the water pollution problem. There have been heated discussions in recent years over the propriety of using them in large quantities. Questions have been raised also as to whether the oceans should be used for the dumping of nuclear wastes and for undersea nuclear explosions.

Land Pollution

Land pollution results from the dumping of a wide variety of wastes on the terrain and from tearing up Earth's surface through such activities as strip mining. Highways are littered with refuse thrown from passing automobiles. Junkyards grow as we scrap millions of automobiles per year, to say nothing of the prodigious amounts of other machinery and appliances that are retired from use. Garbage dumps and landfills grow as towns and cities dispose of the solid wastes they collect and accumulate. Even more troubling are hazardous waste sites, many of which are located in densely populated states. Examples include New Jersey with 115 sites, Pennsylvania with 96, New York with 91, and California with 98.[2] All these reduce the capacity of the terrain to render environmental services.

MARKETS, RESOURCE ALLOCATION, AND SOCIAL WELL-BEING: A RECAP AND EXTENSION

Before we can fully appreciate the economic effects of pollution, we must summarize and extend what we have learned about markets, resource allocation, and social well-being. Thus far, we have examined social well-being from two different perspectives. In Chapter 2, we considered social well-being within the context of the market model of supply and demand. From this perspective we conclude that a market equilibrium occurs when consumers feel that producers have used precisely the correct portion of society's scarce resources in a particular production process. And since we believe the consuming public to be the best judge of what yields well-being, their satisfaction with the market outcome leads us to conclude that the market-determined equilibrium reflects that allocation of resources which maximizes social well-being. Were this not true, consumers would not be satisfied with the outcome.

A second perspective on the issue of maximizing social well-being was first introduced in Chapter 1 and has been used regularly since. From this perspective and relying on cost-benefit analysis, we say that social well-being is enhanced when an increase in the production of a good or service benefits society at least as much as it costs. Consequently, social well-being is as high as is possible when production of all goods or services is carried to the point where marginal social benefit (*MSB*) equals marginal social cost (*MSC*).

---

[2]U.S. Department of Commerce, Bureau of the Census, *Statistical Abstract of the United States, 2003,* Table 381.

Now, we must bridge these two ways of looking at resource allocation and social well-being. To do so, we must bring the cost-benefit analysis comparison of marginal social benefit and marginal social cost into the demand-supply analysis of the market model.

Demand, Marginal Private Benefit, and Marginal Social Benefit

Consider first the demand side of a market. As consumers, we make purchases for the satisfaction, or benefit, that consumption brings. If our goal in these purchases is to maximize our own well-being, given our income constraints, cost-benefit analysis suggests that we should not make a particular purchase unless the benefit to us from the purchase is at least as great as its cost.

Is this logic found in a demand curve? Typically we think of a demand curve as indicating the maximum quantity of a good or service that consumers will buy at various prices, other things being equal. An equally valid way of looking at demand is as the maximum price that consumers would be willing to pay for each successive unit of a good or service, other things being equal. For simplicity, consider one person's individual demand for a good such as pizza. Suppose Jim's demand curve for pizza indicates that the maximum he is willing to pay for one pizza during a given week is $10. Why $10? Jim could spend his $10 on a pizza or anything else that $10 would buy. If he chooses to buy a pizza for $10, based on the logic of cost-benefit analysis, we can conclude that the expected satisfaction, or benefit, from eating the pizza is at least as great as the satisfaction that any other $10 purchase would bring. Were this not so, Jim would simply buy something else with his $10. The benefit to Jim, then, of the first pizza is roughly worth $10. We call this Jim's marginal benefit of the first pizza.

Having consumed the first pizza, what's a second pizza worth to Jim? The downward, to the right, slope of his demand curve indicates that the maximum price he is willing to pay for a second pizza is less than $10, perhaps only $8. That is, having eaten one pizza during the week, the marginal benefit Jim anticipates from consuming a second pizza falls. Does this make sense to you? Consider which gives you more satisfaction, the first glass of orange juice at breakfast or the second? The first mug of cold beer after a difficult day of exams or the second? And so on. Experience suggests, and Jim's demand curve points out, that typically marginal benefit, as measured by willingness to pay, declines as more of something is consumed.

marginal private benefit (*MPB*) The benefit that accrues to the direct consumers of a good or service resulting from a one-unit increase in consumption as is reflected in the demand curve for the good or service.

This of course applies to market demand curves as well as to that of an individual. For each successive unit of a good or service, the market demand curve indicates the maximum price consumers are willing to pay. And the maximum price of necessity will be dictated by the benefit in terms of added satisfaction, or simply the marginal benefit, that consumers anticipate from consuming each unit of the good or service. Consequently, a market demand curve can correctly be thought of as a marginal benefit curve for the consumers of a good or service. More precisely, since the market demand is based on the benefits expected by the direct consumers of the product, it reflects the **marginal private benefit (*MPB*)** of consumption.

Recall that we are trying to bridge the market model of supply and demand with the notions of marginal social benefit and cost. We are nearly halfway there. That is, we now know that the market demand is a marginal private benefit curve. But is it the marginal social benefit curve? That is, are the benefits to the direct consumers of a good or service as reflected in the demand curve the same as the benefits to society from the item? Under most circumstances they are. Usually, there are no benefits from consuming a particular good or service other than the benefits that accrue to the direct consumer. In these typical circumstances the market demand curve is both the marginal private and marginal social benefit curve. Unfortunately, this will not always be the case. Suppose, for example, a vaccine is developed which effectively eliminates the risk of contracting a dreaded and contagious disease such as HIV. Clearly, the primary benefit of being vaccinated accrues to the direct consumer, the person being vaccinated. This direct benefit of consumption is properly called the marginal private benefit of the vaccine and is reflected in the demand curve for the product. And this marginal private benefit is necessarily part of the marginal social benefit of the vaccination since the individual being vaccinated is part of society. But, equally clearly, others in society also benefit even if they do not receive the vaccination since there is at least one person fewer, the one who does receive the vaccination, from whom they could possibly contract the illness. As such, there is a spillover of benefits from the vaccine to third parties, that is, to those in society other than the direct consumer of the vaccine. This spillover of benefits to those not directly involved in consuming the good is referred to as an **externality in consumption.**

externality in consumption
A change in satisfaction, which can be either positive or negative, for someone other than the direct consumer of an item.

Many other examples of externalities in consumption exist. Suppose, for example, my wealthy neighbor hires an orchestra to play at her garden party to which I am not invited. She pays for the pleasure of her guests, and they directly benefit from the experience. This is the marginal private benefit of the orchestra's work. But who is to stop me, a lover of beautiful music, from listening to the orchestra's haunting strains from my side of the property line? Similarly, consider the case of my neighbor incurring the costs of new and beautiful landscaping. The primary and direct benefits go to my neighbor, but I also benefit both in terms of the aesthetic quality of my neighborhood and, perhaps, in terms of enhanced property values in the neighborhood. In each of these cases, the externality in consumption has a positive effect on the part of society that does not directly consume the good or service. That is, in each of these cases, the marginal social benefit of the product will be greater than the marginal private benefit by the value of the externality in consumption. In such a circumstance, the market demand curve is not the marginal social benefit curve since it only reflects the marginal private benefit of consumption and ignores the spillover of benefits to nonconsumers.

Of course, third parties can also be adversely affected when someone consumes a product. A good example involves cigarette smoking. While the smoker receives the direct benefit of smoking, those who wheeze through the secondhand smoke clearly lose satisfaction. In this and other similar cases, the marginal social benefit will be less than the marginal private benefit by the value of the lost satisfaction of those enduring the secondhand smoke.

To summarize, when an externality in consumption exists:

$$\text{Marginal social benefit} = \text{Marginal private benefit} \pm \text{Externality}$$

Given the possible existence of externalities in consumption, it is essential to note that the market demand curve is simply the marginal private benefit curve. This demand curve reflects marginal social benefit only when there are no externalities in consumption. That is, market demand curves are both marginal private and marginal social benefit curves only in those instances where there are no externalities in consumption.

Supply, Marginal Private Cost, and Marginal Social Cost

Now consider a standard supply curve. As presented in Chapter 2, a supply curve shows us the maximum quantity of a good or service that sellers are willing to offer for sale at various prices, other things being equal. Once again we can turn this around to say that supply indicates the minimum price necessary to induce sellers to offer each unit for sale, other things being equal. Suppose, for example, that to induce an individual seller to offer a first pizza for sale, a customer must be willing to pay at least $5. Why is $5 the minimum that the seller will take? Again, apply cost-benefit analysis. The benefit side of the transaction is the $5 the seller will take in as revenue if the sale is made. The cost side is simply the cost to produce the pizza. If the seller wishes to make as much profit as possible, he will produce and sell the first pizza only if it brings in at least as much revenue as it cost to produce. If the seller is willing to take no less than $5 for the first pizza, we can conclude that the cost to produce it is $5. That is, we can conclude that $5 is the marginal cost to produce the first pizza. Consequently, the supply curve, by showing the minimum price necessary to induce the seller to offer each successive unit of the good or service for sale, can correctly be thought of as the producer's marginal cost curve or, simply, the **marginal private cost (*MPC*)** curve.

marginal private cost (*MPC*)
The increase in total cost that producers incur when output is increased by one unit as is reflected in the supply curve for the good or service.

Consider a second pizza. Supply curves slope upward to the right; thus, in order to induce the seller to offer a second pizza for sale, a price greater than $5 must be offered. In other words, the marginal cost to produce must be rising. Why? Recall from Chapter 1 the concept of increasing opportunity costs. That is—just as is true for society as a whole—as the firms of an individual industry attempt to increase output they must eventually begin to pay more for additional resources since these resources have to be attracted from increasingly valuable alternative employments. Perhaps initially a pizza maker in a college town can hire labor very cheaply since there is a large pool of student workers to draw from who have limited alternative earning power. As production expands, eventually the pizza maker will run out of relatively cheap labor to hire, and the marginal cost to produce rises. The same will occur for all other resources used as well.

Consequently, whether you are looking at the supply curve of one seller or the combined supply curve of a group of sellers, supply can correctly be thought of as a marginal private cost curve. But is the marginal private cost borne by producers necessarily the same as marginal social cost? That is, can the market supply curve be thought of as the marginal social cost curve? In most production processes, the actual producer of a product in fact bears all costs of producing the product. In this typical case, marginal private cost is the same as marginal social cost and, thus, each is reflected in the market supply curve of the product. There are circumstances, however, when this will not be true. Consider, for example, the case of cattle raised as a food source. While most parts of the cow find their way into food uses, the hides typically do not. Cowhides do, however, find their way into the production of a wide variety of leather products. The availability of such large supplies of cowhides leads to a very large reduction in the cost to produce leather products relative to the cost that would exist were there no or few cattle being raised as food sources. Thus, the existence of the market for cattle as food reduces the cost of producing leather products. This reduction in the cost to produce leather goods is a positive **externality in production** of cattle as food. In this case, the marginal private cost of producing cattle as food will exceed the marginal social cost by the value of the reduction in the cost of producing leather products.

externality in production
The production of one good or service leading to cost changes, either positive or negative, in the production of other items.

Perhaps more commonly, externalities in the production of one product can have adverse cost effects on the production of other goods. For example, strip mining operations may make it more difficult and expensive to prepare a particular piece of land for other uses. In this case, the marginal private cost of extracting the minerals through strip mining understates the true marginal social cost of the operation.

To summarize, when an externality in production exists:

$$\text{Marginal social cost} = \text{Marginal private cost} \pm \text{Externality}$$

Given the possibility of externalities in production, it is essential to remember that the market supply curve is simply the marginal private cost curve. It will be the marginal social cost curve only in those typical circumstances in which no externality in production exists.

The Market and Social Well-Being

With demand and supply curves redefined as marginal private benefit and marginal private cost curves, what can we say about the equilibrium that a market reaches? By equating demand and supply, the market leads to an equilibrium in which the marginal private benefit to consumers is exactly equal to the marginal private cost of producers. And if there are no externalities in either consumption or production, the market outcome also gives an equilibrium where marginal social benefit equals marginal social cost, the condition necessary for proving that social well-being is maximized. Given this, when we, as in Chapter 2, conclude that a market equilibrium of necessity leads to the resource allocation that maximizes social well-being, we are implicitly making the assumption of no externalities in consumption or production. Fortunately, such externalities are either rare or, at least, of such modest size as to be unimportant. When they exist in significant size, however, the equilibrium outcome of the market will not embody an allocation of resources which maximizes social well-being. We refer to such situations as cases of market failure. With this in mind, let's return to the case of pollution and see how it is an example of **market failure** caused by an externality in production.

market failure
Occurs when markets, operating on their own, do not lead to a socially optimal allocation of resources.

ECONOMICS OF POLLUTION

No one likes pollution. Almost everyone would like to see something done about it. Toward this end, we consider in this section the fundamental economics of the pollution problem. First we will examine the reasons pollution occurs, analyze the effects of pollution on resource allocation, look at the costs of pollution control, and identify its benefits. Then we will attempt to establish criteria for determining the appropriate level of control.

Why Polluters Pollute

Why is it that pollution occurs? What is there about the environment that causes consumers and producers to use it as a dumping ground? Ordinarily, pollution results from one or both of two basic factors: (1) property rights in the environment being polluted are either nonexistent or not enforced and/or (2) much of the environment's services are shared by the entire population.

If no one owns a portion of the environment or if an owner cannot police it or have it policed, then it becomes possible for people to use a river, a lake, the air, or an area of land as a wastebasket without being charged for doing so. Because no one owns the air above city streets and highways, automobile owners can dump combustion gases into it without paying for the privilege of doing so. Similarly, a paper mill may be able to dump its wastes into a river without charge because no one owns the river. But even ownership of the environment may not be enough to keep pollution from occurring. How many times have you seen litter accumulate on a vacant lot or junk dumped in a ditch in a pasture away from town because the owner was not there to prevent the dumping?

In addition, many environmental services are used by the entire population, as a group. In such cases, it is hard to single out and determine the value of the air that one person—or an automobile—uses. Similarly, it is often difficult to attach a value to the water deterioration caused by one industrial plant when thousands dump their wastes into a given river. Would any one person be willing to pay someone not to take an action that destroys a beautiful view across the countryside? When values cannot be placed on the amounts of environmental services used by any one person, it is difficult to induce people not to pollute by charging them for doing so.

Pollution and Resource Allocation

Supply curves indicate the marginal private cost of producing a good or service. Before we go further, however, we need a better understanding of what is actually being referred to when we discuss the costs of producing a good or service. It is particularly important to note that the economic measurement of production costs does not necessarily coincide with accounting measures. As an example, consider a small family-owned grocery for which the labor is provided by the owning family. A large part of the costs of resources used by the store—costs of grocery stocks, utilities, and the like—is indeed accounting costs, but some resource costs may be omitted from the accounting records. For example, the costs of the owners' labor are not likely to be listed. Similarly, amortization and depreciation costs on the land, building, furniture, and fixtures may also be omitted. The family may simply take what is left after the out-of-pocket expenses are paid, calling this remainder profit.

The costs of resources bought or hired for carrying on the business are called the **explicit costs** of production. These are the economic costs that are most likely to be taken into account by the business, since they are usually actual cost outlays. The costs of self-owned, self-employed resources (like the labor of the family in the grocery example) are called **implicit costs** of production. These economic costs tend to be hidden or ignored as costs since there is no actual cost outlay. As such, the true cost to society of producing a good or service, what we call the opportunity cost or economic cost, can be accurately measured only if one takes into account both the explicit and implicit costs of the activity.

Always recall, although accounting costs are often readily available, they are reliable measures of opportunity costs only if an activity involves no implicit costs.

With this as background, the marginal private cost curve, or supply curve, includes *both* the explicit costs for resources firms hire to produce their product and the implicit costs associated with any resources used in production that are owned by the firms. What would not be included in the private costs would be entries for resources used that firms do not pay for, either explicitly or implicitly. For example, if firms use a local river or stream for waste disposal and do not pay for the right to do so, no charge is incurred by the firms.

Although the use of the river for waste disposal does not show up on the firms' cost ledger, society as a whole is not so lucky. The use of the river for waste disposal creates a negative externality in production; thus, the marginal social cost of production will be greater than the marginal private cost. To see this more clearly and to fully appreciate the implications, suppose that two industries are located along a riverbank. An industry producing paper is located upstream, while downstream there is an industry producing electric power. Further, suppose that the paper producers discharge a great deal of waste into the river and that this is particularly problematic for the power-generating firms since they need large quantities of clean water for cooling purposes. What impact does the pollution from paper production have on resource allocation and social well-being?

Consider first the paper-producing market as shown in Figure 4.1. The demand curve D_rD_r is also labeled MPB_r, for the reasons discussed above. Further, let's suppose that there are no social spillovers in consumption so that $MPB_r = MSB_r$; that is, the demand curve is both the MPB and MSB curves. The supply curve S_rS_r reflects the marginal private cost to the producers of paper, so we label it MPC_r. This curve indicates the cost that the firms producing paper incur for the resources they use in the production of paper. These costs are therefore part of the marginal social cost to produce paper. But society also bears the burden of the negative externality created by the firms' use of the river as a sewer since so using the river reduces its value to other users. Thus, MSC_r exceeds MPC_r, with the difference being the value of the externality in production. As shown, we assume that the damage done to the river, and thus to society, grows at an increasing rate as the production of paper is expanded.

explicit costs
The costs of production incurred by the producer to buy or hire the resources required to carry on business.

implicit costs
The costs of production incurred by the producer for the use of self-owned, self-employed resources required to carry on business.

FIGURE 4.1 **Effects of Water Pollution on the Polluter**

The market for paper is in equilibrium when r_1 reams of paper per day are produced and sold for $9 per ream. At this level of production, MSC is greater than MSB; thus, social well-being would be enhanced if production were reduced to the r_0 level. The value of well-being lost by the overproduction of paper is equal to the area of the shaded triangle ABC.

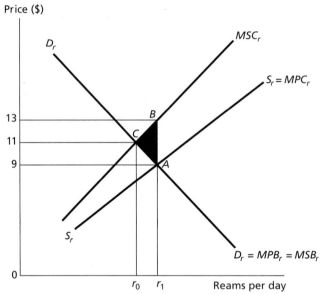

Markets bring together producers and consumers to create an equilibrium at which the price of paper is $9 per ream and resources necessary to produce r_1 reams are employed. But is this market outcome socially optimal? Recall that social well-being is maximized when marginal social cost equals marginal social benefit. What does the market give? At equilibrium, $MSB_r = MPC_r$, but due to the externality in production, MSB_r is not equal to MSC_r. In fact, at equilibrium, while the marginal benefit to society of paper is $9 per ream, the cost to produce it, from society's perspective, is $13. But what do these numbers tell us? The marginal social benefit side is straightforward: The resources needed to produce the r_1 ream of paper will yield $9 of benefits to society if used to produce that ream of paper. The marginal social cost side is a bit more complex. The resources needed to produce the r_1 ream cost society $13 if used to produce paper. But recall, we measure cost in an opportunity cost context. Thus, when we say that the marginal social cost to produce the r_1 ream of paper is $13, what we are in reality saying is that if the resources were used in their best alternative employment rather than in the production of paper, they would produce goods and/or services worth $13 in benefits to society. In other words, by producing the r_1 unit of paper, the paper producers use resources that have an opportunity cost of $13 but which yield only $9 of satisfaction to society. Society's well-being, then, falls by $4 from what it could have been when the r_1 ream is produced. Graphically, this is the vertical distance between A and B in Figure 4.1.

FIGURE 4.2   Effects of Water Pollution on Water Users
The market for electric power is in equilibrium when e_0 kilowatt-hours per day are produced and sold for 12 cents per kilowatt-hour. At this level of production, MSB is greater than MSC; thus, social well-being would be enhanced if production increased to the e_1 level. The value of well-being lost by the underproduction of power is equal to the area of the shaded triangle ABC.

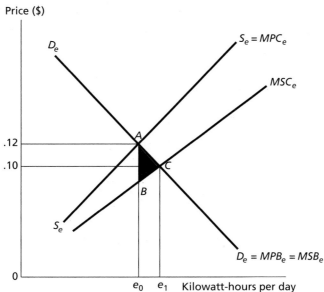

The same reasoning suggests that when each unit of paper from r_0 to r_1 is produced, social well-being is sacrificed. The total value of the lost well-being due to the overproduction of paper is equal to the area of the shaded triangle ABC. If social well-being is to be maximized, production of paper should stop at the r_0 level with the price—which covers all costs of all resources used—being $11 per ream.

What happened here? That is, why did the market outcome not maximize social well-being? The problem came about because the private paper producers were not required to bear the full cost of their production. They were able to shift some of their cost onto society as a whole. And this artificial reduction in the cost to produce paper induced an overproduction of paper. You should see this as an application of the *law of supply*. For this reason we say that polluters face an incentive to overproduce, that is, to use relatively too much of society's scarce resources. This overproduction causes social well-being to be restricted below its maximum potential level.

This, as bad as it is, is not the end of the story. Consider the market for electric power, as depicted in Figure 4.2. Once again, the supply curve S_eS_e (or MPC_e curve) reflects the total explicit and implicit cost that the power producers bear. Note, however, that MSC_e is less for each unit of output than is MPC_e. The difference is that, from society's perspective, the cost of cleaning the river's water before it can be used for cooling by the power generators is properly considered a cost of producing paper, not a cost of producing power. As such, the true cost to society of producing electric power is best measured as the cost that would exist were the river not polluted by the paper producers. While society as a whole has the luxury of looking at cost in this light, the power producers do not. They have to clean the river's water before using it, so this cost is part of MPC_e.

The market equilibrium occurs at a price of 12 cents per kilowatt-hour, and resources necessary to produce e_0 kilowatts per day are hired. But, from society's perspective, each unit of power between e_0 and e_1 should be produced because the benefit to society, MSB_e, is greater than the cost, MSC_e. Once again, well-being is restricted by the market outcome. In this case, the area of the shaded triangle ABC shows the added well-being that society could enjoy if power production were carried to the socially optimal e_1 level. At this level of production, the price that power users would have to pay in order to cover all the legitimate costs of producing power would be 10 cents per kilowatt-hour.

Why did the market get it wrong? Because the power producers had to bear the added cost of the negative externality, artificially increasing their cost of production, they faced an incentive to underproduce. Again, this is an application of the *law of supply*. Any time the cost of production rises, whether artificially or not, the rational firm reaction is one of reducing supply.

In summary, when a negative externality in production exists, in this case caused by the use of the river for waste disposal by the upstream paper producers, the outcomes in the markets for both paper and electricity do not reflect an allocation of resources that maximizes social well-being. For both the polluting paper producers and the power generators who bear the burden of the pollution, market incentives lead to suboptimal production levels. For the polluter, costs of production are artificially reduced; thus, an incentive exists to overproduce. That is, the ability to use the river without charge causes the polluter to attract too much of society's scarce resources. For the power producers, costs are artificially increased; thus, they face an incentive to underproduce. Since they bear some of the legitimate costs associated with paper production, they tend to attract too few of society's scarce resources. In each market, then, there is resource misallocation. And when resources are misallocated, it is the general public that suffers lost well-being.

The Appropriate Level of Pollution Control

Our reactions to pollution often motivate us to simplistically say, "Let's wipe it out!" We feel that we are entitled to clean air, clean water, and clean land. But how clean is clean? Cleanliness, like goodness, is a relative rather than an absolute quality. To determine the amount of pollution, if any, that should be allowed, we must compare the costs and benefits of keeping the environment clean.

Pollution control is not costless. An industrial plant that scrubs or cleans its combustion gases before discharging them into the atmosphere must use resources in the process. Labor and capital go into the making and operation of antipollution devices, and resources so used are not available to produce other goods and services. The value of the goods and services that must be given up is the cost of the plant's pollution control activities.

The benefits of pollution control consist of the increase in well-being that members of society feel when they have the opportunity to experience a cleaner environment. To measure the benefits of a pollution control activity, the value of the increase in well-being that it generates must be accurately estimated. Suppose that smog permeates a particular metropolitan area but that pollution control activities can reduce it or perhaps even eliminate it. To determine the benefits of, say, a 50 percent reduction in smog, we can ask each individual living in the area how much a reduction would be worth to him or her personally. By totaling the replies, we would arrive at a dollar value of the expected benefits.

Once the costs and benefits of pollution control are determined, it becomes possible to establish the appropriate level of control. If the marginal social benefit of additional control—what cleaner air, for example, is worth to the citizens of the society—exceeds the marginal social cost of the additional control, then pollution control should be expanded. Pollution control should therefore be expanded up to the point where the marginal social benefit just ceases to exceed the marginal social cost. Once again, cost-benefit analysis in action.

As an illustration, consider a community of 10,000 persons that is pervaded by a nauseating stench from an incinerator used to dispose of the community's garbage. Suppose that the odor can be completely eliminated by an expenditure of $100,000 per year for an alternative method of garbage disposal (carrying it away and burying it in a landfill outside the town) and that it can be partially controlled by using various combinations of burning and burying.

Suppose that the costs of different levels of partial control are those of columns (1), (2), and (3) of Table 4.1. For simplicity, suppose that each unit of pollution control costs $10,000. By spending $10,000 on carrying and burying, the community can eliminate 10 percent of the stench; each additional $10,000 expenditure eliminates another 10 percent of the original total stench, until with a $100,000 expenditure the pollution is entirely eliminated.

Column (3) in Table 4.1 lists the marginal social cost of pollution control. Since each increment in pollution control (an increment is defined as 10 percent of the control needed to eliminate the odor) adds $10,000 to the total social cost of pollution control, the marginal social cost of pollution control at each control level is $10,000. The assumption of constant marginal social cost of pollution control is used here merely to facilitate the analysis. The more typical case is for marginal social cost to rise as pollution control is expanded. This case is discussed later in this chapter.

The benefits of pollution control to the community are shown in columns (4), (5), and (6). Before any control is undertaken, each person in the community is asked for an opinion of what a 10 percent reduction in the stench is worth. Suppose each person indicates a willingness to pay $10 for it. We conclude that $100,000 measures the total social benefit yielded by the first 10 percent reduction. Since the benefit exceeds the cost by $90,000, the first 10 percent reduction is clearly warranted.

The question now arises as to whether a second 10 percent reduction in the stench is worthwhile. Since the pollution is not as intense as it was with no control, a second 10 percent reduction is of less value than was the first. Suppose each

TABLE 4.1   Annual Costs and Benefits of Pollution Control

(1) Pollution Control or Eliminated Stench	(2) Total Social Cost of Control ($000)	(3) Marginal Social Cost of Control ($000)	(4) Per-Person Marginal Benefit of Control	(5) Marginal Social Benefit of Control ($000)	(6) Total Social Benefit of Control ($000)	(7) Net Social Benefit of Control ($000)
1st 10%	$ 10	$10	$10.00 ea.	$100	$100	$ 90
2nd 10	20	10	8.00	80	180	160
3rd 10	30	10	6.00	60	240	210
4th 10	40	10	4.00	40	280	240
5th 10	50	10	2.00	20	300	250
6th 10	60	10	1.60	16	316	256
7th 10	70	10	1.20	12	328	258
8th 10	80	10	0.80	8	336	256
9th 10	90	10	0.40	4	340	250
10th 10	100	10	0.20	2	342	242

person values the move from 10 percent control to 20 percent control at $8 so that the community valuation of the extra control—or the marginal social benefit of it—is $80,000. Since the marginal social cost of the additional control is only $10,000, putting it into effect adds $70,000 more to the net social benefit of control and is therefore a good investment for the community.

Column (5) shows the marginal social benefit at different levels of control. Marginal social benefit of pollution control is defined as the *change* in total social benefit per unit *change* in whatever it is that yields the benefit. Note that the total social benefit at any given level of control is obtained by adding up the marginal social benefit as the level of control is increased unit by unit up to that level.

Marginal social benefit, as shown in Table 4.1, declines as the level of pollution control is increased (the level of the stench is decreased). This is what we would expect to happen in the case at hand. The greater the amount of control, or the lower the level of the stench, the less urgent additional control becomes. This will be the usual situation in controlling pollution.

The level of pollution control yielding the maximum net social benefit is that at which the marginal social benefit just ceases to exceed the marginal social cost. The marginal social benefit of the first two 10 percent increments in the total amount of control needed to eliminate the stench exceed the marginal social cost of making them. Thus, net social benefit is increased by increasing control at least to the 20 percent level. The third, fourth, fifth, sixth, and seventh 10 percent increments also yield marginal social benefit exceeding their marginal social cost, and they increase the net social benefit of control. Now consider the eighth 10 percent increment. Marginal social benefit is $8,000, and marginal social cost is $10,000. Extending pollution control from the 70 percent level to the 80 percent level *reduces* net social benefit by $2,000. The eighth 10 percent increment is not worth to the community what it costs.

The principle is perfectly general. Net social benefit, or social well-being, will always be enhanced by increasing control if the marginal social benefit of the increase is greater than the marginal social cost of making it. Net social benefit will fall following an increase in the control level if the marginal social benefit of that increase is less than its marginal social cost. The appropriate level of control is the one that approaches as closely as possible the level where the marginal social benefit equals marginal social cost.

WHAT CAN BE DONE ABOUT POLLUTION?

Human beings often react to problems with their emotions rather than with the capacity for logic with which they are endowed. Policies recommended to control pollution reflect this human characteristic. A typical recommendation calls for direct control of pollution by the state. But this is only one of the possible avenues of reducing pollution problems. Others include indirect control by the state through a system of incentives encouraging potential polluters not to pollute or to limit their pollution, and the creation by the state of markets for the right to pollute.

Direct Controls

An appealing and simple way to control pollution is to have the government ban polluting activities or agents. If phosphates contaminate water, then ban the use of phosphates in detergents. If DDT pollutes water and land, ban the use of DDT. If the burning of fuel oil and coal increases the sulfur dioxide content of the atmosphere, prohibit their use. Require industrial plants to clean the pollutants from whatever it is they discharge into the atmosphere or water. The method is straightforward and, on the face of it, seems eminently fair.

Government agencies, notably the Environmental Protection Agency (EPA) at the federal level, use direct controls to reduce many kinds of polluting activities. They set and attempt to enforce emission standards for such polluters as automobiles, power plants, and steel mills. State regulation of polluters, to the extent that it is accomplished, is, in general, supervised by the EPA.

The case of the city with the terrible stench shows that complete prohibition of pollutants is not likely to be worth its costs. Pollution control uses resources that could have produced other goods and services, and the value of the goods and services forgone is the opportunity cost to society of controlling the pollution. If the damage done by an additional unit of pollution is less than the costs of preventing it from occurring, social well-being is enhanced if it is allowed to occur. Consequently, direct controls usually should aim at a less idealistic goal than a pollution-free environment. They may take the form of controlling the level of pollution by such devices as setting emissions standards or limits for industrial plants, automobiles, and other polluters.

One problem raised by the use of direct controls to limit the amount of pollution is that it presupposes the regulatory body can determine what the economically desirable levels of pollution are. This is not an insurmountable problem. Tolerance limits on the amount of pollution to be allowed can be reasonably well established. Within those limits, overall costs can be weighed continually against benefits to establish an approximation of the desirable levels of pollution.

A second problem is the difficulty facing a regulatory body in achieving an efficient allocation of the permissible pollution among different polluters. For example, it may be more costly for a steel mill to eliminate a unit of sulfur dioxide from its emissions than it is for a power plant. In the interests of economic efficiency, it is best to eliminate pollution where it is least costly to do so. Thus, the power plant should be required to reduce its sulfur dioxide emission before the steel mill is required to do so. This is a difficult kind of decision for a regulatory body to make because it is responsible to a political body for which economic efficiency is not a primary goal. In addition, it is unrealistic to suppose that the regulatory body has a working knowledge of the nature of costs for every polluter.

A third problem is that of enforcing the standards of emissions once it has been determined what those standards should be. Direct controls fail to provide polluters with an economic incentive not to pollute. In fact, it will pay them to seek ways and means to evade the pollution standards set for them. But we should not overstate the enforcement problem. Almost any prohibition of activities that individuals and business firms want to engage in creates enforcement problems.

Indirect Controls

It is possible for the government to control many types of pollution by placing taxes on polluting activities. Where the amounts of polluting discharges can be measured for individual polluters, a tax can be placed directly on each unit of discharge. This will induce the polluter to reduce the amount of pollution that is discharged. In some cases where such measurement is not possible, polluters may be taxed indirectly—for example, automobiles not equipped with pollution control devices can be subjected to a tax on a mileage basis. This would induce their owners either to install pollution control devices or to drive less.

Figure 4.3 illustrates the use of a tax to control the amount of pollutants discharged into the environment. Consider an industrial concern that discharges its polluting wastes into a river. Processes for cleaning the wastes to control the extent of pollution are available, but they are not free. For simplicity, suppose there are no externalities in producing pollution control; thus the marginal cost curve of Figure 4.3 is both the *MPC* and the *MSC* curve. As shown in Figure 4.3, as more of the pollution is suppressed, that is, as we approach 100 percent control, the marginal cost of additional control rises. This is simply the rational firm's response to the problem of eliminating its discharge. For example, suppose that the polluting discharge is a composite of a number of chemical wastes. If the firm is left on its own to clean up the discharge, what strategy will it follow? Given that a number of chemical wastes are involved, the rational firm will choose to first eliminate those wastes that it can eliminate most cheaply. The waste that can be eliminated only at extreme cost will be saved until last. In other cases, the polluting discharge may involve only one offending substance. Here we can also expect the marginal cost of control to rise as control is pressed toward 100 percent. For example, minor

FIGURE 4.3 **Pollution Control by Means of a Tax on Polluting Discharges**
When the tax exceeds the marginal cost of control, a firm will choose to eliminate its polluting discharge and avoid the tax. If the cost and benefits of pollution control can be accurately estimated, a tax can be established that will cause the firm to voluntarily produce the appropriate level of pollution control. In this case, a tax of T^* per unit of polluting discharge will bring about the optimal level of pollution control C^*.

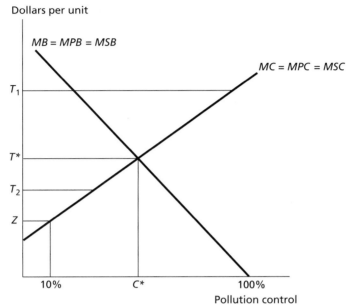

adjustments in the production process might yield modest increases in pollution control, while complete elimination of the polluting discharge may be brought about only by a complete overhaul of the production process. Regardless of the exact reasoning, the marginal cost of pollution control can be expected to rise as the degree of control increases, giving the positively sloped marginal cost curve of Figure 4.3. From the opposite perspective, as we have already discussed, the marginal social benefit of pollution control is likely to fall as the degree of control is increased, giving the negatively sloped marginal social benefit curve of Figure 4.3. As discussed earlier in this chapter, we can identify the appropriate level of pollution control in this situation as C^*, that is, that level at which the benefit of additional control just ceases to outweigh the cost of additional control. If C^* is the desired level of pollution control, how can it be achieved through taxation? As you have probably already guessed, a tax of T^* per unit of polluting discharge will bring about the desired degree of pollution control, C^*. The reason for this is clear: For units of pollution control below C^*, the firm will eliminate its discharge to avoid the tax because the marginal cost of control is less than the tax. For example, the marginal cost of the first 10 percent unit of pollution control is Z dollars. Put differently, the firm can eliminate 10 percent of its polluting discharge if it incurs a cost of Z dollars. In doing so, the firm avoids paying the tax of T^*. Consequently, the firm can save $T^* - Z$ dollars by eliminating the first unit of pollution. Savings of this nature to the firm exist for each unit of pollution control up to the C^* level. Beyond this level, the firm will choose to pay the tax because it is less than the cost of control.

It is equally important to realize that such a tax regimen can lead to less than optimal outcomes. For example, a tax of T_1 per unit will result in too much pollution control effort and, thus, too much of the economy's scarce resources devoted to pollution control, whereas a tax of T_2 per unit will result in too little control and too little of the economy's resources devoted to this purpose. Can you explain why?

The use of taxes to control pollution has its advantages. A major one is that it provides an incentive to the polluter to seek improved ways and means of avoiding or cleaning up its discharge. Another advantage is that it prevents the polluter from shifting some of its production costs (pollution costs) to others; it reduces the incentive to overproduce.

There are also disadvantages. First, to determine the benefits—total and marginal—to society of cleaning the discharge usually is difficult. The criticism should not be carried too far, however, since it applies to any attempt to control pollution. Second, enforcement of such a tax is not easy. Policing is necessary to determine that the discharge is indeed properly cleaned. Third, taxes are levied by political rather than economic bodies, and politics may well get in the way of the enactment of appropriate tax levels.

Creation of Pollution Rights Markets

As was discussed earlier in this chapter, the absence of well-defined property rights to the use of the environment's services is the primary source of pollution problems. Recall the example of the upstream paper industry and the downstream power industry. Since neither owns the river, that is, since neither has a property right to use the river, the paper industry is able to use the river as a sewer for its polluting wastes. And the cost of cleaning the wastes falls on the power industry.

pollution rights market
A market that exists when firms are allowed to buy and sell government-issued licenses granting the holder the right to create a certain amount of pollution.

In many such instances, it is possible to bring about the optimal level of pollution control in a cost-efficient manner through the establishment of a **pollution rights market,** in which firms buy and sell government-issued licenses to pollute. Specifically, the state can determine how much discharge it wishes to allow based on marginal social benefit and marginal social cost analysis, print licenses or permits that in total grant the holders the right to discharge the optimal amount, and then allocate to the polluting firms a share of these licenses.

To see how this might work, suppose that after the market for pollution rights on the river has been in operation for some time, an equilibrium price is established such that a firm can purchase the right to dump 100,000 gallons of discharge into the river for $1,000. Any paper producer capable of making a 100,000-gallon reduction in its discharge for less than $1,000 could increase its profits by making the reduction and then selling a license to dump 100,000 gallons of waste that it holds to another firm. And any firm that could only reduce its discharge by 100,000 gallons at a cost greater than $1,000 would be happy to purchase this license because the difference between the license price of $1,000 and the cost of the reduction in discharge would be directly added to profits. If a decision is made that the overall level of pollution must be reduced, the government would need only to *buy back* some of the licenses it had previously made available to the market. In this way, the state can achieve any particular level of pollution control it wishes and it can be sure that any needed reductions in pollution will be made where it is cheapest to do so. Put differently, through the establishment of a pollution rights market, the state can make certain that any desired level of pollution control can be accomplished in the way that places the least burden on the economy's scarce resources.

Interestingly, the use of pollution rights licenses and the resulting creation of a pollution rights market are not just an academic aside. In the Clean Air Act of 1990, the federal government took its initial steps in this direction by allowing electric companies to trade in sulfur dioxide licenses. Specifically, the act allowed roughly 100 utilities operating principally in the Midwest to produce a certain amount of sulfur dioxide discharge each year. Firms that could reduce their discharge cheaply were allowed to sell their licenses to others. Those who could not reduce their discharge as cheaply could then purchase the right to continue to pollute. While the program has been in effect for just a little more than a decade, it is clearly working in textbook fashion, leading to a fall in sulfur dioxide emissions of more than half, easily surpassing the targets embodied in the program's authorizing legislation. Equally important, these emission reductions have occurred in a cost-effective manner, with some estimates suggesting that the reductions were achieved at about one-fourth the expense predicted at the program's outset.

Summary

The environment provides environmental services that are used by both household units and producing units of the economy. In the processes of consumption and production, wastes are generated. If the ecological system cannot recycle these wastes as fast as they are generated, wastes accumulate. This constitutes pollution.

Economic analysis of pollution provides a perspective on its causes and its effects, along with the costs and benefits of controlling it. Incentives to pollute stem from (1) an absence of property rights in the environment and (2) the fact that many of the environment's services are shared by all of us. Polluters, by polluting, transfer a part of their costs to others. Cost-benefit analysis is useful in determining how much pollution should be allowed. It indicates that forbidding pollution altogether is seldom in the common interest.

There are three main avenues that government pollution control policies can take. First, certain polluting activities may be controlled directly through prohibitions or limitations on polluting activities. Second, they may be controlled indirectly by providing polluters with incentives not to pollute—say, through taxation of polluting activities. Third, in some cases, pollution may be efficiently controlled by allowing for the creation of markets for pollution rights, in which firms buy and sell government-issued licenses to pollute.

Discussion Questions

1. Recent research indicates that secondhand smoke from cigarettes endangers the health of those who are in sustained contact with smokers. Show graphically and explain why the market, operating on its own, will lead to an overproduction and overconsumption of cigarettes.

2. Define and give examples of externalities in consumption. Be sure to list externalities which have both positive and negative effects.

3. Define and give examples of externalities in production. Be sure to list externalities which have both positive and negative effects.

4. Define and list both explicit and implicit costs associated with your taking this class.

5. Distinguish between economic and accounting costs. Which is a better measure of the true cost to society of producing a particular good or service?

6. From an economic perspective, explain why pollution takes place.

7. Show graphically and explain why polluters face an incentive to overproduce their product.

8. Show graphically and explain why those who bear the burden of pollution face an incentive to underproduce their product.

9. Explain how polluting firms effectively force other firms to bear part of their legitimate production costs.

10. The equilibrium reached by a market typically reflects a resource allocation that maximizes social well-being. Explain why this will not be the case when externalities in production exist.

11. Discuss: "The goal for pollution control should be the complete elimination of all polluting discharges."

12. Show graphically and explain how taxes can be used to cause polluting firms to voluntarily cut their polluting discharges to the socially optimal level.

13. Under what circumstances would it make economic sense to eliminate all of a particular type of pollution?

14. Explain how the creation of a pollution rights market might work. Suppose, after a few years, it was decided that too much pollution was being allowed under the plan. What could be done?

15. Relative to using a tax on polluting discharge as a means of pollution control, what advantages does the creation of a market for the right to pollute offer? Are there disadvantages?

Additional Readings

Brown, Stephen P. "Global Warming Policy: Some Economic Implications." *Economic Review*, Federal Reserve Bank of Dallas, 4th Quarter, 1998, p. 26.
Provides a thorough benefit-cost analysis of the Kyoto protocol showing that this protocol, from an economic perspective, leads to excessive reductions in carbon dioxide emissions.

Constanza, Robert, Charles Perrings, and Cutler J. Cleveland. *The Development of Ecological Economics*. The International Library of Critical Writings in Economics 75. Brookfield, VT: Edward Elgar Publishing Company, 1997.
Readings on the history, principles, theories, and assessment of ecological economics.

Council on Environmental Quality. *Annual Report*. Washington DC: Government Printing Office.
An annual and up-to-date set of reports dealing with significant current pollution problems, policy issues, and data on various pollutants.

Goodstein, Eban S. *Economics and the Environment*. Englewood Cliffs, NJ: Prentice Hall, 1995.
This textbook for students in environmental economics and environmental studies classes provides information on global environmental concerns, global warming, environmental regulations, and clean technology.

Joskow, Paul, Richard Schmalensee, and Elizabeth Bailey. "The Market for Sulfur Dioxide Emissions." *American Economic Review*, September 1998, pp. 669–685.
Offers a thorough discussion of the market for sulfur dioxide emissions created within the Clean Air Act of 1990.

The Journal of Economic Perspectives, Summer 1998.
A thorough and accessible treatment of the 1990 Clean Air Act's creation of a sulfur dioxide pollution rights market.

Markandya, Anil, and Julie Richardson, eds. *Environmental Economics: A Reader*. New York: St. Martin's Press, 1992.
Collection of essays that covers all aspects of environmental economics, from an overview to valuation methods and applications and on to international and global environmental problems.

Sankar, Ulaganathan, ed. *Environmental Economics*. Oxford, England: Oxford University Press, 2001.
Fourteen essays on environmental economics by Ronald H. Coase, Harold Hotelling, Robert Solow, and Garrett Hardin, among others.

Taylor, Jeffrey. "Smog Swapping: New Rules Harness Power of Free Markets to Curb Air Pollution." *The Wall Street Journal*, April 14, 1992, p. 1.
Describes ways many companies are beginning to acquire and trade pollution rights following the Clean Air Act of 1990.

Tietenberg, Thomas H. *Economics and Environmental Policy*. 3rd ed. Don Mills, ON: Addison-Wesley Longman, 2000.
Collection of articles discussing theories and applications of economic incentives in environmental policy.

World Wide Web Resources

Center for Sustainable Systems
css.snre.umich.edu/0_1_index.htm

A compendium of education materials designed for university instruction in pollution prevention.

Earth Pledge
www.earthpledge.org/

Earth Pledge is a nonprofit organization that is committed to protect the earth using up-to-date technologies. The Web site includes links to initiatives, publications, ep news, and events.

Environmental Organization Web Directory—Recycling
www.webdirectory.com/Recycling/

Recycling icons for chemical recycling, recycled glass, metals, paper products, petroleum plastics, computer products, and links to other sites.

The Internet Consumer Recycling Guide
www.obviously.com/recycle

Provides links to guides for curbside materials and hard-to-recycle material, an index to local recycling centers, and ways of reducing unwanted mail.

National Center for Environmental Economics (NCEE)
yosemite1.epa.gov/ee/epa/eed.nsf/pages/homepage

The NCEE, maintained by the U.S. Environmental Protection Agency, "analyzes relationships between the economy, environmental health, and environmental pollution control." Has information on publications, grants and funding, events, links, and a search engine.

Sierra Club
www.sierraclub.org/

The Sierra Club is America's oldest, largest, and most influential grassroots environmental organization. Provides links to their publication, *Sierra Magazine*, issues updates, jobs at the Sierra Club, and a search engine.

United States Environmental Protection Agency
www.epa.gov/

Gives links to U.S. laws and regulations, projects and publications, programs, and other resources.

Economics of Crime and Its Prevention
How Much Is Too Much?

Checklist of economic concepts

- Opportunity costs
- Externalities in consumption
- Individually consumed goods and services
- Semicollectively consumed goods and services
- Collectively consumed goods and services
- Free-rider problem
- Public goods
- Cost-benefit analysis
- Marginal social benefit
- Marginal social cost
- Equimarginal principle
- Psychic income
- Psychic costs

On Thursday, March 17, 1988, at 10:45 P.M., in the Bronx, Vernia Brown was killed by stray bullets fired in a dispute over illegal drugs. The 19-year-old mother of one was not involved in the dispute, yet her death was a direct consequence of the "war on drugs." By now, there can be little doubt that most, if not all, "drug-related murders" are the result of drug prohibition. The same type of violence came with the Eighteenth Amendment's ban of alcohol in 1920. The murder rate rose with the start of Prohibition, remained high during Prohibition, and then declined for 11 consecutive years when Prohibition ended. The rate of assaults with a firearm rose with Prohibition and declined for 10 consecutive years after Prohibition. In the last year of Prohibition—1933—there were 12,124 homicides and 7,863 assaults with firearms; by 1941 these figures had declined to 8,048 and 4,525, respectively.

Vernia Brown died because of the policy of drug prohibition. If, then, her death is a "cost" of that policy, what did the "expenditure" of her life "buy"? What benefits has society derived from the policy of prohibition that led to her death? To find the answer, I turned to the experts and to the supporters of drug prohibition.

In 1988, I wrote to Vice President George Bush, then head of the South Florida Drug Task Force; to Education Secretary William Bennett; to Assistant Secretary of State for Drug Policy Ann Wrobleski; to White House drug policy adviser Dr. Donald I. McDonald; and to the public information directors of the Federal Bureau of Investigation, Drug Enforcement Administration, General Accounting Office, National Institute of Justice, and National Institute on Drug Abuse. None of these officials was able to cite any study that demonstrated the beneficial effects of drug prohibition when weighed against its costs. The leaders of the war on drugs are apparently unable to defend on rational cost-benefit grounds their 70-year-old policy, which costs nearly $10 billion per year (out of pocket), imprisons 75,000 Americans, and fills our cities with violent crime. It would seem that Vernia Brown and many others like her have died for nothing.

Source: James Ostrowski, "Thinking about Drug Legalization," *Policy Analysis,* number 121, May 25, 1989, The Cato Institute.

Criminal activities create an important set of social problems in the United States. They affect our general well-being by threatening the loss of property and by generating concern for our physical safety. In addition, a large share of national output is devoted to crime prevention activities, and resources so used become unavailable for other production processes. As crime rates have increased over the years, public support for "getting tough on crime" has grown as well, as evidenced by the fact that most candidates for political office above the level of city dogcatcher have made crime and its prevention a primary part of their campaigns in recent years.

While there is near unanimity on the importance of the topic, we too often seem to approach it with emotion rather than reason. When increases in the crime rate are reported, we immediately demand increases in the budgets of police forces so that the criminals can be apprehended, without considering whether it might be more beneficial to devote the additional resources to ensuring quick trials and certain incarceration. When we feel that too many crimes are being committed by repeat offenders, we demand long mandatory minimum sentences, without reference to the potentially more violent offenders who must be released to make room for those with the mandatory minimums. When we conclude that we would be better off without certain goods or services in society, we simply outlaw their production, distribution, and use, without reference to any potentially negative side effects that outright prohibition might bring.

While our approach to crime and its prevention is typically rooted in emotion, it is unlikely that we will ever be successful unless we begin to look at these issues in a systematic, analytical way. To do so requires the use of economic analysis along with input from other disciplines—especially the social sciences. In this chapter, we focus on the economic aspects of crime and its prevention, addressing six interrelated questions: (1) What is crime? (2) What role should government play in crime prevention? (3) What is the optimal level of crime prevention activities? (4) How should the resources devoted to crime prevention be allocated among the police, courts, and penal system? (5) What are the overall effects of prohibition? (6) What are the causes of criminal activity?

WHAT IS CRIME?

It seems almost silly to raise such a question as "What is crime?" However, if we are to look at crime analytically, we must have a solid base from which to work. The concept of what constitutes criminal activity is often not clear in the mind of any one person and may be ambiguous from one person to another. Some people think of crime in terms of that which is immoral; others think of it in terms of that which is illegal.

Immorality?

Are immoral acts criminal? It is not easy to answer this question. In the first place, many acts do not fall clearly into a moral–immoral classification. In any society, some acts are generally considered immoral—murder and most kinds of theft, for example. But the morality of many other acts depends on who is evaluating them. Examples of such acts include marijuana smoking, drinking alcoholic beverages, betting on horse races, homosexual activities, and adultery. It is clear from these simple examples that the moral–immoral classification helps little in determining whether specific acts are criminal.

Illegality?

A definition that seems to be meaningful and useful analytically is that a criminal act is one the society (or one of its subdivisions) has decided it is better off without and which it has therefore made illegal through laws, ordinances, and the like. It may or may not be immoral. For example, is it immoral to drive 30 miles an hour along a deserted street that is posted for 20 miles an hour, or to run a stop sign at an intersection where there are no other cars, or to catch a fish in a mountain stream before you have obtained a fishing license? As you quickly discover when you are caught, these acts may very well be criminal in nature. On the other hand, if gambling, drinking, and prostitution are immoral, there are many places where they are not illegal and are therefore not criminal.

Acts that are illegal or criminal are designated as such by legislative bodies, such as city councils, state legislatures, and Congress. There are a number of reasons for making certain acts illegal. Some acts may be unacceptably offensive to the moral standards of a majority of legislators and their constituents. Murder, rape, and theft are cases in point. Others may lead to consequences (in the minds of legislators, at least) of which the doer is ignorant. The consumption of alcohol, cocaine, or heroin thus may be made illegal because legislators fear that those who try them may become addicted, with disastrous consequences to the users. Still other acts are designated illegal in order to prevent chaos or to promote order—violation of established traffic rules, for example. Finally, some acts may carry no taint of immorality but may be made illegal because they are considered contrary to the general welfare of the society. Acts of pollution, such as burning your trash within the city limits, illustrate this point.

Classification of Criminal Acts

For purposes of reporting crime rates, the Department of Justice classifies criminal acts as (1) violent crimes and (2) crimes against property. We can add to the classification (3) traffic in illegal goods and services and (4) other crimes. Violent crimes are crimes against persons. They include murder, rape, aggravated assault, and armed robbery. Crimes against property include such things as fraud, burglary, theft, embezzlement, forgery, arson, vandalism, and the like. Traffic in illegal goods and services is made up of dealings in such things as gambling, narcotics, loan-sharking, prostitution, and alcohol. The "other crimes" classification is of course a catchall for everything from nonpayment of alimony to speeding.

Crime is generally thought to be a very serious problem in the United States. In every large city, and in many small ones, people are reluctant to go out at night for fear of being robbed, raped, beaten, or even murdered. Table 5.1 reports the rates of violent, property, and total crime for the period 1980–2001. The data show a pronounced cyclical pattern both for the total crime rate and for the violent and property crime subcategories. Although the turning points are not precisely the same for each category, we can roughly summarize by saying that crime decreased during the early 1980s and continued to fall until about 1985, at which time it increased again until the early 1990s, and has generally declined since.

THE COSTS OF CRIME

That crime has economic costs is certain. The measurement of those costs, however, is at present very inaccurate. First, many criminal activities go unreported. Second, an accurate dollar value cannot be attached to the cost of those crimes that

TABLE 5.1
Crime Rate per
100,000
Inhabitants,
1980–2001

Source: U.S. Department of
Commerce, Bureau of the
Census, *Statistical Abstract
of the United States, 2001,*
Table 305.

Year	Total	Violent Crime	Property Crime
1980	5,950	597	5,353
1981	5,858	594	5,264
1982	5,604	571	5,033
1983	5,175	538	4,637
1984	5,031	539	4,492
1985	5,207	556	4,651
1986	5,480	617	4,863
1987	5,550	610	4,940
1988	5,664	637	5,027
1989	5,741	663	5,078
1990	5,820	732	5,089
1991	5,898	758	5,140
1992	5,660	758	4,903
1993	5,484	747	4,738
1994	5,374	714	4,660
1995	5,278	685	4,593
1996	5,087	637	4,450
1997	4,930	611	4,319
1998	4,619	568	4,052
1999	4,267	523	3,744
2000	4,125	507	3,618
2001	4,161	504	3,656

are reported. Nevertheless, estimates of the costs of crime are necessary if decision making regarding the level of crime prevention activities is to have any degree of economic soundness. The better the estimates, the better the decisions that can be made.

The basis for measuring the cost of crime is the opportunity cost principle. The net economic cost of crime to the society is thus the difference between what the gross domestic product (GDP) would be if there were neither criminal nor crime prevention activities and what GDP currently is, given present criminal and crime prevention activities.

Current reports on crime are concerned solely with the number of crimes committed, not with dollar estimates of their costs. To estimate correctly the cost of violent crime, we would start with the loss of earnings (or value of production services rendered) of the victims and of those close to the victims. Obvious costs of crimes against property are the values of property destroyed or damaged. It is not at all clear that there is a comparable direct cost to society of traffic in illegal goods and services—the production and the sale of these *adds* to the well-being of their consumers but may at the same time impose a negative externality in consumption on society as a whole. Thus, traffic in illegal goods and services imposes a direct cost on society whenever the production and the negative externality in consumption, if any, exceed the addition to consumer well-being, whereas the reverse would indicate that such traffic actually provides a direct benefit to society.

TABLE 5.2

Expenditures on Criminal Justice in the United States by Level of Government, 2000

Level of Government	Direct Expenditure ($ Millions)	Percent
Federal	$ 28,000	20.9
State and local	105,603	79.1
Total	133,603	100.0

Source: U.S. Department of Commerce, Bureau of the Census, *Statistical Abstract of the United States, 2001,* Tables 443 and 476.

Additional costs of the whole range of criminal activities consist of the costs of prevention, apprehension, and correction since resources used for these purposes could have been used to produce alternative goods and services valuable to consumers. Many items thought to be costs are really transfers of purchasing power to the perpetrators of the crimes from their victims. In the case of theft, the thief is made better off at the same time that the person from whom the item is stolen is made worse off. Reprehensible as theft may be, it is difficult to conclude that it represents a large net economic cost to society. It may, however, represent sizable costs to the individual victims.

Criminal activities in the aggregate lower GDP below what it would be without them. *Crime prevention activities* should, if effective, raise GDP above the level that it would be in their absence. Crime prevention activities can thus be considered an economic good or service since GDP is higher with them than it would be without them. We can think of crime prevention activities as using productive resources— labor and capital—going into the production process. The costs of these services are measured by applying the opportunity cost principle: The costs of resources used in crime prevention are equal to the value these resources would have had in their best alternative uses. From Table 5.2, we see that the expenditures of federal, state, and local governments for law enforcement and justice were an estimated $133,603 million for 2000, the latest year for which data are available.

In summary, satisfactory measures of the costs of crime, in terms of GDP lost because of it, have not yet been devised. The costs of crime prevention activities can be estimated with a fair degree of accuracy; however, these figures leave out a substantial part of the total costs of crime.

INDIVIDUALLY AND COLLECTIVELY CONSUMED GOODS

Would a 5 percent increase in the police force of your city be worth anything to you personally? Would an increase in the number of patrol cars on the city's streets affect you directly? Would it benefit you if there were an increase in the number of courts and judges in the system of justice? Your answers to these questions will be, "No," "I don't know," or "Possibly."

Such questions lead us logically to a useful threefold classification of the economy's goods and services. The first includes those that are *individually consumed.* The second includes those that are *semicollectively consumed.* The third is made up of *collectively consumed* goods and services.

Individually Consumed Goods

individually consumed goods and services
Any good or service that gives satisfaction only to the direct consumer.

The concept of **individually consumed goods and services** is straightforward. It includes only those that directly add to the satisfaction of the person who consumes them. Much of what we consume is of this nature—hamburgers, suntan lotion, pencils, and the like. With each, the person doing the consuming is able to identify the satisfaction received. For example, eating a hamburger gives the eater pleasure and reduces hunger pangs. Further, individually consumed goods and services are said to be exclusive in that once they are consumed by one person, they are unavailable for others to consume. Finally, as pointed out in Chapters 2 and 4, a competitive market does a very good job of approximating the socially optimal allocation of resources when we are considering individually consumed goods and services.

Semicollectively Consumed Goods

semicollectively consumed goods and services
Goods and services that yield satisfaction to the direct consumer but also affect the satisfaction of others.

Semicollectively consumed goods and services yield identifiable satisfaction to the one who consumes them, but their consumption also leads to a change in satisfaction for other members of society. My neighbors' consumption of the various items that lead to beautiful landscaping on their property yields satisfaction to me as well as to them. When other people in a democratic society consume the services of primary education—learn to read, write, and do arithmetic—they benefit directly, and I benefit, too, because a literate population improves the functioning of society. When other people purchase sufficient medical care to avoid epidemics, I also benefit from their purchase of health care.

A great many items that people consume and that yield direct satisfaction to them also cause the satisfaction of others to rise as the consumption occurs. These benefits to persons other than the direct consumers were identified in Chapter 4 as positive externalities in consumption. We also noted that the consumption of some semicollectively consumed goods may yield negative externalities in consumption to persons other than the direct consumers. Cigarette smoking in a restaurant or workplace in which there are nonsmokers may be a case in point. In general, when considering semicollectively consumed goods and services, a competitive market will tend to not reach an allocation of resources that maximizes social well-being. In such cases, government intervention *may* improve the functioning of the market. For example, consider the case of cigarette smoking. Suppose the market-determined price for cigarettes is $4 per pack. Yet, when consumed, the cigarettes lead to a fall in satisfaction to those burdened by secondhand smoke equal to about $1 per pack. In this case, a government-imposed tax of $1 per pack will *internalize* the externality. That is, the tax will force the consumers to pay the full cost of the cigarettes and may cause them to voluntarily reduce their smoking toward the socially optimal level. The revenues generated by the tax could then be used in antismoking advertising campaigns, to fund research into smoking-related illnesses, or perhaps to directly fund treatment of these illnesses. It is important to note, however, that in the case of semicollectively consumed goods and services, government need not replace the market. All that is required is for government to assist the market in its attempt to properly allocate resources. And this government interference should be as limited as possible to achieve the goal of maximizing social well-being. An interesting and important application of these principles is presented in Chapter 6, which analyzes the economics of elementary and secondary education.

Collectively Consumed Goods

collectively consumed goods and services
Goods and services that yield benefits to each person within a group and no one person in the group can identify the specific part of the benefit he or she receives. In addition, once provided, the benefits of a collectively consumed good or service cannot be excluded from any member of the group.

Collectively consumed goods and services lie at the opposite extreme from those that are individually consumed; in this case, the individual is not able to isolate or identify a specific personal benefit from consumption. Consider national defense services. What part of the total defense services provided by the economy can you identify as being consumed by you, and what is your estimate of the resulting increase in your satisfaction or well-being? Services such as these contribute to the welfare of the group to which we belong, but it is not possible to pick out the part of the benefit that accrues specifically to any one person. An additional characteristic of a collectively consumed good is that once it is provided, no individual can be excluded from its benefits. Can the government exclude you from the benefits of national defense?

Many kinds of services produced and consumed by a society are collectively consumed. They include national defense, crime prevention, space exploration, some aspects of public health, and most antipollution measures. With collectively consumed goods and services, the market, even if competitively structured, tends to fail in its attempt to reach an allocation of resources that maximizes social well-being. As such, government intervention is usually needed and is typically much more extreme than in the case of semicollectively consumed goods and services.

The Free-Rider Problem

free-rider
An individual who consumes benefits from a collectively consumed good but who pays no part of its cost.

When dealing with collectively consumed goods and services, the market tends to fail due to the natural tendency of some of the beneficiaries of the goods and services to be **free-riders.** The nature of the free-rider problem can be illustrated by an example from the Old West. On the plains of Oklahoma, Texas, Kansas, and other frontier cattle-raising states, cattle rustling was a serious problem. To deal effectively with the problem in one area (say, the Dodge City environs), it was advantageous for the cattle ranchers of the area to band together. They organized vigilante groups of sufficient size to make rustling in the area an exceedingly dangerous business—as those who were caught and hanged would have testified, had they been able. All the ranchers of the area contributed to the cost of organizing and maintaining the vigilante group, in essence forming a market for security services.

As the problem was brought under control, however, the costs of holding the vigilante group together became difficult to meet. Any one rancher was inclined to think that if the others maintained the group, they could not keep the one from benefiting from its activities. If rustlers were afraid to operate in the area, everyone benefited, even those who did not help pay the costs. Each rancher, therefore, had an incentive to withdraw support from the group, becoming a free-rider, since no single producer, even one who did not pay for the protection, could be excluded from its benefits.

Government Production of Collectively Consumed Items

Historically, groups of people have found that in banding together they can do things collectively that they are not able to do as individuals. One of the first things discovered was that the group provides better protection from outsiders than individuals can provide on their own. They also found that group action is well-suited to protecting the members of the group from predators in their midst.

Group action on a voluntary basis is technically possible, of course. The vigilante group of the Old West is an excellent example. But voluntary associations to provide collectively consumed goods have a tendency to fall apart because of the incentives that induce some people to become free-riders, since they cannot be excluded from the benefits of the good. Thus, the voluntary association is at best a tenuous mechanism for this purpose.

Supplanting the voluntary association with the coercive association that we call *government* can effectively remedy the free-rider problem. A coercive government unit (and the power of coercion is an essential feature of government) simply requires that all who receive the benefits of a collectively consumed good or the service pay appropriate taxes for it. Thus, the provision of national defense, crime prevention, pollution prevention and cleanup, and other collectively consumed goods and services becomes a government function. These items are often referred to as **public goods.**

public goods
Collectively consumed goods and services, usually provided by government units.

Most modern governments do not confine their production of goods and services to collectively consumed goods. Name any good or service, and there probably is a government somewhere that produces it. As pointed out in Chapter 2, a major difference between the market and command economic systems is that the government of the latter is responsible for the production of individually consumed as well as collectively consumed and semicollectively consumed items. The government of the former leaves the bulk of individually consumed goods to private business, although it may play a relatively important role in the provision of such semicollectively consumed goods as education.

THE ECONOMICS OF CRIME PREVENTION ACTIVITIES

The "Optimal" Level

What is the appropriate, or optimal, level of expenditures on crime prevention activities by governmental units in the United States? Is the $134 billion level currently being spent roughly optimal? The same question can and should be asked about every category of government activity and expenditure. We gain an important insight when we realize that this is very much the same question that must be addressed regarding the production of any good or service, whether individually, semicollectively, or collectively consumed. Recall from Chapter 1 that we identified the fundamental goal of an economy as being the maximization of social

cost-benefit analysis
A technique for determining the optimal level of an economic activity by considering the relationship between the costs and benefits of the activity. In general, an economic activity should be expanded so long as the resulting increase in benefits is at least as great as the resulting increase in costs.

well-being. Thus, in principle, the optimal level of production for any good or service is that level where the well-being of society is maximum. But how do we find this level of production? Chapter 1 also discussed **cost-benefit analysis.** This widely useful economic tool can help us identify the optimal level of expenditures on crime prevention activities, but it requires good estimates of the benefits and costs of these activities. Once benefits and costs are carefully estimated, cost-benefit analysis indicates that well-being will be enhanced through an increase in crime prevention activities so long as the benefit society derives from the increase is at least as great as the cost of the increased activities.

The framework for such a problem is set up in Table 5.3. Suppose the annual benefits and costs to society of crime prevention at various levels have been investigated thoroughly and the estimates have been recorded in columns (1), (2), and (4). A "unit" of crime prevention is a nebulous concept, a composite of police personnel, patrol cars, courthouses, judges' services, prison costs, and the like. We avoid the problem of defining physical units by using arbitrary $60,000 units of crime prevention, assuming that each $60,000 chunk is spent in the best possible way.

The money expense of crime prevention to society is met by levying taxes. The *economic cost* to society is the value of the goods and services that resources used for crime prevention activities could have produced if they had not been used for crime prevention. The *benefit* to society of crime prevention is society's best estimate of how much better off the suppression of crime will make them—the value of the extra days they can work as a result of not being raped, maimed, or murdered, plus the value of property *not* destroyed, plus the value of the greater personal security they feel, and so on. Obviously, the benefits will be much more difficult to estimate than the costs. In fact, the most difficult and vexing part of the problem is the estimation of the benefits that ensue from various kinds of crime prevention activities.

If the benefits and costs are known, and we assume in Table 5.3 that they are, determination of the optimal level of crime prevention is relatively simple. Consider first whether there should be no crime prevention at all or whether one unit would be worthwhile. One unit of prevention yields benefits to society of $200,000—keeps $200,000 worth of GDP from being destroyed by criminal activities—and it would cost society only $60,000 to obtain it. Obviously, this is better than no prevention; the net benefit to society (total benefit minus total cost) is $140,000.

Now consider two units of prevention versus one unit. The total benefit yielded to society is $380,000. But note that the increase in total benefit yielded in moving from one to two units is $180,000, somewhat less than the increase in total benefits resulting from a movement from zero to one unit. The increase in total benefit to society resulting from a one-unit increase in the amount of crime prevention is called the marginal social benefit of crime prevention. As the number of units of prevention is increased, marginal social benefit can be expected to decline because each one-unit increase would be used to suppress the most serious crimes outstanding. The more units of prevention used, the less serious the crimes to which

TABLE 5.3
Estimated Benefits and Costs of Crime Prevention, Typical U.S. Community ($ Thousands)

(1) Units of Crime Prevention per Year	(2) Total Benefit to Society	(3) Marginal Social Benefit	(4) Total Cost to Society	(5) Marginal Social Cost	(6) Net Benefit to Society
0	$ 0		$ 0		$ 0
		$200		$60	
1	200		60		140
		180		60	
2	380		120		260
		160		60	
3	540		180		360
		140		60	
4	680		240		440
		120		60	
5	800		300		500
		100		60	
6	900		360		540
		80		60	
7	980		420		560
		60		60	
8	1,040		480		560
		40		60	
9	1,080		540		540
		20		60	
10	1,110		600		500

they are applied and, therefore, the less the increase in the benefit to society from each one-unit increase in prevention.

Society is rewarded for moving from the one-unit level to the two-unit level of prevention because the marginal social benefit yielded by the second unit exceeds the marginal social cost of the increase. The marginal social cost of crime prevention is defined as the increase in total cost to society resulting from a one-unit increase in prevention. Marginal social cost of prevention is constant in the example because we are measuring units of prevention in terms of $60,000 chunks. Therefore, the net benefit to society will be increased by $120,000 ($180,000 − $60,000) if the level of prevention is increased from one unit to two units. As such, we can be sure that social well-being is increased when the second unit of crime prevention is added. (Make sure you understand this before you go any further.)

Using the same logic, we can determine that it is worthwhile for society to use the third, fourth, fifth, sixth, and seventh units of crime prevention. For each of these increases, the marginal social benefit is greater than the marginal social cost—that is, each adds more to total benefit than it adds to total cost. Therefore, each brings about an increase in net benefit to society. Net benefit to society, our measure of the increase in social well-being due to crime prevention, reaches a maximum of $560,000 at the seven-unit level. If the level of prevention is raised to eight units, no harm is done. Marginal social benefit equals marginal social cost, and there is no change in net benefit. But if the level is raised to nine units, the net benefit to society will fall to $540,000.

As citizens, we *must* understand the logic underlying determination of the optimal amount of government activity in crime prevention—or in anything else. It is very simple, very important, and usually overlooked. If a small increase in the level of an activity yields additional benefit to society worth more than the additional cost of providing it, it should be expanded. On the other hand, if its marginal social benefit is less than marginal social cost, the activity should be contracted. It follows that the optimal level is that at which marginal social benefit equals marginal social cost. (Study Table 5.3 until you understand this thoroughly.)

The foregoing economic analysis suggests something important about dealing with increasing crime rates. If, when crime prevention activities are stepped up, the cost of an increase in prevention is less than the benefit it realizes, we ought to engage in more crime prevention activities. We are irrational if we do not. However, if a unit of prevention is not worth to us what it costs, then it is equally irrational to attempt to further suppress crime. Complete suppression of crime is never logical from the point of view of economics alone. There will be some level of crime prevention at which the benefits of an additional unit of prevention are simply not worth what they cost. (What about 10 units of prevention in Table 5.3?)

Allocation of the Crime Prevention Budget

Economic analysis also has something to contribute in determining the effectiveness of different facets of crime prevention activities. There are several facets to any well-balanced government crime prevention program. Ideally, it should deter people from engaging in criminal activities. Failing in this—as it surely will—it must first *detect and apprehend* those engaging in criminal activities. This is primarily a police function. To *determine the guilt or innocence* of those charged with criminal acts, the legal system utilizes courts, attorneys, judges, and juries. Those convicted are fined and/or put in prison to *rehabilitate and/or punish* them. Reference to the prison system as a corrections system indicates hope that those incarcerated will somehow be rehabilitated and deterred from engaging in further criminal activities. In practice, the sentences of those convicted of crimes usually take on at least some aspects of punishment.

How much of a governmental unit's crime prevention budget should be allocated to police departments? How much for courts, judges, and prosecutors? How much for corrections, rehabilitation, and punishment? Detection and apprehension of persons thought to be committing criminal acts are of little value unless there are adequate court facilities for trying them. Trying persons apprehended and sentencing those convicted presuppose an adequate system of corrections. No one facet of crime prevention can contribute effectively unless the others are there to back it up.

**equimarginal
principle**
An efficient allocation
of a budget exists
when the last dollar
spent on any one
facet of the budget
yields the same
marginal social
benefit as the last
dollar spent on any
other facet.

The most efficient mix of the different facets of crime prevention is determined logically by what economists call the **equimarginal principle.** The crime budget should be allocated among police, courts, and corrections so that the last dollar spent on any one facet yields the same addition to the benefits of crime prevention as the last dollar spent on the others. Another way of saying this is that the budget should be allocated so that the marginal social benefit from a dollar's worth of police effort equals the marginal social benefit of a dollar's worth of judicial effort and a dollar's worth of corrections in the overall suppression of crime.

As an example, suppose that the crime prevention system is relatively overloaded in the area of detection and apprehension. The courts cannot handle all those who are being arrested, so many of them must be set free without trial or, in the case of plea bargaining, sentenced for a lesser crime than the one committed. The mere fact of arrest will have some crime-deterring effects, but the deterrent effect will be much less than it would be were there adequate court facilities to try the persons apprehended. The contribution to crime prevention of an additional dollar's worth of police activity at this point is low. On the other hand, an expansion of court facilities would increase the likelihood of trial and conviction of those apprehended. We would expect the crime-deterring effect of a dollar's worth of such an expansion to be greater than that of a dollar spent on detection, apprehension, and subsequent freeing of those apprehended. Suppose that taking $1 away from police work brings about enough of a crime increase to cause a 75-cent loss in GDP to society. Now suppose that court activity is increased by $1, and the increased activity deters criminal activity enough to make society better off by $3. Under these circumstances, society will experience a net gain of $2.25 in GDP by a transfer of $1 from police activities to court activities. Such net gains are possible for any dollar transfer among police activities, court activities, and corrections activities when the marginal social benefit of $1 spent on one is less than the marginal social benefit of $1 spent on either of the others. No further gains are possible when the crime prevention budget is so allocated that the marginal social benefit of $1 spent on any one activity equals the marginal social benefit of $1 spent on any one of the other activities.

Changing the Legal Status of Goods and Services

Economic analysis can also be applied to advantage when evaluating the effects of changing the legal status of goods and services. The provision and sale of goods and services in some cases changes, from being generally legal to generally illegal, or vice versa. Good examples include certain drugs, abortion services, certain types of gambling, and prostitution. But the classic example, no doubt, concerns alcohol. Early in the past century, a great deal of controversy surrounded the production, sale, and consumption of alcoholic beverages. Those opposed to alcohol use were eventually able to change the Constitution of the United States when the Eighteenth Amendment ushered in the prohibition era. The legal treatment of alcohol changed again in 1933 with the passage of the Twenty-First Amendment, which repealed prohibition. In many such controversies, the primary arguments turn on issues of morality. Clearly, economists are in no position to offer much insight into the moral issues surrounding the legal status of goods and services. Economic analysis can, however, provide valuable insights into the effects that changing the legal status of goods and services will have on the conditions of sale and use of the products.

Over the past few decades, the legal status of drugs such as marijuana and cocaine has come up for a great deal of public debate. And in general referendums during recent election cycles, the people of California, Arizona, and Washington, among others, voted in favor of allowing the medicinal use of some previously illegal drugs. Opponents, which include the president's drug policy advisers, see such moves as misguided and as inevitably leading to outright legalization of what they view to be very dangerous substances. Such opponents usually argue that the production, traffic in, and use of illegal drugs lead to much of the criminal activity that we see in society today and, furthermore, lead to severe personal consequences, often unexpected, for the users. Proponents of some form of legalization counter that the criminal activity associated with illegal drugs today is not a consequence of the drugs per se but simply a consequence of the drugs' illegal status. Further, they argue that any unintended consequences to users are again due to the drugs being illegal since it is the illegality that limits reliable information about the products being readily available to consumers. This issue is obviously quite complex. However, some important insights can be had when economic analysis is applied to the issue. To do so, let's consider the possible legalization of a physically nonaddictive substance such as marijuana.

In Figure 5.1, suppose that D_1D_1 and S_1S_1 represent the demand and supply conditions for marijuana with its current illegal status. Under this circumstance, the interaction of consumers and producers leads to an equilibrium price of p_1 per ounce and an equilibrium quantity exchanged of M_1 million ounces per year. What can we expect to happen in this market if marijuana production, distribution, and use are all legalized? On the demand side, we can expect to see some increase to a level such as D_2D_2. As shown, the increase in demand is quite modest. The substance's current widespread use—a recent survey of 7th through 12th graders indicates that 40 percent had tried marijuana—and widespread availability— nearly 60 percent reported marijuana to be "easy to obtain"—would seem to confirm the supposition of only a modest increase in demand following legalization. That is, apparently rather few individuals currently avoid using marijuana solely due to its illegality.

The real dramatic effect on the market can be expected on the supply side. We show this as the increase to S_2S_2. Why such a dramatic increase in supply? Recall that the first thing we hold constant when drawing a supply curve is the cost of production. Consider the cost to produce and distribute marijuana when it is illegal versus when it is legal. When the substance is illegal, the grower must either cultivate indoors and lose the productivity of the outside environment or run the added risk of growing outdoors. Given the risk of discovery, outdoor growers must choose remote locations for even modest scale cultivation and then often have to "pack in" supplies such as water. Once harvested, the drug has to be

FIGURE 5.1   **Economic Effects of Making Marijuana Legal**

When marijuana is illegal, the interaction of demand $D_1 D_1$ and supply $S_1 S_1$ leads to an equilibrium price of p_1 and an equilibrium quantity exchanged of M_1. Legalization would lead to a modest increase in demand to $D_2 D_2$ and sharply increased supply to $S_2 S_2$. The result would be a large fall in equilibrium price and a large increase in the quantity exchanged.

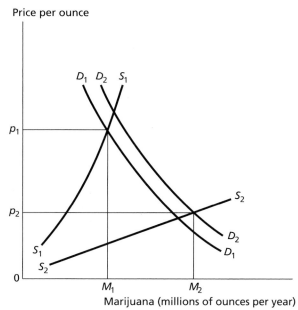

shipped, without detection, to every corner of the country. And, at every step in the process, the producer has to be aware of the legal implications, and the costs, of the operation being discovered. None of this would be necessary were the drug legal. Clearly, then, legalization of marijuana would lead to greatly reduced production costs and, consequently, greatly increased supply.

Taken together, the new demand and supply would lead to a new equilibrium price of p_2 per ounce and an equilibrium quantity exchanged of M_2. That is, we can expect that legalization will lead to a great fall in price and a significant increase in the quantity of the good exchanged and consumed. But might any other outcomes reasonably be expected? Experience with other goods and services suggests that additional outcomes should be expected from legalization. These outcomes might include a significant increase in the quality of marijuana available as suppliers are forced to compete for business, less criminal activity associated with the good since violence rarely is associated with the production and sale of legal goods, and a significant freeing up of resources within the government's crime prevention budget that would then be available for other uses.

Should we legalize drugs such as marijuana, then? Again, keep in mind that economic analysis alone does not provide an answer to this question, especially if the drug in question is highly physically addictive, such as heroin or crack cocaine.

With these types of drugs, the analysis presented above really does not hold since it assumes that the user is making a voluntary choice—is not addicted—when he or she purchases and uses the drug. When we are considering a nonaddictive drug such as marijuana, however, what economic analysis provides is a clear understanding of the economic aspects of the market for a good or service given its legal status. To summarize that analysis, when a good or service is legal, we can expect relatively low prices, high product quality, large quantities available for consumption, and limited illegal activity associated with the production, sale, and use of the good or service. That is, we can expect that, as is generally true, the market will work to the benefit of the consuming public. Should there be moral issues associated with the analysis, these issues, as is appropriately the case, must be left for individual consideration.

Causes of Criminal Activity

Thus far we have looked at the issue of crime and crime prevention from society's perspective. Economic analysis is also helpful in looking at crime from the perspective of the criminal or potential criminal. Specifically, why do some people choose to participate in criminal activities? Clearly the reasons are nearly infinite, and many have little or nothing to do with economics. In many cases violent crimes are the result of unrestrained passions or emotions. Most murders, for example, result from deep-seated, highly intense feelings of some sort between the murderer and the victim. The victim may be a wife, a husband, a lover, or the guy who drives too aggressively on the highway. The level of the murderer's emotion pushes aside the constraints of conscience and law that society has established. While this is often the case, a great deal of criminal activity no doubt has roots that are economic in nature, especially in cases such as trafficking in illegal substances. For these types of criminal activities, economic analysis can offer important insights into the motivations of the individuals involved.

To see the value of economic analysis in understanding why people commit certain crimes, consider the supply side of the market for marijuana as presented above. What are the motivations that lead individuals into the business of growing marijuana even though it is against the law? The key word in this question is *business.* That is, marijuana is grown as a business venture, and as such the motivations to enter this business are much the same as those which exist for any other business—whether legal or illegal. There are, no doubt, many different motivations. Some people enter a particular business because that business offers a lifestyle they greatly value. In other cases, decisions to enter a particular business result from a desire to live in a certain area of the country or world. While these and other motivations exist, it is undeniable that in many, if not most, cases the fundamental reason that someone enters into a business is the pursuit of profit—the difference between income and cost. But does the pursuit of profit as a motivation for entering a particular business necessarily conflict with other motivations, such as perhaps desiring to live and work in a beach community? Not

psychic income
Benefits an individual receives from a business endeavor in the form of personal satisfaction rather than in the form of money.

necessarily. If we broaden our notion of income to include what is known as **psychic income** as well as money income, there is no conflict between these various motivations. That is, while one might be willing to sacrifice money income that could be earned as a big-city public accountant to operate a bicycle shop at a beach, presumably the lost money income is more than offset by the psychic income he or she receives from living and working at the beach. Taking both money and psychic income into account, then, we assume that the decision to enter a particular business is driven by a desire to earn profit. And if this seems reasonable when considering opening a bicycle shop at a beach, why should we believe the situation to be any different for the potential marijuana grower?

For the operation to make a profit for the grower, total income, or revenues, from the sale of marijuana must be greater than the production costs. If this is true, we might conclude that "crime does pay." The revenue side of the operation is straightforward: It is simply the price at which the grower can wholesale his or her produce times the quantity that is sold, plus any psychic income that he or she derives from being in the business. The cost side is a bit more complex. By now you know that economists measure costs in opportunity cost terms. The opportunity cost of operating the marijuana-growing business is made up of both explicit and implicit costs. The explicit costs are likely to include the money paid to secure the property used to grow the product and the costs of electricity, lighting systems (assuming indoor growth), and fertilizers and pesticides needed to actually bring forth a harvest. As is often the case, however, there are going to be implicit costs borne by the marijuana grower. Chief among these is the cost created by the fact that the garden will need tending, and time spent tending cannot be used to earn income in some other way. That is, if the grower spends 20 hours a week tending plants, the income that could have been earned during the 20 hours is an implicit cost of growing marijuana. Equally important, the grower must take into account the implicit cost of getting caught—lost liberty, especially in an environment of mandatory minimum prison sentences. Of course, the cost of getting caught is difficult to estimate. Suppose the penalty for getting caught is highly severe, say, life imprisonment. This would seem to create an extremely significant implicit cost of growing marijuana. But this might not be the case. Whether or not the existence of a severe penalty imposes a great implicit cost depends on the risk of being caught. If the risk is high, the implicit cost imposed is equally high. On the contrary, if the risk of being caught is low or nonexistent, the cost of being caught is proportionately low. Finally, an additional implicit cost to the grower is the loss of social standing. If there is some degree of social stigma attached to being known as a criminal grower, this loss of social standing must be added to the cost side of the marijuana grower's ledger. In this way, the stigma attached to growing marijuana can be thought of as negative psychic income or simply as a **psychic cost** of the business.

psychic costs
Costs an individual incurs in pursuing a business in the form of negative personal satisfaction rather than in the form of money.

Once potential revenues (including both money and psychic income) and potential costs (including all explicit and implicit costs) are estimated as accurately as is possible, the decision to enter the business of marijuana growing becomes a simple application of cost-benefit analysis. If the revenues are reasonably expected to be greater than costs, the individual increases his or her level of well-being by becoming a marijuana grower, that is, by becoming a criminal in the current legal environment. If the reverse is true, the individual finds another line of work.

Although this analysis seems straightforward, we must discuss a couple of other factors. Specifically, let's look more closely at the implicit costs of growing marijuana from an opportunity cost perspective. The most important implicit costs for the grower are likely to be the income that he or she forgoes from other employment in order to grow marijuana and the potential cost of incarceration should the operation be busted. But what if the individual, prior to entering the business, is unemployed and, because of local economic conditions, sees little likelihood of becoming gainfully employed legally? For such a person, the cost side of the equation is much smaller than would be true for someone who is employed in a high-paying job. This is not to say that all, or even most, poor people will enter into a criminal activity such as marijuana growing. But this application of the opportunity cost principle does, for example, seem to explain the widespread growth of marijuana in highly depressed areas of Appalachia, which produce such a large share of the domestically grown marijuana in the United States. When the possibility of earning even a minimal living by legal methods seems dim at best, the field is ripe for criminal activity. But, on the contrary, this does not suggest that the opportunity cost principle is applicable only to criminal activities of the poor. Although the opportunity costs are much greater for someone who is in a good-paying job than for someone who is unemployed or who has a low-paying dead-end job, even someone from the highest strata of society may be tempted to enter into a criminal enterprise if the potential income is great enough—this is, no doubt, the primary cause of white-collar crime.

Thorough consideration of the implicit costs of entering a particular illegal endeavor from the standpoint of the opportunity cost principle provides insights into the causes of certain criminal activities. And these insights can be useful to society in its attempt to reduce criminal activity. That is, to the extent that those in dire economic circumstances turn to criminal activities because their desperate plight lowers the opportunity cost of the activities, many of these individuals may be deterred from turning to crime through improved educational opportunities that can be expected to increase earning power from legal jobs as well as programs such as job training and counseling, community economic development, and relocation in some instances. Similarly effective might be public provision of recreational activities for young people in depressed areas. Each of these types of programs, to the extent that they are successful, tends to increase the opportunity cost of pursuing a criminal activity and, thus, makes it less likely that the individual will so choose. Also important is the implicit cost created by being caught and punished. As pointed out, this cost approaches zero if the risk of capture is very low. In this way, an application of the equimarginal principle might suggest that some people could be convinced not to enter into a particular illegal activity if relatively more resources are put into the quick and certain arrest and conviction of criminals, and relatively fewer resources are put into longer, but less certain, prison terms.

Summary

Criminal activities are defined as activities that are illegal. They may or may not be immoral. They are usually classified as (1) crimes against persons, (2) crimes against property, (3) traffic in illegal goods and services, and (4) other crimes.

Good information on the costs of crime is not available because many criminal activities go unreported and because it is difficult to place dollar values on the results of some kinds of these activities. Some reported "costs" of crime are not really economic costs to the society as a whole but are transfers of income from the victim of the crime to its perpetrator.

In an economic analysis of crime, it is useful to classify goods and services into three categories: (1) individually consumed, (2) semicollectively consumed, and (3) collectively consumed items. Governments, with their coercive powers, are in a unique position to efficiently produce such collectively consumed items as crime prevention. Consequently, collectively consumed services of this type are usually provided by governments.

Cost-benefit analysis can be used to advantage in determining the optimal level of crime prevention activities in a society. The cost of crime prevention can be easily determined, but the benefit—much of which is intangible—is hard to estimate. Conceptually, it is the difference between what GDP would be *with* crime prevention and what it would be *without* such activities. On the basis of the best estimates that can be made, society should seek that level of crime prevention at which the net benefit to society is greatest. This will be the level at which the marginal social benefit of crime prevention is equal to marginal social cost.

Once the level of the government's crime prevention budget is determined, it should be efficiently allocated among the different facets of crime prevention activities. These include detection and apprehension of violators, determination of their guilt or innocence, and corrections. The most efficient allocation of the crime prevention budget among these facets is determined by applying the equimarginal principle. The most efficient allocation will be such that the marginal social benefit from a dollar's worth of detection and apprehension is equal to the marginal social benefit from a dollar's worth of each of the other two facets of crime prevention.

Economic analysis is also helpful in determining whether goods or services should be considered illegal. Typically, when an illegal activity is made legal, both supply and demand increase, although in most cases the increase in supply can be expected to be greater in degree than the increase in demand, leading to a fall in the equilibrium price of the activity and an increase in the equilibrium quantity purchased. Additionally, it is reasonable to expect the quality of the good or service to increase. In each case, just the reverse may be anticipated if a currently legal activity is made illegal.

Economic analysis is also useful in understanding the motivations of individuals to commit certain crimes. A rational individual can be expected to enter into a criminal activity if the revenue generated from the activity is perceived as being greater than the cost. It is important that all revenues (from both money income and psychic income) and all costs (both explicit and implicit) be taken into account. With the balance sheet properly understood, society can make more effective use of the equimarginal principle in its attempt to protect itself from crime.

Discussion Questions

1. Some people think of crime as that which is immoral. Explain why morality helps little in determining whether specific acts should be considered criminal.

2. Goods and services can be assigned to one of three categories: individually consumed, semicollectively consumed, or collectively consumed. Explain the differences, and provide examples of each category.

3. What are free-riders, and how do they influence the ability of markets to allocate resources effectively?

4. Markets have difficulty in providing collectively consumed goods and services. Explain why. Be sure to use the free-rider concept.

5. From a standpoint of the free rider-problem, discuss the likely effectiveness of group assignments. Does the economic analysis based on the free-rider problem seem to match your experiences?

6. Explain how the optimal level of government expenditure on a collectively consumed good or service can be arrived at.

7. Suppose the end of the semester is approaching and you have exams to prepare for in economics, calculus, and history. Further suppose that your primary goal is to maximize your grade point average. Explain how the equimarginal principle might be used to help you allocate your study time.

8. Using abortion services as the example, describe the effects that you would expect were the services to become illegal.

9. Explain how economic analysis can assist in understanding why individuals commit crimes. What does this analysis have to say about attempts to reduce crime?

10. Political pressure remains high for mandatory minimum sentences for those convicted of certain crimes. Based on the analysis of this chapter, discuss the likely consequences of such sentences.

11. Discuss: "The crime associated with the drug trade is due to the illegality of the drugs, not due to drugs per se. As such, if you want to bring down crime in the United States, you should legalize drugs such as marijuana and cocaine."

12. The city of Boca Raton, Florida, recently opened a publicly financed skateboard facility. Using the analysis developed in this chapter, explain this facility's likely impact, if any, on juvenile crime in the city.

13. Relying on the concepts of marginal social benefits and marginal private benefits, show graphically and explain why the market, operating on its own, will tend to cause too many cigarettes to be produced and consumed.

14. Is government production of semicollectively consumed goods necessary to reach the socially optimal allocation of resources?

15. Is government production of collectively consumed goods necessary to reach the socially optimal allocation of resources?

16. Discuss: "When government outlaws a good or service like abortion, it is really making a value judgment as to who should be allowed to have the service since relatively wealthy people will always be able to find high-quality abortion services even if they are illegal."

Additional Readings

Bayer, Ronald, and Gerald M. Oppenheimer, eds. *Contemporary Drug Policy.* New York: Cambridge University Press, 1993.
A set of essays about drug decriminalization.

Boaz, David, ed. *The Crisis in Drug Prohibition.* Washington, DC: The Cato Institute, 1990.
Taken together, these essays offer an in-depth, thoughtful, and balanced analysis of the question of legalizing drugs.

Eide, Erling. *Economics of Crime: Deterrence and the Rational Offender. Contributions to Economic Analysis.* New York: North Holland, 1994.
Thorough analysis of the economics of criminal activity, although the figures on crime are from Norway.

Federal Bureau of Investigation. *Crime in the United States.* Washington, DC: U.S. Government Printing Office, annual.
Sums up all reported crimes in the United States on an annual basis, providing the most complete statistical data available on the different types of crimes and the people who commit them. Also provides trend data for key types of crime statistics. There is very little analysis of the data.

Forst, Brian, ed. *The Socio-Economics of Crime and Justice.* Armonk, NY: Sharpe, 1993.
Chapter 3 presents an economist's perspective on criminality; sociologists, psychologists, and law professors present their own perspectives in other chapters.

Miller, Roger L., Daniel K. Benjamin, and Douglass C. North. *Economics of Public Issues.* 13th ed. Don Mills, OH: Addison-Wesley Longman, 2002.
Discusses the economic gains from legalizing prostitution, the economic nature of criminal activity, and other issues. The authors argue that to reduce crime, the price paid (punishment) by the criminal must be increased.

Myers, Samuel L., Jr., and Margaret C. Simms, eds. *The Economics of Race and Crime.* New Brunswick, NJ: Transaction Books, 1988.
Combination of historical and contemporary articles discussing blacks, crime, unemployment, and other issues.

Naylor, R. T. *Wages of Crime: Black Markets, Illegal Finance, and the Underworld Economy.* Ithaca, NY: Cornell University Press, 2002.
Discusses the economic aspects of crime, including black markets, guerrilla groups, money laundering, and the mafia.

Schaler, Jeffrey A., ed. *Drugs: Should We Legalize, Decriminalize, or Deregulate?* Amhurst, NY: Prometheus Books, 1998.
Defines addictions, shows the relationship between drugs and crime, and discusses U.S. laws regarding illegal substances.

World Wide Web Resources

Bureau of Justice Statistics

www.ojp.usdoj.gov/bjs/

Provides latest national statistics on crimes and victims. Links to information about the U.S. justice system and other justice-related databases.

Economics and Crime in the States

www.frbatlanta.org/frbatlanta/filelegacydocs/zbecsi.pdf

This article from the Federal Reserve Bank of Atlanta's *Economic Review*, First Quarter, 1999, discusses the "regional differences and trends in the patterns of crime" in the Unites States.

Federal Bureau of Investigation

www.fbi.gov/

Provides access to *Uniform Crime Reports* and gives statistics on crime rates, violent crimes, and other figures.

National Archive of Criminal Justice Data

www.icpsr.umich.edu/NACJD/

Provides links to over 550 data collections of statistics, prevention, specialized training sites, and more.

National Crime Prevention Council (NCPC)

www.ncpc.org/ncpc/ncpc

The NCPC, an educational nonprofit organization, sponsors the McGruff crime dog advertisements. Their Web page has links to coalition membership, youth safety corps, topics in crime prevention, and more.

United States Department of Justice

www.usdoj.gov/

Has links to publications, employment, fugitives and missing persons, and justice for kids and youth.

World's Most Wanted

www.mostwanted.org/

World's Most Wanted, Inc., a not-for-profit corporation, provides a home page to help law enforcement agencies use the Internet more effectively. Provides links to child support, bail jumpers, U.S. listings by state, and other sites.

The Economics of Education
Crisis and Reform

Checklist of economic concepts

- Demand
- Supply
- Marginal private benefits
- Marginal social benefits
- Marginal private costs
- Marginal social costs
- Externalities in consumption
- Market failure

WASHINGTON—If you are a high school student thinking about college, consider this: Someone with a bachelor's degree earns nearly $1 million more over his or her lifetime than a high school graduate.

A Census Bureau survey released today shows a college graduate can expect to earn $2.1 million working full-time between ages 25 and 64, which demographers call a typical work-life period.

A master's degree–holder is projected to earn $2.5 million, while someone with a professional degree, such as a doctor or lawyer, could make even more— $4.4 million.

In contrast, a high school graduate can expect to make $1.2 million during the working years, according to the bureau report that tracked the influence of education on lifetime earnings.

Not all students look at college as an investment, "but I'm sure parents do," said Jacqueline King, policy analyst with the American Council on Education, a higher education advocacy group. "The challenge is to convince those high school students on the margin that it is really worth their time to go to college."

Source: Excerpt from Genero C. Armas, "Survey: Education Affects Earnings," posted 7/18/02 at TheState.com (*http://www.thestate.com/mld/thestate/3684141.htm*).

The importance of effective primary and secondary education (kindergarten through 12th grade, or simply K–12) cannot be overstated, either from the perspective of students and their families or from that of the overall economy. From the individual's perspective, gone, or at least nearly gone, are the days when one could eke out even a modest living through the effort of muscle alone. Even the most basic jobs in today's information-hungry world require workers to be able to read, write, and do simple arithmetic—and most jobs require a great deal more. The young adult entering the job market today, lacking at least a solid K–12 education, will most likely live life in or very close to poverty. Stated positively, as noted in the opening vignette, college graduates can expect to earn fully $1 million more over their working lifetimes than someone who goes no further than high school. This outcome is not a criticism of our market-oriented economy: As discussed in Chapter 3, in a competitive market economy, workers tend to be paid based on the value that their work creates for their employer, in terms of added revenues. That is, the greater the revenue that a worker brings to the firm, the more the worker is paid. And this clearly shows the importance of a good system of K–12 education to the economy as a whole: The better educated and trained and, thus, the more productive the workforce, the more efficient will be individual firms and, taken together, the faster will the overall economy grow. As you recall from Chapter 1, a primary way in which an economy's production possibilities curve can be shifted outward, reducing the effects of scarcity in society, is through improving the quality of the economy's productive resources, the most important of which is its workers.

The United States has a long and, by all accounts, generally successful history with broad-based basic education. Yet, in recent years, many have come to question the effectiveness of K–12 education as it is now delivered. Although some of the problems plaguing the current K–12 system are social or political in nature, many have very significant economic components. Most important are questions such as: How much K–12 education should be provided? Who should pay for it? What institutional structure should be employed to provide it? We will concern ourselves with these questions in this chapter. We will not even arrive at arguably defensible answers, however, until we have a clear grasp of what is meant by the "crisis in K–12."

THE CRISIS IN K–12

Throughout much of the twentieth century, the system of K–12 education in the United States was held in very high public esteem. This started to change in the 1960s and 1970s as we began to witness the relatively low status of American students in international assessments of educational outcomes, declining scores on college entrance exams, and an increasing sense that our K–12 graduates lacked the educational foundation, skills, and training needed to succeed in the workplace. Perhaps most troubling is the accumulating evidence that high school graduates in the United States are being systematically outperformed internationally in the all-important areas of science and math training. The plight of American high school graduates, relative to their international peers, is presented in Table 6.1. The data in Table 6.1 are taken from the Third International Mathematics and Science Study (TIMSS), which was completed in 1995. As you see, taken as a group, high school graduates in the United States do not fare particularly well in either math or science. In fact, not only do our graduates suffer when compared with those in other advanced, relatively wealthy economies; they barely hold up against their counterparts in the less well-developed parts of the world. Of the 11 countries listed, U.S. students were fourth from the bottom in science and, even worse, next to the bottom in math.

The data in Table 6.1 are quite persuasive, but the use of the TIMSS data to make international comparisons is not without shortcomings. Notable among these are differences between countries in such key factors as curriculum, teacher preparation, and the length of both school days and school years. As an example of the difficulty involved with such international comparisons, consider differences in the average length of the school year. Students in the United States average about 180 days per year in school. By contrast, the school year is 192 days in England, 195 days in Canada, 208 days in Russia, 240 days in Germany, and 243 days in Japan. Clearly, were it possible to fully correct for this and other shortcomings, international comparisons of student achievement might show students in the United States faring a bit better. With this said, however, a cautious way of looking at

TABLE 6.1
American High School Graduates versus the World, 1995: Average Scores for Secondary School Graduates

Source: Third International Mathematics and Science Study (TIMSS) of 1994–1995, as presented in the *Digest of Education Statistics, 2001*, Tables 407 and 408, available at *http://nces.gov.*

Country	Math	Science
United States	461	480
Australia	522	527
Canada	519	532
Cyprus	446	448
Czech Republic	466	448
Denmark	547	509
France	523	487
Germany	495	497
Italy	476	475
Sweden	552	559
Switzerland	540	583

Table 6.1 is to see a picture of U.S. educational achievement that one should not expect from the world's richest country. That is, shouldn't the world's richest country enjoy educational achievement that is clearly second to none?

Achievement is, of course, only part of the story. The other side of the coin is a country's commitment to education as expressed in its expenditures on education. That is, the outcomes for achievement listed above might be understandable and even acceptable if it were shown that the United States is failing to keep up, internationally, on education expenditures. Table 6.2 shows education expenditures for selected countries, both in absolute dollars per secondary school student and in terms of total expenditures on all K–12 students as a percentage of GDP.

As Table 6.2 points out, in terms of expenditures per secondary school pupil, the United States comes in at the higher end of the international distribution. The $8,157 per pupil the United States spends on its secondary school students is certainly great enough, comparatively speaking, to refute the idea that the achievement outcomes noted above are simply a by-product of generally poor educational funding. From a pure efficiency perspective, it would seem that we are not getting the "bang for the buck" that other listed countries' K–12 systems are delivering. This point is further driven home by considering the percentage of GDP devoted to all K–12 education internationally. By this measure, the United States is in the middle to upper part of the pack. Not a bad place to be, perhaps, were we achieving middle to upper results, but of course we are not. Taken together, Tables 6.1 and 6.2 suggest that the K–12 system in the United States is, for the observed achievement outcomes, simply a relatively expensive system. But why is this so?

Kindergarten through 12th-grade education in the United States is delivered within a composite system of primarily public, but, increasingly important, private elementary and secondary schools. In 2000, some 90 percent of the 50 million school-aged children in the United States attended a public school funded through

TABLE 6.2
International Comparisons of Education Expenditures, 1999

Source: Digest of Education Statistics, 2001, Tables 413 and 414, available at http://nces.ed.gov.

Country	Expenditures per Student ($)	Expenditures as a Percentage of GDP
United States	$8,157	3.5%
Australia	$6,850	3.8
Denmark	$7,626	4.8
France	$7,141	4.2
Germany	$6,603	3.0
Italy	$6,518	3.2
Sweden	$5,911	5.1
Switzerland	$9,756	4.0

various taxes. The remaining students took advantage of a variety of private school offerings. The key distinguishing characteristic between the two types of schools is that a much greater direct financial burden is placed on the families of the private school students than exists in the normally zero-tuition public schools. It is within this institutional context that we must find answers to our three key questions: How much educational service should be produced? Who should pay for it? What is the most appropriate institutional framework for offering that education? As a first step in answering these, we will consider what a purely private market for K–12 would yield.

K–12 AS A PURELY PRIVATE MARKET

Set aside, for the moment, all you know of K–12 as it exists now in the United States. That is, suppose that there were (1) no public schools, (2) no public monies spent on education, and (3) no public regulations requiring attendance in school for any child, regardless of age. How would that system look? Consider first the family side of the equation. In general terms, families would decide whether their children would attend some form of school and for how many years. This decision would be based, like all other spending decisions, on family income, prices of education and all other goods and services, and the value placed on education by the family. What is it that determines the value that a family places on the education of one of its children? The primary benefits to both the child and the family from K–12 education come from the advantages one receives due first to the achievement of basic literacy and then to the knowledge and perspective that flow from building on that base of literacy. Much of this can be measured through the additional earning power that accrues to the individual as education is extended. But we should not overlook the intangibles of education as well—better decision making within families concerning health, hygiene, and financial matters; perhaps greater understanding in interpersonal relations; and the pure satisfaction that learning can bring. In each case, the value of an additional year of education most likely can be expected to decline as more education is consumed. That is, the early years of education, moving the child from illiteracy to literacy, are likely to yield a greater marginal benefit, in terms of both earning power and education's intangibles, than later years, which simply serve to extend and refine the child's knowledge.

As you probably realize, we just traced out, in words, the family's demand for education. It is much like the family's demand for housing, food, transportation, or anything else it consumes. All else held constant, the family's demand for education reflects the marginal private benefit it receives as its children move through K–12. Initial years of education, yielding the greatest benefit, are worth most to the family. As the child moves through K–12, additional years, at the margin, become progressively less valuable. The family's demand for K–12 is, consequently, accurately reflected in the demand curve *D* of Figure 6.1. As is typically the case for demand curves, *D* shows that, other things held constant, a falling price for schooling—lower tuition rates—will cause families to opt for additional years of education for their children. Finally, it should be noted that *D* is also labeled *MPB*, indicating that, as is typical, the demand for K–12 expressed in *D* accurately reflects the benefit to the child and family, or the marginal private benefit, of each successive year of education.

Now let's examine the supply side of a purely private market for K–12. With no public schools, no public money spent on K–12, and no regulations requiring attendance, would there be providers of K–12? Too often, we seem to think not. But of course this is simply a kneejerk reaction to our having been raised in an environment in which government plays such a predominant role in K–12. Were there no government footprint at all in K–12, what would we have? A market. That is, as is true for any good or service, so long as consumers are willing to pay at least what it costs to produce an item, private, profit-seeking individuals and groups will step up to offer the item. Those that do so profitably and to the satisfaction of the consumers will thrive and expand, while those that do not will contract and either change to meet consumer demands profitably or cease to exist. In fact, this fairly accurately describes the landscape for basic education in the United States up through the mid-1800s. Perhaps one of the most important lessons of basic economics is at play here: If there is an effective demand for an item (a willingness to pay at least as much as the cost of production), there will be a supply.

At this point, you are probably asking who will be involved in supplying K–12 and how quality can be ensured without government involvement. It is true that in the current environment government both provides K–12 and is charged with ensuring its quality through direct oversight and regulation. But if government were taken out of the mix, would there be no effective oversight of K–12 designed to ensure the quality of educational opportunities that our children deserve? Two points must be made here. First, to believe that without government oversight of schools there would be no effective quality control requires one to believe that markets, in general, have no mechanisms to ensure quality. This is, of course, not the case. What happens when a supplier offers a subpar good or service? Is government required to correct the situation? Typically not: We simply take our business elsewhere, and the supplier either improves or goes out of business. It

FIGURE 6.1   **K–12 as a Purely Private Market**
A purely private market for K–12 would function like most markets, leading to an equilibrium at which $D = S$ and, alternatively, where $MPB = MPC$. This occurs at point b with an enrollment level of E_1.

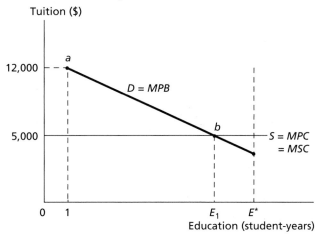

cannot be stressed strongly enough that private markets are not without mechanisms to ensure quality. In fact, they have the strongest, most effective, and quickest quality control mechanism possible: the ability of consumers to simply take their business elsewhere. Equally important, however, it should be noted that the existing quality control mechanism of direct government control is apparently not working effectively—recall the data of Tables 6.1 and 6.2. Were this not true, you would not be reading this chapter.

Before considering the market graphically, however, we are going to make four simplifying assumptions:

1. We assume that the market is competitively structured.
2. We assume that there are no externalities in producing K–12; thus, the supply curve is both the marginal private and marginal social cost of providing the education.
3. For simplicity, we assume that the cost of providing additional years of education is constant, yielding a supply curve S that is horizontal at this constant cost, say, $5,000 per student-year. This $5,000 is also the price or tuition that the students' families must pay for each year of schooling.
4. We have to take into account that once all children complete the K–12 program, there is no further demand for the service. We identify this as occurring when enrollments reach the E^* level.

Given these assumptions, we have the market for K–12 in Figure 6.1, as it would appear without any government participation. What does the demand curve of Figure 6.1 indicate? It indicates the value that the family, in terms of both the tangible benefit of increased earning power and the less-tangible benefits of better family decision making and lifestyle issues, places on each year of K–12 for its children. As drawn, the demand curve indicates a positive marginal private benefit for the 12th year of education, even for the very last potential student who finishes 12th grade. The fact that the *MPB* is positive at the E^* level, which is reached when all children complete K–12, reflects the belief that, if nothing else, finishing a 12th year of schooling allows the individual access to jobs requiring a high school diploma and is thus of some positive value. There are likely some intangibles associated with this very last possible year of K–12 as well.

Consider the education decision-making process that would exist within a particular family. For example, suppose we are talking about the very first child to receive the first year of training within a given family. Why does her family choose to purchase this year for its daughter? The answer is clear: By doing so, the family's well-being is increased. To see this, recall that the demand curve of Figure 6.1 is also the marginal private benefit curve. It shows the maximum price that consumers are willing to pay for each unit of a good or service and, as such, indicates the value or benefit consumers expect from consuming the item. In this case, as is captured at point *a*, the family is willing to pay $12,000 for the first year's education. Consequently, we say the benefit of the first year's schooling to the family is expected to be $12,000. While the benefit to the family is $12,000, this first year's training can be purchased for the constant tuition rate of $5,000. Should it be purchased? If the family's goal is to use its resources in the way that increases family well-being as much as is possible, it certainly should. By consuming this year of education, the family has essentially taken $5,000 and turned it into $12,000 of value. Not a bad deal at all. And the family's good fortune does not translate into bad fortune for the private schools. Had the suppliers been losing money, that is, had the suppliers not been able to cover production costs at a price of $5,000, they simply would not have been willing to enter into the deal. Remember, a voluntary exchange between two parties happens only if neither is made worse off by the exchange.

Just as this first student-year is both profitably produced (from the standpoint of the schools) and beneficially consumed (from the standpoint of the student and family), all years out to an enrollment of E_1 will be produced and exchanged, giving an equilibrium at point *b*. For each student-year from 0 to E_1, the benefit to the families, and thus their willingness to pay, exceeds the market price and consequently will be produced and consumed. Equally, however, rational families would not pay for student-years beyond E_1. Why not? For each year beyond enrollment level E_1, the benefit of an additional year of schooling is not worth the tuition that the family must pay to consume it, and so it is rejected, as would any other expenditure that failed to yield benefits greater than costs. A family would no more pay $5,000 for a year's schooling that delivers less than $5,000 in benefits than it would if the item wasn't schooling but, rather, a high-end computer, a trip to Fiji, or anything else that $5,000 could buy.

How responsive would we expect this market to be? What if, for example, the overall demand for K–12 increased as reflected in the shift from D to D_1 in Figure 6.2? This might come about due to either an increase in the monetary or less-tangible side of the benefit structure or, perhaps, increases in family income. Regardless, it suggests that families want relatively more of the economy's scarce

FIGURE 6.2   **How Responsive Might a Purely Private Market for K–12 Be?**
A purely private market for K–12 can be expected to be responsive to changes arising from both the demand and supply sides of the market. Should demand rise (fall), enrollments will rise (fall). At the same time, should the cost of production fall (rise), enrollments will rise (fall).

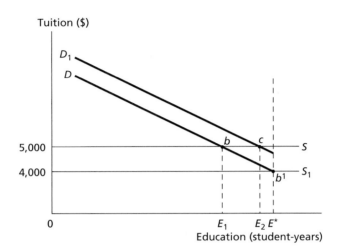

resources drawn into the K–12 market. How will the market react? Resources will be drawn into K–12, and production and consumption will increase to the new equilibrium at point c, which shows an enrollment level of E_2. When the economy's families want more K–12, they get it. Of course, should they want less, they would get less, with overall demand and the resulting enrollment falling. And, most important, this happens without any mention whatsoever of government.

It seems clear that a purely private K–12 market would be responsive to changes in family desires, but can we expect the market to be as responsive to changes coming from the production side of K–12? Suppose first that the original demand D reflects the demand for K–12 yielding an equilibrium at point b. Further suppose, for example, new learning technologies are developed which significantly lower the cost of providing K–12, perhaps to $4,000 per student-year. Graphically, we would find the cost curve S in Figure 6.2 shifting to this new level S_1. The outcome would be more output of educational services, that is, more school years consumed, since the equilibrium is now at point b^1—interestingly, at this equilibrium, we have the full enrollment level, E^*. In other words, we can expect that a competitive, purely private market for K–12 would serve the function all properly structured markets serve: to allocate resources in accordance with the desires of the consuming public. Schools that can both keep costs down and exceed the expectations of families will survive and even thrive. As with all markets, however, those that do not meet the family's expectations or do not do so in a cost-effective manner simply lose revenues as they lose students to schools that are performing better.

POTENTIAL SHORTCOMINGS OF A PURELY PRIVATE MARKET FOR K–12

Numerous potential shortcomings exist for the hypothetical purely private market model outlined above. Some can be easily corrected within the confines of the market, and others cannot. In addressing these shortcomings, we find ourselves in a better position to evaluate reforms being proposed and implemented within the existing K–12 system.

Positive Externalities in Consumption

positive externality in consumption
An increase in the satisfaction of one person caused by the consumption of a good or service by another person; education, especially K–12, is said to create such externalities.

Perhaps the most obvious potential shortcoming of the purely private K–12 market as presented concerns an assumption made in that presentation. Specifically, we assumed that the entire benefit of schooling accrues to the student and his or her family. This is the case for most individually consumed goods or services, such as hamburgers or home furnishings. But, as was discussed in Chapter 4, in some cases part of the overall benefit of a good or service *spills over* to third parties who were not at all part of the original exchange. This spillover to others is called a **positive externality in consumption.** And, since people other than the direct consumer of the item find their well-being enhanced by the direct consumer's use of it, it is said to be semicollectively consumed. An example is an inoculation for a particular illness, such as measles. When my child is inoculated, she receives the primary benefit of the medicine in that she will not contract the disease. But she is not the only one to benefit from the injection. Specifically, all the children with whom she comes into contact will also receive some benefit in that there is one fewer child from whom they can contract the disease. This spillover of benefits, or positive externality in consumption, creates a divergence between the marginal private and marginal social benefit of the inoculation, with the *MSB* being greater than *MPB* by the value of the externality. Since the externality causes the private market to undervalue inoculations by not taking into account the value of the spillover, the market will underproduce inoculations.

Are there similar spillover benefits or positive externalities in consumption from education, in general, and from K–12, in particular? Those who believe there are positive externalities argue that benefits accrue to society as a whole, over and above the benefits of education to the family and the student. They suggest a whole array of possible positive externalities such as more rapid economic growth, better functioning democratic processes, improved public safety and hygiene, and greater charitable giving as the average years of education increases in society. Less obvious but equally important, some believe that a better-educated society will lead to improved economic decision making in general, which, in turn, leads to more efficiently operating markets. Moreover, some benefits typically thought to accrue solely to the student and his or her family may carry with them further positive externalities to society as a whole. For example, proponents of this view point out that an increase in the average level of schooling in society might lead to better nutritional and health care choices, which benefit both the individual and, by extension, society as a whole by obviating the need for extremely expensive health services. The same argument would hold for the positive relation between the years of parents' education and the years-choice made for the family's children or the negative relation between years of education and the likelihood of an individual choosing to participate in criminal activities. Regardless of the source, it does seem clear that there is at least the potential for a significant spillover of benefits from K–12 education to society in general.

Whereas the potential existence of such positive externalities is clear, the size of the spillovers is rather muddy. There is no consensus as to the size of any such positive externalities arising from K–12, at least once even moderate levels of enrollment have been reached. That is, opponents of the externalities argument suggest that although society probably does benefit in the ways described when all children move through the first few years of K–12, by the time all children reach the later years of schooling, no benefits accrue to society other than the direct benefit to the student and family. Each side of this argument seems unpersuaded by the other, but new research may yield a more accurate estimate of any existing positive externalities. One issue on which all agree, however, is the notion that the absolute size of the positive externalities coming from one's moving through the K–12 system declines with each passing year of education. The greatest value of the positive externalities accruing to society from a child moving through the K–12 system is likely to occur in the earlier years of K–12, as the student moves from illiteracy to literacy.

Figure 6.3 reproduces the original demand D and original supply curve S from Figure 6.1. Again, the supply curve is labeled as the marginal private and marginal social cost curve while the demand is labeled as the marginal private benefit curve. Above the MPB curve are three new curves, MSB_0, MSB_1, and MSB_2. For now, ignore all but the middle curve, MSB_0. This curve shows the value to society of the provision and consumption of the various school-years of education. You will recall from Chapter 4 that MSB, in the case of a positive externality in consumption, is the sum of the MPB and the positive externality arising from consuming the service:

$$MSB = MPB + \text{Positive Externality}$$

MSB is a composite of the benefits accruing both to the families of students and, over and above that, to society in general due to the students' education. It differs from MPB by the value of any externality in consumption that might exist. If no externality is present, $MSB = MPB$. Here we assume there are positive externalities in consumption. As such, the vertical distance between the MPB and MSB_0 in Figure 6.3 is our best guess of the value of the externality. Notice that MSB declines more rapidly than does MPB since the marginal value of the spillover is expected to decline as years of education consumed increases. What's the importance of all this? This framework allows us both to offer a valid criticism of purely private market provision of K–12 education and to answer our first key question of how much K–12 should be provided.

FIGURE 6.3 **Positive Externalities and a Purely Private Market for K–12**

Positive externalities in consumption drive a wedge between *MPB* and *MSB*. If this difference between *MPB* and *MSB* is great enough, as in the case of MSB_0 and MSB_1, the market will not produce the socially optimal level of K–12 on its own.

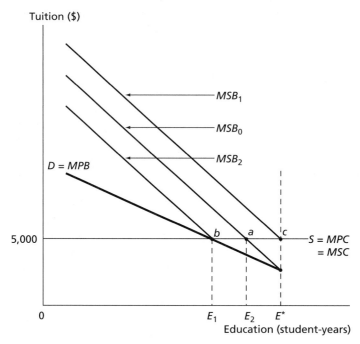

Ask yourself how much of this service should be provided. By now you should readily be able to answer this question by stating that the provision of K–12 should be extended to the point where social well-being is maximized, which occurs when $MSB = MSC$. To see this general principle, consider again the family decision-making process concerning the years of education their children should receive. We said that the student's family would happily pay for the first year of schooling since it yielded $12,000 in direct benefits to the family and cost only $5,000—an increase of $7,000 in family well-being. Since the benefit to the family was greater than the cost, the family's interest was served by taking this year of education. The same is true from society's perspective—*MSB* of that first year of schooling far outpaces *MSC*—so that both family and social well-being are enhanced by the provision and consumption of this first year of education. And this same logic of expanding production and consumption so long as $MSB > MSC$ would lead society to find its well-being at a maximum once E_2 student-years are provided since, at point *a*, $MSB = MSC$. Obviously, this enrollment level is somewhat greater than the E_1 level that the purely private market would lead to, at point *b*. The criticism of this market outcome is that since the market is incapable of taking into account the spillover of benefits from K–12 to society as a whole, it will necessarily undervalue K–12, leading to a level of enrollment too low to maximize social well-being.

The significance of this criticism depends on the size assumed for the social spillover. Figure 6.3 depicts three alternatives. The one we have addressed, MSB_0, shows an intermediate value of the externality leading to a social well-being–maximizing level of enrollment of E_2. In this case, the market gets it wrong in that it underproduces K–12. By the same token, should the spillover be greater as identified along MSB_1, 100 percent enrollment through 12th grade, at enrollment level E^*, would be the proper outcome for society. That is, $MSB = MSC$ at point c. On the other hand, should the spillover be such that MSB_2 is appropriate, the market outcome will maximize the well-being of the family as well as social well-being, since the externality is assumed to have fully evaporated at the market-determined enrollment level E_1, as is identified at point b. The importance of this criticism, consequently, hinges on one's beliefs concerning the value of any existing externality to society from K–12 education. To the extent that it is relatively large, the private market, operating on its own, will produce too little K–12. This does not, however, indicate that the private market cannot be used in the production of K–12, or that government provision is required. Rather, a more appropriate conclusion to draw is that when significant social spillovers are thought to exist, a private education market will fail to produce the socially optimal level of the educational service. Government intervention then *may* improve the functioning of the market. As is always the case, however, before recommending any government action, we must make certain that the action will both do the job and do so in a cost-effective manner.

To consider the role government might play in correcting an existing positive externality within a purely private K–12 market, suppose that there is an initial equilibrium at point b causing the private market to produce, on its own, an enrollment level of E_1 student-years, as in Figure 6.4. At this equilibrium, tuition and the cost of production are $5,000 per year. Further suppose that positive externalities arising from education exist, yielding marginal social benefits of MSB. In this case, the optimal level of enrollment, that is, the level of enrollment at which $MSB = MSC$, is E_2. This is identified as point a. What might government do to encourage production out to the socially optimal level? Consider the student-year E_2. It is in the social interest to have this year produced and consumed since it carries with it MSB that is just equal to MSC, at $5,000. Yet the market will not cause it to be produced because the value to the student's family of this year of schooling is only $4,000, as given by MPB. The problem here is simply that the family's valuation of the year of schooling is $1,000 lower than the market cost (MSC) of providing it. Thus, the student and her family would be unwilling to pay the $5,000 price necessary to cause that unit of education to be produced. Put this way, the $1,000 difference between what the year of education is worth to the student's family and what that same year is worth to society clearly is the problem. If the producers were offered only the family's desired price of $4,000, it would be turned down.

But what if, when the student offered $4,000, the government chipped in another $1,000 in the form of a **tuition subsidy**? Now the private schools will produce the E_2 unit since their cost is covered, and the student will take the additional year because the price she has to pay is exactly equal to the benefit she receives from the year in school. This same logic applies to each unit of education in which

tuition subsidy
A payment made to families or schools by government to encourage additional investments in education; when externalities are present, a tuition subsidy equal in value to the gap between marginal private benefits and marginal social benefits should result in the optimal level of enrollment.

FIGURE 6.4 **Using Subsidies to Correct the Externalities Problem**

Subsidies equal to the value of the spillover from education (the difference between *MPB* and *MSB*) will cause the private market to produce the socially optimal level of education. Here, a subsidy of $1,000 is required to bring about the optimal enrollment level, E_2.

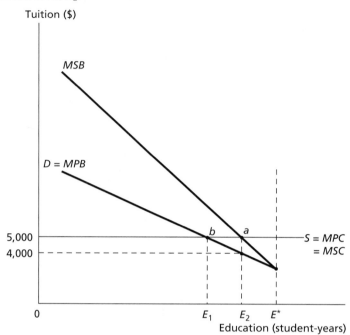

a significant positive externality results from consumption and this situation can typically be corrected through government subsidies. Note, the government need not actually *produce* education; that is, public schools as we now know them are not necessary to correct this market shortcoming. Rather, private provision can still exist; it simply will require some assistance, such as through a government tuition subsidy, to reach the socially optimal level of production of K–12. This outcome gives insight into our third key question concerning the optimal institutional structure to use in producing K–12. Specifically, while government production *may* be used to advantage, such extensive government involvement is not economically required. And, remember, when government intervention is called for within a market economy, that intervention is likely to be most beneficial when kept to the minimum necessary to achieve the desired goal.

But is this approach "fair" to the taxpayers who are going to inevitably have to foot the bill for the subsidy? Once this question is asked, we find the answer to our second key question concerning who should pay for K–12. Specifically, consider again the situation described above at point *a*: The student's family pays $4,000 for the year's education; government pays $1,000, and, in return, the producer offers the year's education. How did we arrive at the division of the $5,000 that was required to induce the producer to offer the additional year? We argued that the student's family, being rational, would always be willing to pay up to the benefit they expect from the year's education, in this case, the *MPB* of $4,000. At this level of enrollment, the *MSB* is $5,000—the $4,000 in private benefits to the student's family and a spillover of benefits of $1,000 to society. When the allocation of the bill for the year's schooling is $4,000 to the student and $1,000 to society, both are simply being asked to pay for the benefit that the year's education yields to them. It is true that, for that student-year, taxpayers are being asked to cover $1,000 of the cost to provide the year's education to the student. However, this is simply the general public's "fair payment" for the benefits it receives from this year of education, over and above the benefits accruing to the student and her family. In this way, both the family and society are paying for the benefits they uniquely receive.

The same would be true, of course, for any year of education that had significant positive externalities in consumption associated with it. In such cases, the socially optimal level of education can be achieved through government subsidies in support of education equal in value to the external benefits of the education that are received by society. The answer to the question of who should pay, then, depends on the value of the externality in consumption arising from K–12. When it is significant, a strong case can be made for significant public funding. If the externality is small, the student and his or her family should be expected to foot most of the bill. As with any good or service, the conclusion with respect to who should pay for K–12 is that all who receive benefits should pay an amount equal to the value of the benefits they receive at the socially optimal output level.

Lost Social and Cultural Cohesion through Segregation

One of the great strengths of the United States is the diversity of its people. A quick glance around the world shows clearly that such diversity is not always a country's strength. History is replete with examples of a country's people breaking apart along racial, ethnic, cultural, or religious fault lines so severely as to pull the country apart. To avoid this fate, the people of a country must share a common experience or set of experiences. In this regard, large port cities such as New York and Boston have served as a socializing experience for many of this country's new arrivals, since people from all corners of the world could be neighbors. By bringing people together in a "melting pot," these cities have served to lessen ignorance and, consequently, increase respect among people of very different backgrounds. An often-noted benefit of a public K–12 system such as that of the United States is that it, too, is a melting pot. Since most children living in a given area attend the same school, it is thought that vitally important lessons on understanding, tolerance, and respect for others are instilled from the very earliest ages through a public K–12 system—yet another example of education's positive spillovers. Further, since there is at least the perception of fairly uniform quality (common curriculums, for example) across the schools of a public system, K–12 serves as a primary tool in facilitating equal opportunity to all children, regardless of racial, ethnic, cultural, or religious background.

If ignorance is the root cause of a society fragmenting along racial, ethnic, cultural, or religious lines, schools are certainly in a unique position to add to social well-being by bridging these gaps through interaction. But what of a purely private market for K–12? Is segregation in this environment inevitable? There is no reason to believe that all or even most families would, if allowed, necessarily select schools for their children that perpetuate any already existing segregation. Unfortunately, however, some families will. And, potentially most harmful to social cohesion, the probability of a family choosing a school that satisfies its racial, ethnic, cultural, or religious tastes in the purely private market for K–12 is likely to be greatest precisely where society needs more, not less, interaction: areas where social cohesion is already beginning to fray. As in all purely private markets, if there is an effective demand expressed for a particular good or service, it will be supplied. That is, if the public, or a significant part of the public, desires to place their children in schools distinguished by their racial, ethnic, cultural, or religious character, such schools will be built and will thrive so long as their customers remain satisfied with the services provided.

It does seem inevitable that a purely private market for K–12 would lead to some degree of segregation, at least a greater degree than would exist in a public K–12 system. So long as parts of the population want their children educated from a particular orientation, or within an environment of students similar to themselves, rational providers of education will tend to specialize in these market niches. In doing so, they are able to differentiate their product, increasing their ability to target and attract customers. And there is some evidence of this. Holland has a K–12 system very different from that of the United States. Three-fourths of its children attend privately operated but publicly funded schools of their family's choosing. As of 1980, in excess of 90 percent of the private schools in Holland were affiliated with or directly sponsored by one of that country's various religious orders. Further, consider K–12 in the United States before and immediately following various steps taken toward desegregation in the 1950s, 1960s, and 1970s. Prior to that time, extreme segregation, mostly based on race, was the rule in many parts of the country, suggesting that a large part of the white population preferred to have their children educated predominantly with those of their own race. What followed desegregation in K–12? The advent and proliferation of a great many private schools offering K–12 services in a de facto segregated way. We are not suggesting that all or even most private K–12 providers operate in this fashion—many offer educational opportunities to a very diverse clientele. But the flight of white middle- and upper-income students following steps toward desegregation in the public sector to what were relatively more segregated private and suburban public K–12 programs cannot be overlooked.

On the other hand, public schools cannot be assumed to lack degrees of social segregation. Clearly, many public school students today attend schools where the student body is disproportionately from one racial or social group or another. Apparently, however, segregation along racial, ethnic, cultural, or religious lines is more likely to exist within a purely private K–12 system than would exist were enrollments in particular schools based solely on communitywide attendance boundaries.

What of Equal Opportunity?

One of the virtues regularly ascribed to the United States is the belief that hard work and perseverance lead to economic success. Countless immigrants have come to the United States expressly for the opportunities provided that they did not enjoy in their home countries. Of course, for there to be an equal opportunity to achieve, there must be something approximating an equal opportunity to receive quality education and training. Without access to quality education and training, the notion of there being an equal opportunity to succeed is an illusion. This is a primary argument in favor of the admittedly rather generic school offerings in the current public system of K–12. That is, while quality differences remain, an attempt is made in the public school system to equalize the educational experience for students across schools. What would happen to the goal of equal opportunity in a purely private market system of K–12? Families have competing needs and wants for income, including the basics of housing, meals, and clothing, in addition to their children's education. In the current K–12 system, available slots in most school systems are allocated, or rationed, based on where one lives. Rationing would, of course, exist in a system of private market-based schools as well. Unlike the public system, however, rationing in a purely market system of K–12 would occur as in any other market, on the basis of the price–quality trade-off the different schools offer. Given that rational families can be expected to place their children in the best learning environment that they can afford, children from relatively wealthy families will likely have far more high-quality options open to them than children in relatively poor families. Rationing based on a price–quality trade-off is likely to lead to segregation of students, much as discussed above, except that this time the segregation is based on income or economic class. Should this extend to the point where the children of the poor are significantly and disproportionately educated in low-cost–low-quality schools compared with the wealthier counterparts, the seeds of growing inequality in society are sown.

Note, however, that to some extent this is also a criticism of the community-based allocation of students to particular schools that occurs now in K–12. Specifically, since there is geographic segregation based on income in our society, it is not surprising to find many public K–12 schools that are rather segregated by income or socioeconomic status. With this in mind, the best conclusion probably is that the problem of segregation, while present in current K–12 system, would likely be aggravated within a purely private K–12 system.

PROPOSALS FOR REFORM IN THE CURRENT K–12 SYSTEM

School Choice and Vouchers

To this point, we have discussed in detail how a purely private market for K–12 education might work. This allowed us to find answers for two of our primary questions about K–12: How much service should be provided? and Who should pay for that service? A purely private market K–12 system, while offering benefits typically associated with competition in markets, may fail to bring about the socially optimal level of K–12 due to education's consumption externalities and may also contribute to segregation along racial, ethnic, cultural, economic, or religious lines. This does not mean that the market system lacks virtue while the current system is above reproach; both approaches have drawbacks. We turn our attention now to some of the proposals for reform of the current K–12 system, along with their underlying analysis, that are designed to improve the functioning of the current system. In particular, these reforms are targeted at the taxpayer-financed, zero-tuition, public elementary and secondary schools in the United States in which about 90 percent of American children receive their formal K–12 education. In the process, we will address the final of our key questions, which concerns the appropriate institutional structure within which to offer K–12.

Many criticisms of the current K–12 system center on its perceived excessive centralization, bureaucracy, and lack of effective parental input. A typical arrangement is for a given state's education department to serve as a central planner for K–12 within the state, setting guidelines to be implemented by local school boards concerning everything from textbook selection and curriculum to teacher qualifications. This state agency is also charged with quality oversight of the local school boards and schools. If this framework sounds familiar, it should. It is quite similar to the centralized model of economic planning discussed in Chapter 2. But recall the outcomes of such centralized planning: limited consumer choice, poor product quality, relatively high prices, and a nearly complete lack of responsiveness on the part of producers to the desires and wishes of the consuming public. For many critics of the current system, this tradition-bound, inflexible, and unresponsive delivery system and its inherent lack of competition have led to the outcomes found in Tables 6.1 and 6.2, that is, an American system of K–12 education that, by international comparisons, achieves relatively little at relatively high cost.

voucher programs
Programs that provide students in poor-performing public schools the opportunity to attend other schools and carry with them the state funding that the poor-performing school would have received for these students.

Many critics of the current system of K–12 favor attempting to increase competition between schools as a means of improving student achievement. **Voucher programs** are an example of just this type of school choice initiative. A voucher program gaining recent popularity gives the parents of a child in a "failing" public school, or a failing public school system, a voucher roughly worth the cost of providing the child's education in the local, community-based public school. This voucher could then be used to buy the child's education from any school other than the one assigned by the school board. These "other" schools may be other public schools, private religious-oriented schools, or private nonsectarian schools. The determination of which schools and systems are failing would generally be made by the state department of education, based on student performance on statewide exams, graduation/promotion rates, dropout rates, or any other measure of performance the state chooses. A voucher program, put simply, suggests that if you find yourself in a situation in which your child is in a school identified as failing, you should be given the opportunity to move your child to a school that you think will provide a better education. Further, when you move your child, you take the money that would have gone to the community-based public school to which your child had been assigned, to help pay for the better education.

Three important elements of existing voucher programs have been omitted in this discussion. The first relates to the schools from which parents can choose. Some programs allow parents to choose from the entire universe of potential providers (for example, the voucher program in Florida), whereas others restrict choice to nonsectarian schools (the original Wisconsin/Milwaukee program). Still others limit choice to public schools (Minnesota and about 30 other states). These programs also make important distinctions concerning which children are eligible to participate in particular programs. In Milwaukee, for example, only children of low-income families have been allowed to take part in the voucher program, whereas in Florida, any child attending a "failing" school, regardless of family income, can participate in that state's voucher program.

charter schools
A relatively new hybrid in which parents or other groups or organizations in a local public school district are permitted to create a new school and are given control over most aspects of the school's operations, creating essentially what are independent, privately operated, publicly funded local schools.

At least one additional option shares some characteristics with vouchers— **charter schools.** In a growing number of states, groups of parents or other organizations have been given direct control, or choice, over their local, community-based public school, creating a new category of public school, the independent public school. In these cases, the families, as a group, are essentially put in the position of being the school board for the charter school, having direct control over curriculum, hiring, performance oversight, and the like. In this way, charter schools can be thought of as a special case of a voucher program. The only difference is that in the standard voucher program students from public schools perceived to be failing are funded to attend various new and existing public and private schools, whereas with the charter approach, a voucher is given to the families, who, as a group, create the alternative educational experience they desire for their children. Note that in many of these cases the parents contract out the actual operations of their schools to private suppliers, creating the hybrid, publicly funded but privately operated charter schools.

These differences in existing voucher programs, and the many more that could be listed, have significant implications for evaluating the effectiveness of vouchers, as will become clear. As a first step, however, consider a generic voucher program that has no limitations on the schools among which families can choose and where the program is open to all students, regardless of their socioeconomic background. Proponents argue that such a voucher program will serve to improve the K–12 system by creating market-based competition between schools as families exercise their power and control over their children's educational choices. It is thought that since 90 percent of students in K–12 attend public schools, and since most of these students are assigned to a school based entirely on where they live, public schools have been in that most favored position of having very little effective competition, which all producers crave. The elementary school in one neighborhood does not have to compete for students with one from another neighborhood—each simply takes in the children in its own neighborhood.

What is the effect of this lack of competition? Suppose we are not talking about K–12, but something a bit easier to sink our teeth into, like pizza. How might you expect prices, service quality, and product quality to change, in a typical town, if it were to evolve from having a single pizza delivery service to many? First, you probably should expect to see falling prices as the new competitors aggressively try to secure for themselves as much of the market as possible. After this continues for a period of time and prices have been pushed down to the point where further reductions might lead to losses, the competitors can probably then be expected to shift to competing with one another, not on the basis of price, but on the basis of the quality of service and product quality—better pizza, faster delivery times, and so on. This is what effective competitive markets give. Proponents of voucher programs ask why, if this is what happens for pizza, wouldn't it apply to K–12 as well? In a voucher environment, should a local public school or system be determined to be failing, many of its students are likely to be moved, by their parents' choice, either to other public schools that the parents feel are doing a better job or to better performing private schools. How would the failing schools react? Their choices are to either improve their achievement outcomes, thus halting the exodus of students and the funding that goes with them, or to continue to repel students through the school's own ongoing poor performance and, consequently, slowly wither away. In this way, proponents argue that the existence of vouchers, whether exercised or not, will lead to an improved general level of K–12 education. That is, if you give parents the choice of where to place their children, poor performing schools will have no option but to improve if they wish to remain open.

Analysis of Existing Voucher/Choice Programs

A key underlying assumption of the voucher/choice approach is that learning will be enhanced through the competition for students that this approach brings to the table. This is, of course, an empirical question. Since very few voucher programs have been in effect either long enough or broadly enough to get reliable results, relatively little research has offered direct evidence of the effectiveness of vouchers. One exception is the voucher program created by the state of Wisconsin in 1990 and implemented in the public schools of Milwaukee (called the Milwaukee Parental Choice Program). The general characteristics of the program are as outlined above with three notable exceptions:

1. Vouchers were made available only to low-income students, defined as those with incomes less than 1.75 times the poverty line. This allowed, for example, a child, in a family of three, with income of about $21,000 per year or less, to apply for the voucher program.
2. The vouchers could be "cashed in" only at nonsectarian, private schools (an exception that has since been dropped from the program).
3. Enrollment in the program—the maximum percentage of school students taking advantage of vouchers—was limited to between 1 and 1.5 percent of the student population in Milwaukee public schools.

Each of these unique aspects of the Milwaukee program, as well as the considerably high and uneven rate of attrition from the program, among other statistical concerns, suggests that definitive answers, of a general nature, probably cannot be found by looking at the Milwaukee program alone. However, with this caveat in mind, what has the Milwaukee experience taught us? Several recent studies have analyzed the performance of students in Milwaukee's voucher program. The most thorough analysis, which does the best job dealing with the statistical challenges posed by the available data, is by Rouse, who concludes that while math scores likely increased for participants in the program, reading scores did not significantly change.[1] That is, there does seem to be some positive effect on student performance in math from the increased choice offered by Milwaukee's voucher program. Since the program was limited, however, to such a small fraction of the public school population in Milwaukee, it was impossible to identify any measurable, positive performance effect in Milwaukee's public schools arising from the new competition they faced from the city's private schools.

A second bit of more general evidence concerning the effectiveness of vouchers and charter schools comes from a recently published book, *Rhetoric versus Reality: What We Know and What We Need to Know about Vouchers and Charter Schools.*[2] The authors survey most existing voucher programs and conclude that although there is enough evidence to suspect that these programs improve student achievement, the effect is uneven, concentrated disproportionately among African-American and economically disadvantaged children, and, even there, quite modest in size. With respect to charter schools, the results are even less clear. The authors' examination of Michigan's fairly new charter school program shows no difference in performance of seventh graders from charters and other traditional public schools and an actual achievement advantage for the traditional schools in fourth grade. Just the opposite is found in Arizona, where students in charter schools do seem to be outperforming traditional public school students, at least in the area of reading. Will later analysis, with the advantage of additional years of educational outcomes from the growing number of voucher/choice programs around the country, come to different and more consistent conclusions? Only time will tell. For now, however, it seems that our best guess is that a voucher program, such as that in Milwaukee, might well show some positive effect on achievement. It also seems clear that much of this positive effect will be enjoyed by minority students, in general, and those of relatively modest means, more specifically. The likely effectiveness of charter schools, however, is to date much less easy to predict.

Downsides to Vouchers/Choice?

The available evidence concerning vouchers offers some hope to the supporters of such programs. Suppose that after a few more years of experience with the Milwaukee program and other voucher programs around the country the assumption that students enrolled in a voucher program do better than public school students who are not in such a program becomes widely accepted. Would this suggest, on its own, that vouchers should receive widespread support? Not necessarily since,

[1]Cecilia Elena Rouse, "Schools and Student Achievement: More Evidence from the Milwaukee Parental Choice Program," *Economic Policy Review,* The Federal Reserve Bank of New York, March 1998, pp. 61–76.

[2]Brian R. Gill, Michael Timpane, Karen E. Ross, and Dominic J. Brewer, *Rhetoric versus Reality: What We Know and What We Need to Know about Vouchers and Charter Schools* (Santa Monica, CA: Rand Education, 2001).

as is always true, you cannot effectively judge a program without considering both its benefits—improved achievement in this case—and its costs. What costs? Opponents of vouchers generally suggest two significant costs that might be associated with a voucher program or any program that provides students and their families with a great deal of choice as to what school children attend.

Cream-Skimming Who is most likely to choose a voucher program? Opponents of vouchers argue that the most likely students to enroll in a voucher program are those who are from families that are relatively well-to-do and who have greater access to information and financial resources, beyond the voucher amount, to defray costs associated with exercising the voucher option, such as added transportation expenses. Further compounding the issue, opponents fear that schools may tend to prefer, and thus select, students from relatively well-off families who have a stronger family tradition of academic accomplishment. The admittedly failing public schools would then be left with a disproportionate share of the community's relatively poor students, often lacking a strong family tradition of schooling.

A general voucher program can address this criticism by restricting eligibility. Recall that in the Milwaukee program enrollment is limited to relatively poor students, thus effectively eliminating the problem of cream-skimming. Although the Milwaukee program's income restriction gets the program around the cream-skimming accusation, such a program is likely to be viewed by ardent supporters of vouchers as being barely "half a loaf" in that it fails to provide any publicly subsidized choice for students from families of greater means. Many of us, no doubt, see a publicly subsidized choice limited to poor families as being inherently unfair. Opponents of opening the program to all income groups argue that those of relatively high incomes already have and, in many cases, already exercise choice in the school their children attend—the choice provided by their own, relatively great resources. When income limits are imposed within the context of a voucher program, the program can be thought of not just as education reform, but also as part of the overall social safety net. Each side of the debate here seems to be able to make a strong case, leaving a final conclusion to each of us.

Social Segregation A similar criticism concerns the potential problem of increased segregation along social, cultural, ethnic, or religious lines. This is the same as the criticism applied to a purely private market K–12 system discussed earlier. That is, within a broad-based voucher system in which parents have a wide range of choices in the schooling of their children, private schools wanting to increase their enrollments will likely try to exploit niches in the market, the best of which may be based on the political, philosophical, religious, ethnic, or cultural differences between families. By doing so, the schools hope that they can create a brand identity and loyalty for their schools. But geographic assignment to community-based K–12 schools, as is typical in public K–12 today, serves the purpose of bringing differing subpopulations together, benefiting all; the specialization that would likely follow the implementation of a broad-based voucher/choice program therefore is troubling.

Contrary to the potential problem of cream-skimming, there would seem to be no easy solution to the segregation argument. This is particularly problematic in that those with special educational needs will tend to find themselves trapped in public schools, whether failing or not, since relatively few private schools provide the specialized, high-cost services needed by these students. Given the elevated costs associated with these students, it is unlikely that they would be attractive to private schools unless they were eligible for voucher amounts larger than those available to standard-needs students. The same argument holds for many vocational and other unique programs that are far less common in private schools than in public.

Are Private Schools More Efficient than Public?

It is commonly assumed that private schools are more cost-efficient than their public school counterparts. Comparing school systems might seem like an easy task, but the typically available data on the issue are difficult, if not impossible, to compare. The basic cost measure available for public schools is expenses per student. In private schools, often the only measure of costs available is the tuition rate. If compared, the private school tuition rate would be found to be much lower, typically, than the per-pupil expenditures of the public schools. However, this comparison overlooks several important facts. First, most private schools rely much more heavily than their public counterparts on fund-raising events, private contributions, and special student fees. Each of these serves to lower the tuition rates of private schools below the actual cost of providing the service. Further, those private schools that are supported by a religious order often employ the labor of both clergy and volunteers at prices below the true market value of those resources. Third, direct cost comparisons between public and private schools are complicated because they tend to present very different options. Specifically, as noted, public schools are much more likely to offer relatively expensive programs such as special and vocational education than are their private counterparts. Finally, transportation, food, and many other services that are on the public schools' cost statements do not show up on the cost statements of private schools, which tend to require surcharges for such items.

Why is the issue of relative costs between public and private schools important? In reality, it is the crux of the matter. That is, if public and private schools are equally efficient, why would we expect competition between the two to lead to a more efficient, overall, system of K–12? Taking all of the above into account, the research on the question suggests, perhaps, a slight cost advantage for private, voucher schools, offering some hope for improved overall K–12 cost performance when vouchers are introduced.

A Conclusion about Vouchers/Choice?

The primary benefit suggested by proponents of choice programs in general and of vouchers in particular is the positive effects of the increased competition between schools following the implementation of a choice program. It is felt that the only "losers" here are those failing public schools that are unable to correct their problems and, as a result, simply wither away. The only solid evidence supporting voucher programs to date is that there are some, admittedly small, achievement gains for students enrolled in voucher programs, especially for minority children and those from families of modest income. On the other hand, opponents point to several potential costs of the voucher programs, including problems associated with cream-skimming and increasing social segregation. It is probably too soon to tell which side of the benefit/cost equation dominates. As is often the case, however, additional experience with vouchers and choice programs will probably show that these programs, though potentially useful, are not the cure-all for the ills of K–12 as the most ardent supporters expect. Similarly, it is highly unlikely that the dire consequences predicted by the staunchest opponents will occur. Thus a final conclusion as to the effectiveness of vouchers and choice programs will require each of us to decide the value we place on issues such as increasing social segregation and families having maximum choice over their children's education. Regardless, it does seem that proponents of vouchers and choice programs, by emphasizing the positive effects of competition and the beneficial effects of providing families with greater educational choices, have brought potentially useful tools to the discussion of K–12 reform.

Class-Size Reductions and Other School Resource Issues

Many have argued that the current system of public K–12 schools is doing a relatively poor job when it comes to student achievement primarily due to perceived severe resource constraints. These constraints, it is argued, lead to low teacher salaries and a resulting high turnover rate as many teachers abandon teaching for more lucrative employment, decaying infrastructure, outdated materials and supplies, and growing class sizes. The class-size issue has become particularly important as a number of reform proposals expressly call for new, lower limits on class size. Public schools, especially, are thought to have average class sizes too large to maximize student achievement, contributing to the reported gap in performance between public and private school students. A typical proposal was embodied in a ballot initiative which voters approved in Florida in 2002, which mandates significant reductions in average class sizes across the Florida public K–12 system. Specifically, Florida public school classes must be limited to 18 children in K–3, 22 in grades 4–8, and 25 in high school, by 2010. Opponents, including the state's governor, Jeb Bush, criticized the proposal as either not likely to increase student performance, calling into question the presumed relationship between smaller classes and enhanced student achievement, or not doing so in a cost-effective manner. The cost of such a program should not be downplayed. The Florida program is estimated to cost anywhere from $10 billion to $25 billion. At such a price, it is not surprising that the debate was lively, to say the least.

The underlying question prompting the debate is straightforward: Do students learn more effectively, on average, in small rather than large classes? Although the question is simple, research results on the question have, until fairly recently, been quite mixed. A number of recent analyses of the question do seem, however, to be tilting the balance of the evidence clearly toward the perspective that student performance can be enhanced by a move to smaller classes. For example, in 1996, California enacted a very aggressive plan that has resulted in more than 90 percent of the state's K–3 students attending classes of no more than 20 students. Early analysis points to modest but significantly improved student achievement in California, and, equally important, these gains remain even after the students move into larger classes above grade 3, which are not covered by the program.[3] Similarly, data from a class size/student performance experiment in Tennessee indicate that, for K–3 students, those in small classes (fewer than 18 students) scored about 5–10 percentile points higher on standardized exams than their peers in larger classes. Further, the students who seemed to have gained most from reduced class sizes were those from relatively low-income families.[4] Equally important, as was found in California, students who benefited from the smaller K–3 classes in Tennessee maintained their performance differential over those students who had not been in the program after moving beyond the third grade into classes that were not limited in size. A similar positive effect of reduced class size has been recently reported based on an analysis of student achievement across 58 countries.[5] Finally, research based on the results of the National Assessment of Educational Progress tests given in math and reading between 1990 and 1996 also show that student achievement, especially in the lower grades, is enhanced through reduced class sizes.[6]

Finally, the Milwaukee voucher program embodies an interesting bit of evidence on this question. In her analysis, Rouse compares the performance of those students taking advantage of the Milwaukee voucher program with those who remained in their assigned public school, as well as considering the effectiveness of one of Wisconsin's other education initiatives.[7] Specifically, a number of local public schools in Wisconsin (Project Rise Schools) whose students are predominantly poor, minority, and low-achieving have been participating in a state program that provides these schools with significantly enhanced financial support for pre-K through grade 5, a program called P–5. The program has, primarily, caused large class-size reductions in the P–5 schools, though other changes have taken root as well. While class size was not the focus of her analysis, it is interesting to note Rouse's summary finding: Students in the P–5 public schools scored as well in both reading and math as those who participated in the city's voucher program. Might this mean that much of the admittedly modest improved performance identified in Milwaukee is due not to the voucher program per se, but rather to the

[3]George W. Bohrnstedt and Brian Stecher, *Class Size Reductions in California: The 1998–1999 Evaluation Findings* (Santa Monica, CA: Rand Education, 2000).

[4]Alan B. Krueger, "Economic Considerations and Class Size," National Bureau of Economic Research, Working Paper 8875, April 2002.

[5]Jong-Wha Lee and Robert J. Barro, "Schooling Quality in a Cross Section of Countries," *Economica* 68 (2001), pp. 465–488.

[6]David W. Grissmer, Ann E. Flanagan, Jennifer H. Kawata, and Stephanie Williamson, *Improving Student Achievement: What State NAEP Test Scores Tell Us* (Santa Monica, CA: Rand Education, 2000).

[7]Rouse, "Schools and Student Achievement."

smaller class sizes that exist in the voucher schools, relative to the standard Milwaukee public school?

While it is becoming increasingly clear that smaller class sizes would likely enhance student achievement, especially for disadvantaged children, there remains the very important question of whether these gains can be achieved in a cost-efficient manner. Relying on data from Texas, Hanushek et al. found student achievement improved as class size shrank, although the improvement was both uneven and modest in scope.[8] Specifically, the effect was found only for low-income fourth and fifth graders and was small enough to cause the authors to conclude that, from a resource perspective, reducing class size to improve the performance of students would likely not be cost-effective. A nearly identical conclusion was reached by Ehrenberg et al., who noted that the dollars expended to reduce average class sizes might boost student achievement more if spent in ways other than reducing class size.[9]

Consequently, while the evidence is beginning to show that smaller class sizes are associated with enhanced learning, the jury is still out on the exact size of the effect, its evenness across students, and whether class-size reductions are cost-effective. The issue of class size is, in reality, just one aspect of a broader controversy concerning the level of funding in public K–12 schools. Put in the blunt terms of one side of the argument, can you improve student performance by simply "throwing money at schools"? To some extent, the answer is, probably, *yes*. There is a rather large body of literature that addresses the relation between school funding (teacher salaries, resources for class-size reductions, and the like) and student achievement. With specific respect to class sizes, the research increasingly is indicating that current resource constraints, as expressed in relatively large class sizes, do seem to be limiting student achievement in public schools, at least to some extent. Equally important, several of the studies discussed here also show that additional money spent, for example, to increase teacher pay, would likely also increase student achievement. Nationally, teacher pay tends to be low relative to the pay of similarly trained professionals. Naturally, this leads many to choose either not to enter the teaching profession or to drop out in favor of more lucrative employment in other fields. And there is an obvious relation between initiatives designed to reduce class sizes and those designed to increase teacher pay that should not be overlooked. Specifically, when efforts are taken to significantly reduce average class sizes, additional teachers will be required to staff the new smaller classes. Therefore, class-size reductions that are not accompanied by increases in teacher pay will lead to both an overall shortage of teachers and a fall in the average quality of teachers (as measured by factors such as the extent of academic preparation and the average years of experience), neither of which is likely to be a boon for student achievement. A similar link exists between class-size reductions and funding for new school construction since smaller classes necessarily require an increase in the number of schools, at least in the typical school system

[8]Eric A. Hanushek, John F. Kain, and Steven G. Rivkin, "Teachers, Schools, and Academic Achievement," National Bureau of Economic Research, Working Paper 6691, August 1998.

[9]Ronald G. Ehrenberg, Dominic J. Brewer, Adam Gamoran, and J. Douglas Wilms, "Class Size and Student Achievement," *Psychological Science in the Public Interest,* May 2001, pp. 1–30.

that is operating near capacity now. From this perspective, then, additional money spent on K–12, if properly targeted and efficiently administered, should be expected to improve student achievement. Whether that improvement is cost-efficient, however, remains an unanswered question.

Reform Proposals: A Postscript

As you read through these reform proposals, you may have concluded that there is very little agreement as to where we are, where we should go, and how we should get there, with respect to improving K–12 in the United States. In reality, a great deal is agreed upon. First, our K–12 system is not providing great enough value, in terms of student achievement per dollar spent. Second, education analysts agree that reform of K–12 is essential if the United States wishes to have the high-level human capital needed to maintain its position on the world stage in the future. Third, although there may be little agreement as to the overall effectiveness of vouchers, there is growing support for the notion that bringing added competition into K–12 would likely lead to better education outcomes than we now have. Finally, there is something close to agreement that, at least in some states and in particular areas of specific states, increasing funding levels for initiatives such as those to reduce class sizes especially in the lower grades and to increase teacher pay will likely be a required part of an effective, overall reform of K–12. This is most likely to be true in areas of states marked by high levels of poverty, since research on the topic consistently suggests that such initiatives have the greatest impact on student achievement for children from such disadvantaged environments. Put differently, if one's primary concern is ensuring the cost-effectiveness of initiatives that require increased public funding, targeting those programs to disadvantaged children would yield the greatest "bang for the new buck."

Summary

As with individuals and families, countries have resources at their disposal which can be devoted to a wide variety of endeavors. From the perspective either of individuals and families or of entire economies, resources to provide basic education are of paramount importance. Without a solid, broad-based, and modern basic education, neither the individual nor the overall economy can reach its full growth potential. Yet in the United States there is a crisis in K–12 in that the K–12 system is too expensive relative to its produced achievement outcomes. We are simply not getting the "bang for the buck" out of K–12 that other nations are enjoying.

The K–12 system in the United States is a predominantly publicly financed and operated system, with about 90 percent of children attending a school located in their community. This is not to suggest that the problem in K–12 is simply its public orientation. In fact, it is clear that a purely private, market-based system of K–12 would not be without its shortcomings. Most important of these are the likelihood that such a system would underproduce K–12 since it is incapable of assessing the existence of and making the needed output adjustments resulting from any positive externalities in consumption that K–12 might yield. Also troubling within a purely private market system is the possibility that it would evolve in a way that leads to even greater social segregation than we now suffer.

Where are we, then? We have a predominantly public system of K–12 that is not working well. Yet a purely private system seems to carry with it significant costs. Taken together, it seems that what we need is reform within the current system, especially reforms that are designed to take advantage of the positive elements of markets and our growing understanding of how students learn. Numerous reforms along these lines that proponents feel address the fundamental shortcomings of the existing system and which offer the hope of improved student achievement have been discussed, with some implementation. The most frequently addressed of these is a voucher program in which children in a failing local public school are allowed to enroll in another, possibly private school and take their public funding with them. The benefits of competition on which the voucher idea is based have an undeniable economic appeal since we enjoy the same benefits of competition in so many other areas of our lives. Troubling, however, are the arguments of voucher opponents who suggest that such programs would likely end up "skimming the cream" of the public school students, leaving public schools with a disproportionate share of lower-income children and children with special learning needs. Further, as with a private system, opponents of vouchers suggest that increased social stratification may be an inevitable by-product of a voucher program.

Another area of proposed reform that gets much attention concerns funding levels in the existing public K–12 schools. Research in the area is beginning to suggest that increased funding for initiatives such as reduced class sizes and increased teacher pay can be expected to yield measurable achievement gains. This appears to be particularly true in the lower grades and for disadvantaged children.

What can we conclude? In the United States, K–12 is broken and must be reformed to provide the high-level human capital necessary to maintain our preeminent international position into the future. However, a great deal of experimentation and analysis of those experiments must take place before definitive answers to the question of where and how reform should proceed can be reached.

Discussion Questions

1. Drawing on the data presented in this chapter, discuss the crisis in K–12.
2. Show graphically and explain how a purely private market for K–12 might work. How responsive would such a system be?
3. Relying on the concepts of marginal private and social benefits, explain why a purely private system of K–12 might not lead to enrollment levels that maximize social well-being.
4. List and briefly explain any externalities in consumption that you think exist for K–12.
5. How does the existence of externalities in consumption arising from K–12 influence the question of who should pay for schooling?

6. How might tuition subsidies be used to cause a purely private system of K–12 to produce the socially optimal enrollment level?

7. Explain the arguments in favor of a voucher program. Now explain the arguments against such a program. What evidence is there in support of each view?

8. Discuss: "Class size matters little to student achievement."

9. Discuss: "Because of the extensive externalities arising from K–12, government production of K–12 is economically called for."

10. What role, if any, do you think teacher pay might play in an effective reform of K–12?

11. Suppose the legislature of the state that you live in decides to invest an additional $100 million in K–12 education in hopes of improving student performance. Which of the following ways of spending the money would you expect to be most successful:

    a. Dividing the money equally among the schools in the state to increase teacher salaries.

    b. Dividing the money equally among the schools in the state to reduce class sizes in all grades.

    c. Dividing the money equally among the schools in the state to reduce class sizes in the lower grades.

    d. Using the money to reduce class sizes in the lower grades and giving a disproportionate share to schools in the state's poorer areas.

12. The existence of positive externalities in consumption from K–12 education leads one to conclude that public subsidies of K–12 may be economically appropriate. If this is correct, are such subsidies as defensible for private as for public schools?

13. Discuss: "You cannot correct the problems of K–12 in the U.S. by simply 'throwing money' at the schools."

14. If a state decides to significantly reduce class sizes and wants to maintain instructor qualifications, why will it likely be required to increase teacher salaries?

Additional Readings

Bohrnstedt, George W., and Brian Stecher. *Class Size Reductions in California: The 1998–1999 Evaluation Findings.* Santa Monica, CA: Rand Education, 2000.
An excellent summary of the overall effects of California's class-size reduction initiative.

Card, David, and Alan B. Krueger. "School Resources and Student Outcomes: An Overview of the Literature and New Evidence from North and South Carolina." *Journal of Economic Perspectives,* Autumn 1996, pp. 31–50.
The two states' vastly different treatment of black students (and thus white students as well) in the early 1900s allows for an excellent examination of the issue of school resources and student performance.

Ehrenberg, Ronald G., Dominic J. Brewer, Adam Gamoran, and J. Douglas Wilms. "Class Size and Student Achievement." *Psychological Science in the Public Interest*, May 2001, pp. 1–30.
An excellent and thorough overview of the large and growing literature on the effects of class size on student achievement.

Gill, Brian R., Michael Timpane, Karen E. Ross, and Dominic J. Brewer. *Rhetoric versus Reality: What We Know and What We Need to Know about Vouchers and Charter Schools*. Santa Monica, CA: Rand Education, 2001.
Perhaps the most thorough treatment of school choice programs available today.

Grissmer, David W., Ann E. Flanagan, Jennifer H. Kawata, and Stephanie Williamson. *Improving Student Achievement: What State NAEP Test Scores Tell Us*. Santa Monica, CA: Rand Education, 2000.
Provides a great deal of insight into issues like the effectiveness of various reform initiatives and funding levels based on a three-year study of state-level National Assessment of Educational Progress testing outcomes.

Hanushek, Eric A., John F. Kain, and Steven G. Rivkin. "Teachers, Schools, and Academic Achievement." National Bureau of Economic Research, Working Paper 6691, August 1998, available at *http://nber.org*.
A thorough treatment of the school-specific characteristics that affect student performance.

Krueger, Alan B. "Economic Considerations and Class Size." National Bureau of Economic Research, Working Paper 8875, April 2002, available at *http:// nber.org*.
Offers a thorough review of the issue of class size and student performance as well as an analysis of the Tennessee STAR class-size experiment.

Lee, Jong-Wha, and Robert J. Barro. "Schooling Quality in a Cross Section of Countries." *Economica* (2001), pp. 465–488.
Analyzing data for 58 countries, the authors offer evidence concerning the role of both family inputs (such as family income and parents' education) and school resources (most notably class size and teacher salaries) in producing quality education outcomes.

Levin, Henry M. "Educational Vouchers: Effectiveness, Choice, and Costs." *Journal of Policy Analysis and Management* 17, no. 3 (1998), pp. 373–392.
By now a bit dated, this still offers a thoughtful treatment of the many issues raised by voucher programs.

Rouse, Cecilia Elena. "Schools and Student Achievement: More Evidence from the Milwaukee Parental Choice Program." *Economic Policy Review*, Federal Reserve Bank of New York, March 1998, pp. 61–76.
Offers a very accessible analysis of the Milwaukee experience with vouchers.

Wolfe, Barbara, and Robert Haveman. "Social and Nonmarket Benefits from Education in an Advanced Economy." Working Paper, as presented at the Federal

Reserve Bank of Boston's June 2002 conference, *Education in the 21st Century: Meeting the Challenges of a Changing World*, available at *http:// www.bos.frb.org/ economic/conf/conf47/*.

Perhaps the most thorough and contemporary treatment of the externalities arising from education available today.

World Wide Web Resources

Digest of Education Statistics, 2001

www.nces.ed.gov/pubs2002/digest2001

The Digest of Education Statistics is a publication of the National Center for Education Statistics. Has links to chapters on elementary and secondary education, postsecondary education, and outcomes of education.

Economic Education Web

www.ecedweb.unomaha.edu/home2.htm

The mission of EcEdWeb is to provide support for economic education in all forms and at all levels. Has links to K–12, college, data and information, and other Web sites.

National Council on Economic Education (NCEE)

www.ncee.net

The NCEE promotes economic literacy nationally and internationally. Links include online lessons, campaign for economic literacy, and the NASDAQ teaching awards.

Resources on Private School Vouchers

www.weac.org/resource/vouchpg.htm

The Wisconsin Education Association Council provides links to web pages on background material and news stories about private school vouchers.

School Vouchers

www.adl.org/vouchers/vouchers%5Fmain.html

The Anti-Defamation League maintains this site. The essay's title is "School Vouchers: The Wrong Choice for Public Education."

U.S. Department of Education

www.ed.gov/index.jsp

Has information on the national program No Child Left Behind, information for students, parents and families, teachers, financial information, and other links.

Poverty Problems and Discrimination
Why Are So Many Still Poor?

Checklist of economic concepts

- Poverty
- Determinants of income distribution
- Lorenz curve
- Income inequality
- Marginal revenue product of labor
- Ownership pattern of resources
- Discrimination
- Unemployment
- Tax policy
- Negative income tax

JULY 7, 2002—When asked whether welfare reform changed her life for the better, Jacqueline Brewer looks at her bag of free groceries and chuckles. It's that "you gotta be kidding me" expression of a woman who smiles to keep from crying. Brewer, 37, is upset that welfare reform plucked her out of community college and put her through a string of job preparation programs that didn't lead to a job. She's hard-working, and a voice of reassurance when taking calls on the Hunger Hotline for the Alameda County Community Food Bank. It is the volunteer job the county assigned her as a "workfare" slot—an idea of last resort to give people on welfare workplace experience if they can't find employment.

The promises of welfare reform—the stable job, the independence and the subsidized child care—are still not a part of Brewer's daily life. She manages to remain upbeat, partly because her work puts her in a position to comfort those in worse situations than hers. "Wow, that's some heavy stuff, girl," she tells one caller who has been kicked off welfare and has no money for food. Brewer knows what it means to want. Her welfare check for Anthony, her 11-year-old son, is $548 a month, and the rent on her West Oakland apartment where she has lived for over a decade is $500. She has to decide between heat and a telephone, so she chooses heat.

Keeping a job is harder without a car or a phone, but Brewer has a long resume. From the time Anthony was born in 1990, she has worked as a cashier at Toys 'R' Us, Walgreens, Sears and Rite Aid, and waitressed at Denny's and H's Lordships Restaurant in Berkeley. She worked as a security guard, and as a teller at Wells Fargo Bank. She does hair and nails on the side. Between jobs, when she could spare the $13 per course credit, she took business computer classes at Laney College in Oakland.

When California's version of welfare reform—CalWorks—arrived in 1998, she was one semester away from a proficiency degree in business management. She received a letter telling her to come in and sign her welfare-to-work plan with the Alameda County Social Services Agency. The letter explained that she could lose her welfare check if she failed to sign up for CalWorks. With her expenses so tight, she thought it best not to argue, and quit school to attend a county class on how to write a resume. The county welfare department next assigned her to a fashion design course, to teach the women how to make their own patterns and design clothes for a dressmaker certificate. As part of the class, she had to go to a sewing factory. One day the factory boss showed up with a pile of cloth for AC Transit bus driver uniforms. Brewer was the only one who spoke up, and threatened to tell her social worker that he was using the women for free labor. He relented, and she finished the course. "I'm the kind of person who thinks it's better to make the best of any situation, so I figured I'll just do this sewing thing and get it over with," Brewer said.

A year went by and still Brewer had no job. The welfare department sent her to the Urban League, where she wound up in another resume writing workshop. She then went to another job search program, this time one run by the state Employment Development Department. Almost two years into welfare reform, she was still learning the ABCs of how to get a job. Frustrated, she stayed after class and searched the Internet until she found a job as a security guard for Pacific Gas and Electric Co. It lasted only a month. "The welfare department had some problem with my paperwork and sent me a letter to come in, with only a day's notice," she said. "My boss said I didn't give him enough notice, and he was right. So he fired me."

Her situation is complicated, because without a phone, the welfare department must alert her to meetings by mail. Often, by the time she gets the notice, the meeting has passed or is the next day, leaving her little time to alert her bosses. She has to take nearly an entire workday off to navigate public transportation to and from the meeting, she said. "I've lost three or four jobs because of this," she said.

Brewer is trying to figure out a way to go back to Laney at night. Her main obstacle is finding someone to watch her son. Although welfare reform promised struggling mothers child care subsidies, Brewer says the welfare department keeps telling her to wait in line. Anthony spends four hours after school in two different after-school programs, both free. The second program drives him home at 6 P.M., an hour after Brewer gets home from the food bank.

It's a constant struggle to keep a positive attitude. "I think about leaving the Bay Area. It's so hard to survive here. I keep thinking there's gotta be something better than this. Maybe I should go back to my family in New Orleans or my sister in Arkansas. But then I think . . . all this fighting, for what? I've been struggling so long, if I leave, it's like admitting I lost." Her luck changed recently when she parlayed her phone skills into a part-time customer service job at Pacific Bell. She's hoping this one lasts.

Source: *San Francisco Chronicle* (July 7, 2002), "Jumping Through Reform's Hoops Makes It Hard to Hold Job Down," by Meredith May.

Copyright 2002 by San Francisco Chronicle. Reproduced with permission of San Francisco Chronicle in the format Textbook via Copyright Clearance Center.

"Poverty amidst plenty" exists in America. In the world's richest nation millions are poor, and millions more not in poverty are *relatively* poor. Not the American dream, this is the American paradox.

Poverty may be a more serious problem in our society than in less affluent societies. Poverty amidst poverty is easier to understand and even condone. But in a land of abundance, it is difficult to comprehend why some people are inadequately fed, clothed, and sheltered.

We approach our study of poverty in the United States in two ways. First, we examine poverty in reference to *absolute* income levels, which permits the identification of people who live below a designated poverty level of income. Second, we study it in terms of income distribution, that is, the share, or percentage, of national income that people receive.

POVERTY IN TERMS OF ABSOLUTE INCOME LEVELS

In today's American economy, poverty is essentially an income distribution problem. The U.S. economy generates enough income to go around so that no one has to live in poverty. But enough income does not go to everyone, and some people do live in poverty.

Figure 7.1 illustrates the incidence of poverty in our economy between 1959, when the federal government first began measuring poverty, and 2003. The first official poverty count for 1959 revealed that 22.4 percent of the American population lived in poverty. This statistic meant that almost 40 million people in the world's richest economy suffered from poverty. At the time, these numbers shocked many people, and poverty became one of the major social issues of the turbulent 1960s. The challenge the Kennedy and Johnson administrations took up was to eradicate poverty through a vigorous "war on poverty." Although the ultimate goal was not fully met, new social programs were developed and new initiatives were taken by the federal government that significantly reduced the rate of poverty throughout the 1960s. By 1969, the poverty rate stood at 12.1 percent of the population, a reduction in the rate of 46 percent. This is the legacy of the period that is often referred to as the Great Society. Unfortunately, the downward trend in poverty did not continue into the following decades. As can be seen in Figure 7.1, the poverty rate has fluctuated in a narrow range since the 1970s. After reaching a low of 11.1 percent in 1973, the poverty rate has in general trended upward, peaking above 15 percent in 1983 and 1993. Understandably, these peaks roughly correspond to economic recessions and periods of relatively high unemployment. However, the poverty rate has never fallen back to the levels experienced in the early 1970s, even though the 1990s saw the overall economy grow for an unprecedented period of time and the economy record the lowest rates of unemployment in more than 30 years. In 2003, the overall rate of poverty stood at 12.5 percent.

What Is Poverty?

Poverty is not easily defined. Yet, a precise definition has been implied in the statement that many Americans are poor. We shall use the definition of poverty developed by the government.

Poverty is concerned with the relationship between the minimum needs of people and their ability to satisfy those needs. The difficulty with any definition of poverty involves the meaning of "minimum needs" and the amount of money required to satisfy these needs. The federal government's approach is a two-step process. First, the monetary cost of a nutritionally sound minimum diet is determined. Second, the cost of the minimum diet is multiplied by 3 to allow for expenditures on all other goods and services. The multiplier value of 3 was chosen

FIGURE 7.1
**Poverty in the
United States:
1959–2003**

Source: U.S. Department
of Commerce, Bureau of
the Census, *Statistical
Abstract of the United States,*
various issues.

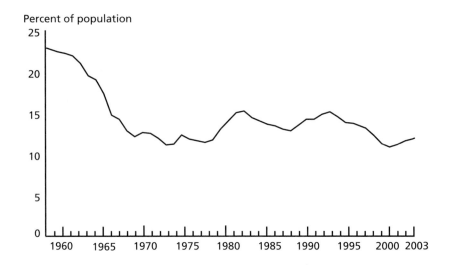

because the cost of food represented about one-third of the average family's after-tax money income when the poverty definition was formulated more than 45 years ago. Each year, the monetary cost of the minimum diet is adjusted for price changes using a price index. (Recall from Chapter 1 how price index numbers can account for the effect of inflation.) Using this process, a set of poverty lines, or thresholds, are calculated for various family sizes and compositions. Separate poverty thresholds are calculated based on the number of adults and children in the household, and for some households, the age of the family head. A person is officially counted as living in poverty when that person's household's annual pre-tax income is less than the threshold for the household's size and composition. Poverty thresholds as defined for different household sizes are listed in Table 7.1.

Since the 1960s, the government's method of calculating poverty thresholds has been criticized. For example, some critics argue that the definition of income should be expanded to include the value of in-kind benefits such as health insurance and day care services received by families. Others argue that changes in living standards call into question the legitimacy of defining poverty based on the relative size of what an average family's food budget was more than 45 years ago. Studies indicate that households today spend less than one-third of their income on groceries. Furthermore, the current poverty definition does not account for different costs of living in different regions of the country. Although numerous refinements and alternatives to the current process of defining poverty have been proposed over the years, none has been officially adopted.

Who Are the Poor?

In 2003, some 7.6 million families, or 10 percent of all families, lived in poverty (Table 7.2). This translates into more than 35.9 million individuals, a staggering number to many Americans who have never been personally touched by poverty.

TABLE 7.1
Poverty Threshold Levels in 2003

Source: U.S. Department of Commerce, Bureau of the Census, Current Population Report, Series P-60, No. 226, *Poverty in the United States: 2003*, p. 39.

Family Size	Threshold Level
1	$ 9,393
2	12,015
3	14,680
4	18,810
5	22,245
6	25,122
7	28,544
8	31,589
9 or more	37,656

Indeed, some have characterized those who live in poverty as the "hidden poor." Who, then, are the poor?

Before examining the characteristics of the poverty population we must first recognize that circumstances and events beyond personal control have the capacity to impoverish *anyone*. In fact, each year many Americans who experience natural disasters, such as hurricanes, tornadoes, floods, and fires, or personal disasters, such as the death of a spouse, find themselves without any means to financially support themselves and their families. Such cases of poverty are often transitory, but recovery from major disasters, or even minor ones, is more difficult for some people than others. Studies have shown that there is a significant turnover in the poverty population: Families and single individuals move into and out of poverty several times throughout the years in response to significant life events. Although no reliable estimate exists for the number of "hardcore poverty" cases, the incidence of poverty can be easily seen to vary dramatically across a number of demographic characteristics.

Poverty rates are higher among families with only one parent or head of household present. In 2003, families headed by a single female exhibited a poverty rate of 28 percent, more than five times the rate for families headed by a married couple. Obviously most single parents have less earning capacity than most married couples, but it is also true that single parents face additional constraints that limit their flexibility and resource base to adapt to unforeseen events and circumstances. These limitations increase the probability of low earnings and income, which results in poverty. Likewise, the number of children in a household is positively related to the incidence of poverty. As recognized by the poverty thresholds reported in Table 7.1, larger families require higher incomes to meet their basic needs.

Poverty is also related to age—those very young and those very old have higher rates of poverty than those in their prime and middle-age years. More than 12.9 million children below the age of 18 lived in impoverished households during the year 2003. In fact, this represented 35.9 percent of the total poverty population for the nation. For children, the source of poverty lies with their parents or guardians and not with themselves; thus many public and private antipoverty programs are designed to specifically target those under the age of 18. At the other end of the age

TABLE 7.2
Selected
Characteristics of
Families below
the Poverty Level,
2003

Source: U.S. Department
of Commerce, Bureau of
the Census, Current
Population Report, Series
P-60, No. 226, *Poverty in
the United States: 2003.*

Characteristics	Number (in Thousands)	Percent
All Family Types		
All	7,607	10.0
White	5,058	8.1
Black	1,986	22.3
Hispanic	1,925	20.8
Married Couples		
All	3,115	5.4
White	2,504	5.0
Black	321	7.8
Hispanic	976	15.7
Female Householder, No Husband Present		
All	3,856	28.0
White	2,171	24.0
Black	1,473	36.9
Hispanic	792	37.0
Male Householder, No Wife Present		
All	636	13.5
White	383	10.8
Black	192	24.5
Hispanic	157	17.3

spectrum, those 65 and over had a poverty rate of 10.2 percent, which was slightly more than 2 percentage points below the overall rate but significantly greater than the rates for middle-aged individuals. Social Security and the advent of employer-provided pension plans have significantly reduced poverty among the elderly during the past several decades. Those individuals between the ages of 18 and 64, which corresponds to the length of an average worker's career, had a poverty rate of 10.8 percent in 2003.

The incidence of poverty in the United States varies across racial and ethnic lines. Minorities, especially blacks and Hispanics, report significantly higher rates of poverty relative to whites. The overall poverty rates for blacks and Hispanic individuals in 2003 were 24.4 percent and 22.5 percent, respectively. These rates were more than twice the white rate of 8.2 percent. Disproportionate differences between racial groups have been consistently observed since the government first started tracking poverty. The persistence and size of the gap are often cited as evidence of racial discrimination in our economy. However, much of the gap can be traced to differences between racial groups in terms of the factors that determine earnings and income. These differences include the average levels of education and training, years of work experience, occupational status, accumulated wealth, and geographic location. It is important to note that many economic studies find that these factors alone cannot explain the whole earnings gap between racial minorities and whites. Encouragingly, the gap between black and white poverty rates has begun to narrow in recent years.

Regional differences in the poverty rate are also apparent. Figure 7.2 is a map presenting the three-year average poverty rate for each of the 50 states. As of the year 2003, New Hampshire had the lowest average rate, 6 percent, and Arkansas had the highest, 18.5 percent. Notice that the average rates in the South and West tend to be greater than those observed in the Northeast and Midwest. It is not surprising that states which have historically offered limited opportunities for economic advancement and have high concentrations of racial minorities and the elderly report higher poverty rates compared to the rest of the country. However, analyses of the long-run trend show that poverty is less regionally concentrated than in the past, but rates remain higher in very rural and inner-city areas throughout the nation.

POVERTY IN TERMS OF INCOME DISTRIBUTION

The second approach to poverty considers the distribution of income in the United States. We have said that the poverty problem in this country is mainly one of income distribution. This means that the level of income in our country is high enough so that a more equal distribution of income should mitigate the poverty problem and reduce its significance.

Income Equality

Lorenz curve
This curve shows the cumulative percentage of total family income that is going to the lowest percentiles of families; it is a way of measuring the degree of income inequality in a country.

Economists usually explain income equality and income inequality by reference to a curve called a **Lorenz curve,** after M. O. Lorenz. Income equality among families means that any given percentage of families receive an equal percentage of family income: 10 percent of families receive 10 percent of income, 20 percent of families receive 20 percent of income, and 100 percent of families receive 100 percent of income. In Figure 7.3, equal percentages of families and incomes can be measured along the two axes. Income equality is shown by a 45-degree line starting at the origin. At any point on the 45-degree line, the percentage of families shown receive an equal percentage of total family income.

Income Inequality

Income inequality can be illustrated graphically by lines that deviate from the line of income equality. A Lorenz curve derived from actual data on income distribution will usually lie to the right of the line of income equality (the 45-degree line). The farther to the right of the 45-degree line it lies, the greater the inequalities in income distribution. Lorenz curves are useful in making income distribution comparisons in a given year among different countries or in the same country over time.

Table 7.3 divides U.S. families into five numerically equal groups, or quintiles, and indicates the distribution of personal income among these groups. The table also shows the income share of the top 5 percent of families. It can be observed that income is very unequally distributed. The highest 20 percent of families received 49.6 percent of income in 2000, and the lowest 20 percent received 3.6 percent. The

FIGURE 7.2 Percentage of People in Poverty by State, Three-Year Average; 2001–2003

Source: U.S. Department of Commerce, Bureau of the Census, Current Population Report, Series P-60, No. 226, *Poverty in the United States: 2003*, p. 23.

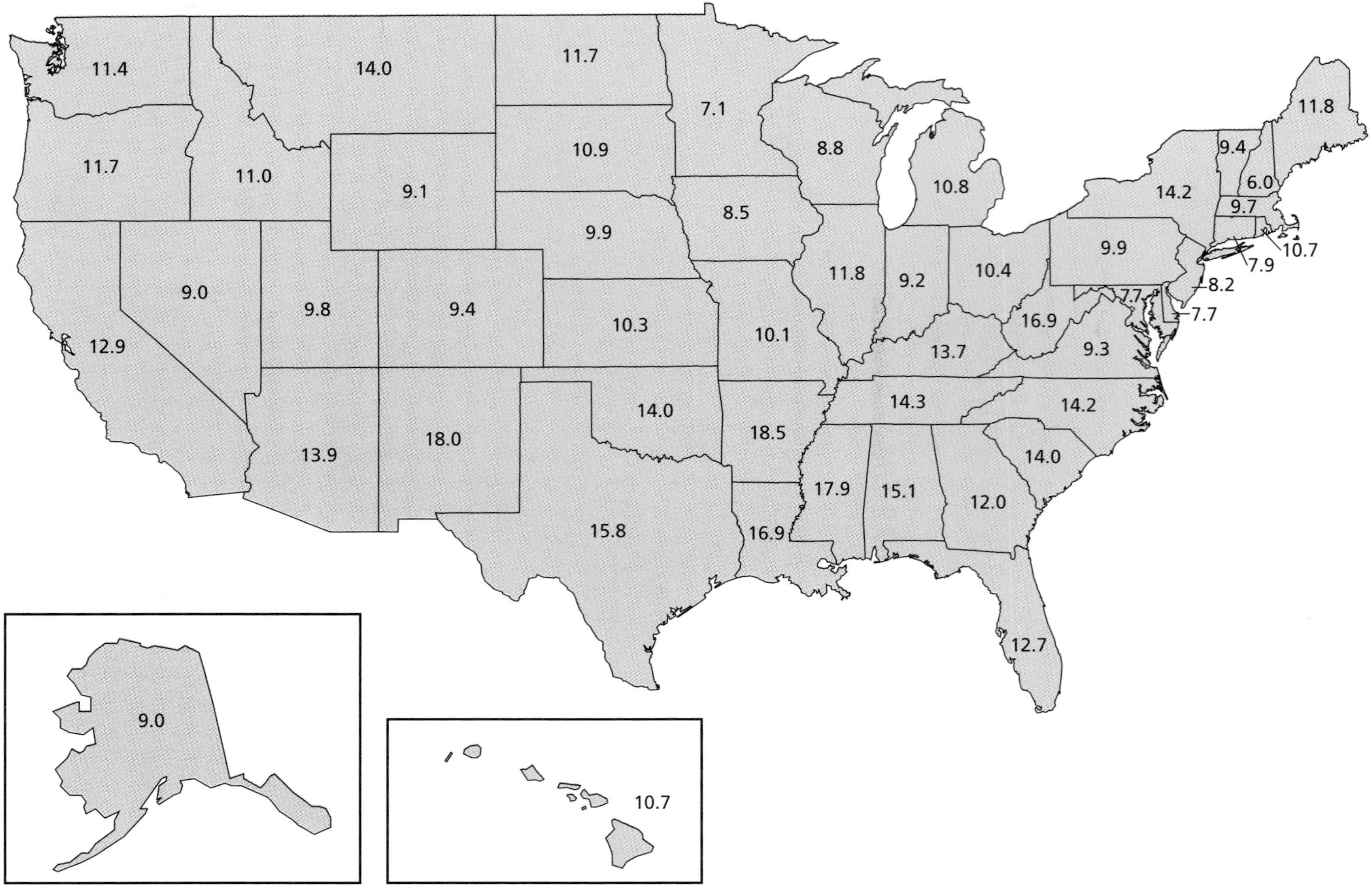

TABLE 7.3
Percentage of Income Received by Each Fifth and the Top 5 Percent of Families, 1960–2000

Source: U.S. Department of Commerce, Bureau of the Census, *Statistical Abstract of the United States*, various issues. *Note:* Column totals may not sum to 100% due to rounding.

Quintile of Families	1960	1970	1980	1990	2000
Lowest fifth	4.8%	5.4%	5.2%	3.9%	3.6%
Second fifth	12.2	12.2	11.5	9.6	8.9
Third fifth	17.8	17.6	17.5	15.9	14.9
Fourth fifth	24.0	23.8	24.3	24.0	23.0
Highest fifth	41.2	40.9	41.5	46.6	49.6
	100.0	100.0	100.0	100.0	100.0
Top 5 percent	15.9	15.6	15.3	18.6	21.9

top 5 percent of families received 21.9 percent of income. These data on income inequality are shown by the Lorenz curve in Figure 7.3.

Income inequality was reduced during the 1930s and the years of World War II. The share of income received by the top 5 percent of the highest 20 percent decreased between 1929 and 1944, while the share received by the lowest 20 percent of families increased. The two main reasons for this trend toward greater income equality are generally agreed on: Property income fell drastically during the Great Depression of the 1930s, and the gap between low-paid and high-paid workers was reduced when full employment was reached during World War II.

In more recent times, income inequality has increased. The share of income going to the top 20 percent income class increased from 46.6 percent to 49.6 percent between 1990 and 2000, an increase of almost 6.5 percent. All the income classes by quintiles with the exception of the highest 20 percent received a smaller share of income in 2000 as compared to 1990 (Table 7.3). A major explanation for this increase in income inequality is tied to the reductions in the progressive federal income tax rates that took effect during this period.

THE ECONOMIC CAUSES OF POVERTY

Determinants of Resource Prices and Employment

Family incomes depend on the quantities of resources that families can place in employment and the prices received for those resources. To understand poverty, then, it is important to understand what determines the prices paid for human and capital resources and what determines the quantities that can be employed.

marginal revenue product of labor
The change in the firm's total revenue resulting from adding or subtracting a unit of labor, say, adding an hour of work or adding another worker. Thus, it indicates the value of a unit of labor to the firm.

Wage Rate Determination

Under competitive market conditions, the basic principle of wage rate determination is that units (person-hours) of any kind of labor tend to be paid a price equal to any one worker's (hourly) contribution to an employer's total receipts. In other words, workers are paid about what they are worth to employers. What a worker is worth to an employer is referred to by economists as the **marginal revenue product of labor.** (Recall our discussion of labor markets in Chapter 3.)

FIGURE 7.3 **Lorenz Curve Plotted with Data on U.S. Family Income, 1997**
The Lorenz curve shows the degree of income inequality. The horizontal axis measures the percentage of families, starting with the poorest. Thus, 20 percent represents the lowest fifth of the families. In 2000, the lowest 20 percent earned 3.6 percent of the total income, and the lowest 40 percent earned 12.5 percent. This means that the second quintile (the families between the 20 percent and 40 percent marks) earned 8.9 percent of the total income (12.5 − 3.6). If perfect income equality existed, the Lorenz curve would be a 45-degree line.

Source: U.S. Department of Commerce, Bureau of the Census, *Statistical Abstract of the United States*, various issues.

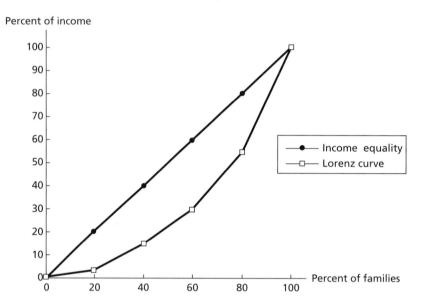

Suppose the marginal revenue product of the worker is $4 per hour; that is, an hour of labor is contributing $4 to the receipts of the employer. Then the worker is worth $4 an hour to the employer and would be paid that amount under competitive conditions. If a worker were paid less than what she or he is worth to an employer, the worker would also be paid less than she or he would be worth to *other* employers. Consequently, other employers would bid for the worker's services, driving the worker's wage rate (hourly wages) up to what she or he *is* worth. On the other hand, rather than pay $5 an hour, an employer would lay a worker off.

This principle can be seen more clearly with reference to Figure 7.4. The demand curve for labor (*DD* in the figure) shows what employers are willing to pay at different quantities of labor (worker-hours per month) or, alternatively, how much a unit of labor is worth at different possible employment levels. The supply curve for labor (*SS* in the figure) shows the quantity of labor that will be placed on the market at different wage rates. Labor is paid less than it is worth at the wage rate w_0. Only q_0 units of labor want to work at this wage rate. However, at this

FIGURE 7.4

Wage Rate Determination under Competition

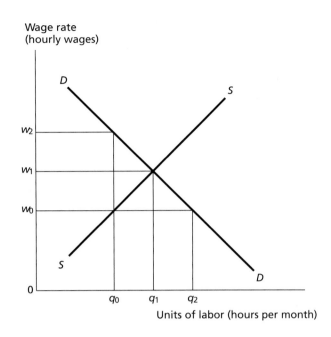

employment level, labor is worth w_2 to any employer. Thus, a shortage exists; that is, at the wage rate w_0, the quantity of labor demanded is greater than the quantity supplied, and the wage rates will be driven up to w_1. Labor is paid about what it is worth at w_1. At a wage rate above w_1, however, the quantity of labor supplied is not worth that wage to employers. A surplus exists; that is, the quantity of labor supplied is greater than the amount demanded. Thus the wage rate will return again to w_1.

The Price of Capital

In a competitive market the price of a unit of capital (say, a machine) is determined in a way similar to the price of a unit of labor. The price of any kind of capital depends on the demand for and supply of units of capital, and, at market equilibrium, the price of capital equals what that capital is worth to its employer.

Determination of Individual or Family Income

The income of a person depends on the *price* he or she receives for his or her resources, labor and capital, and the *quantities* of resources he or she can place in employment. For example, the monthly family income from labor equals the quantity of its labor employed, multiplied by the wage rate. From capital, its income equals the quantity of capital employed, multiplied by the price of each unit of capital. Total monthly family income, then, is a summation of the two monthly income flows.

Determinants of Income Distribution

The distribution of income among individuals and families depends on the distribution of resource ownership and the prices paid for resources of different kinds in different employments. The ownership pattern of resources is unequally distributed among individuals and families. This unequal ownership pattern of resources gives rise to an unequal distribution of income in our society. People at the bottom of the income ladder own a small share of the nation's resources on which the market places a high value.

Causes of Differences in Labor Resource Ownership

Brains and Brawn   The inheritance of mental and physical talents is not equally distributed among people. Some people have greater capabilities than others. Some families' labor resources have exceptional learning abilities; others' labor resources have special talents—acting, singing, playing baseball or football. Other families are not so fortunately endowed.

Skill Levels   Skill levels vary among individuals. Differences in skills among people are primarily due to differences in inherited capabilities, training opportunities, and discrimination. Some inherit specific abilities to do certain tasks better than others. Most often people with high skill levels have acquired them from their training and education. In some instances, people have low skill levels because they have been discriminated against and have not had equal opportunities for training and education. Even with the same training, certain groups, say, women, may not receive the same pay as others, although they perform the same tasks. In general, those with highly developed skills are worth more and, therefore, are paid more in the market than are unskilled or semiskilled workers.

Capacity Utilization Rate   The capacity utilization rate is the ratio of actual earnings to earnings capacity. Utilization rates differ among people for many reasons. Among these reasons are differences among people with respect to their preferences for income and leisure, and with respect to their responsiveness to changes in their income due to, say, taxes and government transfer payments. Also, some people, such as working wives, may have low utilization rates because of certain labor supply barriers. Garfinkel and Haverman found that the major cause of income inequality is due to differences in earnings capacity among people and that not more than 20 percent of income inequality can be explained by differences in capacity utilization rates.[1]

Causes of Differences in Capital Resource Ownership

Inheritance   Some individuals and families inherit real property and claims on real property such as stocks and bonds. These people have a head start on those who do not begin with inherited capital resources.

---

[1]Irwin Garfinkel and Robert H. Haverman, *Earnings Capacity, Poverty, and Inequality* (New York: Academic Press, 1977), p. 39.

Luck   Luck is not evenly distributed among the population. Some families may be at or near the bottom of the income pyramid because of bad luck. A business failure caused by a depression, a prolonged illness, a fatal accident, or a natural disaster may leave persons and families without income or the ability to earn an adequate income.

Propensities to Accumulate   People vary as to their propensities or tendencies to save and accumulate capital resources. Those who are strongly motivated are willing to forgo consumption today in order to enjoy greater income in the future. Others are more concerned about their current consumption standards. They do not save and do not accumulate capital resources.

The Effects of Discrimination on Income

discrimination
The term means that equals are treated unequally or unequals are treated equally.

In addition to their limited human and capital resources, those in poverty sometimes face an additional obstacle to earning an adequate income—discrimination. **Discrimination** as we use it means that equals are treated unequally or that unequals are treated equally. For example, discrimination exists in a labor market when people with equal productivity are paid different wages or people with differences in productivity are paid equal wages. Discrimination can also exist in the product market when consumers pay different prices for the same product.

Market discrimination exists, then, when the terms on which market transactions are based are not the same for all. A seller who charges different prices to different consumers for essentially the same product or service is practicing price discrimination. An employer who pays different wages for identical units of labor provides another illustration. Sellers who cannot sell in a certain market and buyers who cannot buy in a certain market for reasons other than price are examples of complete market discrimination.

Market discrimination may be traced to two primary sources. These are the *power* to discriminate in the market and the *desire* to discriminate.

Monopoly Power

Monopoly power may exist on the selling and buying sides of markets. A monopolistic market is one in which the seller is able to manipulate the product price to his or her own advantage and can keep potential competitors out of the market. A similar problem exists on the buying side of the market when one firm or a group of firms acting as a cartel hires all or most of the available labor in a particular area and of a particular type. An example might be a mill town in western North Carolina or a mining community in rural Kentucky. In this case, the firm or firms are said to be labor market monopolists or simply *monopsonists*. A monopsonist has the power to control the price at which labor is hired. The existence of monopoly power on the buying and selling sides of the market makes it possible for consumers and workers to be exploited. Consumers are exploited when the price of a product is above the cost per unit of producing it, and workers are exploited when the wage rates paid are below their marginal revenue product, that is, below their contributions to the receipts of their employer.

Exploitation may exist without discrimination. For example, both blacks and whites with the same productivity may be paid equal wages that are below their productivity. However, monopoly power is a source of discrimination. In the exercise of monopoly power, a seller may segregate the market and charge consumers different prices for the same product. A monopsonistic buyer may segregate the job market and practice discrimination by paying workers on bases other than merit or productivity.

Desire to Discriminate

Some people have a taste for discrimination and strive to satisfy this taste or desire. An employer who desires to discriminate acts as if nonmonetary costs were connected with hiring those whose skin color, religion, age, gender, or sexual orientation, among other factors, differs from the employer's subjective ideal.

The primary source of an individual's desire to discriminate is personal *prejudice.* Prejudice refers to the biases and unfavorable attitudes that people hold against others who do not share their own personal characteristics or beliefs. Prejudiced individuals may or may not engage in discrimination. However, when unfavorable actions based on personal prejudices are taken against others, discrimination occurs. From an economic perspective, discrimination motivated by prejudice results in resources being allocated on a basis other than productivity. Thus, employment opportunities and incomes of the adversely affected groups are reduced and poverty may result.

THE EVIDENCE FOR DISCRIMINATION IN OUR ECONOMY

In our complex market economy the wages of workers vary widely between industries and firms. Even workers hired by the same employer to perform similar jobs are often paid different wage rates. Given what we know about how wages are determined, it is easy to see why wage differentials exist. Remember, the demand for labor reflects a worker's productivity and the ability to generate revenue for the employing firm. More productive workers can command higher wages because they are more valuable to employers than less productive workers. Workers who differ in skill and ability will not be treated as equals by the labor market. Thus, it is not surprising that today the average college graduate earns approximately 75 percent more than the average high school graduate. Wage differentials between workers that result from different levels of productivity should not be labeled as discrimination.

Another important point to recall is that labor is a derived demand. The demand by consumers for the product or service that workers produce influences the employer's demand for labor. Everything else being the same, product markets with relatively strong demand will result in higher prices than product markets with relatively weak demand. Higher product prices, in turn, imply higher wages for the workers who produce the product. This is true because higher product prices, which increase revenue, make each worker more valuable to the employer.

Thus, wage differentials may exist between industries or firms due to differences in the demand for their products. Once again, when workers vary in their contribution to a firm's revenue, nondiscriminatory wage differences may result.

As we saw earlier, the incidence of poverty is greater among black families and those headed by a female—two groups which may also be victims of discrimination. Do the lower levels of income historically earned by blacks and women reflect various forms of labor market discrimination or merely market-determined wage differentials? This is an important question that economists and policymakers have attempted to answer. Let us look at the evidence.

Wage Discrimination

Full-time working women earn, on average, about 75 percent of what full-time working men earn. The situation is only slightly better for blacks, with the typical full-time black worker earning about 85 percent of the earnings of full-time white workers. These statistics do not, however, suggest that there is a 25 percent discrimination gap in earnings by gender or a 15 percent discrimination gap by race. To determine the importance of discrimination in earnings, we need a better understanding of what constitutes wage discrimination.

The meaning of wage discrimination can be elucidated by the slogan "equal pay for equal work." Suppose a man and a woman complete their accounting degrees at the same time and place, have identical records and recommendations, are hired by the same accounting firm as entry-level staff accountants, and differ in only one respect—the man is paid $35,000 a year and the woman is paid $32,000 a year. This is a case of discrimination. Two workers contribute equally to their employing firm but are paid unequal wages.

It is often difficult to be sure that wage discrimination exists because the person who discriminates typically denies it, and the relative productivities of labor may be difficult to measure. A discriminator may say that qualified blacks cannot be found or that females are paid less than males because their productivity is less. In some instances, discriminators may be right; in others, they may only be trying to hide discriminatory behavior.

The meaning of wage discrimination is clear enough—unequal pay for equal contributions. But proving discrimination depends on being able to distinguish among individuals on the basis of individual efforts and productivity. Generally speaking, human resources, like any other resources, are paid approximately what they are worth in a competitive economy. Thus, wage differences where competition exists reflect differences in labor productivity. Wage discrimination that does exist in the economy means that the market is not working properly in allocating resources among alternative uses.

What can we conclude with regard to the importance of discrimination in earnings gaps according to race and gender? Some part of these gaps is no doubt due to legitimate factors such as differences in productivity and occupations. If we were able to determine the part of the earnings gaps that is due to these factors, the part of the gap that remained would serve as a rough estimate of the degree of discrimination in earnings. Researchers have spent much time doing just this. A general conclusion of this research is that legitimate factors explain only about half of the earnings gaps. In other words, if women were comparable to men with regard to productivity, occupation, and other legitimate factors, they would still earn only about 85 percent of what men earn, while blacks, under the same conditions, would earn about 90 percent of what whites earn.

Employment Discrimination

Employment discrimination means that some people are not hired because of noneconomic characteristics such as race or gender. Two individuals with the same training, education, and experience apply for a job. One is black and one is white. If both do not have the same chance of getting the job, discrimination has entered into the decision-making process.

Employment discrimination, like wage discrimination, is difficult to identify positively. Differences in unemployment rates among whites and minority groups and between males and females may suggest discrimination but do not prove that it exists. However, when you consider all low-productivity families and discover that unemployment rates are much higher among blacks than whites, or when you look at families with identical education levels and find unemployment rates higher among black families than white families, the evidence of employment discrimination becomes more conclusive. For example, in 2002 the unemployment rate of young (16–24 years old) white high school graduates was 8.9 percent, while the unemployment rate of young black high school graduates was 19.3 percent. Although not conclusive, evidence of this nature certainly is suggestive of employment discrimination.

Occupational Discrimination

There is a growing belief that discriminatory differences in pay, especially gender differences in pay, occur largely because of occupational segregation. In general, men work in occupations that employ very few women, and women work in occupations that employ very few men. The economic results of occupational segregation for women are low wages. Women are often relegated to occupations where productivity and experience have little to do with their status and where opportunities for overtime and premium pay are limited.

Why do women fail to enter higher paid male-dominated occupations? It is widely believed that women are socialized into roles that minimize the importance of establishing a career. Women are frequently taught from an early age that their primary roles are as housewives and mothers. In our culture, the division of labor within households often leaves women at home to produce domestic services, such as raising children, whereas men pursue work in the marketplace to provide income for the family. However, the traditional economic roles of men and women changed dramatically during the twentieth century. Two-income households are now the norm, but a woman's job is still most often considered "secondary." Some economists argue that because of our cultural division of labor between the sexes, women *choose* occupations that allow them to simultaneously work and pursue domestic activities. Such occupations generally require less education and training and are therefore lower-paid.

There is some evidence to suggest that women have made major gains in several male-dominated occupations in the last several decades. For example, in 1960, only 3.4 percent of lawyers in the United States were women. By the early 2000s, women accounted for more than one-fourth of all lawyers. However, such dramatic changes have not occurred in all occupations, and very little movement of men into traditionally female jobs has been observed. More than 90 percent of registered nurses, secretaries, and child care workers continue to be female. Clearly, a large degree of occupational segregation still exists in our economy.

GOVERNMENT ATTEMPTS TO ALLEVIATE POVERTY

Two approaches to poverty are suggested by the foregoing analysis. First, the productivity of the employable poor can be increased. This can be accomplished through subsidized education of the children of the poor, adult training and education programs, counseling and guidance, job placement programs, and the elimination of discrimination. Second, a minimum annual income can be guaranteed. Some people, such as the very young, the very old, the disabled, and the ill, are poor because they cannot produce at all, and others are poor because they cannot produce enough. Income-support programs are required to aid those who are unproductive and those who have low productivity.

Although the federal government continues to fight poverty using both approaches, a close examination reveals an emphasis on income support rather than comprehensive human capital development. The government programs designed to alleviate poverty and to help the poor are often referred to as "public welfare." However, it is important to realize that there has never been just one federal welfare program, but rather a loose system of programs, each targeted to those people with specific characteristics and needs. For example, some programs subsidize the income needs of single-parent households, while others address the health care requirements of the aged and disabled. Many targeted welfare programs have attempted to address the various aspects of poverty during the past 40 years. Even though some of the programs have been successful, in recent years the voting public has called for welfare reform to reduce the federal government's role in assistance to the poor. In the next sections we briefly examine some of the major federal antipoverty programs as they existed prior to 1997 and some of their inherent problems. Following that, we turn our attention to an analysis of the ongoing welfare reform that places a new emphasis on work.

The Old Federal Welfare System

Since the War on Poverty began in the 1960s, numerous federal programs have been designed and undertaken specifically to benefit low-income groups in our society. Most welfare programs prior to 1997 were to a large extent centralized by the federal government. Although the daily operation of the programs may have been handled by state or local agencies, everyone followed the rules established by the federal government. Thus, eligibility requirements and degrees of assistance were generally set according to national guidelines. The most important of these centralized programs were those that provided income support to poor female-headed households and the disabled. Others included health care provision, housing services, and nutritional assistance. Many of these continue under the ongoing welfare reform measures but with new rules and a decentralized administrative structure.

Income Support

The first federal welfare program to provide income support to the poor was the Aid to Families with Dependent Children (AFDC) program, which was introduced in 1935 along with the establishment of Social Security. AFDC provided direct income transfers to poor families with only one parent living in the household. In practice, this usually meant female-headed households with children under the age of 18. (Some states severely restricted or prohibited AFDC payments to single male-headed households.) AFDC was a *means-tested* program in which families became eligible only if family income and assets fell below some predetermined level. Federal guidelines allowed each state to set its own needs standards for families of different sizes and living locations. Funding for AFDC was shared by the federal government and the states.

Members of families receiving AFDC were allowed, but not required, to work. AFDC benefits were reduced as family income increased. The reduction in benefits was less than dollar-for-dollar, which allowed total family income to rise when gainful employment was maintained. Total annual AFDC payments varied across each of the 50 states, but no state paid benefits sufficient to bring a family above the established poverty line. In the mid-1990s, the average annual AFDC benefit amounted to only 38 percent of the poverty threshold. Because of this, families receiving AFDC were automatically eligible for other federally supported assistance programs, including Medicaid and food stamps.

A second major income support program was enacted in 1972 with the signing of the Supplemental Social Insurance Act by President Richard Nixon. Benefits under this program, known as supplemental security income (SSI), were originally targeted to the elderly who did not qualify for Social Security and the blind and disabled whose income and assets fell below specified thresholds. The federal act provided for uniform national guidelines and benefit levels. This program continues to exist under the welfare reform provisions of 1996, with stricter requirements for continuing eligibility.

Health Care Support

The major health care support program targeted toward the poor was, and continues to be, Medicaid. Under the old welfare system, all families who qualified for AFDC or SSI were automatically entitled to Medicaid benefits. In addition, Medicaid was designed to pay the major costs of both hospital care and physician services for low-income pregnant women and children who were not otherwise eligible for public assistance. Prior to the recent welfare reform provisions affecting Medicaid, more than 32 million persons were annually served by the program.

Funding for Medicaid is shared by the federal and state governments. States with lower average incomes receive more federal dollars than high-income states. The federal government's share of Medicaid funding averages between 50 and about 80 percent of the total program cost. The rising cost of health care accounted for more than one-half of the growth in all federal dollars directed toward the poor during the early 1990s.

Food and Nutrition Assistance

Historically, the primary program providing food and nutrition assistance to the poor has been the federal Food Stamp program. Families receiving food stamps are able to redeem vouchers for the purchase of food in order to maintain a nutritious and healthy diet. Interestingly this program was, and continues to be, administered by the Department of Agriculture as a program to support the demand for food and agricultural products produced by American farmers. Under the old welfare system, recipients of AFDC automatically qualified for food stamps, with the level of support being determined by a means test. By the mid-1990s, more than 25 million people received the benefits of food stamps at an annual outlay of almost $30 billion. In addition to food stamps, the federal government has maintained programs to support lunches for low-income public school children and meals in other institutionalized settings since the welfare reforms of 1996.

Housing Assistance

Housing assistance for the poor has most commonly been provided in the form of rent subsidies. Over the years, a number of federal programs provided direct subsidies for the construction and rental of housing units for the poor in both rural and urban areas. More recently, emphasis has been on housing assistance in the form of rent vouchers. The major problem most low-income families face is not the lack of available housing but a lack of income to afford decent housing. Rent vouchers address this problem directly by giving low-income families the opportunity to choose among publicly and privately owned rental units.

Other Social Services

A number of federal programs provide a variety of social services for the poor. These programs target low-income groups such as the elderly, the disabled, dependent children and youths, and Native Americans. The mix of social services provided includes day care, foster care, child abuse intervention, job placement, health counseling, and emergency shelter. The recent welfare reforms have significantly reduced funding for such services, and greater emphasis is being placed on private charities to meet these needs.

Training and Employment

A number of federally sponsored training and employment programs have been undertaken since the 1960s. These programs generally take the form of grants to states for the purpose of assisting people who have difficulties in the job market.

Target groups include workers displaced by technology, teenagers, and those on other forms of public assistance. The most comprehensive current training and employment program was established by the Job Training and Partnership Act (JTPA), which encourages local businesses to become involved in delivering training and support. Although each state has responsibility for running its JTPA projects, the federal government requires that a major portion of the funding be used for training the economically disadvantaged. Other federal programs include support for each state's Employment Service (job banks) and subsidized summer employment projects for youths.

Problems with the Old Welfare System

Over the years, economists, social workers, and the general public alike widely criticized the old welfare system. This criticism was grounded in the frustration of growing budget requirements for programs that did not appear to reduce the rate of poverty. The inability of the welfare system to significantly lower the incidence of poverty, even during periods of economic expansion, led many to conclude that the system was flawed. It was argued that most of the programs placed an emphasis on financial support and did not encourage recipients to remedy the causes of their poverty. Furthermore, many argued that the programs were structured in ways that created a "welfare dependency" that resulted in a permanent culture of poverty. These criticisms eventually led to the welfare reform initiatives of the late 1990s.

The most important criticism of the old welfare system is rooted in basic economic theory. In Chapter 3 we discussed the *income effect* of a wage change. Recall that the income effect measures the change in hours of work supplied by an individual when there is a change in income, other things being equal. Because leisure is a normal good, a person will demand more leisure time, and therefore work fewer hours, when income rises—if everything else remains the same. Under the old welfare system, recipients were provided income (in the form of cash, food stamps, rent vouchers, etc.) without a work or training requirement. This tended to create a pure income effect. When receiving welfare, recipients increased their income while everything else remained the same. Thus, the income effect reduced the hours of work supplied to the labor market by those receiving welfare benefits. Numerous empirical studies have demonstrated that programs such as AFDC did generate significant reductions in hours of work by recipients. However, because of the low wages available to most workers on welfare, it is problematic to conclude that this disincentive to work kept large numbers of people on the welfare rolls.

The most controversial criticism of AFDC and its related programs was that they created an economic incentive for those on welfare to establish and maintain single-parent households and to have babies. Under the old system, the highest levels of benefits were available only to unmarried, separated, or divorced women with dependent children. In most states the benefit levels increased directly with the number of children present in the household. Critics of the system viewed this as public support for unwed motherhood and single-parent families. Although there has been an alarming increase in the number of unwed births and female-headed households, economic studies have not found strong evidence to correlate this trend with the availability and level of welfare payments. Contrary to popular perceptions, the marginal increase in welfare benefits to a single mother who has an additional child was far less than the expected marginal costs of caring for the child. Thus, it was not "profitable" to continue having babies while on welfare.

Most welfare programs were designed to provide temporary stopgap relief for those who found themselves in an economic emergency due to some event outside their control. However, studies indicate that only about one-quarter of welfare recipients left the welfare rolls within a year, and many of these returned at a later date. Furthermore, the probability of leaving the welfare system was found to decrease with the amount of time spent on welfare. In other words, the longer a person remained on welfare, the lower the likelihood that he or she would exit. Long-run studies of AFDC indicated that as many as one-fourth of the recipients spent at least 10 years on welfare. Results such as these pointed to a permanent welfare class and led policymakers to conclude that the old system needed to be reformed.

Welfare Reform and the New System

When President Bill Clinton signed the Personal Responsibility and Work Opportunity Reconciliation Act during the fall of 1996, he claimed that it would "end welfare as we have known it." This piece of legislation made broad, sweeping changes in the organizational structure and daily operations of our public assistance system. Most important, the bill eliminated the open-ended AFDC program and replaced it with block grants to the states for time-limited income support programs. It also modified various aspects of SSI, food stamps, and other social service programs targeted to the poor. Based on the criticisms of the old welfare system, two important themes are reflected throughout the 1996 welfare reform legislation: (1) the act places time limits on how long a person or family may receive benefits, and (2) the act requires those who receive public assistance to work.

The major differences between the old welfare system and the new are highlighted in Table 7.4. Some of the most important aspects of the new system are reviewed below, followed by a brief discussion of some potential problems.

Income Support

In 1997 the old AFDC program was phased out and replaced by state-designed and state-operated Temporary Assistance for Needy Families (TANF) programs. These programs are financed by block grants from the federal government and state revenues. To qualify for the federal money, each state program must adhere to specific guidelines concerning time limits for assistance and work requirements for able-bodied adults. With these two exceptions, states have a nearly free hand in setting their own eligibility requirements and level of support.

Under the TANF programs, adults who are not working must participate in community service within two months of receiving benefits. All adults in families receiving income support must work or be engaged in training after 24 months or

TABLE 7.4 Major Changes in the Welfare System Mandated by the Personal Responsibility and Work Opportunity Reconciliation Act of 1996

At Issue	Old System	New System
Cash assistance	AFDC* had no limits on how long income support could be received.	TANF† allows no more than two years of assistance without working and sets a five-year lifetime limit for adults.
Cash assistance	No work requirement to remain eligible for AFDC.	Adults in families receiving TANF are required to participate in work activities after 24 months of assistance.
Medicaid	AFDC recipients automatically qualified for Medicaid.	States may set their own eligibility requirements within specified guidelines.
Food stamps	No time limit for those who qualified.	Able-bodied adults may receive food stamps for only 3 months in every 36-month period unless they work.
SSI	Developmentally disabled children qualified.	Stricter diagnosis of developmentally disabled children required, and behavioral disorders no longer qualify.
Citizenship	Noncitizens qualified for a wide variety of programs.	New immigrants cannot receive benefits in their first 5 years; no food stamps or SSI for those who have not paid taxes for 10 years or served in the military; illegal immigrants ineligible for most benefits.
Child support	Female recipients not required to name father of their children.	Female recipients required to cooperate in identifying father and seeking child support.

*AFDC: Aid to Families with Dependent Children.
†TANF: Temporary Assistance for Needy Families.

lose their eligibility for assistance. Also, TANF recipients are subject to a lifetime limit of 60 months (five years) of benefits. To ensure that each state designed a TANF program that encouraged work, the 1996 legislation set minimum standards for annual work participation rates of families receiving assistance. These minimums increase over time, and states that fail to meet the mark are penalized through reductions in their block grants. States that meet or exceed the goals are eligible for performance bonuses in the form of additional financial support.

Medicaid

Under the old system, all recipients of AFDC automatically qualified for Medicaid benefits. The welfare reform legislation of 1996 severs this automatic link and allows states to set their own eligibility requirements within a set of guidelines. States also have the option of denying Medicaid to persons who are not citizens of the United States and those denied income support because of refusal to work. States are required to provide coverage to needy pregnant women and minor children.

Food Stamps

The welfare reform measures retain the basic structure of the Food Stamp program. However, new work requirements have been established for those receiving benefits under the program. Able-bodied adults between 18 and 50 years of age may receive food stamps for only 3 months during every 36-month period unless they are engaged in work or are training for work. Special exemptions can be made only on a limited basis for hardship cases. Recipients who work at least 20 hours per week can continue to receive benefits for an uncapped period of time.

Supplemental Security Income and Other Social Services

The welfare reforms established new disability standards for those receiving and applying for SSI benefits. Changes in the criteria used to establish disability make it more difficult to qualify for income support. For example, under the new system, children with developmental maladaptive behavior problems are no longer considered handicapped and are not eligible for assistance.

The Personal Responsibility and Work Opportunity Reconciliation Act also addresses the issue of citizenship. Most programs in the old welfare system did not give consideration to citizenship or even legal resident status. Programs under the new system may take these factors into consideration. New immigrants must live in the United States for five years before benefits become available from most programs. The residency requirement is even stricter for food stamps: 10 years of paying taxes or some service in the U.S. military.

A number of other requirements are included as part of the welfare reform. For example, single mothers who receive benefits must identify the fathers of their dependent children and assist in seeking child care support from them. Also, those convicted on felony drug charges are prohibited from receiving benefits from most programs. In addition to these changes, a variety of training programs, child nutrition programs, health care counseling, and other social service programs were affected by the welfare reform legislation.

USING TAX POLICY TO FIGHT POVERTY

For a long time, many economists have argued that the most efficient way of transferring dollars to the poor is to use the national income tax system. As our national tax collector, the Internal Revenue Service (IRS) has in place an elaborate system that tracks household income and distributes checks, and by carefully designing our tax policy, it is possible to take advantage of these characteristics in a way that will improve the economic position of the poor. In fact, we have been doing just that for about 25 years. The major program that accomplishes this is the Earned Income Tax Credit (EITC), and as we shall see, its principles are very similar to a more comprehensive approach that policymakers have debated and considered for several years: the negative income tax proposal.

The Earned Income Tax Credit

The EITC was established in 1975 as a modest program designed to offset the negative effects of the Social Security and Medicare payroll taxes paid by the working poor. Because Social Security and Medicare taxes are levied from the first dollar earned and because there are no personal deductions or exemptions, low-wage workers tend to bear a greater burden from these taxes than from other income taxes. The basic idea of the EITC is to reduce the total taxes paid by poor workers by providing them a refundable credit against their annual federal income tax liability. By reducing the total tax liability of the poor, the EITC increases the annual take-home pay of low-income workers and creates a stronger incentive for them to remain active members of the labor force. Because of these positive aspects of the EITC, Congress has expanded the program several times, most recently in 1993.

The EITC is administered by the IRS as part of the federal income tax system. Individuals and families with modest earned incomes, up to a specified limit, are eligible to claim the credit. Since the EITC is a *refundable* tax credit, if a family's tax liability is less than the credit, it will receive a check from the IRS for the difference. For example, if you owe the federal government $1,000 in income taxes but you are also eligible for a $1,500 tax credit, then you could claim a $500 refund from the IRS. For people in this circumstance, the EITC is like cash—it increases their disposable income.

Unlike more traditional income assistance programs that reduce benefits for every dollar earned by the recipient, the EITC increases in value as earnings rise up to some point and then it is phased out once an earnings threshold is reached. Figure 7.5 illustrates the 2004 EITC structure for a family with two or more dependents. Such families are eligible for a 40 percent tax credit on all wages and salaries up to an income of about $10,000. Thus, the maximum EITC is 0.40 × $10,500, or $4,200. This amount can be claimed by families earning up to about $14,750 where the phase-out threshold has been established. Families earning more than $14,750 have their EITC reduced by a rate of 21 percent for every dollar of earnings. Therefore, as can be seen in Figure 7.5, the value of the EITC falls until $34,700 is reached. Families earning more than this are not eligible to receive the tax credit. (All numbers have been rounded for simplicity.)

As a result of the legislative expansions of the program, more than 20 million American households now receive the EITC benefit. Comparison of Figure 7.5 with the poverty thresholds shown earlier in Table 7.1 reveals that the largest tax credits will go to those working families with earnings below the poverty line. This fact makes it more likely that the EITC will lift families out of poverty than programs that target families with little or no income. Proponents of the EITC point out that its design is consistent with the recent welfare reform measures in that it increases the net earnings of those who leave the welfare rolls to take jobs in the private economy. In fact, because the EITC is refundable, it can be considered a wage supplement for the working poor. However, once the phase-out threshold is reached, this wage supplement begins to decline at a relatively high rate. The current rate of reduction in the phase-out range, 21 percent, is higher than the

FIGURE 7.5 The Earned Income Tax Credit, 2004

Families with two or more children may claim a refundable tax credit of 40 percent on earnings up to approximately $10,500. This results in a maximum credit of $4,200. Once earnings exceed about $14,750, the tax credit is reduced by 21 percent for each additional dollar earned. The tax credit is thus exhausted at an earnings level of $34,700. (All numbers have been rounded for simplicity.)

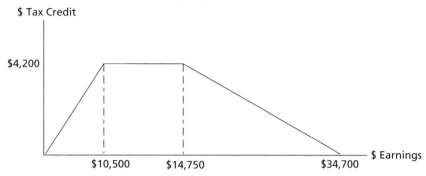

ordinary income tax rate of 15 percent, which is applied to the lowest levels of taxable income. Critics have suggested that this element of the EITC may create disincentives to work for those who find themselves in the phase-out range. To date, however, research into this facet of the program has not revealed a significant reduction in work effort for the affected group of beneficiaries.

Even though the EITC plays an important role in lifting families above the poverty threshold, its impact is not reflected in the official poverty statistics because of the way the government measures household income. Recall that a household's poverty status is determined by comparing its *pretax* income to the appropriate poverty threshold based on family size. Thus, income is measured before any tax credits are applied. Because this approach overlooks the effect of tax credits, economists have devoted considerable research into determining the impact of the EITC on poverty. A recent study published by the Center for Budget and Policy Priorities found that more than 5 million people are lifted out of poverty status by the EITC each year. Furthermore, the researchers found that families were more likely to be pushed above their poverty threshold by the EITC than by other more traditional income transfer programs. The EITC approach has become a popular way to combat poverty. Today, 16 states offer their own EITC programs in addition to the federal one.

Clearly, the EITC has become an important component in our nation's policy to fight poverty. However, some experts argue that the EITC is too complicated and that its cumbersome eligibility rules encourage families with modest incomes to cheat the system. Indeed, the IRS has estimated that in recent years more than 20 percent of EITC benefits were paid in error. For many years, some economists and policymakers have advocated that the way to avoid such problems yet maintain the antipoverty benefits of refundable tax credits is to institute a true negative income tax system.

FIGURE 7.6 A Negative Income Tax

Under a negative income tax system all households are guaranteed a minimum level of income. This is shown as point G. Households with no income would receive a subsidy check from the government equal to that amount. As household income rises, the amount of the subsidy declines at a rate equal to the normal tax rate. Point B represents the level of income where the subsidy is exhausted. Beyond this break-even level of income, households are subject to a positive tax liability.

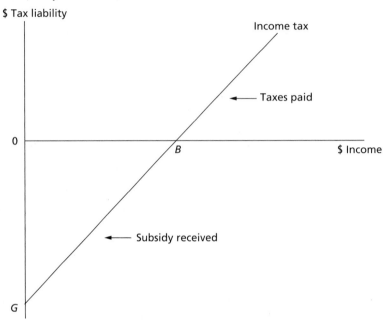

The Negative Income Tax Proposal

Under a negative income tax system, households with income below a predetermined level would not be subject to an income tax liability but would instead receive a subsidy based on their income and the normal tax rate. This type of tax structure involves three important variables: a guaranteed level of income, an income tax rate, and a break-even level of income. Figure 7.6 illustrates how a negative income tax structure works.

In Figure 7.6, a household's income is measured on the horizontal axis and its income tax liability on the vertical axis. Thus, the amount of income taxes owed the government is shown as the upward-sloping line. The slope of this line is determined by the income tax rate. With a negative income tax structure in place, all households are guaranteed a minimum level of income equal to the absolute value of point G. Households with zero income therefore have a negative tax liability equal to G. This means that instead of paying income taxes, the government sends to the household a check equal to G. As seen in Figure 7.6, this subsidy declines by the rate of the income tax as household earnings rise. At point B the subsidy is exhausted. Point B is the break-even level of income above which households face a positive tax liability. In other words, after point B is reached, households no longer receive a check *from* the government; rather, they must pay an income tax *to* the government.

The negative income tax proposal has several attractive features. It is based on the idea that when a household has income above its poverty threshold, the household pays positive taxes; and when a household has income below its poverty threshold, the household owes negative taxes and receives a subsidy check from the government. Because the subsidy check increases total household income, people are always better off if they earn income than they are if they do not earn it; and the more they earn, the better off they will be. In this way, the negative income tax encourages low-income beneficiaries to work. This scheme is designed for individuals and families that have one and only one characteristic: They live in poverty. It is not necessary to be old and poor or blind and poor. To be eligible, you need only be poor. Thus, a negative income tax system is much simpler and probably easier to administer than the vast array of current antipoverty programs. Because of these positive attributes, the negative income tax proposal has been advocated by many influential economists, such as Nobel Prize winner Milton Friedman.

It is important to note that the refundable EITC incorporates some of the same features of the negative income tax proposal into our existing tax structure. Just as under a negative income tax system, low-income households may receive a check from the federal government. However, the EITC program is not a true negative income tax because to qualify a household must have earnings. Families with no one working, perhaps due to disability or other reasons, cannot apply for the EITC. Today, families without earnings must rely on other welfare programs for support. With a true negative income tax system, however, these families would receive cash benefits. Thus, many of the more traditional income transfer programs could be downsized or even eliminated if the negative income tax proposal were adopted.

WHAT CAN BE DONE ABOUT DISCRIMINATION?

The problems of poverty are compounded by the existence of discrimination in our economy. Antipoverty programs and policies will be less effective if those in poverty are also victims of discriminatory practices in the marketplace. Thus, actions to reduce poverty must also be accompanied by actions to reduce discrimination. What can we do to accomplish this?

Reduce Tastes for Discrimination

If tastes for discrimination are to be reduced, people must be persuaded that they should alter their views and behavior. These tastes and desires may be reduced by education, by legislation, and by the use of government subsidies to discourage discrimination.

Education

One task of education is to teach people to understand one another so they will not be prejudiced. Unfortunately, this task of education is hampered by discrimination in education itself, especially in regard to the allocation of resources for primary and secondary education. Although not a panacea, a more equal distribution of resources for public education would reduce inequality in per-pupil educational services, and it could contribute toward reducing tastes for discrimination.

Legislation

Changing the tastes of people by coercion, that is, by passing laws, is difficult. Laws usually are effective only when they are supported by or coincide with people's beliefs. However, the framework for reducing tastes for discrimination can be established by laws. The Equal Pay Act of 1963 was the first major federal attempt to control discrimination. The act makes it illegal for employers to pay different wage rates for "equal work." Since the Equal Pay Act applies only to wage discrimination, it is quite limited. To broaden the impact on discrimination, the Civil Rights Act of 1964 was enacted.

The Civil Rights Act covers discrimination against workers based on race, color, gender, religion, or national origin. Additional antidiscrimination laws have been enacted since the mid-1960s to include other minority groups. The Age Discrimination in Employment Act covers older workers, and the Americans with Disabilities Act (ADA) protects "qualified" workers with physical or mental disabilities. The federal laws that protect workers from discrimination are administered by the Equal Employment Opportunity Commission (EEOC), which has the power to pursue court action on behalf of workers.

Federal law now requires not only equal treatment in wages but also equal treatment in hiring, promotion, and ultimately firing. The law may reduce discrimination by imposing greater risks and higher costs on discriminators. For example, a person who satisfies a taste for discrimination by refusing to sell a house to a black breaks the law and risks prosecution.

Government Subsidies

If the sole goal is to eliminate discrimination, government subsidy payments may be used to encourage employers not to discriminate. Subsidy payments would be made to employers who do not practice discrimination in hiring, wages, and promotions. Employers who discriminate would be sacrificing subsidy payments. Thus, an incentive is provided not to discriminate. Government subsidy payments will reduce discrimination if the subsidy payments are equal to or greater than the nonmonetary gain the discriminator receives from discrimination. Although no direct subsidy payment program currently exists, an implicit subsidy occurs when the federal government grants preferences to contractors who meet equal employment opportunity standards.

Reduce Market Imperfections

Market defects such as scarce labor market information, imperfect competition, and immobility of labor constitute a major source of market discrimination. Some people receive low wages, that is, wages below what they could earn in alternative employment, because they are unaware of other job openings. Better access to job information would make it less likely for a person to receive income below what he or she would be paid on a similar job.

The market for goods and the market for resources may not work well at all if there is little competition in these markets. In imperfect markets, discrimination may be prevalent. A seller or a buyer has control over the price of what he or she sells or buys in highly monopolized markets. Other potential sellers or buyers are shut out of the market. Price, wage, employment, and occupational discrimination may remain unchallenged in the absence of competitive forces and in the presence of monopolistic controls. Antitrust action to strengthen competition and reduce barriers to entry into markets would be an important way to eliminate or at least lessen discriminatory market behavior.

The government has an important role to play in the elimination of discrimination when it is due to the use of monopoly power. It is the responsibility of the government to reduce monopoly power and restore competition in markets where competition is lacking through the vigorous use of antimonopoly laws. In Chapter 8, we more closely examine how markets operate when sellers have monopoly powers, and in Chapter 9 we explore the behavior of monopsonistic employers of labor.

Reduce Discrimination in Development of Human Capital

Investment in human capital, that is, spending on education, training, and health, provides a high rate of return in the form of increased productivity and income. Blacks and other minority groups generally do not and cannot invest enough in human capital, and public investment in human capital is unequally distributed. The elimination of human capital discrimination would tend to make most forms of market discrimination, such as wage and employment discrimination, less effective. The reason is that if human resources are productive and have access to other jobs, treating them unequally would be difficult.

Reduce Occupational Segregation

Occupational segregation results in overrepresentation of blacks, other minorities, and women in the low-wage sectors of the economy. The effect of segregation by occupations is twofold. First, the supply of labor is increased in those occupations restricted to minority groups, depressing wages in those occupations. Second, the supply of labor is decreased in those occupations closed off to minority groups, thus increasing wages in those occupations. The result of these effects is to create a wider gap between low- and high-wage occupations.

In addition, if a member of the minority group crosses over into segregated occupations usually closed to members of the group, he or she has typically not received equal pay for equal work. For example, a black male with a Ph.D. in chemistry who works as a research chemist for an oil company may be discriminated against in wages and opportunities for advancement because he has a position typically reserved for whites. In recent years this situation has been reversed in many cases by the Equal Employment Opportunities Act. Employers are virtually required to bid for minority group personnel. The small supplies available of these workers who are qualified ensure that they will receive salaries above those of white employees.

However, segregation by occupations would be difficult to maintain if minority groups were relatively well educated and well trained. Education and training open up job opportunities. Those who have job opportunities cannot easily be forced into designated occupations; they are mobile and can cut across occupations. Providing improved job opportunities for minority groups is one way to break up segregation by occupations.

Summary

The number of people living in poverty in the United States was significantly reduced by the War on Poverty during the 1960s. This downward trend in poverty did not continue in the following decades. It is somewhat understandable that the number of poor persons and the poverty rate were not reduced in the 1970s, for the economy was essentially stagnant and confronted with other problems during the period. However, this was not the situation after the early 1980s. The economy was in a record-breaking period of expansion. Under these conditions, it would be expected that the incidence of poverty would have been reduced.

Poverty rates vary a great deal among different family groupings. The poverty rate among all families was 10 percent in 2003. The poverty rate, however, was very much higher than this among families with a single female head of the household—approximately 3 times higher. Other demographic characteristics are also associated with relatively higher rates of poverty. Racial and ethnic minorities, the very old and the very young, and those living in remote rural and inner-city areas are more likely to become victims of poverty. The incidence of poverty is also higher in states located in the South and West compared to those in the Northeast and Midwest.

To deal with problems of poverty and low income, programs should be designed to (1) increase the upward mobility of the poor and near-poor and (2) guarantee a minimum annual income to families and individuals who cannot work and those who cannot earn a minimum income when they do work.

Over time, the government has undertaken a wide variety of efforts to reduce poverty, including direct assistance for the needy and tax policies to increase disposable income. Many of the federal programs developed piecemeal, and some were not originally designed strictly for the poor. Critics of the old welfare system claimed that the government programs created negative work incentives for the poor and created a culture of poverty. Welfare reform measures in the mid-1990s established a new system of assistance that ties benefits to work and training and places time limits on eligibility. Whether the economy can successfully create enough jobs for welfare workers is yet to be seen. The existence of discriminatory practices, particularly in labor markets, compounds the problems of poverty. The groups with the highest rates of poverty, black families and those headed by a female, are also groups that are susceptible to being victims of discrimination. Thus, antipoverty programs and policies must be supplemented by actions to reduce discrimination if they are to be effective in the long run.

Discussion Questions

1. What is the difference between "absolute poverty" and "relative poverty"? Provide examples of each.

2. How does the incidence of poverty vary across demographic groups in the United States? Why do we see differences in poverty rates between racial and ethnic groups? Which groups are least likely to experience poverty and why?

3. Discuss the issues that determine the distribution of income in an economy. What has been the primary trend in the U.S. income distribution in recent years? Explain why we see this trend.

4. What factors explain why some people earn very low incomes? Who controls these factors? Can governments through public policy influence all the factors that result in poverty?

5. Explain why some critics claimed that the old welfare system created a "culture of poverty." Using economic reasoning, explain the negative incentive to work that results from cash assistance.

6. Is it possible to provide people with income support without also creating a negative effect on their hours of work? Explain.

7. How do the welfare reform measures address the criticisms of the old system? What problem confronts the new system?

8. How does the Earned Income Tax Credit (EITC) help alleviate the problems of poverty for low-income families? Can the effect of the EITC be seen in the official poverty statistics? Explain.

9. In what ways are the EITC and the negative income tax proposal alike? In what ways are they different? Do you think the United States will ever have a negative income tax system? Why or why not?

10. Explain how a negative income tax differs from more traditional antipoverty programs.

11. Are wage differentials a natural outcome of a market economy? Explain. Under what circumstances do wage differentials reflect discrimination?

12. Discuss the economic costs of discrimination to individuals and to society. How does discrimination compound the problems of poverty?

13. How has government attempted to reduce the incidence and effects of market discrimination in our society? In your opinion, have these efforts been successful? Why or why not?

14. How did the recession of 2001 affect the outcomes of the welfare policy reforms initiated in the late 1990s? Have the reforms been successful? Defend your answer.

Additional Readings

Darity, William Jr., ed. *Economics and Discrimination.* 2 vols. Brookfield, VT: Edward Elgar Publishing Company, 1995.
This two-volume set thoroughly discusses a variety of issues related to the economics of discrimination, including (*a*) neoclassical economics and the theory of discrimination; (*b*) competition, culture, and alternative approaches to the

economics of discrimination; and (c) identification of winners and losers from discrimination.

Ehrenreich, Barbara. *Nickel and Dimed: On (Not) Getting By in America*. New York: Metropolitan Books, 2001.
The author worked as a waitress, a maid, a nurse's aide, and a sales associate for a discount store to see if she could live on minimum wages. It is a fascinating account of her jobs and living arrangements while working at a poverty level of income.

Gans, Herbert J. *The War against the Poor: The Underclass and Antipoverty Policy*. Cambridge, MA: Perseus Publishing, 1996.
The author explores the history of how American society has stigmatized "the underclass" and how the labels we use to describe the problems of poverty perpetuate a division between the poor and the middle class. Gans calls for the media to debunk the popularly held stereotypes about the poor and offers a set of innovative ideas for public policy reform.

Herrnstein, Richard J., and Charles Murray. *The Bell Curve: Intelligence and Class Structure in American Life*. New York: Free Press, 1994.
Controversial book purporting to show that many economic differences between groups in American society may be explained by differences in measured intelligence, and not overt discrimination.

Jacobsen, Joyce P. *The Economics of Gender*. 2nd ed. Malden, MA: Blackwell, 1998.
Discusses how and why men and women are different, and how these differences affect people's economic choices and outcomes.

Kuttner, Robert, ed. *Making Work Pay: America after Welfare*. New York: The New Press, 2002.
These articles first appeared in *The American Prospect*, and discuss, among other issues, the Earned Income Tax Credit, the Leave No Child Behind Act, welfare reform, and day care.

Levitan, Sar A. *Programs in Aid of the Poor*. 8th ed. Baltimore: The Johns Hopkins University Press, 2003.
Thorough analysis of programs in aid of the poor. Especially recommended for further reading are chapters on programs for the next generation and strategies to combat poverty.

Murray, Charles. *Losing Ground*. 10th ed. New York: Basic Books, 1994.
Provocative book examining the effects of traditional antipoverty programs. The author was a leader in the conservative approach to "welfare reform" during the 1990s.

National Research Council. *Measuring Poverty: A New Approach*. Washington, DC: National Academy Press, 1996.
This book reviews the problems and flaws with the current methodology the federal government uses to determine the extent of poverty in our economy.

Alternative conceptual and practical measures of poverty are evaluated, and proposals for a new system are presented.

Nelson, Julie A. *Feminism, Objectivity, and Economics.* New York: Routledge, 1996.
Discusses the economic aspects of sex discrimination against women.

Padavic, Irene, and Barbara Reskin. *Women and Men at Work.* 2nd ed. Thousand Oaks, CA: Pine Forge Press, 2002.
The authors argue that "the amount of sex inequality in a workplace depends on how employers organize work, the tasks involved, organizational leadership, and the existence of external pressures, among other features."

Robbins, Philip K., Robert G. Spiegelman, and Samuel Weiner, eds. *A Guaranteed Annual Income: Evidence from a Social Experiment.* New York: Academic Press, 1980.
The focus of this selection of essays is on the issues of welfare reform and the effects of welfare reform alternatives based on experiments, especially experiments with negative income tax plans.

Rodgers, Harrell R., Jr. *Poor Women, Poor Families.* Armonk, NY: M. E. Sharpe, 1996.
Good account of the economic plight of families headed by females.

World Wide Web Resources

American Public Human Services Association
www.aphsa.org

Provides an in-depth history of welfare reform. Links to other welfare-related sites and the latest news concerning public policy debates.

Center on Budget and Policy Priorities
www.cbpp.org

The Center on Budget and Policy Priorities is a nonpartisan research organization and policy institute that conducts research and analysis on a range of government policies and programs, with an emphasis on those affecting low- and moderate-income people.

Economic Policy Institute Issue Guide: Poverty and Family Budgets
www.epinet.org/content.cfm/issueguides_poverty_poverty

EPI, a nonpartisan, nonprofit think tank, produces issues guides, online resources that provide data, charts, fact sheets, and links to relevant publications on a variety of topics. This is on poverty measurement and basic family budgets.

Health and Human Services Poverty Guidelines
www.dol.gov/esa/whd/flsa

Provides explanation of the official federal poverty thresholds, as well as information on current poverty research programs.

Institute for Research on Poverty

www.ssc.wisc.edu/irp

IRP is a nonprofit university-based center for research into the causes and consequences of poverty and inequality in the United States. Site provides links to research reports and other poverty study resources.

Office of Civil Rights

www.gsa.gov/eeo

The General Services Administration maintains this page. Explains what EEO is and who the regional EEO officers are, and gives links to EEO sites and other information.

United States Census Bureau

www.census.gov

Click on *Subjects A–Z*, type in **poverty,** and a screen about poverty will appear. Gives statistics on poverty by year, historical data, poverty measurements, and other data.

U.S. Department of Housing and Urban Development's Homes and Communities

www.hud.gov

Gives links to housing options for people with low incomes, fair housing and equal opportunity, and other sites.

U.S. Employment Discrimination Law

www.law.cornell.edu/topics/employment_discrimination.html

Provides an overview of the major antidiscrimination labor laws and a menu of sources and related materials.

The Economics of Big Business
Who Does What to Whom?

Checklist of economic concepts

- Market, monopolistic
- Market, imperfectly competitive
- Market, competitive
- Concentration ratio
- Demand
- Demand curve facing a firm
- Marginal revenue
- Marginal cost
- Profit-maximizing output
- Supply
- Supply curve of a firm
- Marginal social benefit
- Marginal social cost
- Deadweight welfare loss
- Entry barriers
- Network economies
- Nonprice competition
- Average cost
- Economies of scale
- Diseconomies of scale
- Natural monopoly
- Corporation
- Agency problem
- Stock options

When federal judge Thomas Penfield Jackson threw the whole book and the kitchen sink at Microsoft Monday night, it was the perfect ending to a catastrophic day that saw Microsoft's capitalized market value plummet by $80 billion. What gives? Answer: market investors are saying that if the government can stick it to Microsoft, then they can stick it to anyone. What's bad for the goose could be even worse for the gander. No one can be sure what additional regulatory shoes may fall in the future. After the Jackson decision came down, Assistant Attorney-General Joel Klein piled on. Here's a revealing quote: "It will benefit America's consumers by opening the door to competition, increased innovation and increased consumer choice in the software industry. This landmark opinion will also set the ground rules for enforcement in the Information Age."

Benefit consumers? Set the ground rules for enforcement? It is exactly these regulatory attitudes that sent a very cold chill down the spine of the stock market, including dozens of company shares whose CEOs thought they might benefit from Microsoft's regulatory and legal demise. Think again, fellas. When Uncle Sam starts on a trust-busting tear, plenty of unsuspecting victims fall prey to its anti-market and anti-growth illogic. This was the case one hundred years ago under Theodore Roosevelt and William Howard Taft; it also happened during Franklin Roosevelt's 1930s and again during the Jimmy Carter 1970s. Stock markets and the economy suffered mightily. When government thinks it knows best, stocks and the economy perform least.

The Microsoft revolution of the 1990s has been the backbone of our high growth and low inflation economic miracle. Software output has expanded, prices have fallen, and the economy flourished. In the past four years, as the software revolution evolved into the Internet economy, the high-tech Nasdaq index appreciated 33 percent yearly. This pulled the old economy S&P and Dow indexes up 22 percent annually. Nearly 100 million investors gained extraordinary wealth. Does this picture really need fixing? Even computer klutzes like myself were able to learn Internet Explorer. Software applications such as Excel, Word and PowerPoint made everything simpler and easier to understand and execute. Netscape sold plenty of software but Microsoft proved to be more popular. Meanwhile, the standardized integration of Microsoft software, bundled together with their browser, substantially lowered transaction costs and raised productivity everywhere. Benefit consumers? Maybe consumers don't really want to be saved. No one in their right mind wants Uncle Sam to regulate technology companies that have become the engine of U.S. economic growth. If, however, trust busting is to dominate economic policy now, then the economic growth boom may be coming to an end.[*]

* * *

Recently the impossible became reality: Microsoft failed to bully its way out of trouble thus losing the anti-trust suit which was brought against it by the U.S. Justice Department. Who'd a thunk it? For many years we've watched Microsoft get away with (the business equivalent of) murder and go scot-free while the cash, profits—and market dominance—piled up, and competitor after competitor bit the dust. When I first got heavily involved with computers about 10 years ago, it was an exciting field with lots of players in the home user market: there was Ami Pro, dBase, Paradox, Borland, Corel, Microsoft, Lotus 1-2-3, MS-DOS and other flavours, the newly-emerging Windows 3.1 but also IBM's OS/2 Warp and Apple machines, office suites (three of them!)—in other words, there was competition. You could go to the software store and choose from competing products. Try that today and what will you see? Microsoft products. Competition brought innovation, new features, improvement, enhancements: could someone please tell me what enhancements have been made to Microsoft Word lately?

With the benefit of hindsight it seems almost ridiculous to think that any other conclusion could have been reached in this trial: Microsoft is a monopoly, and it has used its monopoly power to continue its dominance and drive others from the market. Any other interpretation of the evidence is just plain foolishness, and the evidence really does speak for itself. There was a time when those of us who made such claims were deemed—and sometimes dismissed as Microsoft bashers and sore losers and jealous and whatnot. Microsoft still continues to talk about how it just wants to "innovate" and continue to do that despite the (subtext: horribly unfair!) lawsuit brought against it by the U.S. government. It presents itself as a leader in innovation that has been unfairly victimized by legal technicalities.

Since Microsoft has won the "browser war," what has become of its browser? Has the company continued to "innovate" for the benefit of customers or do we have the same browser with a few modifications here and there? Name any product and the result is the same: once it has achieved market saturation and the competition has been put to bed, the product stagnates. Once a year or so a few enhancements are added, a new name is given, and it's sold as an upgrade. And curiously enough, the file formats keep changing (ask any Microsoft Word user), so droves of people are forced to "upgrade" so as to be able to read the new file formats. Is that what Microsoft means by innovation? And isn't innovation doing something new, rather than copying what others have done and then bullying them out of the market?

The verdict in this case has already been appealed by Microsoft, and no doubt the saga will continue. Microsoft bashers—I prefer to think of them as folks interested in competition and all the benefits it brings—can take heart from the fact that their oft-repeated concerns have finally found an amiable hearing. In the meantime, until the case is settled once and for all, Microsoft is free to innovate all it wants. I can't, for the life of me, think of anyone else left in the business to crush and destroy, but you never know.**

In the late 1970s a group of college friends started a new business, and less than 25 years later that business had become the largest and most powerful software company on the planet—Microsoft. By the late 1990s Microsoft had grown so large that one of its founders, Bill Gates, became the richest man in America (and one of the richest in the world). Microsoft has been so successful that well more than 80 percent of all home and office computers run a version of its Windows operating system. This dominance of the market, along with a variety of its business strategies, caused the U.S. Justice Department to file antitrust charges against Microsoft, and in 2000 the court declared that Microsoft was indeed a monopoly and should be broken into separate and competing firms. Later, the presiding appeals court ruled that while the conclusion of the lower court as to Microsoft's monopoly status was correct, the lower court had to assess a penalty that did not involve breaking up the company. After a few months of bargaining, all sides agreed to a settlement that imposed a broad range of restrictions on Microsoft's business practices to be monitored by an independent, on-site, three-member panel of computer industry experts. This did not end Microsoft's legal problems, however; in early 2004 the European Union also won a judgment, with an accompanying fine of $613 million, against Microsoft for what the European court called the company's abuse of its "near monopoly" with respect to its Windows operating system. As can be seen in the two editorials above, which were written in response to the U.S. court's ruling in 2000, there are strong public opinions on both sides of those cases. Clearly, millions of computer users benefit from the operating systems and software applications developed and sold by Microsoft. However, throughout history, Americans have demonstrated a suspicion of the concentration of power. Whether it's the expansion of government, the political influence of special interest groups, or the consolidation of markets by large firms, the general public often expresses its apprehension about, and in extreme cases outright hostility toward, those who are believed to hold undue influence. Are these concerns justified in a market setting? Why do consumers fear big businesses and why do governments outlaw monopolies?

In this chapter, our focus is on the economic performance of big businesses. Care should be taken before concluding that big business naturally results in negative outcomes for the consuming public, for two important reasons. First, firms need not be large to engage in such actions. Conversely, many truly enormous firms with long histories have never even been accused of wrongdoing. Second, recall that a large share of the innovations and inventions which yield great satisfaction to the consuming public results from large and powerful firms. Given this, the primary questions we wish to consider in this chapter are: (1) Should we fear bigness in the business world? (2) What role, if any, should government play in counteracting the growth of bigness?

THE ECONOMICS OF MONOPOLY POWER

A frequently made assumption is that if a firm grows very large, it must have monopoly power which will eventually be exercised against the public. "Big business" and "monopoly," however, are not synonymous. The first step in evaluating the performance of big business is to understand what distinguishes big business from monopoly. Having more carefully identified the source of the problem, we turn our attention to the actual performance of firms that possess monopoly power.

What Is Monopoly Power?

As we noted in Chapter 2, *monopoly* in its strictest sense means there is a single seller of a good or service. Not many big businesses fit the full condition of this definition, however. Most large enterprises operate in markets in which there are several other firms producing and selling the product. In Chapter 2, we labeled such a market structure one of *imperfect competition*. It is the monopoly power exercised by firms in imperfectly competitive as well as monopolistic markets that people worry about and to which we address ourselves in this chapter.

The monopoly power of a firm refers to the extent of its control over the supply of the product that is produced by the industry of which it is a part. The more firms there are producing and selling a given product, the less control any one of the firms can exercise over industry supply. If there are enough firms in an industry so that one firm's output and its control over industry supply are insignificant, we have a market that should tend to be competitive. On the other hand, if there is only one firm producing and selling the product, we have a market of pure monopoly. The monopoly power of a firm in an imperfectly competitive market is greater the larger the firm's output is relative to the output of the industry as a whole. It is less the smaller the firm's output is relative to the output of the entire industry. As such, it is not the absolute size of the firm that gives it monopoly power, but rather its size relative to its rivals that is important.

concentration ratio
The percentage of industry sales accounted for by the four (or eight) largest firms in an industry; a measure of monopoly power.

To determine the degree of monopoly power in imperfectly competitive markets, we often use **concentration ratios.** The most common is the four-firm concentration ratio, which indicates the percentage of industry sales controlled by the four largest firms in an industry. Thus, an imperfectly competitive industry with four, or fewer than four, firms would have a concentration ratio of 100 percent and would be thought to have a very high degree of monopoly power. However, an industry with a large number of small firms might have a concentration ratio of 10 or 20 percent and would be thought to have very little monopoly power. Typically, one might suspect a significant degree of monopoly power when the concentration ratio reaches 70 or 80 percent. Table 8.1 shows four-firm concentration ratios for selected industries. As an example, consider the cereal breakfast foods industry. The concentration ratio of 86.7 percent indicates that 86.7 percent of the sales of cereal breakfast foods is controlled by the industry's four largest firms. Consequently, this industry probably resembles the pure monopoly model more closely than the pure competition model.

The rather high degrees of concentration indicated in Table 8.1 might suggest that the economy is composed of highly monopolistic markets. However, we should be careful before drawing such a conclusion. Although concentration ratios are valuable and do indicate the potential for monopoly power, they have some limitations. Consider the automobile manufacturing industry. The concentration ratio for this industry is 79.5 percent. In reality, however, the industry is not quite

TABLE 8.1

Selected
Four-Firm
Concentration
Ratios

Source: U.S. Department
of Commerce, Bureau of
the Census, *Census of
Manufacturers, 1997,
Concentration Ratios in
Manufacturing*, EC97M315-
CR (Washington, DC: U.S.
Government Printing
Office, 2001).

Industry	Concentration Ratio
Cigarettes	98.9
Cane sugar refining	98.7
Breweries	89.7
Cereal breakfast foods	86.7
Automobile manufacturing	79.5
Aircraft engines	77.2
Soap and other detergents	65.6
Primary aluminum	63.6
Snack foods	57.2
Electronic computers	45.4
Synthetic rubber	39.0
Cement	34.5
Petroleum refineries	34.1
Apparel manufacturing	17.6

so concentrated because the ratio does not take into account the sales of imported cars. With the sales of imports included, this industry might have a four-firm concentration ratio less than 60 percent. As an example of an opposite limitation, consider the cement industry. The concentration ratio is 34.5 percent, indicating that 34.5 percent of cement sales nationally is controlled by the four largest cement firms. The problem with this number is that due to the product's inherent characteristics, cement producers compete only with other cement producers who are located in the same geographic area. That is, for cement, we should be interested in the percentage of cement sales in one geographic area controlled by the four largest cement producers in that area. If this were done, the cement industry would appear much more concentrated than Table 8.1 suggests.

How, then, should the data in Table 8.1 be interpreted? Bearing in mind the limitations of concentration ratios, perhaps a reasonable conclusion might be that there is some evidence of monopoly power in the U.S. economy. We turn our attention now to identifying the impact of monopoly power on firm performance and, ultimately, on the overall performance of the economy.

Outputs and Prices

What impact does monopoly power have on the price a firm charges and on the output level it produces and sells? A useful approach to this question is to contrast the price and output of a firm that exercises monopoly power with those of a firm that does not—that is, with those of a competitive firm.

Demand

We look first at demand for the product being sold. Figure 8.1 illustrates a typical market demand curve. It can be established immediately that with any market structure—competitive, monopolized, or imperfectly competitive—sellers must take into account what buyers will do. For quantity x_1 per unit of time, buyers will

FIGURE 8.1   A Market Demand Curve

A market demand curve is downward-sloping to the right like DD. Consumers will not pay more than p_1 per unit for an output of x_1 per unit of time. In order to sell at a price of p_2 the total sales level must be reduced to x_2 per unit of time. If four firms of equal size were producing output level x_1, one of the four could cause the product price to rise to p' only by cutting its output and sales to zero.

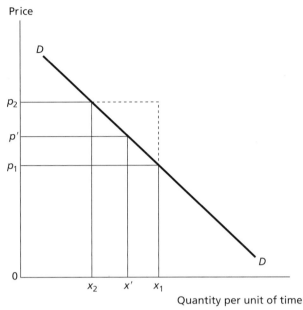

pay a price not higher than p_1. If sellers try to raise the price above p_1, say, to p_2, they cannot sell quantity x_1. At the higher price they can sell quantity x_2 only. Consequently, we conclude that the price which sellers are able to charge is always limited by what buyers are willing to pay. Sellers cannot escape the *law of demand*.

The more sellers there are in the market for a product, the less control any one seller has over the price that it can charge. Suppose, for example, that in Figure 8.1 four sellers of approximately equal size are selling a total quantity of x_1. By how much can any one of the four raise product price? If one firm reduces its output and sales to zero, the other three firms would be selling a total of approximately x' per unit of time, and the price would be p'. Price p', then, is the highest level to which any one of the four firms acting independently can force the price, and it can do this only if it ceases to produce. To stay in business it must of necessity charge less than price p'.

Similarly, if there were 100 sellers of about the same size in the market, the power of one seller to raise the price would be much less. If there were 1,000 sellers of similar size, one seller would not be able to affect the market price of the product at all. If it were to drop out of the market, the total amount sold would decrease by only $1/1,000$ of x_1, which is not enough to cause the price to rise perceptibly. This latter case is typical of a competitive selling market.

Profit Maximization

Economic entities, such as consumers, resource owners, and business firms, like to do the best they can with what they have. Consumers like to get as much satisfaction as possible from spending their annual incomes. As resource owners, we like to get as much income as possible from selling or hiring out the labor and the capital we own. Similarly, business firms try to set prices and output levels so as to make as much profit as possible. The profit maximization principle is simply the business manifestation of a principle that affects most of us—we prefer more to less.

Profit maximization is not a goal peculiar to firms that have monopoly power. It tends to be a major objective of firms in all types of market structures. It is simply the logical conclusion that economic entities reach because they too prefer more to less and make their choices accordingly. Although profit maximization is undoubtedly a major goal of business firms, it is not necessarily the only goal. Firms may also want to build up goodwill in a community, to do right by their employees, or to be known for a quality product. They may also want to get rid of their rivals, collude to raise prices, or block entry into the industry.

In any case, prices and outputs tend to be set so as to maximize profits (or minimize losses) regardless of whether firms producing and selling the product are competitive or have monopoly power. But monopoly power, as we shall see, has important implications for what those prices and outputs will be.

Price and Output in a Competitive Market

How does a firm in a competitive market determine what price to charge and what output to produce? Consider the market diagram in Figure 8.2. This is an ordinary market demand-supply diagram. The market price is p_x and the market output is X. But one individual firm selling this product has *no price-setting capabilities whatsoever* since it supplies an insignificant part of the total market supply. The individual competitive firm can determine only the quantity per unit of time to sell at the market price p_x.

The competitive firm thus faces the *horizontal demand curve dd* for its possible outputs. Its level is determined by the market price of the product. Suppose the market price is $14. In Table 8.2 columns (1) and (4) represent the demand schedule facing the firm, and column (5) shows the firm's total revenue (*TR*) at output levels up to 10 units per day. Although the numbers in column (6) are the same as those in column (4), the concept of marginal revenue for the firm differs from the concept of price. **Marginal revenue (*MR*)** is defined as the change in total revenue resulting from a one-unit change in the output level. The significance of this concept will become apparent shortly.

marginal revenue (MR)
The increase in revenue accruing to the firm from selling an additional unit of its product.

On the cost side, let column (2) in Table 8.2 represent the firm's total costs (*TC*) at different daily output levels. Marginal cost (*MC*), what we referred to as marginal private cost in Chapter 4, is the change in the firm's total cost resulting from a one-unit change in the output level.

profits
The difference between total revenue and total cost; maximized by producing the output at which marginal revenue equals marginal cost.

Determination of the output level that maximizes the firm's profits is easy once we know its *TC* and its *TR* at each possible output. **Profits** are the difference between *TR* and *TC* at any given output level and are listed in column (7). Profits are maximum at either six or seven units of output per day.

FIGURE 8.2 **Price and Output Determination in a Competitive Market**
Product price p_x is determined in the market by the interaction of all buyers and all sellers. The individual firm faces the horizontal demand curve dd, which is also the firm's MR curve. The firm maximizes profits by producing output level x. Altogether the many firms in the market produce output X in the market diagram. The market quantity scale is highly compressed relative to the firm quantity scale. The price scale is the same in both diagrams.

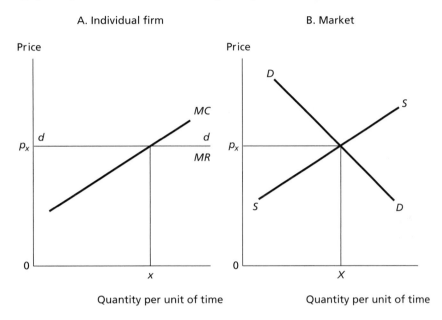

An alternative means of identifying the firm's profit-maximizing output is to find the output at which MR equals MC. Consider any output below the six-unit level (say, three units). A one-unit increase in output would increase TR by $14, or by the amount of MR. It would increase TC by $11, or by the amount of MC. Therefore, it would increase profits by $3, the difference between the MR and the MC of the fourth unit of output. Check the accuracy of this computation in the profit column. We have discovered an important principle: When MR is greater than MC, an increase in the output level will increase profits. (Do you see how this is yet another application of cost-benefit analysis?) Further increases in output through five and six units also increase profits since MR is greater than MC for each of the increases. An increase in output from six to seven units per day adds nothing to profits since $MR = MC = \$14$. However, it does not cause profits to decrease. If output is increased from seven to eight or more units per day, MR is less than MC, and profits decrease—another important principle. But the most important principle of all is that profits are maximized by producing the output level at which MR equals MC. In Table 8.2 profits are maximum at an output level of seven units per day. To be sure, profits are also maximum at six units of product per day, but it will be easier to remember—and always correct—to settle on the output level at which MR equals MC.

TABLE 8.2   Outputs, Revenues, Costs, and Profits for a Competitive Firm

(1) Output (X per Day)	(2) Total Cost (TC)	(3) Marginal Cost (MC)	(4) Price (P_x)	(5) Total Revenue (TR)	(6) Marginal Revenue (MR)	(7) Profits
0	$ 0		$14	$ 0		$ 0
		$ 8			$14	
1	8		14	14		6
		9			4	
2	17		14	28		11
		10			14	
3	27		14	42		15
		11			14	
4	38		14	56		18
		12			14	
5	50		14	70		20
		13			14	
6	63		14	84		21
		14			14	
7	77		14	98		21
		15			14	
8	92		14	112		20
		16			14	
9	108		14	126		18
		17			14	
10	125		14	140		15

The individual-firm diagram of Figure 8.2 shows output x as the firm's profit-maximizing output. Note from Table 8.2 that if a firm's MR is plotted for each output, it will be a horizontal line coinciding with the firm's demand curve dd. The firm's MC curve can be thought of as column (3) of Table 8.2 plotted against output. The output level at which profits are maximum is the one at which MR equals MC.

Recall from Chapter 4 that the MC curve of the firm is the *firm's supply curve* for x, showing how much the firm will place on the market at alternative possible prices, other things being equal. In Figure 8.3 ignore for the present the market diagram and consider the individual-firm diagram only. At a price of $14, seven units per day will be produced and sold by the firm. What would the firm do if the price were $10 instead of $14? The firm's demand curve and MR curve become d_1d_1 and MR_1, respectively. The profit-maximizing output level falls to three units per day. Since the firm seeks to maximize its profits, whatever the market price happens to be, the firm will try to produce the output at which MC equals MR. For a competitive firm, MR and p_x are always equal, so in producing the output level at which MC equals MR, the firm is also producing the output level at which MC

FIGURE 8.3   Marginal Costs and Supply in a Competitive Industry
Since an individual firm produces the output at which $MC = MR = p_x$ in order to maximize profits, the firm's MC curve shows how much it will place on the market at alternative price levels like $10 and $14. The market supply curve shows the combined quantities that all firms in the market will supply at each alternative price. It is the horizontal summation of the MC curves of all the individual firms and is thus a market MC curve for the market as a whole.

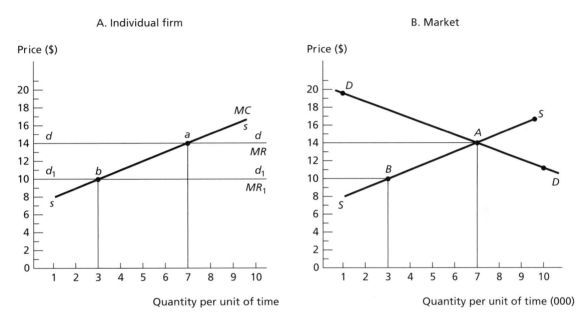

A. Individual firm

B. Market

Quantity per unit of time

Quantity per unit of time (000)

equals p_x. Thus, the outputs that will be produced at alternative price levels are shown by the MC curve, making it the firm's supply curve for the product.

By adding the quantities that all firms in the market will place on the market at each possible price, we get the *market supply curve*. For example, in Figure 8.3 if one of 1,000 identical firms in the market will place seven units of product per day on the market at a price of $14, all firms together will place 7,000 units per day on the market. In Figure 8.3 at the $14 price, the firm would be at point *a* on its supply curve. The market as a whole would be at point *A*. Similarly, at a $10 price level the firm would be at point *b*, and the market as a whole would be at point *B*. The market SS curve is said to be the *horizontal summation* of the individual firm MC or ss curves. It is really a market marginal cost curve for all firms together.

The simultaneous determination of the market price of a product, the individual-firm level of output, and the market level of output for a competitive market now fall neatly into place. In Figure 8.3 let the market demand curve be DD and the market supply curve be SS. The price of $14 is determined by the interaction of buyers and sellers in the market as a whole. It is this price that any one firm in the market takes as given and cannot change. To maximize profits, the firm chooses the output level at which MC equals MR—seven units in this case. The market

TABLE 8.3   Outputs, Revenues, Costs, and Profits for a Competitive Firm

(1)	(2)	(3)	(4)	(5)	(6)	(7)
				Total		
Output (X per Day) ($000)	Total Cost (TC) ($000)	Marginal Cost (MC)	Price (P_x)	Revenue (TR) ($000)	Marginal Revenue (MR)	Profits ($000)
0	$0		$20	$0		$0
		$8			$20	
1	8		20	20		12
		9			18	
2	17		19	38		21
		10			16	
3	27		18	54		27
		11			14	
4	38		17	68		30
		12			12	
5	50		16	80		30
		13			10	
6	63		15	90		27
		14			8	
7	77		14	98		21
		15			6	
8	92		13	104		12
		16			4	
9	108		12	108		0
		17			2	
10	125		11	110		−15

output level of 7,000 units is, of course, the sum of the output levels of all firms producing the product when they are confronted with a $14 product price.

Pricing and Output in a Monopolized Market

To show the effects of monopoly power on the price and the quantity produced of a product, we will suppose that the purely competitive market just discussed becomes monopolized. Consider first the competitive market. The market demand curve *DD* of Figure 8.3 is listed as a demand schedule in columns (1) and (4) of Table 8.3. Similarly, the horizontal summation of the *MC* curves of the 1,000 individual competitive firms, which comprises the supply curve *SS* in Figure 8.3, is listed in columns (1) and (3) of Table 8.3. This information is presented again as *DD* and *SS* in Figure 8.4. As noted in the preceding section, the market price of producing *X* is $14, and the quantity produced and sold is 7,000 units per day.

Now let the 1,000 competitive firms be merged into one gigantic monopoly. Suppose that all the production facilities of the 1,000 firms are taken over in their entireties and that they can be operated by the monopolistic firm with no loss in efficiency. What happens to the output of the industry and the price of the product?

FIGURE 8.4 Comparison of Pricing and Output in Competitive and Monopolized Markets
If the market is competitive, the market price will be $14 and the output will be 7,000 units. Each of the 1,000 firms in the market faces a horizontal demand curve and marginal revenue curve at the $14 level and maximizes profits by producing the output at which its *MR* equals *MC*. Monopolization of the market causes the firm to see *DD* as the demand curve it faces. Since *DD* slopes downward to the right, *MR* lies below *DD*. The profit-maximizing output for the monopolistic firm becomes 5,000 units, which will be sold at a price of $16 per unit.

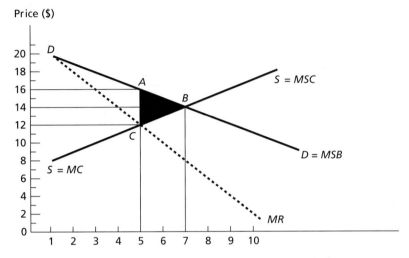

Keep in mind the quantities the competitive firms were producing as they maximized their profits. Each firm found itself looking at a $14 product price that it could not change. Each firm saw a horizontal demand curve for its own output at the $14 level. Each firm viewed marginal revenue as constant at the $14 level—equal to the product price. Each firm produced an output level at which its *MC* was equal to *MR and product price*. Each firm's output level was seven units per day, and the total industry output was 7,000 units per day.

All of that is changed by monopolization of the industry. The monopolist faces the market demand curve *DD*, which is downward-sloping to the right instead of horizontal. This fact has important implications for marginal revenue. Any firm that faces a demand curve that is sloping downward to the right will find that its *marginal revenue is less than product price* at any given output level. We demonstrate this principle in Table 8.3. If the monopolist were to sell 2,000 units of product per day and were to increase sales from 2,000 to 3,000 per day, total revenue of the firm would increase from $38,000 ($19 × 2,000) to $54,000 ($18 × 3,000). Since the 1,000-unit addition to output increases total receipts by $16,000, each one-unit increase in output has increased *TR* by $16. So marginal revenue for the firm in moving from the 2,000-unit to the 3,000-unit level of output is $16 and is less than the price of $18 at which each of the 3,000 units is sold. Marginal revenue in column (6) is computed in the same way for each output level listed in column (1). Compare price and marginal revenue at each level of output. Marginal revenue is plotted as the *MR* curve in Figure 8.4.

If you were the monopolist, what output would you produce and at what price would you sell if your objective were to maximize profits? You would reduce output and sales from 7,000 units per day to 5,000 units per day. You would raise the price from $14 to $16. You would do this because it would increase your profits from $21,000 per day to $30,000 per day as column (7) indicates. At the 5,000-unit output level, *MC* equals *MR* for the monopolist.

To recapitulate the analysis, in a monopolized market the price of the product tends to be higher and output tends to be less than it would be if the industry could be and were competitive. This is not because the managements of monopolized firms are inherently evil while those of competitive firms are not. The managements of firms in both types of markets seek the same general goal—profits. The monopolistic firm restricts output and charges a higher price because its managers see a different relationship between marginal revenue and price than do the managers of competitive firms.

Refer back to Figures 8.3 and 8.4. These figures show that managers of competitive firms face demand curves horizontal at the market price of the product. Consequently, they see marginal revenue curves that are also horizontal and that coincide with the demand curves. To maximize its profits, the competitive firm chooses the output level at which $MC = MR = p_x$. In the diagrams this occurs at the seven-unit output level for each firm. Since all firms in the market maximize profits in the same way, the market output is 7,000 units.

If the market is monopolized and the monopolist continues with the 7,000-unit output level, the monopolist's *MC* would be equal to the product price of $14. But *MR* for the monopolist at that output level is only $8 because the monopolist faces a downward-sloping demand curve. To maximize profits, the monopolist cuts the output back to 5,000 units per day and raises the product price to $16. The monopolist's $MC = MR = \$12$ at that output level.

Since the monopolist causes the output of the product to fall below the competitive level, resources are misallocated. Here, the resources that should be used to produce the 2,000 units between the monopolistic and competitive production levels are forced to be used where they yield less satisfaction to society or, perhaps, are even forced into temporary unemployment. And as we saw previously, when resources are misallocated, social well-being is restricted. For this reason, monopoly is included along with externalities such as pollution in the list of possible market failures that can plague the market economy. To see this clearly, we must apply the tools that we developed in the analysis of pollution in Chapter 4. Specifically, we need to bring the cost-benefit analysis of social well-being maximization into Figure 8.4. Consider first the market demand curve *DD*. This demand curve indicates the maximum price that consumers are willing to pay for each unit of the good or service. And as discussed in Chapter 4, since it can be reasonably assumed that the maximum price consumers are willing to pay for a particular unit is dictated by the satisfaction they anticipate from consuming the item, the market demand curve is also the marginal private benefit curve. For simplicity, let's suppose that the good being considered is individually consumed; that is, let's suppose that there are no externalities in consumption. Given this, the demand curve of Figure 8.4 is both the marginal private benefit and marginal social benefit curve, and so we label it *MSB*.

Now consider the market supply curve, *SS*, in Figure 8.4. This curve reflects the marginal cost of production borne by the producers, and so it is labeled *MC*. In the terms of Chapter 4, this curve is the marginal private cost curve. And if we assume that this good is produced without externalities in production, this curve also reflects the marginal social cost of producing the product. For simplicity, we make this assumption, and so we also label the supply curve as the marginal social cost curve (*MSC*).

We now have in Figure 8.4 curves indicating both the marginal social benefit from consuming this product and the marginal social cost of producing it. What quantity of the good should be produced? By now you know that the answer is that production should be carried to the point where social well-being is maximized, that is, to the point where *MSB* = *MSC*. In Figure 8.4, *MSB* = *MSC* at the 7,000-unit output level. As has been pointed out, this is the quantity that the market would cause to be produced if it were competitively structured. However, if the industry is monopolized, output is restricted to the 5,000 level. Now consider each unit of output between the monopolistic and competitive levels. For each of these 2,000 units, the benefit to society (*MSB*) of consuming the unit is greater than the cost to society (*MSC*) of producing it. As such, if these units are produced, social well-being would be enhanced by the difference between *MSB* and *MSC*. The total value of this enhancement in social well-being is given by the area of the shaded triangle *ABC* in Figure 8.4. Since these units are not produced by the monopolist, social well-being is restricted by the area of this triangle. We call this the **deadweight welfare loss due to monopoly.**

Entry Restrictions

Prices, costs, profits, and losses in a market economy provide the incentives for a continuous reallocation of resources from uses where they contribute less to uses where they contribute more to social well-being. In industries where demand is falling or costs are rising, investors will eventually receive less-than-average returns on their investments. Firms in these industries are said to be incurring economic *losses.* As it becomes possible for them to do so, investors and the firms producing those products will leave the industry, reducing supplies and raising prices relative to costs, until the returns to remaining investors are average for the economy as a whole.

In areas where demand is increasing or costs are falling, investors receive higher-than-average returns, or economic *profits.* New investment and new firms have incentives to enter the industry. If they are successful in doing so, product supplies increase, and prices fall relative to costs until the return on investment is again average. The profit-and-loss mechanism is thus the prime force for contracting productive capacity and output where these are not so urgently desired and for expanding them where they are more urgently desired.

deadweight welfare loss due to monopoly
The reduction in social welfare due to the exercise of monopoly power.

Monopoly power tends to throw sand in the gears of the reallocation mechanism. Over time, firms with monopoly power in profitable industries, those that yield higher-than-average rates of return to investors, may be able to impede or block the entry of new investment and new firms into those industries. To the extent that they are able to do so, outputs will be lower, prices will be higher, and profits will be greater than they would be if entry were open, free, and easy. Such **barriers to entry** can be classified conveniently into (1) private barriers, and (2) government barriers.

barriers to entry
Impediments to the entry of new firms into a market, such as product differentiation and government licensing, usually used by monopolists to protect their favored positions.

Private Barriers

Private entry barriers arise from the nature of markets themselves or from marketplace actions of the firms that enjoy their fruits. There are many privately imposed restrictions on entry into specific industries. We shall list some of the more important ones—not necessarily in the order of their importance. First, consider a situation in which a firm or the firms already in a market own or control most of some key raw material needed for making the product. All they must do to restrict entry is deny potential entrants access to it. Second, suppose that when new firms are in the process of entering, the existing firms threaten to lower prices to the extent that the newcomers would experience substantial losses. This threat tends to discourage entry. It is also difficult on those already in the market, but they may be able to withstand temporary losses better than the potential entrants can. Third, product differentiation may be successful in retarding entry in some instances.

Firms often try to differentiate their products from those of their rivals. Once the products are differentiated, firms then attempt to convince the public that their products are not just different, but superior. Consumers tend to prefer the old tried-and-true brands and to be skeptical of new entrants. Product differentiation reinforces this attitude and makes it tougher for potential entrants to actually enter certain markets. This is no doubt one factor that discourages entry into the automobile industry. A similar barrier to entry can be created through product proliferation. Perhaps the best example of this practice is found in the cereal aisle of your local grocery. As pointed out earlier in this chapter, the four largest cereal producers control almost 87 percent of the breakfast cereal market. Yet a walk through the cereal aisle will certainly turn up dozens of different products. Why do the "big four" offer so many varieties? One answer might be that they are attempting to respond to consumer tastes. A more skeptical answer is that by offering so many versions of their product, any potential entrant's job is made more difficult since, to effectively compete, the newcomer must also offer a wide variety. Product proliferation, then, can have either positive or negative effects on social well-being. To the extent that it exists to serve the varied tastes of consumers, proliferation enhances well-being. When it exists to protect monopoly power, its impact is negative.

network economies
Situation in which the value of a product to a consumer is enhanced when others also choose to consume the same product.

In addition to these traditional private barriers, modern technologies have increased the incidence and importance of another factor which can severely limit market entry. This factor is often referred to as **network economies.** Network economies exist when the value of a product to a consumer is enhanced when others also choose to consume the same product. Microsoft's Windows operating system is a classic example of how network economies act as a barrier to entry. Windows and its companion software applications make it easier for a user to benefit from a personal computer, but the value of the computer's power is increased manifold when other users can share and access the same data files and programs. Today, a computer that cannot share files and programs with other computers has very limited uses. Because of this, it is in the best interest of computer users to adopt software standards that facilitate communications among them. Over time, Microsoft Windows became the de facto standard for home and office computers, which means that a new entrant into the operating system market would have to convince millions of users to make a switch or give up one of the most valuable aspects of their computers. This is one of the primary reasons that Microsoft has not faced serious competition in the operating system market.

Other factors could be added to our list of private barriers as they are limited only by the realities of the marketplace and the imagination of the firms that wish to protect their monopoly positions.

Government Barriers

The firms already in specific industries have difficulty in policing and enforcing restrictions on entry. Consequently, they frequently turn to the government for help. They get city councils, state legislatures, and Congress to pass legislation restricting entry into their markets. Often those government units seem not at all reluctant to take actions that confer monopoly power on certain special interest groups and help them to maintain it over time.

First, in some industries such as railroads, trucking, airlines, and communications, regulatory commissions have established entry-blocking rules that have all the force of law. Initially, regulatory commissions such as the Interstate Commerce Commission and the Federal Communications Commission were established to protect customers from certain practices of monopolistic firms. Over time, however, the range of commissions' activities has expanded to include control of entry into the industries they are regulating. In recent years one could well suspect that their primary function is to protect the firms from consumers. Fortunately, in many of these cases, the regulatory apparatus has been dismantled through deregulation. We discuss the issues of regulation and deregulation in detail later in this chapter.

Second, individual states have many occupational licensing laws on the books licensing plumbers, undertakers, physicians, barbers, and a host of other occupations. Whatever else such laws may do, one thing is certain—they restrict entry into the licensed occupations. Licensing standards and licensing examinations usually are controlled by licensed members of the occupation concerned, that is, by those who are already in it and who have a vested interest in keeping the number of new entrants relatively low.

A number of other forms of government-imposed entry barriers exist. Import duties and import restrictions limit the entry of foreign firms into many of our markets. Patent and copyright laws impede entry. Exclusive franchises to taxicab companies and casinos block the entry of new firms. Zoning ordinances and building codes are used to restrict entry into certain housing markets. Like that of private barriers, the list of government-imposed barriers to entry is a lengthy one.

Nonprice Competition

A common practice in industries containing only a few firms is for firms to compete on grounds other than price. Each such firm in a given industry can increase its profits if it can increase its monopoly power at the expense of its rivals—that is, if it can increase its own share of the total market for the product. One obvious way for a firm to increase its market share is to reduce the price at which it sells its brand of the product relative to the prices charged by the other firms in the industry. But price-cutting presents dangers to the firm that does it. The other firms can cut their prices, too, thus preventing the firm from accomplishing what it set out to do. Worse yet, all firms could end up with lower prices, a larger industry output, and smaller profits. So firms in imperfectly competitive markets are reluctant to use price-cutting to increase their individual market shares. Usually they attempt to increase their degrees of monopoly power through nonprice competition.

Advertising is a major form of nonprice competition. Although it may provide consumers with important information about a firm's product, its major objective is to increase the market share or the monopoly power of the firm that does it. Unlike a price cut by the firm, a successful advertising campaign is hard for other firms to duplicate. Other firms will try to duplicate or match the advertising campaign of the first firm, but they need time to do so. Meanwhile, the first firm reaps the rewards of its efforts. Eventually, if other firms succeed with effective campaigns of their own, all may end up with approximately the same market shares they had before. Much of the advertising effort will have been wasted, and since the resources used for advertising purposes are not available to produce other goods and services, consumers receive a smaller total output from the economy as a whole.

Periodic change in the design and quality of the product is another major form of nonprice competition. The annual model changes of cars fall into this category. Model changes may incorporate new technological developments, and to the extent that they do so, they enable given quantities of resources to make greater contributions to consumer satisfaction. But they may also simply rearrange or change the chrome and the shape, making old models obsolete and new models no better. Another example is the periodic "upgrades" in the software applications industry. To what extent does version 6.2 of a spreadsheet program offer real functional improvements over version 6.1? Successful design and quality innovations by one firm, like successful advertising, may be hard for other firms to imitate immediately and may increase the market share and monopoly power of the firm for a time. However, if other firms are successful over time with their own design and quality changes, all may again end up with approximately the same market shares or with some rearrangement of market shares.

SHOULD WE FEAR BIGNESS?

Does bigness of business enterprises put our economic future in jeopardy? The economic analysis we just completed leads to the conclusion that in industries in which monopoly power is exercised, outputs will be lower and prices will be higher than they would be if the industries were competitive. Profitable firms with monopoly power also may be able to successfully block the entry of additional investment and new firms into their industries. Thus, monopoly power may cause the resources or productive capabilities of the economy to be allocated poorly among alternative uses, with too little of the economy's resources allocated to the production of products made by industries in which monopoly power exists and too much allocated to products that are produced competitively. In addition, monopoly power in imperfectly competitive markets may result in some waste of resources on nonprice competition.

Bigness and Monopoly Power

Before turning our attention to identifying the extent of the economic problems caused by the exercise of monopoly power in the United States, it is essential to bear in mind the difference between the terms *big business* and *monopoly*. In particular, it must be recalled that monopoly power is not determined by a firm's absolute size but rather by its ability to control the output of the industry of which it is a part. Thus a firm that is truly enormous in terms of assets or sales may have comparatively little monopoly power if it happens to operate in a market along with numerous other very large firms. On the other hand, a very small firm might have a great deal of monopoly power if it has few significant rivals.

The distinction depends on the position of the firm in the market in which it operates. For example, the Ford Motor Company is a very large firm in terms of its assets and annual sales volume, yet it likely has very little monopoly power in today's market. If it drops out of the market, other firms will easily take up the slack. If it raises its prices relative to those of other firms in the auto industry, it will very quickly price itself out of the market. It has much actual and potential competition. On the contrary, Stillwater Power and Light Company in Stillwater, Oklahoma, is a small firm in terms of assets and annual volume of sales, but it comes very close to being a pure monopolist. It has no direct rivals, with the possible exception of the local gas company. We must therefore be careful not to confuse bigness with monopoly power. In assessing monopoly power of firms, we must look at specific industries and at individual firms within each industry to see whether they are able to affect significantly market outputs, prices, and buyers' access to the kind of product produced and sold by the industry.

Outputs and Prices

When imperfectly competitive firms restrict output and increase prices, they impose an economic cost on society in the form of reduced social well-being. This reduction in well-being is the deadweight welfare loss due to monopoly. We can better understand the issue of "fearing bigness" if we have a definitive estimate of this loss. While no definitive estimate exists, a consensus estimate places the loss at about 1 percent of gross domestic product per year.[1] That is, monopolistic elements within the economy serve to reduce economic well-being, as measured by GDP, by about 1 percent of GDP per year. And it must be recalled that this loss in well-being comes not from pure monopolists, since pure monopoly is typically illegal, but rather from firms operating in highly concentrated markets.

We know that the consensus places the deadweight welfare loss due to monopoly at about 1 percent of GDP, but how significant is this loss? This decision is for each of us to make. However, we must bear in mind three points when making the decision:

1. A basic economic truth is that while the economy's ability to produce is limited, society's desires for goods and services are unlimited. Consequently, any economic factor that tends to reduce the economy's ability to produce goods and services must be viewed as making an already difficult situation worse.

2. Although 1 percent of GDP may not seem significant, 1 percent of GDP amounted to more than $10.5 billion in 2002.[2] In other words, if all vestiges of monopoly power had been eliminated prior to 2002, during that year society could have consumed $10.5 billion in additional goods and services. For example, if the increased production due to the elimination of monopoly were equally distributed, during 2001 each individual in the United States would have received just over $365 in additional goods and services.

3. A deadweight loss of 1 percent of GDP is the cost to society of monopoly when monopoly is illegal and would be, no doubt, much greater were it not for government attempts to limit the exercise of monopoly power through legal action of the type discussed in the introduction to this chapter.

Entry Restrictions and Resource Allocation

While the estimation of the loss to society of monopoly power in terms of outputs and prices is rather straightforward, identifying the loss caused by *private* barriers to entry is not. In fact, there is no consensus as to the extent of private barriers at all. This does not mean that private barriers do not exist, just that they are very difficult to measure with any precision. A useful informal approach might involve addressing why firms seek to erect barriers to entering their markets in the first place. They do so to protect what they see as their favored relative positions. Any firm successful enough to enjoy significant profits will, of necessity, attract rivals. This is the role profits play in the market economy. In a competitive environment, above-normal profits serve as a signal to resource owners that the consuming public wishes to have the output of industry expanded, which is exactly what new rivals would cause to happen. The existing firms, of course, would prefer to block

[1] William G. Shephard, *The Economics of Industrial Organization* (Upper Saddle River, NJ: Prentice Hall, 1997), p. 109.
[2] Table 1.2.

the entry of the new rivals so that they might continue to enjoy above-normal profits. This leads to the conclusion that significant barriers to entry must exist if both concentration levels *and* profits remain high within a given market for an extended period of time. As an example, consider the cereal breakfast foods industry. As noted in Table 8.1, the four largest firms in this market control about 87 percent of that industry's output. Equally important, these same firms have controlled a similarly large share of this market since the 1940s *and* have enjoyed relatively great profits since that time. Why have there been no significant new entrants? At least part of the answer must be that substantial private barriers to entry exist in this market, with the most likely culprits being the extensive advertising done by the dominant cereal makers and their tendency to proliferate differing brands of their products. Consequently, the combined existence of concentrated markets and relatively high profits over an extended period of time provides at least circumstantial, although not scientific, evidence of the existence of significant private barriers to entry.

Where entry to markets is blocked by law, it is easier to find evidence of resource misallocation. One of the more glaring instances of resources being used in quantities that are relatively too small is the medical profession. Physicians' average net incomes are at the top of the list for professions or occupations. Shortages of medical doctors have been publicly proclaimed for years. Yet, with their tight legal control of entry into medical training programs and into the profession itself, medical doctors continue to deter almost half of the annual qualified applicants to medical schools from entering training. In many local building markets, housing costs have soared, and profits to builders have been high because building codes have inhibited the introduction and use of new technology and prefabrication. In still another industry, try hailing a taxicab in any large city during the morning and evening rush hours.

Nonprice Competition

The impact of nonprice competition on the public is far less clear. The total expenditure on advertising in 2002 amounted to more than $237 billion[3]—somewhere in the neighborhood of 2 percent of current GDP. However, about a fifth of the total was for advertising in local newspapers, a type of advertising that provides information to consumers on what is available, where, and at what price. Another $42 billion was spent for television advertising and is not a total loss to consumers. It is payment—perhaps an overpayment—for the "free" television programs that we see.

We also cannot be sure whether or how much the public loses from product design and quality changes. Many useful innovations are introduced in this way— the self-starter on the automobile, no-frost freezers and refrigerators, word processors, and thousands of other items that make our lives more comfortable. But there

---

[3]U.S. Department of Commerce, Bureau of the Census, *Statistical Abstract of the United States, 2003,* Table 1274.

are many others whose only purpose is to make the previous years' models obsolete.

THE PECULIAR CASE OF NATURAL MONOPOLY

average cost
Ratio of costs to the number of units being produced, sometimes called the per-unit cost.

The analysis presented thus far offers little to commend monopoly. But if we are to be thorough, we must consider evidence of any positive effects of monopoly as well as the negative. And in one circumstance monopoly can actually be defended economically. To see this, we need to add a new concept of firm costs to the total cost and marginal cost concepts that we have been using so far. This concept is the **average cost** of production, which is found by simply dividing the firm's total cost by the number of units being produced. For example, if a firm is incurring total costs of $500 to produce 50 units of its good, then its average cost is $10 per unit ($500/50 = $10). Assuming that both of the firm's inputs, labor and capital, may be varied, Figure 8.5 presents a typical long-run average cost (AC) for a firm.

The most important characteristic of a long-run average cost curve is its U shape, which indicates that average cost declines initially as output per unit of time increases but eventually turns and increases. When the firm is on the downward-sloping portion of the curve (production levels less than Q_0), it is said to be enjoying **economies of scale.** In this situation, the average cost of production may be reduced simply by increasing the firm's size or scale and producing more of the product. Suppose, for example, that General Motors was constrained to produce only 1,000 cars per year rather than the 3 to 4 million cars it now produces. In such a circumstance, assembly lines would be out of the question. Each car would have to be produced essentially by hand. Also ruled out would be bulk-buying discounts for inputs and any benefits that might be derived from the division and specialization of labor. That is, as Henry Ford realized, producing such a small number of cars rules out the use of numerous production techniques that are capable of radically reducing average cost. Thus, a GM producing only 1,000 cars per year would be clearly operating at a much smaller output level than Q_0. It could enjoy significantly reduced average cost simply by increasing the scale of its operation.

economies of scale
Situation that occurs when long-run average cost can be reduced simply by increasing the firm's size and producing more of the product.

diseconomies of scale
Situation that occurs beyond a certain size and production level, when average cost rises as production is increased.

Such "economies" of large-scale production do not continue over the entire range of output possibilities. As certain as we are that economies of scale exist over some range of output, we are equally certain that if the scale of operation continues to grow, eventually, long-run average cost will turn and go up. When average cost starts increasing (output levels greater than Q_0), we say the firm is encountering **diseconomies of scale.** The most obvious explanation for this phenomenon is that the firm simply becomes too large to be effectively managed, with each increase in size adding an additional layer of bureaucracy to the production process. Elliott Estes, former president of General Motors, said it best: "Chevrolet is such a big monster that you twist its tail and nothing happens at the other end for months and months. It is so gigantic that there isn't any way to really run it."[4]

[4]J. Patrick Wright, *On a Clear Day You Can See General Motors* (Grosse Pointe, MI: Wright Enterprises, 1979), pp. 114–115.

FIGURE 8.5 **Long-Run Average Cost of Production for a Typical Firm**
The long-run average cost of production for a typical firm is U-shaped. For production levels less than Q_0, an increase in production lowers average cost. This is the range of economies of scale. Production increases beyond Q_0 lead to an increasing average cost; thus, this range is referred to as the range of diseconomies of scale.

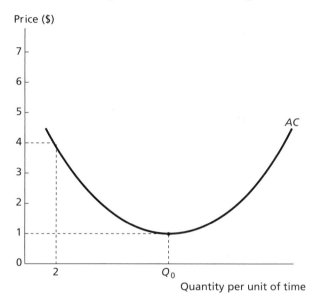

Another factor that might lead to diseconomies of scale is worker boredom. The division and specialization of labor inherent in modern production processes narrows the scope of each worker's job so that the worker is capable of becoming very adept, that is, very efficient at the job. This sort of job narrowing can go too far, however. When it does, boredom is likely to set in and the outcome is reduced, rather than increased, productivity.

A typical situation for a firm, then, is to initially enjoy falling average cost as its size and production level are increased due to economies of scale. Beyond some production level, however, diseconomies of scale arise, which cause average cost to turn and go up. These forces taken together give the long-run average cost curve its U shape.

Now back to the case of natural monopoly. The average cost curve of Figure 8.5 shows that the average cost of producing the product reaches a minimum of $1 per unit when the level of production is Q_0 per unit of time. Suppose that this level of production is 10 units per week. Now consider three separate cases. In the first case, the market for the product is such that 1,000 units may be sold during a week. Here, the market could support 100 firms (1,000/10 = 100), each producing at the minimum possible average cost of $1. In this market, we could expect a high level of competition among a large number of firms, each of which is small relative to the market.

As a second case, suppose the market is such that only 100 units of the product may be sold per week. Here, only 10 efficient firms could be supported. We would say that the concentration and thus the potential for monopoly power is greater in this case than in the first.

Now consider an extreme third case in which only 10 units per week may be sold in the market. In this case, only one efficient firm, a natural monopolist, could be supported. This case is referred to as a **natural monopoly** because no matter how many firms are initially in operation in this market, the largest will have an undeniable average cost advantage over its smaller rivals and should eventually push each of them out of business. That is, when the cost structure of an industry is such that the average cost of production is minimized when only one firm operates, the industry is a natural monopoly.

natural monopoly
An industry in which the average cost of production is minimized by having only one firm produce the product.

As discussed above, society's interests are well-served when markets are composed of many relatively small firms in competition with one another. When natural monopoly is present, this is not the case. To see this point, return to Figure 8.5 and assume that output level Q_0 occurs at 10 units of production per week. Would society be better served by having the 10 units of output produced by one firm or by five firms? With one firm, a natural monopolist, the average cost of production is \$1. With five firms, each producing two units per week, the average cost is \$4 per unit. Thus, requiring "competition," that is, insisting on the existence of five firms rather than a monopolist, causes the product to be produced at an average cost four times greater than necessary. In an opportunity cost sense, this implies that the value of resources needed to produce 10 units of the good when production is distributed among five firms is four times that required when production is concentrated in the natural monopolist. In this case, the benefits to society of allowing the monopolist to exist are clear.

Although these benefits are undeniable, as we have seen, monopolists tend to impose costs on society as well in the form of reduced output and increased prices. Thus resource misallocation appears to be inevitable. If we allow the market to operate on its own, natural monopoly will result and we reap a deadweight welfare loss due to the monopolist's tendency to reduce output below the socially optimal level. Conversely, if we choose through government intervention to require numerous firms to exist, we cause the product to be produced at an average cost above that which is possible. For most of this century, we in the United States have chosen a third policy option, government regulation.

When Should Government Regulate Business?

Numerous justifications have been offered for government regulation of business. Although most of these have economic aspects, they are often primarily an outgrowth of social and political forces. Experience with various attempts at regulation has taught that regulation works best, and is most likely to be successful, when it is limited to those cases in which its primary justification is economic. In general, government regulation of business may be called for when two conditions exist in the private market. First, there must be market failure; that is, a situation must exist where the market, operating on its own, fails to provide a well-being–maximizing allocation of resources. Second, and perhaps more important, there must be reason to believe that the market outcome can be improved through some degree of government control over the market in a cost-effective manner. This second condition is particularly crucial. Regulation is not cheap. Regulatory agencies, commissions, inspector services, and other bureaucracies must be established. And the firms being regulated must also expend much energy in complying with the regulations. In each case, resources are used, and being so used, they become unavailable for other production processes. Consequently, in a given case, although some degree of market failure may be present in a market, regulation may not be appropriate if the cost of regulation outweighs the benefit to society of correcting the failure.

Consider again natural monopoly. If the market is left to its own devices, monopoly results—inevitably leading to a deadweight welfare loss due to the monopolist's tendency to restrict output. And forcing competition, which in this case would increase the average cost of production, is no bargain for society either. It is this trade-off that might justify government regulation. That is, regulation might be designed to allow the monopolist to exist (yielding the benefit of a low average cost of production), while attempting to force the monopolist to produce at the competitive output level and charge the competitive price (to avoid the cost imposed by the deadweight welfare loss). Thus the process of regulation is not guaranteed to succeed in increasing social well-being above the level that the market would provide. Potential pitfalls include the problems associated with estimating the competitive output and price levels as well as the costs associated with administering and complying with the regulation. Social well-being is certainly not enhanced if the cost of the regulation outweighs the benefit of correcting the market failure. Fortunately, relatively few markets have cost structures that yield economies of scale sufficient to justify their being viewed as natural monopolies. Examples might include local distribution of natural gas and electricity and, perhaps, local telephone and cable television service.

If natural monopoly is so rare, you might wonder why we have had so much government regulation of business in the United States. Without doubt, the primary answer to this question is that much of government regulation was inappropriately applied originally. For this reason a strong deregulation movement began in the late 1970s that has led to the dismantling of the existing regulatory apparatus in industries such as airlines and trucking. And, in general, since these regulations were never economically justified, the outcomes for consumers from deregulation have been positive. But this is not to say that all regulation of business is inappropriate and should be eliminated. The rare case of natural monopoly shows that, in some instances, regulation can work to the benefit of society. And we implicitly addressed two other cases in previous chapters.

The first of these concerns circumstances in which consumers lack significant information about a particular good or service. That is, beginning with Chapter 2, we have assumed that consumers have the information necessary to make informed, well-being–maximizing decisions when they purchase goods and services. When this information is lacking, consumers can make choices that maximize neither their nor society's well-being. Suppose, for example, that the rear door of a certain minivan has an unreasonably high tendency to fly open if hit from behind, and this fact is unknown to consumers. The market demand curve would reflect the benefits that consumers anticipate from the minivans, but their anticipations would prove incorrect. In such cases, appropriate regulation might take the form of requiring or actually providing safety testing of all automobiles so that consumers can make informed decisions. In other cases of deficient information, appropriate regulatory tools might include the labeling of specific product ingredients, health and safety codes for products and workplaces, or in extreme cases, the outlawing of items deemed inherently too unsafe for general consumption.

A final circumstance that might prompt economically defensible regulation concerns poorly defined property rights, the classic case of which is the externality of pollution in a production process. Recall that it is the collectively consumed nature of the environment and the absence of property rights to it that cause economic units to pollute. And we indicated that appropriate government responses to the problem might take the form of taxes, direct controls on emissions, outright prohibitions on the use of particular substances, or in some cases, the establishment of markets for pollution rights. A similar problem exists with respect to airwave communications since no individual or group has a property right to broadcast exclusively on a particular frequency. For this reason, the Federal Communications Commission gives radio stations what amounts to a property right to broadcast on a specific frequency within a given geographic area.

In some cases, government regulation may be a useful tool to improve the functioning of failing private markets. Care must be taken, however, before concluding that regulation is appropriate. The cost of regulation must be kept in the forefront: Resources to administer and comply with regulations are not free. Thus, prior to embarking on a regulation, society must be certain that the benefit of regulation is worth its cost. And even if there is strong reason to believe that regulation will be cost-effective—and, as a consequence, regulation is entered into—the process must be closely monitored to ensure that the outcomes serve the interests of the general public. Numerous students of regulation have suggested that in a typical scenario, the regulatory agency is "taken captive" by the industry it was established to control. The reasons for this are unclear. Perhaps the firms of an industry are able to use their political influence to ensure that "friendly" regulators are appointed. Or maybe it occurs simply as an outgrowth of the fact that regulatory bodies have to rely on the firms being regulated for the data they need to carry out their tasks. Regardless, the outcome of this **capture theory,** as it is called, is that the regulatory agency decides on policy based on the interests of the firms being regulated rather than on the interests of the consuming public. Again, the capture theory does not suggest that regulation should be abolished, but simply that it must be very carefully entered into and then closely monitored.

capture theory of regulation
The belief that regulatory agencies, regardless of their initial intentions, eventually come to serve the interests of the firms being regulated rather than the interests of the general public.

Regulation and Corporate Responsibility

A number of high-profile cases in the early 2000s renewed the public's interest in government regulation of business, especially with respect to corporate responsibility and the abuse of market power by large firms. Two of these cases involved firms that operated in industries that had undergone significant deregulation during previous decades, WorldCom in the telecommunications industry and Enron, which brokered the distribution and transmission of electrical power. Both of these large firms commanded significant shares of their respective markets and reported above-normal profits for years prior to the accounting scandals that forced both into bankruptcy and reorganization. In a nutshell, both cases involved improperly reported financial statements that concealed the true costs, and therefore the true profits, of the firm. Some observers argued that the scandals were a result of lax or inadequate government regulation, which created the environment, or even the incentive, to cheat. In response, federal regulations were enacted in 2002 to promote a greater degree of corporate responsibility.

corporations
Firms organized as legal entities separate from their owners, the stockholders, who, by law, have limited liability.

Most large firms in the United States are organized as **corporations.** A corporation is a firm that is considered a legal entity separate from its owners—the stockholders. When you purchase a share of stock in a corporation, you are purchasing a unit of ownership in that firm. By incorporating, firms can finance their operations by pooling the money of thousands, or even millions, of investors. Corporate stocks are attractive to investors because stockholders enjoy limited liability from corporate losses. Stockholders of a corporation, even though they own the firm, cannot by law be held personally responsible for all the debts and actions of the corporation. A stockholder's liability is limited to the value of his or her own stock. Although only about 20 percent of all businesses in the United States are corporations, nearly all big firms are corporations. Corporations account for about 88 percent of all sales nationwide.

The corporate form of business also has some disadvantages. One is that individual stockholders have a limited voice in how the corporation is operated and managed. Most stockholders only have the power to vote for a board of directors who oversee corporate policies and the hiring of top-level managers. (The value of an individual stockholder's vote is based on the number of shares held.) Thus, even though they own the corporation, stockholders do not generally engage in the day-to-day operations of the business. This lack of direct stockholder control often creates what economists call an *agency problem.* In effect, the chief executive officer (CEO) and other top managers of a corporation are agents hired by a board of directors to manage the firm on behalf of the stockholders. An agency problem arises when the managers, or agents, pursue interests and goals that diverge from the interests and goals of the stockholders. For example, although stockholders may desire capital investments that promote long-term growth of sales and profits, a CEO might instead pursue more risky ventures that, if successful, promise a short-term increase in the corporation's stock price. This is a plausible scenario because CEO compensation is often tied to the corporation's stock price, usually in the form of **stock options.** A stock option allows the holder to purchase a set

stock options
Guarantees issued by a corporation which allow the holder to purchase a set number of shares at a fixed price, often called the strike price; stock options are frequently used as a form of managerial compensation.

number of shares at a fixed price, often called the *strike price*. If the stock price rises above the strike price, the holder can exercise the option, purchase the stock, and then sell it on the market at a profit.

Many CEOs and other top managers have been accused of enriching themselves through stock option plans and other means by pursuing corporate policies that were in their own financial interest and not in the best interest of the corporate stockholders. In the WorldCom and Enron cases, agency problems apparently led some executives to misstate the financial position of the corporations. At Enron, this was compounded by the fact that the accounting firm responsible for auditing the corporation's financial statements was the same firm hired to provide consulting services in an effort to achieve greater profits. Remarkably, before the 2002 reforms, no government regulation prevented this clear case of conflicting financial interests. Individual stockholders lost millions of dollars in investments due to the WorldCom and Enron accounting scandals, and in an effort to align the financial interests of CEOs with those of stockholders, the 2002 reforms now require CEOs to sign and personally verify their firms' financial statements. If overt discrepancies are discovered, CEOs now face criminal penalties, including prison terms. Additionally, these reforms, which were designed to produce a greater sense of confidence in corporations by stockholders and investors, also seem to reflect an increasing public acceptance of government regulation of big business.

Summary

Most members of the general public seem to believe that, regardless of how consumer-friendly firms' origins might have been, as firms grow large in size, eventually they will exercise the strength that comes from their bigness to hold back output, raise prices, and waste society's scarce resources. That is, in economic terms the general public fears the monopoly power of large firms. As such, accounts of conspiracies to raise prices such as those noted in the introduction to this chapter come as no surprise. In this chapter, we addressed the issue of fearing bigness in the business world from a systematic, analytical perspective. One of the most important conclusions from this analysis is that bigness, by itself, is not a good predictor of the types of behavior one might expect from monopolies. Specifically, it was determined that for a firm to have and exercise monopoly power, it need not be large in absolute terms. Rather, monopoly power exists when a firm is large relative to the total output of the industry in which it operates. Thus, an enormous firm like the Ford Motor Company may have rather little monopoly power since it is surrounded by numerous equally large rivals. At the same time, your local cable company, although only a tiny fraction of the size of Ford, enjoys the position of being nearly a pure monopolist. Consequently, the question we addressed is whether the public is correct in fearing the monopoly power of firms, regardless of their absolute size.

From a theoretical perspective, there is little to commend with respect to monopoly power. Monopoly power induces firms to produce smaller outputs and charge higher prices than would be the case if the markets in which they operate were competitive. Further, firms with monopoly power are frequently able to restrict entry into their industries, thus compounding the output restriction and higher-price problem and inhibiting movement of resources from less valuable to more valuable uses. Finally, they may also engage in nonprice competition that results in the waste of some of the economy's scarce resources.

Empirically, there is evidence that monopolistic elements within the U.S. economy have imposed, and continue to impose, an economic cost on society in terms of reduced social welfare. Much of the loss in well-being may come from rather small firms. Estimates of the deadweight welfare loss due to monopoly place it at about 1 percent of GDP per year. In terms of real 2002 GDP, this implies that monopolistic elements within the economy were responsible for a $10.5 billion reduction in GDP during that year. Consequently, it is important to keep a close watch on existing and potential monopoly problems. The more competition the market economy can sustain, the better the price mechanism will operate in allocating the economy's scarce resources among their many uses. The primary pro-competition tools at government's disposal are the existing antitrust laws. Of particular importance are the Sherman Act and the Clayton Act, which effectively outlaw both monopoly and anticompetitive behaviors deemed injurious to public well-being.

In the unusual case of natural monopoly, however, the impact of monopoly on social well-being is mixed. This circumstance and the problems caused by poorly defined property rights and consumers having deficient information about products can lead to calls for government regulation of private business. Care must be taken prior to entering into regulation to ensure that the benefit of the regulation is at least as great as its cost. Further, even in those cases where regulation seems cost-effective, the regulatory process must be closely monitored to avoid the problems associated with the capture theory of regulation.

Discussion Questions

1. Explain what a concentration ratio measures and how it can be used to indicate whether a firm is operating in a competitive industry or an industry that is close to the monopolistic model. What shortcomings do concentration ratios have?

2. The profit-maximizing condition for a competitive firm requires production to be carried to the point where marginal revenue is equal to marginal cost. Explain why. Is this condition the same for firms with monopoly power?

3. What are barriers to entry, and how do they inhibit the proper functioning of a market?

4. A merger of formerly competing firms forming a monopoly invariably leads to a fall in industry output. Why?

5. Using the deadweight welfare loss diagram, compare and contrast the outcomes of competition and monopoly.

6. Explain why bigness and monopoly power are not necessarily the same.

7. What is natural monopoly, and what dilemma does it pose for public policy? Give examples of natural monopoly.

8. The typical firm's long-run average cost curve is U-shaped. Why?

9. List and discuss the three economic justifications for government regulation. If one of these exists, does that mean that regulation should be imposed?

10. Define and explain the capture theory of regulation.

11. Explain how agency problems contribute to the abuse of market power by managers of large corporations. Can regulation prevent agency problems? Discuss.

12. What are stock options? Stock option plans are often used as an incentive to hire top-level managers, but do they always create the right incentives for managerial behavior? Explain.

13. In Chapter 3, you learned the concept of diminishing returns. In this chapter, the concept of diseconomies of scale was presented. Compare/contrast these two concepts.

14. Suppose two industries exist, A and B, both of which have concentration ratios of 80 percent. In A, the four largest firms control the following shares of the market, respectively: 60 percent, 10 percent, 7 percent, and 3 percent. In B, the four largest each have a 20 percent share of the market. In which would you expect more potential for monopoly power? What does this say about using concentration ratios as a measure of the potential for monopoly power?

15. Suppose that the market for (extremely) high-end sports cars is such that no more than 100,000 can be sold per year and that at this level of production, the industry's long-run average cost curve is declining. Why will this market most likely naturally gravitate to having only one producer?

Additional Readings

Adams, Walter, and James W. Brock. *The Structure of American Industry*. 10th ed. New York: Prentice Hall, 2000.
A thorough economic analysis of various industries. Although this title has been out of print for some time, it remains a classic.

Adams, Walter, and James W. Brock. *The Bigness Complex: Industry, Labor, and Government in the American Economy*. 2nd ed. Palo Alto, CA: Stanford University Press, 2004.

Best, Michael H. *The New Competitive Advantage: The Renewal of American Industry*. Oxford: Oxford University Press, 2001.
Discusses the resurgence of the competitiveness of American industry in the 1990s.

Lo, Andrew W., ed. *The Industrial Organization and Regulation of the Securities Industry*. National Bureau of Economic Research Project Report. Chicago: University of Chicago Press, 1996.
Collection of papers from an NBER conference, discussing the regulation of the securities industry. Comments by other authors appear at the end of each paper.

Rosenbaum, David I., ed. *Market Dominance: How Firms Gain, Hold, or Lose It and the Impact on Economic Performance.* Westport, CT: Praeger Publishers, 1998.
Each chapter highlights a different American big business which has dominated its industry, from Alcoa to IBM to Microsoft, and discusses its impact on consumers and the economy.

Viscusi, W. Kip, John M. Vernon, and Joseph E. Harrington, Jr. *Economics of Regulation and Antitrust.* 2nd ed. Cambridge, MA: MIT Press, 1996.
Thorough examination of both antitrust and regulation issues, such as airline, cable television, and product safety regulations, and cartels, mergers, and antitrust laws.

World Wide Web Resources

Antitrust and Competition Law
www.hg.org/antitrust.html

Created by Hieros Gamos, one of the first legal and government sites on the Internet. The site provides links to national and international antitrust Web pages, including government organizations and other issues.

Antitrust Policy
www.antitrust.org/

Has up-to-the-minute antitrust headlines, research topics, and antitrust cases based on subjects such as collusion and price discrimination.

Federal Communications Commission (FCC) Home Page
www.fcc.gov/

The mission of this independent government agency is to encourage competition in all communication markets and to protect the public interest. Has headlines, links to bureaus and offices, a consumer center, and major initiatives of the commission.

Federal Trade Commission
www.ftc.gov/

Provides links to consumer protection, antitrust/competition, economic issues, and regional offices.

Supreme Court Antitrust Debates Introduction
www.ripon.edu/faculty/bowenj/antitrust/INTRO.htm

The Supreme Court Antitrust Debates is "a collection of excerpts from 72 of the Court's antitrust opinions from 1895 through 1993."

United States Securities and Exchange (SEC) Commission
www.sec.gov/

Search the EDGAR database for financial information on publicly owned companies.

The Economics of Professional Sports

What Is the Real Score?

Checklist of economic concepts

- Markets, imperfectly competitive
- Product markets
- Resource markets
- Cartels
- Antitrust laws
- Demand and supply
- Marginal revenue
- Marginal costs
- Monopsony
- Supply of labor
- Marginal cost of labor
- Marginal revenue product
- Monopsonistic profit
- Profit maximization

What is the most subsidized industry in all of America? Arguably, it is an industry dominated by small and mid-sized businesses. I would say that the kings of the subsidies game are the four major league sports—the National Football League (NFL), Major League Baseball (MLB), National Basketball Association (NBA), and the National Hockey League (NHL)—along with minor league baseball and hockey. After all, what other industries—other than those actually operated by government, like public schools—have the government subsidize almost all of the buildings in which they operate? Answer: None. It's only pro sports.

From 1990 to 2000, 10 new NFL stadiums opened at a total cost of $2.677 billion (in inflation-adjusted 2000 estimated dollars), with taxpayers financing 77%, or $2.057 billion (again in estimated 2000 dollars). And these numbers do not include tens of millions of dollars more in stadium renovations. During the 2001 and 2002 seasons, an estimated $2.1 billion will be spent on six new NFL stadiums, with taxpayers picking up about $1.2 billion, or 57%, of the costs.

Football teams and leagues are just like any other businesses. If certain teams have a tough time competing against others due to different markets or stadiums, that's a problem for team owners and league officials to resolve. The taxpayers should not be asked to bail them out. For good measure, there are no economic benefits to subsidizing football teams. The money spent at a game would be spent on recreational activities whether a football team resides nearby or not. And while a few businesses around a new stadium might see some benefits, that is generally offset by the net negative for businesses elsewhere. In addition, all businesses and individuals suffer from higher taxes tied to football subsidies.

The only individuals deriving big benefits from sports subsidies are the team owners and the players. Their bottom lines are being padded at the expense of the taxpayers. Football teams, and other sports franchises, should pay for their own facilities, compete in the marketplace, and let consumers decide what they are worth in the end. After all, that's what other businesses have to do.

Source: Raymond J. Keating, "Taxpayers, Are You Ready for Some Football?" Small Business Survival Committee, Weekly Cybercolumn, The Entrepreneurial View #116, September 7, 2000 (*http://www.sbsc.org/*).

THE PROFESSIONAL SPORTS BUSINESS

As the editorial above clearly indicates, the business of professional sports is a major social issue in cities across the United States. In some American cities voters have been asked to choose higher taxes or face the prospect of losing their local professional sports team to another city willing to provide a new stadium or arena.

Furthermore, have you noticed that the sports pages of your favorite newspaper often resemble the business section? Articles concerning labor disputes, ticket prices, television contracts, club relocations, changes in ownership and management, and, of course, player salaries can easily outnumber reports concerning the latest games and scores. Why do the happenings in the boardroom gather as much attention as the happenings on the field or the court? Examination of the economics of professional team sports reveals why following the business of athletics has itself become a major spectator sport for many people.

Professional sports in the United States is a multibillion-dollar business that provides entertainment to millions of fans each year. As do all business firms, professional sports clubs face a myriad of economic decisions in their quest to earn profits. And many sports clubs are very profitable. For example, the Dallas Cowboys of the National Football League have earned as much as $24 million annually in recent years. However, professional sports clubs are unlike most other business firms in at least two important ways: The organizational structure of the professional team sports industry and the unique relationship between the sports clubs and their most important employees, the players, have created a number of economic and social issues that have captured public attention.

Organizational Structure

Today, four major team sports are played professionally in the United States: baseball, basketball, football, and hockey. Each of these sports has a long and colorful history. Although details vary somewhat between sports, a similar organizational structure has evolved within each of the four professional team sports.

In most cases, individual teams, or clubs, are owned and operated for profit by private individuals or partnerships. The team owners are entrepreneurs who hire and fire the managers, coaches, and players; rent or build the stadium; and sell the tickets and broadcast rights to games. The owners of a sports club are ultimately responsible for the economic decisions necessary to the daily operation of the organization.

The spirit of all sports is competition. To attract ticket-buying fans, a sports club must compete on the field or the court against other teams. Thus, sports clubs cannot operate independently but must cooperate with one another in order to sell their entertainment services to the public. The necessary cooperation is institutionalized through the professional sports leagues—the American League (AL) and National League (NL) in baseball, collectively known as Major League Baseball (MLB), the National Basketball Association (NBA), the National Football League (NFL), and the National Hockey League (NHL). The leagues are formal organizations of individual clubs.

All the major sports leagues currently have more than two dozen member clubs. Sports clubs are located in major metropolitan areas scattered throughout the country. The baseball, hockey, and basketball leagues also have clubs located in Canada. The professional sports leagues serve as the mechanism for the cooperation that is necessary between the geographically dispersed teams.

Teams that are members of a professional sports league are contractually obligated to one another. Member clubs agree to abide by the rules and guidelines of the league. Among other things, the league determines the annual schedule of games, makes and enforces the game rules, and sets the guidelines for hiring new players. Because the league also determines when a new team will be admitted to the league and allowed to compete with its members, clubs are often referred to as *league franchises*. In general, the professional sports leagues are controlled by the club owners who hire an outside (nonowner) "commissioner" and staff to oversee the league's operations. The decisions made by the commissioner of a professional sports league are intended to be made in the best interest of the sport, not to favor any individual owner or group of owners.

The rules and guidelines adopted by a professional sports league have important economic implications for the individual member clubs. For most clubs, the rules with the greatest consequences on operating costs and revenues are those that govern the relationship between the teams and their players.

Teams and Players

The relationship between professional sports clubs and their players is perhaps unlike any other employer–employee relationship in our economy. Nowhere else is a worker's productivity so visible to so many and so easily measured. Productive workers in most firms do not receive the cheers of tens of thousands for a job well done or have the quality of their work publicly reviewed in the press. Likewise, most workers who make a mistake on the job (and who hasn't made a mistake?) do not hear the boos and catcalls of an upset crowd. The productivity of a professional athlete is constantly monitored by fans through a myriad of statistics —runs batted in, touchdowns scored, field goal percentage, and so on. Although the performance of professional athletes may be objectively measured and compared by the vast quantities of statistics compiled by sports analysts, controversy still surrounds the salaries earned in professional sports.

The general public is still shocked when a star player signs a multimillion-dollar contract to play baseball or basketball, yet many professional athletes claim they are underpaid by the team's owners. Further, it is not uncommon for one player to earn 10 or even 20 times more than other players on the same team. Ironically, rules imposed by each of the major sports leagues to promote competition on the playing field contribute to the seemingly inconsistent economics of players' salaries.

Each of the major professional sports leagues has very specific and detailed rules that govern the employment of players by the member clubs. Competition on the field would diminish if any club had the ability to hoard the best athletic talent. Thus, league rules are designed to ensure that each club has the opportunity to employ and retain quality players. In essence, the leagues establish the procedures whereby member clubs acquire the "property rights" to contract with specific players. Because specific clubs may hold the exclusive right to contract with a player, athletes are not always free to work for the highest bidder.

Economic Analysis and Professional Sports

Economic analysis provides a means of understanding the issues and controversies surrounding the business of professional team sports. Likewise, professional sports can serve as an example of how market structures and institutional arrangements can influence the economic behavior of firms in an industry.

product market
Buyers and sellers engage in the exchange of final goods and services.

The preceding discussion suggests that professional sports teams operate in imperfect markets. In fact, sports clubs sell their services in an imperfect **product market** and hire their players in an imperfect **resource market.** A product market exists when buyers and sellers engage in the exchange of final goods and services. When a sports club sells you a ticket for a game or a jacket emblazoned with the team logo, the transaction takes place in a product market. On the other hand, a resource market exists when buyers and sellers engage in the exchange of the factors of production. Thus, when a sports club hires a new player or builds a new stadium, the transaction takes place in a resource market. (Later, in Chapter 11, we will see how product and resource markets are related in the overall aggregate economy.)

resource market
Buyers and sellers engage in the exchange of the factors of production.

A closer examination of the product and resource markets in professional team sports can help us to better understand many of the economic issues discussed daily in sports columns across the nation. But perhaps even more important, our study of professional sports will provide us with general conclusions about how imperfect markets affect consumers and employees.

THE PRODUCT MARKET

Cooperation among Teams

As we noted earlier, the essence of sports is competition. However, it is in the best interest of professional sports clubs for this competition to occur on the playing field and not in the marketplace. The reason is easily observable. Imagine that sports clubs competed for fans in purely competitive markets. The more successful clubs would sell more tickets and team merchandise and would naturally earn higher profits, which, in turn, would allow these clubs to attract the best players through higher salaries. Over time, these clubs would become so much stronger than the less successful teams that competition on the playing field would deteriorate and become boring for spectators. Weak teams would eventually be forced into bankruptcy, and strong teams would lose fans. Thus, a professional sports club's economic decisions are inherently interdependent with those of its rivals.

cartel
A group of firms that formally agree to coordinate their production and pricing decisions in a manner that maximizes joint profits.

To remain in business and earn profits for their owners, professional sports clubs must avoid the above scenario. How are they able to do this? The answer is through coordination of economic decisions through league rules and guidelines. The alliance of teams through league organizations coordinates and restrains economic competition among member clubs. In many ways, professional sports leagues resemble market cartels. A **cartel** is a group of firms that formally agrees to coordinate its production and pricing decisions in a manner that maximizes joint profits. Thus, a cartel can be viewed as a group of firms behaving as if they were one firm—a shared monopoly.

In the United States, antitrust laws make it illegal, in most cases, for firms to monopolize an industry through the formation of a cartel. The business of professional sports is a unique exception. In 1922, the U.S. Supreme Court ruled that major league baseball did not meet the legal definition of interstate commerce and was therefore not subject to the restrictions of antitrust law (*The Federal Baseball Club of Baltimore v. The National League of Professional Baseball Clubs*). This precedent has been upheld by the courts in numerous cases since then. Although the antitrust exemption for baseball has not been fully extended to the other professional sports leagues, a variety of cases and legislative acts have granted limited protection to the collective action of clubs in other sports. (As examples, the Sports Broadcasting Act of 1961 allows professional sports leagues to sell the broadcast rights of games as a "package deal" in lieu of individual teams competing against one another for airtime, and the Football Merger Act of 1966 paved the way for the upstart American Football League to be absorbed into the NFL's established cartel.) The law implicitly recognizes that a professional sports team can profitably survive only as long as its league survives.

Cartels

The unique status of the professional sports leagues helps them avoid many of the problems faced by illegal cartels in other industries. Professional sports leagues have been able to maintain economic cooperation between member teams over long periods of time. For any cartel to be successful, several requirements must be met.

First, the cartel members must be responsible for most of the output produced in their market. The greater the proportion of total market output generated by the cartel members as a group, the greater the cartel's degree of monopoly power. Further, in order to maintain monopoly power, the cartel must be able to prevent new competitors from entering the market, or be able to integrate new competitors into the cartel. Each of the major sports leagues has been successful in eliminating competition from teams outside its cartel. By controlling the contracts of star players and holding exclusive contracts to play in major stadiums and arenas, the existing leagues have restricted the ability of newly formed rival leagues to compete for the fans' attention. In several instances, new competitors have been driven out of the market. A recent example was the demise of the Xtreme Football League (XFL) after only one season of competition. In other cases, rival leagues were successful in finding new market territories that had been overlooked by the established leagues. When this occurred, the established leagues found it beneficial to invite the upstarts to join their cartel. Over the past 40 years, we have witnessed the mergers of the American Football League (AFL) with the NFL, the American Basketball Association (ABA) with the NBA, and teams from the World Hockey League (WHL) with the NHL. These mergers helped the leagues maintain their shared monopoly power in their respective sports.

A second requirement of a successful cartel is the production of fairly homogeneous outputs by the member firms. That is, each firm in a cartel should produce outputs that are substitutes for the outputs produced by the other member firms. Pricing and output agreements are easier to enforce and maintain if all member firms are producing the same goods and services. If each cartel firm produced different products, special agreements would have to be made for each output. Within a professional sports league, all clubs do produce the same primary output—entertainment for fans who watch the games. The league structures ensure that all the games played by member clubs are fairly homogeneous. All teams must follow a common set of game rules and regulations enforced by referees and umpires hired by the league. Further, some leagues like the NFL determine the schedule of games whereby each club plays other clubs based on the competitive strength of the teams. This is done in a manner to promote greater parity on the playing field. Thus, common game rules and league-determined schedules help reinforce the appeal of sports and help the leagues maintain their cartel arrangements.

A third requirement for a successful cartel is the ability to divide the market into territories controlled by each member and to establish production quotas. In essence, the cartel members must agree on how their combined monopoly power will be shared among themselves. In professional sports, the market territories and output quotas are determined through the league structure. Each club's territory is protected from inside competition by the league. The location of new expansion teams and the ability of established teams to relocate are determined through league rules and normally require the agreement of a majority of the clubs' owners. Likewise, the production of games is controlled by the league offices, which set the schedule for each season. All teams are given an equal share of the total output during normal seasons by playing an equal number of games. These actions by the professional sports leagues grant local monopoly power to each team and help maintain the shared monopoly of the cartel.

Fourth, in order to succeed, the cartel must have the power to prevent "cheating" by member clubs. In many cartel situations, an incentive to cheat on the agreement exists for member firms. Some firms may find it profitable to break production quotas or enter another member's sales territory in an effort to capture more than the agreed-upon share of the monopoly. Because most nonsports cartel arrangements are illegal, it is virtually impossible for members to enforce their agreements. However, in professional sports the league offices have the contractual power to enforce league rules and guidelines. In each of the major sports, the league's commissioner is empowered to sanction and levy fines against member clubs that do not adhere to the rules. Again, the unique legal status of professional sports leagues reinforces the ability of clubs to maintain monopoly power through the enforcement of cartel agreements.

Coordinated Behavior

The most obvious forms of cartel behavior among a league's member clubs involve various methods of joint marketing and revenue sharing. A professional sports club receives revenue from three major sources: ticket and concession sales, merchandising rights for team souvenirs and novelties, and radio and television broadcast rights. Professional sports clubs cooperate with one another in each of these three areas through their respective league organizations.

Each of the sports leagues has specific rules for dividing the revenue generated through ticket sales between the host home team and the visiting team. Although the formulas vary between leagues, in most circumstances each team is guaranteed a percentage of the gate receipts for the games in which it plays. For example, in the NFL the home team receives 60 percent and the visiting team receives 40 percent of ticket sales.

The league organizations also regulate the business of merchandising products that carry team logos and trademarks. One reason for doing so is to discourage counterfeiters, but it also allows the league to promote entire lines of merchandise for all the member clubs and to minimize interclub competition in this area. If you look hard enough, you can find almost anything from T-shirts to toilet bowl lids in your favorite team's colors with its name and logo. There is a growing global market for products that carry the widely recognized "brands" of the professional sports leagues. In recent years, all four of the major leagues have earned more than $1 billion annually from merchandise sales. In fact, the most financially successful league, the NFL, generates more than $3 billion each year in revenue from retail sales of its licensed merchandise.

Today, the primary source of revenue for most sports clubs is the sale of broadcast rights to television and radio. This is the area in which sports clubs have been most successful in jointly selling their entertainment services through their respective leagues. Each league sells the national television and radio broadcast rights to all the games played by its members as "package deals" to the highest bidder. The revenue raised from selling all the league's games as a package is then evenly divided among the member clubs. Thus, teams in large media markets do not gain an economic advantage over the clubs in smaller cities. The practice of teams pooling their broadcast rights dates back to 1964, when the NFL sold its games to network television for $14.1 million. The revenues raised from selling the broadcast rights to professional sports have dramatically increased over the years. In 1998, the NFL signed a media broadcasting deal with ABC, CBS, Fox, and ESPN that will pay the league a combined $18 *billion* over eight years.

Pricing and Output for Broadcast Rights

To see the effect of cartel behavior on the pricing and output of broadcast rights to professional sporting events, consider Table 9.1 and Figure 9.1. The hypothetical data reflect the output, revenue, and cost figures a sports league faces in the provision of broadcast rights over a period of time, in this case, one month. The league faces the demand schedule reported in columns (1) and (4) of Table 9.1, which is shown as demand curve DD in Figure 9.1. DD represents the summation of the downward-sloping demand curves for broadcast rights faced by each club in the league. Given its monopoly power, the league's marginal revenue curve, MR, lies below the league's demand curve. The league's marginal cost curve, MC, is the horizontal summation of the marginal cost schedules each team would face if it

TABLE 9.1   Monthly Broadcast Output, Costs, Revenues, and Profits for a Professional Sports League

(1) Units of Output	(2) Total Cost ($000)	(3) Marginal Cost ($000)	(4) Price ($000)	(5) Total Revenue ($000)	(6) Marginal Revenue ($000)	(7) Profits ($000)
0	$ 0		$100	$ 0		$ 0
		$40			$100	
1	40		100	100		60
		45			90	
2	85		95	190		105
		50			80	
3	135		90	270		135
		55			70	
4	190		85	340		150
		60			60	
5	250		80	400		150
		65			50	
6	315		75	450		135
		70			40	
7	385		70	490		105
		75			30	
8	460		65	520		60
		80			20	
9	540		60	540		0
		85			10	
10	625		55	550		275

individually and competitively provided broadcast rights to its games. Thus, columns (1) and (3) in Table 9.1 list the total marginal cost schedule for the league as a whole.

   If a cartel agreement did not exist and teams competed against one another in the market for broadcast rights, each club would maximize its profits by selling up to the point where its own *MC* equaled its own *MR*. Because each individual club is a local monopoly facing its own unique demand and cost schedules, it is likely that the profit-maximizing level of output will vary among clubs. But how many total games would be broadcast across all clubs without a cartel agreement? Recall from Chapter 8 that the *MC* curve can be considered the supply curve for an individual competitive firm. Thus, in Figure 9.1, because *MC* represents the summation of marginal costs across all clubs, *MC* can be thought of as the competitive market supply schedule. Likewise, *DD* represents the market demand schedule. Without a cartel agreement, the market would reach equilibrium at point *A*, where *DD* intersects *MC*. The market equilibrium price for the rights to broadcast a game would be $70,000, and seven games would be broadcast in total each month. On average, each broadcast would generate marginal revenue of $70,000 for the team selling the game. Examination of Table 9.1 reveals that the competitive solution

FIGURE 9.1   Pricing and Output for a Cartel

As a shared monopoly, cartel members collectively face demand *DD* and marginal revenue *MR*. Just like a single monopoly firm, the cartel can maximize market profits by producing output such that marginal cost *MC* equals *MR*. In this case, the cartel output is 5, with a price of $80,000. If cartel members competed with one another, the market would reach equilibrium at an output of 7 and an average price of $70,000.

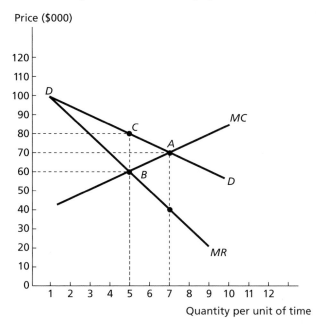

would result in $490,000 of total revenue and $105,000 in average profits each month for the clubs that sold games.

It is important to note that this analysis does not indicate how the profits would be distributed among the clubs in the absence of a cartel agreement. In the short run, teams of poorer quality might find it difficult or impossible to sell the broadcast rights for their games. In this case, the quality of athletic competition would decline as teams that were successful in selling their broadcast rights earned more profits and could afford to hire the best players. Thus, in the long run, less successful clubs would be forced to shut down, leaving the league with fewer teams.

By agreeing to collectively sell their national broadcast rights as a league, and not as individual firms, the clubs effectively enter an agreement to share their monopoly power and behave as if they were one firm. Each team would no longer examine its own demand and costs schedules to determine its profit-maximizing output, but would accept a share of the overall market profits. As a cartel, the teams in the league collectively face demand curve *DD* and marginal revenue curve *MR* in Figure 9.1. Just like a single monopolistic firm, the cartel can maximize profits by producing the level of output where marginal revenues equal marginal costs. Table 9.1 reveals that marginal revenue is equal to marginal cost when the broadcast rights to five games are provided each month. Marginal revenue and marginal cost are $60,000 at this level of output. This can be seen in Figure 9.1 as point *B*, where the *MR* curve intersects with the *MC* curve. The demand schedule in Table 9.1 indicates that buyers will pay $80,000 per game for five games (point *C* in Figure 9.1). Profit maximization can therefore be achieved by selling the rights to five games each month for $80,000 per game. This is verified in column (7) of Table 9.1, which shows that this output and price combination maximizes the cartel's collective profit at $150,000 per month.

The cartel agreement to sell broadcast rights as a league affects both price and quantity. In this example, the cartel will provide five games for broadcast at $80,000 per game, whereas individual teams in competition with one another will provide seven games for $70,000 each. Given the costs of producing additional games for broadcast, the cartel agreement increases total profits across all the league members from $105,000 to $150,000. Without the cartel agreement, the distribution of profits favors the teams with relatively greater athletic success. With the cartel agreement, the distribution of profits is determined by the league's rules and guidelines. Today, most revenue from the sale of broadcast rights is equally divided among a league's member clubs. Even teams that rarely appear on national television or radio receive the same share of revenues from the sale of the league's broadcast rights.

Through the formation of a cartel, professional sports clubs have found it in their best economic interest to cooperate in the competition for the fans' dollars. By restricting output below competitive levels and raising price, overall profits for cartel members can be increased and a degree of stability in the number of teams can be achieved.

The Number and Location of Teams

Today another of the most controversial issues in professional sports concerns the number and location of teams within each league. Recall that a successful cartel must be able to divide the market between its members and to share joint profits. Thus, from each cartel member's perspective there is an incentive to restrict the number of new members. By limiting cartel membership, each existing cartel member will be guaranteed a larger slice of the profit pie. This is clearly seen in professional sports, where, compared to other industries, expansion has been relatively slow. For example, during the past 35 years, Major League Baseball has added only four new teams (Florida, Colorado, Tampa Bay, and Arizona). All four of the major sports leagues stick to a very strict and rigorous process in allowing new members to enter the market. When expansion franchises are granted entry, they are required to pay the existing teams an entry fee that compensates these teams for lost market share.

In late 2001, MLB commissioner Bud Selig started a major controversy when he announced plans to close two professional baseball clubs (Minnesota and Montreal). Baseball owners claimed that these "small-market" teams were unprofitable and that both the American and National leagues would be stronger and more competitive with fewer teams. Many fans and public officials took exception to this argument when in fact MLB had added two teams only three years earlier in 1998. Given that a sizable portion of each individual team's revenues is derived from fixed leaguewide broadcast fees, a reduction in the number of teams overall would leave owners of the remaining teams with larger shares of the overall profits. Stringent restrictions on the number of members who share in the pool of joint profits is a classic form of cartel behavior. Intense public pressure and lawsuits prevented the closure of the two clubs in question. However, the other team owners collectively bought out the owner of the Montreal Expos and collectively ran the club for two seasons until a new owner in a larger market was found.

One consequence of the restricted growth in the number of teams is the incentive for existing teams to relocate to new markets. Over the past several decades, the demand for sports entertainment has grown dramatically in the United States and Canada. Economists have estimated that approximately 50 major metropolitan areas in North America are capable of profitably supporting professional sports teams. However, the largest professional sports league, the NFL, has only 32 teams. There are more cities with fans who want their own teams than teams in each league. Clearly, a shortage of teams exists.

As we learned earlier, whenever a shortage occurs, the market price will rise; this is also true of professional sports. Prospective owners and tax-paying fans in cities without teams will often offer attractive financial deals to teams that are willing to relocate. These deals take the form of publicly built and supported stadiums and arenas, tax abatements, loans, and outright financial payments. In some cases, cities have openly bid on teams that have indicated their willingness to move. Examples include the relocation of the NFL's Los Angeles Rams to St. Louis and the Houston Oilers to Nashville (where they became the Tennessee Titans). Of course, teams that relocate must receive league permission and must share their newfound profits with the cartel membership. Other teams have been successful in garnering new public facilities and tax breaks by simply indicating that they are willing to move elsewhere. Tax-paying fans who were afraid of losing their hometown teams have recently financed new stadiums in Tampa Bay, Seattle, and Milwaukee.

The Stadium Controversy

As we saw in the editorial which opened this chapter, billions of local tax dollars have been spent in recent years on the construction of new stadiums and sports arenas for professional sports teams. A majority of the NFL's 32 teams play in stadiums that were built and opened after 1990. Furthermore, most of the remaining stadiums have also undergone major renovations and expansions. It has been estimated that almost $4 out of every $5 spent during this stadium construction boom came from public sources. Taxpayer support for profit-making enterprises is a hotly debated issue in cities across the country which are trying to attract a new team or hold on to an existing one.

Why are taxpayers and elected public officials willing to financially support a professional sports franchise? The most obvious answer to this question is the desire to satisfy the local public's demand for sports entertainment. However, this is most likely secondary in importance. The primary reason cities seek to attract and maintain a professional sports team is the "major league" status that it brings to the community. A sports team places a city "on the map" and generates national publicity and public relations opportunities for other businesses located there. City officials often claim that a professional sports franchise will generate jobs and tax revenue as new businesses are attracted to the area. (In some sense the nationally recognized status and prestige granted to a city by the existence of a successful professional sports franchise is a collectively consumed good.) After its expansion team had completed only two seasons in the NFL, a spokesperson for the Jacksonville Chamber of Commerce said, "What the Jaguars are doing for us is worth millions, maybe tens of millions of dollars in advertising and exposure."[1]

Undoubtedly the Jacksonville Jaguars did improve the image and visibility of their city, but is a professional sports team a wise investment for economic development? Maybe not. According to economist Andrew Zimbalist, a professional sports team has about as much economic impact as a new Macy's department store.[2] When the Jaguars entered the league, the average revenue for an NFL team was approximately $65 million. In the case of Jacksonville, the metropolitan area's disposable income at the time was about $11 billion. Thus, the NFL contributed only about 0.6 percent to the community's purchasing power. (The figure would be even less for other cities because Jacksonville is the smallest NFL market.) Further, most of the jobs directly created by a professional sports franchise are low-paying service sector jobs that are often seasonal. Most of the high-paying jobs are held by small groups of players and management, who may not live in the local community year-round. Finally, when a new sports team arrives in town, a substitution effect will occur with respect to consumer spending. Local fans who purchase tickets, concessions, parking, and souvenirs will have less to spend on other forms of entertainment. Thus, fewer dollars are available for spending at businesses such as local restaurants, theaters, and bowling centers.

Even though professional sports seem to permeate many aspects of our modern society, individual sports teams are actually *small* businesses. Today the average per-team revenue for sports clubs ranges from about $55 to $60 million in the NHL to a little over $100 million in the NFL. By the standards of corporate America, where revenues of market-leading firms are often measured in the billions of dollars, these are small numbers. In fact, if you are attending a midsized or large public university, there is a very good chance that your institution spends more each year than your favorite professional team. Numerous impact studies have concluded that the direct economic benefits of building a new stadium or arena are very low for the local community. Because voters continue to accept public financing for such construction, we must conclude that a majority of taxpayers believe the intrinsic value of being the host city for a professional sports team is greater than the burden of increased public debt.

Because the primary benefits of a professional sports team to its local community are intangible and hard to measure (how much is civic pride worth?), the debate concerning the use of public funds to support professional sports is likely to

[1]Jason Cole, "Jags Well on Road Toward Recognition," *ESPNET,* January 8, 1997, pp. 1–2.
[2]Federal Reserve Bank of Atlanta, "Does the Bouncing Ball Lead to Economic Growth?" *Regional Update* 8, no. 3 (July/August 1996), pp. 1–8.

continue. However, many economists argue that public investments in new factories and schools would generate greater and longer-term economic returns to the community than investments in new stadiums and arenas.

THE RESOURCE MARKET

The Employment of Players

Perhaps one of the most controversial economic aspects of professional team sports involves the leagues' rules that govern the hiring and employment of players. Each of the major professional leagues strictly controls the methods by which teams hire and fire their player-employees. The employment contracts between clubs and players must meet the very specific guidelines imposed by the league. The rules are rigidly enforced to ensure that no club can gain a competitive athletic advantage due to its employment practices.

The most visible of a league's employment rules involve the procedures used to allocate new players among the league's member clubs. In an effort to generate a competitive playing balance among teams (sometimes referred to as *parity*) and to prevent any single club from hoarding quality players, each sport conducts an annual draft of the new players who enter the market. Although the specific procedures are different in each sport, the basic design of each league's draft is the same. In a predetermined order, clubs take turns choosing (drafting) players from the available pool of new players. The drafting order is normally determined by the previous season's league standings. In general, teams with relatively poor records choose first, and relatively strong teams choose last. Under league rules, when a club drafts a player, that club has exclusive rights to sign the player to a contract. No club can hire a player drafted by another team unless that team first sells or trades away its exclusive rights to hire the player. In most cases, league rules dictate that once a drafted player signs a contract with a club, that club maintains its exclusive right to the player's services for a specified number of seasons. Thus, new players become the "property" of their employing clubs and do not have an open opportunity to offer their skills to the highest bidder. League rules also forbid a team from "tampering" with a rival team's players by offering them employment opportunities while they are still under contract.

For decades, professional athletes who were drafted had virtually no ability to choose the team for which they played. Players could change teams only if their employing club chose to trade their contract for the contract of a player owned by another club, or if another club purchased their contract. If an athlete wished to play professional sports, he had to agree to these terms as imposed by the leagues. Thus, players had little, if any, real bargaining power when salaries were determined. Obviously, this situation provided owners with the opportunity to pay their players relatively low wages.

Even though professional sports league employment rules are designed to increase the quality of competition on the playing field, the preceding description clearly shows that drafts and hiring restrictions reduce the quality of competition

monopsony
A market with only
one buyer or
employer.

in the market for ballplayers. When league rules allow the member clubs to own the property rights to new player contracts, an imperfect factor market called a **monopsony** is created.

Monopsony

A monopsony is a market with only one buyer or employer. When only one club, according to league rules, has the right to contract with a specific player, that club becomes a pure monopsony from the player's perspective. In an even broader sense, the leagues themselves can be considered joint monopsonies. For example, if you want to play professional football in the United States, you must play in the NFL. There are no other buyers for the specific athletic talents of football players. (Arena football leagues demand players with similar skills; however, the rules of the game are different and arena football teams are increasingly serving as minor league development opportunities for future NFL players.) A league's draft and employment rules reinforce and strengthen the monopsony powers collectively held by its member clubs.

Two major factors create monopsony power for professional sports clubs and leagues. The first factor is the immobility of new players who have been drafted. New draftees who wish to play professional sports are required to sign contracts that bind them to their teams for a specified number of years as determined by league rules. Once a player has entered the league and signed a contract, he does not have the option of negotiating with other clubs. In fact, because of the draft structures, new players who are drafted often never have the option of offering their services to the highest bidder. Thus, from a legal perspective, the mobility of players is severely limited. New players become "locked in" to their teams for the period specified in the contracts sanctioned by the leagues. Because new players are contractually obligated, the employing clubs become the only potential buyer of the players' athletic talents in the league.

The second factor that generates monopsony power in professional sports is the highly specialized athletic talents and skills possessed by the players. Athletes who are qualified to play a professional sport have invested many years in training and instruction to learn their craft. The athletic skills and knowledge acquired during this preparation by a professional athlete are in most cases very specific to his or her sport and are not readily transferable to other sports or employment situations. Very few athletes have the ability to excel at more than one professional sport. (Deion Sanders and Bo Jackson are rare exceptions.) Recall that basketball great Michael Jordan failed to advance beyond the minor leagues in his attempt to play professional baseball. Players who possess only very specialized skills have employment opportunities limited to only those employers who require such skills. The talents of a player who has trained and studied to be a professional quarterback are demanded by only 32 NFL clubs. Since each club employs only two or three quarterbacks, fewer than 100 individuals in the United States earn their living in this highly specialized occupation. Compare this with the nearly 4 million people who are schoolteachers or even the 125,000 people who are professional economists! Teachers and economists are more generally trained than quarterbacks and have many

TABLE 9.2
Wages, Costs, and the Marginal Revenue Product of Professional Baseball Pitchers

(1) Number of Players	(2) Wage ($000)	(3) Total Cost of Labor ($000)	(4) Marginal Cost of Labor ($000)	(5) Marginal Revenue Product ($000)
0	$ 0	$ 0		
			$ 300	$1,500
1	300	300		
			500	1,300
2	400	800		
			700	1,100
3	500	1,500		
			900	900
4	600	2,400		
			1,100	700
5	700	3,500		
			1,300	500
6	800	4,800		

more options in the labor market. It is easy to see that the specialized talents of professional athletes contribute to the monopsony power of their employers.

Wages and Employment in a Monopsony

The effects of monopsony power on wages and employment are illustrated in Table 9.2. Because a monopsony is the single buyer of labor in its market, it faces a positively sloped market supply curve of labor. Thus, in order to attract additional workers, a monopsony must increase its wage offer as it hires additional employees. This is seen in column (2) of Table 9.2. The monopsony baseball club in this example can hire two pitchers for an average wage of $400,000 each, but to hire three pitchers it must pay a wage of $500,000 each. Columns (1) and (2) are plotted in Figure 9.2 as the market supply curve SS.

Because a monopsony firm must raise the wage along the market supply of labor schedule in order to hire additional workers, the monopsony firm will experience a change in its total labor costs that is in excess of the wage. This fact can be seen in Table 9.2. Columns (2) and (3) report that when two pitchers are hired at $400,000 each, the total cost of labor is $800,000. However, in order to hire a third pitcher, the wage of $500,000 must be paid to each. This raises the total cost of labor to $1,500,000. By hiring a third pitcher, the club experiences a change in its total labor cost of $700,000. The change in the total labor cost of a firm due to hiring an additional worker is known as the **marginal cost of labor (MCL).** The MCL is reported in column (4) of the table. Notice that the MCL is greater than the wage beyond the first player hired. This is because a monopsony must pay a higher wage to the additional worker as well as all workers previously hired. The MCL curve is plotted in Figure 9.2 using the numbers from columns (1) and (4) of Table 9.2. Graphically, the MCL curve lies above the supply of labor curve and is more steeply sloped.

marginal cost of labor (MCL)
The change that occurs in a firm's total labor costs due to hiring an additional worker, per unit of time.

FIGURE 9.2   Wage and Employment Determination for a Monopsonist

As the single employer of labor, the monopsony faces the market supply of labor curve *SS*. The marginal cost of labor curve *MCL* reflects the addition to costs the firm experiences by hiring an additional worker. The monopsonist will hire workers up to the point where *MCL* equals *MRP*. In this case, the firm will hire four workers at a wage of $600,000.

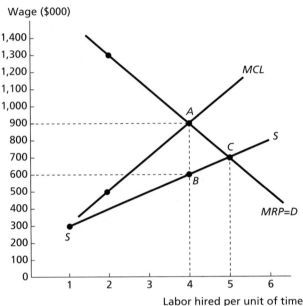

Column (5) of Table 9.2 reports the marginal revenue product (*MRP*) for the pitchers hired by the ball club. Recall that *MRP* is the change in revenue experienced by a firm when it employs an additional worker. As additional pitchers are hired by the ball club, the team can produce more games and other entertainment services that generate revenue for the club. However, just like any other business firm, the ball club experiences diminishing returns from hiring additional workers. Thus, as more pitchers are added to the team's roster, team output and revenue increase at a declining rate. This is seen in column (5), which shows *MRP* falling as the number of pitchers hired increases. Recall that the *MRP* schedule represents the demand for workers.

How many pitchers will the ball club's management decide to hire, and what wage will they be paid? To answer these questions, first compare columns (4) and (5) of Table 9.2. When the *MCL* in column (4) is less than the *MRP* in column (5), the ball club adds less to its labor costs by hiring an additional pitcher than it adds to its revenues. In this case, it is obviously profitable to go ahead and hire. However, when the *MCL* in column (4) is greater than the *MRP* in column (5), the ball club adds more to its labor costs by hiring an additional pitcher than it adds to its revenues. In this case, the ball club would reduce its profits by hiring. Thus, the ball club will continue to hire pitchers up to the point where *MCL* = *MRP*. In our example, this occurs when four pitchers are hired and MCL and MRP are both equal to $900,000. Note that if the ball club hires more than four pitchers, MCL is greater than MRP and the club would experience a loss of profitability.

As our example illustrates, for a monopsony, the optimum quantity of labor to hire is found at the point where $MCL = MRP.$ This is shown in Figure 9.2 as point A, where the MCL curve intersects with the MRP curve. Point A indicates that MCL and MRP are equal at $900,000 when four pitchers are hired. However, according to the market supply schedule, the ball club can attract and hire four pitchers for a wage of $600,000 each. This occurs at point B on the supply curve SS in Figure 9.2. Thus, even though a pitcher's contribution to the club's revenues (MRP) is $900,000, each pitcher will be paid a wage of only $600,000. In a monopsony, the difference between a worker's contribution to the firm's receipts and the wage is known as **monopsonistic profit.** In our example, the ball club earns a monopsonistic profit of $300,000 for each of the four pitchers hired for a total of $1,200,000. This is the additional profit earned by the ball club because of its monopsony power.

monopsonistic profit
The difference between the workers' contribution to a monopsonistic firm's receipts and their wages.

Recall that, in competitive labor markets, additional workers are hired up to the point where the wage is equal to $MRP.$ If the ball club in our example operated in a competitive labor market, it would hire more than four pitchers. According to Table 9.2, the wage rate is equal to MRP when five pitchers are hired. This is seen in Figure 9.2 as point C, where the supply curve SS intersects with the MRP curve. If the labor market was competitive, five workers would be hired for $700,000 each and their MRP would also be $700,000. Thus, in a competitive labor market, a firm does not earn a monopsonistic profit.

As our example illustrates, a monopsony hires fewer workers than a competitive firm and pays a lower wage than a competitive firm. Because of these two economic outcomes, it is often said that monopsonies "exploit" their workers. If firms with monopsony power are made to purchase labor under more competitive conditions, we should expect to see more workers hired and wages rise. In fact, in recent years, professional sports leagues have been forced to give up some of their monopsony powers and we have seen dramatic increases in player salaries.

Free Agency

For many years, all professional baseball players were asked to sign a basic playing contract that included what came to be known as the reserve clause. This part of the contract reserved the right of the employing ball club to perpetually hold exclusive rights to the players' services. Players could not move freely among clubs. A player could change teams only if his employer traded or sold the rights to his contract to another team. The reserve clause arrangement gave baseball clubs monopsony power over the players they hired.

Realizing that the reserve clause kept salaries below what could be obtained in a competitive market, baseball players organized and fought the owners in antitrust court. In 1975, an independent arbitrator overturned the reserve clause in Major League Baseball. The players and owners eventually reached a compromise whereby the employing club can hold exclusive rights to a player's contract for a specified number of years after which the player can declare "free agency" and sell his services to the highest bidder. A free agent is a player whose contract is no longer exclusively held by one club.

Each of the major sports leagues has very specific rules concerning when a player can declare free agency. In baseball, a player must have at least six years of playing experience and not be under contract with any ball club. In 1993, football players entered into an agreement with the owners of the NFL that gives unrestricted free agency status to uncontracted players with five years of experience. In both the baseball and football leagues, some clubs have openly opposed free agency and players have accused team owners of secretly agreeing not to hire certain free agents. However, the advent of free agency has greatly reduced the degree of monopsonistic exploitation in professional sports.

The impact of free agency on player salaries has been dramatic. Figure 9.3 reports the increase in the average salaries for baseball players since the inception of free agency. In 1976, the average Major League Baseball player earned $52,300. By 2004, the average player was earning more than $2.48 million! Wages and prices in the overall economy also increased during this time, but not to the same extent. For example, the average weekly earnings of a full-time worker in the U.S. economy increased by about 150 percent while the average salary of a major league baseball player increased more than 45-fold.

As another point of comparison, consider the "plight" of professional football players. Until 1993, football players had very limited access to free agency status. In 1992, before the new free agency rules, the average NFL starting player's salary was $660,092—about half of the average comparable salary in baseball at that time. Within 10 years the average salary in the NFL reached $1.1 million. Free agency clearly reduces the degree of monopsonistic exploitation in professional sports. In fact, most informed observers would argue that the average salaries across the four major sports leagues vary proportionally with the degree of free agency allowed, which in turn varies directly with the strength of the respective players' union. (In 2004, average salaries were $4.54 million in the NBA, $2.48 million in MLB, $1.64 million in the NHL, and $1.25 million in the NFL.)

Labor Disputes

labor union
A formal organization of workers that bargains on behalf of its members over the terms and conditions of employment.

Professional athletes have fought for many years against monopsonistic employment rules, such as the reserve clause, enforced by the leagues. In opposing the restrictive employment practices of team owners, players in all four major sports have united to form labor unions. A **labor union** is a formal organization of workers that bargains on behalf of its members over the terms and conditions of employment. Player unions negotiate with team owners to determine the standards that are applied to all player contracts.

Disagreements between the team owners and the players' unions have resulted in a number of labor disputes in the past several years. Baseball has been particularly affected by labor disputes; since the early 1970s, MLB has suffered eight major work stoppages, and in 2002 a ninth work stoppage was narrowly averted. In 1994, the Major League Baseball Players Association (the players' union which represents baseball players in both the American and National leagues) called a

FIGURE 9.3
Mean Major League Baseball Salary for Selected Years since Free Agency

Source: Major League Baseball.

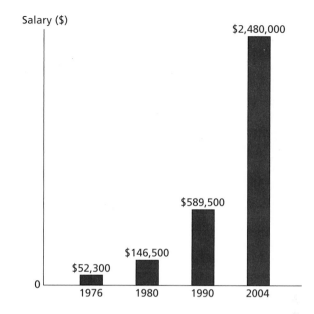

strike
A work stoppage initiated by labor.

lockout
A work stoppage initiated by management.

strike that forced the cancellation of hundreds of games, including the World Series. Later in the same year, the team owners of the NHL canceled half a season by enforcing a **lockout** against professional hockey players. In 2005, the entire NHL season was canceled due to a lockout. In each of these cases the major points of disagreement concerned the mechanics of how players would be paid and the conditions necessary for players to become free agents.

The shortened baseball and hockey seasons of 1994 resulted from the players' resistance to the owners' proposed "salary caps." A salary cap is a rule that limits the amount of money that any team can spend on player compensation. The owners argued that player salaries were too high for them to make a "fair profit" on their investments and that limits needed to be placed on their spending to ensure parity. However, a salary cap also prevents owners from bidding against one another for the services of talented players. Therefore, baseball and hockey players argued that a salary cap would keep their salaries artificially low. Basketball players took up this same cry before the 1998–1999 NBA season, which was also partially canceled due to a lockout by the owners.

In terms of the analysis presented in this chapter, a salary cap can be viewed as a mechanism for owners to enforce the monopsonistic employment of players leaguewide. In other words, a salary cap is just another cartel rule, which is intended to maximize the joint profits of the leagues. In every league, players have actively spoken out against the salary cap rules. It is likely that future labor disputes will occur unless the players and owners can agree on how profits should be divided among themselves.

In 2002, a strike called by the MLB players' union was canceled at the last minute when team owners and players agreed to a new multiyear contract which adjusted the distribution of revenue between teams and put into place new rules on the determination of player salaries. The major points of conflict between the owners and players in 2002 concerned the formula for how revenues are shared between the "large-market" teams (like New York and Los Angeles) and the "small-market" teams (like Kansas City and Minneapolis) and the imposition of a "luxury tax" on teams with relatively high player payrolls. The first of these issues is clearly a question faced by any cartel: How will jointly produced revenues be shared among its members? The question is more difficult to answer in a professional sports context because team revenues directly affect the ability of franchises to build and maintain a competitive team, and without some degree of competitive balance on the playing field the league as a whole would suffer and profits would decline for everyone. In an effort to create a greater degree of parity, the 2002 contract increased the relative shares of revenue received by the small-market teams at the expense of the large-market teams. The luxury tax included in the 2002 contract forces teams that exceed a predetermined team payroll limit ($128 million in 2005) to make a payment to the league, which will be shared by those teams that are not penalized. This scheme creates an incentive for individual teams to curb their spending on expensive high-performance players; therefore, it can be considered as just another form of a salary cap. In return for concessions on the luxury tax, the players' union negotiated an increase in the minimum starting salary for new players ($300,000 in 2004) and a promise that neither baseball league would contract by closing teams. Although the 2002 agreement avoided a strike and the cancellation of games, the negotiations were very intense and clearly illustrated the importance of economic issues in the world of professional sports.

Do Professional Athletes Earn Their Pay?

The competition among teams for free agents and the insistence by owners on salary caps have caused many people to wonder why professional athletes command such lofty salaries. The premier players in each sport can easily earn several million dollars a year. How can someone earn millions of dollars playing a game when the median household income in the United States is only about $42,000?

Recall that as long as an employer experiences an increase in revenue that is greater than the increase in costs due to hiring an additional worker, the employer can increase profits with a new hire. Stated another way, profits increase as long as the marginal revenue product is greater than the marginal cost of labor. Therefore, a club can make a profit and pay its players millions of dollars if those players generate even more millions of dollars in revenues. For example, in 1988, the Los Angeles Kings of the NHL paid $15 million to the Edmonton Oilers for the right to hire Wayne Gretzky. The Kings then signed Gretzky to an eight-year, $20 million contract. Was this a good deal? It has been estimated that Gretzky increased the Kings' revenues over the eight years by as much as $52,150,000 through increases in season ticket sales, game attendance, and cable television rights.[3] Thus, due to Gretsky's

---

[3]Robert J. Downs and Paul M. Sommers, "Is the Great One Slipping? Not on the Ice," *Journal of Recreational Mathematics* 23, no. 1 (1991), pp. 1–5.

contract, the Kings experienced a change in total costs of $35 million, but revenues increased by even more. The Kings made more than $17 million from the deal.

The salaries of professional athletes reflect their contribution to the club's revenue. The same is true for all workers in a market economy. The more a worker contributes to an employer's revenues, the more that worker can be paid. Workers with relatively large *MRP*s will command higher wages, and those with relatively small *MRP*s will command lower wages. Why doesn't the average doctor or teacher have a multimillion-dollar contract? Because they do not generate millions of dollars in revenues for their employers. Salaries in a market system are not determined by a worker's contribution to the public's health or overall well-being but by the worker's contribution to his or her employer's revenues. Professional athletes earn their salaries because fans are willing to pay to enjoy their performances.

Illicit Drugs and Professional Sports

Over the past several years, one of the most controversial issues in professional sports has been the use of drugs by athletes. Each of the major professional leagues has a substance abuse policy that prohibits the use of illegal "recreational" drugs such as marijuana and cocaine. Furthermore, the leagues also ban athletes from using performance-enhancing drugs that may or may not be legally produced. Some classes of drugs, such as steroids, do have legitimate medicinal uses but are often taken illicitly by athletes for their body-building side effects. Each league maintains a list of drugs and substances that players are banned from using. The collective bargaining agreements between the leagues and the players' unions outline the policies and procedures that teams and players must follow to identify and confirm the use of banned substances by individual athletes. Does economic analysis have anything to say about why some professional athletes run the risk of losing their well-paying jobs, their health, and in some extreme cases, their lives by taking illicit drugs? Yes, it does.

Recall that economic analysis indicates that people make choices by comparing their marginal private benefits to their marginal private costs. What are these benefits and costs? From a player's perspective, the benefits are obvious; by consuming illicit substances a professional athlete is able to artificially enhance his or her game performance, which will ultimately attract more fans and thereby increase the player's *MRP*. Of course, a higher *MRP* means that the player will command a higher salary. Thus, if there were no costs, an economic incentive would clearly exist for professional athletes to consume performance-enhancing drugs. However, there are costs. The leagues view the use of performance-enhancing drugs as a form of cheating and enforce collective rules against their consumption. If detected, a player who consumes substances banned by his league is subject to fines and possible suspensions. Each league imposes a graduated scale of punishment for players who violate the substance abuse policies. In multiple repeat-offender cases a player can even be expelled from a league. Furthermore, professional athletes who consume large quantities of illicit drugs also run the risk of permanently damaging their health and jeopardizing their future well-being.

When a professional athlete chooses to consume a banned substance, the player must believe that the marginal benefits outweigh the marginal costs. Extremely large differences in pay separate the average professional athlete from the superstar athlete. It is not uncommon for superstar athletes to earn 10 or even 20 times the amount paid each season for a rookie or backup player. Given such disparity, it is easy to see why some athletes are tempted to find a chemical shortcut to superstar status. While the economic benefits of illicit drug consumption are quite large, the potential costs may not appear to be as significant. Not all consumers of illicit drugs are detected by the leagues. Each league enforces formal drug-testing policies, but no procedure is foolproof and some players avoid detection through deception and other means. Historically, the leagues' punishments for violating substance abuse policies were not very severe. Even today, the fines and suspensions for first-time offenders are usually small in comparison to an athlete's annual salary.

It is not surprising that the use of illicit drugs occurs in the professional sports industry. The potential marginal private benefits of future earnings is often quite large in comparison to the probability of detection and enforcement of league sanctions against substance abuse. Economic analysis suggests that professional sports leagues have two avenues to address the substance abuse problem. First, the leagues could find ways to reduce the economic reward of those who are found to use performance-enhancing drugs. For example, standard contracts could be written whereby athletes forfeit a significant portion of their salaries if the use of illicit drugs is detected. Second, the leagues could find ways to increase the probability of detecting the consumption of illicit drugs and increase the relative severity of sanctions. In fact, the leagues are already doing this. Although they have been opposed by the players' unions, in recent years each of the major sports leagues has strengthened its drug-testing procedures and implemented stronger penalties for those who violate them.

Given the potential rewards, it is unlikely that the use of performance-enhancing drugs will completely disappear from professional team sports—there will always be some athletes who choose to gamble and take the risk. However, by recognizing that the choice to consume illicit drugs is similar to other personal choices, the leagues can structure contracts and devise policies and sanctions that will reduce its prevalence.

The Case of Major League Soccer

The most popular professional team sport in the world is soccer (known outside the United States as football). However, professional soccer has struggled to capture the attention, and dollars, of the average American fan for years. Entrepreneurs several times have attempted to establish a soccer league modeled after those of the big four sports in the U.S. market. The most successful was the North American Soccer League (NASL), which operated from the late 1960s through 1985. The inability to maintain a profitable professional soccer league within the traditional business structure—independent team owners contractually obligated to each other under a league umbrella—resulted in a radically new type of structure when Major League Soccer (MLS) was launched in 1996.

MLS is a *single-entity league.* A single-entity league is organized as one corporation rather than as a group of individually owned teams. Instead of each team being a separate business with its unique set of owners, all MLS teams are part of one larger corporation owned jointly by a group of investors who buy corporate stock in the league. In this manner all MLS investors share in the ownership of all teams competing in the league. Some investors also buy a special class of stock that designates them as "investor-operators" and provides them with operating control over a team. The amount of control investor-operators can exert over a team is limited to day-to-day operations and management, since all employment contracts are between a player and the league and not between a player and a team. (All broadcast rights, licensing, and merchandising are also centrally controlled.) The league hires all players and then allocates them to the teams. By limiting the budget spent to hire each team's players the league directly enforces an equal salary cap on each team. Players do not have the ability to sell their skills to the highest bidder since there is only one bidder in the market, the MLS league office.

Clearly, under the single-entity structure MLS has even greater monopsony power over players than that exercised by the four major established leagues. An examination of soccer player salaries bears this out. While the average professional athlete in the major basketball, baseball, hockey, and football leagues commands salaries in the millions of dollars, the *maximum* salary offered by MLS to its top stars is "only" $280,000 a year. In fact, the salary cap imposed by MLS is approximately $2 million *per team* with the average player salary below the $100,000 mark. To put this in perspective, the average NBA *player* salary is about twice the salary cap for two MLS *teams.*

A close examination of the professional soccer market in the United States can explain why much of this observed salary disparity exists between soccer and the more established sports. In a nutshell, soccer is far less popular with American sports fans than basketball, baseball, football, or even hockey. Despite a national network contract, broadcasts of MLS games draw far fewer television viewers than any other major professional team sport. Furthermore, MLS games are played in smaller stadiums in front of smaller crowds. Since the league's inception, attendance has averaged around only 15,000 fans for each game. Thus MLS has a much smaller fan base from which to draw revenue than other professional team sports. In terms of our analysis in this chapter, all MLS players have a potential *MRP* that is significantly less than their counterparts in the other sports. Of course, lower *MRP*s imply that an employer, in this case the MLS central office, has less revenue to pay the employees, in this case the players.

But does the smaller market explain *all* of the gap between MLS and the other leagues? From the beginning, soccer players did not accept the small-market argument, and in the league's second year of existence they sued MLS, claiming that the league's business structure created a monopsony and that it exercised its market power to restrict wages to an artificially low level. In late 2000, the court ruled in favor of the MLS investor-owners. The court ruling was based on what constituted the relevant labor market for professional soccer players. Given that American players have always had the option to sell their services to professional leagues in Europe, South America, and Asia, the court declared that the single-entity structure of MLS did not technically result in a monopsony market for soccer players. The court held that the market for soccer players is a global market and that MLS competes for players with professional leagues in other nations. This fact, which allowed the MLS investor-owners to prevail in court, is ironically also a major stumbling block for the growth and development of the league. Star soccer players can command millions of dollars in Europe's premier leagues, making it very difficult for MLS to hire and keep the top-quality players it needs to develop a larger fan base and revenue stream.

Given the court ruling on the single-entity status of MLS, some have argued that team owners in the other leagues may consider restructuring plans to take advantage of the ability to centrally control the escalation of salaries through competitive bidding for athletic talent. In fact, NBA owners used the single-entity structure when they developed the first successful major women's basketball league, the WNBA. Whether the single-entity status is the wave of the future in professional team sports is not yet clear, but more antitrust cases are likely to be filed in the years to come by players seeking to earn what they consider to be their market worth.

Summary

The business of professional team sports provides an example of imperfect market structures. A unique characteristic of professional sports is the interdependence of teams. A professional team can be successful only if its competitors are successful. Each team must have rivals to play games and attract fans. To ensure their mutual success, ball clubs are organized into professional leagues. These leagues have important economic implications in both the product and resource markets.

Professional sports leagues are economic cartels. Through the leagues, teams formally agree to behave as if they were one firm—a shared monopoly. By forming cartels, sports clubs can increase the joint profits for all members of the league by restricting output and increasing price relative to a competitive market. By sharing the joint profits from the sale of their output, leagues can ensure the long-term survival of member teams.

In the resource market, professional sports leagues enforce employment rules that grant member clubs exclusive rights to player contracts. When a club holds the exclusive rights to contract with an athlete, the club is a monopsony—the single buyer of labor in the market. A monopsony is able to employ workers at wages below what would be observed in a competitive market. In recent years, professional athletes have won the right to free agency, which reduces the monopsony power of the clubs. In response to free agency, the average salaries of professional athletes have dramatically increased. The size of a professional athlete's paycheck reflects the player's contribution to his club's revenue.

Discussion Questions

1. Explain why professional sports teams must cooperate with one another in order to produce competitive games for fans.

2. What is a cartel? What industry characteristics are necessary for the successful formation and operation of a cartel?

3. Professional baseball enjoys a special legal exemption in the United States. What is this exemption, and why does it exist? Does it apply to other sports leagues?

4. Explain how professional sports leagues maximize joint profits through coordinated behavior in the product market. Will each team earn the same amount of profit under a cartel agreement as it would if market competition prevailed?

5. Why does a cartel's marginal revenue curve lie below its demand curve? Explain with a numerical example and a graph.

6. Why do taxpayers continue to support the public financing of new stadiums and arenas for professional sports teams? Are new stadiums and arenas good investments for a metropolitan area? Why or why not?

7. Discuss the economic pressures and incentives for professional sports teams to relocate. Are professional sports teams an important tool for a city's economic development? Explain why or why not.

8. What is a monopsony? What conditions give rise to a monopsony? How can professional sports teams be considered monopsonies?

9. What is free agency? How has it eroded the monopsonistic power of professional sports teams?

10. For many years professional football players have earned on average less than half of what professional baseball players earn. Using economic reasoning, how can this fact be explained?

11. Why do team owners rigorously regulate the number of teams in their league? Under what circumstances would team owners vote for an expansion in the number of teams? When would they vote for a reduction in the number of teams?

12. What is the difference between a strike and a lockout? Why are labor disputes so common in the professional sports industry?

13. Define what is known as monopsonistic profit. How is it different from normal profit? If an employer is earning monopsonistic profit, are workers being "underpaid"? Why or why not?

14. From an economic perspective, explain why some professional athletes choose to consume performance-enhancing drugs. What can professional sports leagues do to reduce the incidence of illicit substance use among players?

15. From an economic perspective, are professional sports players worth their multimillion-dollar salaries? Explain.

Additional Readings

Danielson, Michael N. *Home Team*. Princeton, NJ: Princeton University Press, 1997.
Excellent book that details the impact professional sports has on urban areas, with one chapter devoted to how stadiums affect where teams play.

Euchner, Charles C. *Playing the Field: Why Sports Teams Move and Cities Fight to Keep Them*. Baltimore: Johns Hopkins University Press, 1993.
Explores the competition between major cities to attract and keep professional sports franchises. Examines the economics and the politics of team relocation.

Fizel, John, Elizabeth Gustafson, and Lawrence Hadley, eds. *Sports Economics: Current Research*. Westport, CT: Praeger, 1999.
This collection of essays addresses sports leagues and markets, the location of teams and stadiums, and labor market issues in team sports.

Jones, Michael E. *Sports Law*. Upper Saddle River, NJ: Prentice Hall, 1998.
An interesting textbook that introduces the reader to a myriad of legal issues surrounding all aspects of professional and amateur sports in the United States. Specific chapters discuss labor and antitrust issues and the business of professional sports teams.

Lupica, Mike. *Mad as Hell: How Sports Got Away from the Fans and How We Get It Back*. New York: Putnam, 1996.
Irreverent and sometimes sarcastic examination of the business of professional sports from the fans' perspective.

Noll, Roger C., and Andrew Zimbalist, eds. *Sports, Jobs and Taxes: The Economic Impact of Sports Teams and Stadiums*. Washington, DC: The Brookings Institution, 1997.
A selection of articles examining the controversies surrounding the economics, finance, and politics of the sports facilities boom and its impact on local communities.

Quirk, James, and Rodney D. Fort. *Pay Dirt: The Business of Professional Team Sports*. 2nd ed. Princeton, NJ: Princeton University Press, 1997.
Inside look at the modern business of professional sports. Includes a detailed bibliographic reference section.

Rosentraub, Mark S. *Major League Losers: The Real Costs of Sports and Who's Paying for It*. Rev. ed. New York: Basic Books, 1999.
Discusses subsidizing sports, how governments make money from sports, how sports affect economic development in Canada, and other issues.

Scully, Gerald W. *The Business of Major League Baseball*. Chicago: University of Chicago Press, 1989.
In-depth economic analysis of the many facets of major league baseball.

Scully, Gerald W. *The Market Structure of Sports.* Chicago: University of Chicago Press, 1995.
Examines the market structure of professional sports leagues in the United States and provides an overview of the historical and current context of anti-competitive practices in the industry.

Sheehan, Richard G. *Keeping Score: The Economics of Big-Time Sports.* South Bend, IN: Diamond Communications, 1996.
In-depth and critical economic analysis of almost every major facet of modern professional sports. Also examines major college sports and the NCAA. Lots of numbers and statistics.

Staudohar, Paul D. *Playing for Dollars: Labor Relations and the Sports Business.* Ithaca, NY: ILR/Cornell Paperbacks, 1996.
The author describes the mechanics of contract and salary negotiations, including the issue of free agency. He also explores how unions became established in the four major American professional sports leagues and how they have affected the escalation of salaries.

Weiner, Jay. *Stadium Games: Fifty Years of Big League Greed and Bush League Boondoggles.* Minneapolis: University of Minnesota Press, 2000.
Weiner, a reporter for the Minneapolis-St. Paul *Star Tribune,* discusses the history of Minnesota stadiums from 1952 to 2000.

World Wide Web Resources

EconEdLink
www.econedlink.org/lessons/index.cfm?lesson=NN104

EconEdLink, maintained by the National Council on Economic Education, has links to "Underpaid Millionaires?" "If You Build It, Will They Come?" and "Comparative Advantage and Specialization," which are lessons in the economics of sports.

ESPN
www.espn.go.com

Provides daily sports news and commentary on the sports industry.

Major League Baseball
mlb.com

The official site of Major League Baseball. Gives statistics, scoreboards, standings, players, links to teams, and other information.

National Basketball Association
www.nba.com

League home page, which provides access to standings, statistics, news, and team pages.

National Football League

www.nfl.com

Provides access to standings, statistics, news, and team pages.

National Hockey League

www.nhl.com

Provides access to standings, statistics, news, and team pages.

SI.COM: Sports Illustrated

www.sportsillustrated.cnn.com

Created by CNN and *Sports Illustrated*. A Web-based sports page with links to professional and college sports, top stories, features, and *Sports Illustrated* for kids.

SportsEconomics

www.sportseconomics.com

www.SportsEconomics, a sports business consulting firm, fosters communication between researchers, professionals, and the public on a wide variety of sports economic topics. The site has links to data exchange, citations of industry research, and other information.

Protectionism versus Free Trade

Can We Restrict Ourselves into Prosperity?

Checklist of economic concepts

- Imports
- Exports
- Production possibilities curve
- Consumption possibilities curve
- Terms of trade
- Comparative advantage
- Comparative disadvantage
- Exchange rates
- Demand
- Supply
- Current account transactions
- Capital account transactions
- Balance of trade (merchandise)
- Balance of payments
- Tariffs
- Quotas
- Voluntary restraint agreements
- Embargoes
- Dumping
- Customs union
- Free trade area

Stunned by violent street protests resulting in scores of arrests, delegates to a 135-nation trade gathering insisted they would push ahead today with efforts to launch a new round of talks aimed at breaking down barriers to global commerce—and the city officials vowed to back them up. President Clinton was scheduled to address ministers today in the conference he has been banking on heavily, but was heading into a trashed downtown where officials sought to restore order with an overnight curfew and officers in riot gear. Washington Gov. Gary Locke ordered as many as 200 members of the National Guard and 300 state troopers to the city, where they will serve as backup to police who battled rampaging protesters with tear gas and pepper spray.

City officials declared a no-protest zone for nearly all of the city's downtown core, about 50 city blocks, acknowledging they were caught unaware by the magnitude of the disturbance. Police moved in swiftly to break up pockets of demonstrators and arrested about 250 of them, bringing in transit buses to take them away. Most of the protesters were nonviolent, going limp as police tried to pick them up. "This conference will be a success. The issues are far too important to be ignored," said Mike Moore, director general of the World Trade Organization.

WTO delegates long had expected protests, but nothing like the storm that hit Seattle when at least 40,000 activists took to the streets on the day the conference was to open. Some 5,000 protesters confronted police, with a handful launching an assault on the downtown business area. Windows were shattered everywhere from NikeTown to Santa's Village outside of Nordstrom. A Starbucks coffee shop was broken into and looted.

News of the violence generated headlines across Asia: "Demonstrators overrun Seattle," said a page-one headline in the *Times of India,* one of India's top national newspapers. In Tokyo, Yasushi Abe, an official at Japan's Ministry of International Trade and Industry, said he had anticipated protests. "But the scale of demonstrations and reported violence were beyond imagination," he said in an interview in Tokyo.

The protesters are unhappy with the Geneva-based organization that sets the rules for global trade, charging that it too often considers only the needs of giant multinational corporations at the expense of protecting the environment and worker rights. Some of the more moderate opponents want the WTO to include tougher labor and environmental standards in any trade deal—an idea strongly opposed by developing nations in Asia and Latin America that depend on cheap labor to make economic gains.

The wild protests drew angry responses from some WTO delegates. Colombia's external trade minister, Marta Lucia Ramirez, was jostled and shaken up, officials said, though apparently she was not seriously harmed. As other trade ministers dined at a gala miles away, police in body armor and gas masks fired tear gas and pepper spray to clear demonstrators from the downtown core. Hundreds ran choking from heavy clouds of gas. Seventeen minor injuries were reported, and 68 people had been arrested.

Source: George Tibbits, "WTO Session Disrupted, Ministers Insist They Will Carry On," Associated Press Wire Report, December 2, 1999.

THE CONTROVERSY OVER INTERNATIONAL TRADE

Once again, at the dawn of a new century, issues surrounding the trade of goods and services between nations have risen to the forefront of social consciousness. In fact, as the newspaper story above clearly reveals, people are so concerned about some of the perceived impacts of international trade that they are willing to riot in the streets to demonstrate for change. And these passions are not limited to the United States; during the past several years demonstrations over trade issues have taken place in Europe, Asia, and elsewhere. Today, international trade is an international social issue. Historically, since the human race has organized itself into geographic groups and engaged in trade among those groups, conflict has emerged between those wanting to suppress trade relationships and those wanting to promote them. The U.S. government severely restricted product imports right up to the end of World War II. Since the late 1940s, import restrictions have tended to fall slowly and steadily. The pace of the fall in the United States and the rest of the world, for that matter, has recently increased with the enactment of various multinational trade accords, such as the North American Free Trade Agreement and the World Trade Organization. Opposition remains keen, however. What underlies this conflict between *protectionists* and *free traders?* It is useful to consider the polar positions, recognizing that within the United States one finds all shades of intermediate positions—people who are free traders in some respects and protectionists in others.

The Protectionist Viewpoint

First, protectionists want to reduce foreign competition against U.S. goods and services. They see the importation and sale of foreign goods crowding U.S. goods out of the markets in such areas as stereo and video equipment, automobiles, steel, footwear, and textiles. They note that shrinking markets for U.S. goods means less demand for U.S. labor and higher domestic unemployment rates. Our industries cannot compete successfully, in the protectionists' view, against those in other countries that pay only a fraction of the wage rates that U.S. producers pay. The argument usually gains force during recession periods as unemployment increases. It also received much attention during the debates surrounding the North American Free Trade Agreement because that accord leads to the elimination of tariffs on imports from the notoriously low-wage economy of Mexico.

A second argument advanced by protectionists is that import restrictions are necessary to remedy balance of trade and balance of payments problems. They point to the continuing deficits in the U.S. balance of trade, noting how much more we pay out for our imports than we receive for our exports of goods. Sometimes, as was the case in the first half of the 1970s, these deficits are viewed as driving the dollar prices of foreign currencies up, making the dollar worth less. In this case, if we were to reduce our imports, the dollar demand for foreign currencies would also be reduced, decreasing the balance of trade deficits and protecting the value of the dollar. At other times, as during the early 1980s, the causal relationships are turned around. A strengthening dollar was seen as causing balance of trade deficits because it encourages imports and discourages exports. Protectionism is then advocated to block foreign competition from merchandise sales in the United States.

Another protectionist argument is that certain key industries in the United States are vital to our security and to our economic welfare. Among such industries we find automobiles, aerospace, steel, petroleum energy, and nuclear energy. We cannot depend on foreign suppliers during times of war. To be superior to other countries in technology of key industries, we must encourage their development and growth by restricting imports of those products from other countries.

Finally, a new set of protectionist arguments has gained widespread support in recent years. Adherents of this new perspective contend that trade barriers are necessary to protect Earth's natural environment and to prevent the exploitation of the world's impoverished workers. In fact, these were the primary issues which led to the Seattle riots and other notable recent demonstrations. It is argued that to remain globally competitive, large multinational corporations seek profits by pursuing low-cost, environmentally damaging production processes and monopsonistically reduce wages in markets where workers have severely limited job opportunities. Some blame the growth of international trade for the destruction of the South American rainforests and the inhumane working conditions found in the sweatshops of southeast Asia. To prevent such abuses, it is argued that strict labor regulations should be imposed on multinational corporations and that restrictions should be placed on trade in markets that are environmentally sensitive.

The Free Trade Viewpoint

Free traders generally maintain that the interests of consumers worldwide are best served if economic units in all countries are free to engage in whatever voluntary exchanges they believe will be advantageous to them. They see trade among nations conferring the same benefits on the exchanging parties as trade among individuals in any one country. If all parties to a potential voluntary exchange fail to see gain for themselves in it, then it will never be consummated. So why inhibit economic activity—voluntary exchange—that takes place only if all participants gain? We are all made better off, they argue, through specialization and voluntary exchange.

THE ECONOMICS OF INTERNATIONAL TRADE

What can economic theory contribute toward resolving the conflict of viewpoints? It is useful to learn and apply to the problem (1) the underlying mechanics of international trade, (2) the production and consumption possibilities of a country, without trade and with trade, (3) the principle of comparative advantage, (4) the financing of international trade, and (5) the economics of international trade restrictions. The world is increasingly becoming a global marketplace, and it is vitally important to understand how international trade affects our economy and our own standard of living.

How Trade Takes Place

It takes two to tango. A country cannot unilaterally import unless it also exports goods. Neither can it export unless it also imports goods.

Suppose the *only* potential international transaction that exists, now and forever, between the United States and the rest of the world is the importation by me of a German BMW automobile. This assumption is ridiculous, but it illustrates an important point. Where would I get the euros to make the purchase? The answer is obvious. There are and will be none available. Or, looking at it from the other side of the water, if I want to pay in dollars, what would the Germans do with dollars? They would have no use for dollars and, consequently, would not accept them. The transaction would never take place.

Suppose now that I want to import a BMW, and Cessna Aircraft wants to export a Cessna to a German citizen. If Cessna can sell the airplane for euros, then I can buy euros from Cessna for dollars, using the euros in turn to purchase the BMW. In order for people in one country to import, it is also necessary that they export. There is no escape from this fundamental proposition.

Production and Consumption Possibilities

In general, why do people in different countries want to engage in exchange? The underlying reason is that it enables them to increase the levels of well-being they can get from their resources. Recall from Chapter 1 that an economy's production possibilities curve shows the maximum quantities of goods and services that can be produced when the economy's resources are used efficiently. Given this, the production possibilities curve may also be thought of as a **consumption possibilities curve** because, in the absence of trade, the economy can consume no more than it produces. With trade, however, it becomes possible to consume more than is produced domestically. That is, trade can cause the consumption possibilities curve to shift outward, beyond the production possibilities curve. Thus, trade enables the totality of consumers in each country to achieve higher satisfaction levels with the complement of labor, capital, and technology available to them. Let's see how it works for two countries, Alpha and Omega, that can engage in trade with each other and with other countries of the world.

consumption possibilities curve Graph of the maximum quantities of two goods and/or services that can be consumed in an economy when its resources are used efficiently.

Without Trade

Consider the production and consumption possibilities of Alpha in the absence of international trade. Given Alpha's resources and techniques, suppose its economic system can produce either 100 million loaves of bread or 200 million gallons of milk. Assuming that its resources are unspecialized to either product, the trade-off between the two products is one for two. By giving up 1 million loaves of bread, the resources released can always be used to produce an additional 2 million gallons of milk. So Alpha alone can produce and consume any combination of bread and milk on line *AB* in Figure 10.1. Thus, *AB* is both Alpha's production possibilities curve and its consumption possibilities curve in the absence of trade. Suppose its people select combination *C*, containing 50 million loaves of bread and 100 million gallons of milk.

FIGURE 10.1 **Alpha's Production and Consumption Possibilities with and without Trade**
In the absence of trade, Alpha's resources will produce 100 million loaves of bread, or 200 million gallons of milk, or any combination of the two products as shown by *AB*. Given this, *AB* is both the production and consumption possibilities curve for Alpha when there is no trade.

If terms of trade are one for one, with trade Alpha's production possibilities curve remains *AB*, but its consumption possibilities curve rotates outward to A_1B. Alpha can concentrate on milk production and can trade for bread at less than it would cost to produce it in Alpha.

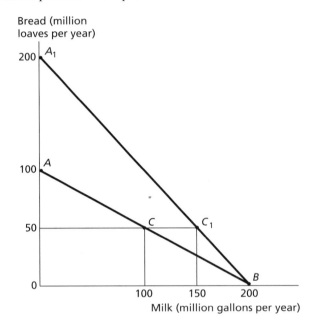

Let Omega's resources differ somewhat from those of Alpha, but consider that they, too, are unspecialized. Suppose that Omega's economy can produce, without trade, either 100 million loaves of bread or 50 million gallons of milk. The trade-off in production between the two products is 0.5 million gallons of milk for 1 million loaves of bread, or 2 million loaves of bread for 1 million gallons of milk. Thus, Omega's production possibilities curve is *MN* in Figure 10.2. Likewise, since there is no trade, *MN* is also Omega's consumption possibilities curve. Suppose its population settles on combination *P*, containing 50 million loaves of bread and 25 million gallons of milk.

With Trade

What would happen if Alpha and Omega were now able to enter into international trade relationships? Under what circumstances would Alpha and Omega be willing to trade bread for milk? Or milk for bread? First, we determine the limits within which the terms of trade must fall if the countries are to engage in trade. Second, we show what trade within the terms of trade limits will do for each country.

FIGURE 10.2   **AOmega's Production and Consumption Possibilities with and without Trade**
In the absence of trade, Omega's resources will produce per year 100 million loaves of bread, or 50 million gallons of milk, or any combination shown on the line *MN*. Given this, *MN* is both the production and consumption possibilities curve for Omega when there is no trade.

If terms of trade are one for one, with trade Omega's production possibilities curve remains *MN*, but its consumption possibilities curve rotates outward to MN_1. Omega can concentrate on bread production and trade for milk at less than it would cost to produce it in Omega.

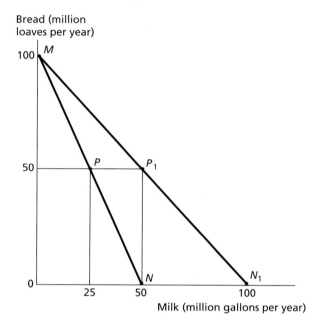

Alpha would refuse to enter into any trade relationships in which the cost of importing 1 gallon of milk exceeds 0.5 loaf of bread, or in which the cost of importing 1 loaf of bread exceeds 2 gallons of milk. A gallon of milk produced domestically costs Alpha only 0.5 loaf of bread. Why import it if the cost per gallon of the import is greater? A loaf of bread produced domestically costs 2 gallons of milk, so Alpha would not be willing to pay more to import it. We summarize these results in Table 10.1.

Omega would not voluntarily engage in trade if the terms of trade exceed 2 loaves of bread for the importation of 1 gallon of milk or 0.5 gallon of milk for the importation of 1 loaf of bread. It could do better producing both domestically. These limits are shown in Table 10.1.

Suppose now that as the countries consider engaging in trade, the terms of trade between bread and milk settle at a gallon of milk for a loaf of bread. Both Alpha and Omega can gain from trade. The reason each can gain is that while trade leaves each country's production possibilities curve unchanged, trade causes their consumption possibilities curves to rotate outward.

TABLE 10.1
Limits to Terms of
Trade between
Bread and Milk,
Alpha and Omega

	Alpha	Omega
Bread	1	2
Milk	2	1

If Alpha produces only milk and trades milk for bread, the population of the country can import one loaf of bread for each gallon of milk it is willing to export. If it were to export all its milk, it could import 200 million loaves of bread. While the production possibilities curve remains *AB*, Alpha's consumption possibilities curve rotates outward to A_1B in Figure 10.1. Thus, the impact of trade is to allow the citizens of Alpha to consume more than can be produced domestically, given their resources and technology.

If Omega concentrates all its resources on breadmaking and trades for milk, it can import a gallon of milk for every loaf of bread it produces and exports. If it exports 100 million loaves of bread, it can import 100 million gallons of milk. Thus, with trade, Omega's production possibilities curve remains *MN*, but its consumption possibilities curve becomes MN_1 in Figure 10.2. That is, as was true for Alpha, trade allows the citizens of Omega to consume more than can be produced domestically, given their resources and technology.

Country Alpha will concentrate on the production of milk, and Country Omega will produce bread. Producing milk only, Alpha's people are not limited to combination *C* of milk and bread, which contains 50 million loaves of bread and 100 million gallons of milk. They can produce 200 million gallons of milk and trade 50 million gallons for 50 million loaves of bread, leaving themselves with combination C_1, containing 150 million gallons of milk and 50 million loaves of bread. They are 50 million gallons of milk better off than they were before the trade.

Country Omega's people will be better off producing only bread and trading for milk. Before trade they chose combination *P*, containing 50 million loaves of bread and 25 million gallons of milk. By specializing in bread, they can produce 100 million loaves, trade 50 million loaves for 50 million gallons of milk, and end up with combination P_1, containing 50 million gallons of milk and 50 million loaves of bread. Trade enables them to obtain a net gain of 25 million gallons of milk.

The Principle of Comparative Advantage

comparative advantage
The ability of a country to produce a good at a lower opportunity cost of producing the good than any other country.

Clearly, specialization and exchange help both Alpha and Omega increase the volumes of goods and services available for their people to consume. It pays any country to specialize in producing those things in which it has a **comparative advantage** and to trade for goods in which it experiences a **comparative disadvantage.**

comparative disadvantage
The inability of a country to produce a good except at a higher opportunity cost of producing the good than another country.

A country has a comparative advantage in the production of any good that it can produce with a smaller sacrifice of some alternative good or goods, that is, at a lower opportunity cost, than can the rest of the trading world. Note that there is no presumption that the country can produce that good at a lower *absolute* cost than can other countries. In terms of the number of units of labor and capital necessary to produce a million gallons of milk, Alpha may use 3 times (or 10 times) more of each than other countries. Yet if Alpha must give up 0.5 million loaves of bread for 1 million gallons of milk and can trade the million gallons of milk for *more* than 0.5 million loaves of bread, Alpha has a comparative advantage in producing milk. Use this same reasoning to determine Omega's comparative advantage product, if any.

Symmetrically, a country has a *comparative disadvantage* in the production of any good that requires a greater sacrifice of some alternative good or goods, that is, it produces at a higher opportunity cost, than is required in the rest of the trading world. Country Alpha in our example has a comparative disadvantage in the production of bread. It must sacrifice 2 gallons of milk for a loaf of bread if it produces bread domestically. But it can import a loaf of bread by giving up only 1 gallon of milk to the international market. In which product does Omega have a comparative disadvantage?

Look again at the complete examples of Alpha and Omega, without and with trade. Note that if a country has a comparative advantage in the production of one good (and it most certainly will have in the real world), it must have a comparative disadvantage in the production of some other good or goods. Usually a country will have comparative advantages in the production of several goods and comparative disadvantages in the production of several others.

The reasons that every country has comparative advantages in the production of some goods and comparative disadvantages in the production of others is that countries differ in their respective resource endowments and in their states of technology. Some countries are short on certain mineral deposits such as oil, coal, and copper, but they may have relatively large quantities of good capital equipment and high levels of technological know-how. Such a country, Japan, for example, will likely have comparative advantages in the production and sale of goods embodying high technology and good stocks of capital with which to work. Some countries have vast quantities of good agricultural land while others do not. Some are particularly well-suited in terms of climate, terrain, and soil to grow outstanding wine grapes. Some excel in coffee production, and others in growing tea. A beef industry seldom thrives in densely populated, mountainous countries. Some countries have high literacy rates. In others the bulk of the population may be illiterate. All these differences, and many more, confer on each country or region of a country certain comparative advantages and disadvantages that make specialization and exchange worthwhile.

How International Trade Is Financed

International trade has two important characteristics that set it apart from trade within the boundaries of any given country. First, each country, or group of countries, has its own currency. Producers in any given country want to be paid in that currency, and buyers want to use it to pay for goods and services. Second, nationalism, regionalism, and political objectives are invariably injected into trade

TABLE 10.2
Dollar Exchange Rates for Selected Foreign Currencies, Winter 2005

Source: The Wall Street Journal, January 19, 2005, p. C14.

Country	Dollars	Foreign Currency Unit
Argentina	0.3406	1 peso
Australia	0.7556	1 dollar
Britain	1.8669	1 pound
Canada	0.8169	1 dollar
Denmark	0.1750	1 krone
European Union	1.3023	1 euro
Japan	0.0097	1 yen
Mexico	0.0889	1 peso
Saudi Arabia	0.2666	1 riyal
South Africa	0.1643	1 rand
South Korea	0.0009	1 won
Switzerland	0.8435	1 franc
Taiwan	0.3136	1 dollar

relationships among nations. All sorts of impediments to trade are enacted by governments to further political ends even though the trade, if allowed, would have been in the best economic interests of the trading parties. Remember that voluntary exchange will occur only if *all* parties to the exchange expect to gain. In this section we concentrate mostly on the problems arising from the different currency units used by different countries.

The link between the currencies of any two trading countries is the exchange rate. An **exchange rate** is the price of one country's currency in terms of the monetary units of another. It is useful for us to think of it as the dollar price of another country's currency. We list a recent sample of such exchange rates in Table 10.2. The dollar exchange rate for the British pound of $1.55 is the highest one listed. The lowest one listed is $0.0008 for the South Korean won (this amounts to 8 one-hundredths of a cent).

Exchange rates, in the absence of intervention by governments, are determined in exchange markets that arise from millions of such transactions as the importation of a BMW automobile into the United States or the export of a Cessna airplane to Germany. The existence of exchange markets makes the pairing of individual import transactions with individual export transactions unnecessary. Anyone in the United States can buy foreign currency with dollars and can use it to import that country's goods. Similarly, anyone with excess amounts of a foreign currency on hand from selling goods abroad, or for any other reason, can sell that currency for dollars in the foreign exchange market.

In the absence of government intervention, the exchange rate of any home country currency for a foreign currency is determined, like any other price, by the forces of demand for and supply of the foreign currency. To understand the demand for and supply of foreign currency, remember that people in the home country demand foreign currency so that they might purchase goods from the foreign country, while foreigners supply foreign currency through their demand for goods produced in the home country. Specifically, the demand curve for the foreign

exchange rate
The price of one country's currency in terms of the monetary units of another country.

FIGURE 10.3   U.S. Demand, Supply, and Exchange Rate for Pounds
Demand for pounds is represented by *DD,* and supply is *SS.* The equilibrium exchange rate is *r* dollars per pound, and the equilibrium quantity of pounds is *q.*

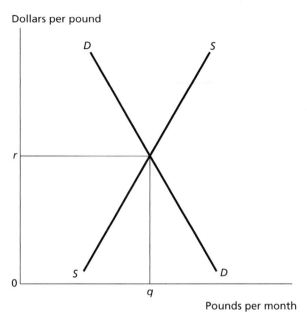

Dollars per pound

Pounds per month

currency is essentially the same as the demand curve for anything else. That is, it slopes downward to the right, like *DD* in Figure 10.3, since it is derived from the demand for foreign goods, which is itself negatively sloped. Similarly, the supply curve *SS* illustrated in Figure 10.3 usually slopes upward to the right because it is derived from the foreign demand for goods produced in the home country. The exchange rate *r* is the equilibrium price. Quantity *q* is the equilibrium quantity exchanged of the foreign currency.

In order to discuss the demand for and supply of foreign currency more formally, consider the summary of U.S. international transactions for 2003, which is presented in Table 10.3. As noted above, our demand for foreign currency arises from our desire for foreign goods. Thus, our demand for foreign currency may be determined by identifying any payments that we want to make abroad. The largest part of our demand for foreign currencies in 2003 arose from imports of goods, shown on line 2. This demand source is straightforward. During 2003 we needed $1,260.67 billion worth of foreign currencies to purchase goods imported from other nations. The second largest part of our demand for foreign currency arose from increases in U.S. investments abroad; this is shown on line 6. When American companies invest abroad, they need foreign currencies to purchase land, build plants, and buy equipment. According to Table 10.3, this amounted to $283.41 billion in 2003. Much smaller but third in importance is the transfer of funds by private individuals and organizations shown on line 5. This figure

TABLE 10.3
U.S. International
Transactions,
Summary, 2003
(billions of current
dollars)

Source: U.S. Department of
Commerce (Bureau of
Economic Analysis) and
Department of the
Treasury.

Transaction Type	Demand for Foreign Currency	Supply of Foreign Currency	Balance
Current Account			
1. Goods exported		713.12	
2. Goods imported	−1,260.67		
3. Net services		51.04	
4. Net investments	−33.28		
5. Transfers	−67.44		
Balance on current account			−597.23
Capital Account			
6. Change in U.S. assets abroad	−283.41		
7. Change in foreign assets in the United States		829.17	
Balance on capital account			545.76
Totals	−1,644.80	1,593.33	51.47
Statistical discrepancy			51.47

represents the foreign currency needed to support cash gifts and grants made to relatives, friends, and organizations abroad. Finally, line 4 of Table 10.3 reports the demand for foreign currency needed to support interest payments, dividends, and capital gains on investments held in the United States by foreigners. This amounted to $33.28 billion in 2003. Summing all the sources of demand results in a total demand for foreign currency of $1,644.80 billion during 2003.

Supplies of foreign currencies, as one would expect, arise from transactions reciprocal to those generating demand. A significant source of foreign currency in 2003 was the export of goods. Line 1 of Table 10.3 indicates that this amounted to $713.12 billion. Also of importance was the change in assets within the United States held by foreigners. This represents new investments here by foreign companies and individuals. Examples of such investments include the Japanese building a new car plant or the Dutch buying U.S. property or financial securities. The level of foreign investment in the United States has been increasing in recent years. Line 7 of Table 10.3 reports that $829.17 billion in new foreign investment occurred in 2003. A third source of foreign currency was the net export of services. This includes transactions undertaken by the military abroad, travel and transportation receipts from foreigners, and other services produced by Americans while overseas. In 2003 net services accounted for $51.04 billion in our supply of foreign currencies. Adding together each source of foreign currency results in a total supply of $1,593.33 billion during 2003.

The separation of transactions in Table 10.3 into "current account" and "capital account" categories is simply a classification convenience. Current account items are more or less immediate and short term in character. A transaction is consummated, and that is the end of it. Other transactions of a similar nature are occurring concurrently and over time. Capital account items are long-term transactions that will persist into the future and yield continuing influence on the demand for and supply of foreign exchange.

Notice the difference between the total demand for and the total supply of foreign exchanges listed in Table 10.3. It amounted to $51.47 billion, a sizable pocketful of change, but it is simply a statistical discrepancy: a failure to get all international transactions on record. Such a discrepancy is not a cause for concern.

International Trade Restrictions

Despite the strong arguments that favor the free exchange of goods and services between countries, governments often impose restrictions on international trade. Protectionist laws that tax and regulate the flow of goods between nations have a long and colorful world history. International trade has been a controversial social issue for centuries. In fact, the philosophical debates concerning the English "corn laws" of the eighteenth century, which restricted the trade of food grains, were instrumental in the development of classical economics. In today's global economy, international trade restrictions generally fall into one of four broad categories: (1) tariffs, (2) quotas, (3) voluntary restraint agreements, and (4) embargoes. In this section we briefly describe each category and examine the economic effects of international trade restrictions.

Tariffs

tariff
A tax placed on internationally traded goods, usually imports.

A **tariff** is a tax placed on internationally traded goods, usually imports. Tariffs are the oldest and most common form of international trade restriction. In the United States, tariffs have been imposed on imported goods since the American Revolution. Throughout much of our history, tariffs were an important source of federal government revenue. Since the Great Depression, tariffs have been imposed primarily to protect domestic jobs and production, not as a means of generating tax revenue. Today, revenue from tariffs represents an insignificant portion of the total U.S. budget.

The economic effects of a tariff are shown in Figure 10.4. *DD* represents the demand curve for a specific brand of imported Japanese cars, and *SS* represents the supply curve of these cars exported from Japan to the United States. Without a tariff, or other form of trade restriction, 10,000 cars per year will be sold at the domestic market equilibrium price of $20,000. When a tariff of $5,000 is placed on cars imported from Japan, the supply curve shifts back by the amount of the tariff. The new supply curve reflecting the tariff is shown as S_1S_1 in Figure 10.4. In effect, the tariff increases the marginal cost of producing and exporting the Japanese cars to the United States. With the tariff in place, a new market equilibrium will be established at the intersection of the S_1S_1 curve and the *DD* curve. Notice that the tariff results in a higher price for consumers and a lower number of imported car sales. In our example, the tariff raises the price to $22,500, an increase of $2,500, and lowers the quantity sold to 8,000, a decrease of 2,000 cars per year.

FIGURE 10.4　The Economic Effects of an Import Tariff
The *DD* and *SS* curves represent the demand and supply curves for cars imported from Japan. Without a tariff, 10,000 cars will be sold per year at an equilibrium price of $20,000. A $5,000 tariff reduces supply to $S_1 S_1$. With the tariff, only 8,000 cars will be sold per year at a price of $22,500. In this case, the burden of the tariff is shared equally by the Japanese producers and the domestic consumers.

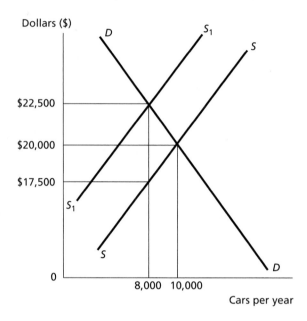

Why is the increase in price ($2,500) less than the tariff ($5,000)? The answer is that the burden of the tariff is shared by the consumers and producers. Buyers pay the Japanese car producers $22,500 for each car, but in turn the producers must pay the U.S. government a $5,000 tariff per sale. Thus, the net revenue to the producer is only $17,500 per car ($22,500 − $5,000). Without the tariff, producers would have kept the entire $20,000 original selling price. Thus, in our example, the burden of the tariff is equally shared. Producers receive $2,500 less in revenue, and consumers pay $2,500 more in terms of a higher price. In practice, the relative shares of the tariff burden depend on the relative shapes of the demand and supply curves.

The government will collect revenue from the tariff equal to the amount of the tariff times the number of cars sold. In our example, this would be $5,000 × 8,000 = $4,000,000. Therefore, the government receives $4 million in new revenue from the imposition of the tariff. Tariff revenues are often referred to as *import duties* and are generally collected by customs agencies when goods are physically brought into the country.

Tariffs also have an effect on domestic producers. Because tariffs reduce the quantity of foreign-produced goods and raise their price, the demand for domestically produced products increases. In our example, tariffs on Japanese cars will increase the demand for American-made Chevrolets and Fords. As the demand for domestically produced cars increases, so too will their prices. The end result is higher prices for both Japanese and American cars.

Tariffs and their economic effects made headlines in the spring of 2002 when President Bush announced his approval of a plan to impose tariffs of up to 30 percent on steel imported into the United States. Previously, President Bush had advocated lower tariffs and freer international trade as part of his administration's standing economic policy. The economic rationale cited by the administration for contradicting this policy centered on arguments concerning the protection of American jobs and the safeguarding of a key domestic industry—two arguments that are almost universally cited to justify taxing imported goods (as we shall see shortly). Over the two decades prior to Bush's announcement, total employment in the U.S. steel industry fell from about 450,000 to around 150,000. Much of this decline resulted from improvements in productivity and the dissemination of technological advances throughout the industry. Over this period some domestic jobs were undoubtedly lost to foreign competition, but during the three years immediately preceding the announcement of new steel tariffs, domestic steel producers were reclaiming previously lost sales as the market share held by foreign steel producers fell from 28 to only 21 percent.

The new steel tariffs were not warmly received by U.S. trading partners around the world, who threatened to retaliate by imposing tariffs of their own on American-made goods. Many domestic consumer groups also protested the tariffs, citing the fear that the new taxes would translate into higher costs for cars, appliances, and other consumer goods. The standard economic analysis of tariffs as discussed in this section indicates that such fears are well founded. In fact, estimates indicate that the average American family will pay more than $200 a year in higher prices due to the new steel tariffs. Although a relatively small amount, to many consumers this seemed to be an excessively high price to pay to save 8,000 to 10,000 jobs. As is the case in the implementation of most international trade restrictions, the costs of the steel tariffs will be spread throughout the entire economy while the benefits will be concentrated among a select group. This makes tariffs and other trade restrictions politically appealing to elected officials even though they are generally economically unattractive.

Quotas

quota
A regulation that limits by law the quantity of specific foreign goods or services that may be imported during a period of time.

A second method by which governments can restrict international trade is called a **quota.** A quota limits by law the quantity of specific foreign goods or services that may be imported during a period of time. Quotas are used less often than tariffs, but they are still a common form of international trade restriction. Examples of quotas imposed by the United States include those on peanuts, cotton, and sugar.

Figure 10.5 illustrates the economic effects of a quota. In this example, *DD* represents the demand curve for sugar imported into the United States from Brazil, and *SS* represents the supply curve of sugar exported from Brazil to the United States. Without a quota or other form of trade restriction, the market equilibrium price would be $30 per ton, and 1,000 tons of Brazilian sugar would be purchased by U.S. consumers. Now, assume that a quota of 750 tons per year is imposed. This

FIGURE 10.5 **The Economic Effects of an Import Quota**

The *DD* and *SS* curves represent the demand and supply curves for sugar imported from Brazil. Without a quota, 1,000 tons of sugar will be sold per year at an equilibrium price of $30 per ton. A quota of 750 tons per year reduces supply to S_1S_1. This new supply curve is vertical because only 750 tons can be sold per year regardless of price. Given *DD*, the equilibrium price with the quota will be $35 per ton. Because Brazilian suppliers of sugar are willing to sell 750 tons per year for $25 per ton, holders of import licenses will earn an extra $10 per ton in profits due to the quota.

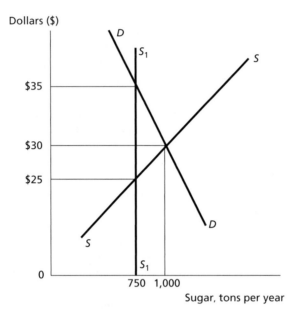

results in a new vertical supply curve at the quota limit, as shown by the S_1S_1 curve in Figure 10.5. The new supply curve is vertical because only 750 tons of Brazilian sugar can be sold in the United States—regardless of the market price. The quota results in the establishment of a new market equilibrium at the intersection of the *DD* and S_1S_1 curves. Thus, in Figure 10.5, the price of Brazilian sugar in the United States will rise to $35 per ton.

According to the original supply curve *SS* in Figure 10.5, Brazilian suppliers of sugar are willing to sell 750 tons of sugar to the United States at a price of $25. What, then, is the difference between the price that consumers must pay with the quota ($35) and the price received by Brazilian suppliers ($25)? This $10 per ton of sugar is extra profit earned by the holders of the quota rights. Often licenses will be granted to foreign governments or companies that give them the right to export specific quantities of products to the United States. The owners of these licenses therefore receive the profits generated by the quota restrictions. Notice that the source of these profits is divided between the foreign suppliers and American consumers in a manner similar to the shared burden of import tariffs. (Foreign suppliers receive $5 per ton less than what they would receive with free trade, and American consumers pay $5 per ton more than they would with free trade.)

Quotas also increase the price of domestically produced goods. As quotas restrict the quantity of foreign goods and raise their price, the demand for substitutes made in the United States will increase. If all else is held constant, an increase in the demand for these domestically produced goods will result in higher prices. Quotas, therefore, also result in higher prices for both foreign and domestically produced goods.

Voluntary Restraint Agreements

voluntary restraint agreement
An international treaty whereby one nation "volunteers" to restrict its exports of a product that it sells to another nation.

In recent years, a new form of international trade restriction has emerged. A **voluntary restraint agreement** occurs when one nation "volunteers" to restrict its exports of a product that it sells to another nation. In essence, a voluntary restraint agreement is a quota without the effect of law. In the United States, tariffs and quotas must be approved by Congress, but voluntary restraint agreements can be negotiated by the president. Voluntary restraint agreements became popular when the United States negotiated an agreement with Japan in the 1980s that placed voluntary limits on the number of cars that Japanese companies sold in America.

Because they do not have the force of law, voluntary restraint agreements are negotiated when one nation places economic or political pressure on another. In this sense, such agreements may not always be voluntary. For example, Japan agreed to limit the sales of cars in the United States due to the threat of new heavy tariffs and quotas in other sectors of the economy.

The economic effects of voluntary restraint agreements are similar to those of a quota. Foreign producers must coordinate their export activity, as if they were monopolists, in order to maintain the voluntary limits. The result once again is a restriction in the number of foreign-produced goods and an increase in the price for domestic consumers.

Embargoes

embargo
Government provision formally preventing one nation from trading goods and services with another nation or group of nations, intended to eliminate international trade between the countries in question.

The most extreme form of international trade restriction is an embargo. An **embargo** occurs when one nation is formally prevented from trading goods and services with another nation or group of nations. Effectively, an embargo is an import and export quota set at zero. Most embargoes result from political disputes between countries, but they may be imposed for economic reasons as well. The United States has been the target of embargoes, such as the one imposed by the Organization of Petroleum-Exporting Countries (OPEC) in the 1970s, and it has also implemented embargoes against other nations. A classic example of an embargo imposed by the United States is the longstanding embargo against commercial trade with Cuba. This embargo was imposed against Castro's dictatorship with the hopes of destabilizing the communist government and bringing about democratic reforms. The Cuban embargo has not met its political goals, but the economic effects have been dramatic.

To understand the economic effects of an embargo recall our example at the beginning of this chapter. We saw that nations which engage in trade can increase their levels of consumption beyond their levels of domestic production through the principle of comparative advantage. The overall level of well-being derived from existing resources rises in each country when trade occurs. An enforced embargo that prohibits trade between countries, therefore, prevents potential trading partners from enjoying the mutual benefits of trade which derive from the principle of comparative advantage. An embargo limits consumption possibilities to the level determined by production possibilities (refer back to Figures 10.1 and 10.2) in both countries. Clearly, then, an embargo is a trade policy that imposes not only an economic cost on the target nation but also a significant cost on the nation implementing the trading ban. This is certainly true in the case of the U.S. embargo against Cuba. Because of the embargo, Cubans forgo a host of American-made goods and American consumers are prevented from savoring Cuban cigars or purchasing Cuban sugar and fruits at U.S. supermarkets. As with any quota, prices are higher and total output available is less in the United States for those goods which could be imported, as in this case, from Cuba. In 2002, the U.S. Congress opened holes in the embargo to allow the exportation of agricultural products to the island as a humanitarian gesture of goodwill. However, Cuba was required to pay for these exports in cash with American dollars. The Cuban government's immediate purchase of millions of dollars of foodstuffs produced in the United States indicates that the embargo had not stopped the flow of dollars into Cuba through international trade with third-party countries and through international remittances by Cuban-Americans to relatives and friends still living in Cuba.

ANALYSIS OF THE CONTROVERSY

In light of this brief survey of the economics of international trade, what light is shed on the controversy between protectionists and free traders? Should we protect ourselves from imports of Japanese and European automobiles and steel? Is it wise to limit textile imports from South Korea, Taiwan, and China? Is the importation of Japanese motorcycles a threat to our prosperity? Will the expansion of a global marketplace destroy the environment and exploit impoverished workers in the lesser developed countries? In analyzing these issues, it is important that we separate economic from political considerations. Economic analysis provides insight primarily into the former.

Protection from Cheap Foreign Goods

The principle of comparative advantage and the economic gains ensuing from specialization and exchange make it reasonably clear that a country's population as a whole will lose from import restrictions. They will have less of all goods and services to consume. Real per capita income and living standards will be lower than they would be if all potential international voluntary exchanges are allowed to be consummated. Foreign goods cannot displace all or even a large part of the domestic production and sale of goods. A country cannot import unless, by selling domestic goods and services or other kinds of domestic assets to foreigners, it earns foreign exchange with which to buy those imports. International trade is a two-way street enabling those countries that engage in it to shift their consumption possibilities curves outward. It serves to *increase* the real per capita income and living standards in the trading countries.

Free trade may indeed injure *segments* of a country's economy. It is concern for that part of the population investing in and working in the injured segments that prompts most protectionist efforts. Import quotas and/or high tariffs on steel and automobiles keep the demands for the outputs of domestic steel and automobile manufacturers higher than they would otherwise be, thus supporting profits, wages, and employment in those industries. Free trade enables foreign competitors to enter the domestic producers' markets, resulting in lower domestic profits, wages, and employment levels in those industries.

Consequently, the imposition of import restrictions leads to winners (those investing and working in the protected sector) and losers (consumers who must pay higher prices for the protected good). But do the winners "win" by more than the losers "lose"? In other words, do the benefits of the import restrictions outweigh the costs? Considering the case of automobiles will help us see that in the typical case, the costs of import restrictions far outweigh the benefits. In the early 1980s, in response to poor domestic auto sales, the Reagan administration was successful in getting Japan to voluntarily limit auto exports to the United States. The major benefit of the import restriction was the significant number of jobs saved in the auto sector (at the expense of jobs lost in the export sector). The cost of the program increased the price that consumers had to pay for autos. Which was greater? One estimate suggests that the voluntary import restriction imposed a cost of $160,000 per job saved.[1] That is, in an effort to save a job paying $30,000 to $40,000, we spent $160,000. Even more startling and costly outcomes have been found for protectionistic practices in areas as divergent as the importation of luggage, ceramic tiles, and peanuts. Table 10.4 provides a look at the estimated costs of protecting American jobs through recent trade restriction policies.

If the benefits of import restrictions rarely outweigh the costs, why is protectionism so popular? The gains from free trade, because they are spread over the entire consuming population, tend to be unnoticed by the average individual. The same is not true with respect to those injured by free trade. Had the import restrictions on Japanese autos not been in effect, numerous individuals would have lost their jobs. Significant personal losses of this nature are easily noticed by the entire population. Consequently, it is not strange to find that "free traders win the arguments, but protectionists win the elections," as the anonymous saying goes.

Outsourcing of Service Jobs

In recent years, protectionists have added a new element in their call for trade restrictions. Along with the centuries-old argument for protection against cheap foreign *goods,* modern protectionists also argue that the increased importation of *services* damages the American economy. This is the "outsourcing" controversy

---

[1]Robert W. Crandall, "Import Quotas and the Automobile Industry: The Costs of Protection," *Brookings Review,* Summer 1984, p. 8.

TABLE 10.4

Estimated Costs of Protecting American Jobs from Foreign Competition

Source: G. C. Hufbauer and K. A. Elliott, *Measuring the Costs of Protection in the United States* (Washington, DC: Institute for International Economics, 1994), pp. 11–13.

Protected Industry	Number of Jobs Saved	Total Cost (in Millions)	Annual Cost per Job Saved
Luggage	226	$ 290	$1,285,078
Sugar	2,261	1,868	826,104
Frozen concentrated orange juice	609	387	635,103
Ceramic tiles	347	191	551,367
Canned tuna	390	100	247,889
Peanuts	397	74	187,223
Women's fashion footwear	3,702	142	132,870

that first captured the public's attention during the economic downturn of 2001. With the advent of the Internet and other advances in modern telecommunications, it became possible for businesses to move some routine service operations overseas, where wages and overhead costs are lower. Thus, consumers soon found out that the clerk who took their catalog order over the phone was located in India and not in Indiana. Software companies and accounting firms also found it profitable to hire programmers and bookkeepers physically located overseas in other nations. Of course, when such service jobs are moved "offshore," these jobs are lost domestically. It is estimated that between 2000 and 2003, between 155,000 and 215,000 service jobs were shifted overseas.

Is the loss of a couple of hundred thousand service jobs detrimental to the overall health of the American economy? As presented in this chapter, economic theory suggests not. Although the outsourcing of jobs overseas will impose short-run costs on those workers whose jobs are initially lost, in the long run the domestic economy benefits from the trade. When a computer programming job is outsourced to India, India must have a comparative advantage in the production of that service. Remember, a nation imports from those trading partners that produce more efficiently at a lower cost. Thus, domestic prices for software are lower than those that would exist without trade. Furthermore, domestic resources are freed up for employment in other areas where the United States maintains a comparative advantage. As we have seen, international trade, based on comparative advantage, always benefits both trading partners. Efforts to prohibit or limit the outsourcing of service jobs would impose significant costs and inefficiencies on the American economy similar to the costs of protectionist policies against the importation of goods.

Payments Problems

Protectionism for balance of trade problems appears to stem from a less than complete view of the whole set of a country's international transactions. In the United States, we are reminded by the news media every month of the balance of trade deficit for that month. We are warned by many members of Congress of the dire consequences of the continuing trade balance deficits unless we curb our appetites for foreign-made goods. What seems to be overlooked is that the trade deficit doesn't really matter in the overall set of international transactions.

From current account transactions alone, the U.S. population could reasonably expect to import a greater value of goods than it exports for almost as far as one can see into the future. For a great many years, we have earned much larger investment income abroad than foreigners have earned in the United States. Net investment income alone would enable us to import more than we export, even if we were to maintain a current account balance of zero. The merchandise trade balance simply doesn't tell us much.

When we take capital account transactions into consideration, the merchandise trade balance becomes even less important. Foreign investments in the United States provide us with foreign currencies to import goods if we so desire. U.S. investments abroad use supplies of foreign currencies, leaving smaller quantities available for importing merchandise. And, since much trade and investment is done by private economic units without the need of government supervision, blessing, or curse, a great many transactions never get in the official record.

Trade deficits are important only to the extent that they lead to overall balance of payments deficits. A balance of payments deficit means that a country, during a given year, is short of sufficient foreign currencies to meet its obligations. Government setting or pegging of the country's exchange rate would be necessary for such a shortage to occur.

The circumstances creating a foreign exchange shortage are illustrated in Figure 10.6. Let the equilibrium exchange rate be $1.75 for £1 (one pound sterling). If the U.S. government sets an exchange rate ceiling on the pound at $1.50 each, the British will want smaller quantities of our exports (which are now more expensive to them), and we will want to import more from them (because British goods are now cheaper for us). A shortage of q_1q_2 pounds per month occurs. Such a shortage is generally referred to as a *balance of payments deficit*.

The deficit can persist only if the lid is kept on the price of the pound. The $1.50 ceiling overvalues the dollar relative to the pound. If it is removed, the shortage of pounds will induce buyers of British goods to bid against each other for the available supply of pounds. The price of the pound will move toward its equilibrium level of $1.75, and the dollar will depreciate relative to the pound.

The free trade position and a free exchange rate position go hand in hand. In general, the argument runs that with free trade a freely flexible exchange market will appropriately value the currencies of different countries with respect to each other. Shortages or surpluses of foreign exchange will be short-term transitional phenomena. On the other hand, a fixed exchange rate will result in incentives to restrict trade. In Figure 10.6, for example, with the ceiling of $1.50 for the pound, the shortage of pounds gives Congress an incentive to restrict imports. Import restriction would move the *DD* curve to the left, reducing the shortage of pounds.

Protection of Key and Infant Industries

One of the oldest and most frequently cited protectionist arguments concerns the need to shelter key and infant industries from foreign competition. A key industry is generally defined as one that is important and vital to national security or health. Infant industries are new industries producing cutting-edge products and

FIGURE 10.6   **The Effects of Pegging an Exchange Rate below the Equilibrium Level**
If a country pegs its exchange rate for another country's currency below the equilibrium level, the effect is the same as it is for the imposition of any effective price ceiling. There will be a shortage. If the exchange rate is fixed at $1.50 per pound, the shortage is $q_1 q_2$ pounds per month.

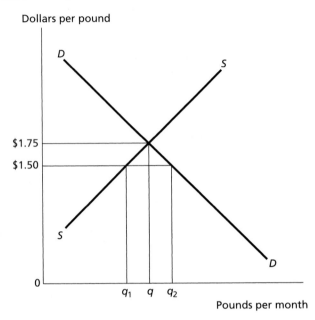

services in an emerging market. In today's economy, infant industries can be found in the high-tech areas of the computer and electronics sector of the economy.

In an uncertain political world the protectionist viewpoint for key and infant industries may be more frequently recommended. But the arguments are political rather than economic. It is very difficult to draw the line between what constitutes an absolutely indispensable industry for military purposes and what does not. Even in times of war, allied countries depend on one another for strategic arms and other war material.

Any one country finds it very difficult and very costly to be self-sufficient in all types of military goods. In determining where to draw the line, there should be a very careful weighing of the benefits of self-sufficiency against its costs.

Protection of the Environment and Human Rights

Recently, those in favor of protectionist trade policies have gained allies from the movements to protect the environment and to secure human rights around the globe. A number of leading environmental organizations have openly expressed opposition to international treaties and policies which lower the barriers to free trade. These environmentalists have been joined by human rights activists in their fight against a more open global marketplace. The arguments made by these two groups are similar and have gained wide acceptance, not only in the United States but in several other industrialized nations. (As demonstrated by the antitrade protests held in various cities around the world in recent years.) What dangers do these groups see in international trade, and is there a solid economic basis for their arguments?

The basic position held by the antitrade environmentalists and human rights activists is that business firms, particularly large multinational corporations, will take advantage of the prevailing conditions in the lesser developed countries and exploit their natural and human resources in a quest to earn greater profits through trade with the industrialized nations. Thus, from this perspective, international trade is viewed as encouraging corporations to pursue low-cost but environmentally damaging production processes and the perpetuation of low-wage jobs in the world's poorest regions. This argument carries a strong political appeal in support of tariffs and other barriers to trade; however, its economic foundations are less than clear.

As we learned earlier, when property rights do not exist or are not enforced, profit-maximizing firms may pollute the collectively consumed parts of the environment. To the extent that international trade expands production, additional negative externalities may be created through pollution and environmental damage. But the root cause of this cost to society is not trade itself, but the failure of governments to properly assign environmental property rights or otherwise regulate polluting activities. Although it is true that the world's resources will be misallocated if some nations force producers to bear the costs of environmentally damaging production processes and others do not, the imposition of international trade barriers may only further the misallocation and distort the true picture. Marginal analysis suggests that it is in the best interest of each of the world's societies to determine the extent of pollution control that they are willing to pay for relative to the costs that must be borne. However, when environmental damage imposes externality costs on other societies, such as atmospheric pollution, there is a need for international cooperation in setting equitable standards of conduct and responsibility. Such ideas have been incorporated into a number of international environmental treaties and pacts during recent years and have been implemented through the trading guidelines supported by the World Trade Organization (as discussed later in this chapter).

Some human rights activists claim that protectionist policies are needed to prevent the exploitation of workers in the lesser developed countries of the world. The inhumane working conditions of sweat shops and factories in many poor regions of the world cannot be denied. But is international trade the *cause* of these deplorable situations? Most likely not. As we saw in Chapter 1, workers in lesser developed countries often find themselves trapped by a limited education, few marketable skills, and institutional or political barriers to the free operations of the marketplace. Again, the enactment of international trade barriers will not solve these fundamental problems but only further distort the allocation of resources. In fact, protectionist policies may only serve to more severely limit the opportunities of workers in many parts of the world while free trade promotes economic growth, which increases job development. Economists with the World Trade

Organization have estimated that the liberalization of international trade between the end of World War II and beginning of the twenty-first century lifted nearly 3 billion people out of poverty.

TODAY'S INTERNATIONAL TRADE ENVIRONMENT

It is often said that the world is fast becoming a "global marketplace." International trade today is more open and free of protectionist restrictions than ever before. In part, this is due to the lessons learned from the past. During the 1930s the United States and Europe engaged in a devastating trade war. Severe restrictions in the form of high tariffs and strict quotas led to a reduction in world trade of more than 75 percent. This downturn contributed significantly to the worldwide Great Depression of that decade. As a result, following World War II, a treaty was signed by 23 industrialized nations, lowering the barriers to international trade. Known as the *General Agreement on Tariffs and Trade* (GATT), this trade treaty was renegotiated over the years as more countries joined the pact. The GATT treaty was instrumental in lowering world tariffs from an average of 40 percent in the 1940s to about 4 percent today. On January 1, 1995, a new international body, the *World Trade Organization* (WTO), took over from GATT; the WTO now oversees international trade relations between member countries.

The World Trade Organization

The World Trade Organization is the permanent institutional foundation for the negotiation of trade agreements and settlement of trade disputes between its 147 member nations. The WTO has outlawed most import quota systems, but tariffs and voluntary restraint agreements remain legal. Members of the WTO must offer all other member countries the same trade concessions as any member country. Thus, all members must treat one another as equals at the bargaining table; this is known as the *most-favored-nation* clause of the WTO agreement. Under the WTO, average worldwide tariffs are expected to fall even further.

The WTO's Dispute Settlement Body is charged with handling trade disagreements between member nations. This body enforces the WTO's provisions on "unfair competition" and violations of the most-favored-nation clause. The most predominant charge of unfair competition involves the practice of **dumping.** Dumping occurs when a producer sells products abroad at a price below cost or below its domestic price. Although dumping charges are frequently filed by domestic producers of products that face strong international competition, such charges are often difficult to prove. In practice, most real dumping occurs during recessions when international producers find themselves with surpluses that cannot be sold at home. Long-term dumping cannot take place unless the producer's economic losses are subsidized. The WTO strictly regulates the practice of export subsidies and treats them as a form of unfair competition.

Additional nations may join the WTO over time. However, each new nation must negotiate its conditions for entry. The WTO provides special concessions for developing countries with emerging economies, but eventually all member

dumping
An international trade practice in which a producer is selling abroad at a price below cost or below its domestic price.

nations must adhere to WTO standards and the most-favored-nation clause. As the premier international organization which governs the terms of trade between member nations, the WTO is one of the world's most visible institutions. Because of this it has been the target of those groups, particularly the environmentalists and human rights activists, which have demonstrated for more protectionist policies. In response to its critics, the WTO explicitly incorporates environmental and human rights considerations into its guidelines and policies. As the economic importance of international trade increases, so too will the importance of the WTO.

Common Markets

The economic benefits of free international trade have led to the creation of multinational treaties where all or most barriers to trade have been lifted. The primary goal of these treaties is to create a "common market" that is shared among the member nations. The two most important common markets are the *European Union* and the zone created by the *North American Free Trade Agreement*. Although these two alliances of nations share a common ideal, they do differ in significant ways.

The European Union (EU)

customs union
A free trade alliance of nations that share common external tariffs.

The European Union is a **customs union** that includes most of the nations in western and central Europe. (See Figure 10.7.) A customs union is a free trade alliance of nations that share common external tariffs. Member nations of the EU have dropped all significant trade barriers between themselves and have devised a common set of rules regarding international trade between the union and other nonmember nations around the world. Today, the EU represents one of the world's largest markets, encompassing 25 member nations with a combined population in excess of 456 million people.

The EU has been successful in increasing the flow of resources and goods between its members. It continues to work toward creating a truly unified single European market, but many nationalistic hurdles still stand in the way. The most ambitious project is the adoption of a new European currency which circulates across national borders. The new currency, known as the euro, was introduced in stages over several years.

On January 1, 1999, the euro became a recognized currency in 11 of the then 15 EU member nations (Denmark, Sweden, and the United Kingdom postponed their decision to adopt the euro, and Greece initially failed to meet the qualification deadline). However, European consumers were not able to make everyday purchases with the euro until January 1, 2002. Until that time, the euro was used only for paper and electronic financial transactions, record keeping, and the sale of public bonds. The original value of the euro was determined by a weighted average of the participating nations' respective currencies. On the first day of trading, the exchange rate for the euro in U.S. dollars was 1.1747. Due to a number of factors, most notably a perceived degree of uncertainty in the ability of a single monetary unit to succeed as common currency for the diverse economies of Europe, the exchange rate for the euro slowly fell during its first two years. By the end of 2002

FIGURE 10.7 **Countries of the European Union**
The European Union consists of 25 nations: Austria, Belgium, Cyprus, the Czech Republic, Denmark, Estonia, Finland, France, Germany, Greece, Hungary, Ireland, Italy, Latvia, Lithuania, Luxembourg, Malta, the Netherlands, Poland, Portugal, Slovakia, Slovenia, Spain, Sweden, and the United Kingdom.

THE EUROPEAN UNION (EU)

Indicates the 25 countries that form the European Union (EU), 2005.

the euro was trading at a few pennies less than one dollar. However, over time the EU was able to demonstrate its power to maintain the stability of the new currency and the euro became more valuable on the world's money markets. By early 2005, the cost of purchasing a euro had climbed to more than $1.30.

During the first six months of 2002, new euro coins and paper money replaced the old national currencies. On July 1, 2002, the old national currencies ceased to officially exist and all transactions had to be made using euros. In the long run, use of the euro is expected to result in an increase in trade between the member nations and to further strengthen Europe's economic standing in the global marketplace. The primary reason for this expectation is very easy to understand: The euro reduces the costs of trade between member nations. Prior to the introduction of the euro, a French citizen would have had to purchase marks before a shopping trip to Berlin, and a German would have had to purchase francs before a vacation on the Riviera. Of course, every time a currency conversion was made, the broker making the exchange demanded a fee for this service. With a common currency such as the euro, these transaction costs, and all the time spent making currency conversions, are eliminated. Thus, the euro reduces the costs of trade. In addition, the euro makes it easier for consumers to understand the true prices they are paying for internationally traded products. For example, French shoppers in Berlin do not have to convert marks to francs in their heads before deciding whether to buy a new car there or to wait until they return home. Prices all across Europe are now posted in euros, and since everyone is also paid in euros, accurate price comparisons can be made easily. Because of this, many expect a greater degree of competition, and therefore efficiency, to emerge in the European economies that use the euro. However, since the euro represents the first time that a common currency has been adopted by so many nations representing such a large share of the world's economy, it is difficult to predict the final outcome of this bold experiment at forming a true common marketplace.

The North American Free Trade Agreement (NAFTA)

free trade area
An alliance of nations without trade barriers between its members.

The North American Free Trade Agreement creates a **free trade area** between the United States, Canada, and Mexico. A free trade area is an alliance of nations without trade barriers between its members. Members within a free trade area are allowed to set their own tariffs with nations outside the alliance. Thus, a free trade area agreement does not require the same degree of cooperation as a customs union.

Mexican tariffs have historically been twice as high as those of the United States, and American exporters have seized on this opportunity. Sales of American-made products in Mexico have increased dramatically since the inception of NAFTA in 1992. However, many Americans have expressed fear that NAFTA creates domestic unemployment. It is true that some unemployment has occurred, but it is also true that new jobs have been created. Remember the principle of comparative advantage: All trading partners gain when they specialize. Thus with NAFTA, the United States gains jobs in the areas in which we specialize and have a comparative advantage and loses jobs in those areas in which Mexico and Canada specialize and have a comparative advantage. Although the *mix* of jobs in each of the three NAFTA nations has changed to some extent, all indications are that more jobs will be created in total than are lost in the long run.

The perceived benefits of NAFTA have been so great that Chile and other Latin American countries have petitioned to join. As international trade barriers fall we can expect to experience lower prices, greater availability, and more diversity of products in our markets and stores for years to come.

The Spread of Common Markets

In general, most world leaders view the economic alliance of nations through common markets in a positive light, as evidenced by the increasing number of common markets around the globe. For example, Australia and New Zealand recently amended the Australia New Zealand Closer Economic Relations Trade Agreement (ANZCERTA) to establish a bilateral free trade zone between them, and 10 nations of southeast Asia are now members of a free trade area allied through the Association of Southeast Asian Nations (ASEAN). Other common markets and trading blocks closer to home now exist in Latin America (through the Latin American Integration Association, or LAIA), South America (through Mercado Común del Cono Sur, or MERCOSUR), Central America (through the Central American Common Market, or CACM), and the Caribbean (through the Caribbean Community and Common Market, or CCCM). In fact, treaties establishing either customs unions or free trade areas are in effect in every populated continent of the world. Virtually every member of the WTO is a participant in one or more common market agreements.

Why have we experienced a proliferation of common market treaties? Clearly, the nations which sign such agreements must expect that membership in a common market yields economic and political benefits. In most cases, almost without exception, the establishment of a common market is a hotly debated issue among the citizens of the participating countries. The traditional protectionist arguments outlined in this chapter have been argued and debated countless times in public forums around the world. However, the promise of economic growth and improved living standards through freer international trade has caused many of the world's citizens to abandon their protectionist points of view and support the common market concept.

Given the trend toward common markets, it seems fair to inquire into the actual effects of such treaties on the economies of member nations. Such an inquiry appears at first straightforward, yet an empirical analysis of a free trade pact is fraught with difficulty. For example, if we are interested in NAFTA's effect on employment patterns, we can observe the employment patterns that exist today now that NAFTA is in place, but we cannot observe what the employment patterns would have been today if NAFTA had not been signed. Thus, researchers must make assumptions about the economic conditions that would have existed in the absence of a common market environment. Of course, different assumptions will lead to different conclusions. This is illustrated in two studies of NAFTA's effect on U.S. jobs that were published only two months apart. A report from the Brookings Institution concluded that NAFTA had created more jobs than it destroyed, while a report published by the Economic Policy Institute concluded that during its first three years NAFTA had eliminated almost 400,000 jobs.[2] Obviously, when conflicting empirical results are published by well-respected policy research institutions, the protectionist versus free trade debate will continue. However, we should note that most economists agree that free trade in the long run is beneficial to both trading partners and that many of the debatable issues concerning common markets lay in the details of the agreements which may give one nation an advantage over another in specific situations. Therefore, as long as common market agreements lead to freer international trade, they will undoubtedly continue to spread around the globe.

Summary

The creation of the North American Free Trade Agreement and the World Trade Organization stepped up the controversy between protectionists and free traders. Protectionists argue that imports should be limited to reduce foreign competition with goods produced in the United States, to remedy balance of trade and balance of payments problems, and to encourage U.S. industries vital to national security and economic welfare. Free traders maintain that the economic welfare of a country is enhanced by voluntary free exchange among countries.

A country's consumption possibilities are greater when it trades with other countries than when it does not. By concentrating on the production of goods in which it has a comparative advantage and trading for goods in which it has a comparative disadvantage, the population of the country will have a larger GDP to consume and/or invest.

International exchange markets arise from international transactions. A country's demands for foreign exchange are generated by imports of goods, investments in other countries, and any other transactions that result in payments made abroad. Supplies of foreign exchange are created by exports, by foreign investments in the country, and by any other transactions that cause payments to be made to the country. Exchange rates are determined by the forces of demand for and supply of currencies used in international trade.

Trade restrictions generally take the form of tariffs, quotas, voluntary restraint agreements, or embargoes—all four of which result in higher prices for imports as well as domestically produced goods and services. Further, trade restrictions reduce the availability of products at the consumer level. Governments can raise revenue through the imposition of tariffs, but quotas result in extra profit for holders of import licenses. Recently, voluntary restraint agreements have become more widespread, but they are difficult to enforce and are often influenced by international political relations.

Economic analysis indicates that a country's population as a whole usually loses as a result of import restrictions. Gains to the protected industries come at the expense of export industries and consumers. Balance of payments problems are

[2]For an overview of these two reports, see David Ensign, "NAFTA: Two Sides of the Coin," *Spectrum: The Journal of State Government* 70, no. 4 (September 22, 1997), p. 1.

essentially exchange rate problems arising when countries attempt to peg exchange rates. It appears that the preferred solution to such problems is exchange rate adjustment rather than protectionism. Protection of key industries may have some merit—if only we could determine which industries properly fall into this category.

In recent years, nations have sought the benefits of free trade by reducing international trade restrictions worldwide. The WTO has been instrumental in minimizing the barriers to trade between member countries. The nations of western Europe formed the EU, and the United States entered into NAFTA in order to reap the benefits of free trade. Other groups of nations around the world have followed suit, forming their own regional customs unions and free trade areas. Many people still support protectionist policies, but the trend is toward more open markets and global economies.

Discussion Questions

1. Why do some people fear international trade? Defend the protectionist viewpoint using sound economic reasoning.
2. Explain the principle of comparative advantage. In what areas do you have a comparative advantage over your classmates? How can this be used to improve your current economic position?
3. Discuss how international trade can improve the social welfare of two nations engaged in exchange. Provide an example.
4. Use diagrams to illustrate how international trade affects both the production possibilities and consumption possibilities of a trading nation.
5. What is today's exchange rate for the British pound? Convert the price of lunch in your school cafeteria to British pounds.
6. Discuss the differences between tariffs and quotas. How are they the same, and how are they different?
7. Using a supply and demand diagram, illustrate the effects of the tariffs imposed on imported steel by the United States. How will these tariffs affect American manufacturers and consumers?
8. Many taxicab drivers in Havana, Cuba, drive automobiles manufactured in the United States 40 or 50 years ago. Why is this, and why are new American cars not exported to Cuba? What is the effect of this policy on the United States? Explain.
9. What is the balance of payments deficit? Is it a major problem? What can be done about it?
10. Discuss the differences between the European Union and the North American Free Trade Agreement. In what ways are they similar?
11. Should American workers fear the long-term effects of NAFTA? Provide a solid economic argument using the economic analysis discussed in this chapter.
12. How do international trade restrictions hurt the American consumer? Provide an example.

13. What is the WTO? Discuss the role that it plays in promoting international trade between participating nations.

14. Why have common market agreements between nations become so prevalent in today's global economy? Have such agreements been successful? Explain why or why not.

Additional Readings

Artis, Mike, and Norman Lee. *The Economics of the European Union: Policy and Analysis*. 2nd ed. Oxford, England: Oxford University Press, 2002.
Volume of 15 articles that provide a comprehensive account of the economics of the European Union. Papers cover the gamut of economic topics, including monetary integration, international trade, environmental policy, and social development.

Bagwell, Kyle, and Robert W. Staiger. *The Economics of the World Trading System*. Cambridge, MA: MIT Press, 2002.
The authors examines the history and design of GATT/WTO, the theory of trade agreements, competition policy, the most-favored-nation clause, and other issues.

Bhagwati, Jagdish. *Free Trade Today*. Princeton, NJ: Princeton University Press, 2002.
This eminent economist discusses current threats and new challenges to free global trade and provides an excellent response to those who argue that trade agreements come at the expense of environmental standards.

Gonnelli, Adam. *The Basics of Foreign Trade and Exchange*. New York: Federal Reserve Bank of New York, 1993.
This short book offers an excellent introduction to the basics of international trade and exchange.

Heilbroner, Robert L., and Lester C. Thurow. *The Economic Problem*. 7th ed. Englewood Cliffs, NJ: Prentice Hall, 1984, Chapters 36 and 37.
Good discussion of the protectionist as well as the free trade point of view.

Kowalczyk, Carsten, ed. *The Theory of Trade Policy Reform*. The International Library of Critical Writings in Economics 127. Northampton, MA: Edward Elgar Publishing Company, 2001.
Discusses the economic impact of trade barriers and analyzes how recent trade policy reforms affect domestic and world welfare.

Miller, Henri, ed. *Free Trade vs. Protectionism*. The Reference Shelf, vol. 68, no. 4. New York: The H. W. Wilson Company, 1996.
Excellent reference source that discusses all the major economic and political aspects of global trade in today's world.

Nivola, Pietro S., ed. *Comparative Disadvantages: Social Regulation and the Global Economy*. Washington, DC: Brookings Institution Press, 1997.
Discusses how several U.S. domestic regulations and policies affect international trade.

Organisation for Economic Cooperation and Development. *Open Markets Matter: The Benefits of Trade and Investment Liberalisation.* Paris: OECD Publications, 1998.
Argues against protectionism and argues for better global social policies, including labor, education, taxation, training, and product market flexibility.

Stiglitz, Joseph E. *Globalization and Its Discontents.* New York: W.W. Norton, 2002.
The Nobel Prize–winner and chairman of the President's Council of Economic Advisors during the Carter administration explores the powers, policies, and social impact of the major international financial institutions, including the World Bank, the International Monetary Fund, and the World Trade Organization.

World Wide Web Resources

Center for Trade Policy Studies (CTPS)

www.freetrade.org

The mission of the Center for Trade Policy Studies, affiliated with the Cato Institute, is to increase public understanding of the benefits of free trade and the costs of protectionism. Scholars at the center focus not only on U.S. protectionism but also on trade barriers around the world. The site has links to key trade issues, publications, jobs and research, and an advanced search engine.

Europa—The European Union's Server

europa.eu.int

Europa, the European Union's Web server, provides access to press releases from EU institutions, basic information about and policies of the EU, and other links.

Federal Reserve Bank of Dallas: The Fruits of Free Trade

www.dallasfed.org/fed/annual/2002/ar02b.html

This report, complete with graphs and charts, is an excellent source of information about the benefits of international trade to American consumers.

National Law Center for Inter-American Free Trade

www.natlaw.com

This nonprofit research and educational institution provides the full text of major international trade treaties through its "Inter-Am Database."

North American Free Trade Agreement (NAFTA)

www-tech.mit.edu/Bulletins/nafta.html

Provides the complete text of the agreement on the Web.

Organization of American States (OAS)

www.oas.org

OAS is the world's oldest international organization. It provides links to the latest news, member states, OAS publications, documents, and reports.

United States Foreign Trade Statistics

www.census.gov/foreign-trade/www

Part of the Census Bureau. Gives links to foreign trade statistics, information, and a searchable index.

United States Trade Representative Home Page

www.ustr.gov

The U.S. Trade Representative and staff are responsible for developing and implementing trade policies with other countries. Site has links to press releases, speeches and testimonies, and reports.

The World Trade Organization

www.wto.org

The WTO's Web site provides an up-to-date listing of member countries and overviews of how the organization is structured and how decisions are made. The site also provides visitors with a history of the WTO and its predecessor treaty, GATT.

Unemployment Issues
Why Do We Waste Our Labor Resources?

Checklist of economic concepts

- Labor force
- Discouraged workers
- Frictional unemployment
- Structural unemployment
- Cyclical unemployment
- Full-employment unemployment rate
- Circular flow of production and income
- Aggregate demand
- Marginal propensity to consume
- Marginal propensity to save
- Psychological law of consumption
- Investment multiplier
- Aggregate supply
- Leakages
- Injections
- Aggregate demand policies
- Aggregate supply policies

I'd get up at five in the morning and head for the waterfront. Outside the Spreckles Sugar Refinery, outside the gates, there would be a thousand men. You know dang well there's only three or four jobs. The guy would come out with two little Pinkerton cops: "I need two guys for the bull gang. Two guys to go into the hole." A thousand men would fight like a pack of Alaskan dogs to get through there. Only four of us would get through. I was too young a punk.

So you'd drift up to Skid Row. There'd be thousands of men there. Guys on baskets, making weird speeches, phony theories on economics. About 11:30, the real leaders would take over. They'd say: OK, we're going to City Hall. The mayor was Angelo Rossi, a dapper little guy. He wore expensive boots and a tight vest. We'd shout around the steps. Finally, he'd come out and tell us nothing.

I remember the demands: We demand work, we demand shelter for our families, we demand groceries, this kind of thing. . . .

I remember as a kid how courageous this seemed to me, the demands, because you knew that society wasn't going to give it to you. They'd demand that they open up unrented houses and give decent shelters for their families. But you just knew society wasn't yielding. There was nothing coming.

Source: Studs Terkel, *Hard Times* (New York: Random House, 1970), p. 30.

COSTS OF UNEMPLOYMENT

Two kinds of costs are related to unemployment. The first is the economic cost, which can be measured rather precisely. The second is the social, or noneconomic, cost, which is just as real as the economic cost but more difficult to assess and measure.

Economic Costs

The economic cost of unemployment to the person unemployed is the loss in income and the resulting decrease in consumption and saving. The economic cost of unemployment to the economy takes the form of a decrease in the production of goods and services because the economy is not operating on its production possibilities curve. It is operating instead inside the production possibilities curve, and the full potential of the economy is not being realized. The sum of the losses in income of the unemployed equals the losses in production and therefore the total economic cost of unemployment.

Another interesting thing to keep in mind regarding the production possibilities curve and the economic cost of unemployment is that the opportunity cost of decreasing unemployment may be low, or even zero. Production can be expanded for a given product without a decrease in the production of other products when the economy is operating inside the production possibilities curve. However, if unemployment is reduced below a certain rate, inflation rears its ugly head. This problem is discussed in the next chapter.

Noneconomic Costs

Unemployment threatens the stability of the family as an economic and social unit. Without income or with a loss of income, the head of the family cannot play the role in which he or she was cast. Family wants and needs are not fulfilled, and family relationships suffer as a consequence. Economic and social dependency and important family ties may be in jeopardy and eventually may be severed by prolonged unemployment. High unemployment rates have been found to be associated with drug abuse, higher divorce rates, and higher crime rates generally.

Human relationships outside the family are also seriously affected by unemployment. An unemployed person loses self-respect and influence among those who are employed, faces possible rejection by working companions, and experiences a possible loss of pride and confidence. In the end, the unemployed may become emotionally disabled.

Some families may be economically and socially prepared for unemployment. Perhaps they have savings set aside just in case of a rainy day, or maybe they can receive financial support from other family members. However, unemployment generally has a profound effect on families the least prepared and capable of withstanding either its economic or its social effects.

WHAT IS UNEMPLOYMENT?

It would seem that unemployment could be easily defined. However, there are many complexities and ramifications concerning its meaning. The first thought about unemployment may be that the unemployed are people without jobs. This may be true, but many people without jobs are not considered officially unemployed. What about a person who prefers leisure to work? Are retired persons over 65 to be considered unemployed? Is a full-time college student included in the unemployment count?

Our approach to unemployment in this section is, first, to give the government's official definition of the labor force and, second, to elucidate the importance of the unemployment problem. The subsequent sections probe deeper into the sources of unemployment.

The Labor Force

To understand how employment is defined and measured, we must first become familiar with the concept of an economy's labor force. A labor force consists of all the human resources currently engaged in, or available for, productive economic activity in an economy. A nation's culture and legal institutions determine which

labor force
All noninstitution-
alized individuals
16 years of age and
older who are
employed for pay,
actively seeking
employment, or
awaiting recall from
a temporary layoff.

human resources will be included in the labor force. In the United States we define the **labor force** as including all noninstitutionalized individuals 16 years of age and older who are employed for pay, actively seeking employment, or awaiting recall from a temporary layoff. This definition is used by the U.S. Department of Labor to measure the size and growth of our labor force over time. Other nations use slightly different definitions, which sometimes make international comparisons difficult.

Several aspects of the official labor force definition are important to understand. First, note that individuals who are institutionalized are not included in the labor force. Institutions include jails, prisons, mental hospitals, and long-term nursing homes. Second, members of the labor force must be at least 16 years of age. In the United States, children under the age of 16 are subject to child labor laws and are not legally available for many types of paid work. Third, note that the labor force includes those who are employed and those who are unemployed. The employed members of the labor force consist of those who are working for pay. Anyone who works at least one hour per week and receives pay is considered to be an employed member of the labor force. Unemployed members of the labor force include those who are actively seeking employment and those waiting to be called back from a layoff.

It is crucial to realize that being without work is not a sufficient condition to be counted as unemployed in the United States. An individual must be actively seeking employment, or available for work during a temporary layoff. Someone who is actively seeking employment undertakes the normal job search activities such as responding to want ads, submitting resumes and job applications, and taking interviews with prospective employers. When someone stops actively searching for a job, he or she no longer satisfies the labor force definition and is therefore not counted as being unemployed. The unemployed who give up their job search activities and officially leave the labor force are called **discouraged workers.** Some economists believe that the official measures of unemployment may underestimate the problem during downturns in the business cycle due to the existence of discouraged workers.

**discouraged
workers**
People not included
in the official
measures of
unemployment
because they have
stopped actively
searching for work
and are no longer in
the labor force.

Today the labor force in the United States is approximately 147.5 million members. The vast majority of the labor force is employed. Still, every month there are millions of Americans who are counted as being unemployed. Why does unemployment occur, and what can be done about it?

Unemployment in a Market Economy

The economic aspect of unemployment originates from a situation in which the quantity of labor demanded is less than the quantity supplied at the market wage rate. This results in unemployment. Unemployment occurs when wage rates are too high, that is, above competitive levels. The solution to unemployment is to expand demand or, if competitive forces are operating, to rely on automatic market forces to drive wage rates down to the level at which the amount of labor demanded equals the amount supplied.

FIGURE 11.1 Unemployment in a Competitive Market
DD = Demand curve for labor
SS = Supply curve for labor
e_0 = Amount of labor demanded at w_1
e_1 = Amount of labor supplied at w_1
$e_1 - e_0$ = Unemployment

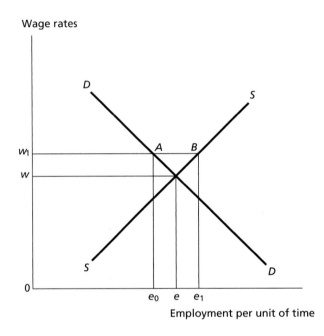

Figure 11.1 clarifies the meaning of unemployment in a competitive economy. DD and SS are the demand and supply curves for labor. The wage rate is w_1. The amount of labor demanded at this wage rate is e_0, and the amount supplied is e_1. This difference between e_0 and e_1 is the unemployment at the wage rate of w_1. In a purely competitive situation, wage rates would be forced down to w, and unemployment would disappear.

ANALYSIS OF THE UNEMPLOYMENT PROBLEM

Types of Unemployment

The meaning of unemployment may be elucidated further by distinguishing between different types of unemployment. Three major types are frictional, structural, and cyclical unemployment.

Frictional Unemployment

frictional unemployment Brief periods of unemployment usually originating on the labor supply side of the market; is transitional, often in the form of people changing and searching for new jobs.

Frictional unemployment is transitional or short run in nature. It usually originates on the labor supply side; that is, labor services are voluntarily not employed. A good illustration is the unemployment that occurs when people are changing jobs or searching for new jobs. The matching of job openings and job seekers does not always take place smoothly in the economy, and, as a consequence, people are without work.

The important thing about frictional unemployment is that it does not last. Frictional unemployment will exist at all times in the economy, but for any one person or family it is transitional. Therefore, frictional unemployment is not considered a significant economic problem, and it can be reduced by improvements in the flow of information concerning job openings.

Structural Unemployment

structural unemployment Unemployment that is caused by fundamental changes in demand for certain kinds of labor due to, say, technological changes or changes in consumers' tastes and preferences.

Structural unemployment is usually long run in nature and usually originates on the demand side of the labor market. Structural unemployment results from economic changes that cause the demand for specific kinds of labor to be low relative to the supply in particular markets and regions of the economy.

A relatively low demand for labor in a given market may be due to several factors. Technological change, although expected to reduce costs and expand the productive capacity of the overall economy, may have devastating effects in a particular market. Changes in consumer preferences for products expand production and employment in some areas but reduce them in others. Immobility of labor prolongs the period of unemployment that may have originated due to technological change and changes in consumers' tastes. A reduction in job opportunities should induce the unemployed to move, but immobility may prevent this from taking place.

Cyclical Unemployment

cyclical unemployment Unemployment caused by a contraction in aggregate demand or total spending in the economy.

Unemployment caused by economic fluctuations is called **cyclical unemployment.** The term comes from the phrase "business cycle," which is commonly used to label the irregular fluctuations in the aggregate economy. (We will look at business cycles more closely in Chapter 13.) Cyclical unemployment is due to reductions in aggregate or total demand for goods and services in the overall economy. A decline in aggregate demand reduces total production and causes general unemployment throughout the economic system. Cyclical unemployment is the culprit when the economy enters a recession.

Further Dimensions of the Unemployment Problem

The Full-Employment Unemployment Rate

Full employment is often defined for policy purposes as an unemployment rate of, for example, 4 or 5 percent. The economy is considered to be operating at less than full employment at unemployment rates above the full-employment rate. The unemployment below the full-employment rate is supposed to measure only frictional and structural unemployment. The unemployment above the full-employment rate is supposed to measure cyclical unemployment, the unemployment that fiscal policy is directed toward reducing or eliminating. An alternative way of viewing the **full-employment unemployment rate** is that it is a rate consistent with price stability. Any policy attempt to reduce the unemployment rate below the full-employment rate, or the *natural rate,* as some economists like to say, will accelerate the rate of inflation. In the 1950s and 1960s, full employment was defined in reference to a 4 percent unemployment rate. In the 1970s the estimated rate was increased to 5 percent, and in the early 1980s it was increased to a range between 5 and 6 percent. Presently, there seems to be a general consensus among economists that a rate of unemployment of 4 to 5 percent is consistent with a nonaccelerating inflation rate. The basic reasons for defining full employment in terms of a higher unemployment rate are the increasing probability of higher inflation rates when unemployment rates fall below a certain rate and a recognition of structural changes in the labor force such as the increasing number of women and teenagers in the labor force and the restructuring of industries in response to technological advances.

full-employment unemployment rate
The rate that reflects frictional and structural unemployment and is consistent with price stability.

Unemployment Rates over Time

Figure 11.2 shows unemployment rates in selected years from 1961 through 2003. The selected years are the high and low unemployment rates during this period. Unemployment rates follow the ups and downs in the economy and are generally above the unemployment rate officially targeted for policy purposes as full employment. The high unemployment rate in the 1960s centered in 1961 when the rate was 6.7 percent. This occurred during the 1960–1961 recession. After 1961, the unemployment rate declined steadily as the economy expanded, reaching a low rate of 3.5 percent in 1969. For four years, 1966 through 1969, during this decade the unemployment rate was under the full-employment target rate of 4 percent. The unemployment rate rose steadily during the first half of the 1970s, reaching a high of 8.5 percent in 1975, which was the last year of the 1973–1975 recession. The rate of unemployment decreased somewhat between 1975 and 1979, falling to 5.8 percent in 1979. With the exception of one year, 1970, the unemployment rate stayed above the rate of 5 percent, which was established as the rate consistent with full employment during this decade. The 1981–1982 contraction in the economy sent the unemployment rate soaring to almost 10 percent in 1982, the highest since the Great Depression of the 1930s. Job opportunities began to improve in 1983 as the economy embarked on a record-breaking economic expansion. The result was a steady decrease in the unemployment rate to 5.3 percent in 1989. The economy began to show signs of a recession in the summer of 1990, and the unemployment rate began to increase. The recession officially began in the third quarter of 1990, when the real GDP fell about 1 percent. This downward trend in the economy continued in the fourth quarter and in the first quarter of 1991 with the real GDP falling 3.2 percent and 2.4 percent, respectively, in these two quarters. The economy turned around in the second quarter of 1991, but the recovery was

FIGURE 11.2

High and Low Unemployment Rates, 1961–2003

Source: Economic Report of the President, February 2004.

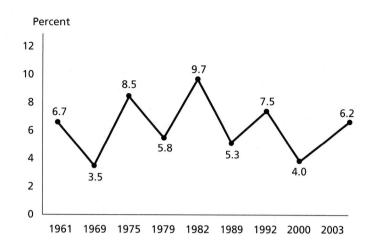

weak. The real GDP grew at a slow rate of less than 2 percent in the remaining quarters of 1991 and did not exceed a 3.5 percent growth rate until the last quarter of 1992. As a result, the unemployment rate continued to rise, reaching 7.5 percent in 1992, before the expansion in the economy was rapid enough to provide new jobs at a pace sufficient to reduce the rate of unemployment. Between 1992 and 2000, as the economy expanded, the unemployment rate fell to 4 percent. Then the economy slowed down, and the unemployment rate increased to 6.2 percent by the middle of 2003.

Who Are the Unemployed?

Just as we learned in Chapter 7 that the overall poverty rate masks the degree of poverty faced by certain family groupings, the general unemployment rate hides the degree of unemployment confronted by persons in different demographic groups. The groups that have a much higher poverty rate than the average generally are the same groups that have higher unemployment rates. In December 2003, for example, when the overall unemployment rate was 5.7 percent, the unemployment rate was 16.1 percent among young persons between the ages of 16 and 19. Further examples of groups that had much higher unemployment rates than the average rate were those who dropped out of high school (8.1 percent) and those of African American heritage (10.3 percent).

WHAT CAUSES PEOPLE TO LOSE THEIR JOBS?

People lose their jobs in a recession when production in the economy is dropping. But what causes the recession? What causes a decline in production? Economists have searched for a single answer and have found many: not enough spending, too much saving, or relatively high wages. Thus, the answer is neither simple nor single. There are many contributory causes; we shall try to explain those that seem to be the most important.

FIGURE 11.3
Flow of
Production and
Income in a
Stationary
Economy

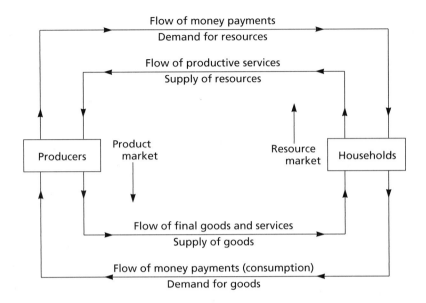

Circular Flow of Economic Activity

To understand why people lose their jobs, it is necessary to understand how jobs are created. This is not difficult in terms of the forces of supply and demand pertaining to products in individual markets. We have established an understanding of equilibrium prices and quantities demanded for individual commodities such as wheat, automobiles, dresses, televisions, ice cream, necklaces, and all other commodities produced in our economy. We now move from demand and supply curves for individual products to a demand-supply curve representing all commodities. Thus, we present an overview of the operation of the economy, which economists call the *circular flow of economic activity.*

The circular flow is illustrated in Figure 11.3. Study this figure carefully, because the relationships it shows are important in understanding the operation of the economy.

Income and jobs are created in a society when goods and services are produced. Owners of resources—labor, capital, and natural resources—sell their productive services to producers who, in turn, pay them money in the form of wages, interest, rent, and profits. The flow of productive services to producers represents the supply of resources, and the flow of money payments from producers represents the demand for resources. Producers transform productive services or resources into goods and services through the production process and sell the goods and services to households. They receive a flow of money payments from households in exchange. The flow from producers to households represents the aggregate supply of goods and services, and the flow of money payments from households to producers represents the aggregate demand for them.

There are several points to remember about the circular flow. First, there are two markets: a resource market and a product market. The prices of resources and employment are determined in the resource market, and the prices of goods and production are determined in the product market. (The product market is seen as the bottom two loops in Figure 11.3, and the resource market is seen as the top two loops.) Second, the resource and product markets are interrelated. The demand for goods creates a demand for the resources that are used to produce goods. The costs of producing goods depend on the prices paid and the quantities of resources used in production. Third, there are two circular flows involved in the economy— a real flow of productive services (labor, capital, and natural resources) and products (autos, dresses, medical services) and a flow of money payments to owners of resources for productive services and to producers for goods and services. Fourth, real income is determined by the physical goods and services produced, and money income is the money value of the physical goods and services produced.

The circular flow of economic activity shows in a simple way how the overall economy operates. It emphasizes the interdependency of economic variables—the dependency of income on production, production on spending, spending on income, demand for resources on the demand for products, and so on. Now we shall turn to the product market in order to find possible reasons why people lose their jobs.

Aggregate Demand

aggregate demand
A schedule showing output demanded at different price levels.

Aggregate demand is a schedule showing total output demanded in the economy at different prices. Since we are concerned with the prices of all goods and services, we must view prices as an average, or as a price level. Since we are also concerned with the quantities of all goods and services, we must view the quantities demanded as composite units of goods and services—each unit composed of shirts, tables, food, fuel, and other items that constitute the real output of the economy.

Aggregate demand is illustrated in Figure 11.4. At the price level p_1, 200 units of goods and services are demanded; at the price level p, output demanded is 400 units, and so on. The output demanded of goods at any price level is the sum of the output of goods and services purchased by *consumers,* such as shoes and steaks; the output purchased by *investors,* such as new plant and equipment; the output purchased by *government,* such as highways and recreational services; and net exports, that is, the difference between foreign purchases of goods and services produced in our country (exports) and American purchases of goods and services produced abroad (imports). A change in the output demanded at a given price level by any of these groups—consumers, investors, government, and the rest of the world—will change aggregate demand. For example, if consumers begin to buy greater quantities of consumer goods at all prices than they did previously, aggregate demand will increase—shift to the right, indicating that greater output is demanded at all prices. Let's now examine the key determinants of aggregate demand.

FIGURE 11.4

Aggregate Demand

DD is an aggregate demand schedule that shows the output demanded at different price levels. For example, at price level p_1, 200 units of goods and services are demanded.

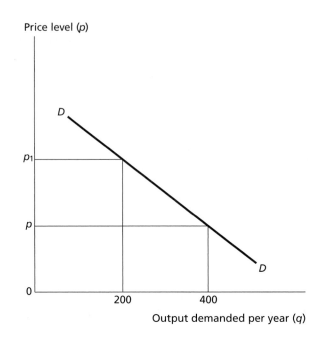

Price level (*p*)

Output demanded per year (*q*)

Consumer Spending (C)

Consumer spending, often abbreviated as simply *C*, is determined by objective factors, such as income, wealth, and the interest rate, and subjective factors, such as tastes and preferences and consumer confidence. Consumer spending is positively related to income and wealth and negatively related to the interest rate; that is to say, we expect that the output demanded by consumers at every price level will be greater when their income and wealth rise due to the increased ability to buy and that it will be lower when the interest rate increases because it would be more costly to buy on credit. Tastes and preferences—and consumer confidence—play an important role because these variables influence the propensity of consumers to spend and save given the income and wealth of consumers. Among all these variables that determine *C*, the income of consumers is generally considered the most important variable. A more logical way of saying this is that *C* depends upon income (*Y*), given these other variables. To extend the relationship between *C* and *Y* further, an important concept to understand is the **marginal propensity to consume (MPC).** The *MPC* is the change in consumption divided by the change in income. Assuming the *MPC* is ⅘, then an increase in *Y* of $100 billion will increase *C* $80 billion and increase saving (*S*) $20 billion. In this instance, the **marginal propensity to save (MPS)** is ⅕, for any part of an increase in income that is not spent on consumer goods and services is saved. The *MPC* plus the *MPS* is always, then, equal to 1. Two general characteristics of the *MPC* are that it is less than 1 and that it tends to be reasonably stable. This last characteristic does not mean that all consumers have the same marginal propensity to consume; low-income consumers will have a higher tendency to spend when their income

marginal propensity to consume
The change in consumption divided by the change in income.

marginal propensity to save
The change in saving divided by the change in income.

increases than high-income consumers. But on the average for all consumers the *MPC* does not vary over time. This first feature of *MPC* means that when income changes, consumption changes, but not as much, which is often referred to as the **psychological law of consumption.** The second feature indicates that when income changes, the change in consumption can usually be accurately predicted. It should be noted that in the discussion above and in the discussion to follow, all the variables mentioned are in real terms or constant prices.

psychological law of consumption
When income changes, consumption changes, but by less than the change in income.

Investment Spending (I)

Investment spending, or simply *I*, is primarily the purchase of new equipment and plant. It is much more volatile than consumer spending and is determined by the rate of interest and the expected rate of return from new investment. When the expected rate of return from investment is greater than the interest rate, the inducement to invest is strong and, hence, investment will increase because it is more profitable to invest than to lend. When the expected rate of return from investment is less than the rate of interest, then the reverse is true—the inducement to buy new equipment is weak and investment will fall. It follows, then, that when the expected rate of return or the expected profit rate is equal to the interest rate, the level of investment is determined; that is, investment spending will not increase or decrease under these circumstances. Expectations play a strategic role in the determination of investment spending. It is not the current profit rate that determines investment but the "expected" profit rate. New investment has to compete with old investment. The fact that the current rate on some existing investment is greater than the rate of interest does not ensure that new investment will be profitable. An increase in the supply of apartments for rent, for example, will tend to decrease the rent that may be charged for apartments and reduce the net income flow from such an investment. Under such circumstances, the profit rate from investments in rental apartments would be expected to be reduced, and, depending upon the rate of interest, this may result in a decision not to invest. It is the role of expectation in making investment decisions, along with the state of confidence of investors, that causes the output demanded by investors to follow a cyclical pattern over time.

Investment Multiplier

There is another aspect of investment spending that calls for special analysis. An increase in investment of $1 will increase income or output demanded by more than $1. This is easy to understand. Suppose an automobile plant was constructed in your town with the cost of the plant and equipment at $100 million. In addition to the output demanded by this investment, a chain of consumer spending will be set off by this investment, resulting in an increase in output demanded or income greater than the cost of the investment. The connecting link between a given change in investment and the resulting change in income is the **investment multiplier.** The multiplier is a numerical coefficient such as 3, 4, or 5. It is the reciprocal of 1 minus the marginal propensity to consume, or simply the reciprocal of the marginal propensity to save. For an example, if the *MPC* is ⅘, the multiplier

investment multiplier
The reciprocal of 1 minus the marginal propensity to consume.

is 5 $[1/(1 - \frac{4}{5})]$. The investment multiplier times the change in investment spending will equal the change in income. In the illustration of the investment in the auto plant, income will increase $500 million as a result of an investment of $100 million, assuming an *MPC* of $\frac{4}{5}$. The increase in income or output demanded of $500 million will be composed of an increase in output demanded by investors of $100 million and an increase in output demanded by consumers of $400 million. The increase in income, assuming an *MPC* of $\frac{3}{4}$, would be $400 million (4 × $100 million), assuming again an increase in investment of $100 million. The breakdown between the increase in investment spending and consumer spending in this instance would be an increase in investment spending of $100 million and an increase in consumer spending of $300 million. The increase in consumption, resulting from increase in investment, will always be the marginal propensity to consume times the change in income.

Government Purchases (G)

Government purchases are the final output of goods and services demanded by government. Government purchases have an impact on income or output demanded similar to the impact of investment; that is, an increase in *G* will have a multiplier effect on income. With respect to the multiplier, it is necessary to distinguish between government spending in the form of purchases of final goods and services and in the form of transfer payments. Government transfer payments such as Social Security payments are payments to individuals and do not directly increase output demanded. Income or output demanded is indirectly affected by transfer payments, for the recipients of the transfer payments will have an increase in their disposable income and will increase their consumption as a consequence. Thus, an increase in government transfer payments will set into action a higher flow of consumer spending, but the multiplier effect will be smaller than an equal increase in *G* due to the fact that transfer payments per se do not increase output demanded. More specifically, the transfer payment multiplier is the regular multiplier minus 1. For example, if the regular multiplier is 5, the transfer payment multiplier is 4. Government lump-sum taxes (taxes that do not vary with income) have an impact on income exactly the same as transfer payments, except that the impact is in the opposite direction. An increase in transfer payments, then, financed by an equal increase in lump-sum taxes, will not change output demanded. On the other hand, an increase in *G* financed by an equal increase in the same kind of taxes will increase output demanded. The increase in output demanded is equal to the increase in *G* because the difference between the government purchase multiplier and the tax multiplier is equal to 1.

Exports and Imports

The final two variables that influence output demanded in the economy are exports and imports. Exports increase output demanded, and imports reduce output demanded. The net effect of international trade on output demanded, therefore, can be measured by the difference between our exports and imports, or net exports. When net exports are increasing, the effect is to increase output demanded, and when net exports are decreasing, the effect is to decrease output

FIGURE 11.5 **Aggregate Supply**

Aggregate supply shows the output supplied at different price levels. At the price level p, output supplied is q, given aggregate supply SS, and q_1, given aggregate S_1S_1. Aggregate supply S_1S_1 represents a greater aggregate supply.

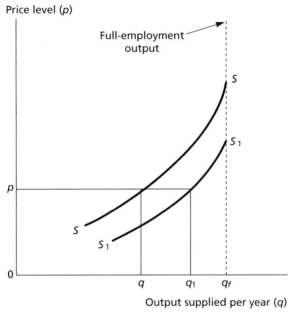

trade deficit
Occurs when the
value of a nation's
imports exceeds the
value of the nation's
exports.

demanded. A so-called **trade deficit** means that net exports are negative or that exports are less than imports. A **trade surplus** means the reverse—that exports are greater than imports.

Aggregate Supply

trade surplus
Occurs when the
value of a nation's
exports exceeds the
value of the nation's
imports.

Aggregate supply is a schedule showing the output supplied at different price levels. It is generally shown as an upward-sloping curve, reflecting increasing marginal costs of producing higher levels of national output. It is profitable to produce higher levels of national output only at higher price levels when higher marginal costs are associated with higher levels of national output.

aggregate supply
A schedule showing
the output supplied
at different price
levels.

The determinants of aggregate supply are the same as the determinants of individual supply curves, namely, resource prices and techniques of production. Aggregate supply varies inversely with resource prices; that is, higher resource prices decrease aggregate supply, and lower resource prices increase aggregate supply. Improvements in production techniques that increase the productivity of resources increase aggregate supply.

Two aggregate supply curves, SS and S_1S_1, are shown in Figure 11.5. Both these supply curves indicate the positive relationship between output supplied and the price level. At the price level p, output supplied is q given SS and q_1 given S_1S_1. In reference to aggregate supply SS, aggregate supply S_1S_1 indicates an increase in aggregate supply. The output supplied at q_f is full employment.

FIGURE 11.6 Aggregate Demand and Supply

Starting with *DD* and *SS*, the equilibrium price level is *p* and the national output is *q*. Full-employment output q_f can be reached by an increase in aggregate demand to D_2D_2. Full-employment output can be reached at a lower demand D_1D_1 if aggregate supply can be increased to S_1S_1.

Aggregate Demand and Supply

Employment and job opportunities depend on both aggregate demand and supply. Figure 11.6 shows three aggregate demand curves and two aggregate supply curves. Beginning with aggregate demand *DD* and aggregate supply *SS*, the equilibrium price level is *p*, and output demanded and supplied is *q*. The economy is experiencing unemployment at this equilibrium level of national output, as indicated by the difference between *q* and q_f, the full-employment level of output. Given aggregate supply *SS*, the economy could reach full-employment output only with a greater aggregate demand as represented by D_2D_2. At this level of aggregate demand, the equilibrium price level is p_2—much higher than it was at the lower level of aggregate demand. However, given the higher level of aggregate supply S_1S_1 and the higher level of aggregate demand D_1D_1, full employment could be reached at the price level *p*.

It can be said that at price level *p* and at the output level *q*, both aggregate demand and aggregate supply are deficient, for the economy is not operating at full employment when *DD* and *SS* represent the strength of aggregate demand and supply. What are some of the reasons for a relatively weak aggregate demand and supply?

FIGURE 11.7   **Breaks in the Circular Flow of Economic Activity: Leakages and Injections**

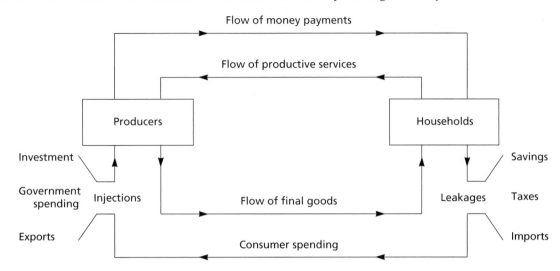

Reasons for Deficient Aggregate Demand

Aggregate demand may not be high enough to provide for a full-employment economy for many reasons. A deficient aggregate demand may be due to an inadequate level of output demanded by consumers. Consumers may reduce their rate of spending for the many reasons that have been discussed, such as changes in tastes, reductions in real income and wealth, and rising interest rates. The weakness in aggregate demand may be traced to the level of investment spending that falls short of the investment spending that would be required for a full-employment economy due to a fall in the expected profit rate and/or a rise in the interest rate. The deficiency in aggregate demand may be related to reductions in government purchases or increases in taxes that discourage private spending. Finally, aggregate demand may be deficient because of a high level of imports relative to exports. All or any of these reasons may explain why the economy may not operate at its full potential.

To understand more thoroughly why the economy may not operate at full employment, let's return to the circular flow of economic activity. The circular flow of economic activity shows that income is created in the process of production and that income created in production may return to producers in the form of spending for the products produced. However, there may be breaks in the circular flow.

These breaks are called *leakages* and *injections*. Figure 11.7 shows the leakages and injections in the circular flow of economic activity. Leakages, or withdrawals from the flow of economic activity, may be offset by injections to the flow of economic activity. An example of a leakage is *saving*, and an example of an injection is *investment*. Saving means that people are not spending part of the income created in production on the purchase of consumer goods such as radios, apples, cigarettes, ties, or refrigerators. This may turn out all right. Saving is required for the economy to invest in new plant and equipment and to grow. If the rate of saving at full employment returns to the circular flow of economic activity through investment (that is, the purchase of investment goods such as plant and equipment), aggregate demand will be sufficient to buy all the goods and services produced. If full-employment saving is greater than full-employment investment, then aggregate demand will be deficient unless other injections into the circular flow are greater than other leakages by the amount of difference between saving and investment. When aggregate demand is deficient, part of the income created by production does not return to producers in the form of spending. This results in surpluses at current market prices and employment levels. Producers respond to a surplus market situation by reducing production (and, therefore, income), causing people to lose their jobs.

Another example of a leakage is government taxes, and the corresponding example of an injection is *government purchases.* Taxes are similar to saving in the sense that they represent a withdrawal from the circular flow of economic activity. Taxes reduce private spending and, therefore, reduce aggregate demand. Aggregate demand may be deficient because taxes are too high in relation to government purchases.

Do you know why many Americans have been so concerned about the *deficit* in the U.S. international balance of payments? A deficit in international trade, as you know, means we are buying more products and services from other countries than they are buying from us. An *import* is a **leakage** from the circular flow of economic activity, and an *export* is an **injection.** A deficit, an excess of imports over exports, will decrease aggregate demand and contributes to the difficulty of reaching the level of aggregate demand required for full employment.

Reasons for Weak Aggregate Supply

We have said that aggregate supply depends essentially on resource prices and techniques of production. The weakness or strength of aggregate supply depends, then, on these two factors. Suppose the price of a resource such as labor increases and is not offset by productivity increases. Under these circumstances, as we said before, aggregate supply would decrease and cause unemployment. As we also said previously, the weakness in aggregate supply may be attributable to the low productivity of labor.

The motivating force behind aggregate supply in a market economy is the profit motive. Producers are not going to expand output if it is not profitable to do so. The relationship between employment and wages and productivity may be extended further. It is profitable to expand employment out to the point where the real wage equals the marginal productivity of labor. In Figure 11.8, with the demand or the marginal product of labor shown by DD and the real wage equal to w, the equilibrium or profitable level of employment is equal to n. There are two ways in which it would be profitable to expand output and increase employment to n_1. One way is for the real wage to decrease to w_1. The second way is for the

leakages
Withdrawals from an economy's circular flow which include savings, taxes, and imports.

injections
Additions to an economy's circular flow which include investments, government spending, and exports.

FIGURE 11.8   Real Wages, Marginal Product of Labor, and Employment

Given the demand or marginal product of labor DD, and the real wage w, the level of employment is n. There are two ways to increase employment to n_1. One way is to reduce the real wage to w_1. The second way is to increase the marginal product of labor to D_1D_1.

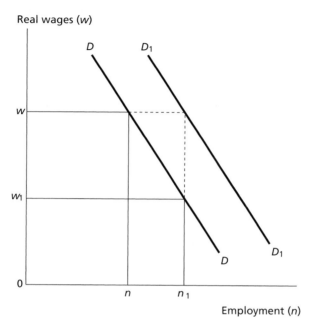

marginal product of labor to increase to D_1D_1. Again, the weakness of aggregate supply is closely linked to wages and productivity.

The weakness of aggregate supply can be related to incentives to save and work. The stock of real capital assets in the economy cannot increase unless there is an adequate flow of savings to finance real investment. It is the stock of real capital assets that determines the general productivity of the economy. If incentives to save are seriously reduced, say, by taxes, saving could be inadequate to provide for the replacement, modernization, and additions to the economy's capital stock. Certain taxes and certain government expenditure programs may reduce incentives to work by lowering the relative price of leisure. As a consequence, people may work less and take more leisure, resulting in a decrease in the supply of labor and a weaker aggregate supply.

COMBATING UNEMPLOYMENT

Unemployment has to be approached from both sides of the market since it may arise from the demand side or the supply side of the market. In the 1950s, 1960s, and 1970s, an aggregate demand approach was taken to cope with unemployment. More attention has been given to the supply approach in recent years because of some aggregate demand policy failures and because recent bouts with unemployment appear to stem more from that side of the market.

Aggregate Demand Policies

Aggregate demand policies are based on aggregate demand theory. This theory develops and explains the determinants of private consumer and investment spending. Two policy views have emerged from this theory. The first view is to stabilize aggregate demand over the business cycle. This means that government spending would be increased and/or taxes cut when private spending is contracting, and government spending would be decreased and/or taxes increased when private spending is expanding. The effect of these changes in government spending and taxes would be to smooth out economic fluctuations in the economy by stabilizing aggregate demand over time. The second policy view is to stabilize aggregate demand at a high level of employment and production, say, at the full-employment level, which means that government spending would be increased and/or taxes decreased any time the economy was not operating at the full-employment production level. This view dominated the policy thinking during the 1960s and most of the 1970s.

The aggregate demand approach to unemployment is to increase aggregate demand directly by increasing government purchases and to increase aggregate demand indirectly by reducing taxes. Policies based on this approach have not been an unqualified success. The economy experienced a long period of growth and low unemployment rates in the 1960s under aggregate demand policies. However, the inflation rate increased in the late 1960s and very little was done about it, and what was done was done too late. After the 1973–1975 recession, the economy expanded but encountered strong inflationary pressures that erupted into an inflation rate above 10 percent in 1979 and 1980. Then, the economy fell into a sharp recession in 1981–1982, primarily in response to contractionary economic policies that were necessary to rid the economy of inflationary forces that were permitted to build up in the latter part of the 1970s. This set the stage for the introduction of aggregate supply policies to cope with the problem of unemployment.

Aggregate Supply Policies and the Economy in the 1980s

Aggregate supply policies are based on aggregate supply theory. This theory provides the framework for analyzing the determinants of aggregate supply. The implication of the theory is that an alternative approach to unemployment is to pursue policies that would increase aggregate supply. The drawback to the supply-side approach is not in the theory but in the difficulty of designing a policy that will increase aggregate supply. What sort of economic policy will reduce resource prices and increase productivity in the economy?

The Reagan administration set into action, beginning in 1981, policies that were inspired by supply-side thinking, even though the policies had an impact on aggregate demand as well as aggregate supply. The most significant policy from a supply-side viewpoint was the reduction in federal tax rates, especially the reduction in the marginal income tax rate from 70 to 50 percent, and then (in 1986) to 28 percent. The stated purpose of these marginal tax rate reductions was to increase aggregate supply by increasing incentives to save, work, and invest.

The economy responded well to these policy incentives (and to other underlying forces in the market) and started to expand in 1983. The real growth rate in the gross domestic product (GDP) was 3.9 percent and 6.2 percent in 1983 and 1984, respectively. The expansion continued during the rest of the 1980s but at a slower growth rate. The growth rate was 2.5 percent in 1989.

Consumer spending played an important role in bringing the economy out of the 1982 recession and in sustaining the expansion into 1990. Consumption was maintained, even during the recession, and increased steadily from 1982 to 1990. Investment, as usual, was more volatile in nature, decreasing and contributing to the recessionary forces in 1982 but increasing and contributing to the rapid real growth in the economy during 1983 and 1984. Between 1984 and 1990, investment remained at about the same rate. Government (federal, state, and local) purchases of goods and services were a stimulating force throughout the expansionary period from 1983 to 1990, increasing in real terms $263 billion over this time span. On the other hand, net exports (exports − imports) were a contractionary force during the first part of the period. Export deficits increased from $63 billion in 1983 to $164 billion in 1986. The export deficit was reduced over the remaining expansionary period to $62 billion in 1990. Even though there were trade deficits in each year from 1986 to 1990, exports increased faster than imports during these years, contributing to the expansion.

What role did federal economic policy play in the economic expansion that began in 1983? The cut in income tax rates and the increase in federal purchases of goods and services together stimulated both aggregate demand and supply. However, the private sector not only had to respond to these policies and other market forces, such as the decline in oil prices, but it also had to introduce new products and services and efficiently supply them in order for the economic expansion to have been as long-lasting.

The Recession, Recovery, and Record-Breaking Expansion of the 1990s

The 1983–1990 economic expansion came to an end in 1990. Beginning in the third quarter of 1990, the economy began to contract, causing more than 3 million people to lose their jobs. During this contraction, the unemployment rate increased from 5.1 percent to 7.1 percent. The contraction ended in the first quarter of 1991, and a new expansion began which continued into the first quarter of 2001. This expansion broke all previous records, reaching 117 months in December 2000. The unemployment rate reached its lowest rate in over three decades.

An important question needs to be answered: What are the underlying forces explaining the duration of this economic expansion? Table 11.1 compares the late expansion economy in the 1960s and in the 1990s. The economic expansion in the 1960s was the longest expansion until the expansion in the 1990s. In the late period

TABLE 11.1
The Late-Expansion Economy in the 1960s and in the 1990s (average annual percent change)

Item	1967 Q4 to 1969 Q4	1997 Q4 to 1999 Q4
Real GDP per capita	2.5	3.4
Unemployment rate	3.5	4.4
Productivity (output per hour worked)	1.3	3.0
Real business fixed investment	6.0	10.0
Consumer Price Index	5.3	2.0

Source: Economic Report of the President, February 2000, p. 78.

(fourth quarter 1967 to fourth quarter 1969) of the expansion in the 1960s, real GDP was growing at an average annual rate of 2.5 percent, the unemployment rate was 3.5 percent, productivity (output per hour worked) was 1.3 percent, business fixed investment was 6 percent, and the inflation rate was 5.3 percent. Compare this same economic data with the data with reference to the late period in the 1990s. An important difference was the much higher productivity rate in the 1990s, a productivity rate of 3 percent in the 1990s compared to 1.3 percent in the 1960s (131 percent difference). A factor that can terminate an expansion is rising labor costs. This can be offset by an increase in labor productivity. This was taking place in the late expansion of the 1990s, and not taking place in the late expansion of the 1960s.

Another factor related to labor productivity is that if increases in money wages are not offset by increases in labor productivity, prices are going to increase, and the result will be an increase in the rate of inflation. The inflation rate was 5.3 percent in the late-expansion period in the 60s and only 2 percent in the late-expansion period of the 90s. Still another factor connected to labor productivity is business fixed investment. There is no doubt that labor is more productive when there is an increase in the ratio of capital to labor. Table 11.1 shows that real business investment was growing at a 67 percent faster growth rate in the late expansion in the 90s than in the 60s. In conclusion, why the expansion in the 60s came to an end and why the expansion period in the 90s exceeded the expansion period in the 60s seems clear.

The 2001 Recession

A recession is defined as a period when the real gross domestic product decreases for two consecutive quarters. The economy was in a recession in the first three quarters in 2001. This was a mild recession, since the real GDP declined less than 1 percent in the first and third quarters and less than 2 percent in the second quarter. The economy returned to an expansion path in the fourth quarter and continued on this path into 2002 and beyond.

A major cause of the 2001 recession was the decline in the growth rate in private investment spending, which decreased in every quarter in 2001. However, if private investment spending is to be blamed for the recession in 2001 it should be given some credit for the recovery and expansion in 2002, for private investment spending started growing at a rapid rate again in 2002. As usual, there are many forces operating in the economy to alleviate a recession and move the economy toward an expansionary direction.

Even though the U.S. economy grew at a modest rate throughout 2002 and 2003, many workers experienced a "jobless recovery" as unemployment rates crept back up. The unemployment rate peaked at 6.3 percent in June of 2003 before following a downward trend over the rest of that year and through 2004. Although a number of factors may have been responsible for this bump up in unemployment, the one issue that received the most attention was the trend for outsourcing service jobs overseas. However, as we learned in the last chapter, the number of service jobs lost to international competition is not large enough to significantly affect the overall rate of unemployment. The return to the labor market of workers who had dropped out of the labor force during the recession and the ongoing restructuring of jobs due to technological change most likely had greater impacts on the unemployment rate than outsourcing.

Summary

Unemployment has both economic and social effects. The economic effect involves the waste and loss of goods and services when resources are unemployed. The social effect involves the breaking up of human relationships within the family and outside it.

There are three types of unemployment—frictional, structural, and cyclical. Frictional unemployment is transitional in nature and is not a major economic issue. Structural and cyclical unemployment are major economic issues. Structural unemployment results from fundamental changes in demand and supply for products in specific sectors of the economy. Cyclical unemployment is associated with the ups and downs in the overall economy.

Aggregate demand and supply theories are developed to explain why people lose their jobs. Aggregate demand is composed of the output demanded by consumers, investors, and government. The determinants of consumer spending are prices, income, wealth, and rate of interest. At a given price level, the output demanded by consumers will vary directly with income and wealth, and inversely with the rate of interest. The determinants of investment spending are the expected profit rate and the rate of interest, with investment spending related directly to the expected profit rate and inversely with the interest rate. Government purchases, the final part of aggregate demand, depend on social priorities and policies.

A deficient aggregate demand or a weak aggregate supply may explain why the economy may operate at less than full employment. An aggregate demand approach to unemployment would pursue fiscal policies that would increase aggregate demand, namely, increase government expenditures related to taxes. An aggregate supply approach would pursue policies that would increase aggregate supply, namely, policies that would increase the productivity of resources and decrease the price of resources. The best possible approach is to pursue consistent aggregate demand and supply policies because unemployment may be caused by both a deficient aggregate demand and a weak aggregate supply.

The 1990s began with the economy in a recession but ended with the economy expanding into the new millennium, breaking the expansionary duration record of the 1960s. The economy went into recession and came out during 2001. The early 2000s indicated that the forces of aggregate demand and aggregate supply will continue to fluctuate over time as the economy responds to the ever-changing world. It is inevitable that any market-based economy will experience swings in its rate of unemployment and that unemployment will always be a potential problem to be faced by policymakers.

Discussion Questions

1. Discuss the economic and noneconomic costs of unemployment.
2. Explain the meaning of *labor force*. Are the unemployed included in the definition of the labor force? What about discouraged workers?
3. Discuss the different types of unemployment. Include in your discussion the type of unemployment that may be reduced without causing inflation.
4. Draw the circular-flow-of-economic-activity diagram. In reference to the diagram, explain the relationship between the product market and the resource market.
5. What are the components of aggregate demand? Discuss the marginal propensity to consume and save and the investment multiplier principle.
6. Explain the causes for increases in aggregate demand and supply.
7. Explain why the economy will contract when leakages from the circular flow of economic activity are greater than the injections into the flow of economic activity.
8. Compare and contrast aggregate demand policies and aggregate supply policies with respect to attempting to maintain a full-employment economy without inflation.
9. Discuss the 1990–1991 recession, the 1991–1992 recovery, and the 1992–2000 expansion.
10. Discuss the recession in 2001. Why was it so short in your opinion?
11. Explain the differences between aggregate demand and aggregate supply policies. Are there situations where one approach should be favored over the other? Discuss.
12. If aggregate demand remains constant and the economy suffers a reduction in the level of aggregate supply, what will happen to the unemployment rate? What will happen to prices? How does this situation differ from a period of deficient aggregate demand?

Additional Readings

Carson, Robert B., Wade L. Thomas, and Jason Hecht. *Macroeconomic Issues Today: Alternative Approaches.* 7th ed. Armonk, NY: M. E. Sharpe, 2002.
The authors present conservative, liberal, and radical views for a variety of economic topics, including unemployment, inflation, and balancing the federal budget.

Cottle, Thomas J. *Hardest Times: The Trauma of Long-Term Unemployment.* Westport, CT: Praeger, 2001.
The author interviewed many long-term unemployed men and recorded their stories.

Froyen, Richard T. *Macroeconomics Theories and Policies.* 8th ed. Upper Saddle River, NJ: Prentice Hall, 2004.
Includes a chapter which develops aggregate demand theory in detail and discusses aggregate demand policies.

Hicks, Alexander M. *Social Democracy and Welfare Capitalism: A Century of Income Security Politics.* Ithaca, NY: Cornell University Press, 1999.
Provides a history of public welfare, social security, welfare economics, and the labor movement.

Jenkinson, Tim, ed. *Readings in Macroeconomics.* New York: Oxford University Press, 1996.
The editor devotes four chapters to inflation and unemployment, discussing wage determination and inflation policy and explaining unemployment.

Layard, Richard, Stephen Nickell, and Richard Jackman. *The Unemployment Crisis.* New York: Oxford University Press, 1994.
Addresses the rise in unemployment over the last few years and the reasons behind the fluctuations.

Munger, Frank, ed. *Laboring below the Line: The New Ethnography of Poverty, Low-Wage Work, and Survival in the Global Economy.* New York: Russell Sage Foundation, 2002.
These contributors examine various issues dealing with poverty, low-wage employment, and survival in the global economy.

Reducing Unemployment. Symposium by the Federal Reserve Bank of Kansas City. Jackson Hole, Wyoming, August 25–27, 1994. Kansas City, MO: Federal Reserve Bank of Kansas City, 1994.
Alan Greenspan, Martin Feldstein, John P. Martin, and others contributed to this symposium on the causes of and the policies to reduce unemployment.

World Wide Web Resources

Best Jobs USA
www.bestjobsusa.com
Provides links to job ads all over the country.

Bureau of Labor Statistics
www.bls.gov

An agency within the U.S. Department of Labor. Provides data on unemployment and other statistics.

Current Population Survey (CPS) Main Page
www.bls.census.gov/cps/cpsmain.htm

CPS is a joint project between the Bureau of Labor Statistics and the Bureau of the Census. Provides links to unemployment figures.

Economic Report of the President
www.access.gpo.gov/eop

Annual report prepared by the chairman of the President's Council of Economic Advisors. Discusses current unemployment situation.

United States Department of Labor
www.dol.gov

Provides links to labor-related data and information on the department's programs and activities.

The White House: Economic Statistics Briefing Room
www.whitehouse.gov/fsbr/employment.html

Provides up-to-date charts and figures for the country's civilian labor force.

Inflation
How to Gain and Lose at the Same Time

Checklist of economic concepts

- Inflation
- Price index numbers
- Equity
- Efficiency
- Money supply
- Creating money
- Money multiplier
- Legal reserve ratio
- Discount rate
- Open-market operation
- Equation of exchange
- Quantity theory of money
- Demand-pull inflation
- Cost-push inflation
- Incomes policy

We had sold out almost our entire inventory and, to our amazement, had nothing to show for it except a worthless bank account and a few suitcases full of currency not even good enough to paper our walls with. We tried at first to sell and then buy again as quickly as possible—but the inflation easily overtook us. The lag before we got paid was too long; while we waited, the value of money fell so fast that even our most profitable sale turned into a loss. Only after we began to pay with promissory notes could we maintain our position. Even so, we are making no real profit now, but at least we can live. Since every enterprise in Germany is financed in this fashion, the Reichsbank naturally has to keep on printing unsecured currency and so the mark falls faster and faster. The government apparently doesn't care; all it loses in this way is the national debt. Those who are ruined are the people who cannot pay with notes, the people who have property they are forced to sell, small shopkeepers, day laborers, people with small incomes who see their private savings and their bank accounts melting away, and government officials and employees who have to survive on salaries that no longer allow them to buy so much as a new pair of shoes. The ones who profit are the exchange kings, the profiteers, the foreigners who buy what they like with a few dollars, kronen, or zlotys, and the big entrepreneurs, the manufacturers, and the speculators on the exchange whose property and stocks increase without limit. For them practically everything is free. It is the great sellout of thrift, honest effort, and respectability. The vultures flock from all sides, and the only ones who come out on top are those who accumulate debts. The debts disappear of themselves.

Source: *The Black Obelisk* by Erich Maria Remarque. Copyright © 1957 by Erich Maria Remarque. Copyright renewed © 1985 by Paulette Goddard Remarque.

Most people consider inflation as equal to or second only to unemployment among the nation's major aggregate economic problems. In almost every presidential campaign, candidates call inflation a bad thing and vow to control it once elected. The rising cost of groceries, gasoline, medical services, clothes, travel, and everything else is a main topic of conversation among consumers. Business firms realize that higher prices for materials, labor, equipment, and other things they buy will reduce business profits unless they are successful in passing these higher costs on to the consumer in the form of higher consumer prices. Inflation is a prime bargaining consideration in labor union negotiations. A stated national goal of government economic policy is to stabilize the price level. All groups composing the population—consumers, business firms, and government—are concerned about inflation.

MEANING AND MEASUREMENT OF INFLATION

Most people have a good idea of what is meant by inflation. They know that it causes a sack full of groceries to cost more money. They know that buying Christmas presents costs more. They know that it is more expensive to eat out, to go to a movie, to take a vacation, or to buy a car. They know they will be generally worse off in the future unless their pay can keep up with inflation.

What Is Inflation?

inflation
A continuing rise in the general level of prices.

Inflation is a continuing rise in the general level of prices. This is in sharp contrast to a simple one-shot increase in the price level to a higher equilibrium level. An equilibrium price level is not reached when there is inflation since forces are continuing to move prices upward. During inflation some commodities may be falling in price and some may be rising, but the commodities that are rising are dominant, and they exert an upward force on the general price level.

Inflation has *dynamic, self-sustaining* properties. Increases in the price level induce economic groups to react to rising prices, causing further increases in prices. For example, consumers expecting increases in prices may increase current consumer spending, causing current market prices to rise. During periods of rising prices, producers are not inclined to resist increases in wages and other costs, since higher production costs may be shifted forward to consumers in the form of higher prices. These increases in prices, however, become the basis for further increases in production costs and still higher prices.

Rising prices, however, are *not* always observable in inflation. It may be suppressed, as market prices may not always reflect the inflationary forces operating in the economy. *Suppressed inflation* is usually associated with an attempt on the part of government to control prices. During the control period, market prices remain the same. Inflationary forces, however, persist because the government is not doing anything to alter the underlying inflationary forces in the market. Under these circumstances, it is difficult to keep prices under control, and prices in general will rise rapidly when price controls are lifted.

How Is Inflation Measured?

Inflation is measured by price index numbers. Recall that price index numbers indicate the general level of prices in reference to a base year. For example, the consumer price index in 2004 was 110, using 1999 as the base year. This means that consumer prices on average increased 10 percent between the base year (1999 = 100) and 2004. The consumer price index was 108 in 2003. What was the rate of inflation between 2003 and 2004? The answer is 1.85 percent. This was derived as follows:

$$\text{Inflation rate} = \frac{110 - 108}{108} = 0.0185$$

Price Indexes

The Consumer Price Index, or CPI, sometimes referred to as the *cost-of-living index*, includes commodities that city wage earners and clerical workers buy, such as food, housing, utilities, transportation, clothing, health services, and recreation. The wholesale price index includes hundreds of commodities such as farm products and processed foods, as well as industrial commodities such as textiles, fuel, chemicals, rubber, lumber, paper, metals, machinery, furniture, nonmetallic minerals, and transportation equipment. Another price index that is used often by economists is the *implicit price deflator*. The implicit price deflator includes the components of the GDP—consumer services, durable and nondurable goods, residential and nonresidential fixed investment, exports and imports, and goods and services purchased by governments.

Construction of a Price Index

Since inflation is measured by price index numbers, it is important to understand how price index numbers are derived. Although we briefly explored price indices in Chapter 1, it is important for us to thoroughly review the process of constructing a price index. A simple illustration can point out the essential underlying principles. Suppose a family spends $20,000, $21,000, and $22,000 in 2008, 2009, and 2010, respectively, for identical baskets of goods. If 2008 is used as the base year, the index number for the goods for that year is 100. It is 105 for 2009, calculated by dividing the cost of the basket in the base year ($20,000) into the cost in 2009 ($21,000) and multiplying by 100 in order to remove the decimal. By the same procedure, the index number in 2010 is 110, or

$$\frac{\text{Cost of market basket (2010)}}{\text{Cost of market basket (2008)}} \times 100 = \frac{\$22,000}{\$20,000} \times 100 = 110$$

The basket of goods used to compute price index numbers is a representative sample of the quantities of each good in the basket—the number of dresses, shirts, loaves of bread, gallons of gasoline, movie tickets, television sets, autos, and so forth—bought during the year specified. The sum of the price times the quantity of each good in the basket gives the value of the basket. After the value of the basket is calculated, the final step in the construction of a price index is to select the base year and compute the index numbers as illustrated.

A set of price index numbers is not a perfect measure of inflation. Only a sample of commodities is included in the index. What constitutes a representative sample is difficult to determine, and it changes over time in response to changes in tastes and preferences of people. It is also difficult to account for changes in the quality of goods that occur over time; for some goods and services, higher index numbers reflect higher costs for a better commodity rather than higher costs for the same commodity. An even more difficult problem arises when improved technology results in *lower prices* for higher-quality goods (example: personal computers). Despite these imperfections, price index numbers are still useful indicators of trends in the level of prices.

FIGURE 12.1   **Average Annual Inflation Rate in Selected Periods, 1960–2004**

Source: Economic Report of the President, February 2004.

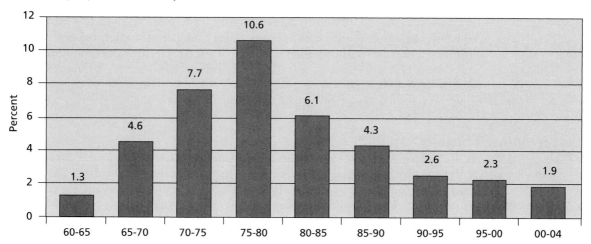

Rate of Inflation

Figure 12.1 shows the average inflation rate over five-year intervals from 1960 to 2004. The first half of the 1960s was a period when prices were almost stable, with consumer prices on average increasing only 1.3 percent each year. The inflation scenario was different in the last half of the decade. The economy reached full employment in 1965, and inflationary forces began to mount. The result was an average annual inflation rate between 1965 and 1970 of more than three times the rate of the earlier period (4.6 percent). The decade of the 1970s started with a high rate of inflation of about 6 percent and ended with a much higher rate of over 10 percent. What happened? How did the policymakers let inflation get out of control? First, nothing was done to stem the inflationary forces in the late 1960s. The most effective way to control a serious inflation is to not let it happen in the first place. Second, wage and price controls were enacted in the early 1970s to cope with the inflationary problem. Wage and price controls treat only the symptoms of inflation, not the basic cause of inflation. The year controls were removed, 1974, the inflation rate was 11 percent. A final factor that has to be taken into consideration in the assessment of the rampant inflation of this period is the increase in energy prices. An increase in an important input like energy increases the cost of producing most goods and services. In part, then, the high annual rate of inflation of 10.6 percent between 1975 and 1980 reflects the higher costs of producing goods and services.

Inflationary forces were brought under control in the 1980s. However, it took a serious recession in 1981 and 1982 to do so. A recession after a long period of inflation can usually be expected, for the economy must slow down or decline in order for inflationary forces to be eliminated. The average annual inflation rate was

6.1 percent between 1980 and 1985. The annual rate of inflation was reduced to 4.3 percent in the 1985–1990 period, and fell further to 2.6 percent in 1990–1995. By 2000–2004, inflation was averaging only 1.9 percent per year, based on the CPI. The lesson to be learned from history is that very high inflation rates reflect the failure of resolving the problem of inflation when it first arises in the economy. Inflationary forces feed upon themselves and can cause people to expect inflation and behave in a way that causes inflation. The causes and cures of inflation will be discussed in subsequent sections.

ECONOMIC EFFECTS OF INFLATION

equity effects of inflation
The effects of inflation on the distribution of income.

Inflation affects the distribution of income, the allocation of resources, and the national output. The effects of inflation on the distribution of income are referred to as the **equity effects,** and the effects on resource allocation and national output are called the *efficiency* and *output effects* of inflation, respectively.

Equity Effects

The impact of inflation is uneven. Some people benefit from inflation, and some suffer economic harm. Because inflation alters the distribution of income, a major concern is the degree of equity, or fairness, in the distribution of income.

Anyone who is on a fixed income is hurt by inflation since it reduces real income. For example, a person who earns $20,000 a year during an inflationary period in which there is a 25 percent increase in the price level suffers a cut in real income equivalent to the rate of inflation—$5,000 in this illustration. Examples of those whose incomes often do not rise as fast as the price level are retired people on pensions, white-collar workers, civil servants, people on public assistance, and workers in declining industries.

People who hold assets in the form of money and who have fixed claims on money may be made worse off by inflation. Suppose a person deposits $1,000 in a savings account and receives a 5 percent interest rate, or $50, during the year. If the rate of inflation is in excess of 5 percent, the real value of the original savings of $1,000 plus the $50 earned on the savings for a year is reduced to less than the original $1,000. Creditors and owners of mortgages and life insurance policies are hurt by inflation, since the real value of their fixed money claims is reduced. People who bought government savings bonds for $18.75 and were paid $25.00 at maturity 10 years later have sometimes discovered that the $25.00 would not buy the same quantity of goods and services that the $18.75 would have bought 10 years earlier.

The prices of some goods and resources, due to inflation, may rise faster than the general level of prices. Wages and salaries of workers in rapidly growing industries are likely to rise faster than the price level. Strong unions are sometimes successful in bargaining for wage increases that are greater than the increases in the price level. People who depend on income in the form of profits—owners of stocks and business enterprises—may have increases in real income, depending upon the rate of increase in profits in comparison to prices. The value of land and improvements on land may rise during inflation; if they rise in value faster than the rate of inflation, the owners of land will be relatively better off.

In summary, if inflation is not anticipated and people therefore cannot adjust their economic behavior, inflation alters the distribution of income and wealth. Inflation is like a tax to some people and like a subsidy to others. People whose real incomes are reduced by inflation are those who have fixed incomes and hold assets in the form of money. People whose real incomes are increased by inflation are those who have money income that increases faster than prices and hold real assets that appreciate in value faster than inflation. The arbitrary manner in which inflation may change the pattern of income distribution gives support to the claim that inflation is inequitable.

Efficiency Effects

efficiency effects of inflation
The effects of inflation on the pattern of resource allocation.

Inflation tends to change the pattern of resource allocation. In a competitive market, the prices of different goods and services reflect differences in consumer valuations of the quantities made available. Inflation causes demands for different goods and services to increase, but demands for some increase more rapidly than those for others. Increases in demands evoke supply responses, the extent of which vary from product to product. Thus, inflation changes relative demands, relative supplies, and relative prices of different goods and services. The pattern of resource allocation, then, is not the same pattern that would exist in the absence of inflation. The pattern of resource allocation with inflation is not necessarily less efficient (that is, results in lower economic welfare) than the pattern without inflation. However, many economists argue that inflation distorts the pattern of resource allocation, implying a less efficient allocation of resources.

Inflation encourages economic groups to spend time and resources in an attempt to adjust to inflation. Since inflation reduces the purchasing power of money, it encourages everyone to economize or minimize their money balances, that is, assets held in the form of money. The time spent and the resources used in adjusting to inflation could have been used to produce goods and services. Inflation, by encouraging everyone to make adjustments and divert time and resources away from production, reduces economic efficiency.

Output Effects

output effects of inflation
The effects of inflation on the level of production.

The preceding discussion of the equity and efficiency effects of inflation assumes that the levels of real output and production lie on the economy's production possibilities curve. This assumption is made in order to focus attention on how inflation may alter the distribution of real income among people (equity effects) and the allocation of resources (efficiency effects). Simply stated, a certain-size pie is assumed in the previous discussion, and our concern was the way inflation alters the slices of pie and affects the use of resources in making the pie. Now we consider the effects of inflation on the size of the pie. What are the effects of inflation on the level of output of goods and services?

Inflation may have a stimulating effect on production and employment in the economy. The argument in support of this proposition can be presented as follows. During inflation, money wages lag behind price increases. Real profit income is increased. Under the stimulus of higher profits, producers expand production and employ more people.

The argument that inflation may stimulate production and employment should be qualified. Runaway inflation, or hyperinflation, may depreciate the value of money so drastically that it loses its acceptability as a medium of exchange. Under these circumstances, a barter economy develops, accompanied by lower production levels and higher unemployment. If the economy is operating at full capacity and full employment, then, of course, inflation cannot stimulate them further. Inflation at full employment is usually referred to as *pure inflation.*

The impact of inflation differs depending on whether inflation is associated with increases in production and employment. As long as production is rising, there is a check on inflation because, although lagging behind demand, supply is increasing and inflationary forces are mitigated. The equity effects of inflation are also minimized if production and employment are rising. However, as the economy approaches full employment, the seriousness of inflation increases. The possibility of an accelerated rate of inflation is nearer, and the possible beneficial effects of inflation on production and employment are remote.

WHAT IS MONEY?

Inflation is sometimes described as a situation in which "too much" money is chasing "too few" goods. As a first step to understanding this notion we need to be able to answer the question: What is money?

Money is anything that is generally accepted as a means of payment for goods, services, and debt. Many things have been used for money, such as seashells, bullets, and metals. Money is much more than just cash. There are several measures of money, and what is included in the money supply and the functions of money are the points of interest in this section.

medium of exchange
The use of money for the payment of goods and services and for the payment of debt.

measure of value
The use of money to measure the value of goods and services.

store of value
The use of money as an asset to hold.

Functions of Money

Money serves three basic functions: a medium of exchange, a measure of value, and a store of value. Goods and services are paid for in money, and debts are incurred and paid off in money. Without money, economic transactions would have to take place on a barter basis, that is, one good traded for another good. Thus, the use of money as the **medium of exchange** simplifies and facilitates the exchange process. Second, the values of economic goods and services are measured in money. Money as a **measure of value** makes possible value comparisons of goods and services and the summation of quantities of goods and services on a value basis. It is not possible to add apples and oranges, but *it is possible* to add the *values* of apples and oranges. Third, wealth and assets may be held in the form of money. Money serves as a **store of value.**

The Money Supply (M1 and M2) in the United States

Money is an asset that is completely liquid; that is, you do not have to sell money in order to buy goods, services, and other assets. The money supply, then, is composed of assets that are 100 percent liquid or come so close to meeting this liquidity criterion that they are considered to be money. Several definitions of the money supply exist. The narrowest, called **M1** for short, includes currency and coins in circulation, nonbank traveler's checks, demand deposits at financial institutions, and other checkable deposits such as NOW accounts, ATS accounts, and credit-union share drafts. NOW accounts are negotiable orders of withdrawal, and ATS accounts are automatic transfers of savings accounts. NOW and ATS accounts are similar to a regular checking account in the sense that goods and services can be paid for by writing checks on these accounts. In the case of ATS accounts, a bank will automatically transfer from savings to checking accounts when it is necessary to cover checks that have been written. The effect is the same as if all balances were held in a regular checking account. Credit-union share drafts are also the same as regular checking accounts at commercial banks.

M1

Currency and coins in circulation, nonbank traveler's checks, demand deposits, and other checkable accounts such as NOW accounts.

The second definition of the money supply, **M2,** is broader and includes M1 plus savings and time deposits of small denomination (less than $100,000) and money-market mutual funds. A phone call or a trip to the bank is often the only difference between a demand deposit and a time deposit, especially a time deposit of a small denomination. Some savings accounts may have more stringent conditions placed on them, such as the loss of interest if they are withdrawn early, but, in general, savings accounts are like money. Many people find it convenient and can earn more interest by buying shares of money-market mutual funds. These funds are invested in almost riskless, interest-yielding assets, namely, U.S. Treasury bills. Money-market mutual funds are easily accessible and, under certain conditions, checks can be written against these funds.

M2

M1 plus savings and time deposits of small denomination and money-market mutual funds.

There are still broader definitions of money referred to as M3 and L. Time deposits of $100,000 and over plus M2 are included in the definition of M3, and L includes M3 plus other liquid assets such as commercial paper, banker's acceptances, and Treasury bills. The major purpose of these broader measures of money is to have a measure of money and near-money and, therefore, a measure of the overall liquidity in the economy. The money supply M2 is the definition of the money supply that is the generally more acceptable definition, especially from a policy viewpoint. This definition of the money supply includes assets that are 100 percent liquid for all practical purposes and is a broader definition than the restrictive M1. For example, the dollar value of M2 in December of 2003 was $6,044.6 billion, while the value of M1 was only $1,287.1 billion. Although the Federal Reserve keeps track of the growth rate of M1 and the broader definitions of money, the Federal Reserve has officially announced that the growth rate in M2 is the primary target to watch closely and keep within a stated range of control.

Figure 12.2 shows the high and low M2 growth rates during each decade over the 1960–2003 period. Ideally the money supply should grow at a steady growth rate, varying generally only within a range, say, of 4 to 6 percent. During the 1960s, the growth rate of M2 stayed reasonably close to this range, with a high rate of growth

FIGURE 12.2 **High and Low M2 Growth Rates in the Decades 1960–2003**

Source: *Economic Report of the President*, February 2004.

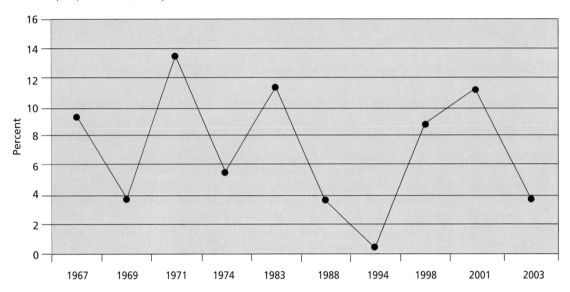

of slightly over 9 percent in 1967 and a low growth rate in 1969 of slightly under 4 percent. The growth rate in M2 got out of control in the early 1970s, reaching the highest rate of growth for the entire period under review of 13.4 percent in 1971. The low M2 growth rate in the decade of the 70s was 5.5 percent. The 1980s experienced much improvement in economic conditions compared to the preceding decade. The high M2 growth rate was 11.2 percent in 1983, and the low M2 growth rate was 3.6 percent in 1988. The stage was set for an expanding economy without an inflationary problem in the 1990s. The low growth rate in M2 was less than 1 percent in 1994, and the high growth rate was 8.8 percent in 1998, which then dropped to 6.1 percent in the last year of the decade. This growth rate in M2 of 6.1 percent was the same growth rate in the year 2000. However, in 2001, M2 accelerated to a growth rate of 10.4 percent. The increase in the growth rate of M2 could not have occurred at a better time since, as you may recall from Chapter 11, the economy slid into a decline in the first three quarters of 2001. This increase in the growth rate in M2 contributed to the expansionary forces operating in the economy, which moved the economy in an upward direction again in the last quarter of 2001 and into the year 2002. By 2003, after the recovery had begun, the M2 growth rate fell to 3.9 percent.

THE PROCESS OF CREATING MONEY

The major part of the money supply is in the form of checkable deposits. Checkable deposits are held in commercial banks and other depository institutions, namely, savings and loan associations, mutual savings banks, and credit unions. In this section, the focus is on the way these deposits are created and destroyed.

Commercial Banks and Other Depository Institutions

There are about 8,000 commercial banks in the United States. Banks are private firms that are in business to make a profit by providing a full range of financial services, including checking accounts, savings accounts, loans, automatic transfers from savings to checking accounts, and electronic banking services. Commercial banks are either state banks or national banks. State banks receive their charters to engage in the banking business from the state, whereas national banks receive their charters from the federal government.

The traditional distinctions between commercial banks and other depository institutions or banks are disappearing. The Monetary Control Act of 1980 allows more flexibility in providing services. Prior to this act, savings and loan associations and mutual savings banks were restricted to offering savings accounts. These institutions now offer checking accounts and are expanding other banking services. Historically, savings deposits of savings and loan associations were used primarily to finance the purchase of homes. Now with checking deposits, savings and loan associations can make other types of loans as well. Mutual savings banks are very much like savings and loan associations; however, they were originally intended to serve small savers and used their funds for different purposes, such as investment in stocks and bonds.

Another depository institution is the credit union. A credit union is a cooperative banking venture in which members or owners have a common employer or union. Credit unions have savings and checking accounts and use their funds primarily for small consumer loans. The services of credit unions can be expected to expand in the future.

Banking Regulation

Banks have been subject to a great deal of both federal and state government regulations. The idea behind the regulations was to make banks safe and sound. One of the early and important federal acts was the passage of the Banking Act of 1933, better known as the Glass-Steagall Act, which restricted commercial banks from providing insurance and brokerage services. This act was controversial because it prevented banks from expanding services to meet the demands of their customers, and it was finally laid to rest in 1999 with the passage of the Gramm-Leach-Bliley Act. This act opened the door for banks to underwrite and sell insurance and securities, conduct both commercial and merchant banking, invest in and develop real estate, and provide other financial activities. This expansion of services provided by commercial banks and the deregulation movement led to a wave of mergers throughout the 1990s. By the early 2000s, some policymakers began to worry that deregulation had created an undesirable concentration of financial clout held by the large banks' holding companies which resulted from the mergers. It is possible that the pendulum of bank regulation may swing back again in the future.

Balance Sheet of a Bank

A balance sheet of a bank shows the relationship among the bank's assets, liabilities, and net worth. The important feature of a balance sheet is

$$\text{Assets} = \text{Liabilities} + \text{Net worth}$$

When there is a change on one side of the equation, there is an offsetting change either on the same side of the equation or on the other side of the equation. For example, if there is an increase in a liability of $10,000, there is a decrease of $10,000 in another liability or net worth, or an increase in an asset of $10,000.

The major assets of a bank are cash reserves, loans and investments, and fixed investments, such as a building and equipment. The major liabilities of banks are demand or checking deposits and time or savings deposits. The net worth of a bank is the owner's equity or the capital stock of the bank.

The balance sheet of a bank appears as follows:

Assets	Liabilities and Net Worth
Reserves: 　Legal reserves 　Excess reserves Loans and investments Fixed investments	Liabilities: 　Demand deposits 　Time deposits Net worth

To focus on the way money is created, we are concerned only with reserves and loans of banks on the asset side and demand or checking deposits on the liability side.

The Fractional Reserve Banking System

Banks are required by law to keep only a part of their deposits in reserves. These reserves are held primarily in the form of deposits at Federal Reserve Banks but also include the cash that banks have on hand, sometimes referred to as *vault cash*. The legal reserve requirement is expressed in percentage terms and is called the *reserve ratio* since it is the ratio of required reserves to bank deposits. For example, if the reserve ratio for a particular bank with demand deposits of $40 million is 10 percent, this bank must have in legal reserves 10 percent of $40 million, or $4 million.

Banks may have *excess reserves,* that is, reserves above what is required to meet the legal reserve requirement. Banks must have excess reserves to make new loans. When banks as a group expand loans, they create demand deposits; and when banks as a group contract loans, they destroy demand deposits. Now let's turn more specifically to the process of creating and destroying demand deposits or money.

Demand Deposit Creation

Suppose there is a new demand deposit of $10,000, and the reserve ratio is 10 percent. The demand deposits of the bank increase $10,000, and reserves increase $10,000. If the new deposit was made from withdrawing currency in circulation, there is no change in the money supply since the money supply is composed of currency in circulation and demand deposits. Given a 10 percent reserve ratio, the bank has to keep $1,000 in legal reserves and has $9,000 in excess reserves.

Now, let's say you go to the bank and borrow $9,000 in order to buy a car. You sign a piece of paper called a *promissory note* agreeing to pay back the loan plus interest over a period of time in monthly installments. The new auto is used as collateral for the loan. After you sign the promissory note, the bank increases your checking account by the amount of the loan, or $9,000. You write a check for $9,000 to pay for the new auto. Your balance at the bank remains what it was prior to obtaining the loan. Demand deposits at another bank increase $9,000 when the auto dealer deposits your check. A loan of $9,000 to pay for a new auto has created new demand deposits of $9,000 in the banking system.

The process of demand deposit creation does not have to end after your loan of $9,000 creates new demand deposits of $9,000. With the assumed legal reserve ratio of 10 percent, $900 ($9,000 × 0.10) is required to meet the legal reserve requirement. Thus, excess reserves of $8,100 remain in the system. By the same process as your loan, a new loan of $8,100 may be made that creates a new deposit of $8,100. This process may be repeated over and over again until excess reserves become zero.

The multiple expansion of demand deposits from a $10,000 deposit withdrawn from currency in circulation assuming a reserve ratio of 10 percent is shown through four stages in Table 12.1. Could you continue the stages through five, six, seven, and so on? In the final stage, observe demand deposits are $100,000, but the maximum demand deposit *increase* or money supply increase is $90,000, since $10,000 is currency withdrawn from circulation. In a symmetrical way, there may be a multiple contraction in demand deposits and the money supply when demand deposits are reduced in the banking system by a new currency withdrawal of $10,000.

money multiplier
A numerical coefficient derived from the legal reserve ratio and equal to the reciprocal of the legal reserve ratio. The money multiplier multiplied by a change in excess cash reserves of banks gives the maximum change in the money supply.

The maximum demand deposit creation possible from a given new demand deposit can be calculated using the equation

$$D = E \times 1/r$$

where D = maximum deposit creation

E = excess legal reserves

r = reserve ratio

In our illustration, the $10,000 new demand deposit increases legal reserves $1,000 and excess reserves $9,000. The increase in excess reserves times the reciprocal of the reserve ratio, or the **money multiplier,** equals the maximum deposit creation possible ($9,000 × 10 = $90,000).

THE ISSUE OF CONTROL

It is apparent that with a fractional reserve banking system, the money supply can expand and contract rapidly. The system works well when money growth is controlled. The Federal Reserve Act of 1913 established the Federal Reserve System (the Fed). The main purpose of the Fed is to control the money supply.

TABLE 12.1

A $10,000 New Deposit Is Made from Currency in Circulation (legal reserve ratio = 10%)

Assets		Liabilities
	Stage 1: Bank 1	
Reserves: Legal + $1,000 Excess + $9,000		Demand deposits + $10,000
	A $9,000 loan is made Stage 2: Bank 2	
Reserves: Legal + $900 Excess + $8,100		Demand deposits + $9,000
	An $8,100 loan is made Stage 3: Bank 3	
Reserves: Legal + $810 Excess + $7,290		Demand deposits + $8,100
	A $7,290 loan is made Stage 4: Bank 4	
Reserves: Legal + $729 Excess + $6,561		Demand deposits + $7,290
	At the end of Stage 4: Sum total of loans + $24,390	
Reserves: Legal + $3,439 Excess + $6,561		Demand deposits + $34,390
	Final stage: Sum total of all stages Sum total of loans + $90,000	
Reserves: Legal + $10,000 Excess $0		Demand deposits + $100,000

The Federal Reserve System

There are 12 Federal Reserve Banks located in various regions of the country. Each Federal Reserve Bank acts as a central bank for private banks in it's region. A central bank is a bank for private banks. Just as a private bank provides you with a full range of banking services, the Fed provides private banks with many services. Among these services are clearing checks, holding bank reserves or deposits, providing currency, and extending loans to private banks.

The Board of Governors manages the Federal Reserve System. The board consists of seven members appointed by the president and confirmed by Congress. The appointments are for 14 years, and reappointments are prohibited if a member served a full term. The president selects the chairman of the board, who is the chief spokesperson and architect of Fed policy. The current chairman of the board, Alan Greenspan, was appointed by President Reagan in 1987 and has continued to be reappointed by the president in office.

An influential policy committee is the Federal Reserve Open Market Committee (FOMC). This committee is composed of all seven members of the Board of Governors plus five regional Reserve Bank presidents. The FOMC meets about once a month in Washington, D.C., to discuss and determine open-market operations. Open-market operations are the buying and selling of government securities in order to influence the level of bank reserves.

The Monetary Control Act of 1980 brought all banks and depository institutions under the regulations of the Fed. Prior to this act, state-chartered banks could choose whether they wanted to be "members" of the Fed. This distinction between member and nonmember banks no longer has economic significance. All banks are subject to the Federal Reserve legal reserve requirements, and all banks are provided with Fed services.

Federal Reserve Controls

The Federal Reserve has three major policy instruments: the legal reserve requirement, the discount rate, and open-market operations. Each control influences excess reserves and the lending ability of banks. The discount rate is not generally a powerful control but is important because it may indicate the direction of the Federal Reserve policy with respect to interest rates. The legal reserve ratio is a powerful weapon, but changes in the legal reserve ratio are not made frequently. Open-market operations have a direct impact on excess reserves and are the most important way the Fed controls the money supply.

Legal Reserve Ratio

legal reserve ratio
The ratio of cash reserves to demand deposits that banks are required to maintain.

The **legal reserve ratio** is the ratio of reserves that banks are required to maintain to demand deposits. An increase in this ratio reduces excess reserves and the lending potential of banks. Banks that are fully loaned out, that is, banks with zero excess reserves, are required to reduce loans and borrow from the Fed or from other banks with excess reserves in order to meet a higher reserve requirement. A decrease in the legal reserve ratio increases excess reserves and the lending potential of banks. Thus, a contractionary Federal Reserve monetary policy could be in the form of increasing the legal reserve ratio, and an expansionary policy could be in the form of reducing the ratio.

Discount Rate

discount rate
The rate of interest that Federal Reserve Banks charge when banks borrow from the Fed.

The **discount rate** is the rate of interest that Federal Reserve Banks charge when banks borrow from the Fed. The amount that a bank borrows from the Fed counts as legal reserves for that bank. An increase in the discount rate tends to discourage bank borrowing from the Fed, which will lower its reserves, and to increase interest rates on bank loans generally. The Fed increases the discount rate when it desires to tighten credit and slow down growth in the money supply. In contrast, the Fed decreases the discount rate when it desires to ease money and credit. Sometimes, changes in the discount rate are viewed as signals indicating whether the Federal Reserve is pursuing or planning to pursue a policy of monetary ease or monetary tightness. A change in the discount rate not supported by appropriate changes in other monetary weapons may not have much impact on the economy.

Open-Market Operations

open-market operations
The purchases and sales of government securities by the Federal Reserve Open Market Committee in order to control the growth in the money supply.

The Federal Reserve Open Market Committee (FOMC) buys and sells federal securities in order to influence bank reserves, loans, and demand deposits. An open-market purchase means that the Fed is buying federal securities from banks or from the nonbank public. In either case, banks' excess reserves are increased. The primary impact of the purchase of federal securities from banks is to increase excess reserves and decrease federal securities held by banks. The primary impact of an open-market purchase from nonbanks is to increase demand deposits and excess reserves of banks. The FOMC makes the decision to buy federal securities when it desires to expand the money supply. An open-market sale has the opposite effect. Excess reserves and the lending ability of banks are reduced by open-market sales. Thus, the FOMC makes the decision to sell federal securities when it desires to contract growth in the money supply.

Federal Reserve Targets

The two most often discussed monetary policy targets are the interest rate target and the money growth rate target. Federal Reserve policy has often focused on interest rates. When interest rates were believed to be "too high," the Fed pursued a policy of monetary ease; when interest rates were believed to be "too low," the Fed pursued a policy of monetary tightness. These policy actions are sometimes referred to as a policy of *fine tuning,* that is, pursuing a policy which in effect changes the growth rate in the money supply in order to maintain interest rates at a level that will promote economic stability and growth. This focus on interest rates as the prime basis of Fed policy has at times led to serious inflationary problems. During periods of economic expansion, interest rates generally rise because of the increase in the demand for money and credit. To prevent interest rates from rising in these circumstances, the Fed may pursue a policy that increases the money growth rate. Also, political pressures on the Fed to keep interest rates low or to prevent interest rates from rising tend to increase inflationary expectations and eventually lead to a higher money growth rate and inflation. The major criticism of using interest rates as the main policy target is that the Fed would be relinquishing control over growth in the money supply.

Primarily in response to the high rate of inflation in the late 1970s, the Federal Reserve began in October 1979 to focus on money growth as the prime policy target. Money growth rates were established for the various measures of money. In the early 1990s, the target growth rate set for M2 was a range between 2½ and 6½ percent. The target range for the growth rate in M2 was changed to 1 to 5 percent in the mid-1990s. The actual growth rate in M2 was above this new target range in 1998 and 1999, with the M2 growth rate exceeding 10 percent in 2001 (Figure 12.2). However, by 2003 M2 was back within its target range when it grew at only 3.9 percent for the year.

A growing number of economists support the money growth rate target. They make two major points: First, they argue that it is the growth in the money supply that ultimately determines the inflation rate. Second, they argue that erratic movements in the money growth rate are primarily responsible for the economic instability in the economy. For these reasons, a Fed policy that concentrates on a stable money growth rate is favored by these economists.

Another policy issue related to the money growth target is the ability or inability of the Fed to pursue a *stable* money growth rate policy. In some periods, money growth rates vary widely on a monthly basis from the established targets. Critics of Fed policy believed that the Fed was not focusing on controlling the money supply and was basing policy on other considerations. It may be that this criticism was in part justified. It may also be that money growth rates cannot be precisely controlled in the very short run.

In summary, the issue of the appropriate monetary policy target is not resolved among policymakers. Among economists, there is somewhat more agreement that monetary stability can be best accomplished by a Federal Reserve policy that strives to maintain a stable and reasonable money growth rate.

INFLATIONARY CAUSES AND CURES

Two approaches will be taken to explain the causes of inflation and to present possible methods of stopping it. The quantity theory of money is the first approach. This theory stresses the importance of money in the inflationary process. Aggregate demand-supply analysis provides a framework for approaching the causes of inflation.

Quantity Theory of Money

equation of exchange
An identity in which the money supply times velocity equals total spending (left-hand side) and the price level times the quantity of final goods and services produced equals the value of these goods and services produced (right-hand side).

The starting point for the quantity theory of money is the **equation of exchange:**

$$MV = PQ$$

where M = money supply

V = income velocity of money or number of times, on average, a dollar is used to buy final goods and services in a year

P = price level or average price of final goods and services

Q = quantity of final goods and services produced during year

The left-hand side of the equation, the money supply (M) times the velocity or turnover of money (V), measures total money spending in the economy. The right-hand side of the equation, the price level (P) times the national output (Q), equals the money value of the national output or nominal income. The two sides of the equation are equal since the total spending for goods and services is the same as the total sales value of goods and services.

The quantity theory of money states that increases and decreases in M cause increases and decreases in P and Q, respectively. The assumption of this theory is that V is relatively constant. If it is further assumed that the nation's output is fixed, it follows that the price level will rise or fall at the same rate that M rises or falls. More relevant than this extreme assumption concerning output is that,

FIGURE 12.3 Average Annual Inflation Rate and Money Supply Growth Rate in Selected Time Periods, 1960–2004

Source: *Economic Report of the President*, February 2004.

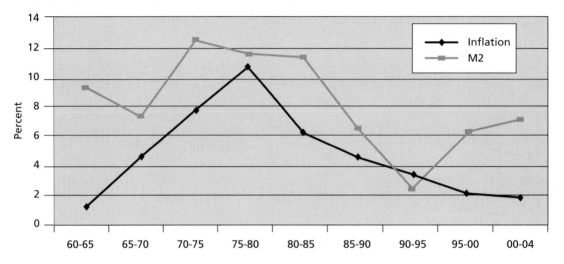

given a constant or relatively constant *V,* the inflation rate is closely connected with the growth rate in the money supply as the economy expands and nears full employment.

An increase in the money supply will certainly increase prices unless velocity of money decreases and/or output increases. In the event of no changes in *V* and *Q,* the price level is the equilibrium variable that moves the economy toward a new equilibrium where the increase in *M* is offset by an increase in *P*. That is to say, when "excess money" is created by an increase in *M,* the excess money (assuming a constant *V*) flows into the final goods market, resulting in inflation. A decrease in *V* or an increase in *Q* could partially or wholly eliminate the excess money and, therefore, could partially or wholly offset the inflationary pressure. The quantity theory of money teaches, however, that growth in the money supply is the basic cause of inflation, and the cure for inflation is to control the growth in the money supply. The control can be achieved, of course, through appropriate use of Federal Reserve controls over the money supply.

In view of the quantity theory of money, let's examine further the growth rates in the money supply and inflation over the time periods between 1960 and 2004 (Figure 12.3). The average annual growth rates in the money supply and inflation certainly appear to be closely related. In general, the average annual growth rates in the money supply and inflation move in the same direction with the growth rate in the money supply above the inflation growth rate. An exception to this pattern is seen over the past decade and a half. In the final period, 2000–2004, the average growth rate in the money supply was 7.0 percent and the inflation rate was only 1.9 percent. A partial explanation for this recent experience is the recession of 2001 and the slow recovery that followed. Recessionary pressures kept inflation in check, but expansionary fiscal policies, such as the tax cut, stimulated spending and the demand for money. Although the quantity theory of money should not be ignored, an alternative approach, which takes into consideration more variables that may have an impact on inflation, needs to be considered.

Demand-Pull Inflation

An alternative approach to the quantity theory of money is the aggregate demand approach. This approach stresses excess demand as the major cause of inflation. The two approaches are similar in most important respects, with some differences in points of emphasis and in policy recommendations. The aggregate demand approach places more emphasis on total consumer, investment, and government spending in the economy (MV) and less emphasis on growth in the money supply. The money supply is viewed primarily as an *accommodating* variable instead of an *initiating* variable. According to aggregate demand analysis, **demand-pull inflation** is initiated by an increase in aggregate demand and is self-enforcing by further increases in aggregate demand. A demand-pull inflation is associated with increases in production and employment until the economy reaches full employment. Once full employment is reached, further increases in demand increase prices only.

Figure 12.4 depicts demand-pull inflation. Beginning at the price level p and production q, an increase in aggregate demand to D_1 means that all of demand cannot be satisfied at p. Thus, the price level rises to p_1, and production rises to q_f. An increase in demand to D_2 causes the price level to rise further to p_2. This inflationary process continues as long as aggregate demand increases, since all of demand can be satisfied only at higher prices. Pure inflation, an increase in the price level without an increase in output, is shown when aggregate demand increases to D_2.

demand-pull inflation
Increases in total consumer, investment, and government spending cause rightward shifts in the aggregate demand curve.

Cures for Demand-Pull Inflation

Demand-pull inflation can be stopped by the appropriate use of Federal Reserve monetary policy and federal fiscal policy. We know now that demand-pull inflations are caused by "excess money" leading to excess spending or that they are caused by "excess demand" accommodated by expansions in the money supply. In either case, this type of inflation can be slowed down or stopped completely by Federal Reserve policy that slows down the growth in the money supply: a policy employing a combination of Fed controls that reduce excess reserves in the banking system and the ability of banks to expand loans and create money.

The appropriate federal fiscal policy in periods of demand-pull inflations is some combination of government expenditure cuts and tax increases; that is, federal budget deficits should be reduced. A decrease in government purchases directly reduces total spending in the economy. A decrease in government transfer payments or an increase in taxes indirectly reduces aggregate demand by decreasing private spending. In addition, increases in the federal debt brought about by budget deficits should be financed in a way that does not create money.

FIGURE 12.4   **Demand-Pull Inflation**

Demand-pull inflation is due to increases in aggregate demand from DD to D_1D_1 to D_2D_2.

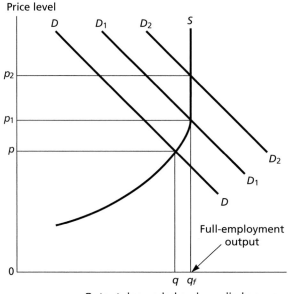

Output demanded and supplied per year

Demand-pull inflations are difficult to stop without causing unemployment. The same economic forces causing inflation also increase production and employment. The secret to controlling demand-pull inflation is not to let it develop in the first place. Once inflation develops and is out of control, as in the late 1960s and 1970s, it seems almost inevitable that the opportunity cost to stop inflation is rising unemployment.

Cost-Push Inflation

Some of the inflationary periods in the 1960s and 1970s cannot be explained only on the basis of demand-pull inflation. The economy has experienced both inflation and recession together at certain times. How can this be? Demand-pull inflation is characterized by rising prices and rising production until full employment is reached. Inflation and recession at the same time mean rising prices and falling production.

The only way the economy can experience simultaneous inflation and recession is for inflation to be initiated by a decrease in aggregate supply. This type of inflation is called **cost-push inflation.** Increases in costs cause aggregate supply to decrease, reducing the quantity of goods produced and increasing prices.

Figure 12.5 illustrates cost-push inflation. Beginning at price level p and production q_f, aggregate supply decreases to S_1. Now all of demand cannot be satisfied at p; that is, aggregate output demanded is greater than aggregate output supplied. As a consequence, the price level rises to p_1. Aggregate supply decreases further to S_2.

cost-push inflation
Increases in the costs of producing goods and services cause leftward shifts in the aggregate supply curve.

FIGURE 12.5 **Cost-Push Inflation**

Cost-push inflation is due to a decrease in aggregate supply from SS to SS_1 and SS_2.

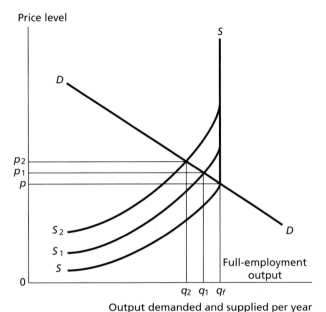

Again, all of demand cannot be satisfied, and price rises to p_2. This inflationary process continues until there are no further decreases in aggregate supply. In Figure 12.5, cost-push inflation is characterized by rising prices and falling production.

Cost-push inflation occurs because of decreases in aggregate supply. But what causes aggregate supply to decrease? The answer is an increase in resource prices not offset by productivity increases. If a resource, such as energy, increases in price, producing the same levels of output at the same price levels is not profitable unless the higher energy costs are offset. For another illustration, an increase in the price of labor increases labor unit costs and, therefore, decreases output supplied at every price level. Sometimes the blame for cost-push inflation is placed on monopoly power—the power of unions to negotiate successfully for wage gains in excess of productivity gains and the market power of monopoly firms to restrict output and increase prices. In the absence of inflationary demand pressures, the monopoly powers of unions and producers to bring about cost-push inflations are exaggerated. The major point to remember about cost-push inflations is that they are caused by resource price increases or productivity decreases regardless of the reason or reasons why these things may occur.

Demand-Pull and Then Cost-Push Inflation

Viewing demand-pull and cost-push as two separate inflationary processes may be misleading. In fact, a single inflationary period may result from both demand-pull and cost-push pressures. Increases in aggregate demand start the inflationary process. Prices, production, and employment rise in response to the pull of demand. Money wages rise, but they still lag behind prices. Unions realize eventually that wages have lagged behind prices and begin to try to catch up by demanding wage increases in excess of productivity increases. Once this happens, cost-push pressures begin to reinforce demand pressures.

The end of an inflationary process may not coincide with the moment that demand-pull pressures no longer exist. Prices may continue to rise for a period because of cost-push pressures. These pressures operating alone sustain the inflation temporarily, even though production and employment are falling. However, without demand-pull pressures, inflation eventually stops.

Is There a Cure for Cost-Push Inflation?

Monetary and fiscal policies can deal, theoretically anyway, with demand-type problems. They are more designed for these purposes. However, they cannot cope effectively with cost-push inflationary pressures. Certain other policies have been advocated by some economists to deal with cost-push inflationary pressures that stem from wage and price increases connected with monopoly power of unions and business firms. These policies are often referred to as **incomes policies.**

incomes policies
Government policies designed to deal with cost-push inflationary pressures associated with imperfect labor and product markets by establishing wage and price ceilings, and some mechanism for their enforcement.

An incomes policy may range from the president of the United States inviting labor and business leaders to the White House in order to persuade them to use wage and price restraint to wage and price controls. President John F. Kennedy adopted a policy of wage and price guidelines in the early 1960s. President Lyndon Johnson abandoned guidelines for jawboning when inflationary pressures mounted in the late 1960s. President Richard Nixon resorted to wage and price controls between 1971 and 1974. President Jimmy Carter announced voluntary wage-price standards in 1978. Presidents Ronald Reagan, George H. W. Bush, and Bill Clinton did not have to deal with cost-push inflationary pressures during their terms of office. There were no strong cost-push forces operating in the economy during the 1983–1990 economic expansion or the 1991–2001 economic boom. However, the war on terror and the resulting spike in oil prices around the world may cause cost-push inflationary pressures to rise again in the early 2000s.

Incomes policies have been far from successful thus far. The main criticism of almost any incomes policy is that it does not eliminate the cause of inflation. Assuming that the monopoly power of unions and business firms is the major cause of cost-push inflationary pressures, these pressures do not disappear unless this cause is eliminated. Also, the monopoly power of unions and business firms cannot be effectively used unless expansionary monetary and fiscal policies cause inflationary pressures.

An incomes policy that has not been tried but has support among some economists is called a *tax-based incomes policy (TIP)*. The general economic thinking behind a tax-based incomes policy is that prices are determined by an average markup of prices over labor unit costs. When labor unit costs rise, say, because of wage increases in excess of productivity increases, prices generally rise in the economy. In the TIP proposal, incentives are provided to discourage "excess wage" increases.

The TIP proposal would work simply as follows. A wage increase guideline would be established, say, 5 percent, at the beginning of the year. At the same time, the government would announce a TIP tax schedule. Suppose the tax schedule is that for each percentage point a corporate firm grants over the wage guideline, 4 percentage points are added to the corporate income tax rate. A firm giving a 6 percent increase in wages, then, would be subject to a 4 percent added tax to its income tax rate.

There are variants to the TIP proposal. One variant is to reward firms that give wage increases less than the wage guideline. Another alternative is to apply the reward-and-penalty system to prices or to both wages and prices. The innovating feature of the TIP proposal and its variants is the use of an incentive system that would tend to foster noninflationary wage and price behavior. However, the effectiveness of a tax-based incomes policy implemented sometime in the future remains questionable.

Summary

Inflation means that the general level of prices is rising, and it takes more money to buy the same quantity of goods and services. Inflation may be suppressed. This occurs when output demanded is greater than output supplied at the current price level, but the price level does not rise because of government price controls.

The three effects of inflation are the equity, efficiency, and output effects. The equity effects are the results of inflation on income distribution. The people who lose during inflation are those who receive fixed incomes and have fixed money claims. The people who gain during inflation are those whose money incomes rise faster than prices and who hold assets that rise in value more than the increase in prices of goods and services.

The efficiency effects of inflation are the results of inflation on the allocation of resources. Inflation changes the allocation of resources, since inflation alters relative commodity prices. It is not certain that this change in resource allocation is a less efficient allocation. However, some economists argue that the allocation of resources is distorted by inflation and results in a less efficient allocation.

The impact of inflation on the national production of goods and services may be to encourage production. Before the economy reaches full employment, rising prices tend to go hand in hand with rising production. The same forces that cause prices to rise cause production to rise. However, the continuation of inflationary forces at full employment leads to pure inflation—that is, rising prices not associated with rising production.

Money plays an essential role in the economy. Money is anything that is generally accepted as a means of payment for goods, services, and debt. Money serves three functions: (1) as a medium of exchange; (2) as a measure of the value of goods and services; and (3) as a store of value. The supply of money in the economy includes currency and coins in circulation, traveler's checks, demand deposits at banks, saving and time deposits of small denominations, and other checkable deposits. There are broader measures of the money supply that include other near-money assets.

The money supply expands when banks as a group expand loans, and contracts when banks as a group contract loans. The Federal Reserve System, which has the responsibility of controlling the money supply, attempts to fulfill this responsibility through the use of policy controls over excess cash reserves of banks. The three policy controls are the legal reserve ratio, the discount rate, and open-market operations. When the Federal Reserve thinks it is desirable to slow down growth in the money supply, the Fed can increase the legal reserves ratio, increase the discount rate, and increase open-market sales of government securities. These policy actions decrease excess cash reserves and reduce the lending ability of banks. The opposite policy actions can be taken if it is desirable to increase the growth in the money supply—namely, decrease the legal reserve rate, decrease the discount rate, and increase open-market purchases of government securities. These actions increase excess cash reserves and increase the lending ability of banks.

Two approaches are taken to explain the causes of inflation and the cures to inflation. The first approach is the quantity theory of money. This theory stresses the importance of money in the inflationary process. The second approach is an aggregate demand-supply approach. The central message of the quantity theory of money is that behind every inflation there is a rapid growth in the money supply, and the way to stop inflation is to control the growth in the money supply. In a demand-pull inflation, excess aggregate demand initiates and causes inflation. In a cost-push inflation, aggregate supply decreases, resulting in upward pressures on prices. The cure for demand-pull inflation is the appropriate use of monetary and fiscal policies. There is no certain solution to cost-push inflationary pressures other than restoring competitive markets and making sure that inflationary pressures do not exist because of an excessive growth in the money supply. An incomes policy that provides incentives to foster competitive wage and price behavior has been recommended as a possible solution to cost-push inflation but has not yet been implemented.

Discussion Questions

1. Discuss the meaning and measurement of inflation. Include in your discussion the process used to create a price index.
2. Explain the differences in the equity, efficiency, and output effects of inflation. Why do the output effects of inflation encourage inflationary policies?
3. What are the functions of money? Discuss the different definitions of money.
4. Assume a new demand deposit of $1,000 and a legal reserve requirement of 10 percent. Explain in detail how money is created, and show the final balance sheet of the banking system, assuming the maximum increase in the money supply.
5. Discuss the major policy controls of the Federal Reserve. Include in your discussion the relative effectiveness of open-market operations, the discount rate, and the legal reserve requirement.

6. Explain the quantity theory of money. What is the starting point for the theory? Is this theory supported by empirical data? Discuss.

7. Explain the differences between a demand-pull inflation and a cost-push inflation.

8. Discuss the most effective way to cure a demand-pull inflation and a cost-push inflation.

9. How did the Federal Reserve eliminate the high rates of inflation which occurred in the late 1970s and early 1980s? What was the economic cost of this policy?

10. During the recent war in Iraq, the price of oil on the world market nearly doubled. Which type of inflationary pressures did this situation create? Illustrate with a graph and discuss.

Additional Readings

Beckner, Steven, K. *Back from the Brink: The Greenspan Years*. New York: John Wiley & Sons, 1996.
This is a biography of Alan Greenspan and his impact on the Board of Governors of the Federal Reserve System.

Board of Governors of the Federal Reserve System. *The Federal Reserve System: Purposes and Functions*. 8th ed. Washington, DC: Board of Governors of the Federal Reserve System, 1994.
Discusses the roles and responsibilities of the Federal Reserve System in the country's monetary policies.

Kindleberger, Charles P. *Manias, Panics, and Crashes: A History of Financial Crises*. 4th ed. New York: John Wiley & Sons, 2000.
Provides a historical overview of economic panics and crashes from the 1600s to the present.

Mishkin, Frederic S. *The Economics of Money, Banking, and Financial Markets*. 7th ed. Glenview, IL: Scott, Foresman, 2003.
Includes an examination of the German hyperinflation in 1921–1923 and discusses different views of inflation.

Mishkin, Frederic S. *Strategies for Controlling Inflation*. NBER Working Paper Series 6122. Cambridge, MA: National Bureau of Economic Research, 1997.
Examines four basic strategies policymakers use to combat inflation.

Romer, Christina D., and David H. Romer, eds. *Reducing Inflation: Motivation and Strategy*. Chicago: University of Chicago Press, 1997.
Discusses the effects of inflation, improving the conduct of monetary policy, and the contributions of monetary institutions.

Siklos, Pierre, ed. *Great Inflations of the 20th Century: Theories, Policies, and Evidence*. Brookfield, VT: Edward Elgar Publishing, 1995.
Has chapters on hyperinflation, conditions conducive to high inflation, and conditions to end hyperinflation.

Weintraub, Sidney. *Capitalism's Inflation and Unemployment Crisis*. Reading, MA: Addison-Wesley, 1978.
Sidney Weintraub is one of the pioneers of the tax-based incomes policy. Chapter 3 presents the underlying theory behind the TIP proposal; Chapter 6 discusses the proposal.

Williams, Jonathan, ed. *Money: A History*. New York: St. Martin's Press, 1997.
An excellent account of the history of money, from Mesopotamia to the modern period, replete with pictures of coins and currency from all over the world.

Woodward, Bob. *Maestro: Greenspan's Fed and the American Boom*. New York: Simon Schuster, 2000.
Woodward, assistant managing editor at the *Washington Post*, writes an engaging story of Alan Greenspan's role as chairman of the Federal Reserve System and his influence on the American economy.

World Wide Web Resources

Board of Governors of the Federal Reserve System

www.federalreserve.gov/

This Fed Web site has links to breaking news, banking information and regulation, consumer information, and economic research and data.

Consumer Prices Indexes

www.b/s.gov/cpihome.htm

Gives links to data, news releases, publications and other documentation, FAQs, and other information.

Economic Report of the President

www.access.gpo.gov/eop

Sponsored by the Executive Office of the President. Enter search terms to find statistical information on banks and banking.

Federal Deposit Insurance Corporation (FDIC)

www.fdic.gov

Gives access to consumer information, banking information, statistical information, and asset information.

Federal Reserve Bank of St. Louis

www.stls.frb.org/index.html

Click on Economic Research from the main page to get more information about U.S. monetary policy.

United States Department of the Treasury: Currency and Coins

www.ustreas.gov/topics/currency/index.html

The U.S. Department of the Treasury, under the Bureau of Printing and Engraving, and the U.S. Mint are responsible for designing and printing Federal Reserve notes and issuing coins. Subtopics for this site include links to currency, coins, and anticounterfeiting measures.

Economic Growth
Are We Living In a "New Economy"?

Chapter outline

The Concept of Economic Growth
What Is Economic Growth?
The Rate of Growth

Short-Run Fluctuations in Economic Growth
What Are Business Cycles?
Theories of the Business Cycle

The Determinants of Economic Growth
Availability of Economic Resources
Productivity Factors

The New Economy

The Recent Slowdown in Growth
Contributing Factors
The 2001 Recession
Where Do We Go from Here?

Summary

Checklist of economic concepts

- Economic growth
- Real gross domestic product
- Business cycles
- Expansion
- Peak
- Contraction
- Trough
- Economic boom
- Economic recession
- Leading Economic Indicators Index
- Labor
- Capital
- Productivity
- Average product of labor
- Human capital
- Technology
- Investment

Washington—The stock market was booming. Companies were fighting their way into fast-growing foreign markets. Technology was transforming many industries. A blue chip panel of business leaders, economists, and government officials hailed "the dynamic equilibrium of recent years," and the "organic balance of economic forces." Their report on the nation's economic outlook concluded: "Our situation is fortunate, our momentum remarkable."

The time was mid-1929.

Economists have never displayed much skill in predicting recessions. But one thing is common, historians have found, to most periods just before a downturn —the emergence of a widespread belief that this time we have found the magic elixir to produce an extended period of prosperity.

So it may be tempting fate now that so many economists, policymakers, and business executives, looking out over an economic landscape defined by years of moderate growth and low inflation, are willing to judge the business cycle tempered if not tamed. But for all the risk of incurring the wrath of the economic gods—and with the important caveat that recessions can never be completely ruled out—it is clear that the economy has undergone such sweeping changes that it is arguably better equipped to maintain its long-run equilibrium.

Still, to the extent that bumps along the economic road have been smoothed over, stability has come at a substantial cost. Improvements in productivity in recent years have come in part from wide-scale layoffs, creating a new level of anxiety in the workforce. And among business and political leaders, there are those who argue that stability has been bought at the price of forgone growth and opportunity.

Moreover, a more moderate business cycle does not necessarily foster progress in dealing with other deep-rooted problems, like income inequality. Most emphatically, it does not mean that individual companies or entire industries will escape upheaval.

Source: Richard V. Stevenson, "Those Vicious Business Cycles: Tamed but Not Quite Slain," *The New York Times,* January 2, 1997. Copyright 1997 by The New York Times Co. Reprinted by permission.

The American economy closed out the twentieth century with an unprecedented string of 10 straight years of growing prosperity. Indeed, after a mild setback in 1991, it appeared that nothing could go wrong with the U.S. economy; unemployment rates fell to a 30-year low, inflation remained in check, corporate profits rose, and the stock market reached an all-time high. For many Americans, all of this good economic news meant increased household income and wealth, resulting in an improved standard of living. In fact, because economic performance had become so spectacular, some experts began to claim that we had entered a "new economy." But were the factors that generated the economic growth of the 1990s really new? The realities of the first few years of the twenty-first century indicate that the new economy looks a lot like the old one and that we are still susceptible to the periodic swings of the business cycle. In this chapter we focus on understanding the process of economic growth over time and why it is so important to our future well-being.

Almost every night on the evening news broadcasts you hear a report about the performance of the economy. The media constantly monitor and report on the economy's health and speculate about where it is headed. Routinely we are provided with the latest statistics on and forecasts of what the economic future will hold. Business leaders, politicians, and professional economists are always eager to offer their views on the economy's performance and what it all means. Why are we so concerned with economic performance and growth? The answer is obvious: A growing economy implies more jobs, greater output, better incomes, and an opportunity for each of us to achieve a higher standard of living. A growing economy gives us more choices and opportunities to better ourselves. Furthermore, the overall performance of the economy is directly related to many of the social issues discussed throughout this book. For example, a healthy, growing economy generally experiences lower rates of unemployment, poverty, and crime. Similarly, these problems are often exacerbated when the economy is in decline. Clearly, economic growth is an important issue to study and understand in its own right.

As we will see, economic growth is not always a smooth ride, and many issues make it difficult to accurately forecast our economy's future health.

THE CONCEPT OF ECONOMIC GROWTH

A growing economy is a sign of prosperity and the chance to improve our quality of life. Almost everyone agrees that a growing economy is preferred to one that is shrinking. But a number of important questions surround this issue. To begin, how do we measure economic growth, and how fast or slow should the economy grow?

What Is Economic Growth?

economic growth
A long-run process that results from a compounding of economic events over time.

Economists view **economic growth** as a *long-run process*. It is not the result of a single event but the compounding of many events. For the economy to grow, a number of things must occur. Take, for example, an announcement that the unemployment rate has fallen over the past month. Does this mean that the economy is growing? Maybe, or maybe not. A reduction in unemployment may mean more people are working. However, this increased work must then result in an increase in output and production. In turn, this increase in output must be met by an increase in sales, perhaps through higher levels of aggregate demand. Any break in this chain of events, or an intervention from some other factor that affects the economy's ability to produce, and real economic growth will not occur. Thus, we cannot look at a single monthly or quarterly announcement concerning employment to determine if the economy is growing. We must examine the trends in the events that describe the *overall* level of economic performance over time.

FIGURE 13.1 **Growth of the U.S. Economy since 1960; Real GDP by Year (2000 = base year)**
Since 1960 the U.S. economy has grown at an average annual rate of just above 3 percent. Note that long-run growth is not always steady or even. Recessions occurred in 1970, 1974–1975, 1980, 1982, 1991, and 2001. These recessions can be seen as negative deviations from the long-run trend suggested in this graph.

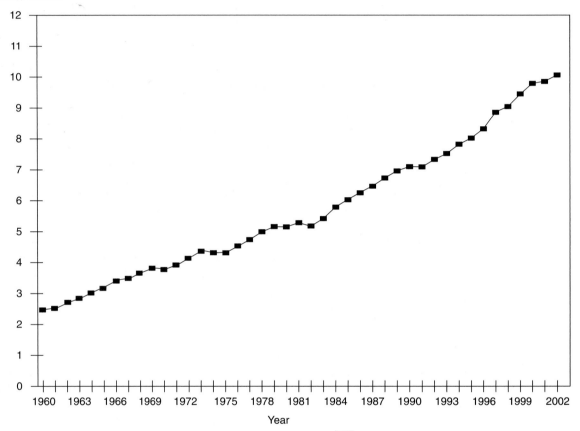

The most frequently used measurement of economic growth is changes in real gross domestic product (GDP). Recall that GDP is the total value of all final goods and services produced in an economy during one year. Also recall that real GDP accounts for changes in the price level. Thus, changes in real GDP reflect changes in the economy's actual production of goods and services. A growing economy is characterized by increases in its real GDP over time.

Figure 13.1 is a graphical representation of how the U.S. economy has grown since 1960. Clearly, our economy has experienced dramatic growth over the past four decades. In fact, between 1960 and 2001, real GDP in the United States more than tripled. Notice in Figure 13.1 that the long-run trend in real GDP is clearly upward over time. However, the graph also shows us that the rate of growth is not constant. Close examination of Figure 13.1 reveals short-run deviations from the long-run trend. In some years the economy appears to grow faster than in others, and in a few instances the economy does not appear to grow at all. In fact, there are years when real GDP actually falls.

Economic growth is sometimes a bumpy ride. Many factors may block the road to continued economic growth. Before we examine these bumps in the road, let's turn our attention to the importance of the *rate* of economic growth.

The Rate of Growth

How fast the economy is growing at any point in time is very important. Small differences in growth rates today can translate into significant differences in the level of economic activity in the future because economic growth *compounds* year after year. This concept is easily illustrated by the following example.

Let's assume we have two economies, Nation A and Nation B, and that each economy has a real GDP of $100 billion. However, Nation A's economy is growing at 3 percent per year, and Nation B's is growing at only 2 percent per year. After one year, Nation A has a real GDP equal to $103 billion ($100 × 1.03), and Nation B has a real GDP equal to $102 billion ($100 × 1.02). In the next year, Nation A produces a real GDP of $106.09 billion ($103 × 1.03), while Nation B achieves a real GDP of only $104.04 billion ($102 × 1.02). Notice that the gap between the two nations' real GDP is wider in the second year than in the first because each successive year provides Nation A with a higher level of GDP on which to build. Table 13.1 shows the level of real GDP for Nations A and B over a 25-year span assuming a constant 3 and 2 percent annual growth rate, respectively. Each year Nation B falls further and further behind Nation A. As seen in Table 13.1, after 24 years Nation A's GDP has more than doubled its original $100 billion level, while Nation B's economy is only 1.6 times its original level. (In fact, it will be another 12 years before Nation B's economy will have doubled!)

This example illustrates that the rate of economic growth is of vital importance and that very small changes in the rate can have long-run consequences on the performance of the economy. Given this, you are probably wondering how fast the U.S. economy has been growing. Table 13.2 shows the annual rate of growth in real GDP for the U.S. economy over the 1960–2002 time span. (The table also reports the level of real GDP for each year during this period.) Again, we see that economic growth is not constant and that the rate of growth in real GDP varies from year to year. According to Table 13.2, the annual growth in real GDP ranges from more than 6.5 percent in the mid-1960s to a *negative* 1.92 percent in 1982. However, if we average the annual rate of growth over the entire period, we find that the U.S. economy has grown at an annual rate of 3.38 percent. This healthy long-run average rate of economic growth is why the size of real GDP has more than tripled since 1960.

Although the data in Table 13.2 reflect a healthy long-run growth path for the U.S. economy over the past four decades, the numbers also indicate a somewhat disturbing trend. When you calculate the average annual growth rate by decade, the evidence suggests that our rate of economic growth is declining. Based on the

TABLE 13.1
Comparison of the
Effect of Different
Rates of Growth
on Long-Run
Economic
Performance

Year	Nation A Real GDP ($ Billions), 3%	Nation B Real GDP ($ Billions), 2%
0	100.00	100.00
1	103.00	102.00
2	106.09	104.04
3	109.27	106.12
4	112.55	108.24
5	115.93	110.41
6	119.41	112.62
7	122.99	114.87
8	126.68	117.17
9	130.48	119.51
10	134.39	121.90
11	138.42	124.34
12	142.58	126.82
13	146.85	129.36
14	151.26	131.95
15	155.80	134.59
16	160.47	137.28
17	165.28	140.02
18	170.24	142.82
19	175.35	145.68
20	180.61	148.59
21	186.03	151.57
22	191.61	154.60
23	197.36	157.69
24	203.28	160.84

data in Table 13.2, the average annual rate of growth in the 1960s was 4.44 percent, in the 1970s it was 3.26 percent, and in the 1980s and the 1990s economic growth averaged only between 3.07 and 3.11 percent. Furthermore, since 2000 the economy has averaged only a 2.12 percent growth rate in real GDP. Given how small changes in growth rates translate into significant long-run differences in economic output, is this downward trend cause for alarm? Before we examine this question, let's look at the short-run fluctuations in economic activity that underlie the long-run trend.

SHORT-RUN FLUCTUATIONS IN ECONOMIC GROWTH

For almost as long as markets have existed, people have been aware of fluctuations in the level of economic activity over time. Every market-based economy on record has experienced historical periods of growth and prosperity followed by periods of declining production and incomes. These fluctuations have come to be popularly known as business cycles.

TABLE 13.2
Economic Growth 1960–2002; Real GDP by Year (2000 base year)

Source: Bureau of Economic Analysis, 2004.

Year	Real GDP ($ Billions)	Growth Rate
1960	2,501.80	2.48
1961	2,560.00	2.33
1962	2,715.20	6.06
1963	2,834.00	4.38
1964	2,998.60	5.81
1965	3,191.10	6.42
1966	3,399.10	6.52
1967	3,484.60	2.52
1968	3,652.70	4.82
1969	3,765.40	3.09
Decade average		**4.44**
1970	3,771.90	0.17
1971	3,898.60	3.36
1972	4,105.00	5.29
1973	4,341.50	5.76
1974	4,319.60	−0.50
1975	4,311.20	−0.19
1976	4,540.90	5.33
1977	4,750.50	4.62
1978	5,015.00	5.57
1979	5,173.40	3.16
Decade average		**3.26**
1980	5.160.00	−0.26
1981	5,290.70	2.53
1982	5,188.90	−1.92
1983	5,423.60	4.52
1984	5,813.20	7.18
1985	6,054.10	4.14
1986	6,263.60	3.46
1987	6,475.60	3.38
1988	6,743.00	4.13
1989	6,981.20	3.53
Decade average		**3.07**
1990	7,112.50	1.88
1991	7,100.70	−0.17
1992	7,336.10	3.32
1993	7,532.70	2.68
1994	7,835.40	4.02
1995	8,031.40	2.50
1996	8,329.10	3.71
1997	8,890.20	6.74
1998	9,067.10	1.99
1999	9,470.10	4.44
Decade average		**3.11**
2000	9,817.00	3.66
2001	9,866.90	0.51
2002	10,082.50	2.19
Decade average		**2.12**
Overall average		**3.38**

What Are Business Cycles?

business cycle
An erratic short-run fluctuation in economic activity around the economy's long-run growth trend. Every business cycle has four distinct phases: expansion, peak, contraction, and trough.

A **business cycle** is an erratic short-run fluctuation in economic activity around the economy's long-run growth trend. Every business cycle is composed of four distinct phases: expansion, peak, contraction, and trough. These four phases are illustrated in Figure 13.2. During *expansion,* the economy experiences a positive rate of growth. An expansion generally brings the level of economic output above the long-run growth trend for the economy. An exceptionally strong or prolonged expansion is sometimes called an *economic boom.* The end of an expansion or boom is called the *peak,* which occurs when the level of economic output reaches a short-run relative high. The third phase of a business cycle, a *contraction,* is characterized by a decline in the level of economic activity and output. An exceptionally strong and prolonged contraction is known as a *recession.* The final phase of a business cycle, the *trough,* occurs when economic output hits a short-run relative low. The next cycle begins when the economy grows out of the trough and a new expansion phase begins.

Business cycles are characterized as erratic because no two business cycles are exactly alike. Business cycles vary in duration and the magnitude of their swings around the economy's long-run growth trend. Since 1960, the U.S. economy has experienced six complete business cycles: Recessions occurred in 1970, 1974–1975, 1980, 1982, 1991, and 2001. These recessions are shown in Figure 13.1 and Table 13.2 as the negative deviations in the long-run trend of real GDP. These recent recessions have been relatively mild when compared to those of previous generations. The deepest and most severe recession in modern times was the Great Depression of the 1930s. Although there is no formal definition for a depression, all economists agree that the United States has not experienced one since the 1930s.

When measured trough to trough, the typical business cycle in the U.S. economy since World War II has averaged approximately 60 months. Historical data suggest that the average length of the business cycle may be increasing, primarily because of longer expansion phases. The 1960s saw an until then unprecedented expansion of 117 months, and in the 1980s we experienced an expansion that lasted nearly eight full years. The longest expansion in modern times lasted from March 1991 through March 2001, a full decade of positive economic growth.

The National Bureau of Economic Research (NBER) tracks the performance of the U.S. economy and announces the official dates for each phase of a business cycle. Because we cannot look into the future to see exactly when an expansion becomes a peak or when a contraction becomes a trough, we generally do not know when the economy moves into the next phase until after it has already begun. Predicting the turning points in the business cycle has become a big business in itself. Many economists earn their living by developing forecasts and predictions about future economic events.

How can you predict what the business cycle will do? Economists have developed a number of techniques to forecast changes in economic growth. The most commonly used tool is the *Leading Economic Indicators Index* developed by the U. S. Department of Commerce and maintained by the Conference Board, a business

FIGURE 13.2   Business Cycles Represent Short-Run Fluctuations in Economic Growth
Economists have classified four phases of the business cycle: expansion, peak, contraction, and trough. An exceptionally high expansion is sometimes called an economic boom. An exceptionally deep and prolonged contraction is known as a recession. Since 1960, the United States has experienced six complete business cycles.

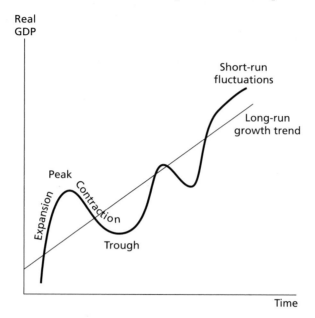

forecasting organization. As the title implies, this is a composite index of economic variables that tend to move in the same direction as overall economic output but do so prior to changes in real GDP. Thus, changes in the index lead changes in real GDP. Table 13.3 lists the current 10 components of the Leading Economic Indicators Index. Even though the relationship between this index and short-term economic growth is relatively stable, it has one major drawback: It takes a great deal of time to collect and compile all the data that go into creating the index. The Leading Economic Indicators Index for a month is generally announced on the last day of the *following* month (for example, the index for January is announced at the end of February). Furthermore, the index is often revised as new data become available. The index tends to lead the turning points in the cycle by six months; however, we may not know when we have turned a corner until after it is far behind us.

Theories of the Business Cycle

Historically, economists viewed business cycles as an inherent characteristic of a market-based economy. In a system where all buyers and sellers are free to make their own choices, it seemed reasonable to expect that the level of economic activity would rise and fall as changing situations influenced decision making. Since the Great Depression of the 1930s, economists have closely studied the business cycle and have expounded several theories to explain its occurrence.

TABLE 13.3
Components of the Leading Economic Indicators Index

Source: The Conference Board, 2004.

1. Stock market prices
2. Real money supply
3. An index of consumer expectations
4. Average workweek for production workers in manufacturing
5. Interest rate spread (10-year Treasury bonds less federal funds)
6. Initial claims for unemployment insurance
7. New building permits granted
8. New orders for consumer goods and materials
9. Contracts and orders for plant and equipment
10. Vendors' performance index for delivery of inputs

Theories of Expectations

Many business cycle theories are based on the belief that economic activity follows general trends of optimism and pessimism. For example, if business owners are optimistic about the future and expect economic growth, they may hire new workers and increase production. This increased employment and output generate higher levels of income, which may then be spent or invested in the marketplace, and the economy grows. When this occurs, the economy will continue to expand as long as people remain confident and optimistic about the future. If business owners begin to worry about how long such an expansion can last, they may begin to reduce their employment and output. This pessimism is self-fulfilling because a lower level of employment reduces income and spending in the economy, and growth declines. Thus, actions based on a pessimistic expectation of the future may generate an economic contraction. The next cycle begins when people regain their confidence in the economy and act on their optimistic expectations.

Expectations about the future influence people's economic decisions every day, and these influences can have very important effects in the aggregate. The role of psychological factors that influence economic behavior cannot be dismissed. Notice that one leading economic indicator in Table 13.3 is an index of consumer confidence in the economy.

Theory of Innovations

One of the most widely acclaimed theories of the business cycle was developed by economist Joseph Schumpeter during the early 1900s. Schumpeter believed that the business cycle was based on waves of innovations that changed the structure of the economy over time. According to his theory, new innovations in products and services would start the economy on an expansionary path. New industries would develop to support these innovations, and the economy would grow. Schumpeter believed that this growth inherently led to economic surpluses as imitators entered the market and tried to cash in on the potential profits. A contraction would naturally occur because of this new excess capacity in the marketplace. The next cycle would begin only after the introduction of the next major wave of innovations. Given the length of time necessary for major innovations to have such effects, Schumpeter's theory is often called a "long-cycle theory."

Inventory Theories

Inventory theories of the business cycle are based on the relationship between the level of inventories held by businesses and the rate of economic growth. These theories assume businesses have a predetermined level of inventories that they want to maintain. During an economic expansion, the demand for goods and services may increase faster than the businesses' ability to increase production. Because it takes time to expand productive capacity and to hire more workers, business inventories may fall as owners try to meet the rising level of demand for their products. To maintain their desired level of inventories, business owners place orders with their suppliers, who in turn must gear up production to meet this demand. As suppliers increase employment and output, incomes rise and aggregate demand increases, further expanding the economy. Eventually, however, businesses will regain their desired level of inventories and reduce their orders with suppliers. As this occurs, suppliers are forced to cut back their output and employment and, eventually, incomes begin to fall. This development begins the contractionary phase of the cycle. The economy will continue to decline until inventories are sold down below the desired level and the cycle begins again.

Monetary Theories

The several monetary theories of the business cycle that have been proposed concern how the monetary authorities react during the various phases of the business cycle. For example, during a period of economic growth, increases in aggregate demand may generate inflationary pressures in the economy. (Recall the discussion of demand-pull inflation in Chapter 12.) In response to this inflation, the Federal Reserve may reduce the growth of the money supply and thereby lower the level of spending in the economy. In addition to reducing inflation, this lower level of spending reduces incomes and output and causes an economic contraction. When the Federal Reserve is satisfied that it has controlled inflation, it may allow the money supply to once again grow at a faster rate. Of course, this action will tend to stimulate aggregate demand, and the economy begins a new round of expansion.

Proponents of the monetary business cycle theories point to the recessions of the early 1980s as support of their argument. In response to historically high rates of inflation, the Federal Reserve significantly reduced the growth rate in the money supply. The results included the minor recession of 1980 and the severe recession of 1982. However, the Fed accomplished its task, and inflationary pressures were abated. When the money supply was later loosened, the economy began an extended period of economic growth.

Real Business Cycle Theories

In recent years new business cycle theories have been developed that focus on economic fluctuations around the level of real potential GDP. Potential GDP can be considered the level of aggregate output that would exist if the economy operated at its natural rate of unemployment (see Chapter 11). According to these theories, the business cycle includes not only short-run economic fluctuations around the long-run growth trend but also movements in the long-run growth trend itself around the level of real potential GDP. This perspective of economic fluctuations is known as the real business cycle school of thought.

Real business cycle theorists postulate that economic fluctuations, in both the short and long run, are primarily due to changes in aggregate supply. It is hypothesized that as the growth of an economy's aggregate supply increases or contracts over time, so too does the overall level of economic activity. Furthermore, changes in technology are viewed as being the principal determinant of changes in aggregate supply. Thus, according to the real business cycle perspective, to ensure real economic expansion, an economy should invest in technological advancement and promote other policies that support the growth of aggregate supply. This emphasis on aggregate supply, rather than aggregate demand, is what sets real business cycle theories apart from other theories.

Exogenous Theories

Exogenous theories of the business cycle postulate that factors *outside* the economic system are responsible for short-run economic fluctuations. For example, a war or major international event may set into motion changes in the growth rate of economic output. Certainly, World War II was the major cause of the significant and prolonged economic expansion during the 1940s. Similarly, the international oil embargo by the OPEC nations has been cited as a major determining factor of the 1974–1975 recession. Other exogenous factors credited with influencing the business cycles of economies around the world include natural disasters such as earthquakes, hurricanes, volcano eruptions, and tidal waves. Just about any external event that can significantly disrupt economic activity may influence the erratic pattern of business cycles.

At this point, let us not neglect the first business cycle theory developed by an economist. Nearly 200 years ago, William Stanley Jevons proposed that solar storms were responsible for disrupting economic activity on Earth. This exogenous theory became known as the *sunspot theory of business cycles.* The preindustrial economy during Jevons's time was dependent on agriculture, and because sunspots influence weather patterns and therefore crop production, the theory had a minor degree of validity. We no longer study solar storms to forecast the business cycle, but Jevons's ideas are important because they suggest that exogenous factors outside our control can influence economic growth.

Which of these theories is correct? Each has something important to say about how business cycles behave, but no one theory can explain every short-run fluctuation in economic activity. The economy is very complex, and any number of factors may divert us from our long-run growth path. With each business cycle, we need to carefully examine the accompanying economic and social circumstances before choosing a theory to explain what happened.

THE DETERMINANTS OF ECONOMIC GROWTH

To understand the long-run process of economic growth, we must look beyond the short-run fluctuations of the business cycle. What primary factors drive the economy forward over the long run? Economists have identified a number of important factors that determine an economy's rate of growth. These determinants of economic growth can be classified into two major groups: (1) availability of economic resources and (2) productivity factors. Let's look closely at each group.

Availability of Economic Resources

Recall from Chapter 1 that an economy's productive resources can be classified as either labor or capital. Economic production cannot occur without the use of these two types of input. All the goods and services that make up an economy's real GDP are produced from labor and capital resources. Without labor and capital, production could not take place. Thus, the availability of resources is essential to economic growth. The greater the availability of resources, the greater the opportunity to produce and grow. Increasing the quantity of labor and the quantity of capital over time are two paths toward economic growth.

The Quantity of Labor

The quantity of labor available for productive uses in an economy is measured by the size of the labor force. In Chapter 11 we learned that the labor force is a specifically defined subset of the population. Remember, not everyone in an economy is available for employment. In the United States, the labor force is defined as those noninstitutionalized individuals 16 years of age and older who are employed for pay, actively seeking employment, or awaiting recall from a layoff. When the number of people who meet this definition increases, the economy has a greater quantity of labor resources to work with. As the labor force increases, the capacity for the economy to produce increases.

The effect of an increase in the availability of labor resources can be shown using a production possibilities graph, such as the one in Figure 13.3. A larger labor force implies that the economy can employ more workers in each production alternative. Thus, in Figure 13.3, the production possibilities frontier shifts outward from *AB* to *CD* in response to an increase in the labor force. The increased availability of labor now provides the economy with a greater set of choices between the two alternative goods. If the economy fully utilizes all its resources, it can produce more of both goods than it did before.

At this point you may be wondering if our labor force has been growing over time. The short answer is a resounding yes. During the past several decades, the American labor force has grown dramatically. In 1950, the U.S. labor force was composed of 63.4 million people; by late 2004, this number had increased to more than 147 million. Thus, the labor force more than *doubled* during this 54-year period. This tremendous increase in the number of American workers has had an important positive impact on our long-run economic growth.

The Quantity of Capital

An economy's capital resources include all the nonhuman elements of production, such as natural resources like land for agricultural production, water, forests, and mineral deposits and man-made tools of production like buildings and equipment. In most cases, the availability of natural resources is determined by a nation's geographical and political boundaries. Some nations have been blessed with a strong

FIGURE 13.3 **Effect of an Increase in the Availability of Labor Resources on an Economy's Production Possibilities**

An increase in the availability of labor resources results in an outward shift of the production possibilities frontier for an economy. If all resources are fully utilized, the economy can produce more of both goods than it did before.

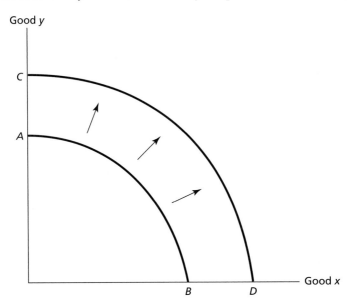

natural resource base, while others have not. To increase its availability of natural resources, a nation generally has to expand its physical territory. The quest for additional resources has been the driving force behind many explorations and international wars throughout history. For our purposes, we assume that the quantity of a nation's natural resources is generally fixed by its geographical characteristics and political borders with other nations. Thus, our discussion of capital focuses on the man-made tools of production.

It is important to understand that man-made capital resources such as factories or forklifts are themselves produced through the use of other resources. Spending on capital equipment therefore increases an economy's ability to produce additional tools of production, which in turn can be used to produce more tools, as well as more goods and services. Increases in the quantity of capital tools and equipment today therefore will lead to increases in the capacity of the economy to produce in the future. Because of this relationship between spending on capital and future productive capacity, economists use the term *investment* to describe the purchase of capital by businesses in an economy. (Refer to our discussion of investment in Chapter 12.)

The effect of capital investment on a economy can also be illustrated via the production possibilities model. The production possibilities curve *AB* in Figure 13.4 represents the alternative combinations of capital goods and consumer goods

FIGURE 13.4   **Effect of Capital Accumulation on an Economy's Possibilities**
When an economy chooses to produce a relatively large amount of capital, such as at point *C* on production possibilities curve *AB*, over time capital will accumulate, which increases the ability of the economy to produce both
capital and consumer goods in the future. This implies that the production possibilities frontier shifts outward,
say, to *EF*.

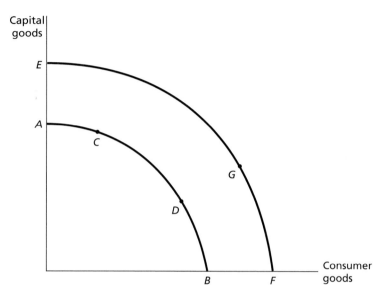

currently available to an economy. If the economy chooses a combination that results in a relatively high quantity of capital goods, such as point *C*, in the future
more capital tools will be available for the production of both capital and consumer goods. Of course, to undertake this investment the economy must bear the
opportunity cost of fewer consumer goods while capital accumulates. Over time,
the investment in capital goods shifts the production possibilities curve outward,
and a new frontier, like *EF*, offers the economy combinations of capital and consumer goods that were previously unobtainable. Eventually, the economy could
choose a point like *G* on the new frontier to satisfy the pent-up demand for consumer goods. (Of course, such a choice implies fewer capital goods will now be
available for future productive pursuits.)

The former Soviet Union and other eastern bloc countries relied on long-run
growth strategies that stressed the production and accumulation of capital over
the long run. Sometimes the planners of these economies seemed to favor capital
goods almost to the exclusion of consumer goods. In fact, this approach was
largely successful in making the Soviet Union a world power. However, the
tremendous opportunity cost of forsaken consumer goods and the other inherent
problems of a command economy eventually took their political toll, and the system collapsed.

The quantity of capital resources in the U.S. economy has grown at an even faster rate than the labor force. According to data from the Department of Commerce, the real net value of the capital stock held by manufacturers in the United States increased more than fivefold between 1950 and 2000. As the number of productive tools available increases, so too does the economy's ability to generate output. Investment in capital is clearly an important determinant of long-run economic growth.

Productivity Factors

productivity
The average amount of output that can be produced with a given set of inputs. It can be calculated as the ratio of output to input.

average product of labor
The total output of labor divided by the total number of labor units used in production. The average product of labor is a measure of labor productivity.

In addition to the availability of resources, factors that affect the productivity of resources are also important determinants of economic growth. **Productivity** is a measure of how efficiently resources are converted into goods and services through a production process. Productivity is usually measured as the average amount of output that can be produced with a given set of inputs. In practice, productivity can be calculated as the ratio of output to input. Thus, the productivity of labor is the output produced per unit of labor, which is calculated as total output produced divided by the total units of labor employed. Economists call this ratio the **average product of labor.** The average product of a resource is a direct measure of its productivity.

The productivity of any resource depends in part on its relationship with other inputs in the production process. For example, a worker equipped with the right set of tools will be more productive than a worker without any tools. Consequently, the productivity of resources can be thought of as being interdependent. Recall that the law of diminishing returns dictates that increases in output will eventually decline as more and more of one input is combined with a given amount of another input. Thus, at some point the provision of additional tools will not significantly enhance a worker's productivity. The productivity of one resource therefore must be evaluated within the context of the availability of other resources.

In addition to these inherent relationships between resources, economists have identified two major factors that influence productivity: (1) human capital and (2) technology. Let's look closely at both factors and examine their impact on economic growth.

Human Capital

Recall that human capital refers to a worker's investment in education and training. Education and training enhance the *quality* of labor. Given the same amount of time and capital equipment, any given number of workers who have been trained and are highly skilled will produce a greater quantity of output than the same number of workers who are untrained and unskilled. In the aggregate, the average product of labor increases due to investment in human capital. Thus, human capital has a positive effect on productivity. Recent studies have shown that human capital investments that improve the quality of an economy's labor force are similar in effect to investments in physical capital that increase the stock of tools and equipment used in production.

American workers have invested heavily in human capital over the past several decades. Between 1950 and today, the percentage of adults who completed high school increased from about 35 percent to approximately 84 percent. During this same period, those who attained a college education increased from about 6 percent to about 26 percent of the adult population. Because they increase productivity, these increases in human capital are a major contributing factor to the long-run growth of the economy.

Technology

Technology refers to the means and methods of production. Normally we think of capital resources when discussing technology because technological change often involves improvements in our tools and equipment. However, technological advances may be more subtle than the latest multitasking automated assembly robot. Technological advances also include changes in the organization or manner in which production takes place. A classic case is the innovation of the assembly line. Henry Ford's workers still used the same tools to build cars, they just built them in a different manner than before. So investments in technology include not only the creation of new "high-tech" tools but also the way we organize production and manage economic resources.

Businesses adopt technological innovations when the new tools or techniques increase productivity. The development of technology allows for the creation of more goods and services from any given quantity of resources. Thus, technological advances can be responsible for outward shifts in an economy's production possibilities frontier over time (not unlike an increase in the quantity of resources). New technologies increase the potential output for an economy. When new technologies become available and are utilized in production, an economy's aggregate supply increases. The link between technology and economic growth is evident.

To accurately quantify technological change over time is difficult. However, by any standard of measure, technology has dramatically improved productivity in modern times. The tools, equipment, and organizational methods used today are far superior to those of past generations. Obviously, some sectors of the economy, such as agriculture, have benefited to a greater extent than others. At the turn of the twentieth century, nearly 40 percent of the labor force was devoted to agricultural production. Because modern farming technologies, which are capital-intensive, have so improved agricultural productivity, only about 3 percent of the workforce is employed in this sector today. To some extent, the same story holds true throughout the economy: Today, fewer workers are required to produce greater quantities of output than in the past. Technological advances continue to be made and contribute to our overall economic growth.

THE NEW ECONOMY

Each determinant of economic growth has contributed to the ongoing expansion of the American economy—both the quantity and quality of our labor and capital resources continue to increase, which fuels economic progress. As we noted earlier, the economic expansion which characterized the 1990s was the longest sustained period of economic growth without recession in modern times. (And as we learned in Chapter 11, this expansion produced the lowest national unemployment rates in more than three decades.) In addition to its longevity, what distinguished this expansion from those in the past was the relatively low rates of inflation that accompanied it. An expanding economy is naturally characterized by increasing levels of aggregate demand, and as we learned in the last chapter, increases in aggregate demand are associated with demand-pull inflation, if everything else remains the same. Thus, the long-run expansion of the 1990s could have resulted in significant increases in the economy's overall price level. However, inflation remained low throughout the decade as consumer prices rose at an average annual rate of less than 3 percent according to the official CPI. Some have heralded this period of strong economic growth and low inflation as the beginning of a "new economy." Have we entered a new economic era? How could the economy experience such a long period of economic expansion with so little inflation?

Only time will tell if the answer to the first question is yes, but we are able to shed some light on the second and more central question. A partial explanation for the low inflation rates of the 1990s is the prudent actions of the Federal Reserve. On several occasions the Federal Reserve responded to inflationary pressures by pursuing policies to raise interest rates in order to slow consumer spending and business investment. While these actions resulted in their intended consequences, over time the economy continued to expand and unemployment rates fell to record low levels. Thus, aggregate demand continued to increase, but only at a slower rate. Recall that during an economic expansion, increases in aggregate demand shift the *AD* curve to the right, "pulling" prices up along the *AS* curve (refer back to Figure 12.4). As aggregate demand increases close to full employment, output expands and the overall price level rises. Then what could allow aggregate demand to increase without causing prices to rise? The answer: contemporaneous increases in aggregate supply due to improvements in productivity. When producers find ways to increase the productivity of their resources, more output can be supplied to the market at the same or lower cost than before. Thus, when an economy experiences simultaneous increases in aggregate demand and aggregate supply, economic growth with little or no inflation can occur. This helps explain the phenomena experienced during the 1990s since it can be shown that productivity rose during the period in question.

Productivity gains are historically the result of capital investments, improvements in labor quality, or technological progress. The 1990s saw all three of these forces at work, but the most visible was technology; computers and the Internet changed millions of lives during the decade. Today, advanced electronic technologies are everywhere and almost no job has been left untouched by the computer revolution. However, this revolution did not immediately translate into improvements in productivity. Between 1990 and 1995, productivity in the American economy grew at just over 1 percent per year, not a very impressive rate. But during the latter half of the decade, this average rate more than doubled to 2.3 percent annually.[1] During this period innovations in the computer industry resulted in more powerful and cheaper machines, which ultimately infiltrated the American economy. As more and more jobs took advantage of the new technologies, productivity began to rise. It is no coincidence, then, that the economy grew even faster in the late 1990s than it did in the early 1990s.

The productivity gains resulting from technological progress seem unlikely to be sustainable over the very long run. In fact, as we will see below, some economists believe that we may have already reached the point of diminishing returns to our investments in modern technology. We shouldn't be surprised if at some point in the future the new economy turns out to have some of the characteristics of the old economy.

THE RECENT SLOWDOWN IN GROWTH

Earlier we determined that the rate of economic growth in the U.S. economy since 1960 has averaged 3.38 percent per year. Official estimates dating back to the nineteenth century suggest that the historical rate of growth averages between 3 and 3.5 percent per year. Thus, since 1960 we have been well within the historical trend. However, as we also discovered earlier, if we examine the rate of growth by decade, the U.S. economy appears to be slowing down. In the 1960s, economic growth averaged 4.44 percent per year, but in the early 2000s we have seen an average annual growth rate of only 2.12 percent.

Now that we have examined the factors that determine economic growth, can we identify any reasons that may explain this disturbing trend? There is no straightforward answer to this question. Many factors may have contributed to the recent slowdown in economic growth. Let's look at the major factors economists have identified.

Contributing Factors

Technology Slowdown

As remarkable as it may seem, the technological advances of the last few years have had a much smaller impact on overall economic growth than the technological advances experienced by our parents and grandparents. (However, once you give it some thought, it becomes obvious that the initial development and economic integration of a new invention—like the computer in the 1950s and 1960s—should have a stronger marginal effect on the economy than the release of a "new and improved" microprocessor chip today.) According to the U.S. Department of Labor, the rate of technological growth has slowed considerably in recent years when viewed over an extended long-run period. In fact, it has been calculated that technological growth during the 1975–1995 period was about one-sixth of that experienced between 1955 and 1975. During the 1950s and 1960s, technological advances were often the result of research and development undertaken to fight

---

[1]Steve Liesman, "Further Gains in Productivity Are Predicted," *The Wall Street Journal,* August 1, 2000, p. A2.

the Cold War and the space race with the Soviet Union. Although we still devote approximately the same share of GDP to research and development activities, today technological advances appear to be suffering from diminishing returns to production. Some economists have even argued that the slowdown in growth due to technology is the primary factor causing the long-run decline in overall economic growth.

Labor Force Factors

As described earlier, the U.S. labor force continues to grow. However, if we examine the characteristics of the new workers contributing to this growth, we notice that a significant proportion of these workers are young and have less experience and on-the-job-training than the rest of the labor force. Furthermore, an increasing number of workers are seeking only part-time employment or temporary jobs. These trends can have a negative effect on productivity and therefore economic growth. On the other hand, many new labor force entrants are bringing more years of formal education to the market. Over the long run, this improvement in the potential quality of labor will offset some of the slowdown in labor productivity.

Saving and Investment

In the circular flow of the economy, saving is the source of funds for investment in capital resources. As discussed earlier, we must give up current consumption so that we can accumulate capital and achieve greater levels of production in the future. An economy's savings rate thus indicates its willingness to forgo current consumption and determines how many resources are available for investment by businesses. Higher rates of saving contribute to higher rates of capital formation and therefore economic growth. The gross savings rate for the United States has increased slightly in recent years but remains relatively low when compared to other nations. Our savings rate averages about 15–16 percent of GDP, about half the rate of that in Japan. Our tendency to save relatively little may be a contributing factor to the slowdown in economic growth.

The Composition of Output

Another factor contributing to the recent slowdown in economic growth is the changing composition of our national output. Much has been written about the growing importance of the service-producing sectors in our economy. The U.S. economy has evolved from one dominated by the production of goods to one that relies heavily on the production of services. From a historic perspective, we experienced our highest rates of growth during periods where great strides were made in technology and capital formation in the goods-producing sectors of the economy. Given the nature of most services, technology and capital have not contributed as greatly to productivity in the service-producing sectors. When resources are shifted from a high-productivity sector of the economy to a low-productivity sector of the economy, overall average productivity must fall. This is the effect we are now experiencing as resources shift from the production of goods to the production of services.

In addition, the ongoing growth of the service sector makes accurate measurement of productivity more difficult. Some economists argue that part of the observed slowdown in economic growth is merely a measurement problem. It is easy to calculate output and productivity in the goods-producing sector of the economy: Simply count the number of cars, watches, tennis rackets, bushels of grain, etc., produced by workers employed in that part of the economy. However, it is much more difficult to ascertain the productivity of service workers. For example, how do you measure the output of teachers, lawyers, or doctors? How do you calculate the productivity of the technicians who keep our computer and telecommunications networks functioning? These inherent measurement problems may lead to an underestimation of the quantity and value of services produced in our economy. To correct this potential bias, new and better measurement techniques must be developed.

Government: Regulation and Public Debt

Some economists argue that our government is in part responsible for the slowdown in economic growth. They cite two primary factors: regulation of business and the growing public debt.

The first argument centers on the belief that government regulation of business diverts economic resources from the production process. Today, most businesses are subject to some form of government regulation, ranging from the Occupational Safety and Health Administration (OSHA) requirements all the way to the formal licensing and oversight regulations public utilities face. In many cases, the businesses must devote resources to ensure that such regulations are met. Obviously, time spent filling out government forms is time spent not producing. However, the net effect of government regulation is not clear-cut. Some regulations, such as OSHA safety guidelines, may have positive impacts on productivity (for example, less work is lost due to injuries on the job). Regardless of the true net effect of government regulation on productivity and growth, this argument has contributed to an ongoing trend to lessen the regulatory burden of business.

Another avenue through which government action may hinder economic growth is the growing public debt. Some economists argue that financing the national debt through borrowing diverts economic resources from the private sector. From this perspective, funds the public loans to the government are funds no longer available for private investment. Thus, when the government borrows to finance the national debt, fewer dollars are left for private businesses to borrow and use to purchase capital and hire labor. Sometimes this is called the "crowding out" effect of government borrowing. To the extent crowding out occurs, productivity and economic growth are diminished. Again, this problem may not be as great as it first appears. Much government spending goes to support social overhead capital expenditures, such as interstate highways, public schools, and health programs, that have a positive effect on productivity and growth. Unfortunately, the proportion of public spending on these items has been falling as the interest on the debt grows.

The total net effect of government action on the recent slowdown in economic growth remains debatable. However, we must note that the government maintains the responsibility for fostering an economic climate that promotes enhanced productivity and long-run economic growth.

The 2001 Recession

During the last week of November 2001, the NBER's Business Cycle Dating Committee announced that the U.S. economy had officially entered a recession in March of that year. This announcement marked the end of exactly 10 years of economic growth and expansion, the longest such period in modern times. Like most turning points in the business cycle, no single cause or event can be readily identified as pushing the American economy past the peak and into the contraction phase of the cycle. However, a number of factors may have been at work.

Two contributing factors behind the 2001 recession appear to have been a growing level of pessimistic expectations about the economic future and a decline in consumer wealth. A year earlier, during the spring of 2000, stock markets in the United States began to tumble as many Internet- and technology-based corporations failed to realize their earnings and profit projections, which in hindsight were vastly overoptimistic. During the previous decade, which was marked by steadily rising levels of household income, millions of Americans had invested their savings in the stock market. The popularity of 401(k) retirement accounts and other financial instruments created during an era of tax reform and deregulation led many families to hold a significant portion of their wealth in the form of stocks. Stock prices rose dramatically during the 1990s in response to the growing demand and enthusiasm of these new investors. However, once the "bubble" burst and stock prices fell throughout 2000 and 2001, investors found their wealth evaporating at a remarkable rate. Estimates indicate that individual investors may have lost as much as $6 trillion in total over this period. As personal wealth fell, expectations about the future were revised downward and households adjusted their spending accordingly. In turn, lower levels of consumer spending forced businesses to reduce their levels of output and employment, both of which are classic symptoms of an economic recession.

In the fall of 2001, as Congress was debating a fiscal stimulus package of spending and tax cuts proposed by President Bush, the U.S. suffered the terrorist attacks of September 11. Although these attacks cannot be blamed for the recession that began earlier in the year, the disruption of normal business, the resulting wars in Afghanistan and Iraq, and the compounding negative effects on consumer confidence exacerbated the existing economic problems. Other events also unfolded to undermine consumer confidence in the economy, including a number of high-profile cases involving corporate fraud, bankruptcies, and embezzlement. By the end of 2001, only a couple of years removed from a national labor shortage, unemployment rates began to rise once again.

Despite these circumstances, many economists thought that the underlying structure of the U.S. economy remained strong at the beginning of 2002. Indeed, preliminary estimates of several key economic indicators, including industrial production and retail sales, began trending upward during the year. Although this news was promising, by the end of 2002 the NBER was not ready to announce that the economy had passed the trough of the business cycle. Historically, the Business Cycle Dating Committee waits a number of months to make such an announcement, given that the data are often revised as more information comes to light and the possibility that contractionary forces could resume to impact the economy. It was not until July 2003 that the announcement was made to declare the recession had ended in November 2001. The recession had officially lasted only eight months. The delay in declaring the recession over is a classic example of the difficulty of accurately forecasting the economic future or even knowing with certainty the current state of economic affairs.

Where Do We Go from Here?

What does the recent slowdown in economic growth portend for our future? How will it affect our standard of living as we move into the twenty-first century? Can anything be done to enhance economic growth? These important and vital questions concern us all. The concepts and ideas we learned in this chapter give us some insight into answering them.

First, where is the American economy headed? Although no one knows for sure what tomorrow holds, economists have learned that the past is the best predictor of the future. History shows us that the economy is capable of sustaining various rates of growth over an extended number of years. Let's forecast the future level of economic activity based on the previous rates of growth witnessed during the recent past. Recall that the economy grew at an average annual rate of 4.44 percent during the 1960s and at 3.26 percent during the 1970s, but during the first three years of the 2000s, the economy grew at an average of only 2.12 percent per year. Figure 13.5 plots the projected level of real GDP from 2005 to 2025 based on these three possible average annual rates of economic growth. Notice that this simple forecast technique assumes no short-run fluctuations in the long-run trend. Of course, in reality a business cycle or two could throw us off the path. However, there are some interesting things to note in Figure 13.5.

It is clear that the rate of future economic growth determines the level of economic activity actually achieved at some future date. Figure 13.5 illustrates how the compounding of growth can generate very different outcomes as time progresses. If we continue to grow at the rate established during the early 2000s, real GDP will increase from approximately $11 trillion in 2005 to $17 trillion in 2025. However, if the economy could establish and maintain the same rate of growth that was present in the 1960s, the economy would reach an astonishing $27 trillion level of real GDP in 2025. By increasing our rate of growth to 4.44 percent per year, we could more than double the size of real GDP in about 20 years!

It is unlikely that the American economy can quickly increase and sustain a rate of growth equivalent to that of the 1960s. Of our three forecasts, perhaps the one based on the 1970s growth rate is most reasonable. The annual average rate of growth in the 1970s was 3.26 percent, almost the same as the average for the entire 1960–2000 time period. Furthermore, this rate is well within the 3 percent to

FIGURE 13.5   Possible Future Growth Paths of the U.S. Economy, 2005–2025
The top line forecasts the potential growth in real GDP, assuming an annual rate of 4.44 percent, equal to that experienced in the 1960s. The second line represents the potential growth path assuming the 1970s average annual rate of 3.26 percent, and the third line projects the potential growth path following the 2000s average annual growth rate of 2.12 percent.

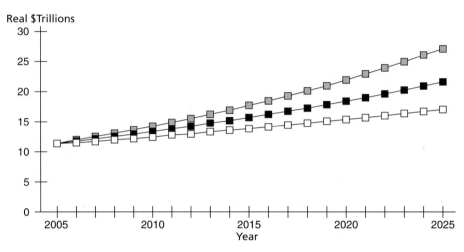

3.5 percent range that history records as the long-run average rate for the economy. According to this projected scenario, the economy would grow to $21.5 trillion by the year 2025. Although this forecast appears reasonable, recall that there are many factors which influence the long-run trend of economic growth and the future can never be foretold with perfect certainty.

What would these projected rates of growth mean for our standard of living? Recall that one economic measure of our standard of living is per capita real GDP. In Chapter 1 we defined this as real GDP divided by the population. Therefore, our measure of living standards depends not only on the growth rate of real GDP but also on the growth rate in the population. Most experts agree that the U.S. population will not grow very fast over the next few decades. The current rate of overall population growth is only an approximate 1 percent per year. Thus, all our forecasts suggest that our standard of living will rise because in all three scenarios, real GDP is expected to increase at a faster rate than the expected rate of population increase.

Even though we can almost be assured of higher levels of per capita real GDP in the future, our different forecasts indicate that a set of very divergent outcomes is possible. Assuming a 1 percent rate of population growth, our optimistic forecast based on a 4.44 percent annual growth rate in real GDP results in a per capita real GDP of $74,000 by 2005. The forecast based on the rate of growth experienced during the early 2000s (2.12 percent) suggests a per capita real GDP of only $47,000 by that year. That is a difference of almost $27,000 for every man, woman, and child in the economy! Clearly, the rate of economic growth over the next two decades will have an important effect on our future standard of living.

Given its importance, is there anything we can do to increase the rate of economic growth? The factors identified in this chapter as being important to economic growth suggest that a number of things can be done. First, overall economic growth can be enhanced by promoting future increases in the size of the American labor force and the long-run accumulation of capital.

The slow but steady increase in the population and the continuing increase in labor market participation by women suggest that the labor force will continue to grow. Policy and institutional changes that encourage more and fuller participation of those currently outside the labor force would support this trend. For example, the opportunity for flexible hours, telecommuting, or other attractive work options and benefits may encourage more prospective workers to enter the market.

With respect to increasing the rate of capital accumulation, one prospective pro-growth policy has received a great deal of attention in recent years: lowering the tax on capital gains. Proponents of this idea argue that by reducing the tax rate investors pay on the appreciation of their capital investments over time, greater incentives will exist for future investments. In essence, a lower tax rate would increase the profitability of capital investments and, therefore, more investment would take place. Congress has debated this issue a number of times, and it is likely to consider the idea again. Another way to encourage capital accumulation is to promote more personal saving. As the pool of savings in the economy increases, more funds become available for investment. In recent years we have seen a number of public policy initiatives that encourage saving, including individual retirement accounts (IRAs) and 401(k) pension plans. Such policies promote long-run economic growth by providing the economy with the funds necessary for investment.

Another approach to promoting economic growth is to enhance the productivity of labor and capital. Numerous public policies encourage the formation of human capital, which increases the productivity of labor. Public funding for education, at all levels, is a clear example. Congress recently implemented a set of new income tax breaks for those who attend college or receive job training. By lowering the tax liability of those in school, the deductions encourage more people to invest in human capital. This education plan is specifically designed to stimulate labor productivity and enhance long-run economic growth.

The government also promotes productivity growth by encouraging technological innovations. Numerous programs financed by the federal government directly support research-and-development activities that have commercial applications. Although the U.S. government spends only less than 1 percent of GDP on research and development each year, that amount is more than any other industrialized nation spends. In addition to these direct outlays, a number of additional public programs and tax laws encourage private investments in new technologies.

Obviously, there are many different paths to economic growth. Even though we cannot always predict what the future will bring, history indicates that the American economy will continue on its upward path.

Summary

Economic growth is defined as a long-run process that results from the compounding of economic events over time. To measure economic growth, economists generally examine the rate of change in real GDP from one year to the next. The average annual rate of growth in the U.S. economy averaged between 3 and 3.5 percent during the twentieth century. Between 1960 and 2002, the rate of growth averaged 3.38 percent.

Long-run economic growth does not occur at a steady rate over time. Short-run fluctuations in economic activity are commonly known as business cycles, which are composed of four distinct phases: expansion, peak, contraction, and trough. Because they are erratic, business cycles are hard to forecast. Significant expansions are referred to as economic booms, and significant contractions are called economic recessions. Historically, business cycles on average last about 60 months but have been getting longer over time because of prolonged expansions. Since 1960, the U.S. economy has completed six business cycles. A number of theories have been proposed to explain business cycles, including those based on expectations, innovations, inventories, monetary institutions, aggregate supply, and exogenous factors.

Two sets of primary determinants of long-run economic growth have been identified: availability of economic resources and productivity factors. Greater quantities of labor and capital increase an economy's productive capacity and shift its production possibilities frontier outward. Investments in human capital and technology enhance the productivity of economic resources, which in turn leads to economic growth.

Close examination of the recent history of real GDP in the United States indicates that the rate of economic growth has been diminishing over time. A number of factors may be contributing to this slowdown, including a technology slowdown, changes in the makeup of the labor force, a relatively low rate of savings, the changing composition of economic output, and government actions.

Any change in the growth rate of the economy will have a great influence on the level of economic activity and per capita real GDP in the future. Public policies can be designed that enhance the determinants of economic growth identified in this chapter. By increasing the rate of economic growth, we can improve our own future standard of living.

Discussion Questions

1. What constitutes economic growth? How can we distinguish long-run economic growth from short-run fluctuations in economic activity?
2. Define what is often called the business cycle. Why is the business cycle so hard to predict?
3. Based on what is currently occurring in the economy, what phase of the business cycle are we now experiencing? When was the last turning point in the cycle?

4. Which theory of the business cycle do you find most convincing? Defend your answer.

5. Find the latest release of the Leading Economic Indicators Index on the World Wide Web. Based on this information, how do you expect the economy to perform over the next 6 to 12 months?

6. What are the major determinants of long-run economic growth? Which of these determinants do you think has been most important during the past couple of years? Explain.

7. Why do we call formal education an investment in human capital? How is it like an investment in physical capital?

8. Use a production possibilities graph to demonstrate an increase in productivity on an economy's productive potential.

9. Explain why economists believe the rate of economic growth has been slowing down. Is this something we should be concerned about? Why or why not?

10. Which of the factors discussed in this chapter do you believe is primarily responsible for the recent slowdown in economic growth? Can you identify any additional factors that were not discussed in this chapter?

11. This chapter presented four projections of economic growth through 2020, each based on historic trends. Which one do you believe is most realistic? Defend your position, and provide specific reasons why the most optimistic projection is unlikely to be met.

12. How is your standard of living related to the overall growth of the economy? Is it possible for the economy to grow too fast? Explain.

13. What is the "new economy"? How did the expansion of the 1990s differ from previous expansions? Explain.

14. How does Schumpeter's theory of innovations relate to the economic expansion of the 1990s? Can it be used to explain the phenomena of the "new economy"? Discuss.

15. What factors contributed to the economic recession which began in the spring of 2001? Of the business cycle theories discussed in this chapter, which one do you believe best explains this latest downturn? Discuss and defend your choice.

Additional Readings

Baumol, William J., Sue Anne Batey Blackman, and Edward N. Wolff. *Productivity and American Leadership: The Long View.* Cambridge: MIT Press, 1991.
This book emphasizes that productivity is a long-term issue. Discusses the factors that affect productivity: savings, investment, education, depletion of natural resources, etc.

Frumkin, Norman. *Guide to Economic Indicators.* 4th ed. Armonk, NY: M. E. Sharpe, 2000.
Provides descriptions, backgrounds, and interpretations of more than 50 economic indicators used to measure and forecast economic performance.

Frumkin, Norman. *Tracking America's Economy*. 4th ed. Armonk, NY: M. E. Sharpe, 2004.
Written for students and the general public, this book is a great way to understand all the issues discussed in this chapter, with easy-to-understand graphs and tables.

Heintz, James, et al. *The Ultimate Field Guide to the U.S. Economy: A Compact and Irreverent Guide to Economic Life in America*. New York: New Press, 2000.
The authors designed this book as an "accessible, concise reference for answering specific questions as well as an informative overview of the U.S. economy."

Jones, Charles I. *Introduction to Economic Growth*. 2nd ed. New York: W.W. Norton, 2001.
A wonderful introduction to understanding the determinants and consequences of economic growth, with a mathematical review in the appendix.

Kindleberger, Charles P. *Manias, Panics, and Crashes: A History of Financial Crises*. 4th ed. New York: John Wiley & Sons, 2000.
A classic examination and telling of the events which surrounded major economic downturns throughout human history from ancient Rome until the present.

Krugman, Paul. *The Age of Diminished Expectations*. 3rd ed. Cambridge, MA: MIT Press, 1997.
Discusses such issues as income distribution, the trade deficit, inflation, the budget deficit, free trade and protectionism, and the savings and loan scandal with respect to their effects on economic growth.

Rogers, R. Mark. *Handbook of Key Economic Indicators*. 2nd ed. New York: McGraw-Hill, 1998.
This book thoroughly reviews the economic indicators that analysts use to construct forecasts and projections of economic growth. Tables and graphs illustrate the dynamic relationships between key variables and economic performance.

Stein, Herbert, and Murray Foss. *The New Illustrated Guide to the American Economy*. 2nd ed. Washington, DC: AEI Press, 1995.
Very accessible guide to the many ways of measuring economic performance over time. Various trends and issues are explored and illustrated with colorful graphs and charts. Fun book for browsing.

Zarnowitz, Victor. *Business Cycles: Theory, History, Indicators, and Forecasting*. NBER Studies in Business Cycles 27. Chicago: University of Chicago Press, 1992.
Excellent source that incorporates all aspects of business cycles, from the trends to the theories to the indicators to forecasting.

World Wide Web Resources

American Entrepreneurs for Economic Growth (AEEG)

www.aeeg.org

"AEEG is dedicated to uniting innovative, emerging growth businesses across industry lines to promote positive national government action that benefits the investment and entrepreneurial communities and stimulates economic growth." Has links to facts, policy, membership, and entrepreneurial resources.

Bureau of Economic Analysis

www.bea.doc.gov

The Bureau of Economic Analysis collects and analyzes national data to measure the current state of the economy and its long-run growth. This site provides access to some of this data and numerous publications, news releases, and links to other related sites.

The Conference Board

www.tcb-indicators.org

This is the home of the Business Cycle Indicators. The Conference Board provides the latest estimates and a wide range of articles and other sources of information about business cycles and economic forecasting.

Economic Growth Research

www.worldbank.org/research/growth

This Web site features published articles and working papers from the World Bank's Research Group, as well as related literature on economic growth from a global perspective.

Economic Report of the President

www.access.gpo.gov/eop

This annual publication, prepared by the President's Council of Economic Advisors, reports on the current state of the national economy. Short articles on the current and long-term economic climate are provided, along with a number of the most important economic data series that measure the economy's performance.

Economic Time Series Page

www.economagic.com

This site provides links to hundreds of data series of economic activity. In addition to a comprehensive listing of time series for the U.S. economy, links are also available for other nations.

National Bureau of Economic Research

www.nber.org

This is the home site for the organization that produces the Leading Economic Indicators Index and determines the "official" dates of U.S. business cycles. The site provides access to a variety of national economic data as well as a table indicating the dates for all U.S. business cycles since 1854.

Government Spending, Taxing, and the National Debt

Who Wins and Who Loses?

Checklist of economic concepts

- Government purchases
- Government transfer payments
- Collective goods
- External benefits and costs
- Equal tax treatment doctrine
- Horizontal equity
- Vertical equity
- Relative tax treatment doctrine
- Ability-to-pay principle of taxation
- Progressive tax rates
- Proportional tax rates
- Benefits-received principle of taxation
- Tax efficiency
- Forward and backward tax shifting
- Price elasticity of demand
- Tax incidence
- Government borrowing
- Government debt repayment

I am reminded of the mythical Midwestern farmer retired Senator Stephen M. Young (D-Ohio) used to tell about.

He rode free to public school on free buses, studied agriculture under the GI bill, bought his home with a VA loan, got his power through Rural Electrification Administration lines and sent his kids to government subsidized colleges on government loans.

He eventually made it big in the farming business, joined the John Birch Society and finally, disgusted with his high taxes, wrote to his senator, one Stephen Young:

"I believe in rugged individualism. People should stand on their own two feet, not expect government aid. I stand on my own two feet. I oppose all those socialistic trends you have been voting for and demand return to the free enterprise system of our forefathers."

Source: William Raspberry, " 'American Way' OK, for the Other Guy," *Tulsa Word*, p. A-13, February 16, 1979.

WHAT ARE PEOPLE AFRAID OF?

A great concern of people seems to be related to the involvement of government in their daily lives in the forms of questionable government services, regulations and controls, and the payment of taxes. As is apparent from the introductory quote, many people do not object when they receive government services free or below the market price, but they do object when others are on the receiving line and when they have to pay taxes to support government. On a broader, more philosophical plane, people fear that the increasing scope of government narrows their individual choices and reduces their individual rights.

Most fears of people are related to the *size of government* and to the *distribution of taxes*. Issues connected to government size and tax distributions are the focal points of this chapter.

Size of Government

People appear to be feeling increasingly that government is too big. If this is so, an argument could certainly be made that government services and taxes should be cut. Is there a basis for this feeling?

Some of the fears of people concerning government size are well-founded. Government activities have extended into areas of society not deemed necessary many decades ago. Taxes have risen to pay for these activities until today almost all families have to part with a significant amount of their income in order to pay taxes. The worry that people have about government waste and the abuse that is connected with government expenditures is not imaginary. People have found out about these things through the various means of communication. A day, a month, and certainly a year rarely pass without a report on unnecessary government expenditures or on abuse of some sort in the operation of one or more government expenditure programs.

Some fears of people concerning government size are not well-founded. Although the history of many government expenditure programs is a story of growth, waste, and some abuse, many government expenditure programs, including the provision of benefits to many people and the fulfillment of the needs of people living in a changing society, have been at least partly successful. For example, since the beginning of the Social Security program in 1936, Social Security taxes have grown rapidly and have become a heavy tax burden to many taxpayers. At the same time, however, this program has been enlarged in scope and coverage and now includes not only retirement income and unemployment benefits to those covered but also health care benefits. (See Chapter 15 for a complete discussion of these issues.) More, not less, public debate and scrutiny of government activities are needed, if unneeded programs are to be eliminated and needed programs are to be improved.

The source of some fears is not specific and concrete but general and philosophical. Fear of too much government is an important aspect of the American heritage. The idea that "the least government is the best government" encourages individual choice and problem solving in the marketplace. A market-oriented economy is based on the supposition that the market will solve problems impersonally and efficiently. It is this belief that underlies the concerns of people when the government interferes in the market.

Tax Inequities

The question of tax equity, that is, tax justice, is also a major concern for many people. *Tax equity* refers to the way taxes are distributed among people. Even if tax collections were exactly the right amount to pay for government goods and services demanded by people, there could be concern that tax distributions were not fair. Some taxpayers may be paying more than what they believe is a fair amount, and some may be paying less than what others believe is a fair amount. So, in addition to the fear that government is too big and taxes too high generally, there is the fear that taxes are "too low" for certain taxpayers and "too high" for certain others.

Ample evidence indicates that there are tax inequities in the tax system at all levels of government. The concept of equity will be developed, and illustrations of tax inequities are presented later in the chapter. It may suffice here to point out that the fears that people have concerning the fairness of tax distributions are in part justifiable.

THE PROBLEM OF SIZE

Our approach to the problem of size is, first, to provide background information concerning this problem and, second, to analyze the problem of size in reference to the economic criteria of efficiency and equity.

FIGURE 14.1   Total Government Expenditures and Federal Government Expenditures as a Percentage of GDP, 1960–2003

Source: Economic Report of the President, February 2004, various tables.

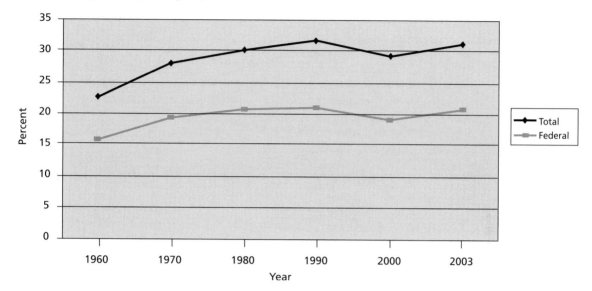

Government Expenditures

People's concern over the size of government is understandable if you just look at the absolute level and growth in government expenditures. Over the 1960–2003 period, government expenditures increased from $120 billion to $3,500 billion. This is an astounding increase. However, a better perspective on the size of government is revealed if the growth in government spending is compared to the growth in the overall economy as measured by the gross domestic product (GDP). Figure 14.1 shows this pattern of growth. Total government expenditures (federal, state, and local government) grew from 23 percent of the GDP in 1960 to 31 percent in 2003. The federal government expenditure share of the GDP grew from 16 percent to 20 percent, and total state and local government expenditure share grew from 7 percent to 11 percent over the same time period.

Two interesting trends are revealed in Figure 14.1. First, total government spending, as a percentage of GDP, rose throughout the 1960s, 1970s, and 1980s. By 1990, total government spending accounted for nearly one-third of the nation's GDP. Then, during the 1990s the concern over big government led to a significant cutback in overall government expenditures. By the year 2000, total government spending stood at less than 30 percent of GDP—a substantial reduction in real terms over a relatively short period of time. As seen in Figure 14.1, the same trend is seen when we look only at federal government expenditures. The second trend revealed in Figure 14.1 is the recent resurgence in the importance of government spending. Between 2000 and 2003, total government spending again increased, up to almost

FIGURE 14.2 Total Government Purchases, Transfer Payments, and Interest Paid as a Percentage of GDP, 1960–2003

Source: Economic Report of the President, February 2004, various tables.

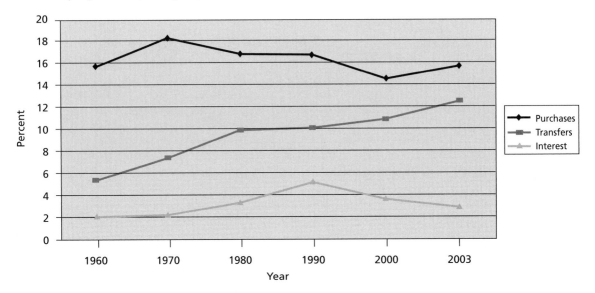

32 percent of GDP. However, much of this new spending was the direct result of homeland security issues and the wars in Afghanistan and Iraq. Once these international issues have been resolved it will be interesting to see if government spending as a share of GDP resumes the downward course observed during the 1990s.

Another matter of interest to some people is the relative importance of the type of government expenditure. Government expenditures may be classified as **transfer payments** or **government purchases of goods and services.** Transfer payments are payments to people who have not made a contribution to the current production of goods and services, whereas government purchases are expenditures for currently produced goods and services. Figure 14.2 shows government purchases and transfer payments as a percentage of the GDP over the 1960–2003 period. Both government purchases and transfer payments increased, as a percentage of GDP, during the 1960s. However, beginning in the 1970s, total government purchases began to fall but transfer payments continued to increase, albeit at a slower rate, throughout the rest of the century. Between the year 2000 and 2003, the share of GDP devoted to government purchases rose for the first time in nearly 40 years. Again, the renewed spending on national security and defense was the primary causal factor in this trend reversal.

Many people are also concerned about the ability of government to finance deficit spending. Figure 14.2 reports the total government expenditures on interest payments as a percent of GDP. These interest payments reflect the costs of government borrowing to finance public debt. As seen in the graph, government interest payments rose throughout the 1960s, 1970s, and 1980s—the years which

transfer payments
Government expenditures in the form of money payments to people who have not contributed to the current production of goods and services.

government purchases of goods and services
Expenditures for currently produced goods and services that are a part of the nation's income.

FIGURE 14.3   Total Government Receipts and Federal Government Receipts as a Percentage of GDP, 1960–2003

Source: *Economic Report of the President*, February 2004, various tables.

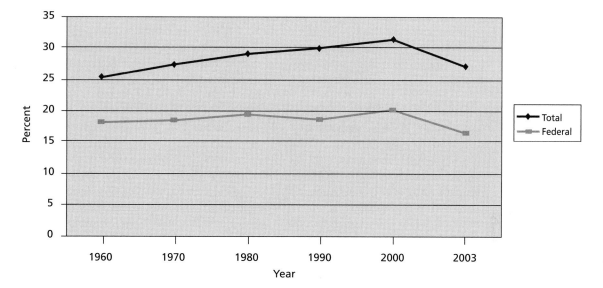

coincided with a growing national debt. Then, the economic boom of the 1990s significantly reduced government's burden to finance its debt. By 2003 interest payments amounted to only 2.8 percent of GDP, down from a high of about 5.1 percent in 1990.

Government Receipts

The other side of the government expenditure-revenue system, receipts, shows a somewhat more stable pattern with respect to its share of GDP. As seen in Figure 14.3, government receipts as a percentage of GDP increased from 25 percent to 32 percent over the entire period from 1960 to 2000. Federal receipts as a percentage of GDP was even more stable, increasing only from 18 percent in 1960 to 21 percent in 2000. The relative stability of government receipts as a percentage of the nation's income compared to the ratio of government expenditures to the nation's income is not surprising, because government receipts tend to be more directly related to changes in the nation's income. This is clearly seen in Figure 14.3 as both total and federal government receipts fell between 2000 and 2003 because of the recession and slow recovery.

ECONOMIC ANALYSIS OF THE PROBLEM OF SIZE

Economic efficiency and equity are two concepts that have been used to analyze many issues previously discussed. Efficiency was the major consideration in the discussion of resource allocation in Chapter 2. It was the basis for evaluation in the examination of the economics of crime and pollution problems. Equity came directly into play in the treatment of poverty. Efficiency in the use of scarce resources of society causes society to produce as many goods and services and to satisfy as many human wants as possible. Equity is concerned with the distribution of goods and services among people. Both equity and efficiency considerations are involved in an analysis of the size of government, for the size of government is determined by expenditure programs aimed at redressing the unequal distribution of income and at providing goods and services that would not be provided at all, or at least would not be provided in efficient quantities, in the marketplace.

An Efficient Level of Government Expenditures

An efficient level of government expenditures is that level at which the *net* benefits to society are maximized, that is, the level at which benefits and costs are equal at the margin. The maximization of net benefits and the equation of marginal benefits and costs were first illustrated in Chapter 4 in analyzing the correct (efficient) level of antipollution activities. This analysis can be applied to government spending in the aggregate. The efficient level of government expenditures would be reached when the marginal benefit per dollar spent in the public sector is equal to the marginal benefit per dollar spent in the private sector.

Although cost-benefit analysis has practical application in many instances and is the guide to an efficient allocation of resources, it must be acknowledged that benefits and costs of government expenditures can seldom be precisely quantified, and often government programs are developed without any attempt to estimate benefits and costs. Thus, there is no way of knowing for certain whether the present size of government is too big or too small. Further insight can be gained, however, into the question of efficiency and the size of government by discussing the proper scope of government.

Pure Public Goods

Earlier we learned that collectively consumed goods and services are also referred to as public goods. Let's take the meaning of a public good a step further in the context of this chapter. A *pure public good* has two distinctive characteristics. The first characteristic is that a pure public good is *nonrival in consumption*—that is, a given amount of the good can be consumed by a person without another person having to decrease his or her consumption of the good. For example, a person may receive the benefits from national defense without affecting the benefits that another person receives. This is in sharp contrast to a private good, which is rival in consumption. For example, a hamburger eaten by one person is not available for another person to consume.

The second characteristic of a pure public good is the *nonexclusion* feature of the good. Private goods are rationed in the market based on the principle of exclusion; that is, you are excluded from the market if you cannot pay the market price. But, in the case of a pure public good, it may not be feasible to exclude people or it may be undesirable to do so. For instance, everyone should receive the benefits from crime prevention activities: No one should be excluded.

The **nonrival in consumption** and the **nonexclusion** features of public goods, such as defense and crime prevention activities, make it difficult, if not impossible, for these goods and services to be supplied and demanded in the marketplace. Remember that (1) the demand for public goods is not generally divisible into small units on the basis of individual quantities demanded and (2) the supply of public goods is not generally divisible into small units. Thus, government provision of pure public goods is widely accepted.

The main issue in the supply of public goods, then, is for the government to supply an efficient amount of these goods. This means that estimates of marginal benefits and costs have to be made. As you know, the efficient level of defense spending is the level where marginal benefits equal marginal costs. How would you derive the demand or the marginal benefits for a public good? The demand for a private good is simply the horizontal summation of the quantities that consumers are willing to buy at each possible price. Now in the case of a public good, the demand for a public good is derived by vertically summing the individual marginal benefits at each quantity. It is much more difficult to determine the efficient level of public goods. In contrast to buyers in the private market, buyers in the market for public goods have an incentive not to reveal their preferences since the quantity available for consumption may not be directly affected.

External Benefits and Costs

The line of demarcation between what government should provide and what private producers should provide would be clear if all goods and services were either collective or private goods and services. However, you have already learned that in the production of certain goods there can be social spillover costs, and in the consumption of certain goods and services there can be social spillover benefits. The existence of **externalities,** that is, social spillovers in production and consumption, broadens the scope of government beyond collective goods and services.

Market demand indicates marginal private benefits (MPB), and market supply indicates marginal private costs (MPC). Assuming no externalities, marginal private benefits and costs equal marginal social benefits and costs. However, if neither external benefits nor costs are present, a divergence will exist between private and social benefits or between private and social costs. This divergence means that government action is required for resources to be used efficiently.

Figure 14.4 shows private demand and supply of good A. Assuming that no external benefits and costs exist, the efficient quantity would be Q, and the price would be P. Suppose, now, that in the consumption of good A, there are external benefits. In Figure 14.4, the demand curve D_T shows both marginal private and external benefits ($MPB + MEB$); that is, D_T shows the total marginal social benefits. The demand curve that indicates all benefits is the relevant one. Thus, the efficient quantity in Figure 14.4 is Q_E, not Q. What can government do to guarantee that the efficient quantity is provided?

The government could consider two choices. One choice would be for the government to produce good A and attempt to produce the efficient quantity. This type of action presumes that government will be an efficient supplier and can

FIGURE 14.4   The Efficient Quantity Assuming External Benefits in Consumption

D represents marginal private benefits (*MPB*), and D_T represents *MPB* and marginal external benefits (*MEB*). Given the supply curve *S*, the optimum or efficient quantity is at Q_E, where *MSB* equals *MSC*. The government could ensure that the efficient quantity would be demanded by giving a subsidy payment to consumers equal to $[(P_E - P_0) \times Q_E]$.

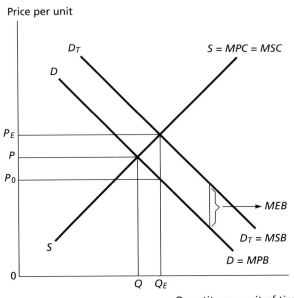

accurately estimate marginal social benefits. The second choice of action does not depend on government's being an efficient supplier but still depends on precise estimates of benefits. Government action could be in the form of subsidies to consumers of good A so that they would be willing to purchase the efficient quantity. In Figure 14.4, consumers would buy the correct amount at P_0 The total subsidy payment would be equal to $[(P_E - P_0) \times Q_E]$. A subsidy payment greater than this would result in too much production of good A, and a subsidy payment smaller would mean that less than the efficient quantity is produced.

The case of external costs in production was examined in Chapter 4 and illustrated in the case of water pollution in the production of paper. In this instance, the market price was too low and the production of paper was too high because external cost in the form of water pollution was not taken into account in the supply of paper. To correct this situation, the government could levy a tax on each unit of paper supplied. The effect of the tax would be to increase the marginal cost of supplying paper and, therefore, to decrease supply. Assuming that the tax equals marginal external costs, an efficient but lower quantity of paper will be supplied at a higher price. The price elasticity of demand for paper will determine how much the price of paper will rise as a result of the tax.

Income Distribution

Government actions thus far have been rationalized on economic efficiency grounds. The scope of government has been greatly extended and defended based on the belief that income inequality needs to be reduced. The distribution of income, and therefore consumption, would be largely based on the productivity of people in a highly competitive economy. A social problem arises because some people have no or low productivity. What should be done to alter the distribution of income so as to help people who cannot work and those who can work little?

Shifting income from those who are relatively productive to those who are relatively unproductive, say, through taxes and subsidies, must be based on the values of people as to what constitutes a fair distribution. It is not surprising that government programs aimed directly or indirectly at altering the distribution of income are under constant attack. Evidently, people generally support programs aimed directly at helping low-income people, such as public assistance and food stamps, and programs that only indirectly help certain low-income groups, such as the Social Security program, for these programs have expanded relative to other government programs. Paralleling this growth has been the increased controversy concerning income transfer programs. Although the debate is not likely to end, the responsibility of government in the area of income redistribution is seemingly established. No private institutions could thoroughly cope with the problem.

Summary

The major ideas that have evolved from our discussion thus far are these: (1) pure public goods and services must be supplied by government; (2) government actions are needed to improve the efficiency of the market system, especially where there are externalities; and (3) government may alter the distribution of income in order to move in the direction of an equitable distribution as determined by the beliefs of people in our society.

TAX PRINCIPLES AND ANALYSIS

equal tax treatment doctrine Taxpayers in the same economic circumstances should be treated equally.

horizontal equity People in identical economic circumstances pay an equal amount of taxes.

The first part of this section develops a theoretical framework based on the criteria of equity and efficiency. The second part examines tax principles pertaining to the shifting and incidence of taxes.

Tax Equity

Everyone agrees that taxes should be just. Not everyone agrees, however, on the exact meaning of justice or fairness in taxation. An idea that runs strongly through Western thought is that tax justice means that taxpayers in equal economic circumstances should be treated equally. This is called the **equal tax treatment doctrine** and pertains to **horizontal equity;** that is, people in identical economic positions should pay equal taxes.

vertical equity
Taxpayers in different economic circumstances are treated unequally based on either the ability to pay or the benefits received.

relative tax treatment doctrine
Taxpayers in different economic circumstances should be treated unequally.

ability-to-pay principle of taxation
Taxes should be distributed among taxpayers based on the ability to pay taxes.

benefits-received principle of taxation
Taxes should be distributed among taxpayers based on the individual benefits received from government goods and services.

In the application of the equal tax treatment doctrine, the best indicator or measure of economic circumstances has to be determined. Generally, economists interpret economic circumstances to mean a person's real income, namely, consumption plus changes in net wealth. Assuming that real income is the best measure of economic circumstances, then horizontal equity is achieved when all taxpayers with the same income pay exactly the same amount in taxes.

What about taxpayers in different economic circumstances? How should they be treated? These questions are related to the idea of **vertical equity,** that is, the tax treatment of taxpayers in different economic circumstances. The **relative tax treatment doctrine** now emerges: Taxpayers in different economic circumstances should be treated differently. But how differently? Two principles of taxation have been developed to shed light on this question—the *ability-to-pay principle* and the *benefits-received principle.*

Ability-to-Pay Principle   The **ability-to-pay principle of taxation** suggests that taxpayers with more ability to pay taxes should pay more taxes. Again, using income as the measure of ability to pay, this means that taxpayers with more income should pay more taxes. But how much more? Progressive and proportional income tax rates are always consistent with the ability-to-pay principle because if the rate of taxation (the percentage of income paid in taxes) is rising as income rises (progressive rates) or constant as income rises (proportional rates), the amount paid in taxes will always be higher as income is higher. On the other hand, regressive tax rates can violate the ability-to-pay principle since the percentage of income paid in taxes decreases as income rises.

Benefits-Received Principle   Do you recall the way the market distributes the costs of producing private goods and services? The market distributes costs based on marginal private benefits. The **benefits-received principle of taxation** is an attempt to apply the rule of the market and is thus a guide to an efficient allocation of taxes rather than to an equitable allocation. However, efficient and equitable tax distributions are not always in conflict, and when equity in the distribution of income is not a concern, the benefits-received principle of taxation is an important tax standard. This principle is more limited than the ability-to-pay principle because private benefits received from government goods and services are usually more difficult to measure than the ability to pay. Illustrations of taxes that are defended on the benefits-received principle are the gasoline tax and local street assessments. The gasoline tax is used primarily to pay for highways. Thus, the demander of highway services, the automobile user, pays for the benefits received from highway services through a tax levied on gallons of gasoline consumed. Similarly, well-maintained local streets benefit property owners by enhancing the value of property. Thus, it is reasoned that property owners should pay in the form of property taxes for the benefits they receive from streets.

Tax Efficiency

Tax efficiency is concerned with the *administration and compliance* cost of taxes. Taxes should be economical to collect and to enforce. They should also be convenient and certain to the taxpayer.

excess tax burden
A measure of tax inefficiency; that is, it measures the nonneutral or the distortionary effects of the tax on relative prices and resource allocation.

A more important aspect of tax efficiency involves minimizing what economists call the **excess burden** from taxes. The idea of an excess burden from taxes can be grasped easily with an illustration. Suppose the government transfers $10 billion worth of resources from the private sector to the public sector via taxes and provides marginal benefits equal to $10 billion. Further, suppose that in the levy of taxes, tax rates are used that discourage incentives to work so that private production is less than what it would have been by $1 billion. This example clearly shows that there is a net loss of $1 billion even though the government is using the resources transferred as efficiently as they would be used in the private sector. This net loss in production resulting from the disincentive effects of taxes is the excess burden that has arisen because of the imposition of taxes.

If there is no excess burden or if the excess burden is small, then we can say that taxes have *neutral* effects or near-neutral effects on the operation of the private economy. Unfortunately, taxes seldom have completely neutral effects. However, certain taxes adhere to the idea of neutrality better than others, and these are the taxes that we are searching for to put into an ideal tax scheme. Taxes that directly alter relative commodity prices or that do so indirectly through altering consumption and income patterns are taxes that have strong nonneutral effects and do not adhere to the concept of tax efficiency. For example, a tax levied on a specific commodity will increase the price of that commodity and result in a shift of spending away from the taxed commodity to nontaxed commodities. Progressive and regressive income tax rates change the pattern of income distribution as well as alter the price of work relative to the price of leisure.

Principles of Shifting and Incidence

forward tax shifting
Situation in which any part of a tax is paid for by consumers in the form of higher prices.

Taxes may be levied on one taxpayer and shifted to another taxpayer. A tax that is shifted **forward** is a tax that falls on the consumer in the form of higher prices; a tax that is shifted **backward** falls on the owners of resources in the form of lower resource prices. The **incidence,** or burden, of a tax that is not shifted, then, remains on the original taxpayer.

backward tax shifting
Situation in which any part of the tax is paid for by the owners of resources in the form of lower resource prices.

Two kinds of tax are to be considered in the following analysis. The first is an output tax, and the second is a tax levied independent of output.

An Output Tax

tax incidence
The burden or the final resting place of the tax.

An output tax is a tax that is levied on each unit of output produced, such as a tax on each pack of cigarettes or on each gallon of gasoline. An output tax increases the cost of producing each unit and, therefore, decreases supply. Given the demand for the taxed commodity, a decrease in supply will increase the price of the commodity. How much of the tax will be shifted forward?

price elasticity of demand
The responsiveness of the quantity demanded of a product to changes in the product's price.

To answer this question, we must first understand a concept economists refer to as the **price elasticity of demand.** By definition the price elasticity of demand is the responsiveness of the quantity demanded of a product to changes in its price. It is measured as the percentage change in quantity demanded divided by the percentage change in price. Anyone who has postponed the decision to buy a product until after it has been discounted during a sale intuitively understands the concept

FIGURE 14.5 **Relative Price Elasticity of Demand**
Both good A and good B initially sell for price P_1. When the price for each product falls to P_2, the quantity demanded of good A increases to Q_A, but the quantity demanded for good B increases all the way out to Q_B. Thus,
the demand for good A is said to be relatively price elastic when compared to good B and the demand for good B
is said to be relatively price inelastic when compared to good A.

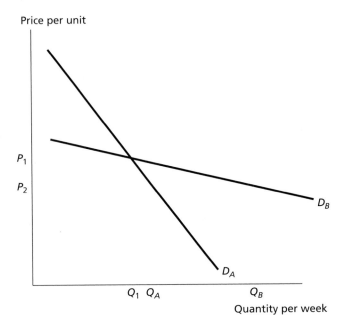

of elasticity. For some items when a seller lowers (raises) prices, consumers will
strongly respond by demanding significantly more (less) than before, holding
everything else the same. A strong response is called an elastic response. However,
for other items when a seller lowers (raises) prices, consumers will only weakly respond by demanding only a little bit more (less) than before, all else being equal.
A weak response is called an inelastic response.

The price elasticity of demand can be measured along the length of every demand curve. For all straight-line demand curves there will be a range where strong
(elastic) responses to changes in price will be observed and a range where weak
(inelastic) responses will prevail. Also, it is often a common practice to compare
the *relative* degree of price elasticity of demand between products. Figure 14.5
illustrates two demand curves, one for product A and one for product B, with different relative degrees of price elasticity. Notice that both curves obey the law of
demand and slope downward to the right. Assume that the initial price for both
good A and good B is equal to P_1 and quantity demanded for each is equal to Q_1.
Now let's see what happens if both sellers lower their price to P_2. Notice that
the quantity demanded for good A increases to Q_A but the quantity demanded
for good B increases all the way out to Q_B. Consumers who purchase good B

FIGURE 14.6   **Perfectly Price Inelastic**

When a demand curve is drawn as a vertical line, the quantity demanded does not respond to changes in price. At a low price such as P_1, the quantity demanded is equal to Q. If the seller raises price to P_2, the quantity demanded remains equal to Q. Thus, in this case the demand curve is called perfectly price inelastic.

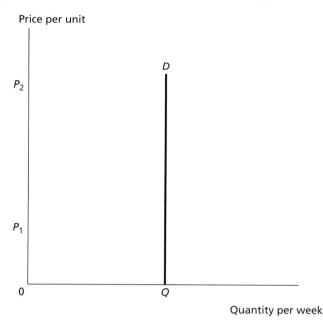

are much more responsive to the price change than are consumers of good A. Thus, we say that the demand for good B is relatively elastic when compared to good A, and that the demand for good A is relatively inelastic when compared to good B.

Both elastic and inelastic responses can be taken to the extreme. For example, we saw earlier in Chapter 8 that firms in perfectly competitive markets are price takers and that if any one firm in the market raised its price, that firm would lose all of its sales. That situation was illustrated with a horizontal demand curve for perfectly competitive firms (see Figure 8.2). Horizontal demand curves are called *perfectly price elastic* demand curves. On the other extreme consider the case where a firm raises its price and there is no response in terms of the quantity demanded. This might be the case where there are no available alternatives for the good or service being sold. This would be illustrated as a vertical demand curve like the one in Figure 14.6. Vertical demand curves are called *perfectly price inelastic* demand curves.

The extent of the forward shifting of an output tax depends essentially on the price elasticity of demand. If demand is *perfectly* inelastic (Figure 14.7), the entire tax is shifted forward. The incidence of the tax, under these circumstances, is *completely* on the consumer in the form of higher prices. If demand is *perfectly* elastic

FIGURE 14.7 **Demand Perfectly Inelastic—Complete Forward Shifting of an Output Tax**
The pretax equilibrium is at a price of P and at a quantity of Q, where supply S intersects demand D. An output tax on each unit produced is levied with the amount of the tax shown above. The effect is to decrease supply to S_1. Thus, price rises to P_1, where S_1 intersects D. The full amount of the tax is shifted forward because the rise in price from P to P_1 equals the amount of the tax.

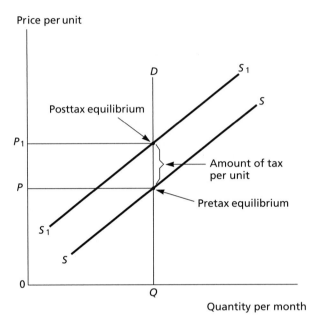

(Figure 14.8), none of the tax is shifted forward; or, in other words, all the tax is shifted backward to resources in the form of lower prices (lower wages, etc.). The elasticity of demand for most products will not be either of these two extremes. We can generalize, then, by saying that an output tax will normally be shifted forward and backward, with more forward shifting when demand is more inelastic and more backward shifting when demand is more elastic.

Independent of Output Tax

A tax levied on income, say, the net income or profits of a business, is a good illustration of a tax that is independent of output. Suppose a business has selected the best output, that is, the output where profits are maximized, before a 25 percent profits tax is imposed. Now, after the tax, is there a better output? The answer is no. If the best output is selected before the tax, it remains the best output after the tax. There is no short-run shifting of a tax levied independently of output. The incidence of such a tax is on the owners of the business in the form of a reduction in profits. The difference between an output tax and a tax independent of output is that the former increases costs and decreases supply, whereas the latter does not. For taxes to be shifted, a change in supply has to occur.

FIGURE 14.8   **Demand Perfectly Elastic—Complete Backward Shifting of an Output Tax**
The pretax equilibrium is at a price of P and a quantity of Q, where supply S intersects demand D. An output tax decreases supply to S_1. The posttax equilibrium is at a price P and a quantity of Q_1, where supply S_1 intersects demand D. There is no forward shifting of the tax because price does not change. Thus, the entire tax is shifted backward to owners of resources.

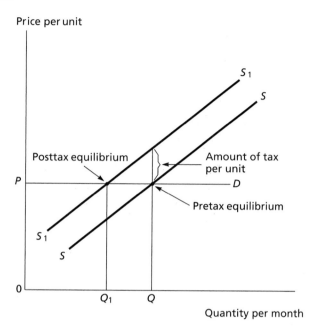

THE AMERICAN TAX SYSTEM

The American tax system is best described as a hybrid system because it relies on taxes levied on income, consumption, and wealth. The major tax sources at the federal level are income taxes, payroll taxes, and excise taxes. At the state level the main tax sources are sales and income taxes, and at the local level property taxes are a vital source of revenue. Two interesting developments over the years have been the increasing importance of payroll taxes at the federal level and of income taxes at the state level. This change has tended to make the federal tax system less progressive and the state system more progressive; however, the federal system is still a more progressive system.

Tax collections in this country were 31.8 percent of the GDP in 2003. This is the smallest share of income gleaned by the government of any modern, industrialized country. Table 14.1 reports the amount of taxes collected as a percentage of GDP for several of these countries. Note that the highest percentages are found in the nations which are members of the European Union, where publicly provided services, like health care, are part of the "social contract" between governments and citizens. In France, more than half (54.4 percent) of GDP is collected as taxes

TABLE 14.1
Tax Share of GDP in Selected Countries, 2003

Source: Statistiques des recettes publiques des pays membres de l'OCDE. OECD, Paris, 2004, various tables.

Nation	Taxes Collected as a % of GDP
Australia	36.4
Canada	38.1
France	54.4
Germany	49.4
Italy	48.5
Japan	38.3
Spain	39.3
United Kingdom	42.8
United States	31.8

TABLE 14.2
Composition of Federal Receipts (% of total receipts)

Source: Statistical Abstract of the United States, 2004, various tables.

Fiscal Year	Individual Income Tax	Corporate Income Tax	Social Insurance Taxes	Excise Tax
1950	39.9	26.5	11.0	19.1
1960	44.0	23.2	15.9	12.6
1970	46.9	17.0	23.0	8.1
1980	47.2	12.5	30.5	4.7
1990	45.3	9.1	36.9	3.4
2000	49.6	10.2	32.2	3.4
2003	46.2	7.8	39.6	3.7

by the French government. The relatively low tax share of GDP in the United States is consistent with the belief that economic decisions are better left to private markets and that government intervention should be limited.

Federal Tax System

Table 14.2 shows the composition of federal receipts on a fiscal year basis from 1950 to 2003. Approximately 85 percent of federal receipts comes from two tax sources, individual income taxes and social insurance taxes, which pay for Social Security benefits and are sometimes referred to as payroll taxes since they are levied on wages and salaries. Individual income taxes have not changed very much in relative importance over the years, although there have been some major changes in the income tax. Corporate income taxes and excise taxes have declined significantly in relative importance over the past four decades. In contrast, social insurance taxes have increased significantly in relative importance over the same time period. The net effect of these changes has made the federal tax system less progressive.

The federal tax system is a progressive tax rate system, meaning that the ratio of taxes paid to income rises as you move up the income ladder. Table 14.3 illustrates the progressive character of the federal tax system. The table reports the effective

TABLE 14.3
Effective Federal Tax Rates by Income Category

Source: Effective Current Tax Rates under Current Law, 2001 to 2014, Congressional Budget Office, 2004.

Income Category	Effective Federal Tax Rate (%)	
	2004	2014
Lowest quintile	6.7	8.3
Second quintile	13.2	14.7
Middle quintile	16.5	18.2
Fourth quintile	20.6	22.4
Highest quintile	27.6	28.8
Overall	22.6	24.1
Top 10 percent	29.3	30.3
Top 5 percent	30.8	31.6
Top 1 percent	33.4	33.6

tax rate paid by households according to their level of income. The distribution of household income is divided into five equal groups, or quintiles, with each group representing 20 percent of the distribution. (Recall that we analyzed the distribution of income in this same manner in Chapter 7 when we examined the issue of American poverty.) Notice that as household income rises, the percentage of income paid as tax to the federal government also rises. In 2004, the federal tax liability for the lowest income quintile was 6.7 percent while households in the highest income quintile paid 27.6 percent in federal taxes. For those households in the top 1 percent of the income distribution the effective tax rate was 33.4 percent that year.

Table 14.3 also shows the expected effective tax rates for 2014 given the reforms that will be phased in over the next several years as part of recent legislative acts. Some of the new tax provisions are controversial because they will disproportionately increase the tax burden of lower income groups. Note in Table 14.3 that the effective tax rate for the lowest quintile will increase from 6.7 percent to 8.3 percent during the 2004–2014 period. This increase of 1.6 percent compares to an increase of only 0.2 for the top 1 percent of households, whose effective rate rises from 33.4 percent to 33.6 percent. Some argue that these projections call into question the equity of the recent reforms.

Most would agree then that the federal tax system meets the ability-to-pay principle of taxation and is generally a fair or equitable tax system. Since the federal tax system is a mildly progressive system, the distribution of income after taxes is more equally distributed.

The Personal Income Tax

As we have already seen, the personal income tax is the single most important source of tax revenue for the federal government of the United States. The enforcement and collection of the personal income tax is the responsibility of the Internal Revenue Service, commonly referred to by its initials as the IRS. The IRS must implement and operationalize a vast array of tax rules and policies as set forth in federal legislation. The federal government often uses the tax code to encourage or discourage certain behaviors. For example, to encourage personal

TABLE 14.4
Federal Personal
Income Tax
Brackets, 2004

Single Taxpayer	Joint Return	Tax Rate, %
$0 to $ 7,000	$0 to $ 14,000	10
$7,001 to $ 28,400	$14,001 to $ 56,800	15
$28,401 to $ 68,800	$56,801 to $114,650	25
$68,801 to $143,500	$114,651 to $174,700	28
$143,501 to $311,950	$174,701 to $311,950	33
$311,951 and up	$311,951 and up	35

savings for education and retirement, Congress has established a number of special investment instruments whereby earnings are tax deferred or even tax exempt. Many other examples exist, from special treatment of interest payments on home loans to tax credits on the adoption of children. So many special rules have been built into the current tax laws that it has become extremely complex for the average taxpayer to understand. An entire industry exists to help households manage their tax liability and file their annual returns.

Although the myriad of details within the current personal income tax law go well beyond the scope of this book, it is important to recognize that the law is based upon a progressive tax framework. This is evident by examining how a household's personal tax liability is levied. A sliding scale of tax rates are applied to taxable income as that income rises. For example, for a husband and wife filing a joint return in 2004, the first $14,000 of their income was taxed at a rate of 10 percent. Income above $14,000 but less than $56,800 was subject to a 15 percent rate of tax. The range of income subject to a specific rate of tax is often called a "tax bracket." Table 14.4 reports the tax brackets for single- and joint-return taxpayers in 2004. The progressive nature of the personal income tax is clearly seen as the marginal rate of taxation rises throughout the brackets by law.

The current set of tax brackets is a legacy of the landmark legislation enacted during the Reagan administration 20 years ago. The 1986 Tax Reform Act broadened the personal income tax base and replaced 14 tax brackets ranging from 11 to 50 percent with only three brackets of 15, 28, and 33 percent. Amendments and recent legislative acts brought the number of tax brackets back up to the current six. The goal of the Reagan reforms was to provide tax relief for the average taxpayer and to encourage work, saving, and investment. The initial result of the tax cuts was a tremendous increase in the federal government's budget deficit and an increase in the national debt. However, the tax cuts did set the stage for the unprecedented economic expansion experienced during the 1990s. By the end of that decade, government budget deficits had disappeared and had been replaced with budget surpluses.

THE BEGINNING OF A NEW CENTURY

The end of the twentieth century found the economy in its longest economic expansion in history, and the federal budget was showing surpluses for the first time in more than three decades. This fiscal budget surplus period, 1998–2001, resulted

TABLE 14.5
Federal Budget
Surplus (+) or
Deficit (−) and
Debt, Fiscal Years
1998–2004
($Billions)

*Source: Economic Report of
the President,* February
2004, various tables.

Year	Surplus or Deficit	Federal Debt
1998	$ 69.2	$3,721.1
1999	125.6	3,632.4
2000	236.4	3,409.8
2001	127.4	3,319.6
2002	−157.8	3,540.4
2003	−375.3	3,913.6
2004	−520.7	4,420.8

in a $401 billion reduction in the federal debt held by the public. Unfortunately, the era of budget surpluses and debt retirement was short lived. The 2001 recession and the necessary increases in government expenditures to support the war on terrorism resulted in the return to budget deficits beginning in fiscal year 2002. Table 14.5 reports the amount of federal government budget surplus or deficit and the resulting impact on the national debt for the 1998 to 2004 time span. Naturally, the swing between debt retirement and deficit spending has important economic implications. Let's first discuss the economic effects of federal government borrowing and the economic effects of the federal government buying some of the debt held by the public. Then we shall briefly discuss recent tax law reforms.

Economic Effects of Government Borrowing

Government borrowing increases the demand for loanable funds and therefore increases the price of loanable funds, that is, the rate of interest. A higher interest rate will decrease the volume of private investment. Alternatively, we could say that government borrowing increases the supply of bonds and, therefore, decreases the price of bonds and increases the interest rate. This inverse relationship between bond prices and the interest rate needs to be discussed further. A bond is a fixed income-yielding asset; that is, a fixed amount of interest is paid annually, say, $1,000. On the other hand, bond prices vary depending on supply and demand. In this example, the government bond has a maturity value of $10,000 and pays an amount of annual interest of $1,000, or a rate of interest of 10 percent ($1,000 divided by $10,000). Now, suppose with an increase in the supply of bonds, the price of the bond falls to $9,000. The interest rate now is 11.1 percent ($1,000 divided by $9,000).

The economic effects of government borrowing should not be confused with the economic effects of a budget deficit. A budget deficit means, of course, that government spending is in excess of tax revenues. The impact of this is to stimulate production and income in the economy. However, the budget deficit leads to government borrowing, which will generally lead to an increase in the interest rate. Now, the question is which way will the economy move? A budget deficit moves the economy in an upward direction, and government borrowing moves it in the downward direction. The answer to the question is that the economy will expand because of the effect of the budget deficit, but it will not expand as much as it otherwise would because of the higher interest rate due to borrowing. In other words, the economy is expanding due to the initial impact of government spending exceeding tax collections. But the increase in the interest rate is a secondary effect resulting from the expansion, and it will generally tend only to slow the expansion.

Economic Effects of Federal Debt Retirement

Federal debt reductions started in the fiscal year 1998, when there was the first budget surplus since 1967. Federal budget surpluses and public debt reductions continued each year until fiscal year 2002, when a return to a budget deficit of $157.8 billion was incurred (Table 14.5).

What are the effects of retiring some of the federal debt held by the public? Government borrowing increases the demand for money, which tends to increase the interest rate and discourage private investment. Retiring the federal debt will have just the opposite effect. It will tend to lower the interest rate and encourage private investment. Another way of saying this is that retiring government debt decreases the supply of government bonds, which increases government bond prices and lowers the interest rate.

Recent Tax Reforms

A major federal tax cut bill, the Economic Growth and Taxpayer Relief Reconciliation Act, was passed by Congress and signed by President George W. Bush on June 7, 2001. Federal tax cuts had been promised by the newly elected president, and the federal budget surplus in 2001, along with that for the three prior years, seemed to make the case for federal income tax cuts stronger. Also, the growth in the economy was slowing down, and the case could be made that federal tax cuts were needed to stimulate the economy. In any event, the 2001 legislation was a landmark act according to some and an act that fell far short of genuine reform according to others. Many of the income tax reforms are not scheduled to take effect until much later in the new decade, but one reform that was immediately put into action was a $300 check for every taxpayer.

The 2001 legislation was followed by two additional tax reform measures, the Job Creation and Worker Assistance Act of 2002 and the Jobs and Growth Tax Relief Act of 2003. Both of these laws further reduced the effective tax rates on income by accelerating some of the provisions provided in the EGTRRA and adjusting downward the tax on income derived from property and financial investments. It is too early to determine the overall long-term impact of these tax measures. However, these reforms have resulted in growing federal budget deficits. The budget deficits of 2003 and 2004 are the largest in nominal terms that the United States has ever experienced. These deficits and the resulting growth in the federal debt will no doubt continue to spark public debate about the proper size of government in a mixed-market economy.

Summary

People are concerned about the size of government and inequities in the distribution of taxes, so this chapter focused on the problems of government size and of tax distributions. After the fears of people were discussed and conclusions were reached that some worries are well-founded and some are not, the problems of government size and tax distributions were approached in the same manner. First, relevant facts were presented; second, an economic framework was developed based essentially on the concepts of efficiency and equity; and finally, policy proposals to deal with these problems were discussed.

In the economic analysis of the problem of size, efficiency considerations justify government expenditures in the form of provisions of collective goods and services, in the form of subsidies to encourage more consumption when external benefits in consumption are present, and in the form of taxes to discourage production when external costs in production are present. Equity considerations justify government programs designed to enhance the economic opportunities of people who do not earn adequate income in the marketplace. The "adequacy" of income as well as the socially accepted distribution of income among people must be based on the beliefs of people.

In the development of tax principles, it was pointed out that an efficient tax is one that has neutral effects on the allocation of resources, and an equitable tax is one that can be defended on the ability-to-pay principle or the benefits-received principle. An equitable system would adhere to the equal tax treatment doctrine and to the relative tax treatment doctrine.

The incidence, or burden, of a tax is the final resting place of the tax. A tax may be shifted forward to consumers in the form of higher prices or backward to the owners of resources in the form of lower resource prices. The shifting of an output type of tax, such as the gasoline tax, depends on the price elasticity of demand. The more inelastic demand is, the more the tax will be shifted to consumers in the form of higher prices. A tax that is independent of output, such as an income tax, does not increase the cost of producing goods and services; therefore, this type of tax is not shifted, at least in the short run. For a tax to be shifted, supply has to decrease.

The Tax Reform Act of 1986 made fundamental changes in the federal income tax system. The income tax base was made much broader by the elimination of many tax deductions, tax exclusions, and tax credits. Many income brackets and tax rates were reduced. The top marginal tax rate was lowered from 50 to 28 percent. Taxpayers in all income classes benefited from the reform, but taxpayers in the lower-income classes benefited the most. The net effect of tax reform was to move the federal income tax system in the direction of a more equitable and efficient tax system.

A new era appeared to emerge when the federal government budget was in a surplus in fiscal year 1998 and continued to be in a surplus in fiscal years 1999, 2000, and 2001. This budget surplus era resulted in the federal government paying off some of the federal debt held by the public, instead of borrowing from the public and going further into debt. This new era of federal budget surpluses came to an end in fiscal year 2002, and federal budget deficits are likely to prevail in the future given recent tax reforms that lower effective tax rates. However, we have seen that a federal budget surplus or a balanced budget is not impossible, and this is desirable in a full-employment economy.

Discussion Questions

1. Discuss people's fears about the size of government. Include in your discussion a historical account of the growth of government expenditures and government revenues. Are these fears justified?

2. What are the characteristics of pure public goods? Explain why these goods cannot be supplied in the private marketplace. What criterion should the government use in determining the quantity of pure public goods?

3. Discuss why externalities on the demand side or the supply side of the market result in an inefficient quantity of goods produced and sold, even in a perfectly competitive market.

4. Assuming externalities on the demand side, explain how the government may pursue a policy that would lead to an efficient quantity produced and sold.

5. Discuss the meaning of tax equity and tax efficiency. Design a federal income tax system based on the two tax criteria of equity and efficiency.

6. What is meant by the shifting and incidence of a tax? Compare and contrast the shifting and incidence of an income type of tax to an output type of tax.

7. Define what is meant by the term "price elasticity of demand." From a tax perspective, why is the price elasticity of demand important? Explain.

8. Compare the tax burden of American taxpayers to those in other industrialized countries. Can you identify why the tax burden varies across national borders?

9. How did the tax reform measures enacted by the Reagan administration in the 1980s affect the marginal rates for the personal income tax? What was the result of these changes?

10. Why was the recent era of federal government budget surplus so short? What factors have contributed to the recent federal government budget deficits?

11. Use the information provided in Table 14.3 to discuss the distribution of the federal tax burden on households in the United States.

12. What are the economic effects of government borrowing and government debt retirement?

Additional Readings

Aaron, Henry J., and Michael J. Boskin, eds. *The Economics of Taxation*. Washington, DC: Brookings Institution, 1980.
Collection of essays on the economics, politics, and legal problems of taxation.

Benavie, Arthur. *Deficit Hysteria: A Common Sense Look at America's Rush to Balance the Budget*. Westport, CT: Praeger, 1998.
Discusses the relationship between the national debt and several issues, such as unemployment, inflation, and social security; outlines several deficit myths.

McCaffery, Edward J. *Fair Not Flat: How to Make the Tax System Better and Simpler*. Chicago: University of Chicago Press, 2002.
The author suggests ways to change the present tax system to make it simpler and fairer to lower-class citizens.

Pechman, Joseph A. "Tax Reform: Theory and Practice." In *Readings in Public Sector Economics*, eds. Samuel H. Baker and Catherine S. Elliot. Lexington, MA: Heath, 1990.
Discusses the Tax Reform Act of 1986 and presents the impact of tax reform on the incidence of income taxes.

Seidman, Laurence S. *Automatic Fiscal Policies to Combat Recessions.* Armonk, NY: M. E. Sharpe, 2003.
The author details, among other issues, the tax rebates the government enacted during the 1975 and 2001 recessions.

Thompson, Kenneth, W., ed. *The Budget Deficit and the National Debt.* Lanham, MD: University Press of America, 1997.
The history, the economics, and the politics of the national debt are discussed.

Zodrow, George R., and Peter Mieszkowski, eds. *United States Tax Reform in the 21st Century.* Cambridge, England: Cambridge University Press, 2002.
This is a collection of essays by tax experts arguing whether a complete overhaul of the tax system is better than a continually slow moving reform of the existing tax system.

World Wide Web Resources

Budget of the United States Government
www.gpoaccess.gov/usbudget

Issued by the Office of Management and Budget (OMB), has the complete current fiscal year budget online. Can also search the budget from 1997 to the present.

Economic Report of the President
www.access.gpo.gov/eop

Sponsored by the Executive Office of the President. Use the Search Terms box to find statistical information on taxes and taxation.

Institute for Research on the Economics of Taxation
www.iret.org

This site analyzes the effects of government tax, budget, and monetary policies. Links are provided for the Institute's publications, reports, and proposals for reform.

NBER Papers in National Government Expenditures and Related Policies
papers.nber.org/jel/H5.html

The National Bureau of Economic Research (NBER) provides links to working papers on a wide variety of economic issues, including taxation.

United States Internal Revenue Service
www.irs.ustreas.gov

Gives tax statistics, electronic services, and taxation relations, forms, and publications.

Social Security and Medicare

How Secure Is Our Safety Net for the Elderly?

Checklist of economic concepts

- Private insurance
- Social insurance
- Fully funded insurance scheme
- Pay-as-you-go insurance scheme
- Cost-of-living allowances (COLAs)
- Substitution effect
- Income effect
- Retirement effect
- Bequest effect
- Wealth substitution effect
- Fee-for-service system
- Managed care system
- Deductible
- Co-insurance
- Prospective payment system

Today, 44 million Americans depend upon Social Security, and for two-thirds of our senior citizens it is the main source of income. For 18 percent of our seniors it is the only source of income. But Social Security is more than just a retirement program. More than one in three of the beneficiaries are not retirees. They are the children and spouses of working people who die in their prime. They are men and women who become disabled, or their children. So Social Security is also a life insurance policy, and a disability policy, as well as a rock-solid guarantee of support in old age. That is why we have to act with care as we make needed repairs to the program occasioned by the huge growth in retirees.

When President Roosevelt signed the bill creating the Social Security system, most seniors in America were poor. A typical elderly person sent a letter to FDR begging him to eliminate "the stark terror of penniless old age." Since then, the elderly poverty rate has dropped sharply. In 1959, the poverty rate was over 35 percent for retirees. In 1979, it had dropped to 15.2 percent. In 1996, the poverty rate was down below 11 percent. Even though most seniors need other sources of income in addition to Social Security to maintain a comfortable lifestyle, if Social Security did not exist, today half of all American retirees would be living in poverty—60 percent of all women. Fifteen million American seniors have been lifted out of poverty through the Social Security system.

Today the system is sound, but the demographic crisis looming is clear. The baby boomers—76 million of us—are now looking ahead to their retirement. And people, clearly, are living longer, so that by 2030, there will be nearly twice as many elderly as there are today. All these trends will impose heavy strains on the system. In 1960, which wasn't so long ago, there were over five people working for every person drawing Social Security. In 1997, there were over three people—3.3 people—working for every person drawing. But by 2030, because of the increasing average age, if present birthrates and immigration rates and retirement rates continue, there will be only two people working for every person drawing Social Security.

Now, here's the bottom line. The Social Security trust fund is sufficient to pay all the obligations of Social Security—both retirement and disability—until [2040], after which it will no longer cover those obligations. Payroll contributions will only be enough to cover 75 cents on the dollar of current benefits. If we act now, we can ensure strong retirement benefits for the baby boom generation without placing an undue burden on our children and grandchildren. . . .

To the older Americans, let me say, you have nothing to worry about. For you Social Security is as strong as ever. To the younger people here today who may believe that you will never see a Social Security check, indeed, I saw a poll which purported to be serious that said that Americans in their twenties thought it was more likely they would see a U.F.O. than that they would ever draw Social Security. That skepticism may have been well founded in the past, but just as we put our fiscal house in order, we can and must put Social Security in order. And above all, to my fellow baby boomers, let me say that none of us wants our own retirement to be a burden to our children and to their efforts to raise our grandchildren. It would be unconscionable if we failed to act, and act now, as one nation renewing the ties that bind us across generations.

Source: Taken from President Bill Clinton's address to a national forum on Social Security in Kansas City, MO, April 7, 1998.

SOCIAL INSURANCE

"What does the future hold?" "What will happen to my family if I become sick or disabled and unable to work?" "Will I be able to afford a secure retirement?" "Can I obtain adequate health care as I grow older?"

We have all asked ourselves such questions, even though they can never be answered with certainty. The world is full of unexpected events that can dramatically change our lives. Accidents, illnesses, and deaths each year interrupt the lives of millions of families. Because some of these events are more likely to occur than others, people may gain some protection for themselves from the known risks of life through the purchase of insurance. **Private insurance** is a contract whereby individuals agree to make payments, often called premiums, to a company in return for a guarantee of financial benefits in the event that some undesired circumstance occurs. In the modern economy, private insurance is common since most people insure their valuable possessions against damage or loss—their cars, their homes, and even their lives. In addition to the availability of private insurance, today most national governments, including the United States, provide their citizens with a variety of social insurance programs. **Social insurance** programs, financed through tax revenues, guarantee citizens financial benefits from the government for events that are beyond an individual's control, such as old age, disability, poor health, and loss of employment.

A number of U.S. federal programs fall under the definition of social insurance; however, the largest and arguably the most popular is Social Security, with its health care companion, Medicare. Today, most workers and employers in the private economy pay taxes to support the Social Security system. Likewise, millions of Americans each year rely on Social Security and Medicare to maintain their quality of life. The program was specifically created to reduce the economic insecurity that often accompanied growing old, but over time it has expanded to provide benefits to other at-risk populations.

Although the evidence indicates that Social Security has been successful in improving the plight of the aged, the program has always been controversial, and soon it will face serious economic problems. As President Clinton noted in his address reprinted above, the demographic trends of the late twentieth century have created a number of significant challenges for the long-run economic stability of the Social Security system. Most notable of these trends is the disparity in the sizes

private insurance
A contract whereby individuals agree to make payments, often called premiums, to a company in return for a guarantee of financial benefits in the event that some undesired circumstance occurs.

social insurance
Government programs, financed through tax revenues, that guarantee citizens financial benefits for events which are beyond an individual's control, such as old age, disability, and poor health.

FIGURE 15.1   **Population Distribution of the United States by Age and Gender**

Source: U.S. Department of Commerce, Bureau of the Census, *Statistical Abstract of the United States*, 1998.

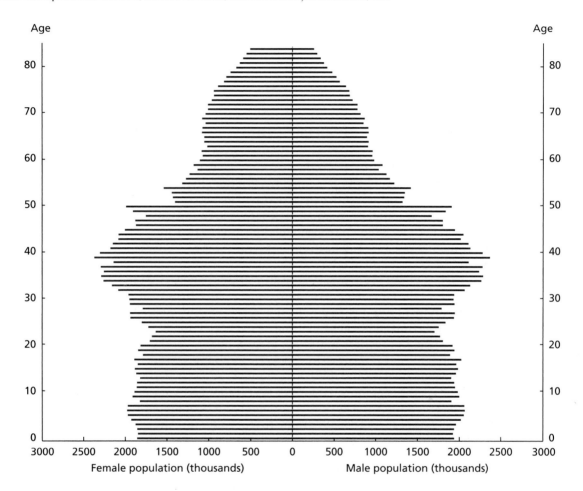

of the "baby boom generation" and the younger generations that follow it. The relative sizes of these groups can be seen in the "population tree" reproduced as Figure 15.1. Notice the bulge created by the large number of people between 30 and 50 and the significantly smaller numbers of people at younger ages. As time passes, more and more baby boomers will reach retirement age and become eligible for Social Security pensions. At current tax rates and level of benefits, the smaller younger generations will not be able to support the Social Security demands of the larger older generation.

In this chapter we will explore the nature and possible solutions of this predicament by investigating the economic and financial structure of our major social insurance programs. Furthermore, given that Social Security and Medicare directly affect the income and purchasing power of a large segment of society, we will discover that social insurance has the ability to significantly influence, or perhaps even distort, economic decision making with regard to issues such as the savings rate, the supply of labor, age at retirement, and the demand for health care. Each of these issues has political and social as well as economic dimensions. This chapter will provide a basic framework within which these economic dimensions can be addressed.

SOCIAL SECURITY

A Brief History of Social Security

The concept of a national social insurance program did not originate in the United States. That distinction belongs to Germany, where in the late 1880s Chancellor Otto von Bismarck implemented his Prussian Plan to provide retirement pensions and other benefits to German workers. The success of the Prussian Plan led to the adoption of similar programs in other western European nations. Although some states and the federal government did provide pensions for civil servants and veterans, a national social insurance program was not established in the United States until 1935.

Throughout the 1930s, American workers experienced the disastrous economic effects of the Great Depression. At some points during this period the national unemployment rate reached almost 25 percent, and most of those lucky enough to hold full-time jobs found that their paychecks purchased very little. Throughout the Great Depression hundreds of commercial banks and financial institutions went bankrupt and were forced to close. Many workers who had saved for personal emergencies and their own retirements lost everything. The future economic security of the average American worker looked very bleak in 1934 when President Franklin D. Roosevelt recommended to Congress the establishment of a national social insurance program. A year later, on August 14, 1935, the president signed into law the Social Security Act.

The original Social Security Act created a program whereby monthly benefits were to be paid to individual workers upon retirement at age 65. The level of benefits received was to be based on each worker's contribution to the program in the form of a payroll tax collected over his or her working lifetime. The federal government began collecting Social Security taxes in 1937, but before the first regular monthly payments to retirees were issued, Congress significantly modified the program. Amendments to the Social Security Act in 1939 created two new categories of beneficiaries that greatly expanded the scope of the program. First, dependents (spouse and children) of a retired worker were extended benefits upon the death of the retiree. Second, surviving family members became entitled to Social Security benefits in the case of the death of a covered worker. These changes shifted the focus of the Social Security program from the individual to the family.

The program's focus on the family is also evident in the next major enhancement of Social Security. In the 1950s and 1960s, amendments to the Social Security Act created benefits for those who became disabled and could no longer work to

TABLE 15.1
The Growth of
Social Security
over Time

Source: Social Security
Administration, various
publications. All numbers
represent the Old Age and
Survivors Insurance and
the Disability Insurance
programs combined.
Dollar figures are reported
in current dollars.

Year	Number of Beneficiaries	Total Benefits Paid
1940	222,000	$ 35,000,000
1950	3,477,000	$ 961,000,000
1960	14,845,000	$ 11,245,000,000
1970	26,229,000	$ 31,863,000,000
1980	35,585,000	$120,511,000,000
1990	39,832,000	$244,135,000,000
2000	45,415,000	$401,367,000,000
2002	46,453,000	$453,601,000,000

support their families. Disability benefits were made available not only for covered workers but also for their dependents. The 1960s also saw the enactment of a new early retirement option, whereby workers could begin receiving reduced Social Security benefits at age 62. The expanded scope of the Social Security Act led to a tremendous growth in the number of Americans receiving benefits. By 1970 Social Security had more than 26 million beneficiaries (see Table 15.1).

Perhaps the most important enhancement to date of the American social insurance system occurred in 1965 when President Lyndon B. Johnson signed the bill that authorized the establishment of Medicare. Medicare is the federal program that provides health care coverage to almost all Americans aged 65 or older. Although many European nations include universal health care coverage as a major element of their social insurance programs, the United States government continues to limit coverage to the elderly and leaves the private sector responsible for providing health care to those below the age of normal retirement. The unique characteristics of the health care industry keep the Medicare program at the forefront of public debate concerning the proper role of government in caring for the welfare of its citizens. (These issues will be discussed later in this chapter.)

Social Security, by any reasonable measure, is one of the most popular and successful federal programs in the United States. By 2004, more than 51 million people received monthly checks from the Social Security Administration, which distributed retirement, survivors, and disability benefits in excess of $431 billion. Many Americans have come to depend on Social Security and view their future benefits, to which covered individuals are legally entitled, as part of their personal wealth. Because of this, Social Security is often referred to as an "entitlement" program. The personal importance that most people place on the Social Security system guarantees that its administration and financial soundness are almost always an issue for public discourse and political debate. This has certainly been true in recent years.

The Current Status of Social Security

The Organizational Structure

Today, the program that most people refer to as Social Security is officially known as the Old Age, Survivors, and Disability Insurance (OASDI) program. OASDI is not only much broader in its scope and coverage than the original Social Security program, it is financed very differently from the way the program was first conceived. Under the original plan, Social Security was to operate in a manner very similar to the way private insurance works. Specifically, individual workers were to make contributions to the program throughout their working lives, and these contributions would be deposited in a fund managed by the government. The fund would accumulate and earn interest over time. Thus, when a worker retired, the interest and principal from the fund would be used to finance the worker's benefits. This type of program, whereby annual benefit expenditures are primarily funded by interest income earned on accumulated payments, is commonly called a **fully funded insurance scheme.** Even though Social Security was originally designed to be a fully funded insurance program, it never operated as such because the immediate pressures to provide benefits to elderly workers who had lost their savings during the Great Depression did not allow the system time to build up an adequate investment fund. In 1939 Social Security was converted to a **pay-as-you-go insurance scheme.** Under this type of plan, annual benefit expenditures are financed from current contributions. In other words, the Social Security benefits paid to current recipients are paid from the tax contributions of those presently working. (Notice that one result of this type of financial structure is an intergenerational transfer of income from taxpaying workers to beneficiaries.)

fully funded insurance scheme Insurance program designed to provide benefits that are financed from the interest income earned on accumulated payments.

pay-as-you-go insurance scheme Insurance program designed to provide benefits that are financed from current payments.

Until recently, OASDI continued to operate as a pay-as-you-go system, whereby one generation's retirees, survivors, and disability beneficiaries were supported by the next generation's workers. During the 1980s and 1990s the baby boom generation swelled the size of the American labor force, and the annual tax contributions the Social Security Administration collected began to significantly exceed the annual amount of benefits paid. The consequence of this action has been the accumulation of a significant surplus that grows each year. This surplus is held in the Social Security trust fund, which will be used in the future to help offset the expected increase in benefits payable as the baby boomers reach retirement age. Therefore, at the present time Social Security is neither a fully funded system nor a pure pay-as-you-go system but rather a hybrid combination of the two schemes. Current Social Security taxes are partially used to finance the payments made to current beneficiaries and are partially invested in the Social Security trust fund. The trust fund will be used to finance the benefits that are payable in the future. In fiscal year 2002, the Social Security trust fund had an increase in its assets of $165.5 billion.

The Way Social Security Works

The vast majority of workers in the private sector of the American economy are now covered by the Social Security system, which is financially supported through the collection of a tax imposed on wages. This payroll tax is a flat percentage of annual gross wages, up to a certain limit, split evenly between the employee and the employer. Although the sharing of the tax bill between the worker and the firm was intended to split the cost equally, it is clear that employers may be able to shift all or part of their burden to the workers in the form of lower wages. Both OASDI and Medicare are financed through this form of payroll tax. The current tax rate is 6.20 percent for OASDI and 1.45 percent for hospital insurance under Medicare.

Therefore, both employees and employers pay a 7.65 percent payroll tax to support Social Security and Medicare. (Most employees have their share of this tax automatically deducted from their paychecks through the Federal Insurance Contributions Act, or FICA.) Workers who are self-employed must pay the combined total of 15.30 percent. In 2004, the payroll tax for OASDI was limited to the first $87,900 in earnings, but there was no earnings ceiling for the tax used to support Medicare's hospital insurance program.

The OASDI benefit structure results in a partial redistribution of income from beneficiaries who earned high wages to those who earned low wages. When a person files a claim with the Social Security Administration, his or her monthly benefits will depend on a number of characteristics, including age, familial status, and, most important, earnings history. Standardized formulas are applied to determine the level of benefits each individual is entitled to receive. (Currently, workers must accumulate 40 "qualifying" quarter years of work to become eligible for pension benefits.) Workers with lower average wages over their lifetimes will receive smaller monthly benefits than those with higher average wages. However, the benefit formulas are designed to provide lower wage workers with a greater percentage of their past earnings than higher wage workers receive. For example, in 1995 it was estimated that Social Security replaced 55.4 percent of earnings for lower wage workers but only 23.5 percent of earnings for higher wage workers. The average earnings replacement rate for Social Security beneficiaries that year was 41.1 percent. Furthermore, the standardized formulas guarantee that recipients with dependents (a spouse and/or children) receive a greater monthly benefit than those recipients who are single. Table 15.2 provides the average monthly Social Security benefits paid to various categories of people in 2003. (If you are interested in the specific rules and formulas used to determine Social Security eligibility and benefit payments, please visit the Social Security Administration Web site referenced at the end of this chapter.)

Under the present rules, workers who retire at age 65 are entitled to full monthly benefits. Workers may choose to retire earlier, beginning at age 62, and receive benefits equal to approximately 80 percent of what they would receive by retiring at 65. Workers may also choose to retire later than 65 and receive an increase in their monthly benefits. Because of financial pressures on the system, which we will discuss later, recent amendments to the law will gradually increase the age of retirement at which workers are entitled to full Social Security benefits. By the year 2022, workers will not be able to receive full Social Security retirement benefits until the age of 67.

Another important feature of Social Security for retirees is that their benefits are influenced by their current earnings from work. Retirees are allowed to earn wages and salaries up to some predetermined limit before their benefits are reduced. The earnings limit is determined each year based on national average wages. A penalty is imposed on earnings above this limit. Currently, Social Security benefits are reduced at a rate of $1 for every $2 earned over the annual limit ($9,600) when a retired person is below the age of full retirement and $1 for every $3 earned over the limit ($15,500) when the beneficiary attains the age of full retirement.

TABLE 15.2
Average Monthly OASDI Benefit Amounts, 2003

Source: Social Security Administration, *Annual Statistical Supplement,* 2003, Table 5-A1.

Type of Beneficiary	Average Monthly Benefits
All beneficiaries	$815
Retired workers	895
Spouses	452
Children	428
Disabled workers	696
Spouses	211
Children	245
Survivors	
Nondisabled	861
Disabled widows and widowers	546
Widowed mothers and fathers	637
Surviving children	584
Parents	770

cost-of-living allowances (COLAs)
The Social Security COLA is equal to the amount of inflation experienced within the economy during the previous year as measured by the Consumer Price Index (CPI).

Every year since 1975, Social Security beneficiaries automatically receive increases in their monthly checks to counter the corrosive effects of inflation. These adjustments are known as **cost-of-living allowances,** or **COLAs.** The Social Security COLA is equal to the amount of inflation experienced within the economy during the previous year as measured by the Consumer Price Index (CPI). (See Chapter 12 for a discussion of the CPI.) In this respect Social Security is more generous than most private pension plans, which seldom incorporate automatic COLAs into their benefit packages. One obvious consequence of this nicety is the growing cost to maintain the program over time.

THE ECONOMIC EFFECTS OF SOCIAL SECURITY

Because Social Security touches almost every American family in one way or another, the program has significant social and economic effects. During the past 65 years economists have closely monitored and studied the impacts of Social Security on individuals and the economy. Studies show that both Social Security taxes and Social Security benefits influence a variety of important economic variables, such as disposable income, the labor supply, and savings. It can be easily postulated that the U.S. economy would look very different today if the Social Security system did not exist.

Income

Perhaps the most obvious economic effects of the modern Social Security system are its impacts on disposable income. First, for those working, the Social Security tax reduces take-home pay and thereby lowers their disposable income. However, for those in the elderly, survivor, and disabled populations who receive benefits, Social Security clearly increases their disposable income. As Table 15.1 indicated,

FIGURE 15.2
Income Sources of the Aged Population, 2001

Source: Social Security Administration, *Fast Facts and Figures,* June 2003 (http://www.ssa.gov).

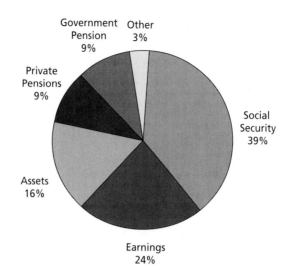

Government Pension 9%

Other 3%

Private Pensions 9%

Social Security 39%

Assets 16%

Earnings 24%

$453 billion in OASDI benefits were distributed in 2002 to about 46.4 million recipients. This amount represents a substantial annual contribution of income to households with traditionally high marginal propensities to consume.

Since its inception, Social Security has grown in its importance as a source of income for the aged population. According to the Social Security Administration, 91 percent of today's elderly households receive Social Security benefits. (An elderly household is defined as one headed by a person aged 65 or older.) To put this into perspective, consider that only 9 percent of elderly households receive private pensions. Clearly, Social Security payments are widely distributed among the older citizens of this country. Furthermore, the relative size of Social Security benefits, compared to other sources of income, continues to grow over time. In fact, 65 percent of household members aged 65 or older who receive Social Security report that it comprises 50 percent or more of their total income. An astonishing 20 percent of elderly households report that Social Security is their *only* source of income. In the aggregate, Social Security income accounts for 39 percent of senior citizens' income. Figure 15.2 illustrates that Social Security is far and away the largest single source of disposable income for this population group.

An additional effect of the distribution of Social Security benefits is its impact on poverty. It is estimated that 10 percent of elderly families live below the poverty threshold; without Social Security this number would rise to 50 percent. Thus, Social Security lessens the need for other, more traditional antipoverty income transfer programs. (Refer to Chapter 7 for a discussion of these programs.)

Social Security benefits represent a significant source of consumption spending that has an obvious positive effect on aggregate demand. By supporting a higher level of aggregate demand, Social Security benefits tend to stimulate overall economic performance and growth. Social Security and the spending it supports are an integral and vital part of the modern economy.

Labor Supply

Both Social Security taxes and Social Security benefits can affect the labor supply decisions of individual workers. The empirical evidence indicates that the overall effect is to cause a net reduction in the size of the labor force. How and why does this happen? The answer is a simple matter of economic incentives that influence the behavior of both the workers who pay Social Security taxes and those who receive Social Security benefits.

First, Social Security is financed through payroll taxes that are unlikely to have a neutral effect on worker behavior. As discussed earlier, the Social Security tax bill is split evenly between workers and their employers. The portion of the tax paid by the worker clearly reduces take-home pay. And this is compounded by the fact that employers could afford to pay higher wages if they were not responsible for their portion of the Social Security tax. Consequently, it is possible for employers to shift all or part of their Social Security tax burden to the worker in the form of lower wages. It seems clear, then, that the Social Security system tends to lead to lower real wages for workers covered by the program. This reduction in the wage can have an important effect on individual labor supply decisions. Recall that changes in the wage rate result in both a substitution effect and an income effect. The substitution effect turns on the fact that the wage rate is effectively the price of an hour of leisure time. (For example, workers making $10 per hour must give up that amount if they desire an additional hour of leisure.) As such, the reduction in the wage brought about by Social Security's payroll tax tends to reduce the price of leisure and causes the rational individual to choose more hours of leisure, that is, to work less. By contrast, the income effect turns on the fact that leisure time is a normal good. Recall from Chapter 2 that the demand for normal goods rises as income rises and declines as income falls. The payroll tax in support of Social Security tends to reduce income and, as such, creates an income effect that causes the individual to desire less leisure, that is, to work more. In theory, which of these effects dominates is not clear. If the substitution effect dominates an individual worker's decision, then the lower wage brought about by the Social Security tax causes the worker to substitute more leisure time for fewer hours of work. On the other hand, if the income effect of the wage reduction dominates, then an individual worker may choose to work more hours and demand less leisure time due to the tax.

Although there is no theoretical answer to the question of which effect dominates, a great deal of empirical research has been conducted on the issue. These studies indicate that the substitution effect of the wage reduction appears to be stronger than the income effect for older workers, possibly because the value of leisure time tends to increase with age. Although other factors have undoubtedly influenced the trend, the effect of Social Security on work and retirement decisions can be seen in the changing labor force participation rates for older Americans. In 1930, before the enactment of the Social Security system, about 50 percent of men over the age of 65 were members of the labor force. Today, the percentage has dropped to 20. Even though economists have yet to determine the exact proportion of this decline caused by Social Security, there is considerable agreement that Social Security does reduce the overall supply of labor available to the economy.

Saving and Investment

Social Security also carries with it the potential to distort saving and investment behavior in a way that may be detrimental to the overall performance of the economy. Understanding this requires insight into the economic incentives and disincentives for saving that are created by the Social Security system. In practice, our Social Security system can influence the saving behavior of households at least three ways.

First, as we saw above, the Social Security system creates an incentive for older workers to reduce their supply of labor by retiring earlier. This implies that workers will enjoy longer periods of retirement than they would if Social Security did not exist. And longer retirements necessarily mean that workers have fewer years to accumulate assets to support their nonworking years. Thus, workers who plan for a lengthier retirement have an incentive to save more than otherwise during their working years. This is often referred to as the **retirement effect** of Social Security on saving.

A second possible way in which Social Security may increase personal saving is known as the **bequest effect.** This effect is based on the assumption that a major reason people save is to leave financial assets to their children after they die. Under the current operating structure, Social Security transfers income from the younger generation to the older generation. Recognizing this, people who wish to leave something to their children must save more during their working lives to compensate for this loss. Therefore, Social Security's bequest effect reinforces the positive impact of the retirement effect on private personal saving.

The third way Social Security influences personal saving works in the opposite direction of the bequest and retirement effects. Because Social Security provides individuals and their families with a guaranteed retirement income in exchange for payroll taxes, workers may view Social Security as a form of saving. The value of future Social Security benefits is a major portion of many Americans' personal wealth. Thus, there is a tendency for workers to substitute the wealth accumulated through their participation in Social Security for other forms of wealth, such as private saving. Essentially, this **wealth substitution effect** accounts for the fact that many workers feel a diminished need to save because they are part of a Social Security system that guarantees them a future return on their tax dollars.

If the retirement effect and the bequest effect induce people to save more and the wealth substitution effect induces people to save less, what is the net impact of Social Security on personal saving? This question has been the center of a number of controversial empirical studies. Based on the evidence, many economists today conclude that the wealth substitution effect dominates the other two. Consequently, it appears that Social Security reduces the total pool of savings in the overall economy. Furthermore, the size of this reduction may be quite large. Some studies indicate that total personal saving is less than half of what would exist without our current social insurance safety net.

retirement effect
The incentive for workers to increase their saving behavior throughout their working lives because Social Security tends to increase the length of retirement.

bequest effect
An increase in saving among people who wish to leave assets to their children as compensation for the losses incurred due to the burden of Social Security taxes.

wealth substitution effect
The reduction in saving as workers substitute the wealth accumulated through participation in Social Security for other forms of private wealth.

FIGURE 15.3 Social Security and Economic Growth

The curve *AD* represents the production possibilities available to an economy. If Social Security causes people to save less and therefore consume more, the economy may find itself at a point such as *C*, where relatively few resources are available for investment. Thus, one cost of Social Security is that it may not be able to move quickly to a higher production possibilities curve and a point like *E*, where more of both consumption and investment goods would be available.

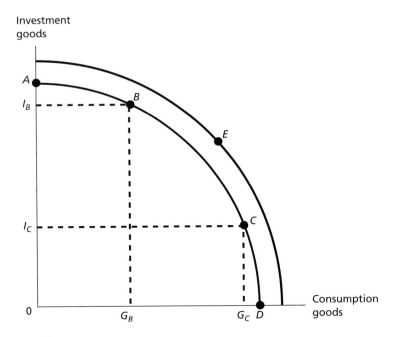

The importance of a reduction in personal savings should not be ignored. In Chapter 11 we learned that saving is necessary to create the pool of funds available for productive investment. If Social Security reduces aggregate saving, fewer dollars are available for businesses to invest in private infrastructure and capital equipment or for individuals to invest in education and training. In this way Social Security may represent a constraint on both current aggregate demand and future economic growth. This concept may be illustrated with the use of a production possibilities model.

In Figure 15.3, the curve *AD* represents the production possibilities available to the economy. The axes are labeled to illustrate the trade-off between consumption goods and investment goods that the economy could produce with its available resources. If Social Security causes people to save less, this implies that they also consume relatively more than would otherwise be the case. Therefore, the economy may find itself at a point such as *C* instead of at a point like *B*, where relatively more resources would be devoted to investment goods. The short-run cost of the reduction in saving brought about by Social Security is the amount of investment goods given up, the distance $I_B I_C$. However, because fewer resources are devoted to investment goods, such as new factories, office buildings, equipment, or educational systems, the economy will not grow as strongly or as quickly as it would if more savings had been available. Thus, the long-run cost is that the economy does not move to a higher production possibilities curve and a point like *E*, where more of both consumption and investment goods would be available.

Even though Social Security may have some negative economic side effects, the social benefits that the system generates in terms of financial support and economic security for the elderly, survivors, and disabled populations clearly outweigh these costs in the minds of the average American. Social Security is something that eventually touches almost everyone in our nation, and it has become a cherished institution that people are willing to protect. As such, it is important for us to identify and quantify these potential negative economic effects and to attempt to deal with them as effectively as possible as the Social Security system evolves. Of perhaps more immediate importance, however, is the heavy pressure that the changing demographics of the American population has placed on the Social Security system.

THE FUTURE OF SOCIAL SECURITY

The Financial Dilemma

In recent years a looming financial crisis facing the Social Security system has become apparent. How can a program with billions of dollars in reserve find its future in jeopardy? The answer is ironic. As baby boomers—those of the generation who worked and paid the taxes that built up the large surplus in the Social Security trust fund—age and begin to retire, the expected payouts in benefits will exceed the expected inflow of tax contributions. When the Social Security Administration's expenditures become greater than its revenue, the trust fund will begin to shrink in size until it is depleted. To make matters worse, once the trust fund is empty, the Social Security system cannot revert back to a strict pay-as-you-go program at current tax and benefit levels because the current generation of workers is not of sufficient size to support the large generation of baby boom retirees and beneficiaries.

Figure 15.4 illustrates the projected future fate of the combined OASI and DI trust fund balance under the intermediate assumption made by the trustees. The 2004 forecast is that tax revenues plus interest earned on the surplus in the Social Security trust fund will exceed expenditures until 2027. In 2027, the trust fund surplus is estimated to reach a maximum of almost $4 trillion. This trust fund balance will then began to fall and become exhausted during 2040. Before this critical point in time is reached, however, modifications in the structure of the Social Security system will have to be implemented to avoid significant tax increases and/or benefit reductions.

Possible Solutions

The public debate concerning how to best fix the looming financial crisis is not likely to go away anytime soon. Two major approaches have been proposed to solve the problem: either modify the current system or establish a new fully

FIGURE 15.4   **Projected OASDI Trust Fund Balance**

Source: 2004 OASDI Trustees Report (http://www.ssa.gov).

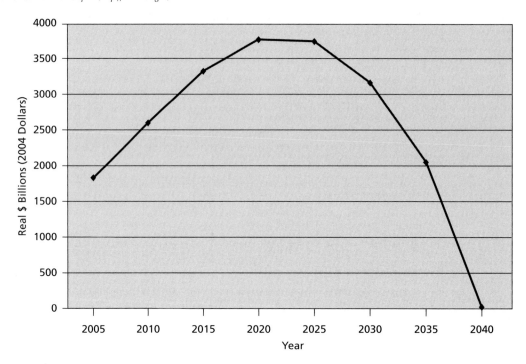

funded system based on private individual accounts. Both approaches have received considerable support, and which way, or combination of ways, we will ultimately choose is unclear.

The most direct way to address Social Security's financial problems is to simply change some of the current rules and operating policies. The most obvious change would be to increase the payroll tax that finances the system. Even though estimates suggest that modest increases in the current rate of taxation would postpone the shortfall in the trust fund by decades, there is very little political support for a tax hike, and therefore a tax increase is not likely to occur anytime soon. Another way to generate more money for Social Security is to transfer more funds from general tax revenues into the system. The federal budget surpluses of the late 1990s could have been used for this purpose, but instead Congress elected to use these funds to retire some of the federal debt held by the public.

If more money cannot be raised for Social Security, the other way to prop up the current system is by reducing its expenditures. Numerous ways have been proposed to do this. In fact, some measures to reduce expenditures have already been put into place, including an increase in the age at which full retirement benefits become available. Most workers now entering the labor force will not be able to receive full Social Security benefits until the age of 67. Other proposed changes not

TABLE 15.3
Total Return on
Stocks, Bonds, and
Treasury Bills,
1950–2000

Source: U.S. Department of
Commerce, Bureau of the
Census. *Statistical Abstract
of the United States,* 2001.

Period	Stocks	Stocks (after Inflation)	Bonds (10-Year)	Treasury Bills
1950–1959	19.28%	16.69%	0.73%	2.02%
1960–1969	7.78%	5.13%	2.42%	4.06%
1970–1979	5.82%	−0.14%	5.84%	6.42%
1980–1989	17.54%	11.87%	13.06%	9.21%
1990–1999	18.17%	15.09%	7.96%	5.01%
2000	−9.1%	−17.08%	7.53%	6.09%

yet adopted include changing the way the annual COLAs are calculated and decreasing the benefits paid for dependent spouses. Undoubtedly, some form of program modifications will be made in the future to slow the growth of Social Security expenditures, but these are also unlikely to yield a lasting long-term solution.

The more innovative approach to addressing Social Security's funding crisis is the proposal to create a new program that would either supplement or replace the current system with personal security accounts (PSAs). The basic idea is to privatize part or all of Social Security. In its most radical form, Social Security payroll taxes would be placed into individual accounts for each worker in the system. Workers would then be given the responsibility to invest these dollars in various financial assets approved by the government, such as stock market funds or money market mutual accounts. When workers reach retirement age, or otherwise become eligible for benefits, they draw upon the savings accumulated in their accounts. Such a system of PSAs essentially represents a compulsory private retirement insurance scheme.

Proponents of the PSA approach argue that such a system would increase the net savings within the economy and make more dollars available for investment. In this way, the privatized system would encourage greater economic growth and provide beneficiaries with a greater financial return. Of course, one obvious drawback of such a system is that it exposes its participants to greater degrees of financial risk. Worker contributions would earn the market rate of return, which cannot be guaranteed during any period of time. Table 15.3 shows the total return on stocks and bonds experienced during the past five decades. Although the long-run return on these financial instruments may be impressive, notice the wide swings in returns between the decades. Most people do not have the luxury to time their retirement or disability needs to correspond to a strong financial market.

How do the rates of return in Table 15.3 compare to the returns experienced by Social Security beneficiaries who pay into the system throughout their working lives? This is a very complicated question to answer. Due to the benefit structure discussed above, obviously the return varies from person to person according to such factors as age, sex, marital status, and earnings history. Furthermore, analysts disagree about whether the financial return to Social Security should be based solely on a person's payroll contributions to the system or include the taxes paid on his or her behalf by employers. Because of these issues, empirical estimates of the return to Social Security vary widely. For example, one study found that the projected real return to Social Security for someone born in 1975 varied from −0.13 percent (for a single high-wage male) to 4.25 percent (for a one-earner low-wage couple).[1] Although such returns are less than the long-run market averages seen in Table 15.3, keep in mind that defined Social Security benefits are more stable over time because they are not subject to the often wild fluctuations of market activity.

Some economists argue that a Social Security system which relies solely on the market is actually one with less security. That is, what if because of poor investment choices or simply because of significant and continued market declines a large proportion of retirees at some point in time find themselves with little or no income from their PSA? Isn't this the situation that Social Security was designed to eliminate?

A few nations, such as Chile, have adopted privatized social insurance programs with remarkable degrees of success, although it must be noted that they generally have done so during times of market prosperity. How successful these programs would have been had they been implemented during a period of prolonged economic stagnation is unclear. Regardless, although Social Security is very unlikely to be replaced by a private system of compulsory saving, elements of the private market may be incorporated into the system at some point in the future. For example, some have advocated that the Social Security Administration be allowed to invest a portion of its trust fund in the stock market or other private financial securities.

THE MARKET FOR HEALTH CARE: A BRIEF OVERVIEW

The OASDI portion of the Social Security program analyzed above is designed to replace earnings lost due to retirement, disability, or early death. This is what most of us think of when we hear the term Social Security. In reality, of course, OASDI is just one part of the overall Social Security program. Another important component of Social Security is Medicare, which is the federal government's health insurance program for those 65 years and older. As discussed above, OASDI faces a funding dilemma created by the demographic shifts resulting from the baby boom generation. The same is true for Medicare since its primary funding source is a payroll tax levied on both workers and their employers. As important as the funding issue is, Medicare also carries with it incentives that have the potential to distort health care markets by contributing to excessive demand. And of course, where there is excessive demand, price increases tend to follow. To fully understand Medicare and how it creates incentives that can lead to inefficiencies in the market for health care, it is useful to be aware of some of the important trends taking place in that market.

---

[1]C. Eugene Steuerle and Jon M. Bakija, *Retooling Social Security for the 21st Century* (Washington, DC: Urban Institute Press, 1994).

FIGURE 15.5   **The Nation's Health Dollar: Where It Came From, 2001**

Source: Health Care Financing Administration, Office of the Actuary, National Health Statistics Group, 2001.

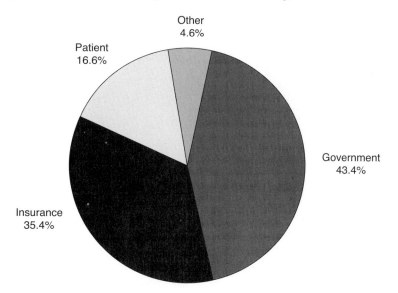

The Nation's Health Dollar: Where It Came From and Where It Went

Overall spending on health care in the United States reached a mind-boggling $1.4 trillion in 2001, or 14.1 percent of the nation's income. Expressed another way, Americans spent $5,035 per person on health care during the year. To better understand this statistic, consider Figures 15.5 and 15.6, which, respectively, show where the typical or average health care dollar came from and where it went in 2001. Figure 15.5 points out one of the most important features of the funding of health care expenditures in the United States. Specifically, only about 17 cents of the typical dollar spent on health care comes from the direct consumer, that is, from the patient. On average, 83 cents of each dollar spent on health care in the United States is contributed by third parties—private health insurance (35 cents), public insurance (43 cents), and private donations (5 cents). Of course, consumers of health care do bear additional costs in the form of health insurance premiums and the like. Nevertheless, the impact of third-party payments on the quantity of health care demanded cannot be overstated. Just imagine how much more you would want of any particular good or service if you had to pay directly only 17 cents out of every dollar it costs. Clearly, a primary impact of any sort of third-party payments is to increase the quantity of health care demand by patients at large, as we detail later in this chapter.

As shown in Figure 15.6, the nation's health dollar went, as you might expect, primarily for hospital care (33 cents), physician services (23 cents), prescriptions (10 cents), and nursing home care (7 cents). The rest of the dollar went for all other

FIGURE 15.6 The Nation's Health Dollar: Where It Went, 2001

Source: Statistical Abstract of the United States, 2003, Table 130.

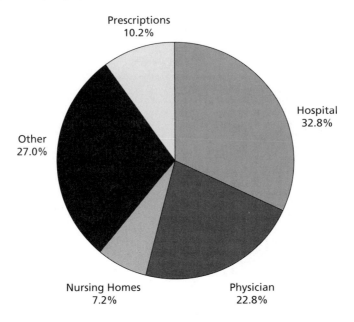

personal health services and other spending, such as the spending on program administration, public health, research, and construction.

Health Expenditure Growth

The average annual growth rate in national health expenditures grew at a steady rate of between 10 and 12 percent for many years since 1960. This growth rate fell drastically in the 1990s to a growth of slightly above 5 percent (Figure 15.7). Then this average annual growth rate in health expenditures increased to 8.7 percent in 2001. As a percentage of the nation's income, expenditures on health care services have remained at around 13 to 14 percent in recent years after increasing from below 10 percent in the 1980s. Thus, the annual growth rate in national health expenditures appears to have leveled off somewhat and is just keeping up with the growth rate in the overall economy.

Government Role in Health Care Financing

The government's role in the financing of health care services has increased steadily and significantly since the inauguration of Medicare in 1965. Prior to the enactment of Medicare, the public sector accounted for only about 25 percent of total health care expenditures. By 1990, the government's share had risen to almost 41 percent, and it has continued to increase. In 2001, government financed 45 percent of health care services provided in the United States.

FIGURE 15.7   National Health Expenditures as a Percentage of GDP and Annual Percentage Growth Rate, 1980–2001

Source: *Statistical Abstract of the United States,* 2003, Table 128.

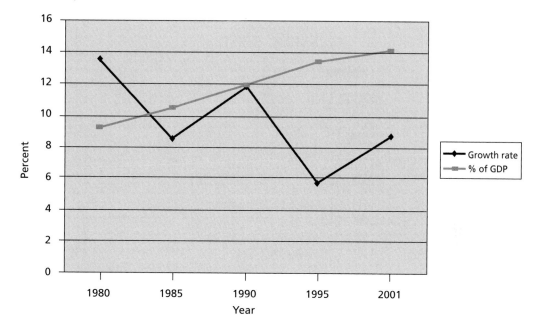

The combined spending on the two primary government health care programs, Medicare and Medicaid, was over $482 billion in 2001. (Recall from Chapter 7 that Medicaid is the federal program which provides health care benefits to the poor and economically disadvantaged.) This amounts to more than one-third of all the spending on health care and about 75 percent of all public spending on health care. Both the Medicare and Medicaid programs enrolled about 40 million citizens in 2001.

The Decline in Importance of Private Health Insurance

Private health insurance financed only about one-third of all health care spending in 2001. While private insurance continues to finance a significant portion of overall health care spending, the annual growth rate in employer-sponsored health insurance has decreased in recent years. Effectively, private health insurance is increasingly being replaced with government-sponsored insurance such as Medicare and Medicaid.

THE MEDICARE PROGRAM

The social insurance program known as Medicare was established in 1965 under Title XVIII of the Social Security Act and was given the name "Health Insurance for the Aged and Disabled." During its first year, 1966, almost 4 million persons

TABLE 15.4   Medicare Coverage, Financing, and Payments

Source: Health Care Financing Administration, November 2000, *http://www.hcfa.gov.*

Coverage	Financing	Provider Payments
Part A: Hospital insurance (HI)		
Inpatient care, skilled nursing care, home health agency, and hospice care	2.9% tax rate levied on wages and salaries; taxes levied on SS benefits; interest earned on invested assets; a deductible ($776 in 2000) and a co-insurance payment ($194 per day in 2000) for hospital stay over 60 days	Prospective payment system (PPS); payment based on patient's diagnosis within a diagnosis-related group (DRG)
Part B: Supplemental medical insurance (SMI)		
Physician and non physician services such as laboratory tests, durable equipment and services, ambulance services, flu vaccinations, some therapy services and prescriptions	Monthly premium ($54.00 in 2002), general tax revenues, an annual deductible (currently $100), and a 20% copayment for covered services	Lesser of submitted charges or a fee schedule based on a relative values scale (RVS); introduction of a prospective payment system in 1997
Part C: Medicare+Choice		
Choice among the following plans: fee-for-service plan, managed care plans, and medical savings accounts	Depends on the plan that is selected. The HI and SMI trust funds are a primary source of revenue. There is some cost sharing depending upon the plan selected	Provider payments are generally determined by the Capitation Payment Methodology; payments vary by plan depending upon the characteristics of the enrolled population

65 and over received some health care benefits under the new program. Medicare was expanded in 1973 to include persons who had qualified for disability benefits for at least 24 months under either the Social Security or Railroad Retirement programs, persons with end-stage renal disease requiring continuing dialysis or kidney transplant, and certain older persons not covered who decided voluntarily to buy into the Medicare program. The Medicare program consists of three parts: A, B, and C. Although each part differs in terms of what and who is covered, each is essentially a public insurance plan. Table 15.4 shows the coverage, the financing, and the form of provider payments for each part of the Medicare program.

Coverage

Medicare Part A is the basic hospital insurance (HI) program for those who qualify. Part A provides beneficiaries with basic insurance coverage for inpatient hospital care, skilled nursing care, and home health agency and hospice care.

Approximately 40 million people were covered under the HI program in 2001 and received benefits totaling $141 billion, or about $2,822 per person. Most Medicare enrollees choose to participate in the optional Part B, which provides supplemental medical insurance (SMI) and covers the cost of many physician and nonphysician services (see Table 15.4) not covered under Part A. In 2001, the SMI program cost $99.5 billion and provided benefits to about 38 million people. Medicare Part C provides optional alternatives to the traditional **fee-for-service** coverage of Part A. The Part C program is known as Medicare+Choice because beneficiaries may choose between the traditional plan, a variety of **managed care plans,** and medical savings accounts (MSAs). Presently, only about 6 million people have selected the Part C program.

Financing

Hospital care services and related services under Medicare are primarily paid from revenues collected through the 2.9 percent payroll tax (split evenly between workers and employers as discussed earlier). In addition, the Medicare program receives revenues from **deductibles, co-insurance payments,** taxes on Social Security benefits, and interest income. These sources of funds finance the medical services covered under Part A. Physician and nonphysician medical services covered under Part B are paid mainly from general tax revenues collected by the U.S. Treasury. In addition, Part B is financially supported by a monthly premium, paid by recipients, that covers about 25 percent of the program's costs. Enrollees of Part B must meet an annual deductible and face a 20 percent copayment to defray overall program spending on medical services. The final Medicare plan, Part C, is financed primarily from the revenue generated by the HI and SMI trust funds. There is also some cost sharing under Part C, depending on whether the enrollee selects a fee-for-service option, a managed care option, or a medical savings account.

Provider Payments

Medicare pays hospitals for their services under a set of guidelines called the **prospective payment system (PPS).** The PPS was established in 1983 in an attempt to slow down the spiraling inflation in the market for hospital care. Under this system, a hospital is not paid the actual cost of providing care but, rather, is paid based on the patient's diagnosis within a diagnosis-related group (DRG). Historically, Medicare paid physicians based on the idea of a "reasonable charge" for their services. This approach was changed in 1992. Since then, physicians have been paid for their services on the basis of the lesser of the submitted charges or a fee schedule known as the relative value scale (RVS). Recent legislation (1997) has authorized the introduction of the PPS in the Medicare payments made to physicians and other health care providers. The way in which providers are paid under the Medicare+Choice plans varies according to the type of option chosen. Health care providers under the traditional fee-for-service options are paid as just described, but under the managed care options, Medicare makes a predetermined per capita payment each year. More will be said about managed care plans later in the chapter.

fee-for-service system
A system in which buyers pay the cost of what they receive.

managed care system
A health care system whereby payments to health care providers are based on a prearranged schedule of fixed fees that has been negotiated between the insurer and the providers.

deductible
The portion of a health services bill that is the responsibility of patient, not the health insurer.

co-insurance
The percentage of the cost above the deductible that the patient is required to pay.

prospective payment system
A health care program whereby the prices of services are fixed in advance by the insurer at a given amount for a given treatment.

THE ECONOMIC EFFECTS OF MEDICARE

The economic effects of Medicare are felt first and most significantly in the general market for health care. With even a little reflection, it should become clear that the health care market is unlikely to operate like the efficient, purely competitive market described in Chapter 2. One important difference is that in a competitive market, would-be buyers are excluded from the market if they cannot or will not pay the equilibrium competitive price for a good or service. It is this exclusion from the market, based on a potential consumer's unwillingness to pay, which ensures that goods and services are consumed by those who place the greatest value on them. Contrary to a competitive market, in the market for health care, it is commonly accepted that no one should be excluded from consumption. This proposition is typically defended either on grounds that many aspects of health care goods and services are semicollectively consumed or purely on grounds of equity. But, no doubt, the most important deviation from the competitive market model that exists in the health care market is its reliance on third-party payments.

Third-party payments, primarily in the form of private and public health insurance, have a major influence on the health care market, shown in Figure 15.8, which reflects the market for physical examinations in a given community. In the absence of health insurance, that is, in a more competitive environment, the equilibrium price is $100 per exam, and 10 exams are provided per day. Now suppose that a health insurance plan is implemented which lowers the cost of an exam to the patient to $40. As the law of demand states, if all else remains the same other than a fall in the price of a good or service, the quantity demanded can be expected to rise. In this case, at a price of $40, the quantity of exams demanded doubles to 20 per day. Of course, suppliers are willing to provide 20 exams per day only if they are paid $200 for each exam. Therefore, third parties—the insurers—pick up the difference between the price the patient pays ($40) and the price paid to physicians ($200). Consequently, in response to the implementation of a health insurance plan, total expenditures on physical examinations rise from $1,000 to $4,000 per day. The impact of health insurance then can be summarized as causing an increase in the quantity of health care demanded, a corresponding increase in health care provided, and an increase in the total cost of providing that care—although the price charged to the patient may decline. Furthermore, whether the insurance is private or social in nature makes no difference. And remember, the government's two primary health insurance programs, Medicare and Medicaid, provide funding for about one-third of the total expenditures on health care in the United States. As such, the role of Medicare in leading to the explosion in the quantity of health care demanded in the United States over the past several decades cannot be overstated. And the link between that increase and the high rates of health care inflation that we in the United States have had should be obvious.

FIGURE 15.8   Third-Party Payments and Their Effects

The price is $100, and the quantity demanded is 10 units per day without third-party payments. Third-party payments reduce the price to the patient to $40, and quantity demanded is 20 units per day. The price has to rise to $200 per unit to meet this increase in the quantity demanded. The effect of third-party payments is to increase medical expenditures per day from $1,000 ($100 × 10) to $4,000 ($200 × 20).

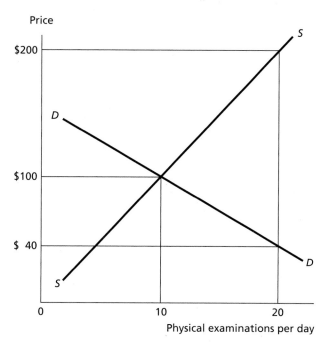

THE FUTURE OF MEDICARE

The Financial Dilemma

The Medicare HI program appears to face no immediate financial problem. Estimates indicate that the HI trust fund will have more income flowing into the fund than the expenditures flowing out of the fund for 15 years. However, the projected HI trust fund income will represent a declining share of expenditures and the HI trust fund would be depleted of assets by the year 2041, according to further estimates. So it is clear that some changes will have to be made in the future to meet the increasing demands of the baby boom generation when they have retired. The Medicare SMI program is in a position to meet future demands for medical care services because the current law already provides for financing based on the current cost per SMI beneficiary.[2]

[2]*HI and SMI Trustees Reports, www.hcfa.gov.*

Possible Solutions

The most obvious way to secure Medicare would be to increase the payroll tax that supports the program. As is true for the general Social Security program, however, any political appetite for even a modest tax increase appears to be lacking. Alternatives to an increase in the tax rate include (1) increasing the insurance monthly premium enrollees have to pay and (2) increasing required cost sharing by increasing existing deductibles and co-insurance payments. These actions, which are also likely to be unpopular, may carry with them an added benefit by reining in some of the excess demand for health care created by widespread insurance.

Although each proposal above will have to be considered and some combination will likely be implemented, other alternatives also attempt to correct some of the inefficiencies created by Medicare. In fact, several of these proposals are already embodied in Medicare's Part C. As was pointed out, Part C allows enrollees to choose among alternatives to Medicare's traditional unrestricted fee-for-service plan. These alternatives include managed care plans and MSAs.

Under a typical managed care plan, payments to providers are based on a pre-arranged schedule of fixed fees that are negotiated between the insurer (known as the managed care organization) and the various health service providers. A managed care plan offers no incentives to provide unnecessary medical services since the fees are predetermined. In contrast, Medicare's traditional fee-for-service system tends to encourage providing excessive services since the provider's income rises with the services given.

Managed care plans, which are not new in the United States, have recently experienced very rapid growth. They are especially common when insurance is employer-sponsored. At present, more than 70 percent of all privately insured employees are covered by a managed care plan. A variety of organizational structures provide managed care plans. The most common are health maintenance organizations (HMOs), preferred provider organizations (PPOs), point-of-service (POS) organizations, and physician networks.

A potential benefit of managed care plans to enrollees is that these plans typically require less cost sharing. Under such a plan, a visit to the office of a doctor may require only a modest fixed fee, say, $10. In addition, some medical services, such as preventive care, may be covered that would not be covered under a traditional plan. However, even though an increasing percentage of the enrollees of Medicare are selecting the managed care option, the vast majority have remained with the traditional fee-for-service plan. In 2001, only 6 million persons with health insurance under Medicare were covered by a managed care plan.

Medicare's MSA plan is unique in that enrollment is restricted to the first five years of eligibility. Under the MSA option the government purchases for a beneficiary a health insurance policy with a very high deductible and then makes an annual deposit into a savings account that is established by the beneficiary. The beneficiary may then use the money in the savings account to pay for health services received before the deductible is met and for other services not covered by the insurance plan. Unlike other Medicare options there are no limits on what health care providers can charge above the amount paid by the Medicare MSA plan. Also, individuals who enroll in MSAs are locked in for the entire year, with a one-time option of withdrawing by December 15 of the year in which they enrolled.

Each approach has merit, especially since they target the excessive demand for health care created by Medicare insurance, but they have not proved popular enough among retirees to have a major impact to date.

The Medicare Modernization Act

In December 2003, President George W. Bush signed into law the Medicare Prescription Drug, Improvement, and Modernization Act, most commonly referred to as simply the Medicare Modernization Act or MMA. Once it is fully implemented, this legislation will result in the most significant changes in the Medicare program since its inception. The most visible of these changes is the inclusion of coverage for prescription medicines. When Medicare was originally conceived in the 1960s, the cost of prescription drugs was only a small fraction of the elderly's medical care expenditures. Over time, as new drugs were developed, the frequency of prescribing medicines increased and prices rose, resulting in prescriptions becoming a major health care expense for many elderly Americans. Although some Medicare beneficiaries had access to other forms of health insurance with prescription drug coverage, many did not. Prior to the enactment of the MMA, studies showed that between one-fourth and one-third of seniors restricted their use of prescription medicines due to their financial limitations. Although the prescription drug benefit will be phased in over a number of years, it is expected that it will significantly reduce the out-of-pocket costs of drugs for the majority of Medicare beneficiaries.

In addition to the prescription drug benefit, the MMA also established new coordinated care plans for those served by Medicare. These plans allow health care providers to establish provision programs that will be responsible for all the health care services needed by beneficiaries, including doctor visits, hospitalization, medicines, therapy, medical devices, and so on. Providers of these plans will be paid a fixed amount per person based on the level of enrollment. Thus, incentives exist for providers to keep costs down and to invest in preventive interventions which will lower future demands for service. Furthermore, given this financial arrangement, coordinated care providers have an incentive to produce and deliver quality service to attract and maintain enrollment.

The MMA also included a number of other reforms in the traditional Medicare insurance program. For example, new enrollees are now able to obtain an initial preventive physical examination and screening tests for diabetes, and cardiovascular problems are now covered. All of these changes are expected to significantly improve the quality of life and to extend the lives of millions of elderly citizens. However, it will be a number of years before the full effects of MMA are understood, particularly those effects on our collective ability to bear the costs of the Medicare program.

Summary

As we saw in this chapter, millions of families rely on Social Security each year to provide income and health care during old age or in the event of disability and death. These social insurance programs have been very successful in providing an economic safety net for the American family. The success of social insurance can be measured by the enormous number of people who are not subjected to the difficulties of poverty or infirmity because they have participated in the system. However, from an economic perspective, the benefits of Social Security and Medicare programs must be viewed alongside their costs. Some costs of social insurance, such as the negative effect of payroll taxes on income, are obvious. Other costs, such as the possible reduction in investment and therefore future economic growth, are not as clearly visible to the average American. The astonishing popularity of Social Security and Medicare indicates that we as a democratic society have decided that the benefits of these programs outweigh their costs.

A major challenge faces us today as we search for a way to restructure our social insurance programs that will guarantee their future financial stability. It is important to recognize that Social Security's financial dilemma has not been caused by an inherent flaw in the concept of social insurance, but rather it is primarily due to the dynamics of changing demographics within the overall population. Although the same factors are at work on the finances of Medicare, the economics of third-party payments for health care services significantly compounds the problem. Given the economics of social insurance, the debate on how to make our programs more financially secure is likely to remain near the top of the public agenda for some time to come.

Discussion Questions

1. What distinguishes private insurance from social insurance? When should governments provide social insurance, and when should insurance be left to private markets?

2. Would the economic effects of a fully funded social insurance program differ from those of a pay-as-you go system? Explain.

3. Evaluate this statement: "The current structure of the American Social Security system results in an intergenerational transfer of income and wealth."

4. Explain how the Social Security system creates economic incentives for early retirement. Is this a positive or negative aspect of the OASDI program? Defend your answer.

5. From a theoretical perspective, explain why Social Security could have either a positive or a negative impact on personal savings.

6. Which current proposal to save the Social Security system do you prefer? Defend your answer using economic reasoning.

7. Explain how health insurance, whether public or private, tends to generate excessive demand for health care.

8. Cost-sharing arrangements in Medicare are designed to limit the growth in demand for health care among enrollees. Explain how this works.

9. Many argue that health care is a right and thus should not be denied to anyone. Evaluate this argument.

10. Explain how managed care plans differ from fee-for-service plans.

11. How would you change the Medicare program to make it financially sound? Be specific, and defend your proposals with economic reasoning.

12. Given that both the Social Security and Medicare programs are facing possible financial insolvency, should we continue to rely on social insurance to meet the needs of the elderly and disadvantaged? Why or why not?

13. How will the Medicare Modernization Act impact a number of elderly Americans? What effects will this have on the financial solvency of Social Security?

14. Will Social Security impact *your* decision as to when to retire? How? Explain your answer using economic reasoning.

Additional Readings

Aaron, Henry J., and Robert D. Reischauer. *Countdown to Reform: The Great Social Security Debate,* rev. ed. New York: Century Foundation Press, 2001.
The authors examine the key issues in the Social Security debate and offer their own suggestions on how to reform the system.

Diamond, Peter A. "Proposals to Restructure Social Security." *Journal of Economic Perspectives* 10 (Summer 1996), pp. 67–88.
Author discusses the economic issues surrounding the most popular proposals to reform Social Security financing. Provides an examination of the Chilean experience with privatizing their social insurance program.

Edelman, Peter, Dallas L. Salisbury, and Pamela J. Larson, eds. *The Future of Social Insurance: Incremental Action or Fundamental Reform?* Washington, DC: National Academy of Social Insurance, 2002.
This book is a compilation of papers addressing such issues as the futures of retirement income, unemployment insurance, and Medicare.

Gramlich, Edward. M. "Different Approaches for Dealing with Social Security." *Journal of Economic Perspectives* 10 (Summer 1996), pp. 55–66.
This article is written by the chairman of a federal advisory council appointed to examine alternative plans to reform the Social Security system. The author provides an analysis of the economic impact of the major proposals recommended by the council.

Kingson, Eric, and James Schullz, eds. *Social Security in the 21st Century.* Oxford, England: Oxford University Press, 1997.
This book is a collection of essays and studies written by leading scholars of social insurance. Emphasis is on the future prospects of the world's social security systems.

Rettenmaier, Andrew J., and Thomas R. Saving. *The Economics of Medicare Reform.* Kalamazoo, MI: Upjohn Institute for Employment Research, 2000.
The authors outline a history of Social Security in America, discuss several different plans for revamping the system, and finally argue for prepaid retirement health insurance.

Rosen, Harvey S. *Public Finance.* 7th ed. New York: McGraw-Hill/Irwin, 2004.
In this advanced textbook, Rosen devotes two complete chapters to the detailed exploration of the economics of social insurance and its effects on consumers and the economy.

Steuerle, C. Eugene, and Jon M. Bakija. *Retooling Social Security for the 21st Century.* Washington, DC: Urban Institute Press, 1994.
In-depth look at the economic and financial problems faced by the Social Security system due to the changing demographics and institutional structure of the U.S. economy. Provides analysis and evaluation of potential approaches to solving the problems.

Thompson, Lawrence. *Older and Wiser: The Economics of Public Pensions.* Washington, DC: Urban Institute Press, 1998.
The author argues that increasing economic growth could increase the cost of supporting future retirees. Discusses the effect of pensions on savings and on the labor supply.

Tynes, Sheryl R. *Turning Points in Social Security: From "Cruel Hoax" to "Sacred Entitlement."* Stanford, CA: Stanford University Press, 1996.
Interesting history of the American Social Security system. Traces the evolution of Social Security from its controversial beginnings to the present time as the most popular federal program.

World Wide Web Resources

Agency for Healthcare Research and Quality (AHRQ)
www.ahcpr.gov

AHRQ is part of the United States Department of Health and Human Services and is charged with conducting research to improve the quality of health care. Gives links to funding opportunities, research findings, quality assessment, data and surveys, and other issues.

Centers for Medicare and Medicaid Services
www.cms.hhs.gov

The CMS is a federal agency within the U.S. Department of Health and Human Services that is responsible for administering Medicare, Medicaid, and the State Children's Health Insurance Program. Their website provides links to these programs, along with news headlines, regulations, statistics, and data.

Social Security Administration
www.ssa.gov

The SSA administers the Social Security and the Supplemental Security Income program. Has links to benefits, online direct services, research and data, the Social Security Law, and other sites.

Social Security Advisory Board
www.ssab.gov

SSAB is an independent, bipartisan board created to advise politicians on matters related to the Social Security and Supplemental Security Income programs. Has links to the members of the board, reports, other websites, and authorizing legislation.

Social Security Information
www.aarp.org/socialsecurity

The American Association of Retired Person (AARP) presents information on the present Social Security System and links to related websites.

United States Department of Health and Human Services
www.os.dhhs.gov

HHS oversees more than 300 programs, including Medicare and Medicaid. Provides links to these two agencies, news and public affairs, and other information.

Glossary

A

Ability-to-pay principle of taxation   The concept that taxpayers with higher incomes should pay more taxes than those with lower incomes.

Aggregate demand   The total quantities of goods and services demanded per unit of time by the economy at various price levels, other things being equal.

Aggregate supply   The total quantities of goods and services supplied per unit of time in the economy at various price levels, other things being equal.

Average cost   The ratio of total costs to units of output of a good or service. Also known as *per-unit* cost.

Average product of labor   The total output of labor divided by the total number of labor units used in production. The average product of labor is a measure of labor productivity.

B

Backward tax shifting   Shifting the burden of a tax to the owners of resources, usually in the form of lower prices paid for their resources.

Balance of payments   The relationship between a country's total monetary obligations per unit of time to other countries and other countries' obligations to the home country.

Balance of trade   The relationship of the value of a country's imports to the value of its exports of goods and services per unit of time. It is in *deficit* when more is owed for imports than is earned by exports; it is in *surplus* when less is owed for imports than is earned by exports.

Balanced budget   A governmental budget is balanced when its total receipts, mainly taxes, are equal to its total expenditures.

Barriers to entry   The various impediments to the entry of new firms into a market, usually classified as (1) private barriers and (2) government barriers.

Benefits-received principle of taxation   The concept that taxpayers should pay taxes in accordance with the benefits they receive from the government.

Bequest effect   The increase in lifetime saving experienced by people who wish to leave assets to their children as compensation for losses incurred due to the burden of Social Security taxes.

Budget deficit   The situation that exists when a government's total receipts, mainly taxes, are less than its total expenditures.

Budget surplus   The situation that exists when a government's total receipts, mainly taxes, are greater than its total expenditures.

Business cycles   Erratic short-run fluctuations in economic activity around the long-run growth trend of the economy. Every business cycle has four distinct phases: expansion, peak, contraction, and trough.

C

Capital account transactions   International trade transactions that are long-term in character, usually investment types of transactions.

Capital resources   All nonhuman ingredients of production. Capital resources can be further divided into natural and man-made categories.

Capture theory of regulation   The belief that regulatory agencies often come to serve the interests of the firms they were established to regulate rather than the interests of the general public.

Cartel   A group of firms which formally agree to coordinate their production and pricing decisions in a manner that maximizes joint profits.

Charter schools   Public schools created, controlled, and managed by parents or other organizations independent of the existing local school district.

Charter schools are essentially privately operated, but publicly funded local schools.

Circular flow of production and income The concept that the expenditures of one group are the incomes for others, who in turn spend and provide income for still others.

Co-insurance The percentage of the cost above the deductible that an insured patient is required to pay.

Collectively consumed goods and services Goods and services that are consumed by a group or groups as a whole and that yield benefits to the group or groups. No individual can single out and value his or her specific benefits.

Comparative advantage The ability of a country to produce a good or service with a smaller sacrifice of alternative goods and services than can the rest of the trading world.

Comparative disadvantage The inability of a country to produce a good or service except at greater sacrifice of alternative goods and services than is necessary for the rest of the trading world.

Concentration ratio A measure of potential monopoly power, defined as the percentage of an industry's sales (or assets or output) controlled by the four (or eight) largest firms in the industry.

Consumption possibilities curve A curve showing the maximum quantities of two goods or services that may be consumed in an economy, given the economy's resources and technology. In the absence of international trade, the consumption possibilities curve is identical to the production possibilities curve.

Corporations Firms organized as legal entities separate from their owners, the stockholders, who, by law, have limited liability.

Cost-of-living allowances (COLAs) Automatic annual increases to insurance benefits or wages equal to the amount of inflation experienced within the economy during the previous year (usually as measured by the Consumer Price Index (CPI)).

Cost-benefit analysis A technique for determining the optimal level of an economic activity. In general, an activity should be expanded as long as the expansion leads to greater benefits than costs.

Cost-push inflation Increases in the average price level initiated by increases in costs of production.

Customs union A free trade alliance of nations that share common external tariffs.

Cyclical unemployment Unemployment caused by economic fluctuations. It results from inadequate levels of aggregate demand.

D

Deadweight welfare loss due to monopoly The reduction in social satisfaction, or welfare, due to the tendency of monopolists to restrict output below the socially optimal level.

Deductible The portion of a health services bill that is the responsibility of the patient, not the health insurer.

Demand The set of quantities of a good or service per unit of time that buyers would be willing to purchase at various alternative prices of the item, other things being equal.

Demand, changes in Shifts in the entire demand schedule or curve for a good or service, resulting from changes in one or more of the "other things being equal." Should not be confused with a movement along a given demand schedule or curve (change in quantity demanded).

Demand, derived The demand for labor is said to be dependent on, or derived from, the demand for the product being produced. In this sense, the demand for labor is a derived demand.

Demand, law of The general rule that at lower prices, buyers will purchase larger amounts per unit of time than they will at higher prices, other things being equal; that is, demand curves slope downward to the right.

Demand-pull inflation Increases in the average price level initiated and continued from increases in aggregate demand.

Developed countries Countries with relatively higher labor quality, relatively larger accumulations of capital, and relatively higher levels of technology, all leading to relatively high living standards.

Diminishing returns, law of The principle that increments of a variable resource used with a fixed resource will lead to smaller and smaller increments in product output.

Discount rate   The rate of interest the Federal Reserve Banks charge commercial banks when commercial banks borrow from the Fed.

Discouraged workers   Those who have stopped actively searching for work are not considered to be part of the labor force. As such, they are classified as discouraged workers rather than unemployed.

Discrimination   Treating equals unequally or unequals equally.

Diseconomies of scale   A situation that occurs when the average cost of producing a good or service rises as output is increased.

Dumping   An "unfair" international trade practice that occurs when a producer is selling abroad at a price below cost or below its domestic price.

E

Economic growth   A long-run process of economic expansion that results from a compounding of economic events over time.

Economies of scale   A situation that occurs when the average cost of producing a good or service falls as output is increased.

Efficiency   The extraction of the greatest possible value of product output from given inputs of resources.

Efficiency effects of inflation   The effects of inflation on the pattern of resource allocation.

Elasticity of demand, price   The responsiveness of the quantity demanded of a product to changes in its price. Measured by the percentage change in quantity divided by the percentage change in price.

Elasticity of supply, price   The responsiveness of the quantity offered of a product to changes in its price. Measured by the percentage change in quantity divided by the percentage change in price.

Embargo   Government provision formally preventing one nation from trading goods and services with another nation or group of nations. The intent of an embargo is the elimination of international trade between the countries in question.

Equal tax treatment doctrine   The concept that taxpayers in equal economic circumstances should be treated equally; that is, people in identical economic positions should pay the same amounts of taxes.

Equation of exchange   The truism that the money supply (M) times the velocity of circulation (V_1) equals quantities of goods and services sold in final form (Q) times the average price level (P).

Equilibrium quantity purchased   The quantity of the product that is actually exchanged at the equilibrium price.

Equimarginal principle   The allocation of spending among different inputs in such a way that the marginal benefits of a dollar spent on any one input is the same as for that spent on any other input.

Equity effects of inflation   The effects of inflation on the distribution of income.

Excess tax burden   The distortionary effects of a tax on relative prices and resource allocation.

Exchange rates   The costs of units of other countries' currencies in terms of units of the home country's currency.

Explicit costs   Costs of production incurred by the purchase or hire of resources by the producing unit.

Exports   Goods and services that economic units in one country sell to other countries.

Externalities   Benefits or costs incurred in the production or consumption of goods and services that do not accrue to the producing or consuming unit, but rather accrue to the remainder of the society.

F

Fee-for-service system   A health care program in which buyers pay the cost of what they receive.

Forward tax shifting   Taxes shifted to consumers in the form of higher product prices.

Free-riders   Those who receive positive social spillovers in consumption benefits without paying the costs of producing the goods or services that yield them.

Free trade area   An alliance of nations without trade barriers between its members.

Frictional unemployment   Brief periods of unemployment experienced by persons moving between jobs or into the labor market; it is not related to basic aggregate demand or aggregate supply problems.

Full-employment unemployment rate   The rate that exists when there is no cyclical unemployment. The full-employment rate of unemployment is consistent with price stability.

Fully funded insurance scheme   An insurance program designed to provide benefits financed from the interest income earned on accumulated payments.

G

Good, inferior   When an increase in income leads to a fall in demand, other things being equal, the good in question is said to be inferior.

Good, normal   When an increase in income leads to an increase in demand, other things being equal, the good in question is said to be normal.

Goods, complementary   Two goods or services are complementary if an increase in the price of one leads to a fall in the demand for the other, other things being equal.

Goods, substitute   Two goods or services are substitutes if an increase in the price of one leads to an increase in the demand for the other, other things being equal.

Government purchases   Government expenditures for currently produced goods and services.

Gross domestic product, current   The market value of all final goods and services produced within an economy during one year. GDP ignores the issue of whether the resources used for the production are owned domestically or are foreign-owned.

Gross domestic product, per capita   Gross domestic product, either current or real, divided by the economy's population.

Gross domestic product, potential   The level of real GDP the economy could produce at full employment.

Gross domestic product, real   Gross domestic product corrected for changes in the price level relative to a base year price level.

H

Horizontal equity   The notion that people in the same economic circumstances should receive the same economic treatment.

Human capital   That part of the productive power of human or labor resources resulting from investment in education and training.

I

Implicit costs   Costs of production incurred by the use of self-owned, self-employed resources.

Imports   Goods and services purchased and brought into a country from abroad.

Income effect   A measure of the change in the hours of work that occurs when there is a change in income, other things being equal.

Incomes policies   Governmental restraints placed on wages and prices intended to reduce cost-push inflation thought to result from the monopolies of labor unions and business firms.

Increasing opportunity costs   As more of a particular good or service is produced, the cost in terms of other goods or services that are given up grows.

Individually consumed goods and services   Goods and services that benefit directly, and only, those persons who consume them.

Inflation   A rising average price level of goods and services.

Infrastructure   All of an economy's basic facilities, such as its roads, power plants, telecommunication systems, schools, and hospitals, necessary for maintaining and promoting normal economic activities.

Injections   New spending in the circular flow, including new investment, new government expenditures, and net exports.

Investment   The purchase by economic units of such real assets as land, buildings, equipment, machinery, and raw and semifinished materials.

Investment multiplier   The reciprocal of 1 minus the marginal propensity to consume.

L

Labor force   All noninstitutionalized individuals 16 years of age and older who are employed for pay, actively seeking employment, or awaiting recall from a temporary layoff.

Labor resources   Human resources, all efforts of mind and muscle, that are ingredients in production processes. They range from unskilled common labor to the highest levels of professional skills.

Labor union   A formal organization of workers which bargains on behalf of its members over the terms and conditions of employment.

Leakages   Withdrawals from spending in the circular flow, including taxes, savings, and imports.

Legal reserve ratio   Ratio of cash reserves to demand deposits that banks are required to maintain.

Lesser developed countries   Countries with relatively low living standards, usually the result of relatively low labor quality, relatively scarce capital, and relatively low levels of technology.

Living standards   The level of economic well-being of a population, usually measured in terms of its per capita real income.

Lockout   A work stoppage initiated by management.

Lorenz curve   This curve shows the cumulative percentage of total family income that is going to the lowest percentiles of families. It is a way of measuring the degree of income inequality in a country.

Losses   The difference between a firm's total costs and its total revenues when total revenues are less than total costs, including as a part of total costs returns to investors in the firm sufficient to yield an average return on their investments.

M

M1   All currency and coins in circulation, nonbank traveler's checks, demand deposits, and other checkable accounts, such as NOW accounts.

M2   M1 plus savings and time deposits of small denomination and money-market mutual funds.

Managed care system   Health care system whereby payments to health care providers are based on a prearranged schedule of fixed fees that has been negotiated between the insurer and the providers.

Marginal benefits   The increase or decrease in the total benefits yielded by an activity from a one-unit change in the amount of the activity carried on.

Marginal cost of labor (*MCL*)   Change that occurs in a firm's total labor costs due to hiring an additional worker, per unit of time.

Marginal costs   The change in total costs resulting from a one-unit change in the output of a good or service.

Marginal private benefit (*MPB*)   The benefit that accrues to the direct consumers of a good or service resulting from a one-unit increase in consumption. The *MPB* is reflected in the demand curve for the good or service.

Marginal private cost (*MPC*)   The increase in total cost that producers incur when output is increased by one unit. The *MPC* is reflected in the supply curve for the good or service.

Marginal product of labor   The change in production that occurs in response to hiring one additional worker.

Marginal propensity to consume (*MPC*)   The change in consumption divided by the change in income.

Marginal propensity to save (*MPS*)   The change in saving divided by the change in income.

Marginal revenue (*MR*)   The change in the total revenue of a seller resulting from a one-unit change in the quantity sold of a good or service.

Marginal revenue product of labor   The change in revenue that occurs in response to hiring one additional worker. Serves as the firm's demand curve for labor.

Marginal social benefit (*MSB*)   The true benefit to society of a one-unit increase in the production of a good or service.

Marginal social cost (*MSC*)   The true, or opportunity, cost borne by society when the production of a good or service is increased by one unit.

Market   The area within which buyers and sellers of a good or service can interact and engage in exchange.

Market, competitive   A market in which there are many sellers and many buyers of a good or service. No one buyer or seller is large enough to be able to affect the price of the product.

Market, imperfect competition   A market that falls between the limits of a competitive market on the one hand and a monopolistic market on the other. It contains elements of both.

Market, monopolistic   A market in which there is a single seller of a good, service, or resource.

Market, product   Buyers and sellers engage in the exchange of final goods and services.

Market, purely competitive   A market with a large number of mobile buyers and sellers of a standardized product. Further, the price of the product is free to move up and down, and there are no obstacles preventing firms from entering or leaving the market.

Market, resource   Buyers and sellers engage in the exchange of the factors of production.

Market failure   Occurs when markets, operating on their own, do not lead to a socially optimal allocation of resources.

Measure of value function of money   The use of money to measure the value of goods and services.

Medium of exchange   The use of money for the payment of goods and services and for the payment of debt.

Minimum wages   Wage rate floors set for specific occupations or groups of workers by governmental units or by labor unions.

Mixed systems   Economies that combine elements of both the pure market and pure command economies.

Money creation   The expansion of demand deposits when banks and other financial institutions, as a group, expand loans.

Money multiplier   A numerical coefficient equal to the reciprocal of the legal reserve ratio.

Money supply (M)   Currency held by the public plus checkable accounts.

Monopoly power   The degree to which sellers can control the supply and hence the price of what they sell.

Monopsonistic profit   The difference between the workers' contribution to a monopsonistic firm's receipts and their wages.

Monopsony   A market with only one buyer or employer of a factor of production.

Monopsony power   The degree to which buyers can control the demand and hence the price of what they purchase.

N

Natural monopoly   When the average cost of producing a product is minimized by having only one firm produce the product, the industry is said to be a natural monopoly.

Near-money   Assets that are easily convertible to cash; they are similar to money because they are very liquid.

Negative income tax   A government subsidy or cash payment to households that qualify because of having income below a minimum or guaranteed level.

Network economies   Network economies exist when the value of a product to a consumer is enhanced when others also choose to consume the same product.

Nonexclusion   For public goods, means it may not be feasible or desirable to exclude people from consuming the good.

Nonprice competition   Competition among firms in matters other than product price. It usually takes the form of (1) advertising and (2) changes in design and quality of the product.

Nonrival in consumption   For public goods, means a given amount of the good can be consumed by a person without another person having to decrease his or her consumption of the good.

O

Open-market operations   Federal Reserve purchases and sales of government securities for the purpose of increasing or decreasing commercial bank reserves.

Opportunity cost principle   The true cost of producing an additional unit of a good or service is the value of other goods or services that must be given up to obtain it.

Output effects of inflation   The effects of inflation on the level of production.

P

Pay-as-you-go insurance scheme   An insurance program designed to provide benefits financed from current payments.

Pollution rights market   When firms are allowed to buy and sell government-issued licenses granting the holder the right to create a certain amount of pollution, the resulting market is called a pollution rights market.

Positive externality in consumption   An increase in the satisfaction of one person caused by the consumption of a good or service by another person. Education, especially K–12, is said to create such externalities.

Price, equilibrium   The price of a product at which buyers are willing to purchase exactly the quantities per unit of time that sellers want to sell.

Price ceiling   A maximum price set for a product, usually by a governmental unit. Sellers of the product are not permitted to charge higher prices.

Price discrimination   The sale of the same product to different persons or groups of persons at different prices.

Price elasticity of demand   The responsiveness of quantity demanded of a product to changes in price.

Price floor   A minimum price set for a product, usually by a governmental unit or a group of sellers. Sellers are not permitted to resell at lower prices.

Price index numbers   A set of numbers showing price level changes relative to some base year.

Private insurance   A contract whereby individuals agree to make payments, often called premiums, to a company in return for a guarantee of financial benefits in the event that some undesired circumstance occurs.

Production   The process of using technology to combine and transform resources to make goods and services.

Production possibilities curve   A graphical representation of the maximum quantities of two goods and/or services that an economy can produce when its resources are used in the most efficient way possible.

Productivity   The average amount of output that can be produced with a given set of inputs. The productivity of any resource can be calculated as the ratio of the units of output to the units of input.

Profit-maximizing output   The output per unit of time at which a firm's total revenue exceeds its total cost by the greatest possible amount. It is the output at which the firm's marginal cost equals its marginal revenue.

Profits   The difference between a firm's total revenue and its total cost when total revenue exceeds total cost, including as a part of total cost returns to investors in the firm sufficient to yield an average rate of return on their investments.

Progressive tax rates   A tax rate schedule that results in an increase in the ratio of tax collections to income as income increases.

Proportional tax rates   A tax rate schedule that results in a constant ratio of tax collections to income as income changes.

Prospective payment system   A health care program whereby the prices of services are fixed in advance by the insurer at a given amount for a given treatment.

Psychic costs   Costs in the form of negative personal satisfaction, rather than monetary loss, that an individual incurs from pursuing an endeavor.

Psychic income   Benefits in the form of personal satisfaction, rather than monetary gain, that an individual receives from pursuing an endeavor.

Psychological law of consumption   A law stating that when income changes, consumption changes but by less than the change in income.

Public goods   Goods and services of a collectively consumed nature, usually provided by governmental units.

Public investments   Government spending for capital goods such as roads, bridges, dams, schools, and hospitals.

Pure command economy   The pure command economy is characterized by state ownership and/or control of resources and centralized resource-use decision making.

Pure market economy   The pure market economy is based on private ownership and control of resources, known as private property rights, and on coordination of resource-use decisions through markets.

Q

Quantity theory of money   The theory that changes in the money supply (M) will tend to cause changes in the same direction of total output (Q) and price level (P).

Quota   A regulation that limits by law the quantity of specific foreign goods or services that may be imported during a period of time.

R

Relative tax treatment doctrine   The theory that taxpayers in different economic circumstances should pay different amounts of taxes.

Retirement effect   The increase in a worker's lifetime saving because Social Security tends to extend the length of retirement.

Reserve ratio, legal (or required)   The ratio of reserves to deposits that banks are required by law to maintain.

Resources   The ingredients that go into the production of goods and services. They consist of labor resources and capital resources.

S

Semicollectively consumed goods and services   Goods and services that yield direct benefits to the consumers of them but that also yield social spillover benefits to others.

Shortage   A situation in which buyers of a product want larger quantities per unit of time than sellers will place on the market. It may be caused by the existence of an effective price ceiling.

Social insurance   Government programs, financed through tax revenues, that guarantee citizens financial benefits against events which are beyond an individual's control, such as old age, disability, and poor health.

Social overhead capital   Capital used by the economy as a whole rather than being limited to use by specific firms. Examples include transportation and communications networks as well as energy and power systems.

Stock options   Guarantees issued by a corporation which allow the holder to purchase a set number of shares at a fixed price, often called the strike price. Stock options are often used as a form of managerial compensation.

Store of value function of money   The use of money as an asset to hold.

Strike   A work stoppage initiated by labor.

Structural unemployment   Unemployment caused by a mismatch between the skills (or locations) of job seekers and the requirements (or locations) of available jobs.

Substitution effects   The effects of a price change of a good or service on the quantity of it purchased because of the substitution of relatively lower priced goods for it when its price increases and the substitution of the item for now relatively higher priced other goods when its price decreases.

Supply   The set of quantities of a good or service per unit of time that sellers would be willing to place on the market at various alternative prices of the item, other things being equal.

Supply, changes in   Shifts in the entire supply schedule or curve for a good or service, resulting from changes in one or more of the "other things being equal." They should not be confused with movements along a given supply schedule or curve (changes in the quantity supplied).

Supply, law of   The higher the price of the product, the larger will be the quantity supplied, and the lower the price, the smaller will be the quantity supplied, other things being equal.

Surplus   A situation in which sellers of a product place larger quantities per unit of time on the market than buyers will take. It may be caused by the existence of a price floor.

T

Tariff   A tax placed on internationally traded goods, usually imports.

Tastes and preferences   Buyers' psychological desires for goods and services—one of the determinants of demand for any one product. A change in consumers' tastes and preferences for a product will shift the demand curve for it.

Tax efficiency   The extent to which a tax has a neutral impact on resource allocation and is economical to collect and enforce, thus minimizing the total tax burden.

Tax incidence   The final resting place or burden of any given tax—who actually pays it.

Technology   The know-how and the means and methods available for combining resources to produce goods and services.

Terms of trade   The cost, in terms of the home country's goods and services, of importing a unit of goods or services from other countries.

Trade deficit   Occurs when the value of a nation's imports exceeds the value of the nation's exports.

Trade surplus   Occurs when the value of a nation's exports exceeds the value of the nation's imports.

Transfer payments   Payments made to persons or economic units that are not for services currently performed. They do not result in new output but simply transfer purchasing power from some persons or units to others.

Transformation curve   *See* Production possibilities curve.

Transitional economy   A nation which is in the process of replacing an economic system of command and control with one based on market principles.

Tuition subsidy   A payment made to families or schools by the government to encourage additional investments in education. When externalities are present, a tuition subsidy equal in value to the gap between marginal private benefits and marginal social benefits should result in the optimal level of enrollment.

Turnover tax   In a command economy, excess demand for goods and services is siphoned off through the addition of, or increase in, a sales tax.

V

Vertical equity   The notion that persons in different economic circumstances should receive different rewards from the economic system.

Voluntary restraint agreement   An international treaty whereby one nation volunteers to restrict the exports of a product that it sells to another nation.

Voucher programs   Programs designed to provide students in poor-performing public schools the opportunity to attend other schools and carry with them the state funding that the poor-performing school would have received for those students.

W

Wage discrimination   Payment of unequal wage rates to persons with equal values of marginal product.

Wants   The unlimited or insatiable desires of humans that generate economic activity.

Wealth substitution effect   The reduction in lifetime saving by workers who substitute the wealth accumulated through participation in Social Security for other forms of private wealth.

Index